WILLIAM KENTRIDGE

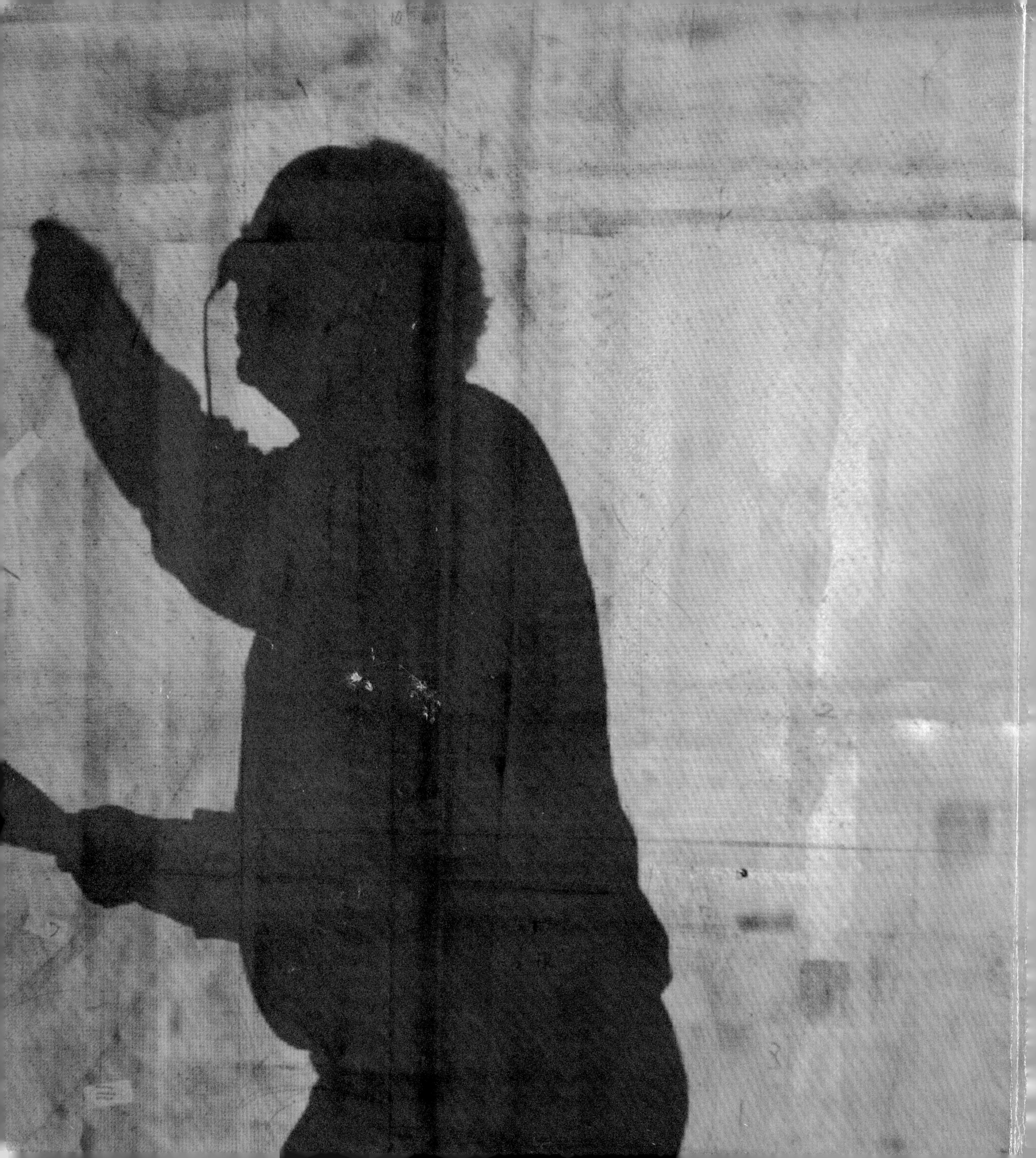

WILLIAM KENTRIDGE

FIVE THEMES

Edited by
MARK ROSENTHAL

With contributions by
MICHAEL AUPING
CORNELIA H. BUTLER, JUDITH B. HECKER, AND KLAUS BIESENBACH
CAROLYN CHRISTOV-BAKARGIEV
RUDOLF FRIELING
WILLIAM KENTRIDGE

San Francisco Museum of Modern Art
Norton Museum of Art
in association with
Yale University Press, New Haven and London

CONTENTS

LENDERS TO THE EXHIBITION

Joan and Richard Barovick
Deutsche Guggenheim/Solomon R. Guggenheim Foundation
Joel and Anne Ehrenkranz
Kenneth and Sherry Endelson
Doris and Donald Fisher
Sally and Michael Gordon
Hirshhorn Museum and Sculpture Garden, Smithsonian Institution
William Kentridge
Aaron and Barbara Levine
Marian Goodman Gallery, New York
Jimmy and Becky Mayer
Lisa and John Miller
Museum of Contemporary Art, Chicago
Museum of Contemporary Art, San Diego
Museum of Modern Art, New York
Norton Museum of Art
Brenda Potter and Michael Sandler
Private collection, Johannesburg
Private collection, New York
Private collection, Ross, California
San Francisco Museum of Modern Art
Heidi L. Steiger
Jennifer and David Stockman
Donna and Howard Stone

DIRECTORS' FOREWORD

The San Francisco Museum of Modern Art and the Norton Museum of Art are proud to have had the honor of co-organizing this sweeping survey of the work of William Kentridge. The artist's last significant American retrospective took place at the start of this decade; overseen by a curatorial team that included Neal Benezra, it was a project that similarly relied upon the skills and resources of two co-organizing institutions. As one might expect, Kentridge's practice has taken a great leap forward since that time. For those familiar with his illustrious earlier work, particularly his Soho Eckstein and Felix Teitlebaum projects of the 1990s, this exhibition may come as something of a surprise. It presents two recent and immersive film installations, one exploring the nature of his creative process in the studio and another inspired by his engagement with the tale of *The Nose,* both the short story by Nikolai Gogol and the opera by Dmitri Shostakovich. The works represent a departure in both scale and aesthetic, one heightened by the installations' juxtaposition with several decades of his earlier films, drawings, and sculptures. We express our profound gratitude to William for entrusting our respective institutions with the responsibility of mounting this exhibition for audiences in the United States, Austria, Israel, and the Netherlands.

The project was conceived by Mark Rosenthal, adjunct curator of modern art at the Norton, who has worked closely with Kentridge to realize this ambitious presentation. Brianna Anderson, curatorial assistant at the Norton, provided tireless support, capably aiding Mark with the myriad details of this complex undertaking. The exhibition's presentation at SFMOMA was expertly overseen by curator of media arts Rudolf Frieling with the help of assistant curator Tanya Zimbardo.

This catalogue, a significant new addition to the literature on Kentridge, has benefited enormously from the generous contributions of the artist himself. The book was produced by SFMOMA under the guidance of Chad Coerver, director of publications. Former managing editor Karen Levine oversaw its every detail, with the indispensable help of publications assistant Amanda Glesmann. The entire publications team extends its gratitude to authors Michael Auping; Cornelia H. Butler, Judith B. Hecker, and Klaus Biesenbach; Carolyn Christov-Bakargiev; Rudolf Frieling; William Kentridge; and Mark Rosenthal for their original contributions. We salute Pentagram's talented Abbott Miller and Kristen Spilman for their highly innovative approach to the catalogue's graphic design. Patricia Fidler, Michelle Komie, and their colleagues at Yale University Press have been the most enthusiastic of partners for the publication. Joshua Shirkey deserves thanks for his painstaking research for the artist's chronology and bibliography, as does Amanda W. Freymann for her skilled oversight of the book's production and printing. SFMOMA publications assistant Laura Heyenga provided vital support in the eleventh hour.

Many individuals at our respective institutions made significant contributions to the project. At SFMOMA, the person most deeply involved has perhaps been Ruth Berson, deputy director, exhibitions and collections. It was Ruth's team, most notably exhibitions coordinator Emily Lewis, that so ably secured the venues and negotiated all details of the extensive tour. Other SFMOMA staff lending their expertise to this undertaking include Olga Charyshyn, registrar; Alexander Cheves, senior museum preparator; Joshua

Churchill, exhibitions technical assistant; Libby Garrison, interim director, marketing and communications; Amanda Hunter Johnson, assistant paper conservator; Sophine Lim, designer; Jennifer Mewha, director of institutional giving; Caitlin Moneypenny-Johnston, marketing associate; Andrea Morgan, associate director of institutional giving, foundation and government relations; Mia Patterson, exhibition and installation design coordinator; Stephanie Pau, manager, interpretation; Jeff Phairas, chief engineer; Kent Roberts, exhibitions design manager and chief preparator; Jennifer Sonderby, head of graphic design; Layna White, head of collections information and access; Dominic Willsdon, Leanne and George Roberts Curator of Education and Public Programs; Greg Wilson, senior preparator; Blair Winn, director of development; and Robyn Wise, public relations associate. Special thanks are due to Steven Dye, exhibitions technical manager, for providing technical advice to all venues, and to Frank Smigiel, associate curator, public programs, for coordinating two related special events in San Francisco: a production of Kentridge's staging of the opera *Il Ritorno d'Ulisse* at Project Artaud Theater and the artist's performance of *I am not me, the horse is not mine* at SFMOMA.

At the Norton, Glenn Tomlinson, curator of education, and Roger Ward, chief curator and curator of European art, have provided invaluable advice and support; registrar Pamela Parry has skillfully managed the logistics of transporting artworks to and from the various tour venues; and Karol Lurie, curatorial administrator, has been involved in myriad aspects of the project. The following individuals are also to be commended for their contributions: Tracy Edling, manager of design and installation; Kipper Lance, director of marketing; Alexia Davis, PR manager; Larry Rosensweig, director of advancement; Graham Russell, associate director of advancement; Natalie Ellis, grants officer; and Kevin Cummins and Dan Leah, art handlers.

Kentridge benefits from having three distinguished galleries working on his behalf. Marian Goodman, founder of Marian Goodman Gallery, New York, has been crucial to the success of this enterprise, and we salute her and her team, especially Agnès Fierobe, director of Marian Goodman Gallery, Paris, and Catherine Belloy, Elaine Budin, and Brian Loftus in New York. No less significant to our success have been Linda Givon, founder of Goodman Gallery, Johannesburg, along with her successor Liza Essers and colleague Kirsty Wesson, and Lia Rumma and her staff, particularly Sofia Bocca and Emma Hedley, at Galleria Lia Rumma, Naples, Italy.

In our efforts to bring together the very best of Kentridge's oeuvre, we have enjoyed the cooperation of some of the artist's most devoted collectors and patrons. We are indebted to our many private and institutional lenders, who have made extraordinary sacrifices in living without their treasured objects for such an extended length of time. In addition to the individuals acknowledged on the list of lenders, we wish to recognize the following institutional colleagues for their kind assistance: Kerry Brougher, acting director and chief curator, the Hirshhorn Museum and Sculpture Garden, Washington, D.C.; Hugh M. Davies, David C. Copley Director, the Museum of Contemporary Art, San Diego; and Madeleine Grynsztejn, Pritzker Director, the Museum of Contemporary Art, Chicago. For their efforts in facilitating important loans we acknowledge Nancy Rosen and Mary Zlot; in addition we thank Sarah Gilmore, Laura Satersmoen, Jennifer Smith, and Robyn Wiley.

After its premiere in San Francisco the exhibition will embark on a lengthy international tour; we extend our warmest thanks to our valued partners at each of the tour venues: Dr. Marla Price, director, and Michael Auping, chief curator, the Modern Art Museum of Fort Worth; Glenn D. Lowry, director, and Klaus Biesenbach, chief curator of media, the Museum of Modern Art, New York; Dr. Klaus Albrecht Schröder, director, the Albertina, Vienna; James Snyder, Anne and Jerome Fisher Director, the Israel Museum, Jerusalem; and Gijs van Tuyl, director, the Stedelijk Museum, Amsterdam.

Generous support for *William Kentridge: Five Themes* is provided by the Koret Foundation; we extend our deepest thanks to Jeffrey A. Farber, the foundation's chief executive officer, and to SFMOMA trustee Richard L. Greene, who played a key role in facilitating the grant. Additional support is provided by the National Endowment for the Arts. We are grateful to both organizations for helping us bring this exhibition to audiences worldwide. The San Francisco presentation is made possible by generous support from Doris and Donald Fisher, the Mimi and Peter Haas Fund, and Nancy and Steven H. Oliver. The West Palm Beach presentation is made possible in part through the generosity of Mr. and Mrs. Ralph Saltzman, the Milton and Sheila Fine Endowment for Contemporary Art, The Dr. Henry and Lois Foster Endowment for the Exhibition of Contemporary Art, and The Contemporary and Modern Art Council of the Norton Museum of Art. Sydelle Meyer of Palm Beach kindly supported the extensive curatorial travel necessary to research the exhibition.

This ambitious project would never have seen completion without the assistance of Anne McIlleron, Natalie Dembo, and Linda Leibowitz at the artist's studio in Johannesburg. We are grateful to Anne in particular for patiently fielding innumerable queries and scouring the archives for the information and images so crucial to this endeavor. John Hodgkiss kindly undertook new photography of Kentridge's films expressly for this catalogue; we thank him for his striking shots of the projections and for his help in ensuring the color accuracy of the book's reproductions. Catherine Meyburgh worked closely with the artist to produce the DVD that is packaged with this publication; we are delighted to be able to share this remarkable video selection, which includes never-before-seen footage of Kentridge at work in the studio, a variety of explorations and studies, and excerpts from his finished films. Thanks are also due to Ronald Hallgren and Jonas Lundquist for their work on the programming and mechanics of *Preparing the Flute* and *Black Box/Chambre Noire,* and for training our technicians to install and maintain these complex works.

These acknowledgments can only conclude with an expression of deepest gratitude to our friend William Kentridge, who has proven himself, as always, a true joy to work with. William has been a thoughtful, generous, and creative collaborator over the several years that this exhibition has been in the making, and we are honored to have had the opportunity to work with him on this project. We thank him for his many contributions to the success of this exhibition and catalogue, but most importantly for his eloquently moving art.

Neal Benezra
Director
San Francisco Museum of Modern Art

Christina Orr-Cahall
CEO and Director
Norton Museum of Art

1

PARCOURS D'ATELIER

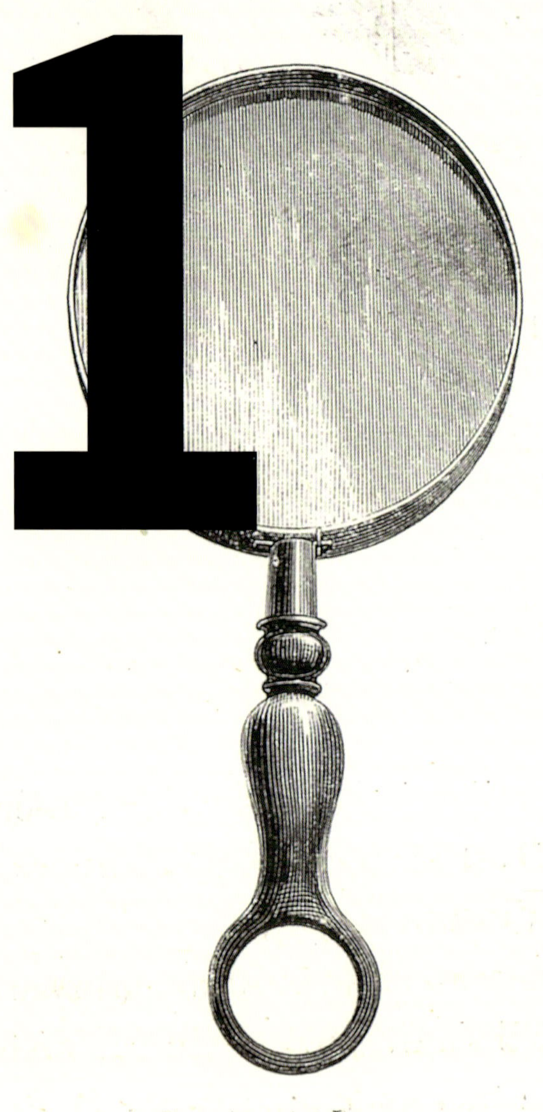

Fig. 83. — Loupe.

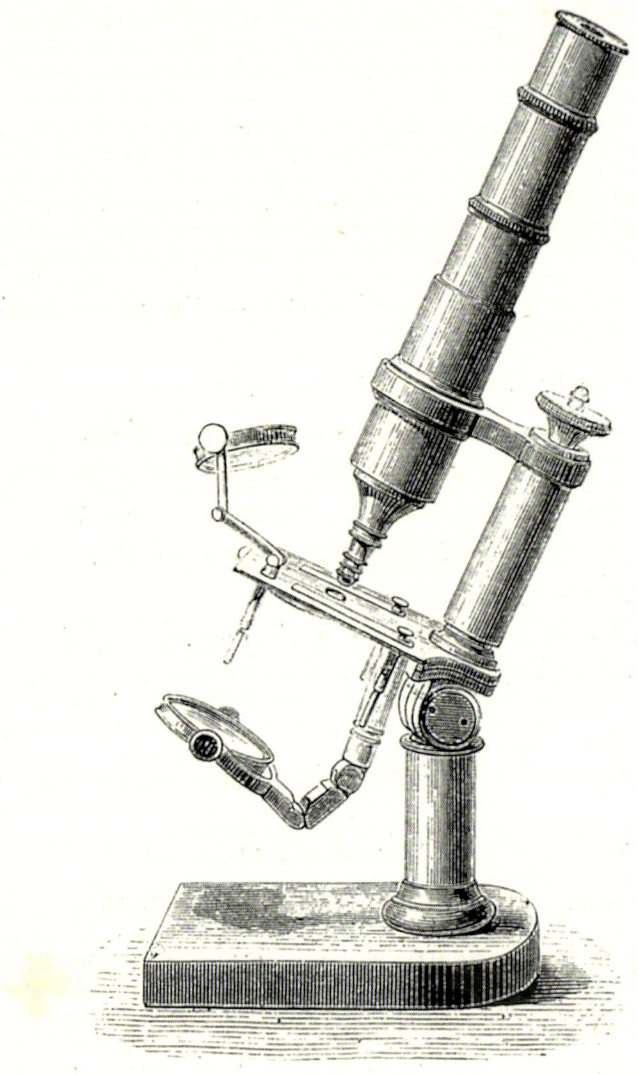

Fig. 84. — Microscope composé.

ARTIST IN THE STUDIO

Walking, thinking, stalking the image. Many of the hours spent in the studio are hours of walking, pacing back and forth across the space gathering the energy, the clarity to make the first mark. It is not so much a period of planning as a time of allowing the ideas surrounding the project to percolate. A space for many different possible trajectories of an image, where sequences can suggest themselves, to be tested as internal projections. This pacing is often in relation to the sheet of paper waiting on the wall. As if the physical presence of the paper is necessary for the internal projections to seem realizable. The physical size and material enforce a scale, a particular starting point, a composition. The myriad of possibilities is called to order. This pacing is sometimes ten minutes, sometimes a morning. (And the pacing is sometimes replaced by sharpening of pencils, gathering of materials, hunting for just the right music—all different forms of productive procrastination.)

It is as if before the work can begin (the visible finished work of the drawing, film, or sculpture), a different, invisible work must be done. A kind of minimalist theater work involving an empty space, a protagonist (the artist walking, or pacing, or stuck immobile), and an antagonist (the paper on the wall). This work, these studio walks, are the subject of the films in *7 Fragments for Georges Méliès*.

The studio is the traditional home of the image, and so works about the studio become about both the activity and the history of image making. The drawings of Anne getting into the bath are an exploration of cinema drawing—successive drawings like successive frames of a film—but also a continuation of Edgar Degas and Pierre Bonnard's images of naked women in the bath (more specifically Bonnard, looking at his wife as model): the model as intimate rather than allegorical, objective, or idealized.

The *Méliès* fragments are both an homage to the early filmmaker and a series of reflections on the studio as subject. There are a series of variations: the studio as model, the artist as model, and of course the model as model. The studio is the subject but also the canvas.

To make his short films Méliès painted his own backdrops in his studio and performed in front of them. And filmed his performances. The films are the combination of his paintings and his performance. He is simultaneously showman, presenter, and actor, rather like Gustave Courbet in his painting *The Artist's Studio*.

In my short films of walking, catching, and falling, I was thinking back too to the early films of Bruce Nauman in his studio, and of course to the footage of Jackson Pollock dripping his painting into existence.

The studio is an enclosed space, not just physically but also psychically, like an enlarged head; the pacing in the studio is the equivalent of ideas spinning round in one's head, as if the brain is a muscle and can be exercised into fitness, into clarity. So the fragments are the internal noise, each finished fragment a demonstration of those impulses that emerge and are abandoned before the work begins.

Journey to the Moon, the one narrative film, follows the story of Méliès's great *Voyage dans la lune*. In the film I use only those objects and drawings in the studio that had been used in the other *Méliès* fragments, as if they were all the preliminary pacing for the final film. The espresso cups for a telescope, the mocha machine as the rocket ship, the saucer for the moon, negative ants as stars. I discovered that the studio, which I had hoped could be a whole universe, became only the enclosed rocket.

I had made the film hoping to escape the confines of the studio but ended up still stuck inside it, looking out through the window of the rocket ship (i.e., staring at a sheet of black paper pinned to the studio wall). **WK**

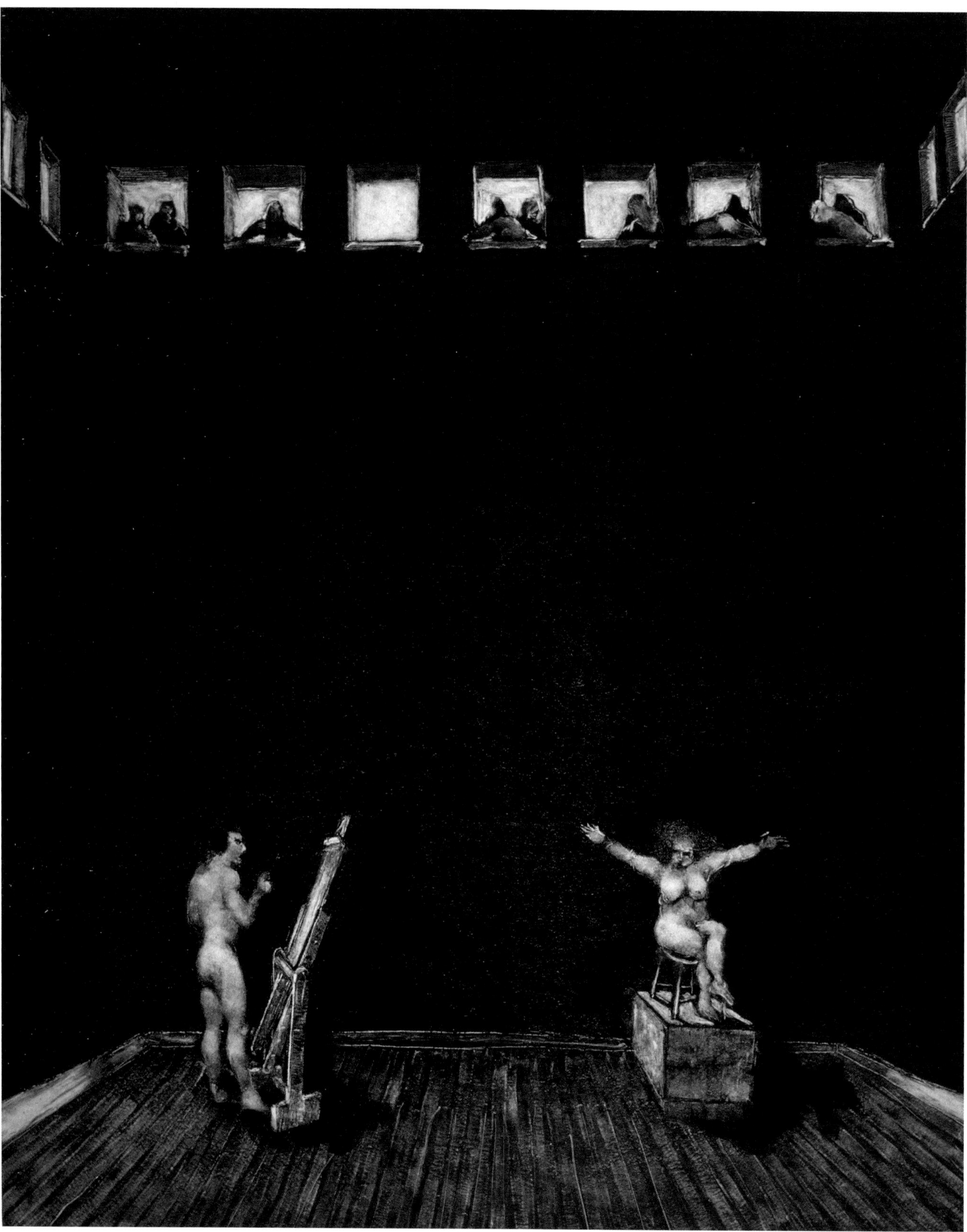

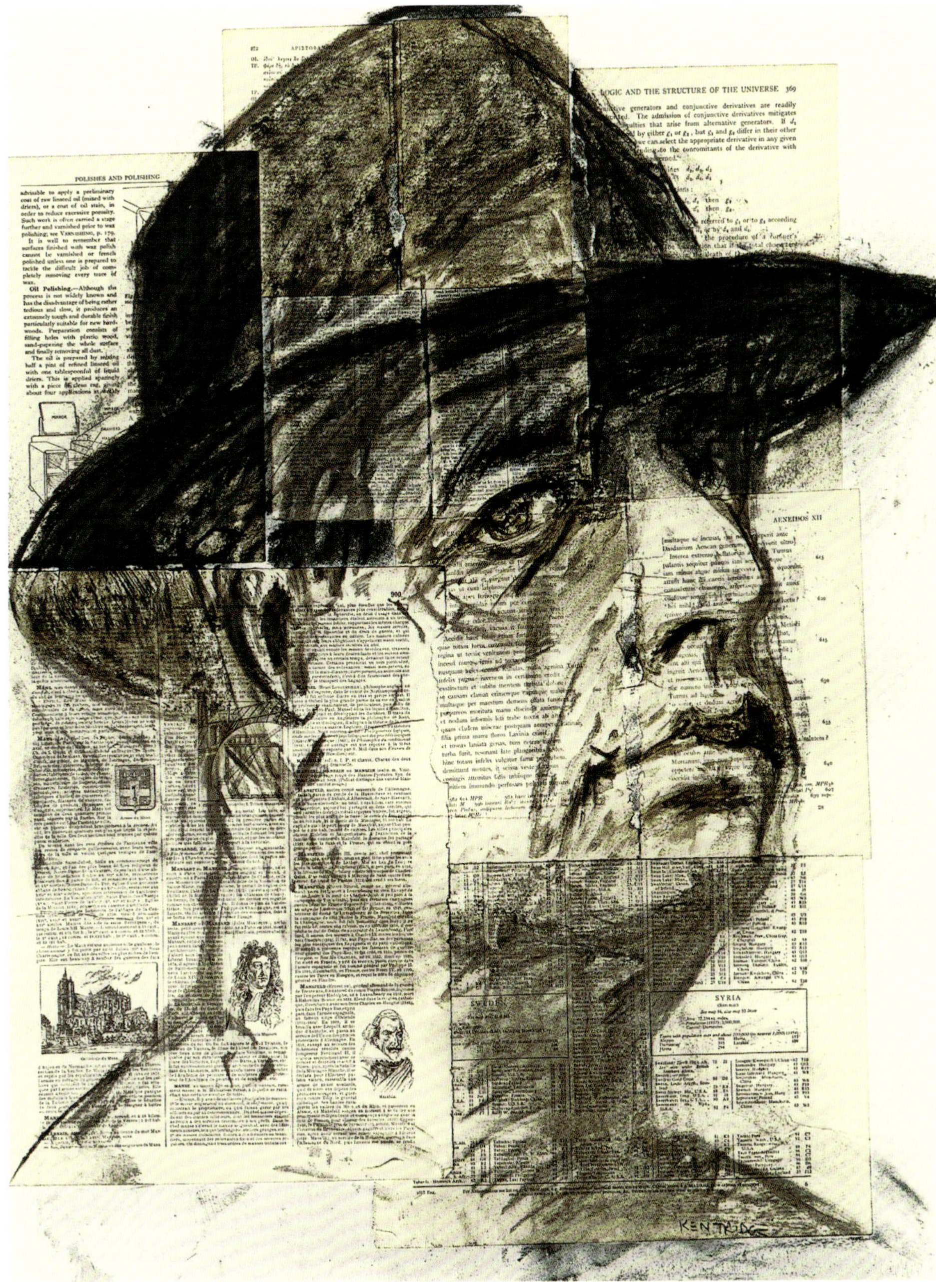

1
***Artist and Model*, from the series *Pit*, 1979**
Monotype
27 1/2 x 19 2/3 in. (70 x 50 cm)
Collection of the artist, courtesy Marian Goodman Gallery, New York, and Goodman Gallery, Johannesburg

2
***Self-portrait (Testing the Library)*, 1998**
Charcoal on paper
26 x 20 in. (66 x 51 cm)
Collection of Brenda Potter and Michael Sandler

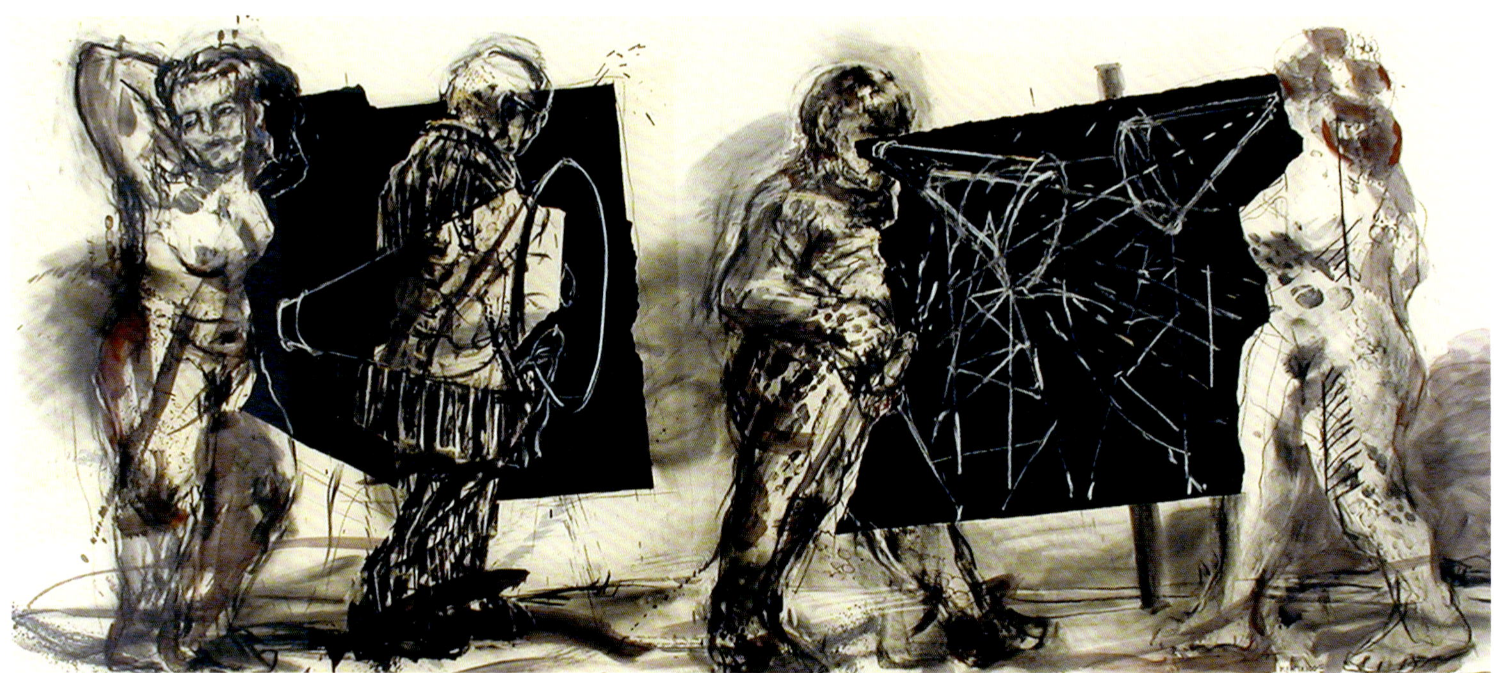

3
Untitled **[Artist and Model Drawings], 2001**
Gouache, dry pigment, charcoal, and pastel on paper
42 1/8 x 100 3/8 in. (107 x 255 cm)
Collection of Jennifer and David Stockman

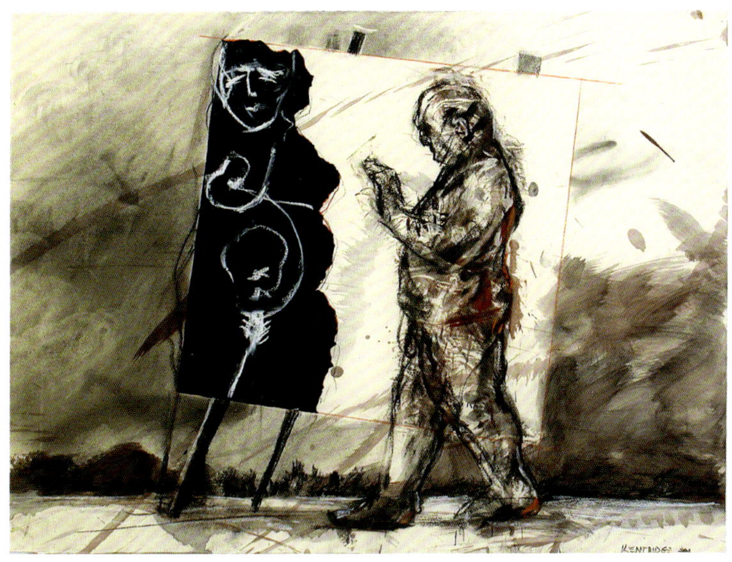

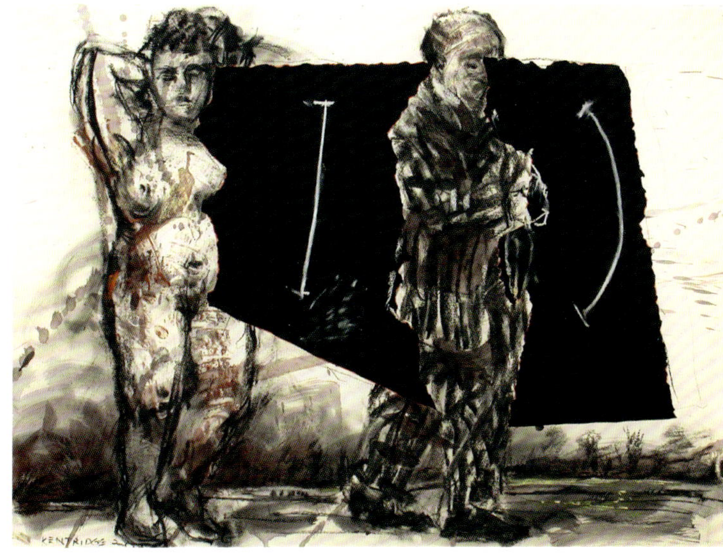

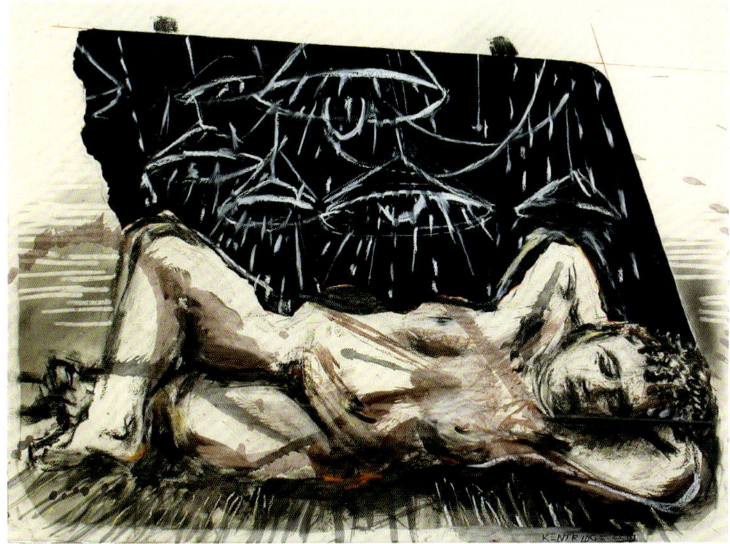

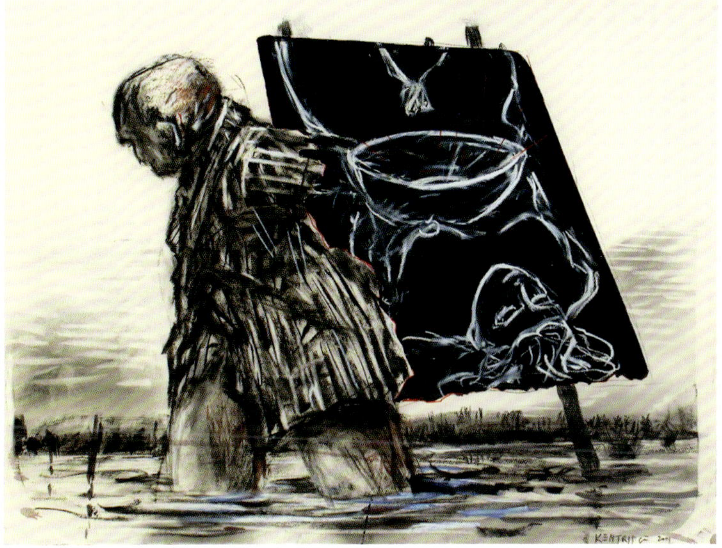

4
***Untitled* [Artist and Model Drawings], 2001**
Gouache, dry pigment, charcoal, and pastel on paper
22 x 29 7/8 in. (55.9 x 75.9 cm)
Collection of Lisa and John Miller

5
***Untitled* [Artist and Model Drawings], 2001**
Gouache, dry pigment, charcoal, and pastel on paper
22 x 29 7/8 in. (55.9 x 75.9 cm)
Collection of Sally and Michael Gordon

6
***Untitled* [Artist and Model Drawings], 2001**
Gouache, dry pigment, charcoal, and pastel on paper
22 x 29 7/8 in. (55.9 x 75.9 cm)
Collection of Sally and Michael Gordon

7
***Untitled* [Artist and Model Drawings], 2001**
Gouache, dry pigment, charcoal, and pastel on paper
22 x 29 7/8 in. (55.9 x 75.9 cm)
Collection of Heidi L. Steiger

8–13
***Invisible Mending*, from *7 Fragments for Georges Méliès*, 2003**
35mm and 16mm animated film transferred to video, 1:20 min.
Collection of the artist, courtesy Marian Goodman Gallery, New York, and Goodman Gallery, Johannesburg

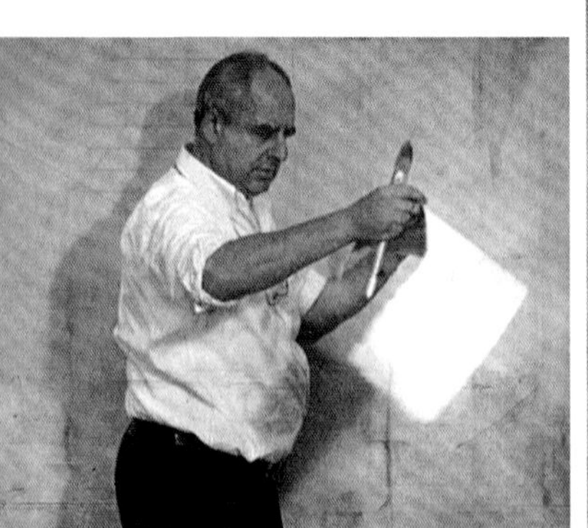

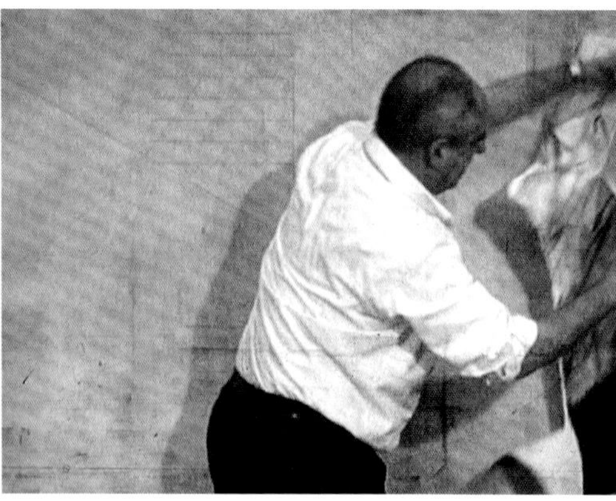

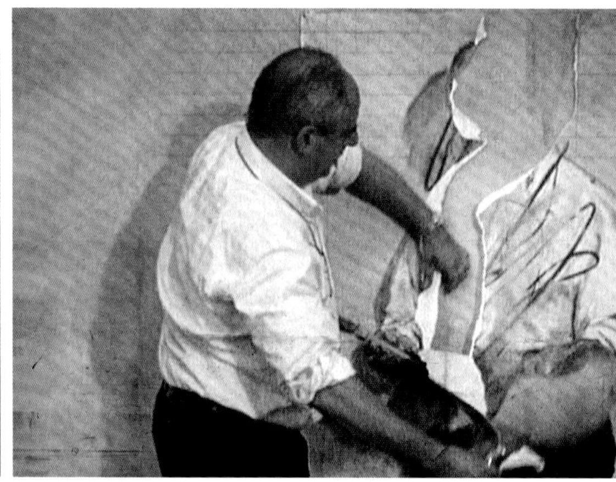

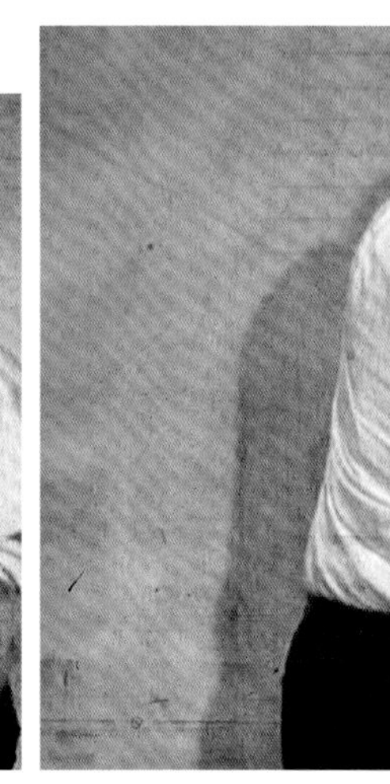

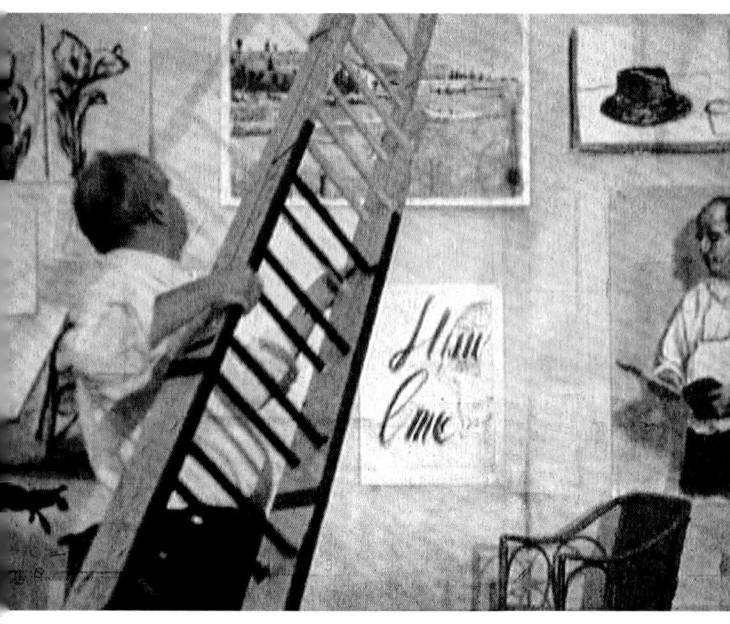

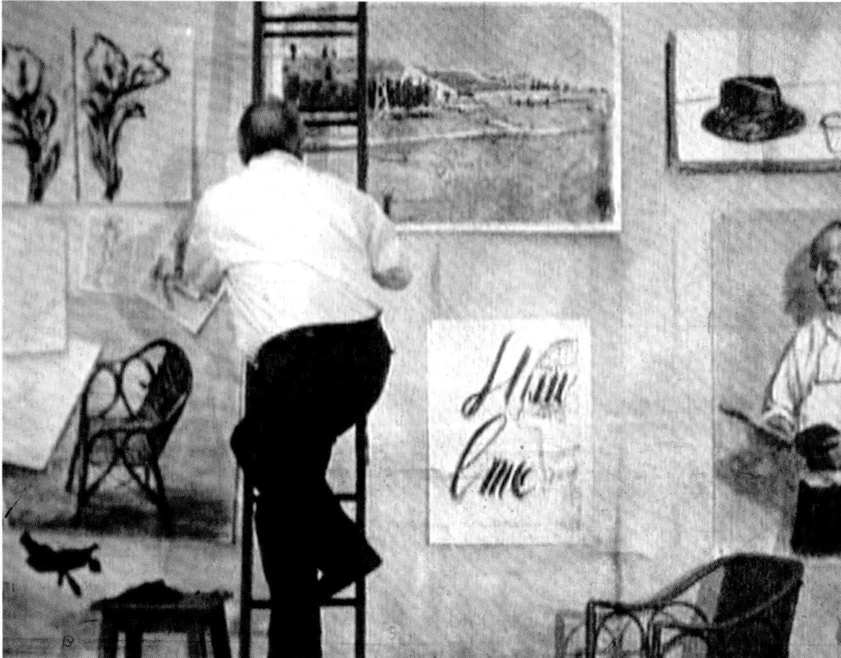

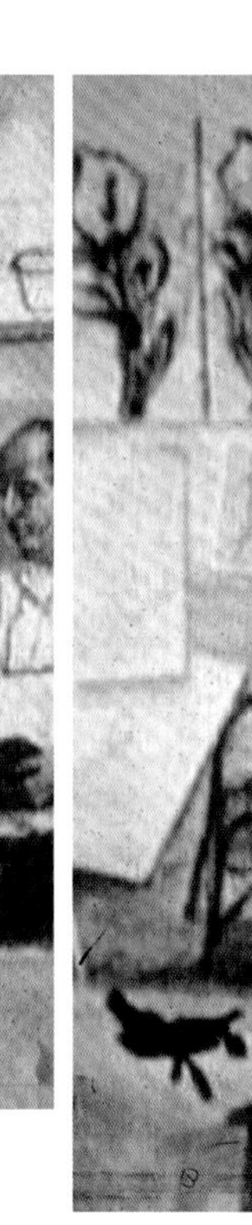

14–17
***Balancing Act*, from *7 Fragments for Georges Méliès*, 2003**
35mm and 16mm animated film transferred to video, 1:20 min.
Collection of the artist, courtesy Marian Goodman Gallery, New York, and Goodman Gallery, Johannesburg

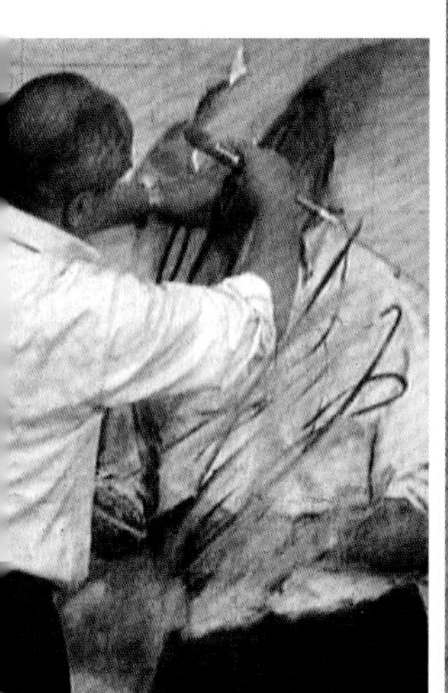

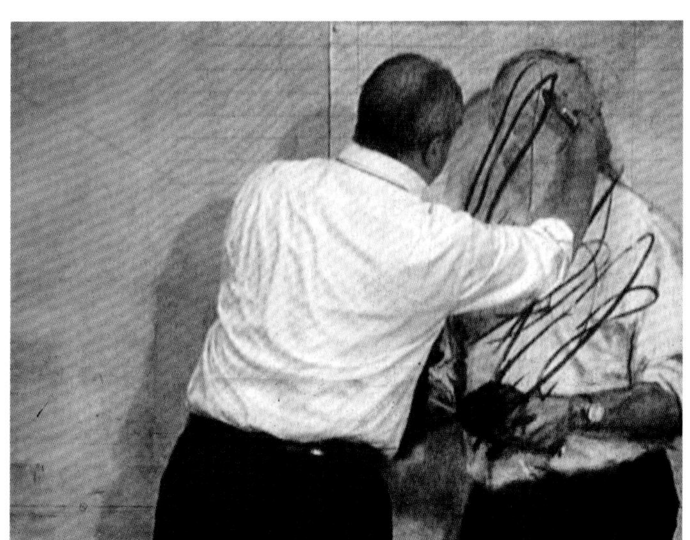

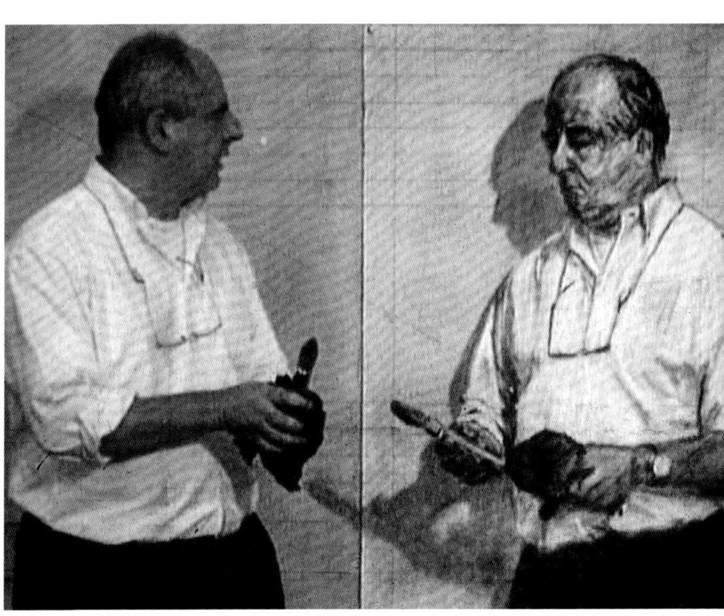

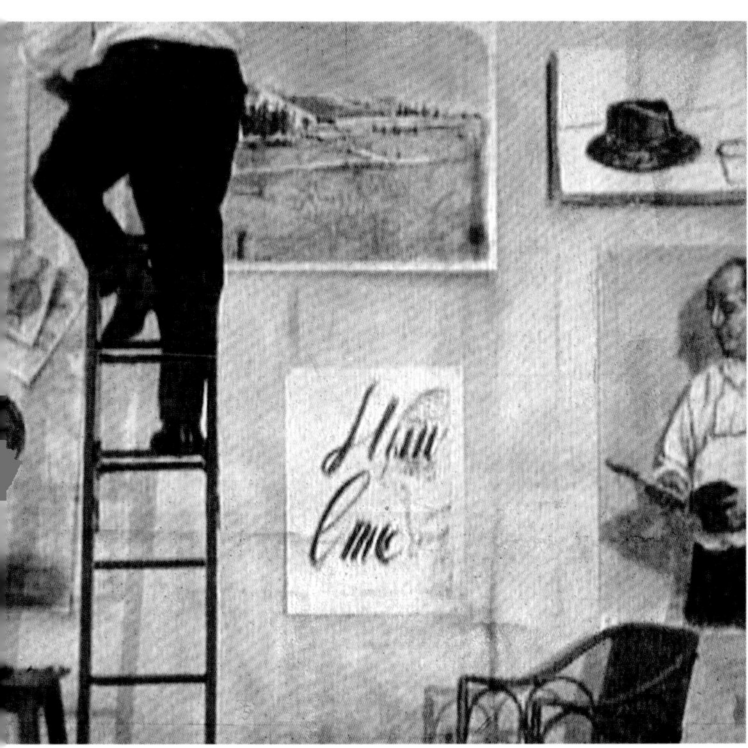

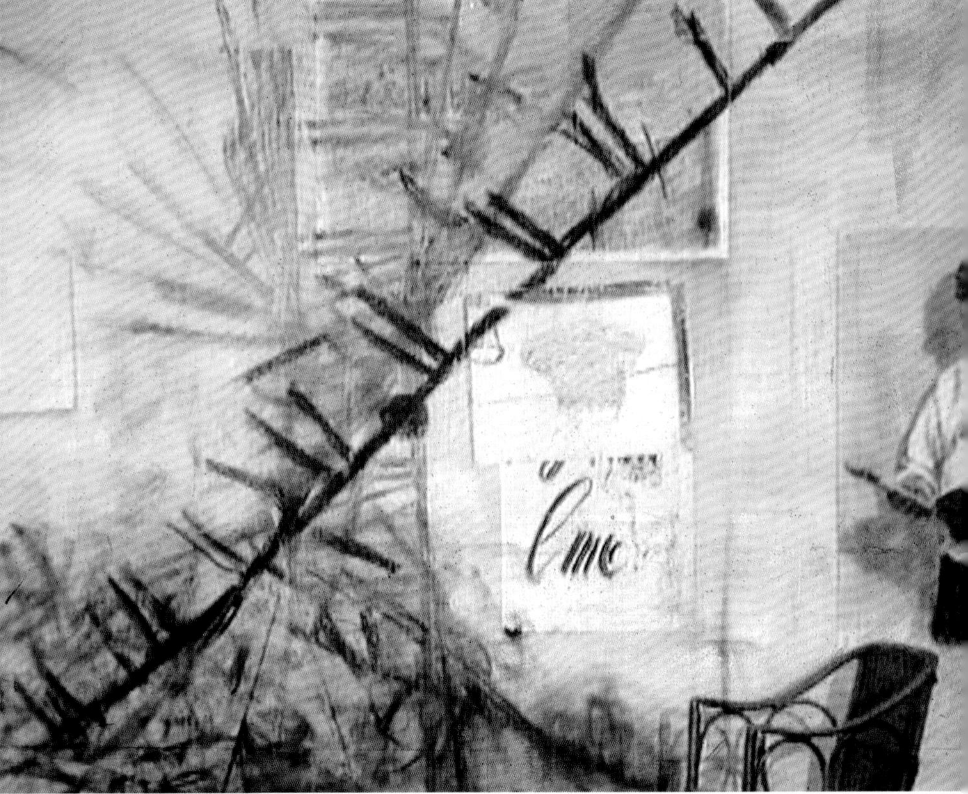

18–23
***Tabula Rasa I*, from *7 Fragments for Georges Méliès*, 2003**
35mm animated film transferred to video, 2:50 min.
Collection of the artist, courtesy Marian Goodman Gallery, New York, and Goodman Gallery, Johannesburg

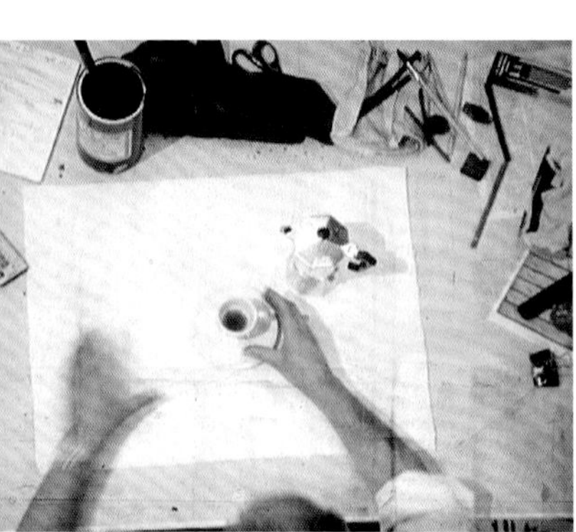
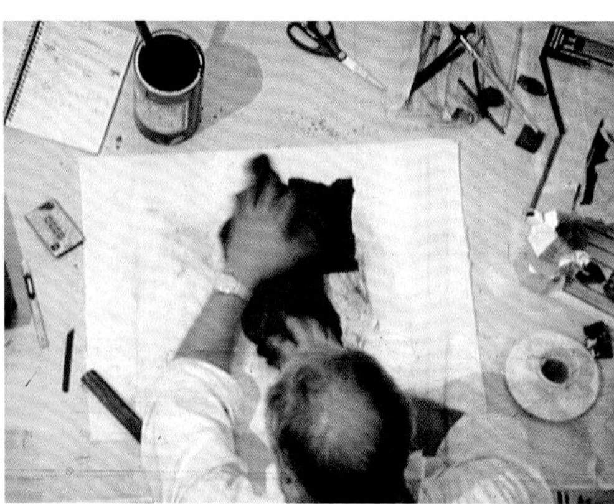
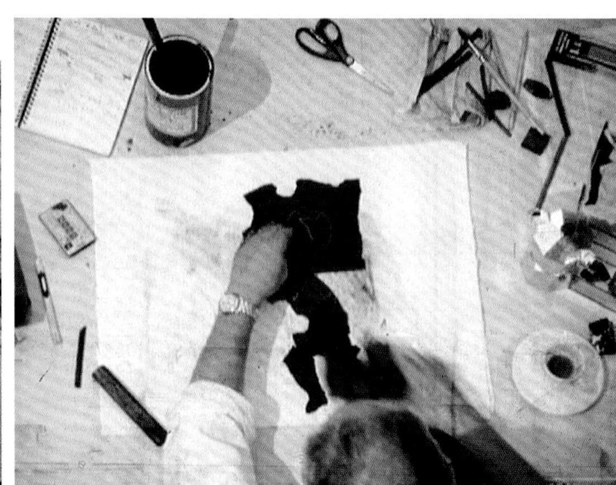
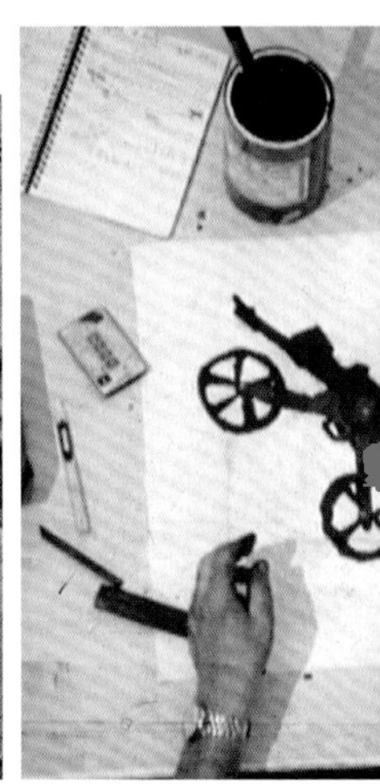
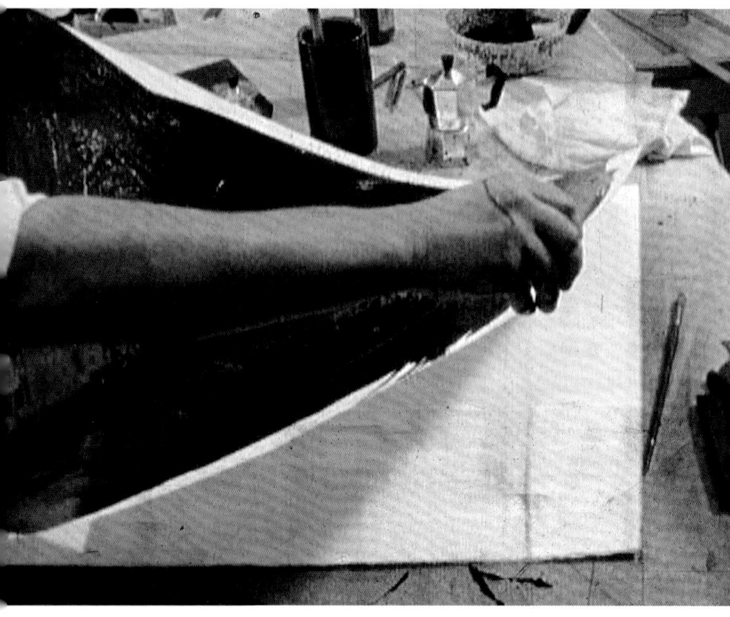
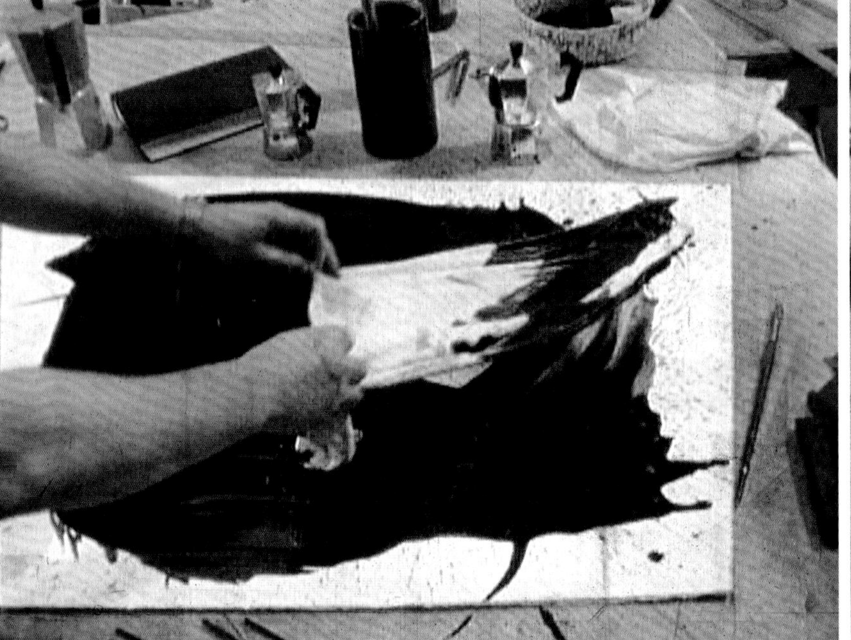

24–27
***Tabula Rasa II*, from *7 Fragments for Georges Méliès*, 2003**
35mm animated film transferred to video, 2:29 min.
Collection of the artist, courtesy Marian Goodman Gallery, New York, and Goodman Gallery, Johannesburg

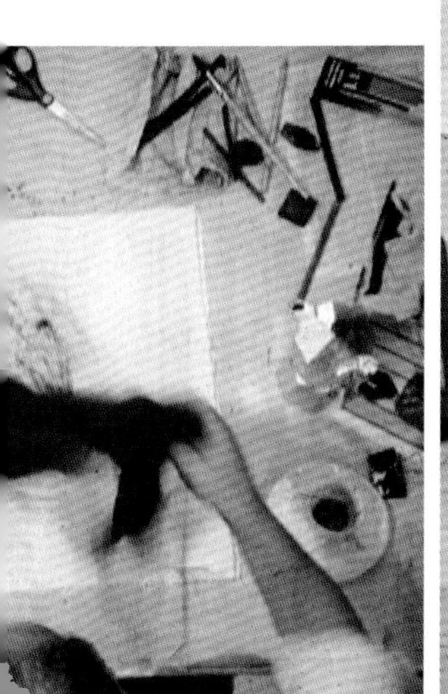

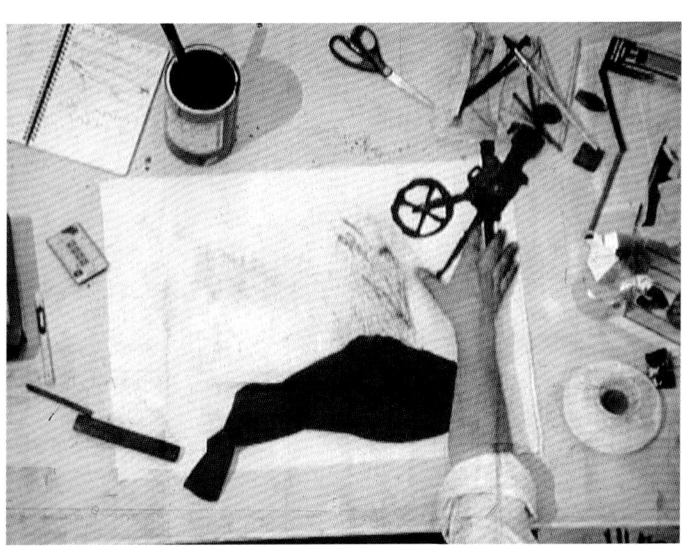

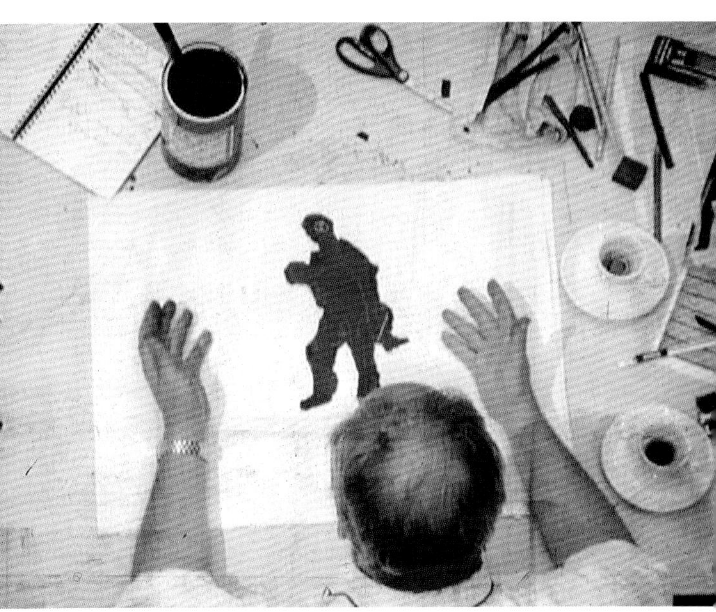

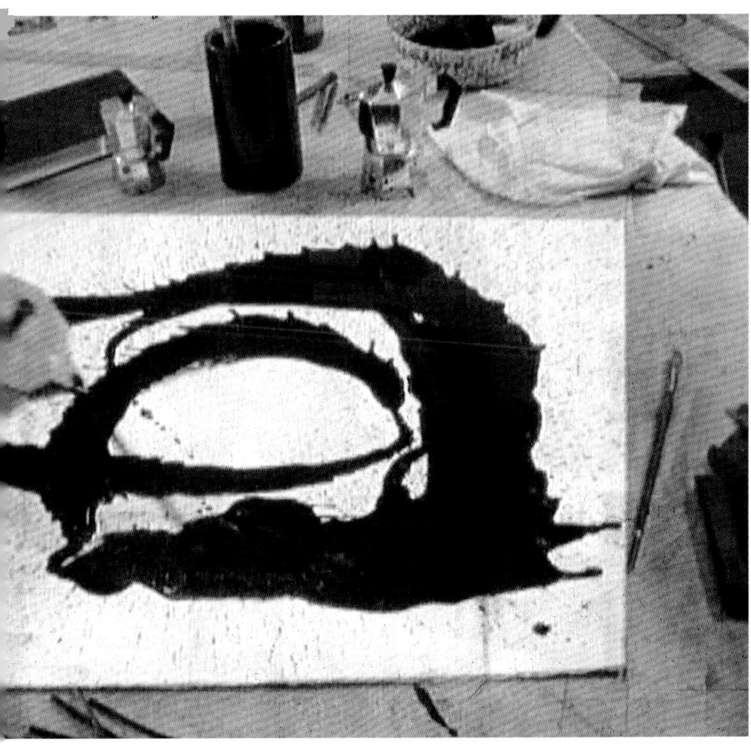

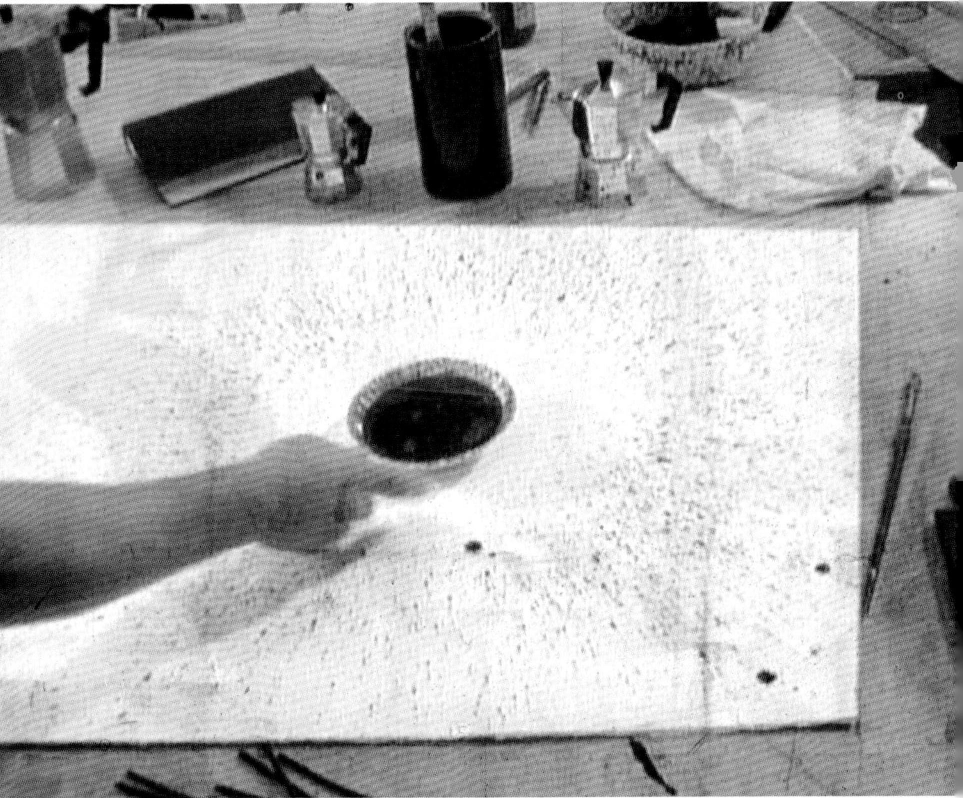

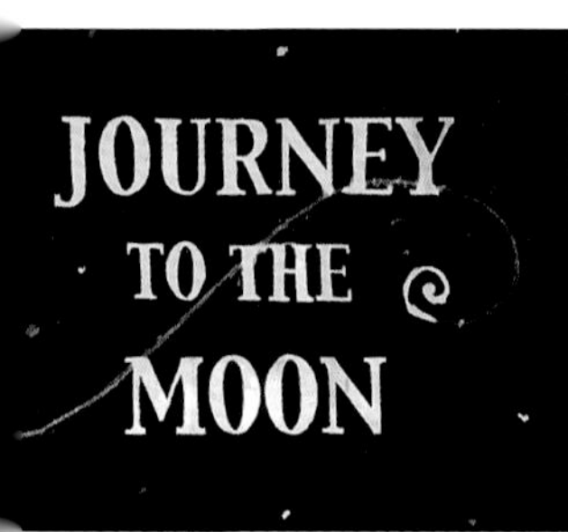
JOURNEY
TO THE
MOON

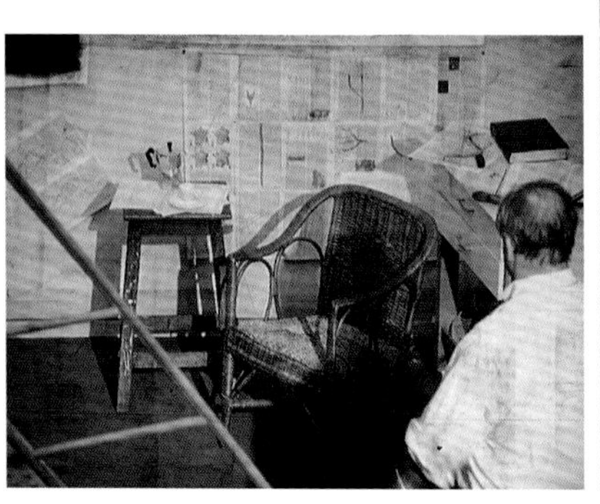

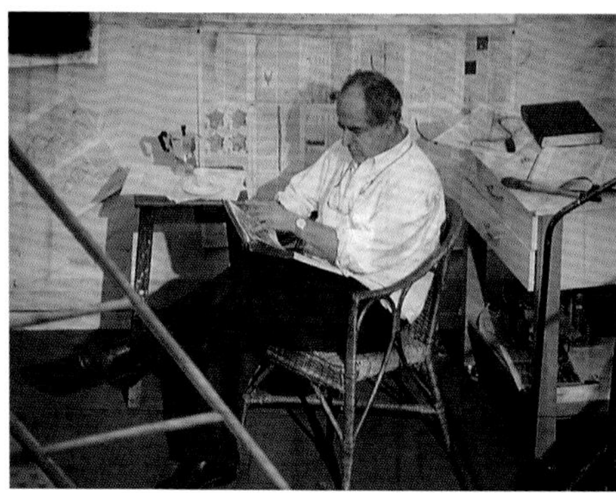

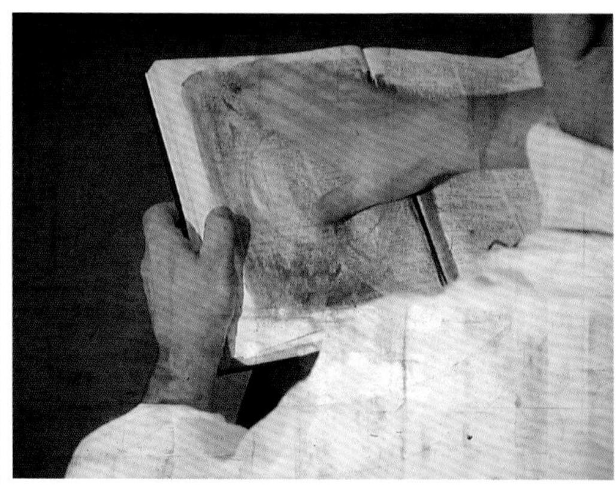

28–47 (THESE AND FOLLOWING PAGES)

***Journey to the Moon*, 2003**

35mm and 16mm animated film transferred to video, 7:10 min.

Collection of the artist, courtesy Marian Goodman Gallery, New York, and Goodman Gallery, Johannesburg

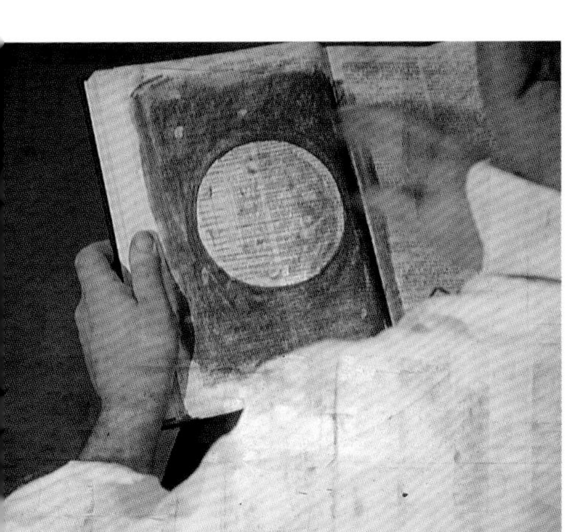

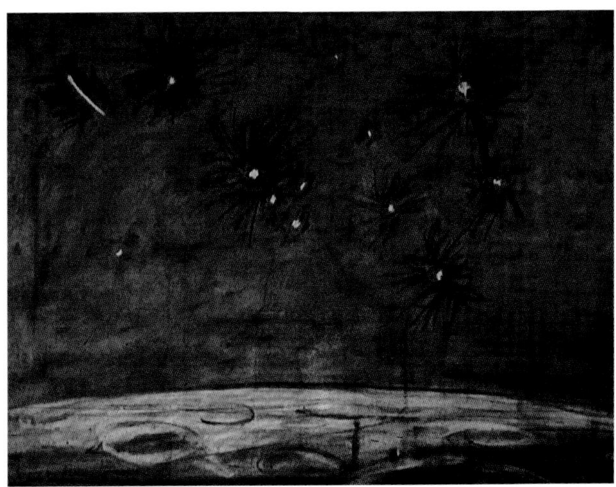

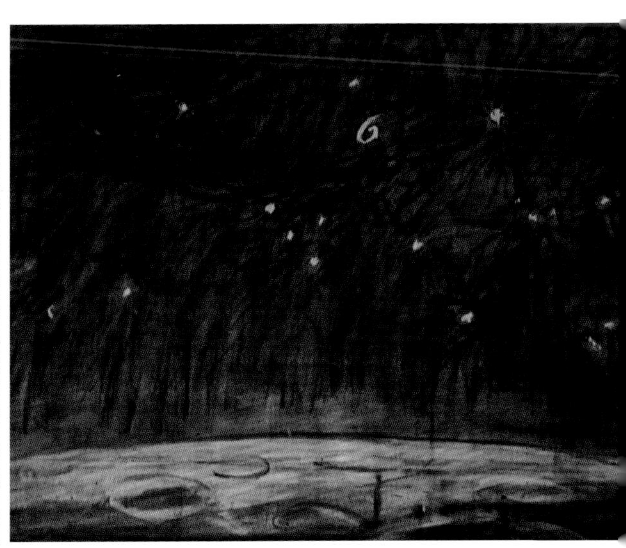

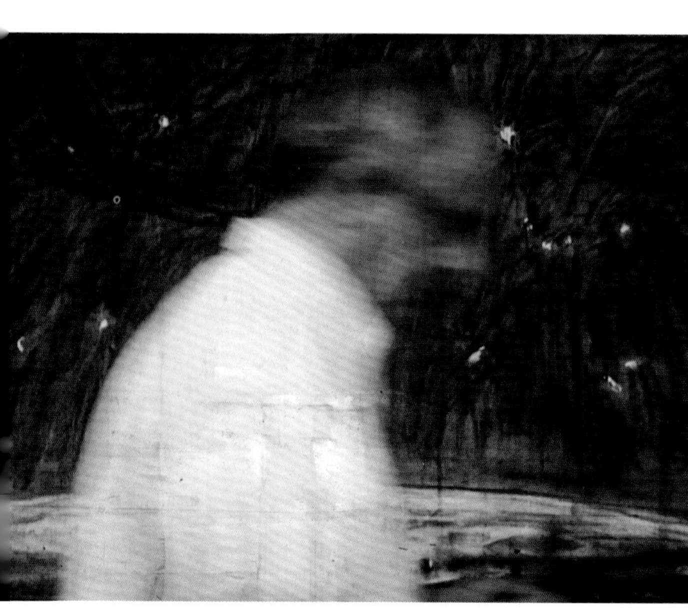

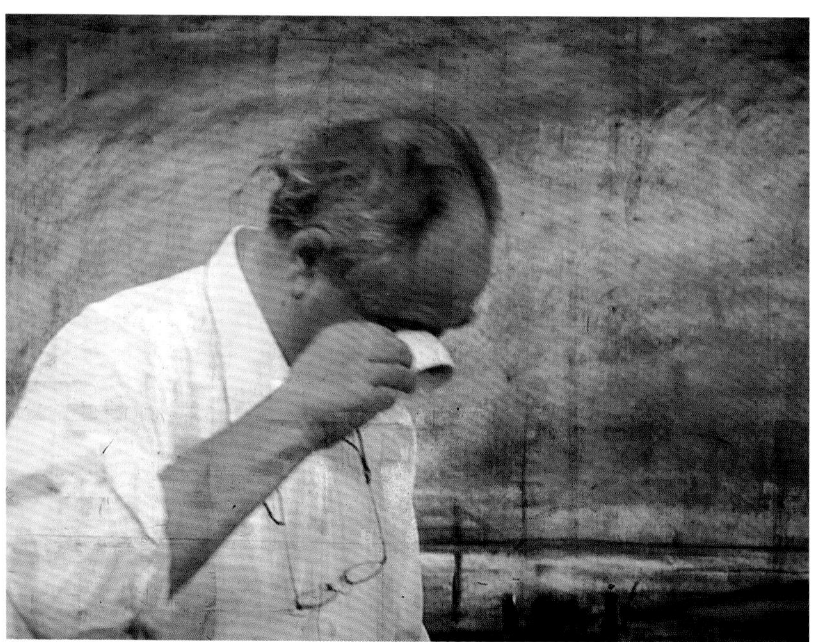

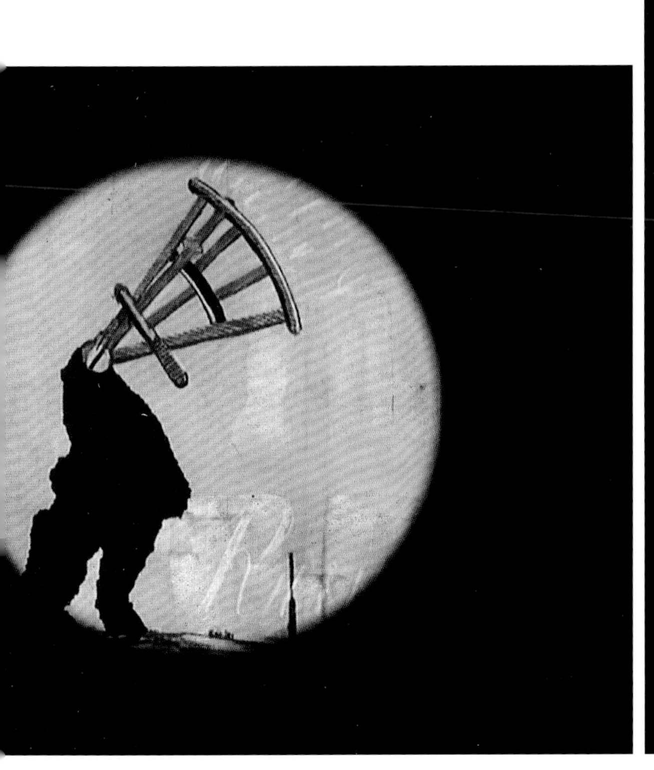

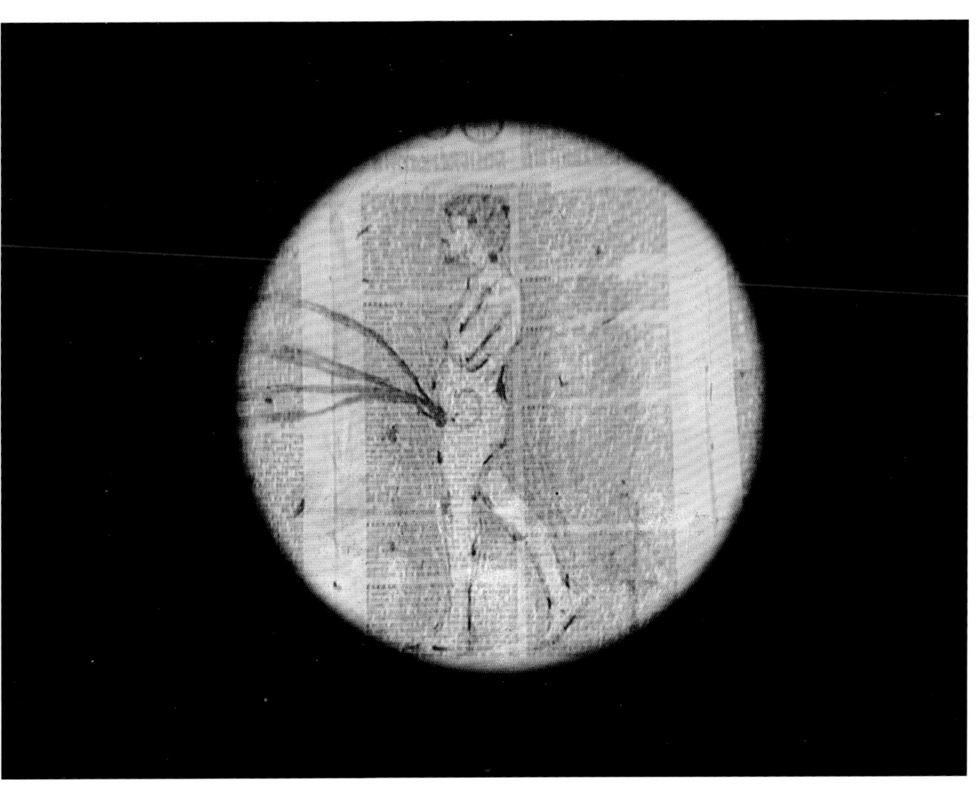

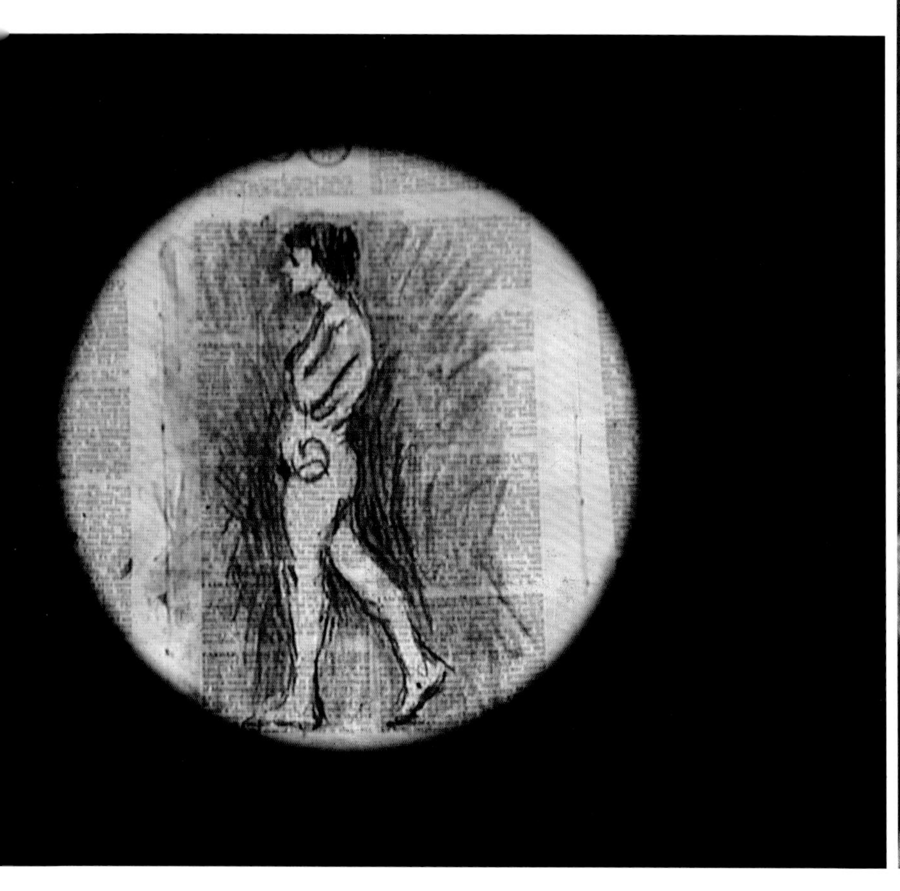

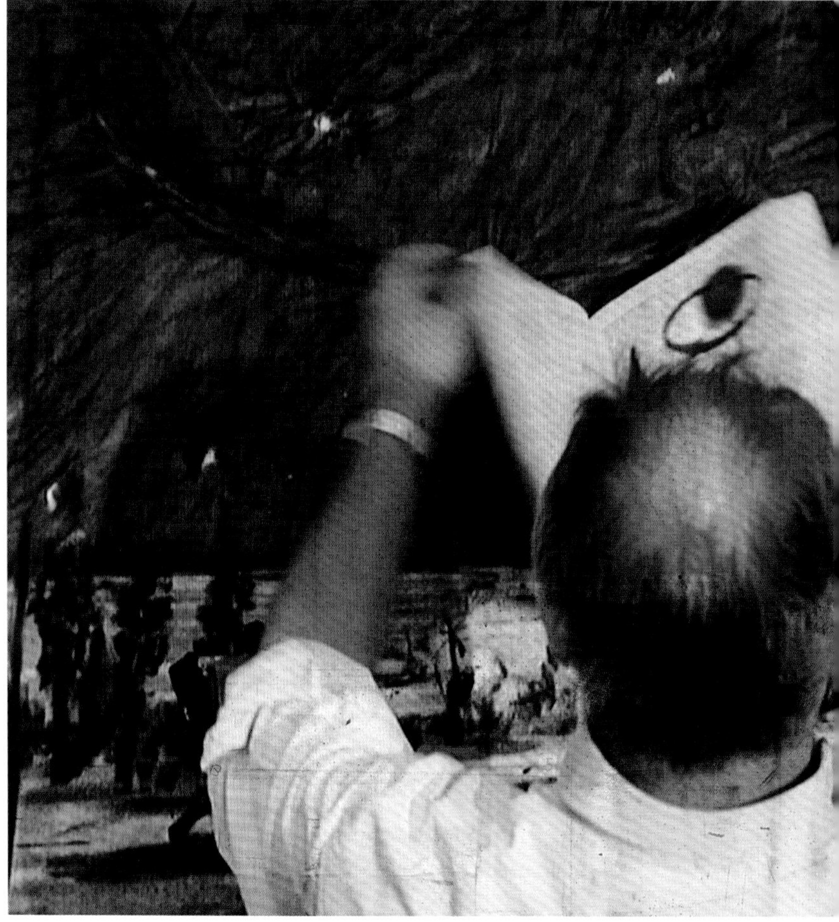

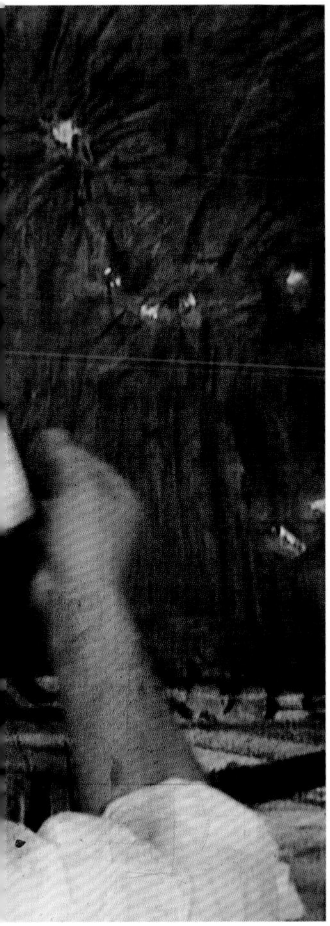

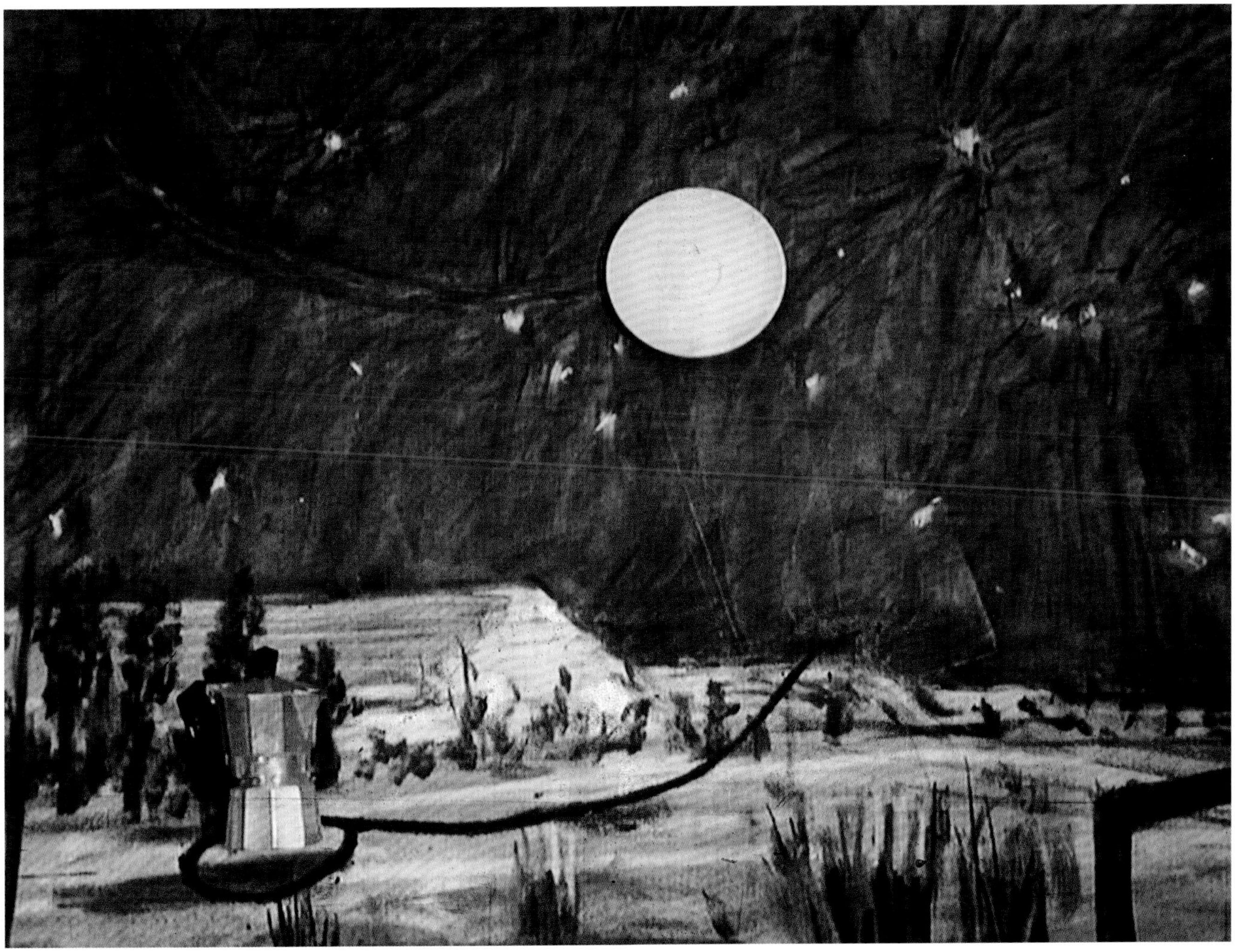

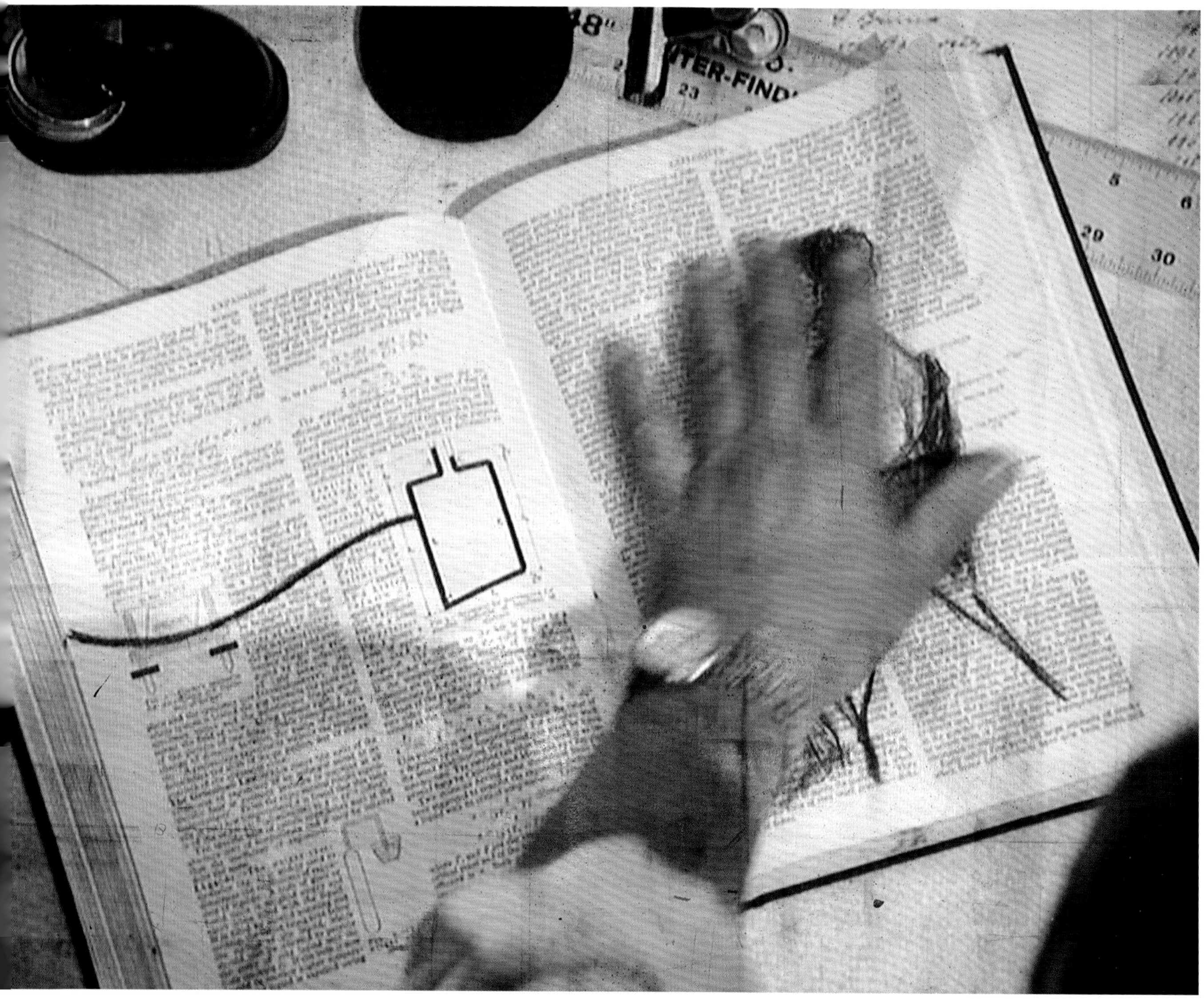

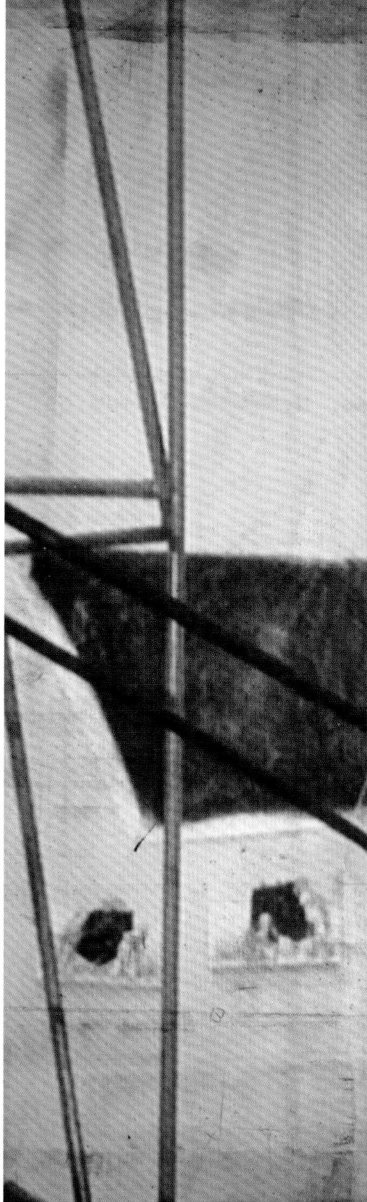

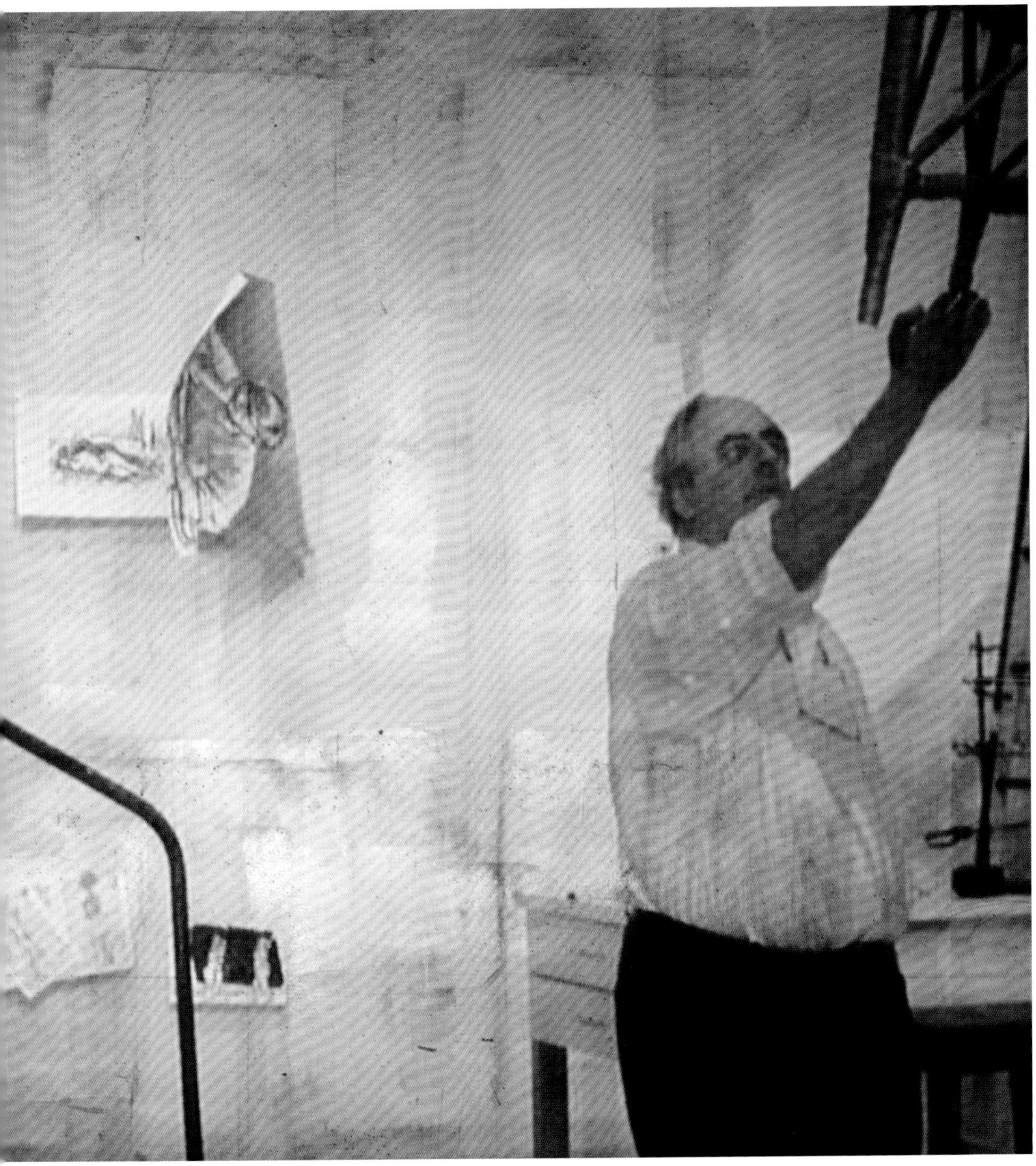

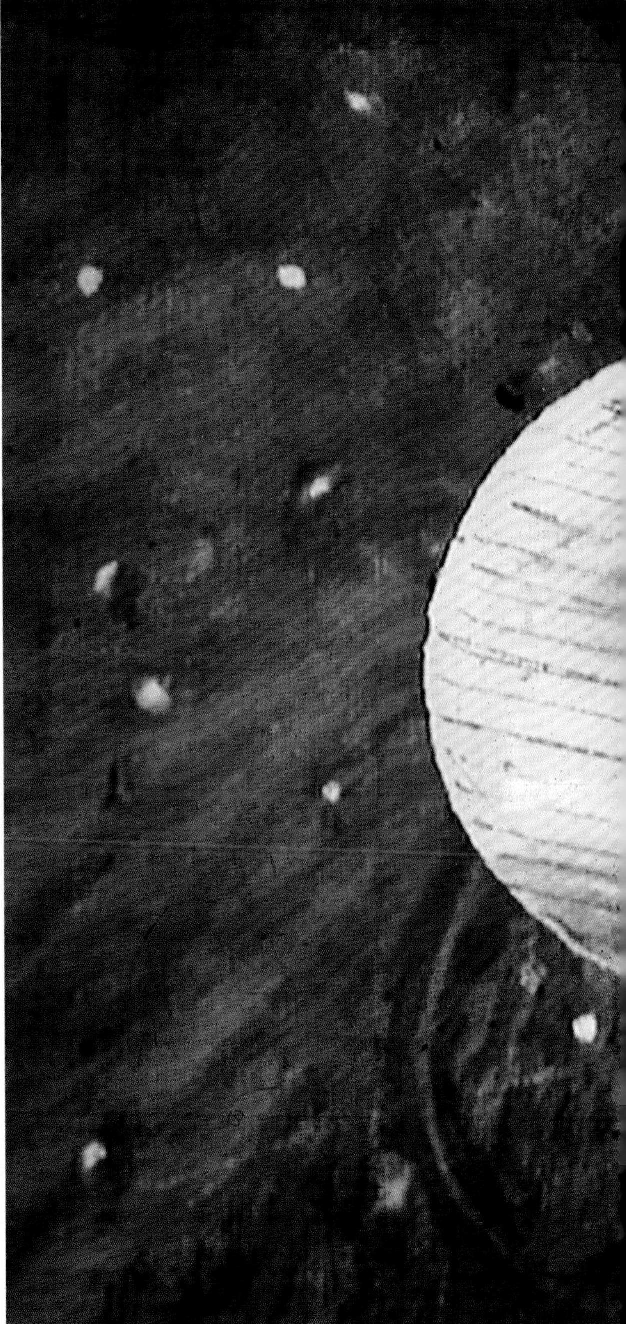

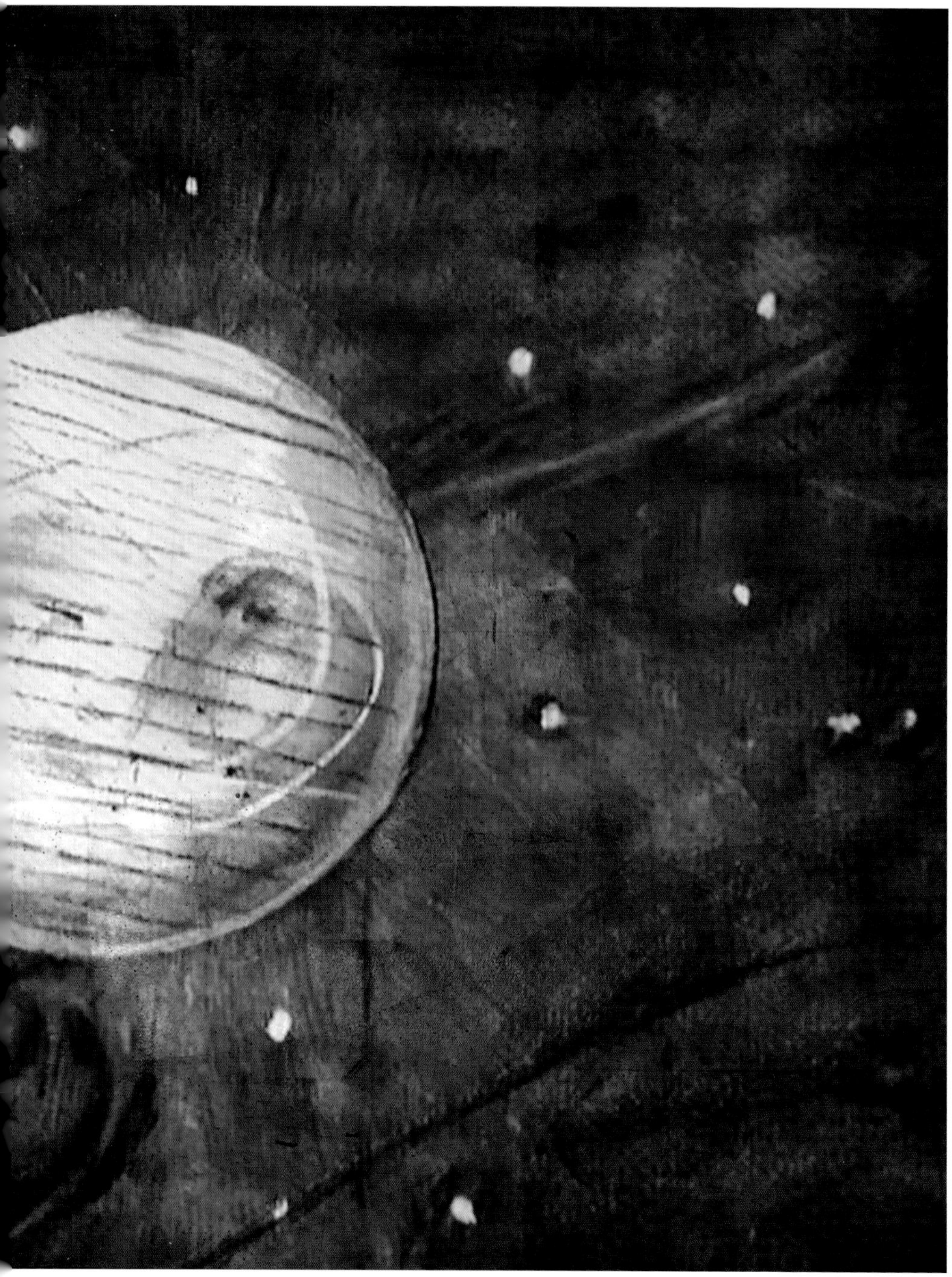

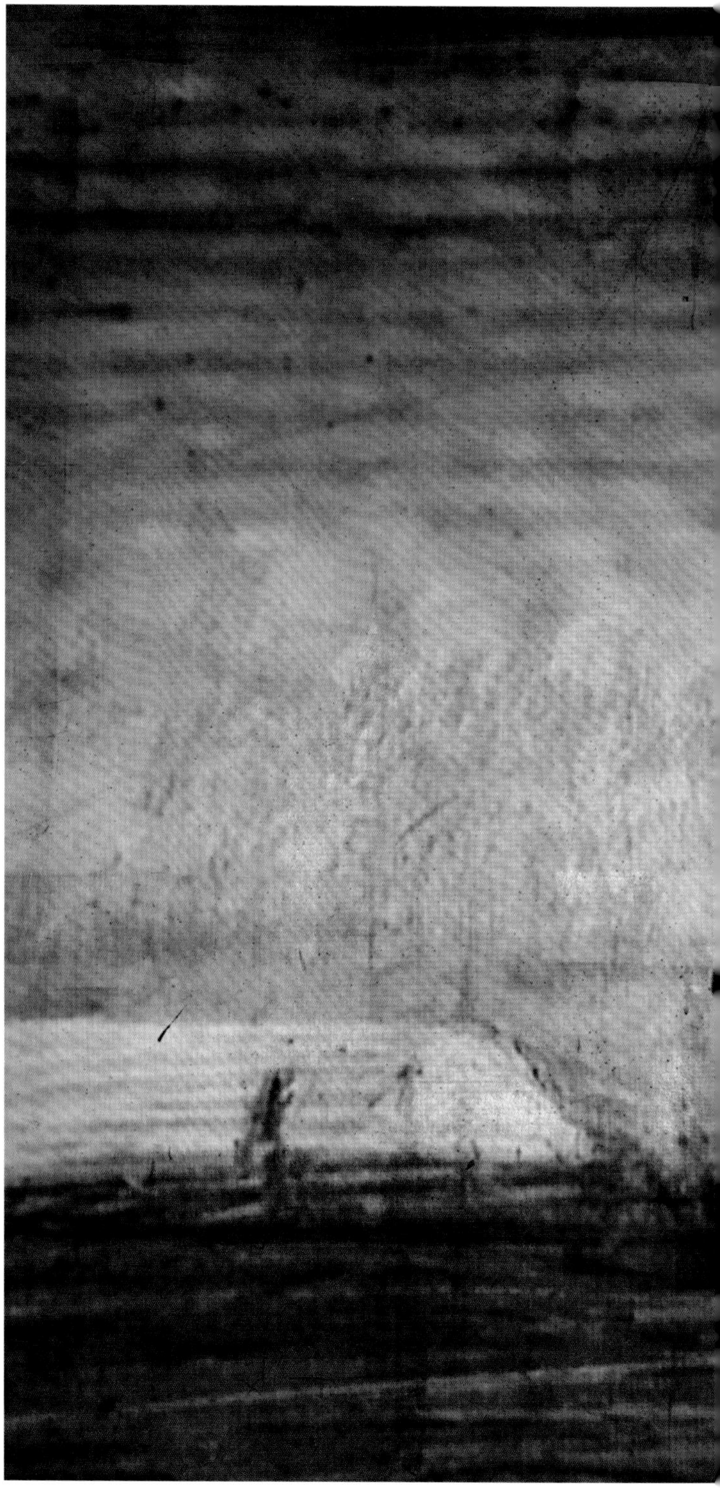

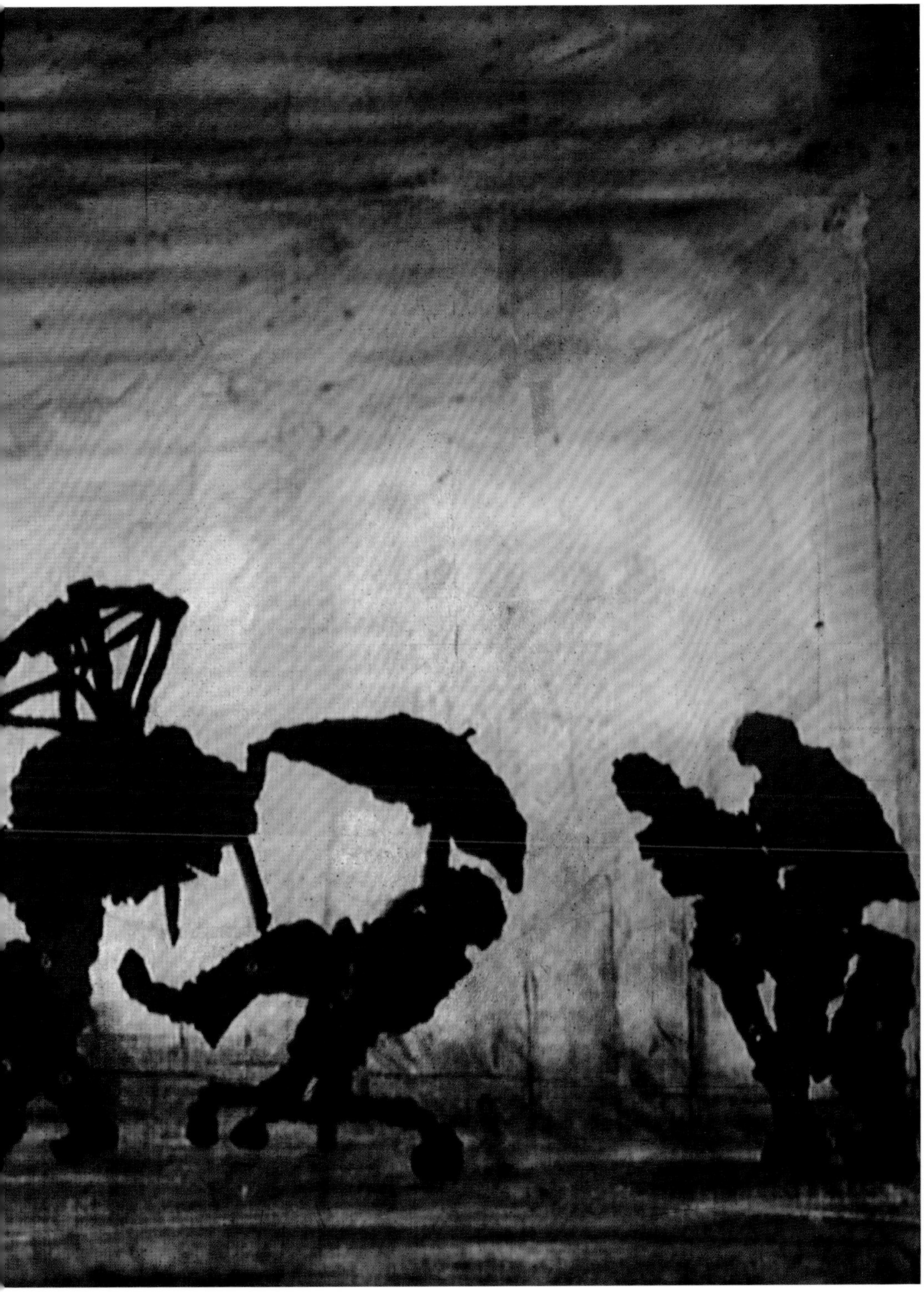

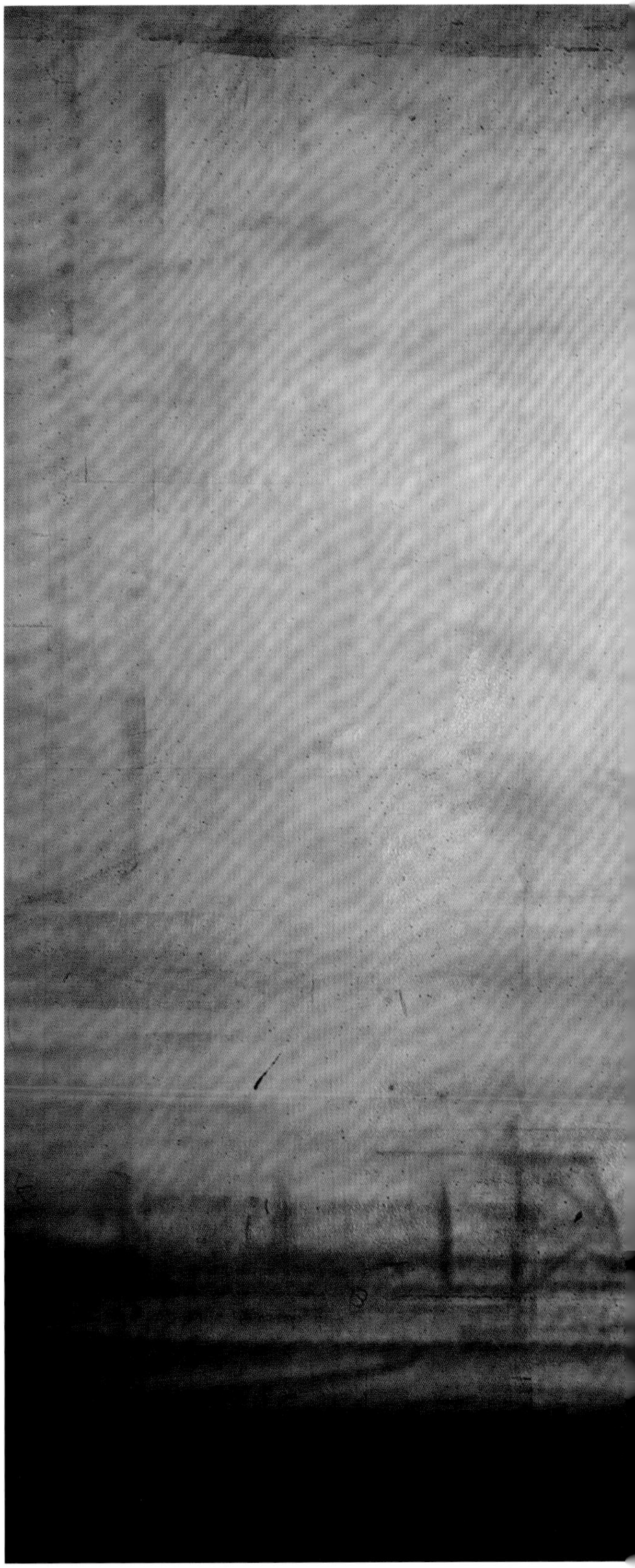

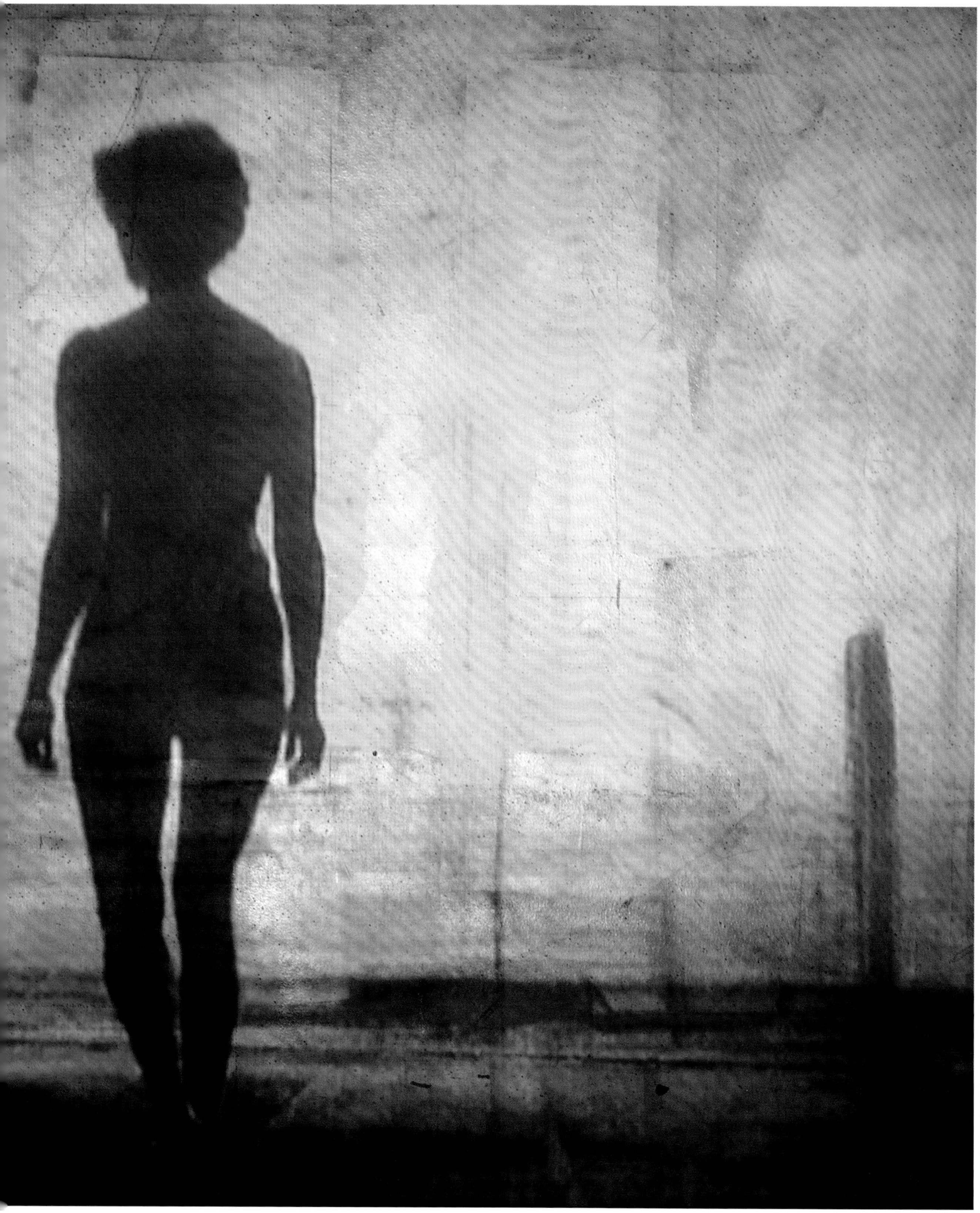

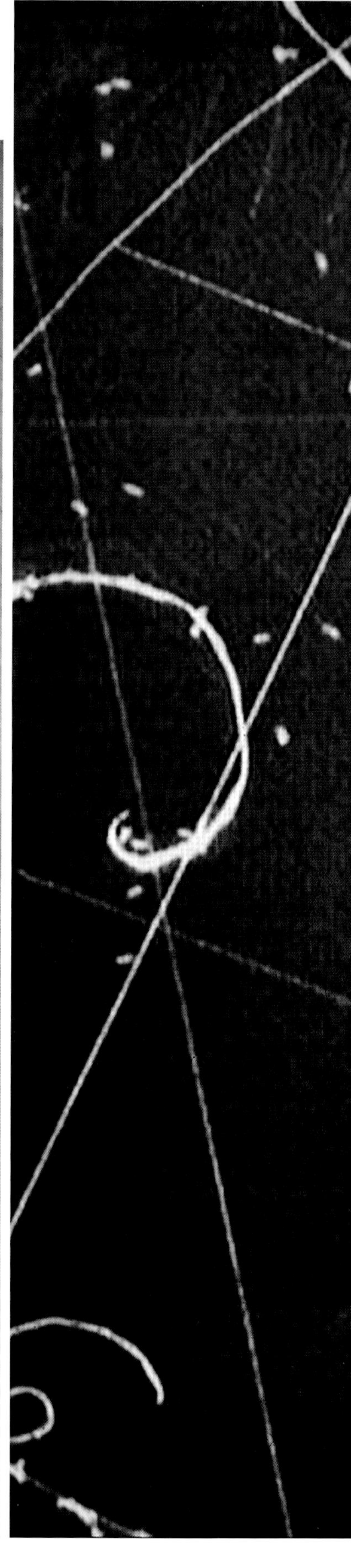

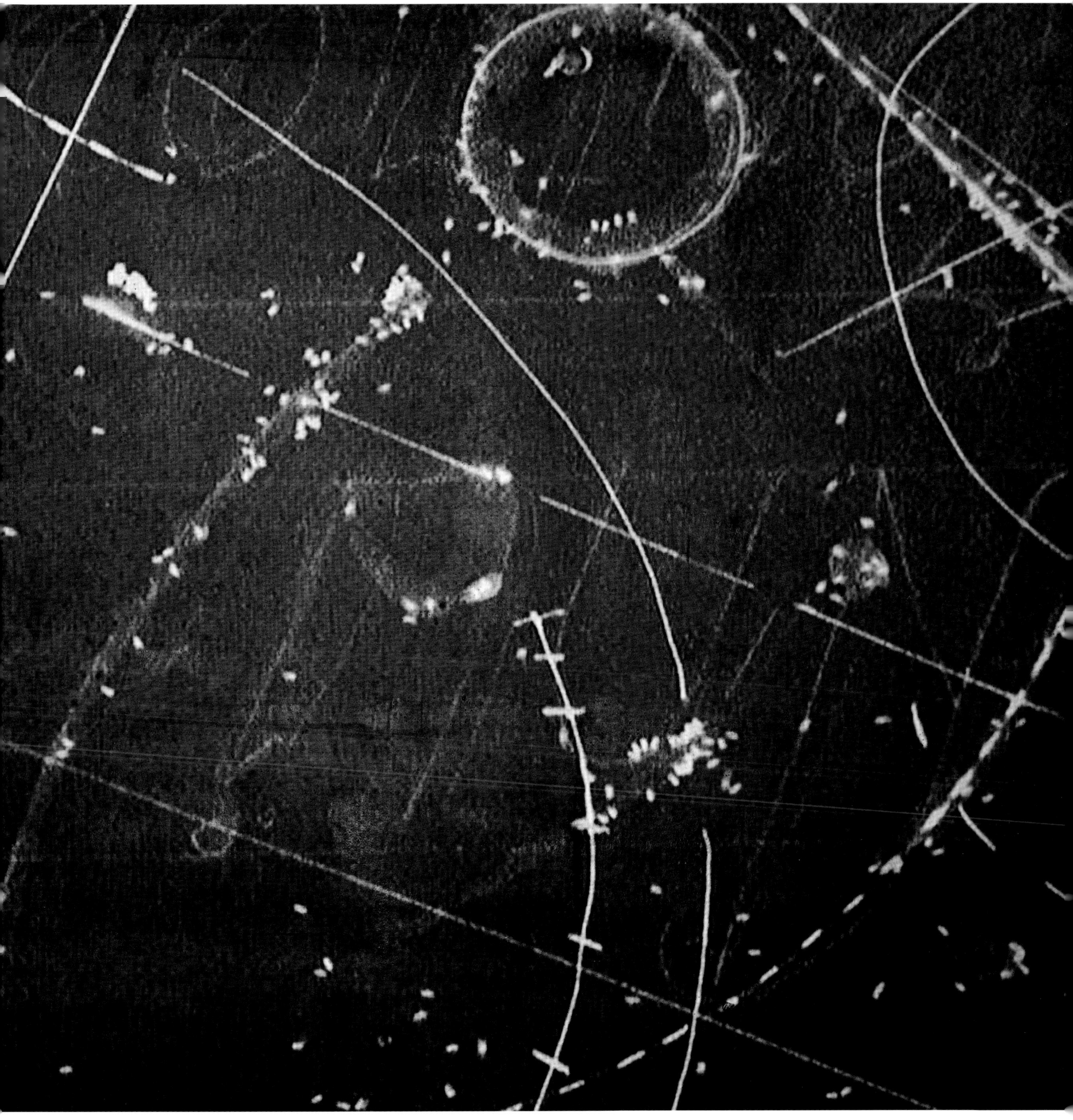

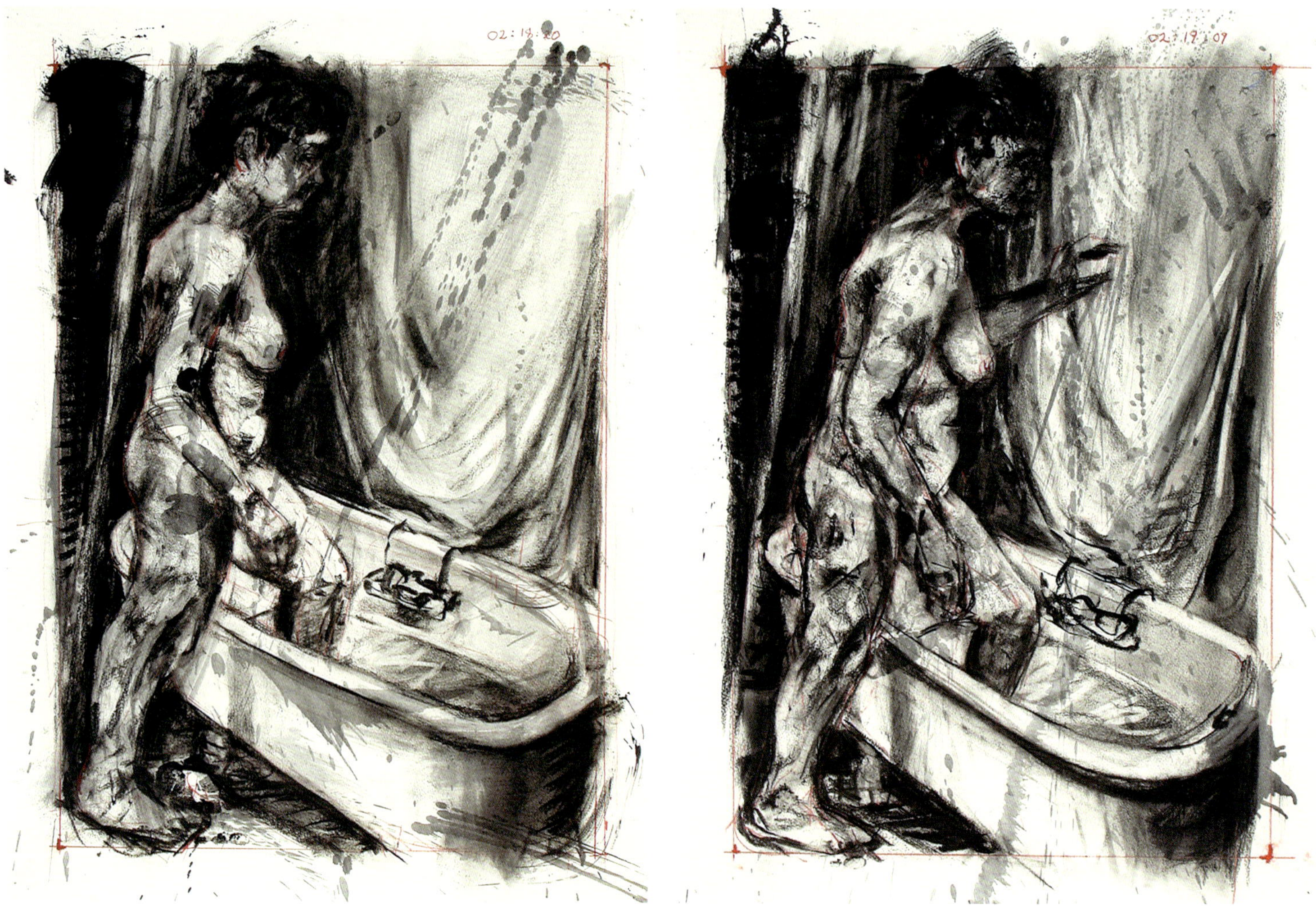

48–51
Untitled (Video Transfers)
[Woman Getting in Bathtub], 2002
Charcoal, dry pigment, and gouache on paper
Nine drawings, each: 31 1/2 x 23 7/8 in. (80 x 60.6 cm)
Courtesy Marian Goodman Gallery, New York

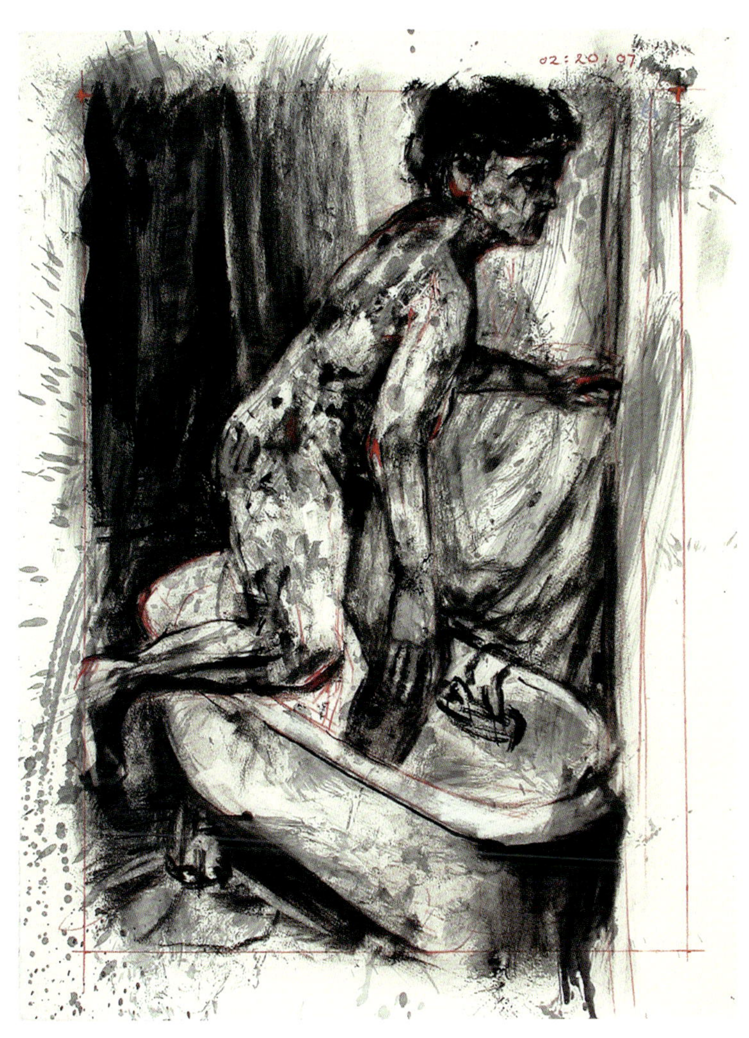
02:20:07

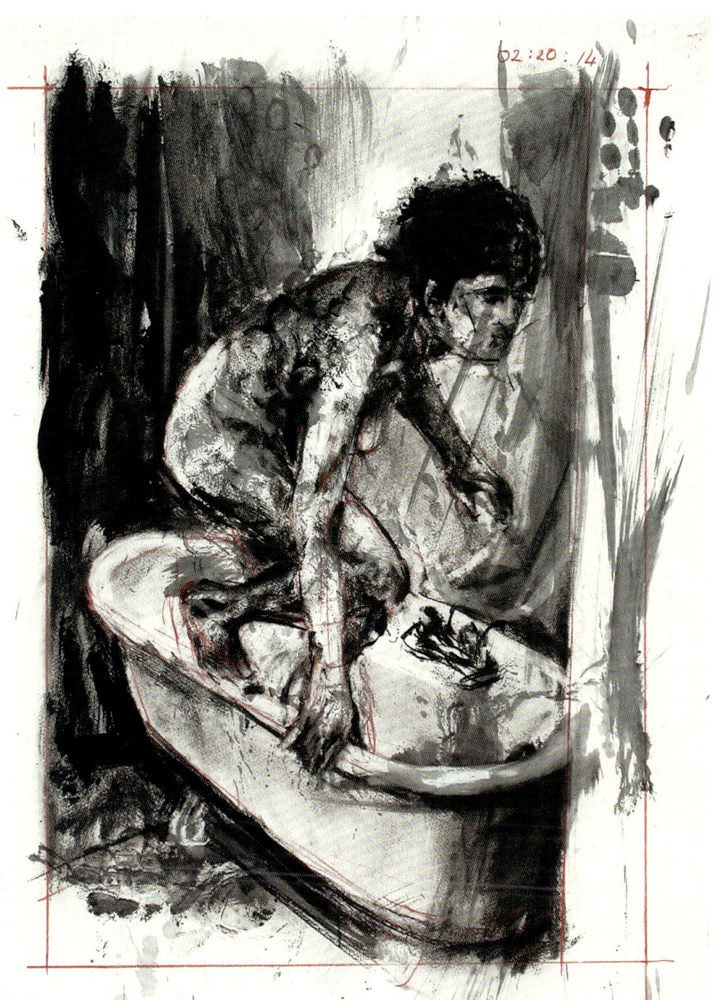
02:20:14

WILLIAM KENTRIDGE
A PORTRAIT OF THE ARTIST

Mark Rosenthal

I DO NOT HAVE THE RIGHT TO BE AN ARTIST.
—WILLIAM KENTRIDGE, 1981[1]

As a young man, William Kentridge imagined art to be a moral and philosophical calling. The right to be an artist was attained only after considerable self-examination and maturation, a process that was separate from finding the appropriate formal means or métier to express one's point of view. As late as 1998, still struggling, he plaintively asked: "How does one bring [about] the entire representation of the world inside one's head?"[2] Some of his self-doubt may have sprung from the fact that his background practically mandated a career in law. To mention the name Kentridge to a South African today is to hear of a nationally celebrated legal family. Turning from the "family business,"[3] as he puts it, was a weighty decision, one that had to be taken with considerable care, regardless of the alternative chosen. Kentridge only made that choice after having first evolved a point of view about the world—and specifically his South African experience.

Kentridge tried many pursuits in his youth, starting in the 1970s with a program in politics and African studies at the University of the Witwatersrand in Johannesburg. He subsequently studied and taught printmaking before going to Paris in the early 1980s to attend classes in mime and theater at the École Jacques Lecoq. Upon returning to Johannesburg he worked in various areas of theater, film, and television. In 1985 he turned to drawing, but his theatrical background continued to have a lasting impact on his art.[4] His work is clearly marked by a predilection for recurring dramatis personae, a taste for large-scale endeavors, and an overall embrace of what was once called multimedia and now falls under the rubric of installation art.

1. William Kentridge and Angela Breidbach, *William Kentridge: Thinking Aloud; Conversations with Angela Breidbach*, Kunstwissenschaftliche Bibliothek, vol. 28, ed. Christian Posthofen (Cologne: Walther König, 2006), 11.

2. Quoted in Carolyn Christov-Bakargiev, *William Kentridge* (Brussels: Société des Expositions du Palais des Beaux-Arts / Vereniging voor Tentoonstellingen van het Paleis voor Schone Kunsten, 1998), 136 (hereafter cited as Christov-Bakargiev, *William Kentridge* [1998]).

3. Kentridge, conversation with the author, July 31, 2008.

4. For Kentridge's take on theatrical influences, see RoseLee Goldberg, "Live Cinema and Life in South Africa: A Telephone Conversation in Chicago, October 21, 2001/Live-Kino und Leben in Südafrika: Telefongespräch vom 21. Oktober 2001 in Chicago," *Parkett* 63 (2001): 99.

With distance, it would appear that Kentridge's initial doubt about calling himself an artist concerned his ability to invest art with his own sentient outlook on South Africa. Born and bred in Johannesburg, with only a one-year stint away from his native city, Kentridge could not put aside this context; "all my work is rooted in this rather desperate provincial city," he says.[5] One might argue that the apartheid system effectively imprisoned each South African in a prescribed role: to be living in misery, a victim of violence; to be maintaining and perpetuating this state of affairs; to be observing; or to be ignoring the fact of apartheid. With regard to his own position vis-à-vis apartheid, Kentridge describes a moral, even religious aspect: "Not to say that one is hoping to make the world a better place.... It is working from the perspective of redemption, rather than working *for* redemption."[6]

Kentridge has characterized the apartheid state as a rock. Frequently depicting this object, he showed it to be long lasting, obdurate, and unfeeling. Moreover, he glumly concluded that "the rock is possessive, and inimical to good work."[7] But it was a mainstay of his existence, and the artist did not leave South Africa during or after apartheid. Indeed, Kentridge's initial rite of passage as an artist concerned an analysis of his position in relation to the overbearing political system. One metaphysical model that describes Kentridge's station is the dialectic of the microcosm and macrocosm. "It is...about how we approach the outside world," he says. "We approach the outside world very much in terms of what is happening inside us."[8] Thus this Jewish, white, male South African lived his individual life within the larger context, defining where he stood with regard to suffering. He described living in a state of "marginality," at the "edge of huge social upheavals yet also removed from them," this for the obvious reason of his skin color.[9] He felt "uncomfortable" and "other," too, because of his Jewish identity in a white Christian world. Yet he knew that the oppression of his Jewish predecessors was not relevant to that of the blacks,[10] and that he would always simply be white in their eyes.

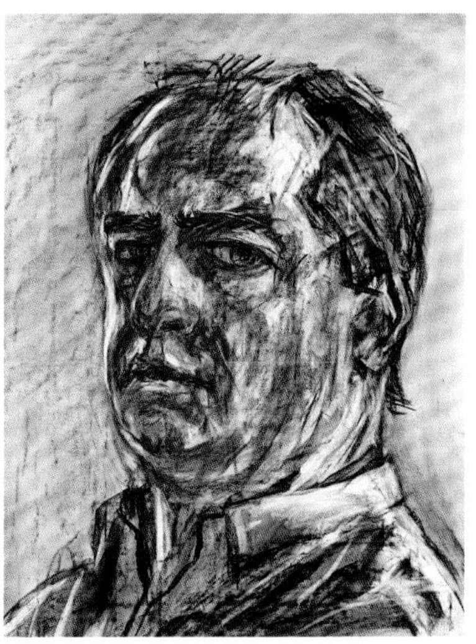

FIG. 1 William Kentridge
Drawing for the film *Medicine Chest* [Self-Portrait], 2000–2001
Charcoal and pastel on paper
47 1/4 x 31 1/2 in. (120 x 80 cm)
San Francisco Museum of Modern Art, gift of Mary and Harold Zlot

It is not only for poetic purposes that the title of this essay refers to *A Portrait of the Artist as a Young Man* by James Joyce; the latter had his own "rock," the oppressive state of Ireland.[11] Just as Kentridge holds the rock of South Africa within himself and Joyce embodied the burden of Ireland, so too did Joseph Beuys suffer within the postwar German state. Kentridge's rock metaphor inevitably recalls Beuys's characterization of his own psychological weight as a "wound." Thus each figure represents in his art a personal and national history as well as a kaleidoscope of micro- to macrocosmic events, the latter to be grappled with, escaped, overcome, or healed, as the case may be. Each of their contexts (the macrocosm) offered a remarkable artistic opportunity. Confronting and struggling with one's position, the artist chooses ways of coping, for instance as a poet, healer, or chronicler. These comparisons are not entirely fortuitous, for Kentridge, from the start of his career, has often positioned himself and his art in relation to his predecessors. He instigates such comparisons so as to better understand his own endeavors and to stand on the shoulders of his forebears, thus making these dialogues part of the content of his work.[12]

5. Quoted in Christov-Bakargiev, *William Kentridge* (1998), 14. Kentridge has spent a good portion of his life in one house and one neighborhood.

6. William Kentridge, "Dear Diary: Suburban Allegories and Other Infections" (1990), in Christov-Bakargiev, *William Kentridge* (1998), 75.

7. Ibid.

8. Kentridge and Breidbach, *William Kentridge: Thinking Aloud*, 91.

9. Dan Cameron, "An Interview with William Kentridge," in *William Kentridge* (Chicago: Museum of Contemporary Art; New York: New Museum of Contemporary Art; New York: Harry N. Abrams, 2001), 72; quoted in Lynne Cooke, "Mundus Inversus, Mundus Perversus," in ibid., 41 (hereafter cited as *William Kentridge* [2001]).

10. See Carolyn Christov-Bakargiev, "On Defectibility as a Resource: William Kentridge's Art of Imperfection, Lack, and Falling Short," in *William Kentridge*, ed. Carolyn Christov-Bakargiev (Rivoli, Italy: Castello di Rivoli; Milan: Skira Editore, 2004), 32 (hereafter cited as Christov-Bakargiev, *William Kentridge* [2004]).

11. Cecilia Alemani refers in passing to the "Joycean hallucinations" of *Black Box/Chambre Noire* (2005) in *William Kentridge* (Milan: Mondadori Electa, 2006), 8. For Kentridge's references to Joyce, see Kentridge and Breidbach, *William Kentridge: Thinking Aloud*, 93.

12. See Cooke, "Mundus Inversus."

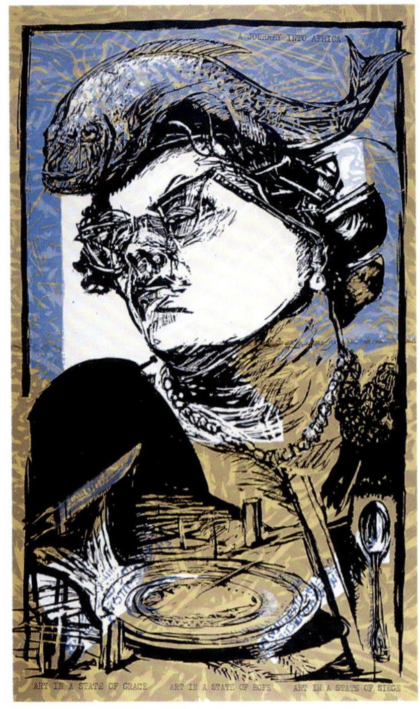

FIG. 2 William Kentridge
***Art in a State of Grace*, 1988**
Silkscreen, ed. of 13
63 x 39 3/8 in. (160 x 100 cm)
University of the Witwatersrand Art Gallery

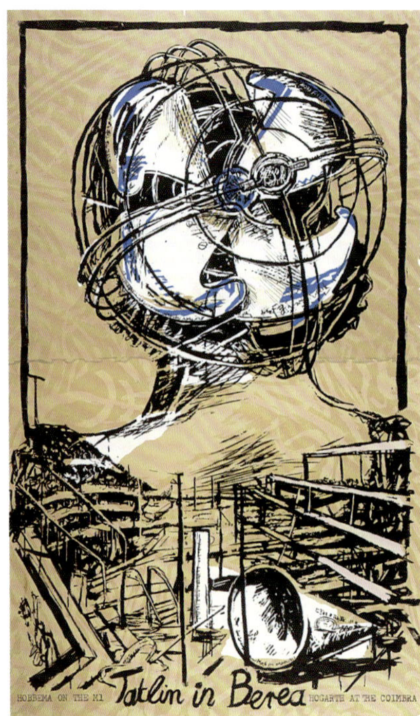

FIG. 3 William Kentridge
***Art in a State of Hope*, 1988**
Silkscreen, ed. of 13
63 x 39 3/8 in. (160 x 100 cm)
Presented by the artist to the University of the Witwatersrand Art Gallery, 1989

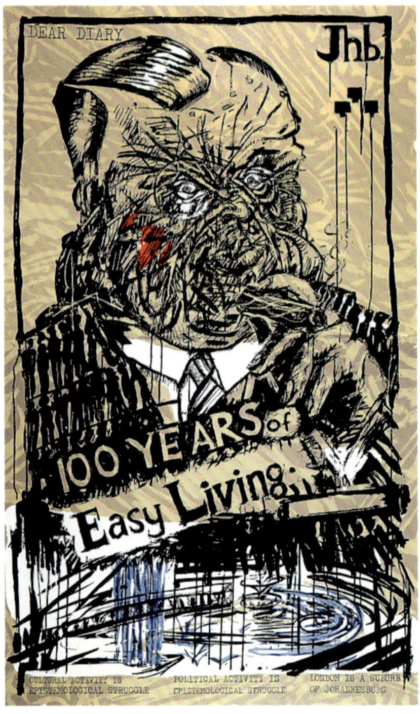

FIG. 4 William Kentridge
***Art in a State of Siege*, 1988**
Silkscreen, ed. of 13
63 x 39 3/8 in. (160 x 100 cm)
University of the Witwatersrand Art Gallery

Kentridge directly addressed his artistic goals and his feelings of inadequacy about becoming an artist in a large graphic triptych of 1988: *Art in a State of Grace, Art in a State of Hope,* and *Art in a State of Siege* (figs. 2–4). The titles convey that Kentridge's attitude toward his work was and is far from art-for-art's-sake; he obviously conceives of art as reflecting the political character of the state in which the work is created. Having spent his entire life in a state of siege (apartheid South Africa), Kentridge has given great thought throughout his career to the history of political art. Within his own country, he looks to the example of David Goldblatt (born 1930), also of Lithuanian-Jewish heritage, whose photographs depict people stoically straining to live dignified lives amid a deeply scarred landscape. Another countryman, Dumile (1939–1991), was particularly inspirational to the teenage Kentridge, who found the older artist's large charcoal drawings of the mid- to late 1960s appealing for their demonic expressionism.[13]

Europe, of course, offered a variety of models for Kentridge's study of political art. One important precedent is the British artist William Hogarth (1697–1764), whose *Industry and Idleness* (1747) moved Kentridge to produce his own version of the series in 1986–87. He also looked to Weimar Germany as "the last (with the exception of the Mexican muralist painters) great flowering of political art."[14] Even early on, Kentridge was seeking to formulate the next flowering of political art, notwithstanding Theodor Adorno's proclamation that after Auschwitz there could be no poetry.[15] He sought through his art to forge a rapprochement with historic events and the lineage of political art, even while taking a new direction: "I am trying to recapture a moral terrain in which there aren't really any heroes, but there are victims. A world in which compassion just isn't enough."[16]

13. Information provided by Kentridge in a conversation with the author, March 2008; see also Christov-Bakargiev, *William Kentridge* (1998), 27.

14. Quoted in Christov-Bakargiev, *William Kentridge* (1998), 16.

15. See Christov-Bakargiev, "On Defectibility as a Resource," 29.

16. Quoted in Christov-Bakargiev, *William Kentridge* (1998), 103.

Kentridge's State of Hope is inspired above all by postrevolutionary Russia and Weimar Germany, milieus that fostered social-engineering experiments intended to produce a kind of heaven on earth. He has frequently looked to these sources, feeling a "distant connectedness"[17] to these spheres and wanting to relate his South African experience to them. Kentridge is attracted to the political optimism of a time before the world was, as he describes it, "exhausted by war and failure. I remember thinking that one had to look backwards—even if quaintness was the price one paid."[18] That "quaintness," in the form of a figurative, expressionistic-looking art, became Kentridge's chosen métier.

In postrevolutionary Russia, artists such as Vladimir Tatlin, with his *Monument to the Third International* (1920), and Kazimir Malevich, with *Black Square* (1915), expressed great hope and idealism through abstraction.[19] The utopian thinking of these individuals, along with the writer Vladimir Mayakovsky (1893–1930) and the filmmaker Dziga Vertov (1896–1954), sustained Kentridge as he sought to define a political art. But the Russian revolutionaries' dream that art would play a central role in daily life was beyond Kentridge's imagination: "I do not know how I would fit into it...with neither a belief in an attained...state of grace, nor a belief in an immanent redemption here."[20] It is therefore understandable that Kentridge has never embraced abstraction in his own work. As explained by Carolyn Christov-Bakargiev, his admiration for his modernist heroes is mediated by the recognition that modernism was the culmination of "the culture of progress and the Enlightenment, but also of colonialism and industrialisation, of idealism and historicism, as well as of scientific thought."[21] He acknowledges the destructive side of modernity even as he chooses from its ranks the artistic sources that helped define his self-described "fox hole."[22] For instance, of his interest in Max Beckmann's 1938 painting *Death,* Kentridge explains: "It accepts the existence of a compromised society....It marks a spot where optimism is kept in check and nihilism is kept at bay. It is in this narrow gap he charts that I see myself working."[23]

Robert Rauschenberg once famously explained that he tried to work in the gap between art and life.[24] For Kentridge, however, art and life have a very intimate and indissoluble relationship. His own "gap"[25] thus represents a political stance: "I am interested in a political art, that is to say, an art of ambiguity, contradiction, uncomplicated gestures and uncertain endings."[26] His interstice is historical, existing between grace and siege, optimism and nihilism. Whereas Rauschenberg was completely comfortable in an aesthetic and ironic gap, Kentridge is forever in a state of moral "disjunction."[27] It is a kind of Joycean limbo—the limbo of hoping against hope.[28] Italo Svevo, whose 1923 novel *Confessions of Zeno* is important to Kentridge, characterized such a state thus: "Life is neither good nor bad; it is original." For Svevo's protagonists, life "is a huge purposeless structure" that "admits no cure." This point of view, in which life is "poisoned to the root," is not at all far from Kentridge's disillusionment and melancholy.[29]

Kentridge has spent much of his career investigating certain themes in depth, turning each over and over to create a plethora of works in a variety of media. It might even be fair to speak of his being consumed by each theme, though that is as much a testament to the richness inherent in his subject matter as it is to his ability to excavate its subtleties. The five themes considered in this essay offer a fascinating overview of the artist's concerns and development. The first two evidence Kentridge's experience as a South African living through the apartheid era. The final three reflect his postapartheid career, wherein he moves outward in his point of view and references.

17. Cameron, "An Interview with William Kentridge," 72.

18. Neal Benezra, "William Kentridge: Drawings for Projection," in *William Kentridge* (2001), 16. For more of the artist's thoughts on Russia, see William Kentridge, "Art in a State of Grace, Art in a State of Hope, Art in a State of Siege" (1986), in Christov-Bakargiev, *William Kentridge* (2004).

19. For Kentridge on Tatlin, see Christov-Bakargiev, *William Kentridge* (1998), 56; Kentridge, "Art in a State of Grace," 68.

20. Kentridge, "Art in a State of Grace," 68.

21. Christov-Bakargiev, *William Kentridge* (1998), 34.

22. Kentridge, "Art in a State of Grace," 68.

23. Ibid.

24. See Dorothy C. Miller, ed., *Sixteen Americans* (New York: Museum of Modern Art, 1959), 58.

25. Kentridge, "Art in a State of Grace," 68.

26. Quoted in Benezra, "William Kentridge," 15.

27. Kentridge, "Art in a State of Grace," 68.

28. See, for example, James Joyce, *A Portrait of the Artist as a Young Man* (New York: Dover Publications, 1994), 172.

29. Italo Svevo, *Confessions of Zeno,* trans. Beryl de Zoete (New York: Vintage International, 1989), 312, 414. Kentridge staged a theatrical production of *Confessions of Zeno* in 2002.

SOHO AND FELIX

In 1989 Kentridge decided to unite his efforts in graphic arts and theater by making the animated film *Johannesburg, 2nd Greatest City after Paris* (1989; pls. 52–56). Though he did not realize it at the time, he had embarked on the first great theme of his career and had found the medium through which to express his complex interests.[30] *Johannesburg* commenced an epic cycle of nine films, an omnibus called *9 Drawings for Projection* that established Kentridge's international fame as a chronicler of the mighty atrocities of apartheid.[31]

Each major work by Kentridge is a synthesis and a summation of what has come earlier. Even before making this film Kentridge had often worked in series of drawings and prints, creating sequences of images that predicted a cinematic approach. He was propelled toward the components of *Johannesburg* by two dreams: "the procession through the wasteland, [and] the fish in one hand."[32] The title of the film and the names of the two central personages came to him in a dream as well.[33]

Does Kentridge truly postulate that Johannesburg is the second greatest city, or is the title an attempt by the artist to establish his locale on the international stage and compare his situation to the European everyman? In other words, is Johannesburg a "desperate provincial city,"[34] or is it a great one? Kentridge depicts his hometown as a busy metropolis, accompanied by lilting Duke Ellington music. It is the setting, the macrocosm, for the predictable yet intensely touching personal drama that unfolds.

Johannesburg begins with an emphasis on Soho Eckstein, a greedy industrialist who takes for granted his wife, a woman whose first name is never given but who is the central love interest of the drama. Emotionally abandoned, she takes up with Felix Teitlebaum, a poetic soul who showers her with erotic attention. The animation consists of slow-moving scenes based on drawings, punctuated by intertitles that advance the story. "Soho takes on the world," we are told; he is an active participant in Johannesburg life, employing huge numbers of people. Felix, meanwhile, is a "captive of the city," a solitary soul and a dreamer. Even Soho's last name references Kentridge's notion of a rocklike South Africa, for its German translation is "cornerstone." Soho is a man in a pinstriped suit, always seen from the front; Felix is nude and viewed from behind. The former seems to lack an inner or emotional life, whereas the latter overflows with feelings. Civilization versus nature, stained versus pure: such are the oppositions implied.

Along with the above-named figures, there is a fourth, generalized character in Kentridge's drama: the nameless individuals who make up a seemingly endless procession of black persons. They dispiritedly advance from the background, the Highveld outside Johannesburg, where the land was degraded by manufacturing and mining, and murders and human suffering were rampant. They are most certainly Soho's prisoners, and he keeps a bookcase holding slaves' heads, as if they were trophies from a safari. When the sound of wailing music is heard from the marchers, he covers his ears and throws food as if attempting to quiet them. Between Soho, Felix, Mrs. Eckstein, and the unnamed masses, Kentridge had arrived at the full complement of dramatis personae for *9 Drawings*.

30. Putting it another way, he sought "a live cinema." William Kentridge, "'Journey to the Moon' and '7 Fragments for Georges Méliès' Including 'Day for Night'" (2003), in Christov-Bakargiev, *William Kentridge* (2004), 193.

31. While making the Soho and Felix films one by one up through 2001, Kentridge never actually showed them together as a block. Then, in the retrospective organized by the New Museum of Contemporary Art, New York, and the Museum of Contemporary Art, Chicago, which premiered in 2001 at the Hirshhorn Museum and Sculpture Garden, Washington, D.C., he finally did so, calling them *Drawings for Projection*. Two years later he made one more film, *Tide Table*, effectively completing the series.

32. Quoted in Jennifer Arlene Stone, *Politeness of Objects: William Kentridge's Noiraille* (New York: Javaribook, 2005), 21.

33. See Kentridge and Breidbach, *William Kentridge: Thinking Aloud*, 66.

34. Quoted in Benezra, "William Kentridge," 20.

In viewing *Johannesburg* it becomes apparent that Soho and Felix resemble each other and the artist himself. The fact that the suited Soho figure was predicted by *Muizenberg 1933,* a 1976 linocut of the artist's grandfather Morris, only deepens these associations.[35] If Soho and Felix are effectively two halves of the same character, intimately intertwined with each other and with their creator and his family, then the drama is very complex indeed. When it was pointed out to Kentridge that the name Felix resembles that of his mother, Felicia, he agreed that this was so.[36] Thus is almost every key player in Kentridge's film a self-portrait.

Kentridge's next films, *Monument* (1990; pls. 60–64) and *Mine* (1991; pls. 66–69), delve further into the perfidious nature of Soho. In the former, Kentridge shows him first as a "civic benefactor" building a monument to a slave. But when the sheet is pulled away we discover a pretentious, oversize sculpture of a heavily burdened, shackled figure—the approbation is for slavery rather than the slave.[37] *Mine* begins with Soho presiding from his bed over the landscape and swarms of workers. The latter sleep in primitive barracks, and in their quarters are showers with uncomfortable Nazi-era associations. Soho's implement of subjugation over these souls is the press of a French coffeepot, which, like a mine drill, inexorably burrows deep into the ground. With a miniature rhinoceros, a symbol of Africa, eating from his hand, Soho lords over his dominion. None of this is subtle; Kentridge is here a political artist in the traditional sense, depicting the perpetrator of horror as a deeply despicable person.

The artist turns back to the love triangle in *Sobriety, Obesity & Growing Old* (1991; pls. 71–76), in which he further delineates Soho and Felix. The former sleeps alone in his pinstriped suit, whereas the nude Felix is found listening to megaphones and loudspeakers—motifs that derive from photographs of Lenin speaking and reveal Felix to be a politically naive idealist.[38] While the lovers embrace in the landscape, Soho's cat, now his only companion, becomes a gas mask.

Seemingly encouraged by the exhortations from the megaphones, marchers besiege Soho's offices. Soho's is an "empire in dissolution." He is clearly more self-aware than before, perhaps even self-destructive, for he seems to cause the building to collapse around him. The unraveling of Soho's empire foreshadows the end of apartheid two years later; Kentridge has described how the fall of the Soviet Union in 1989 was a significant omen predicting the end of South Africa's regime.[39]

35. For a discussion of the artist's grandfather, see Christov-Bakargiev, *William Kentridge* (1998), 13.

36. Kentridge and Breidbach, *William Kentridge: Thinking Aloud*, 66.

37. Kentridge says that the design of the monument derives from a 1930s drawing by Henry Moore. Conversation with the author, July 31, 2008.

38. See William Kentridge, "An Interest in the Making of Things" (1992), in Christov-Bakargiev, *William Kentridge* (1998), 85.

39. Conversation with the author, February 28, 2008.

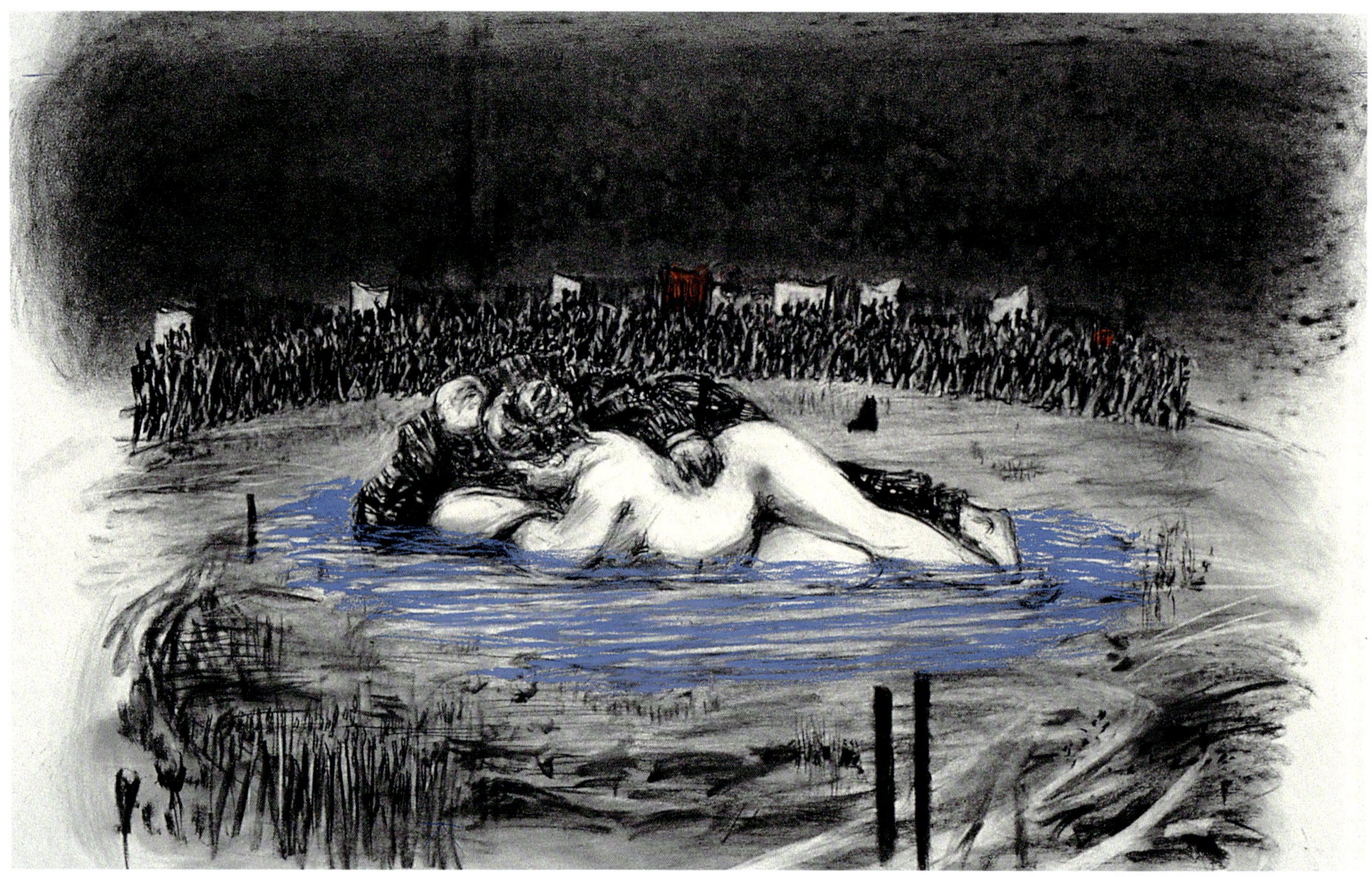

FIG. 5 William Kentridge
Drawing for the film *Sobriety, Obesity & Growing Old* [Soho and Mrs. Eckstein in Pool], 1991
Charcoal and pastel on paper
47 1/4 x 59 in. (120 x 150 cm)
Collection of the artist, courtesy Marian Goodman Gallery, New York, and Goodman Gallery, Johannesburg

The vivid motif of a flood of blue water recurs throughout the film's love scenes and in images of Soho's office. The blue is luxuriant and emotional, in keeping with the extremes of both love and dissolution. Kentridge has observed that the arid state of the Johannesburg region led him to the idea of making a gift of this blue: "a kind of utopian image" of the way his home city might look.[40] The flood of blue suggests the power of love to undo the monstrous Soho, his empire, and by implication the South African regime. Love transforms the stultifying and soulless impact of apartheid; according to Kentridge it represents a state of "domestic redemption."[41]

Kentridge's characterizations pay particular attention to the impact women have on men. Mrs. Eckstein's sensuous embrace of Felix is filled with profound emotion, offering solace and human contact in the midst of the dehumanizing South African context. By contrast, without his wife Soho becomes small and weak; we are told that "her absence filled the world." "Come home," the despondent Soho repeatedly calls across the landscape—and finally she does, leaving Felix alone, listening to his megaphones.

40. Kentridge and Breidbach, *William Kentridge: Thinking Aloud*, 72. He also had a mental image of the Pantheon in Rome flooded with a meter of water, another kind of softening of a hard environment that recalls, after a fashion, Joseph Beuys's idea to add one centimeter to the Berlin Wall for "better proportions." Here, then, is the power of the artist—Kentridge and Beuys, respectively—to idealistically heal an existing state of affairs.

41. Kentridge, conversation with the author, July 31, 2008.

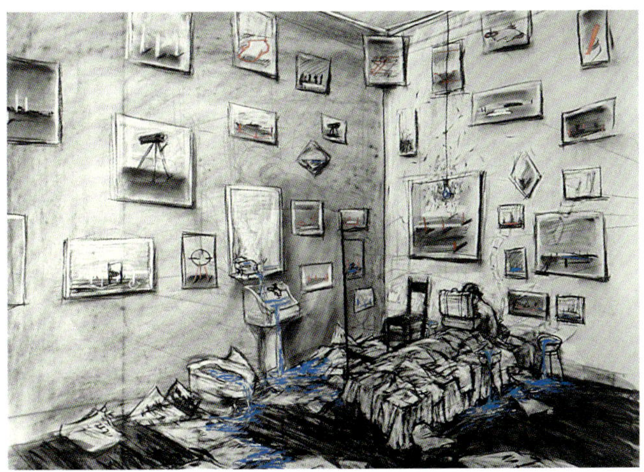

FIG. 6 William Kentridge
Drawing for the film *Felix in Exile* [Felix in Bed], 1994
Charcoal and pastel on paper
47 1/4 x 63 in. (120 x 160 cm)
Billiton Collection, Marshalltown, South Africa

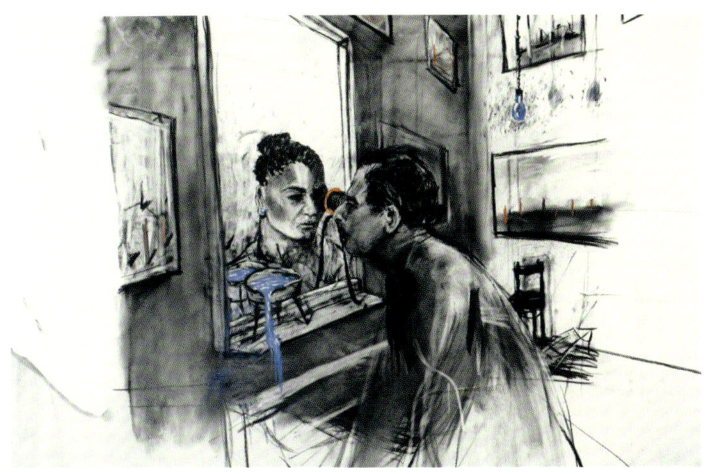

FIG. 7 William Kentridge
Drawing for the film *Felix in Exile* [Eye to Eye], 1994
Charcoal and pastel on paper
47 1/4 x 59 in. (120 x 150 cm)
Kunsthalle Bremen, Germany

Felix in Exile (1994; pls. 77–81) is about Felix's new love affair. Living in a bare room, he quickly fills the space with just-completed drawings (see fig. 6). The room is virtually identical to an often reproduced view of Malevich's 1916 exhibition in Saint Petersburg, *The Last Futurist Exhibition of Paintings "0–10" (Zero–Ten)*. The reference signals a key theme of the film that has to do with the limits of seeing and the care necessary to comprehend. Malevich's *Black Square,* which hangs in one corner of Felix's room, is a monument of abstraction and revolutionary art; it was intended by Malevich to elicit the viewer's perception of the pure emotion that lies within the iconic abstract form. The Russian painter's thesis is the very essence of idealism, and both it and the painting hold great interest for Felix and his lover as the film unfolds.

Felix's love interest, who is black, constantly practices various forms of intense looking. First, using a telescope, she spies a bloody figure lying on a road, covered by wind-blown newspapers. (Kentridge emphasizes the circular eyehole of the telescope, perhaps to contrast it with Malevich's implicit *Black Square.*) Later she makes use of a theodolite, a surveyor's instrument for calculating angles, and turns her attention toward the stars. Both vehicles of sight yield much that might be thought of as unequivocally given and true. On the other hand, when she sees a heavenly constellation that takes the form of faucet handles, which then turn into the fixtures being used by Felix, she invokes a metamorphic or seer's vision. This is reinforced by a number of fascinating scenes at the bathroom mirror, where Felix sees himself and then his lover in the reflection (see fig. 7). He touches her eye, as if in recognition of this powerful metaphor within the film. They look at each other through a telescope that reaches from one side of the mirror to the other. Then she trains her closed eyes on the stars, seeing a mass of black people and a large, rocklike form that transforms into the head of the bleeding figure. Here, then, is the nightmare that might come with closed eyes, a turn from the macrocosm of the heavenly orbs to the microcosm of South Africa.[42]

42. Kentridge reports that his renderings of bodies in a landscape, such as those that appear at the start of *Felix in Exile,* derive from "the body lying on the ground in Goya's *3rd of May 1808.*" William Kentridge, "'Felix in Exile': Geography of Memory" (1994), in Christov-Bakargiev, *William Kentridge* (2004), 100.

Forms of sight are a central theme throughout Kentridge's art and activity. On one hand, there is an apparently objective vision that is attained using a variety of apparatuses. The assumption of truth in what is observed is, however, a highly questionable leap for Kentridge. He relishes Plato's Allegory of the Cave, in which the likelihood of attaining legitimate and accurate sight is turned upside down. He frequently ponders the organ of sight, quoting examples from earlier art. These include the eye that is so famously sliced in Luis Buñuel's film *Un chien andalou* (1929) as well as Man Ray's *Object to Be Destroyed* (1923), a metronome with a photograph of an eye attached to its arm. Also of interest to Kentridge is Malevich's fellow Russian Vertov, in whose films the blinking eye is a metaphor for sight. "There's a hunger in everyone's eyes to understand the world and to look for any clues to create the space," Kentridge observes.[43] Beyond "everyone's eyes," he searches for machines that are involved with various forms of sight. In Kentridge's iconography, coffee is often an aid to achieve acute sight (though a coffee plunger in the hands of Soho can be a malevolent force).

Set against this emphasis on overt sight is inner vision—the dream state and the accompanying possibilities of metamorphosis and hallucination. Kentridge has noted that metamorphosis is what he likes so much about drawing: "I believe that in the indeterminacy of drawing, the contingent way that images arrive in the work, lies some kind of model of how we live our lives."[44] In this zone of indeterminacy, having eyes wide open but not seeing in a conventional manner is highly desirable. This is a classic surrealist plane of experience, and Kentridge often courts surrealistic transformations of images and objects. He adores these manipulations because they show "the persistence and robustness of contradiction"[45]—to which one might add the possibilities inherent in improvisation, irrationality, revolution, and love.

In *Felix in Exile* the mirror is a powerful vehicle for sight and observation, and Kentridge emphasizes this by showing Felix and his lover managing to see and join each other through it. The fact that the artist describes her as "perhaps...a displaced self portrait"[46] adds meaning to the characters' coalescence in the mirror. Reinforcing the implication that Felix holds within himself Kentridge's mother Felicia, the artist asks: "Is that me looking back at my mother in the mirror?...I must have been repressing it for all those years."[47] The mirror accentuates the debatable truth of what we see and how we interpret these observations.[48]

After *Felix in Exile,* the Felix character disappears from *9 Drawings*. However, Soho looks even more like Felix in the next film, *History of the Main Complaint* (1996; pls. 83–86).[49] *History* dates to the year in which the Truth and Reconciliation Commission (TRC) began to meet, ostensibly to heal the wounds of more than three decades. Apartheid (the main complaint) and its ramifications (history) were hardly distant memories, as shown by the TRC's profound impact on contemporary life in South Africa.

43. Kentridge and Breidbach, *William Kentridge: Thinking Aloud*, 7.

44. Quoted in Benezra, "William Kentridge," 12.

45. Cameron, "An Interview with William Kentridge," 68.

46. Quoted in Christov-Bakargiev, *William Kentridge* (1998), 12.

47. Kentridge and Breidbach, *William Kentridge: Thinking Aloud*, 66.

48. Kentridge elaborated on these ideas in *Sleeping on Glass* (1999), an installation in which footage of a sleeping woman is projected onto a mirror. Her physical self and depicted dreams are both seen in the mirror, resulting in an extraordinary outpouring of imagination as sleep becomes the most fertile state of alertness to the possibilities of cognition. Kentridge may have been inspired in this regard by Goya and his *The Sleep of Reason Produces Monsters* (1799).

49. See Staci Boris, "The Process of Change: Landscape, Memory, Animation, and *Felix in Exile*," in *William Kentridge* (2001), 33.

The film finds Soho on a hospital bed, claustrophobically enclosed by a curtain to suggest that it is now he who is in exile. Scanning machines (another mechanism for sight) survey his interior state. Looking very much like their patient, the doctors focus on Soho's stomach with stethoscopes that bore down through him in a manner reminiscent of his French press going into the earth. Soho's illness invokes a white South African's sickly malaise—real, imagined, or emotional—in a nation still dominated by apartheid. Soho has become delirious, entering a coma state in which he recalls past violence.

A recovered Soho is back at his desk at the end of *History,* perhaps no more aware or repentant—that is, until the next film, *WEIGHING... and WANTING* (1998; pls. 89–94). Here, Soho's domestic life unfolds in a house reminiscent of the architectural style of Le Corbusier, thus linking the rapacious businessman with modernist progress.[50] Soho compares, with the aid of a set of scales, a gargantuan rock and the remembered embrace of his wife. Seeking resolution to his dilemma, he uses a coffee cup as a tool for listening and seeing the world. When Soho ultimately chooses the rock, he theatrically embraces the reliable comforts of his past. It is all he has known, after all.

The title of the film comes from the biblical story of Nebuchadnezzar, in which the king is told that he has "been weighed in the balance and found wanting."[51] Neither the king nor Soho is contrite. So entwined is the protagonist with his context, Kentridge explains, "the rock is another way of drawing the inside of Soho's head."[52]

WEIGHING is replete with the motif of the double; having scant faith in certainties of any kind, Kentridge emphasizes a dialectical approach to all things.[53] With his need to present both thesis and antithesis comes a clear acceptance of contradiction as central to his understanding of the world: "Facts are not simple," he says.[54] In Kentridge's work the appearance of a mirror is an explicit invitation to experience a double—the thing and its image—and to question which side of the mirror is accurate. A double encourages our active participation, prompting us to compare and contrast, and much of the richness in Kentridge's art comes from an appreciation of this seemingly basic exercise.

The apartheid state, Kentridge asserts, presents the ultimate stage for a "double life," with each South African having "double understandings" about people.[55] The microcosm inhabited by the artist vis-à-vis the larger South African context is itself a double. And South Africa in relation to the larger world, particularly Europe, represents yet another layer of doubling, as indicated by the title *Johannesburg, 2nd Greatest City after Paris.* Even after apartheid, the positions of blacks and whites are fixed; hence Kentridge describes his position as a "double-bind."[56] To a very real extent, then, he is constantly haunted by knowledge of the double.

50. The house is based on one shown in Sergei Eisenstein's film *The General Line* (1929). It is meant to "evoke Le Corbusier's utopia, but also the lost dream of modernism in contemporary suburban architecture." Christov-Bakargiev, *William Kentridge* (1998), 34.

51. See Kentridge and Breidbach, *William Kentridge: Thinking Aloud,* 112; Christov-Bakargiev, *William Kentridge* (1998), 134.

52. William Kentridge, "The Comfort of a Stone" (1998), in Christov-Bakargiev, *William Kentridge* (2004), 127.

53. Kentridge has stated that he identifies certainty with policemen wielding clubs. See Stone, *Politeness of Objects,* 4.

54. Quoted in Christov-Bakargiev, *William Kentridge* (1998), 17.

55. Goldberg, "Live Cinema and Life in South Africa," 99.

56. Christov-Bakargiev, "On Defectibility as a Resource," 32.

There exist in Kentridge's art a number of verbal circumlocutions pertinent to the theme of the double. For instance, his intertitles for the film *Sleeping on Glass* (1999) couple "amnesia and memory," "adaptability/compliance," and "terminal hurt/terminal longing." Elaborating on these are the already cited optimism and nihilism, not to mention grace and siege. According to Kentridge, the double is, like his South African context, "the medium in which we work."[57] At one moment he might ponder the confusion of the double, simply declaring its existence and naming the components; at another he might attempt "reconciling opposites": "It is not a question of sitting on the fence," he says, "but of removing the fence itself."[58]

The emphasis on doubles is particularly prominent in the film *Stereoscope* (1999; figs. 20, 27, pls. 97–101). By utilizing a split-screen effect to mimic a stereoscopic view, Kentridge was, in effect, hoping to resolve the dueling components of the double. "One understands the double image, the two photographs of a traditional stereoscope, as a true representation of the world," he explains.[59] The viewer must play an active role in bringing the two together.

Tide Table (2003; pls. 105–9), the final film of *9 Drawings,* had as its starting point a 1924 painting by Beckmann entitled *Lido* (fig. 8).[60] Attracted to Beckmann's beach theme, and in keeping with his own interest in water as a potential source of solace, Kentridge was able to imagine a culmination to the life of Soho. Tired, melancholic, and reflective, Soho is shown on a quiet shoreline reading a newspaper containing the tide tables. The sounds of seagulls, lapping waves, and gentle music dominate the scene, though a number of rocks can be seen at low tide. A boy appears on a rock; Soho sees him and is then shown on a rock himself. Cattle skulls lie on the beach, but Soho picks up a stone and skims it across the water. The rocks in the water echo the mighty stone cliffs set back from the beach. Is this narrative, with its dreamy music, a wish fulfillment on Kentridge's part, a vision of forgiveness and goodness set against the unyielding rock?

Kentridge has described the boy in *Tide Table* as having been cared for by a nanny, much as he had been.[61] This degree of identification between the artist and his characters, true throughout *9 Drawings,* is typical of Kentridge, who wants to find himself in and through his work. This process, it would appear, is psychologically driven: his brand of political art is "therapeutic...not an ideological one."[62] This may express a wish for some sort of redemption, if not catharsis, that is clearly autobiographical.[63] Just as Anselm Kiefer depicted himself as a Nazi in order to examine his own capacity for violent behavior, and as Cindy Sherman inhabited any number of female stereotypes to explore her own identity, Kentridge tries out the role of the child in *Tide Table* as well as the characters of Soho and Felix.[64] Moreover, he introduces his grandfather, father, and mother into this lineage, which ultimately becomes one personage.[65] Kentridge, this deeply stoical emanation of his clan, grapples with his South African experience through *9 Drawings,* trying desperately not to give in to his emotions. One might find an example in Mayakovsky, who began his play *A Tragedy* (1913) with the following lines:

> Ladies and gentlemen!
> Patch up my soul
> so the emptiness can't leak out![66]

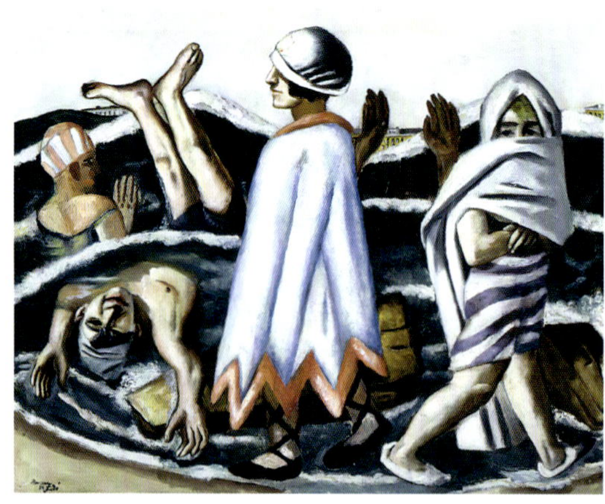

FIG. 8 Max Beckmann
***Lido*, 1924**
Oil on canvas
28 1/2 x 35 5/8 in. (72.4 x 90.5 cm)
Saint Louis Art Museum, bequest of Morton D. May

57. Stone, *Politeness of Objects*, 7.

58. Kentridge, "Art in a State of Grace," 69; Stone, *Politeness of Objects*, 6.

59. Kentridge and Breidbach, *William Kentridge: Thinking Aloud*, 76.

60. Kentridge, conversation with the author, February 28, 2008.

61. See Kentridge and Breidbach, *William Kentridge: Thinking Aloud*, 58–60.

62. Quoted in Christov-Bakargiev, *William Kentridge* (1998), 9.

63. Kentridge says his work is "not necessarily... autobiography"; still, it "functions...like a diary." Quoted in Benezra, "William Kentridge," 20.

64. See Kentridge and Breidbach, *William Kentridge: Thinking Aloud*, 25–26, where Kentridge speaks of projecting oneself into many people in time.

65. Others in this lineage might include Svevo and Mayakovsky.

66. Vladimir Mayakovsky, *A Tragedy* (1913), in *The Complete Plays of Vladimir Mayakovsky*, trans. Guy Daniels (New York: Washington Square Press, 1968), 23.

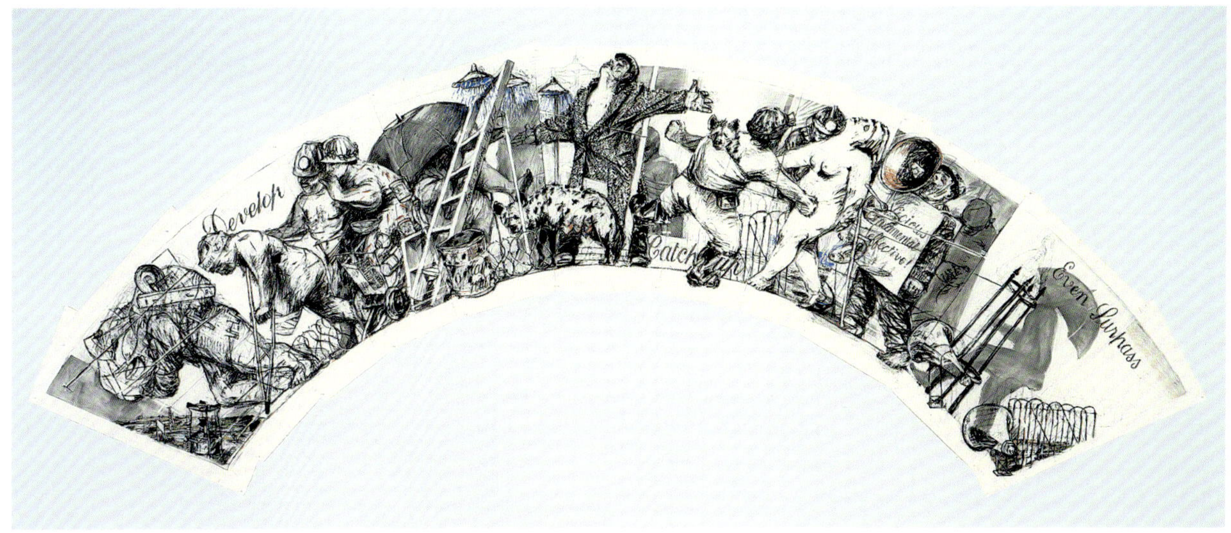

FIG. 9 William Kentridge
***Arc/Procession (Develop, Catch Up, Even Surpass)*, 1990**
Charcoal and pastel on paper
Eleven parts, overall: 118 1/8 x 196 7/8 in. (300 x 500 cm)
Tate Gallery, London

UBU AND THE PROCESSION

All themes overlap in Kentridge's art, hence the second body of work discussed here has close links to Soho and Felix. Ubu is a new embodiment of evil predicted by the character of Soho. And the procession emanates from the start of *9 Drawings* in 1989, when Kentridge began incorporating images of black people in long lines—this at a time of increasing uprisings in South Africa.[67] The ubiquitous procession became a character of equal importance to the others in his art. The finale of this theme is the 1999 film *Shadow Procession,* in which Ubu and the procession come together in dramatic juxtaposition.

Arc Procession (Smoke, Ashes, Fable) (1990; pl. 144), and *Arc/Procession (Develop, Catch Up, Even Surpass)* (1990; fig. 9) are elaborate examples of the procession.[68] This subject refers not only to a South African phenomenon but also to international events. The procession encompasses, in effect, the march of protesters as well as refugees displaced by war. It represents a kind of universal diaspora of people seeking justice, usually far from home.

A diverse mélange of figures march one way and another in *Arc/Procession (Develop, Catch Up, Even Surpass),* a kind of third world version of the assembly on the Parthenon frieze. Reading from left to right, we encounter a weighed-down worker such as those that appeared in the contemporaneous films *Mine* and *Monument*; next is a disabled character with a brutish face, resembling one Kentridge would create for his production of *Woyzeck on the Highveld* two years later. Two more miners follow, then an assortment of high-stepping people joined by animals. A figure with megaphone, a stock participant at political rallies, exhorts the crowd to action; the ladder recalls the iconography of the Deposition from the Cross as well as the imagery of Beckmann. The subtitle, whose words are integrated throughout this sizable work, repeats a slogan that Haile Selassie used to encourage his Ethiopian countrymen.[69] The exaggerated gestures of the figures no doubt resemble actions at Durban political events, which featured marchers and musical performances and were particularly noteworthy to Kentridge.

67. The massing of black people may have begun with imagery Kentridge developed for his first production of *Woyzeck on the Highveld* (1992), according to a May 27, 2008, conversation with the author.

68. See Ari Sitas, "Processions and Public Rituals," in *William Kentridge* (2001); *William Kentridge Tapestries,* ed. Carlos Basualdo (Philadelphia: Philadelphia Museum of Art; New Haven, CT: Yale University Press, 2008).

69. See Benezra, "William Kentridge," 19.

The artist has explained that the crowd scenes in his work are inspired in part by the films of Sergei Eisenstein and in part by Malevich's *Black Square,* which Kentridge interprets as an abstract rendering of the masses participating in the Russian Revolution.[70] He also cites as sources the processions and crowds in Goya's "black paintings," Bernardo Bertolucci's film *Novecento* (1976), and *Men Shoveling Chairs* (1444–50), a drawing from the circle of Rogier van der Weyden that Kentridge encountered at the Metropolitan Museum of Art, New York.[71] In his first depictions of masses of people, as in *Mine,* the procession has not yet emerged, as it were, from the group. Over the course of the 1990s he remained entranced with the theme, depicting the crowd in all manner of situations, including a 1999 projection on the ceiling of Amsterdam's Koninklijk Paleis (fig. 33) and a 2000 installation in a staircase at P.S.1, New York (fig. 23).

These installations contributed toward a new direction in Kentridge's art, whereupon his South African microcosm was explicitly relocated within the European and American context. They marked the start of the large-scale enterprises that, as we will see, soon became the norm for exhibiting his films as well.

A procession literally unfolds in *Portage* (2000; pls. 146–47), a collage on book pages, and it is also the subject of numerous drawings, torn paper collages, prints, sculptures, and tapestries. In some examples, a figure is isolated from the procession and shown burdened by objects; a few appear to be bound, as if captive, while others carry the wounded. A particularly ominous sight is a figure strapped to a chair with an umbrella and a shower above his head—instruments of torture, perhaps. Some figures are metamorphosed from objects on Kentridge's worktable, such as scissors, a typewriter, a compass, or calipers. Anthropomorphized machines also join these processions.

In the midst of producing *9 Drawings* and while focusing on the procession theme, Kentridge reacquainted himself with Alfred Jarry's avant-garde play *Ubu Roi,* first performed in Paris in 1896. "From a South African perspective," Christov-Bakargiev notes, "Ubu is a particularly powerful metaphor for the insane policy of apartheid, presented by the state as a rational system."[72] Having acted, in 1975, in a Johannesburg adaptation called *Ubu Rex,* Kentridge returned to Ubu in 1996 with an intense burst of activity in all of the media in which he works. He began a series of etchings called *Ubu Tells the Truth* (1996; pls. 112–19) and immediately afterward participated in a theatrical production called *Ubu and the Truth Commission,* which synthesized the Jarry play with TRC proceedings. That was followed by an animated film, also called *Ubu Tells the Truth* (1997; figs. 10–11, 21, pls. 120–29), that was based on the etchings. Over the next few years Kentridge monumentalized the Ubu theme in some of his largest drawings and prints to date. In 1997 he made a group of what he termed "messy drawings" for the Bienal de la Habana in Havana. These were followed by the *Sleeper* print series and five very finished drawings (1997–98; pls. 130–34). For all of the work he used source photographs of himself in various positions (see figs. 37–38); over these he made line drawings of the Ubu character. The project marked a breakthrough: no longer would his graphics be in the service of the films—now they were an end unto themselves. Moreover, the human scale of much of the work echoed the increasing dimensions of the film projections, as in the aforementioned installations in Amsterdam and New York.

70. See Cooke, "Mundus Inversus," 42; Christov-Bakargiev, *William Kentridge* (1998), 97. Kentridge also points to his 1989 drawing *Conrad Mauser,* especially as it relates to Nikolai Gogol and the procession. See Christov-Bakargiev, *William Kentridge* (1998), 162.

71. Adding further to this lineage, the figures comprising the procession have been identified by the artist as porters. See Basualdo, *William Kentridge: Tapestries,* 18.

72. Christov-Bakargiev, *William Kentridge* (1998), 118.

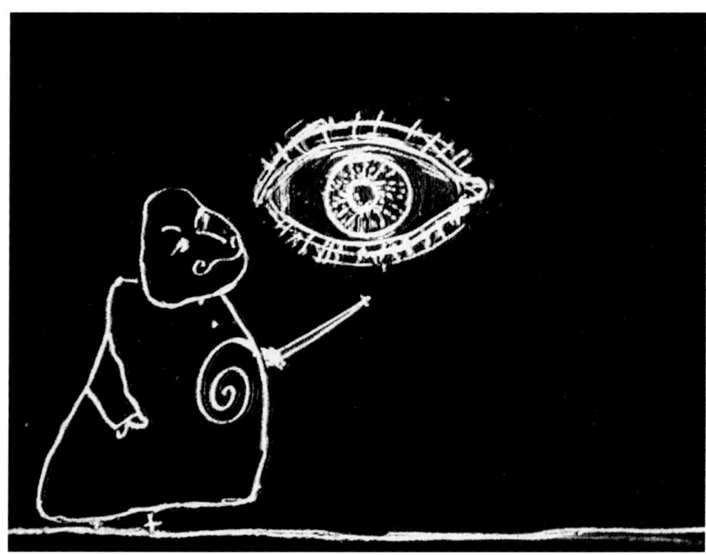

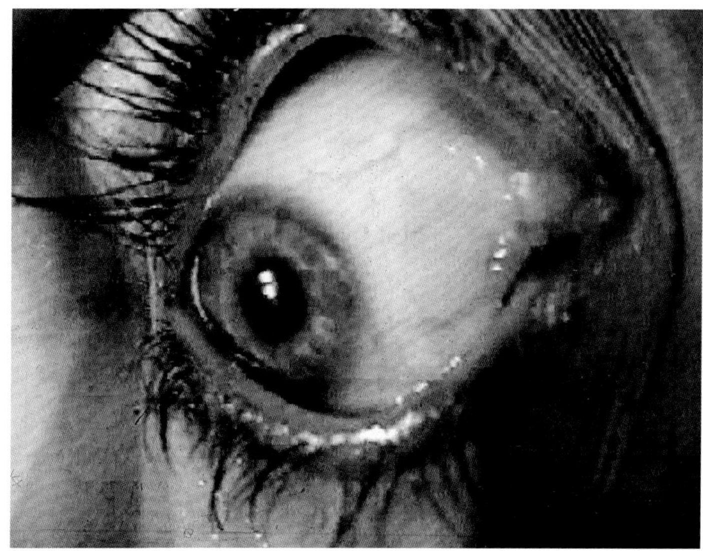

FIGS. 10–11 William Kentridge
***Ubu Tells the Truth*, 1997**
35mm animated film with documentary photographs and 16mm archival film transferred to video, 8 min.
Collection of the artist, courtesy Marian Goodman Gallery, New York, and Goodman Gallery, Johannesburg

The film *Ubu Tells the Truth* begins with the monstrous Ubu himself—identifiable by his pointy head, rotund body, and the spiral on his stomach—strutting and wielding two swords in place of his arms. Applying a very typical Kentridge strategy, the artist relates events in the heavens to those on earth by alternating a drawing of an eye in the sky with film footage of a frightened eye. Ubu grabs the eye and positions it atop his body, which then morphs into a camera on a walking tripod. Recalling the physique of a man holding a megaphone, the camera with tripod serves as Ubu's alter ego or double. It is a leitmotif of the film, suggestive not only of eyewitness accounts but also surveillance techniques and clandestine weaponry, associations that show how this dispassionate instrument of sight can be used for the purpose of evil. *Ubu Tells the Truth* is an ugly, unrelenting compilation of the horrible events (bombings, torture, hangings) that were so graphically described during TRC hearings.[73] In keeping with Kentridge's desire to link Johannesburg to the larger world, he drew on images from news reports of "bombings in Kenya and riots in Mexico and student demonstrations in Cape Town and students being killed in Jakarta."[74]

In the next Ubu film, *Shadow Procession* (1999; pls. 135–43), Kentridge completely integrated the theme with that of the procession.[75] For the first time, the artist based a film not on drawings but on cutouts and silhouettes. It begins with a slow, shadowy procession followed by a more clearly articulated march; we see a sequence of wounded and disabled figures, a structure that might be a gallows, another with a hanging man, a figure pulling a shower, and people carrying belongings, all in a kind of chain gang. Suddenly Ubu rises up, as if from a hole or a casket, and stands under a spotlight. The fearsome maniac starts to dance, one hand a kind of pistol, the other a whip, striking out as if to harass and beat the marchers. The film concludes with another procession, this one accompanied by wild, fast-moving tempos and shouts.

73. Kentridge notes, "To make identification impossible the bodies of those killed by the security forces would be dynamited. After the first explosion the body parts would be gathered together and blown up again. This process of successive fragmentation was known by the police as 'Buddha.' Policemen complained of returning from work smelling of blood and dynamite." See Cooke, "Mundus Inversus," 54.

74. Kentridge and Breidbach, *William Kentridge: Thinking Aloud*, 92.

75. As mentioned earlier, a shadow and its source represent one more double in Kentridge's world. Transplanting the theme to the United States, Kentridge projected *Shadow Procession* in Times Square, New York, in 2001 (see fig. 16).

There is much casting of shadows by the marchers in *Shadow Procession,* raising fresh comparisons to Plato, who, Kentridge has pronounced, "sets the scene for the journey towards knowledge, or away from ideology, or false consciousness, or from appearance to substance."[76] Plato's cave was where prisoners were incarcerated; Kentridge's marchers are by implication prisoners, too. There is, however, a more positive, or double, connotation to the procession. In addition to escaping chaos, the dispossessed are effectively seeking knowledge. In Kentridge's 2001 lecture "In Praise of Shadows," he described Plato's cave and the realm of the procession as spheres in which prisoners seek light.[77] On its own a shadow represents "deep ignorance and primitivism," but it also suggests a path of inquiry, offering the potential for enlightenment.[78] "The question I would want to propose is that of the reverse journey," says Kentridge—one in which we are blinded by the sun and choose to seek knowledge in "the world of shadows."[79]

ARTIST IN THE STUDIO

With the conclusion of *9 Drawings* and the fall of apartheid—a full decade in his rearview mirror, as it were—Kentridge started to think about the possibility of art that might exist apart from the rock that symbolized his country. Joyce's Stephen Dedalus character had to leave Ireland in order to "discover the mode of life or of art whereby [his] spirit could express itself in unfettered freedom."[80] Kentridge ultimately chose not to leave South Africa, but he describes having felt a gradual "dulling of sensibilities,"[81] followed by the emergence of a more expansive purview for his work. This sense of personal change is implicit in his 2006 assertion that South Africa is "not a post-apartheid society but a post-anti-apartheid one."[82] Tellingly, the title he gave to two sections of *7 Fragments for Georges Méliès* (2003; figs. 44–46, 53–55, pls. 8–27), his most important work to follow the South African–themed projects, was *Tabula Rasa.* Kentridge always exhibits *7 Fragments* as a multi-image environment with two additional films, *Journey to the Moon* and *Day for Night* (both 2003) at either end of the room. Notwithstanding the extravagantly large scale of the installation, with its nine films running simultaneously, the project offers an intimate self-portrait of the artist, alone in the studio and making art.

Each of the *7 Fragments* is separately titled, with the first, *Invisible Mending,* setting the prevailing tone for the whole suite. Here we see the artist capturing torn sheets of paper that are flying through the air; he reassembles them on the wall to form a photographic self-portrait, over which lies an abstract drawing that he erases. Between the shadows, images, and drawings, there are effectively four versions of him in the room. After putting the fragments together and admiring his work, he walks away to the left; in his absence, the figure in the photo comes to life and walks off to the right. Through these magical acts of creativity, Kentridge discovered a new way to describe and realize himself through art.

76. William Kentridge, "In Praise of Shadows" (2001), in Christov-Bakargiev, *William Kentridge* (2004), 152.

77. See ibid., 151–61.

78. Stone, *Politeness of Objects,* 9.

79. Quoted in ibid., 10.

80. Joyce, 180.

81. Quoted in Christov-Bakargiev, "On Defectibility as a Resource," 29.

82. Quoted in Rachel Donadio, "Post-Apartheid Fiction," *New York Times Magazine,* December 3, 2006, 50.

In *7 Fragments* the artist emerges from the shadows, much as Diego Velázquez does in *Las Meninas* (1656). But it is not as if Kentridge had withheld himself in his earlier art. He made a series of thirty monotypes in 1979 that included a print on the theme of *Artist and Model* (pl. 1), and the film *Memo* (1994) approached the same subject. In 2001 he made his untitled artist and model charcoal drawings (pls. 3–7); in 2002 a series showing his wife, Anne, entering a bath (see pls. 48–51); and in 2005 the *Middle-Aged Love* series of large-scale drawings (figs. 49–52). The example of Pablo Picasso, with his many pictures documenting his studio and his complex psychological and physical interactions with his models, lies near to this body of Kentridge's work.

The studio milieu of *7 Fragments* seems to have encouraged Kentridge to make deliberate references to other art and artists, aside from the aforementioned connection to Picasso. These include Beuys and his signature hat; Joseph Kosuth and his play on the actual and linguistic identities of a chair; Goya and his love of the Icarus legend; Richard Serra and his obsessive rubbing out of forms in the video *Hands Scraping* (1968); Rauschenberg and his *Erased de Kooning Drawing* (1953); Max Klinger and his *Paraphrase on the Finding of a Glove* (1881); and Bruce Nauman and his references to coffee-addled awareness, including *Photograph for Caffeine Dreams* (1987).

Notwithstanding the freighted art historical layers of *7 Fragments,* much of the work has a madcap, Charlie Chaplin–like quality of play in its depictions of Kentridge's creative activity. Like boomerangs, objects are tossed in the air, reverse direction, and return to their starting point to be caught; others are charmingly transformed, as Kentridge demonstrates for himself and the viewer the ways in which art images come about, or fade from view, against the backdrop of their ostensible reality. Success and failure enchantingly play out before our eyes. *7 Fragments* is a kind of soliloquy about seeing and the power of art and the artist. One moment we are watching Kentridge; the next we are standing beside him observing the world. As he explains, "The excitement and the reason for doing the work (or any drawing) [have] to do with the engagement of being caught between the object and the sheet of paper."[83]

From the confines of the studio to outer space, *7 Fragments* is thematically framed by *Journey to the Moon* and *Day for Night.* The latter title refers to the cinematic technique, known in French as *nuit américaine,* whereby a nighttime scene is simulated during daylight filming. François Truffaut famously used the term as the title of a 1973 film that takes as its subject the process of filmmaking. Depicting mysterious dots in a simulated night sky, Kentridge's own *Day for Night* consists entirely of solar system–type views (see fig. 28). The imagery was inspired by the artist's experience watching ants march around his studio. Realizing the visual potential, he spilled sugar to direct the ants' movements for the camera. At the time, Kentridge explained, he was thinking a great deal about reversals of all kinds—witness the objects' movements in space and, more profoundly, Kentridge's own turn from the rock. In the final image of *Day for Night,* black ants become white as the paper's coloration reverses, befitting the title.[84]

83. William Kentridge, "Two Thoughts on Drawing Beauty," in *Beautiful/Ugly: African and Diaspora Aesthetics,* ed. Sarah Nuttall (Durham, NC: Duke University Press, 2006), 101.

84. See Kentridge, "'Journey to the Moon,'" 190, 192.

Like *7 Fragments,* the title of *Journey to the Moon* directs us to the work of Georges Méliès (1861–1938). A pioneering French filmmaker working at the dawn of the medium, Méliès reveled in technological sleights of hand, visual jokes, and illusions.[85] His best-known film, *Le voyage dans la lune* (A Trip to the Moon, 1902), is a virtuoso demonstration of inventiveness and humor (the rocket, for example, wounds the man in the moon). Kentridge enjoys the fact that in Méliès's work "time is reversed, [showing] what it would be like if we could remember the future,"[86] and has made use of similar effects in his own films.

At the start of *Journey to the Moon* (pls. 28–47) Kentridge is in his studio, drinking from a coffee cup, which he then begins to employ as a magnifying glass or telescope. The coffee cup and pot have magical powers to see through objects and beyond immediate space; indeed, the pot slowly flies off toward the moon, much like the rocket in Méliès's film. Mirror images abound: the ant march and the human procession, the Highveld and the moon, the man in the studio and the man in the moon.

Journey to the Moon is a kind of finale to *7 Fragments,* moving from artistic tricks to a state of melancholy—a mood reinforced by the slowing tempo of the music. The loneliness of life in the studio is the ultimate subject, and the doubled images of the artist indicate multiple or conflicting creative inclinations. Having turned back from the moon to his immediate surroundings, Kentridge starts to pace in a disturbed way. Through the coffee cup he spies the familiar procession in the landscape. A nude muse, a chimera in the person of Kentridge's wife, Anne, appears as part of the procession. Then she is in the studio, consoling the artist with an arm around his shoulders. Kentridge returns the gesture of his muse, but she disappears, whereupon he goes back to pacing. She returns to touch him again; this time he does not seem to feel her hand. With her departure, the ants reappear on a drawing of the cosmos. Kentridge may have had a journey to the moon, but—like Icarus falling to earth—he must return to South Africa. As the artist has explained, Méliès's moon was "a late 19th century colonial moon.... My lunar landscape is... just outside Johannesburg."[87]

85. Kentridge admired these same qualities of trickery in the later films of the Russian Vertov.

86. Quoted in Mick Hartney, "Up-to-Date Conjurer Seeks Vanishing Lady: William Kentridge's *Seven Fragments for Georges Méliès,*" in *William Kentridge: Fragile Identities,* ed. Tom Hickey (Brighton, UK: Faculty of Arts and Architecture, University of Brighton, 2007), 33.

87. Kentridge, "'Journey to the Moon,'" 193.

In the process of making *7 Fragments, Journey to the Moon,* and *Day for Night,* Kentridge achieved a dramatic if momentary shift, seeming to drop his reserve as he revealed himself at work in his studio.[88] He assumed the identity of a cinematic auteur, an aspiration announced by his references to Méliès and Truffaut (Truffaut, of course, being the prototypical auteur). One imagines Kentridge repeating the words of his admired Vertov: "I am kino-eye, I am mechanical eye, I, a machine, show you the world as only I can see it."[89] In addition to these French and Russian models, the South African auteur found parallels in more contemporary visual art. Kentridge acknowledges the powerful impact of Nauman's *Mapping the Studio* (2001), a totally deadpan and continuous filming, Warhol-style, of an empty space in which very few incidents occur, as well as Nauman's earlier films, in which the artist, in frustration, repetitively performs various physical actions.[90] Kentridge recently amplified on the subject: "Nauman is an American artist, i.e. at the centre of the art imperium, with the deep-rooted confidence and arrogance that this gives. The confidence to do the most minimal of actions and believe that they were 'enough'; versus a provincial need to provide more, and in the end find a story." Kentridge was also inspired by "films of artists performing in their studios, Nauman, Pollock, and Méliès each being examples of this."[91] As with all of these precedents, he revels in using his body and improvising actions within the studio context.

Although *7 Fragments* suggests an antic auteur in the style of Méliès or Chaplin, *Journey to the Moon,* with its implied return to earth, gives a more traumatic cast to life in the studio. Notwithstanding the fact that Kentridge sees film reversals as having a "utopian" impact ("from chaos there is return to order"[92]), in this case the return trip restores his South African context. Indeed, he has pointedly said that "*Journey to the Moon* was an attempt to escape."[93] Despite the fact that Kentridge's ability to put aside problems "gnaws"[94] at him, this characteristic has allowed him the space to consider one of the oldest themes of art history—the artist in the studio—and, for the moment, to sidestep the rock.

88. Upon being informed of a statement by Jasper Johns about reaching a point in his career when he might "drop the reserve," Kentridge noted a similarity to his own development. Conversation with the author, May 27, 2008.

89. *Kino-Eye: The Writings of Dziga Vertov,* ed. Annette Michelson (Berkeley: University of California Press, 1984), 17.

90. During his 2002 stay in New York, at Columbia University, Kentridge saw several Nauman exhibitions. See Christov-Bakargiev, "On Defectibility as a Resource," 36. That same year Kentridge was invited to give a lecture on Nauman at Dia Art Foundation, New York; he had previously seen a Nauman exhibition in Zurich.

91. Kentridge, email to the author, March 6, 2006. See also Sitas, "Processions and Public Rituals," 60. Kentridge's mention of Jackson Pollock specifically references Hans Namuth's well-known film of Pollock painting in his studio.

92. Quoted in Stone, *Politeness of Objects,* 17.

93. Quoted in ibid., 19.

94. Kentridge, "Art in a State of Grace," 69.

THE MAGIC FLUTE

In 2003 Kentridge accepted a commission to stage and direct a full production of Mozart's opera *The Magic Flute* for La Monnaie, Brussels. This commission led to a magnificent body of work that includes, in addition to the 2005 staging, a film, two miniature theater pieces, an anamorphic film, and a host of drawings and prints. Once he accepted the commission, Kentridge set to work pondering the narrative, characters, and the meaningful potential of this complex drama.

The first major manifestation was the film *Learning the Flute* (2003; pls. 149–50), in which Kentridge played with some of the key motives of the opera and began interpreting its themes. Informed by his recent experience making *Journey to the Moon,* Kentridge created a cosmic framework from the start. A starry sky, recalling Vincent van Gogh's, is shown to the accompaniment of Mozart's overture. This stirring heavenly setting is immediately compromised by shooting stars that form the menacing Ubu spiral, then a triangle that is transformed into a metronome with an eye (again recalling Man Ray's *Object to Be Destroyed*).[95] In quick succession we glimpse the key elements of the opera, along with now-familiar props such as calipers and a camera on a tripod. We see night and day, darkness and light, all so important in distinguishing the Queen of the Night from Zarastro, the central dichotomy of Mozart's work.[96] Kentridge depicts himself as a shadowy magician, a foreshadower of Papageno, who pulls birds from the air. These brilliant, playful sleights of hand, similar to those demonstrated in Kentridge's studio in *7 Fragments,* are accompanied by Mozart's sparkling music.[97]

In order to enhance the physical presence of the film, Kentridge chose to project *Learning the Flute* onto a blackboard that sits on an easel. In addition to being a pedagogical tool, the blackboard was inspired in part, Kentridge explains, by a Joan Jonas installation entitled *Lines in the Sand* (2002) that he saw at *Documenta* that year. The blackboard also became a very important prop in Kentridge's staging of the opera.

After having completed the first performances of *The Magic Flute* in Brussels, in 2005 Kentridge decided to turn his model stage set into a work of art. This theater-in-miniature, entitled *Preparing the Flute* (2005; pls. 151–54), comprises a computerized lighting system with front and rear projections, a soundtrack, and filmed footage from the staging of the opera. The work reflects the artist's long-held "desire to bring the theater world back into the studio,"[98] and it also represents a novel variation on the installation or large-scale art manifestation, wherein the viewer is immersed in a theatrical experience within the museum milieu.

95. Confirmed by the artist in a conversation with the author, May 27, 2008.

96. For Kentridge on the phenomenon of the eclipse, see Kentridge and Breidbach, *William Kentridge: Thinking Aloud,* 31–33.

97. The film uses Thomas Beecham's 1937 recording with the Berlin State Opera Orchestra, which Kentridge found in Namibia.

98. Kentridge, "'Journey to the Moon,'" 193.

An abridged version of the opera, *Preparing the Flute* is less a narrative than a highly dense compilation of the drama's key strands, both thematic and musical. We see Kentridge himself, having emerged from the studio in *7 Fragments,* light-handedly drawing in space; his magical powers are mirrored by the bird's freedom to attain unfettered flight. The bird, another alter ego, might also serve as a personification of Mozart. Paralleling the bird is a rhino, dangled and manipulated like a marionette. Force lines and heavenly comets are ubiquitous, conjoining and interweaving the various depicted worlds. Adding to the sense of compressed connections, Kentridge turns the entire space into a fast-rotating mass, a formal device that recalls the procession drawings and their theme of continuously repeating patterns of life. The same circular spinning effect is characteristic of the compositions of many of the drawings attendant to *The Magic Flute.*[99]

Preparing the Flute concludes with an explosion of linear bursts, an eye, and a celebration of light, just as Kentridge's opera did. Here is the ostensible ascension of the Enlightenment as epitomized by Sarastro, though Kentridge himself would privilege neither light nor enlightenment: he believes both shadow and light, a thematic double, are necessary to approach full and true knowledge.[100] Much in evidence in the opera staging and in *Preparing the Flute,* a camera remains the key symbol for his ambiguous approach to vision, invoking both the apparent neutrality of objective reporting and the frightening prospect of surveillance. Reinforcing the significance of the camera, Kentridge explains that good and evil are "almost provoked by each other the way a photographic negative and positive [are], they are complementary."[101]

In 2005, for an exhibition at the Deutsche Guggenheim, Berlin, Kentridge created a sequel to his *Magic Flute* suite. *Black Box/Chambre Noire* (fig. 29, pls. 163–69), a second miniature theater, incorporates a number of puppets moving in accordance with computer-programmed light projections.[102] He summarized the thinking behind the work as follows:

> The years since Mozart wrote the opera have made us more wary of philosophical autocrats. The enforced bringing of wisdom has had unintended but calamitous consequences all through the years, not just in the Robespierrian terror of the years immediately after the writing of the opera, but throughout the colonial era, and throughout our own century. Though we may believe in Sarastro's benevolent guidance, in the end we believe in Mozart more, in his mix of the rational, the fantastic, the contradictory.[103]

99. *Living Language,* a 1999 series of prints on gramophone records, prefigured the circles that are so evident in the *Magic Flute* suite.

100. See Stone, *Politeness of Objects,* 10. For Kentridge on the connection between Plato and *The Magic Flute,* see Kentridge and Breidbach, *William Kentridge: Thinking Aloud,* 97.

101. Quoted in Stan Schwartz, "The Modern 'Magic Flute,'" *New York Sun,* March 26, 2007.

102. Kentridge made use of puppets long before making *Black Box,* for example in *Woyzeck on the Highveld,* his 1992 collaboration with Handspring Puppet Company in Johannesburg. Here Kentridge synthesized Anton Bruckner's version of *Woyzeck* (originally written by Georg Büchner) with the contemporary South African context, invented an elaborate lighting system, and projected his drawings onto a backdrop. In *Preparing the Flute* these techniques were made more complex; projections were doubled, from the front and rear, to produce—in conjunction with the puppets—a kaleidoscopic impact. For Kentridge, of course, puppets represent another kind of "quaint" or "stone-age" technique.

103. William Kentridge, exhibition brochure, *William Kentridge: Black Box/Chambre Noire* (Berlin: Deutsche Guggenheim, 2005).

In *Black Box* Kentridge deliberately intermingles manifestations of Enlightenment culture (for instance, Mozart's music) and imagery related to the effects of colonialism, specifically the German occupation of Namibia in the late nineteenth and early twentieth centuries.[104] He references a Berlin conference of 1884–85 during which the European powers divided Africa for the purpose, in Kentridge's words, of "bringing light to...the 'Dark Continent.'"[105] That enlightenment, effected by force, quickly turned to no good. In 1904, when the Namibians rose up against the Germans, the Europeans annihilated approximately 75 percent of the Herero tribe.[106] After the massacre, Kentridge points out, the Germans "washed and cleaned [their victims' skulls] and sent [them] back to Germany to be measured, to prove the superiority of the 'Aryan' skull."[107] The artist's interest in Namibia was fueled by a research trip to that country, where he came across a sinister antique shop filled with Nazi memorabilia. Because Germans continue to live in considerable numbers in Namibia, this might not have been altogether surprising. But what a remarkably disturbing coincidence it was for Kentridge to find there a 1937 recording of *The Magic Flute* by the Berlin State Opera Orchestra.[108]

Kentridge explains that a major theme of *Black Box* is the move away from the "certainty of sunlight" and toward "the illuminating shadow,"[109] statements that reinforce his ongoing interest in Plato's Allegory of the Cave. For Kentridge the Enlightenment—as epitomized by Mozart—was further subsumed in and supplanted by nineteenth-century industrialization, notions of progress, the ostensible security of scientific investigation and thought, and finally modernism.[110] All of this misguided idealism fed into the Namibian massacre.

104. Kentridge's 2005 theatrical production *Faustus in Africa!* had similarly juxtaposed European Enlightenment manifestations and African colonization. See Christov-Bakargiev, *William Kentridge* (1998), 102; Benezra, "William Kentridge," 22. Another forerunner is *Overvloed* (1999), a procession film projected on the ceiling of Amsterdam's Koninklijk Paleis (see fig. 33).

105. William Kentridge, "Black Box: Between the Lens and the Eyepiece," in *William Kentridge: Black Box/Chambre Noire*, by Maria-Christina Villaseñor (Berlin: Deutsche Guggenheim, 2005), 49.

106. See Maria-Christina Villaseñor, "Black Box #3: Flight-Data Recorder," in ibid., 101.

107. Kentridge, "Black Box," 51.

108. See Steven C. Dubin, "Theater of History," *Art in America* 95, no. 4 (April 2007): 131.

109. Kentridge, "Black Box," 51.

110. See Christov-Bakargiev, *William Kentridge* (1998), 34.

111. See Goldberg, "Live Cinema and Life in South Africa," 101.

112. So eloquent is this footage, Kentridge introduced the same newsreel in a later production of *The Magic Flute* at the Brooklyn Academy of Music, long after the initial performances in Brussels. As usual with Kentridge, in *The Magic Flute* there are many parallels and doubles, including shooting stars and shootings, phrenology lines and constellations in a starry sky, a sign indicating *Trauer* ("sadness") and the joy of the hunter, the African woman with her headdress and the female colonist with her hoopskirt, the massacre and the safari, globes and skulls. And through it all are frequent instances of the earth spinning, suggesting that the world's events are ceaselessly repeating.

With *Black Box,* Kentridge frames Namibia and Germany as the latest in a long line of doubles. Nowhere is this more eloquently stated than in his choice of music. Throughout the work, Mozart's brilliant arias are countered by the powerful rhythms of Herero music.[111] If the former might be described as heavenly, utopian, and even birdlike, the latter is stirring and earthy.

The chief protagonist/perpetrator of *Black Box* has a caliper for a body, all the better to stab at his opponents and measure their skulls. One arm thrusts outward in exaggerated mimicry of the Nazi salute. His insignia is an eagle, the symbolic transformation of Mozart's melodic bird into the multiple incarnations of Germany's national emblem. A formidable Herero woman wearing a headdress is his counterpart and, presumably, his victim.

Throughout *Black Box* are numerous beatings, shootings, and showers metamorphosed from lamps and gallows, much reminiscent of concentration camp images. The most poignant moment of violence is perhaps the newsreel film that shows a German hunter and an African tracker on safari. The hunter shoots and kills a symbol of Africa, the rhino, whereupon he triumphantly shakes hands with the tracker—an echo of an earlier scene in which two mechanistic figures inflict a beating and then exchange a handshake. The hunter draws a line on the foot of the rhino, perhaps marking an intention to amputate that part of its body for further study. Afterward, the hunter skips away from the scene in great joy. The filmmaker, however, lingers over the impressive face and body of the animal, perhaps expressing the enormous grief of an African population decimated by colonization.[112]

The title of *Black Box* refers simultaneously to the black box–type theater, a room with no proscenium stage; the interior of a camera, also known as the *chambre noire*; and the cockpit device that records flight data, which is usually consulted only after a disaster.[113] Kentridge summarized the meanings of his title as follows:

> *Black Box* is not really a meditation on what it is to take a photograph. Rather it is about the artificial construction of an image—which is what we do when we look through a camera lens—as a metaphor for what we do when we look through our own lives.... It is not simply a matter of the world coming in to us, but it is constructing the natural world as we understand it.[114]

The black box of a camera is the chamber between the lens and eyepiece, the space "into which light enters and where a kind of meaning is created. Here," notes Kentridge, "are the infinite possibilities of the outside world, but a single image is chosen, fixed upon the plane."[115]

By virtue of his construction of an entire world inside the black box, Kentridge makes himself and his synthetic vision participants in the drama that unfolds there. Moving well beyond the use of Soho and Felix as alter egos, the auteur enters the picture plane, whereupon Kentridge's self-transformation is carried into another dimension. Hence, at the start of his next film, *What Will Come (has already come)* (2007; fig. 18, pls. 170–72), the artist's presence is dramatically invoked by the appearance of his hands, stirring the ingredients of the narrative that follows.

What Will Come is effectively a coda to the *Magic Flute* works.[116] Instead of a camera the apparatus for vision is the process of anamorphosis, and instead of Namibia the field of colonization is Abyssinia (later Ethiopia). The inspiration for the project was the Fascist invasion of Abyssinia by Benito Mussolini in 1935.[117] The native population, led by Haile Selassie, successfully repelled the invaders for much longer than was expected. But then, with the help of Hitler—which eventually led to the formation of the Axis—Italy seized control. Kentridge intended the work as a "riposte" to the German philosopher Hegel, who asserted that "after the pyramids, World Spirit leaves Africa, never to return."[118]

What Will Come, unlike Kentridge's previous films, is projected from the ceiling onto a sheet of circular paper on a round table of the artist's design.[119] The animation is composed of a sequence of anamorphic drawings made by the artist; it is only by watching the mirrored cylinder at the center of the table, which appears to be spinning, that the viewer can read the imagery in a conventional way. Kentridge's interest in anamorphic drawing is longstanding and entirely in

113. See Villaseñor, introduction to *William Kentridge: Black Box/ Chambre Noire,* 33.

114. Bronwyn Law-Viljoen, "Interview," in *William Kentridge: Flute,* ed. Bronwyn Law-Viljoen (Johannesburg: David Krut, 2007), 38.

115. Kentridge, "Black Box," 51.

116. A good discussion of this work is Jane Taylor, "Spherical and Without Exits: Thoughts on William Kentridge's Anamorphic Film *What Will Come (Has Already Come),*" *Art & Australia* 45, no. 4 (Winter 2008): 609–15.

117. Kentridge's 2002 film *Zeno Writing* utilizes many of the same motifs in a World War I, Italian context. In *Confessions of Zeno,* Svevo writes that in the end, after a huge explosion, "the earth will return to its nebulous state and go wandering through the sky, free at last from parasites and disease" (Svevo, *Confessions of Zeno,* 416). This salvation is not imagined by Kentridge.

118. Kentridge quoted Hegel in his 1995 program notes for *Faustus in Africa!* See Christov-Bakargiev, *William Kentridge* (1998), 105.

119. Angela Breidbach claimed that *What Will Come* is the "first anamorphic film in history" (Kentridge and Breidbach, *William Kentridge: Thinking Aloud,* 21), but Kentridge has discounted this contention. Conversation with the author, May 27, 2008.

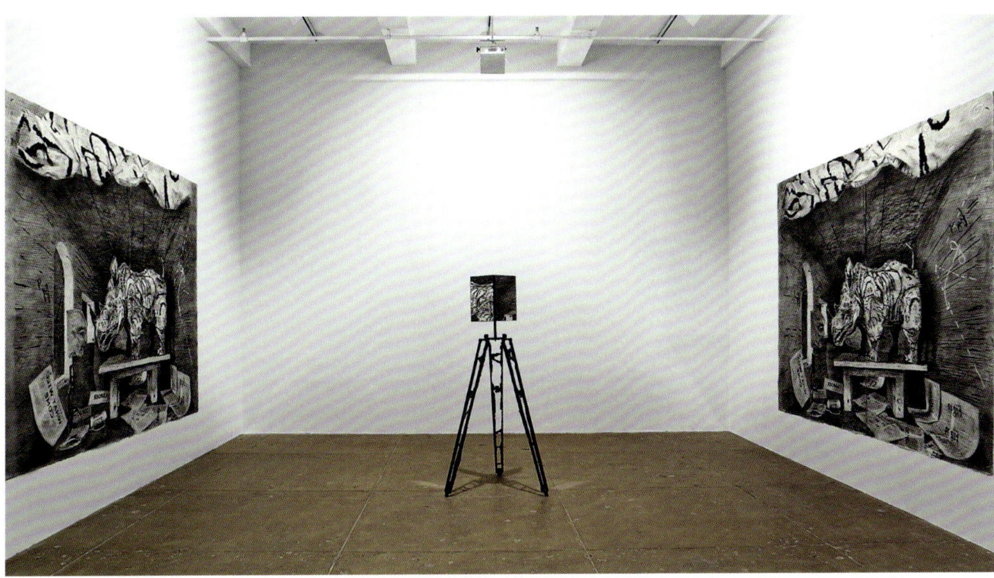

FIG. 12 William Kentridge
***Larder*, 2007**
Drawings (charcoal, pastel, and colored pencil on paper), mirrors, and tripod
Two drawings, each: 84 x 108 1/4 in. (213.5 x 275 cm); overall dimensions variable
Collection of Doris and Donald Fisher

keeping with his fascination with machines and techniques of seeing, including those that might appear quaint or obsolete.[120] Such technologies provide filters through which the world might be newly glimpsed, grasped, or represented, imbuing the viewer with a degree of self-consciousness regarding sight and its need for mediation.[121] Kentridge's emphasis on sight is not just an abstruse preoccupation; it reveals a much deeper investigation into how we perceive and understand the world. For him this is an inquiry that is both psychological and philosophical.

When Kentridge first exhibited *What Will Come* at the Städelmuseum, Frankfurt, in 2007 and subsequently at Marian Goodman Gallery, New York, in 2008, it was with a host of related material; the overall assemblage was like a walk-in experience of the artist's studio. In addition to his demonstration of anamorphic moving images, there were several static examples—anamorphic drawings that lay on special tables to be read on the central cylinders. He also showed a number of stereoscopes with photogravures beneath, so that the double images appeared whole and three-dimensional when viewed through the lenses. Finally, a large installation titled *Larder* (2007; fig. 12) invited the viewer to approach two angled mirrors. Each mirror reflected a drawing on the opposite wall; as the visitor neared the mirrors' point of intersection, the drawings were integrated into a single image, as if seen through a stereo viewer. Revealing the impetus for some of these inquiries, at the Städelmuseum Kentridge included a seventeenth-century anamorphic painting and a series of woodcuts by Albrecht Dürer. The latter's *Draftsman Drawing a Portrait* (1525), which inspired Kentridge to produce a series of variations and recalls his artist and model drawings of 2001, shows an artist constructing a picture of a nude woman whose legs are slightly open. The artist is guided in his prurient portrait by means of a screened grid, creating a composition that predates Marcel Duchamp's *Etant Donnés* by more than four hundred years.

120. See Kentridge, "'Journey to the Moon,'" 180.

121. By way of example, for the 1999 procession projection in Amsterdam, viewers needed small hand mirrors to read the reversed words (see fig. 34).

THE NOSE

In 2005 Kentridge was invited to stage an opera at the Metropolitan Opera in New York. After pondering the matter for more than a year, he and the opera decided on Dmitri Shostakovich's *The Nose,* based on the 1836 short story by Nikolai Gogol and first performed in 1930.[122] The opera's story and context fit many of Kentridge's interests. Set in czarist Russia, it concerns a petty bureaucrat, Major Kovalyov, who awakens one morning to find his nose missing from his face. The story revolves around his comical attempts to retrieve it, even as his nose parades around Saint Petersburg with a higher status than its former owner. Absurd in the extreme, *The Nose* concerns the daily pettiness of hierarchical life, but it also describes the ways in which an individual has multiple sides, public and private, that may or may not interlock.

Kentridge quickly undertook an intensive study of the Gogol story, learning that it was inspired by a Russian translation of Laurence Sterne's *Life and Opinions of Tristram Shandy, Gentleman* (1759), in which the nose is a central motif. Sterne's own inspiration, according to Kentridge, was Miguel de Cervantes's *Don Quixote* (1605). This lineage delights and fascinates the artist, for it indicates the deepening complexity of a single "personage." Cervantes gave Kentridge his second motif: the horse.

As we have seen, Kentridge has a great interest in postrevolutionary Russia; he is particularly fascinated by Stalinism's eventual disapproval of artist-revolutionaries such as Tatlin and Malevich. Shostakovich's traumatic life followed a similar trajectory. Though he started out in favor of—and in the favor of—the authorities, the state eventually rejected the composer. For him, then, Gogol's tale must have demonstrated that Russian pretensions had remained unchanged since prerevolutionary times, a message that would have been clear to Shostakovich's contemporary audiences. Gogol's story, with its burlesque characters, irreverent attitude toward authority, and slapstick atmosphere, was very appealing to Kentridge, offering him an exciting opportunity to exercise his comic gifts. He was also drawn to the ways in which the character of the Nose, by courting transgression and taking an outlaw's attitude toward decorum and rank, encourages anarchy.

Over the past few years Kentridge has embarked on a welter of works that deal, directly or indirectly, with *The Nose.*[123] In prints, drawings, collages, and sculptures, the Nose appears as a character on horseback, a kind of comic-ceremonial monument to the organ of smell.[124] It is frequently combined with processions and other earlier motifs. In 2008, in preparation for the opera and an exhibition at Marian Goodman Gallery, Paris, Kentridge made a large backdrop in his studio. Music (though not by Shostakovich) was performed in front of this work, and a film was projected against it during the Paris showing.

122. The opera is scheduled to premiere in March 2010.

123. The first drawing for *The Nose,* according to the artist, is *Il Communicato N.32 (Making a Place for the Secret)* (2006). Conversation with the author, July 31, 2008.

124. All his life, Kentridge has said, he has wanted to make tabletop monuments; he conceived some of these sculptures as such. Ibid.

The display of the backdrop and film in Paris introduced a number of aspects key to Kentridge's subsequent interpretations of *The Nose*. Specifically, he made use of a collage aesthetic reminiscent of Dada and Russian Constructivism, creating a free-wheeling milieu of images and words. It is a kind of stream-of-consciousness depiction of the Russian streets, full of life and change. Although Kentridge has always formulated surrealistic metamorphoses, he has generally made straightforward, continuous plots. But now, under the sway of a more intuitive approach that embraces chaos, Kentridge's narrative style has changed. Instead of emphasizing sequence, he privileges multiple layers and overlaps. This had been the approach in *7 Fragments* as well, but it has greatly intensified as Kentridge has worked through *The Nose*.

A key statement in the first film associated with *The Nose* is "Every Man His Own Projector"—a proclamation seconded with *William Kentridge: Everyone Their Own Projector*, the artist's book published to accompany the 2008 Paris exhibition. The democratic, all-inclusive tone clearly echoes Beuys's revolutionary "Everyone is an artist." Thus, alongside the aura of flux that is so essential to *The Nose* comes a generous, quasi-all-inclusive philosophy. Leaving behind the rigid hierarchy of traditional Russian society, nothing is fixed. "Refuse the 3 Point Perspective," an injunction printed on one page of the book, could be the anthem of the liberated artist.

For a 2008 exhibition at Annandale Galleries in Sydney, Kentridge gathered a wide-ranging assemblage of *Nose*-related works. Here the Nose became an antic character—a joyous being, free of the earthbound constraints of the body, and a doppelgänger of the artist himself. The show was called *William Kentridge: Telegrams from the Nose*, a title that echoes Fyodor Dostoevsky's *Notes from the Underground*.[125] At the same time, for the Biennale of Sydney, Kentridge was creating what would become the first, and most ambitious, manifestation of his newest consuming theme. Entitled *I am not me, the horse is not mine* (2008), the work comprises eight films that run simultaneously in one room (see figs. 25–26, 35). The title, a Russian peasant saying denying guilt of thievery, calls forth a Gogolian world of paranoia, frantic bewilderment, and unalloyed pathos. Kentridge came across the saying in a Russian trial transcript, the plenum of the Central Committee of February 26, 1937, in which a former Russian operative, Nikolai Bukharin, is interrogated. That event became the subject of one of the work's films, *Prayers of Apology* (pls. 202–8). In it the accused speaks of being beaten with (what else?) a stone; his alleged duplicity is an unsurprising attribute in Kentridge's world of doubles. Pleading his innocence in the film, Bukharin forlornly declares, "No one believes in human feelings anymore"—a comment that is met with laughter.

Opposite *Prayers of Apology* at the biennial was *A Lifetime of Enthusiasm* (pls. 174–81), a procession-themed film that includes the Nose and shows Tatlin's monument being dragged along at the end. Another fragment, *Commissariat for Enlightenment* (pls. 192–96), features the Nose wielding a cane, which it uses to make drawings, then stoops and walks in the manner of Charlie Chaplin or Groucho Marx.

125. There is certainly much to compare between Kentridge's outlook and the writings of Dostoevsky and Gogol. Issued in 1864, not long after the publication of Gogol's "The Nose," *Notes from the Underground* is filled with the same stultifying atmosphere of czarist Russia. Like Gogol's protagonist, Dostoevsky's main character is a collegiate assessor. Though he despises his lot in life, he is proud and revengeful, constantly confronting a "stone wall."

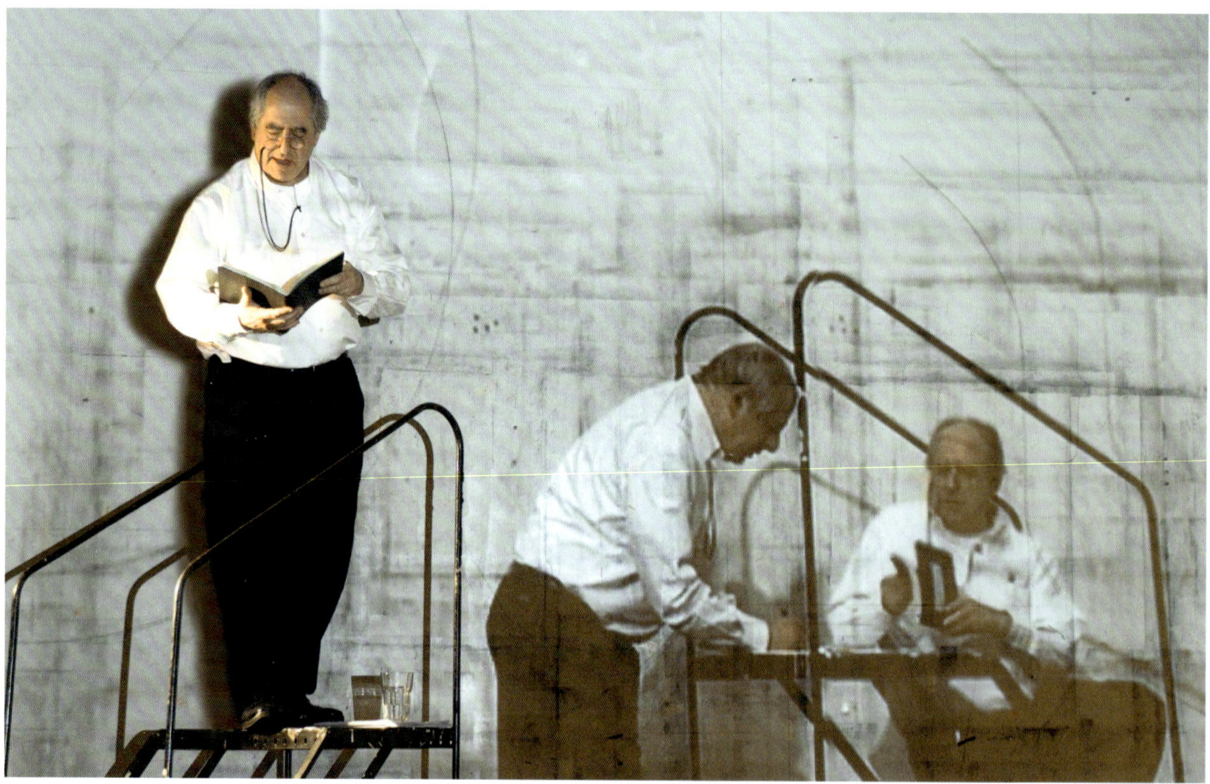

FIG. 13 Kentridge performing ***I am not me, the horse is not mine*** (2008) at the Biennale of Sydney, 2008

The immersive atmosphere of the Sydney installation was replete with a sense of plenitude furthered by the conflicting messages of the films and the cacophony of musical styles. The juxtaposition of African music and Russian context represents a new synthesis of cultures on Kentridge's part. At one point, a rhythmic chant in Zulu repeats the Russian sentiment "where is my nose; bring me back my nose." As was implied by the title *What Will Come (has already come), I am not me, the horse is not mine* suggests the inevitable circularity of life. Kentridge, the auteur, skates above reality to create a raucous and anarchistic version of events. He fights for a territory in which imagination and laughter can coexist. This effectively became the theme of a lecture/performance Kentridge gave at the opening of the biennial in the gallery space where *I am not me* was displayed (see figs. 13, 17, 42).

Bearing the same title as the installation, the performance commenced as an apparent lecture on the Gogol story. With the sudden appearance of a film on the back wall—a projection of the artist performing different actions—Kentridge began a mimed interaction with himself. The projections multiplied, allowing him to reveal the multiple selves that haunt his existence while also illustrating the drama of the Gogol story. Juxtaposed references to utopia, war, and tragedy recalled the Russian context. Notwithstanding the fact that Bukharin speaks of being beaten with a stone, *I am not me,* both installation and lecture, evinces an indomitable extravagance of spirit. With Gogol and Shostakovich as his guides, the immodest Kentridge does battle with the macrocosm of political circumstance.

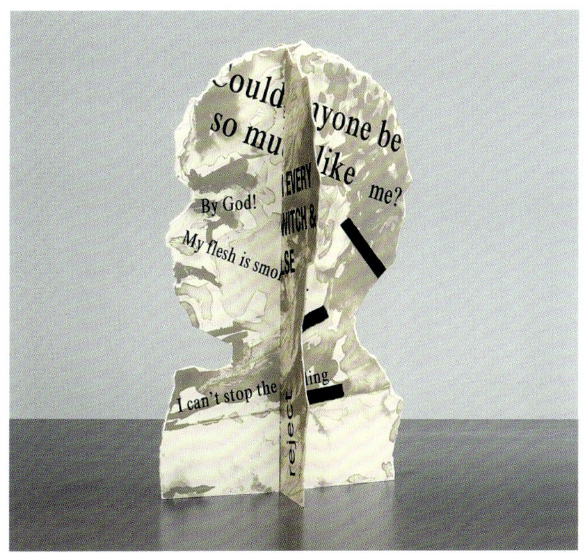

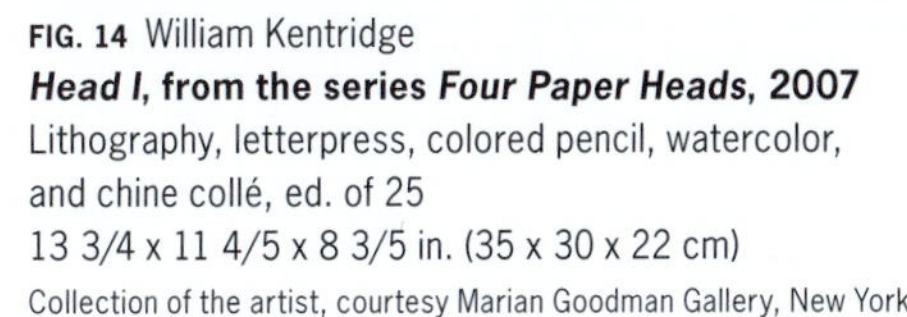
FIG. 14 William Kentridge
***Head I*, from the series *Four Paper Heads*, 2007**
Lithography, letterpress, colored pencil, watercolor, and chine collé, ed. of 25
13 3/4 x 11 4/5 x 8 3/5 in. (35 x 30 x 22 cm)
Collection of the artist, courtesy Marian Goodman Gallery, New York

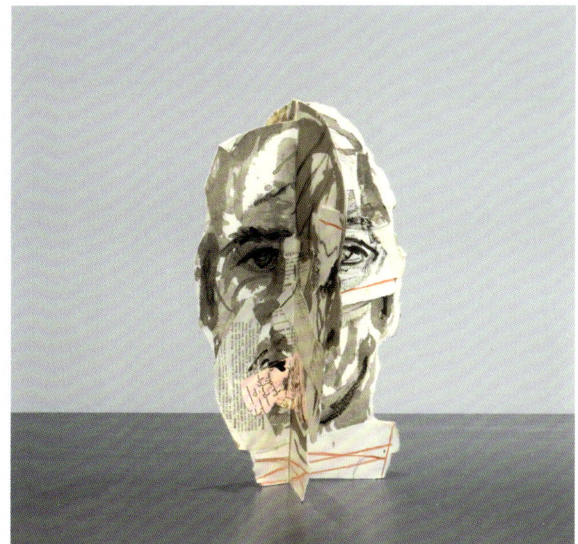

FIG. 15 William Kentridge
***Head IV*, from the series *Four Paper Heads*, 2007**
Lithography, letterpress, colored pencil, watercolor, and chine collé, ed. of 25
14 3/5 x 9 4/5 x 7 4/5 in. (37 x 25 x 20 cm)
Collection of the artist, courtesy Marian Goodman Gallery, New York

THE SUM OF THE PARTS

Kentridge has often, almost with resignation, remarked that he cannot avoid having his work reflect his person and psychological makeup.[126] Having come to terms with this, he was "released...from a paralysis I found myself in regarding what I should be doing, what images I ought to be making."[127] In other words, recalling his early anxiety about being worthy of becoming an artist, his acceptance of the inherently personal content of art may have played a role in his decision to become one.[128] Kentridge has more than one alter ego, though; we have already noted his physical resemblance to Soho and Felix, and he also inscribed himself within the physique of Ubu. In a recent series of busts entitled *Four Paper Heads* (2007; figs. 14–15), Kentridge built his sculptural image on the example of Picasso's *Absinthe Drinker* series of 1914.[129] He had echoed Picasso's practice in his artist and model drawings, but in *Four Paper Heads* he specifically turned to cubist portraiture as a vehicle for compiling personalities, not just visages.

Who, then, is the individual we see in the mirror of Kentridge's art? While it is possible to make too fine a point in answering this query, Kentridge has unapologetically admitted to possessing the extremes of behavior demonstrated by Soho and Felix: "If in the end there is a terrible image of someone there that emerges in the film, then that is part of who I am... whether you like it or not."[130] He reveals a streak of self-conscious and self-deprecating humor but an absence of postmodern irony (a person who explains his position as being somewhere between optimism and nihilism has no use for that sort of thing). In a word, stoical perhaps best describes the psychological makeup of Kentridge and many of his characters—a stoicism belied only by the musical component of his work, where emotion seems to surge forth.

126. See Kentridge and Breidbach, *William Kentridge: Thinking Aloud*, 11, 66. Kentridge often expresses trepidation about psychology and its inquiries, and yet, because he accepts that art will inherently reflect "who you are," he feels he does not need to spend time analyzing himself for "self-knowledge." Ibid., 68. Kentridge's use of puppets may reflect another process of self-awareness, mimicking post-traumatic stress disorder. Just as psychologists encourage children who have suffered traumas of various kinds to reenact their experiences with dolls, Kentridge may have found puppets therapeutic.

127. Stone, *Politeness of Objects*, 4.

128. In this regard, he may also have been influenced by his admiration for the photographer David Goldblatt, whom Kentridge quotes as saying that one's work "reveals your fears and desires." Ibid.

129. Interestingly, there were also four images of Kentridge in the *Invisible Mending* section of *7 Fragments*.

130. Kentridge and Breidbach, *William Kentridge: Thinking Aloud*, 66.

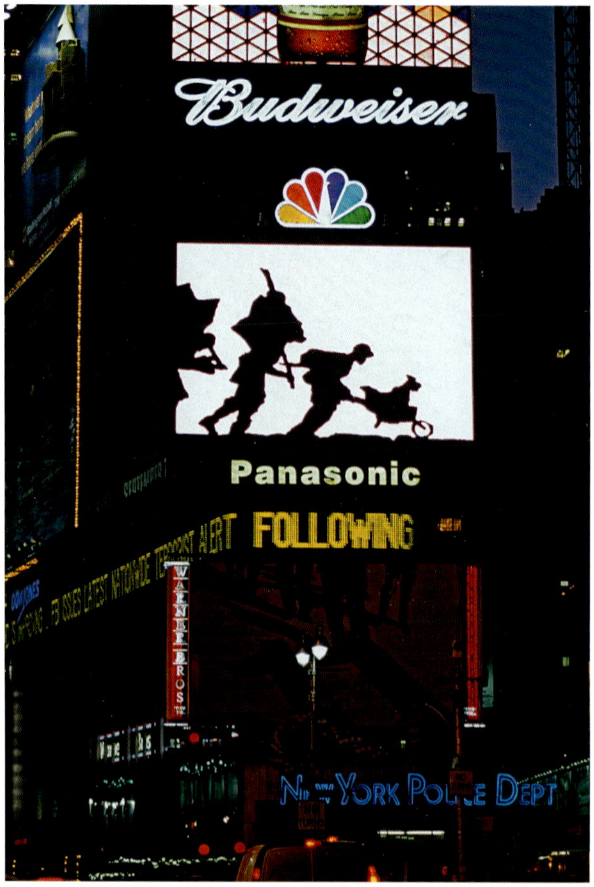

FIG. 16 Installation view of ***Shadow Procession*** (1999) in Times Square, New York, 2001

Kentridge's work is inherently political, for it intimately reflects the conditions of his locale: Johannesburg, the South African state, and Africa in general. The son of a politically minded family, Kentridge was raised on the political ideals of earlier utopian societies. Yet, though his work engages with that of past artists who were deeply involved with political themes, he has moved beyond what is traditionally considered political art. His is an art that does not seek to present (or re-present) tragedies or express outrage, as was the case with Picasso's *Guernica* (1937). Rather, he introduces the perspective of the perceiver-ego. In effect, he is saying that the macrocosm offers only unspeakable horror, whereas the microcosm—the individual—offers possibilities for art.

It is perhaps for these reasons that Kentridge has attracted such a large international audience. When he installs one of his procession works on a giant screen in New York's Times Square (fig. 16), he speaks of much more than South Africa, even as he starts from that context. Reviewing the work of the French literary theorist Pascale Casanova, the critic Louis Menand has written on a recent phenomenon in the evolution and appreciation of artists. At earlier moments of the modern era, he remarks, artists such as Joyce had to go to Paris in order to position themselves vis-à-vis "the standards of the metropole...the eternal center of the literary universe."[131] (Kentridge followed suit with his title *Johannesburg, 2nd Greatest City after Paris.*) But today, says Menand, a new model prevails: being a "national artist" is something to be admired, for "acceptance has shifted from assimilation to differentiation, and differentiation means *not* being modern."[132] It is in this spirit that Kentridge has embraced the quaintness of earlier eras; to be modern in appearance is of no consequence to him. Furthermore, Menand notes the ascendance and appeal of intellectually sophisticated artists who are, nonetheless, steeped in their national identities—a perfect description of Kentridge and his work.

131. Louis Menand, "All That Glitters," *The New Yorker,* December 26, 2005/ January 2, 2006, 139.

132. Ibid.

All of this speaks to the first two-fifths of the material covered in this exhibition—the work that springs from what one might call Kentridge's South African–focused period. However, in the same way that Joyce's writing evolved after his departure from Ireland and the work of Anselm Kiefer, Sigmar Polke, and Gerhard Richter changed with the fall of the Berlin Wall, Kentridge's art has been transformed since the end of apartheid. He no longer has quite so volatile a context. His world was remade, and his work as well. First he turned inward, making himself and his practice the subject of *7 Fragments,* and then he looked beyond his immediate locale to the rest of Africa. At the same time, he dramatically enhanced the physical scale and presence of his art.

Plato's Allegory of the Cave is not the only Platonic concept that might be applied to Kentridge's work. There is also the philosopher-king as articulated in *The Republic*. Plato's king is a wise man who practices dialectical thinking, loves learning, rules over a utopian society, and is guardian of the law. Kentridge might be seen as his artistic counterpart—a stoical dialectician who is highly inquisitive, moral, and alert to his political circumstances. In this guise he certainly does have the right to be an artist, one who is not so modest as to shy away from representing the world. Modesty is not really an issue, at any rate; as Kentridge explains, the moment pencil touches paper, his point of view and self-portrayal are inevitable. On the other hand, sometimes this characterization turns in an unexpected direction, as in the aforementioned *Four Paper Heads,* on which Kentridge wrote the following:

Could anyone be
so much like me?
My flesh is smoking
I can't stop sizzling
By God!
Lightnings all over my body
A million volts
A painter of cups

The first four lines of Kentridge's text are from Mayakovsky's epic poem "What It's About,"[133] but he has appended four lines of his own. Here Kentridge presents an identity that is dialectically opposed to the inquisitive, politically thoughtful, stoical individual described above. Suddenly his inner life explodes into his art with a remarkably personal revelation.

In Mayakovsky's play *A Tragedy,* the protagonist resides in a violent city in which "smoke-blackened mugs of factories feast/on the bones of heaven."[134] Self-pitying in the extreme, this poet/artist/martyr cries out:

Can you understand
why I,
quite calmly,
through a hailstorm of jeers,
carry my soul on a platter
to be dined on in future years?[135]

We rarely see such extreme emotions in Kentridge, but given his admiration of Mayakovsky and his citation of the Russian in *Four Paper Heads,* it is clear that these feelings underlie his multifaceted persona. The portrait that emerges of the self-described "painter of cups" is that of an emotionally taut individual, one of a very few—elected, as it were—able to attend to, describe, and declare the world's true state of affairs. It is doubtful that he conceives of himself as holding the power to heal, as Beuys imagined his own role in postwar Germany. Rather, it is Kentridge looking at himself looking that has sustained him through the five great themes of his art and up to the present moment.

133. Vladimir Mayakovsky, "What It's About," in *Pro eto*, trans. Alexander Lavrentiev (Berlin: Ars Nicolai, 1994), 19, 36.

134. Mayakovsky, *A Tragedy,* 29.

135. Ibid. Kentridge expressed his admiration for Mayakovsky's play in a conversation with the author, October 2005. Other similarities between *A Tragedy* and imagery in Kentridge's work abound. Examples include the frequent companionship of cats and many instances of metamorphoses, such as "bridges wringing their iron hands" or "The sky is weeping" (Kentridge intertitles) and "I, undaunted,/have borne my hatred for sunlight through centuries,/my soul stretched taut as the nerves of a wire" (Mayakovsky, 21).

HIGHLAND
PARK
SOMERSET
JEPPE HIGH BOYS
ROBERTS
ERNEST
LINDEN
SANDOWN EXT.
EXT. 3
EXT. 6
ILKLEY
ATHOLL
YORK ROAD
SOUTH KENSINGTON
NORTHUMBERLAND
HELEN
DAISY ST.
MARIA
KATHERINE
STREET
VALLEY
DRIVE
SCHOOL
WESTMORELAND ROAD
QUEEN ST
SPORTS GROUND
NEW YORK RD
OCEAN
ORION
PANTHER
PATROL
PHOENIX
PROTEA
LANGERMANN
BROAD
NINTH
TENTH
ELEVENTH AVE
WAY
AVE
NAIAD ST.
CUMBERLAND
SCHOOL
CLACTON
CAMBRIDGE
AVENUE
ABERFELDY
ABERDEEN
CARDIFF
ORLANDO ST.
MONTAGU
RHODES PARK
OXFORD
BUCKINGHAM
OSPREY
ORWELL
NOTTINGHAM
KENSINGTON
DERBY
KING EDWARD
SURREY RD
STANMORE RD.
SUFFOLK RD.
MILNER
CRESCENT
NYMPHE
ONYX
NILE
MILDURA ST
MARATHON
MERLIN ST
MINERVA ST.
MERSEY
MEDUSA
JEPPE GIRLS HIGH
ROAD
ISIPINGO
NATAL
JOLLY
DURBAN RD
UMLAZI RD
PADDOCK
WYNDCLIFF RD
STEWART DRIVE
CENTRAL
BELLEVUE
HIGHLANDS
SOUTH ST
PERCY ST
TUDHOPE
BEREA
STIRLING
NOLA
AVON
GIBSON
MARGARET AVE.

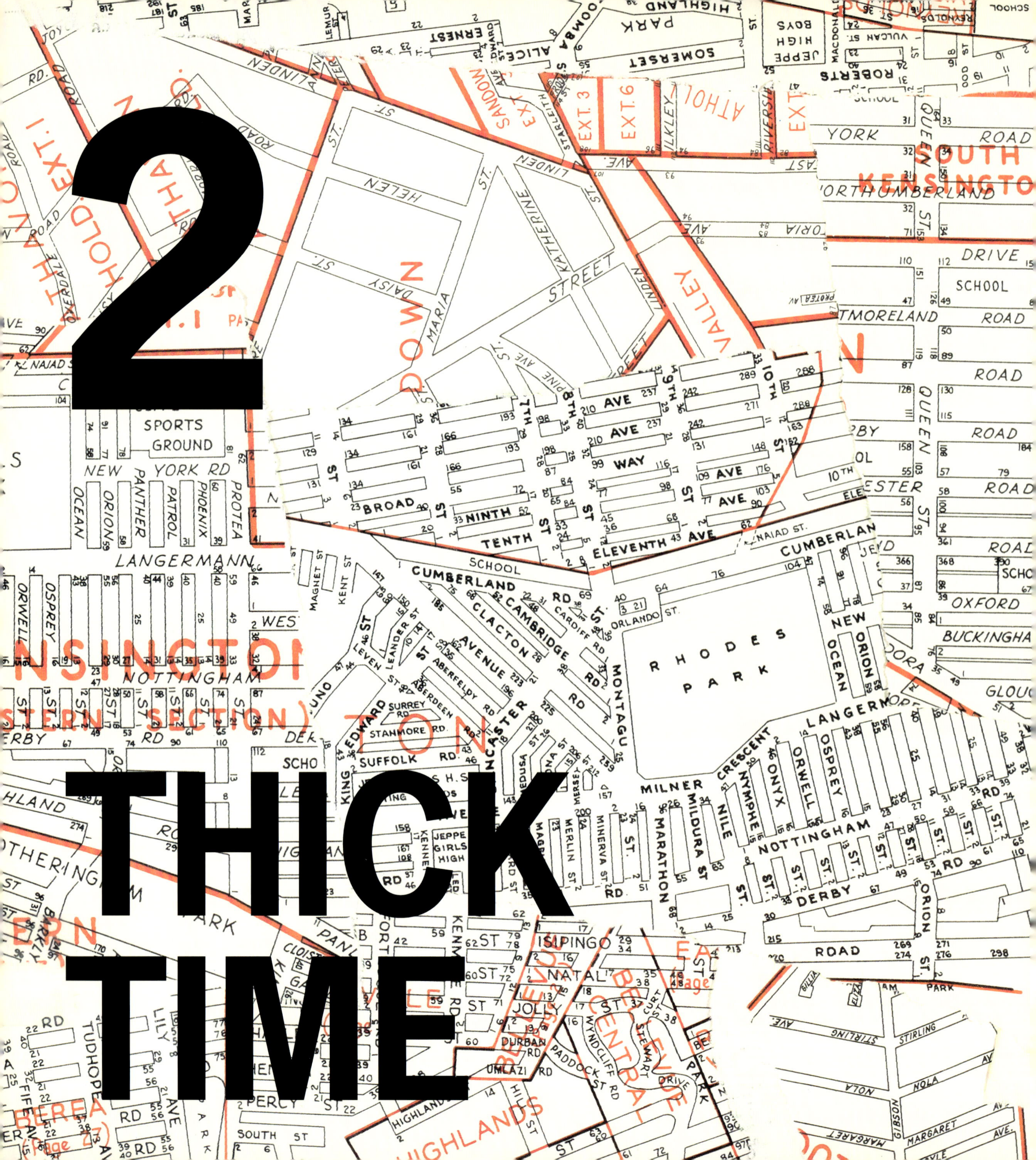

2

THICK TIME

SOHO & FELIX

Everything can be saved. Everything is provisional. A prior action is rescued by that which follows. A drawing abandoned is revived by the next drawing.

The films of Soho Eckstein and Felix Teitlebaum were all made with the principle of NO SCRIPT, NO STORYBOARD. The making of each film was the discovery of what each film was. A first image, phrase, or idea would justify itself in the unfolding of images, phrases, and ideas spawned by the work as it progressed. The imperfect erasures of the successive stages of each drawing become a record of the progress of an idea and a record of the passage of time. The smudges of erasure thicken time in the film, but they also serve as a record of the days and months spent making the film—a record of thinking in slow motion.

A slow trawling of motives, of connections between the characters in the films and in their world—the world of South Africa since the late 1980s. There is if not a deliberate blindness then certainly a bluntness in the progression of the films: bluntness both in the crude charcoal and fat erasures that are inevitable when using these materials, and in the unrefined succession of images. In the expectation or resignation that in the end, crude or sharp, well or ill, the constellation of images, story, and sound will reveal who one is (who I am, although the first person singular feels an impertinence, or at any rate inadequate. One of the things the films showed was that Soho and Felix were both close to me—not so much a self divided, but the artist as mediator between several different factions of the self. In *Stereoscope* Soho divides in two; in *History of the Main Complaint* he becomes eight or nine).

The first Soho film was an indulgence, time out from being an artist, a private pleasure that did not have to make sense to anyone outside the studio. Once the films started to be seen (about three years after the series began), it became harder to reclaim each time the space of not knowing what I was doing. One of the tasks of the years has been to find strategies to keep clarity at a distance. I still rely on a first image, phrase, or idea, but with oceans unknown between them—a sufficient impetus to put the camera in front of the paper and shoot the first frame.

The scale of the drawings (the largest are an arm's span, the smallest about a quarter of that), the materials (charcoal, one or two pastels, an eraser, and a cloth of chamois leather), and the format (film, not 4:3 video) stay the same. The gaps between making the films have become longer. It is now six years since the last one, *Tide Table*. But the start of a new film feels more and more a return to a familiar space—to a refuge for slow time.

The hope (and this is too much to load on the films) is that the succession of images and the connections between them will show not only a way forward for the narrative of the film, not only a revelation of who one is, but also a hint as to how to go forward in the world outside the studio, as if the gradual accretion of marks can somehow lumberingly draw agency into existence. **WK**

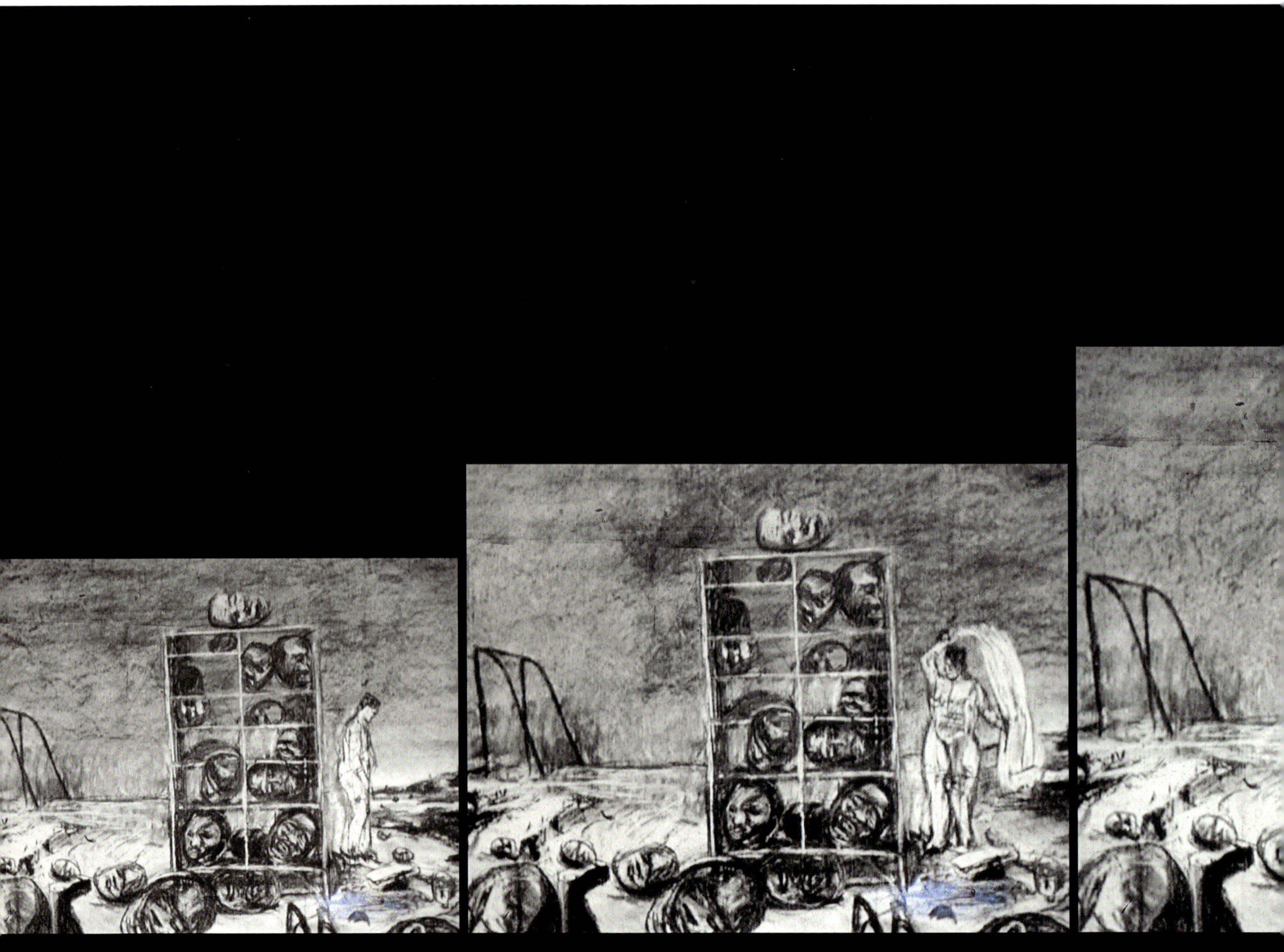

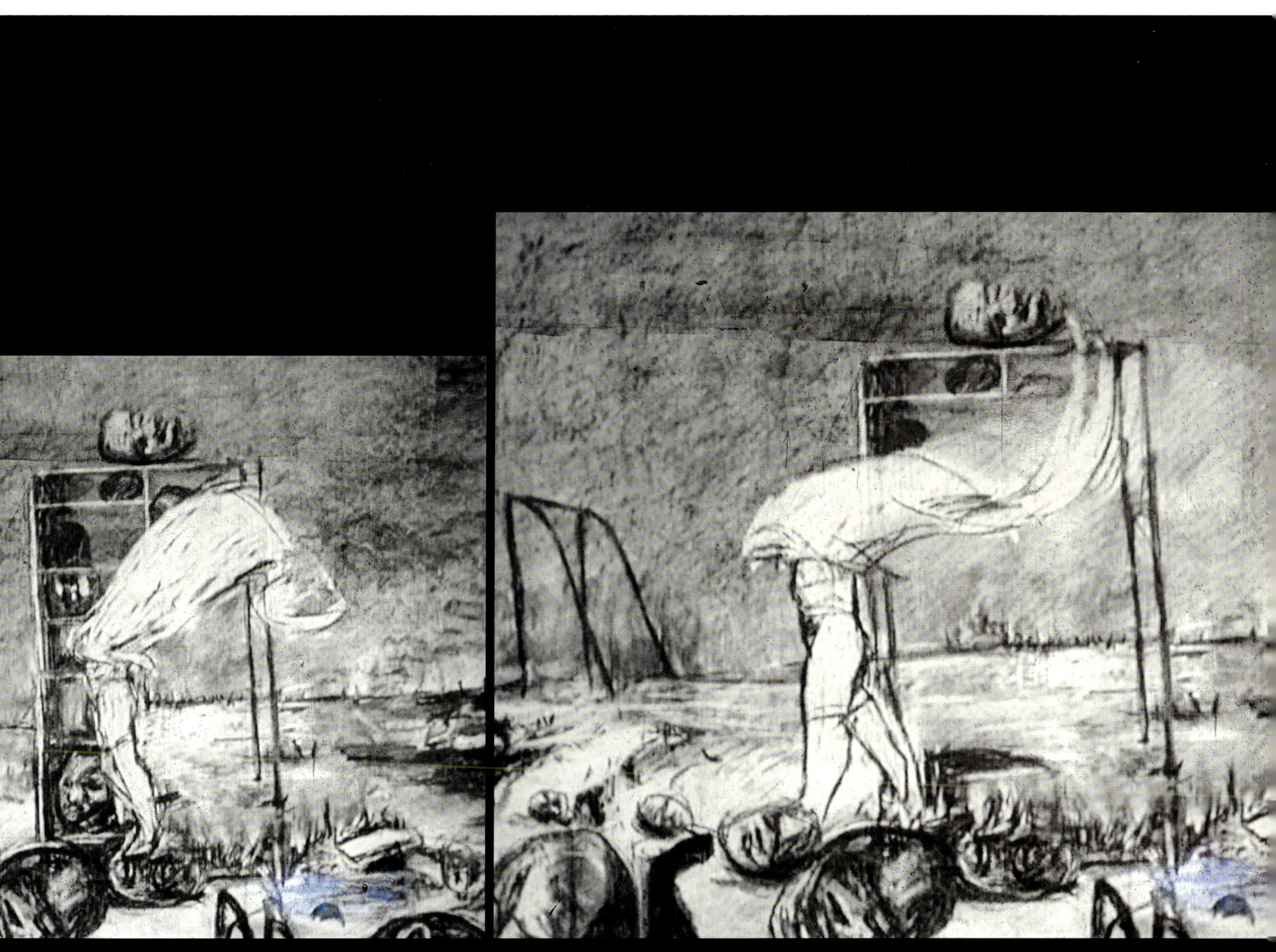

52–56
***Johannesburg, 2nd Greatest City after Paris*, 1989**
16mm animated film transferred to video, 8:02 min.
Collection of the artist, courtesy Marian Goodman Gallery, New York, and Goodman Gallery, Johannesburg

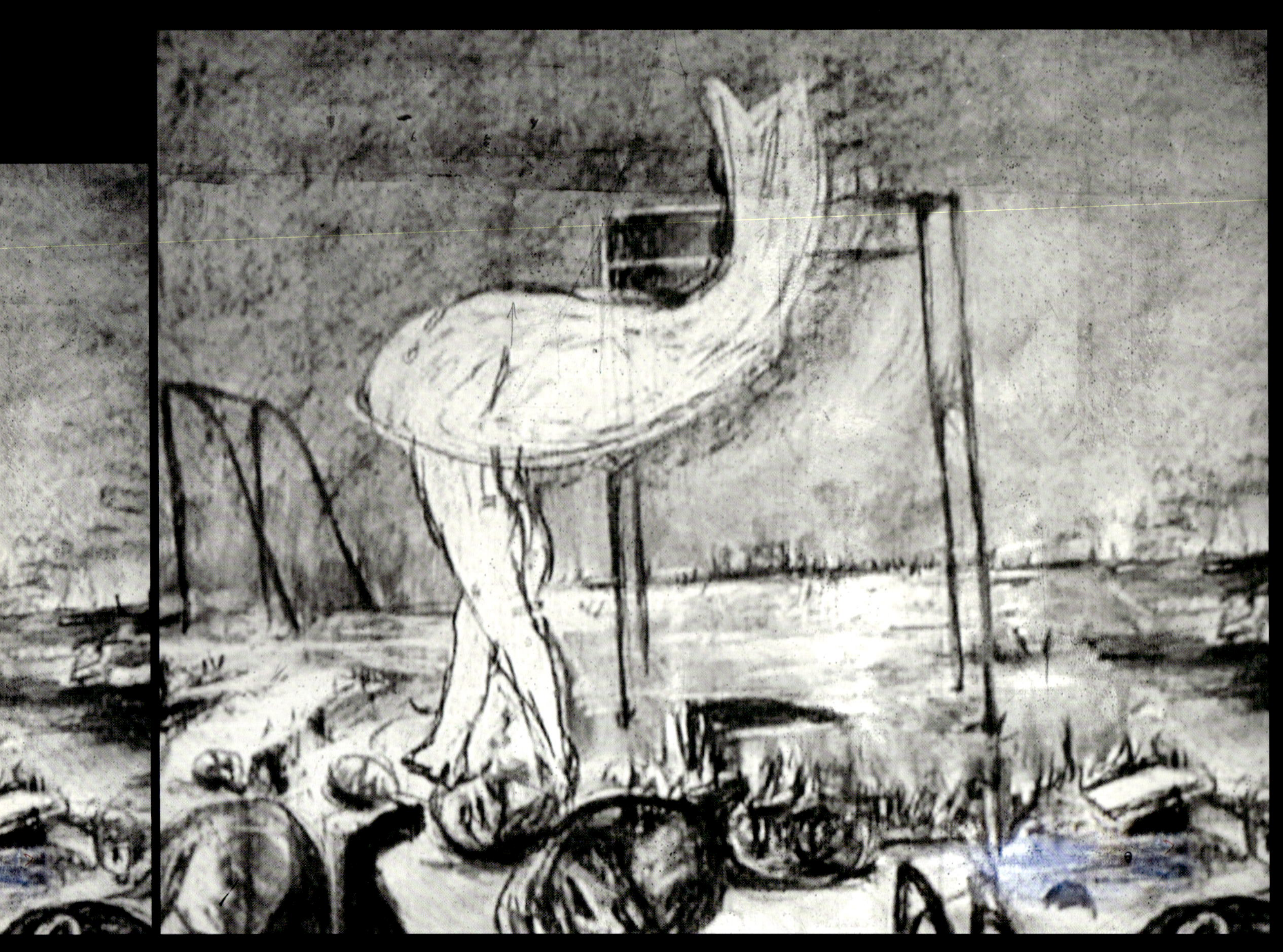

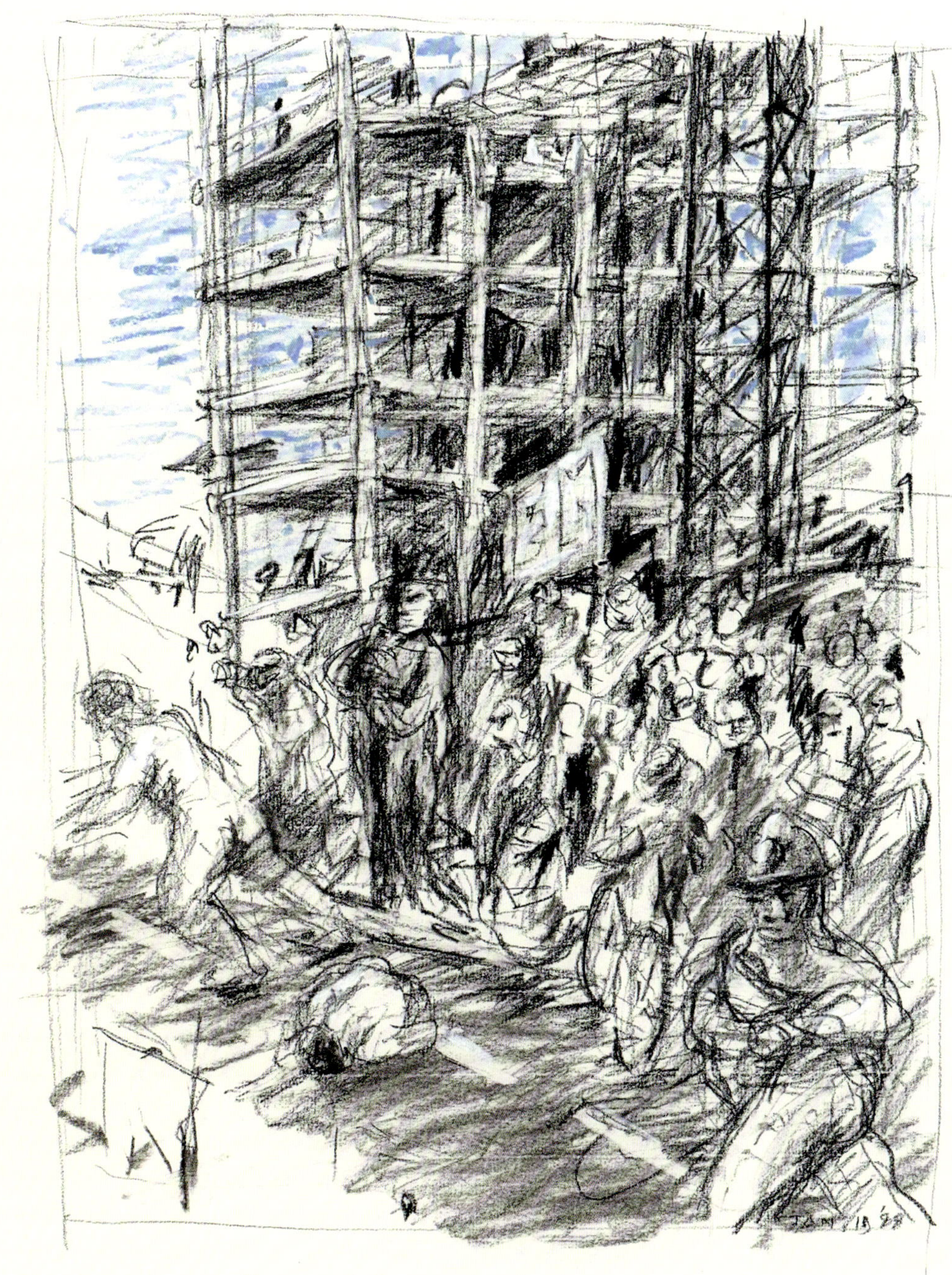

57

Drawing for the film *Johannesburg, 2nd Greatest City after Paris* [Soho Outside His Headquarters], 1989

Charcoal and pastel on paper

19 7/10 x 13 3/4 in. (50 x 35 cm)

Collection of the artist, courtesy Marian Goodman Gallery, New York, and Goodman Gallery, Johannesburg

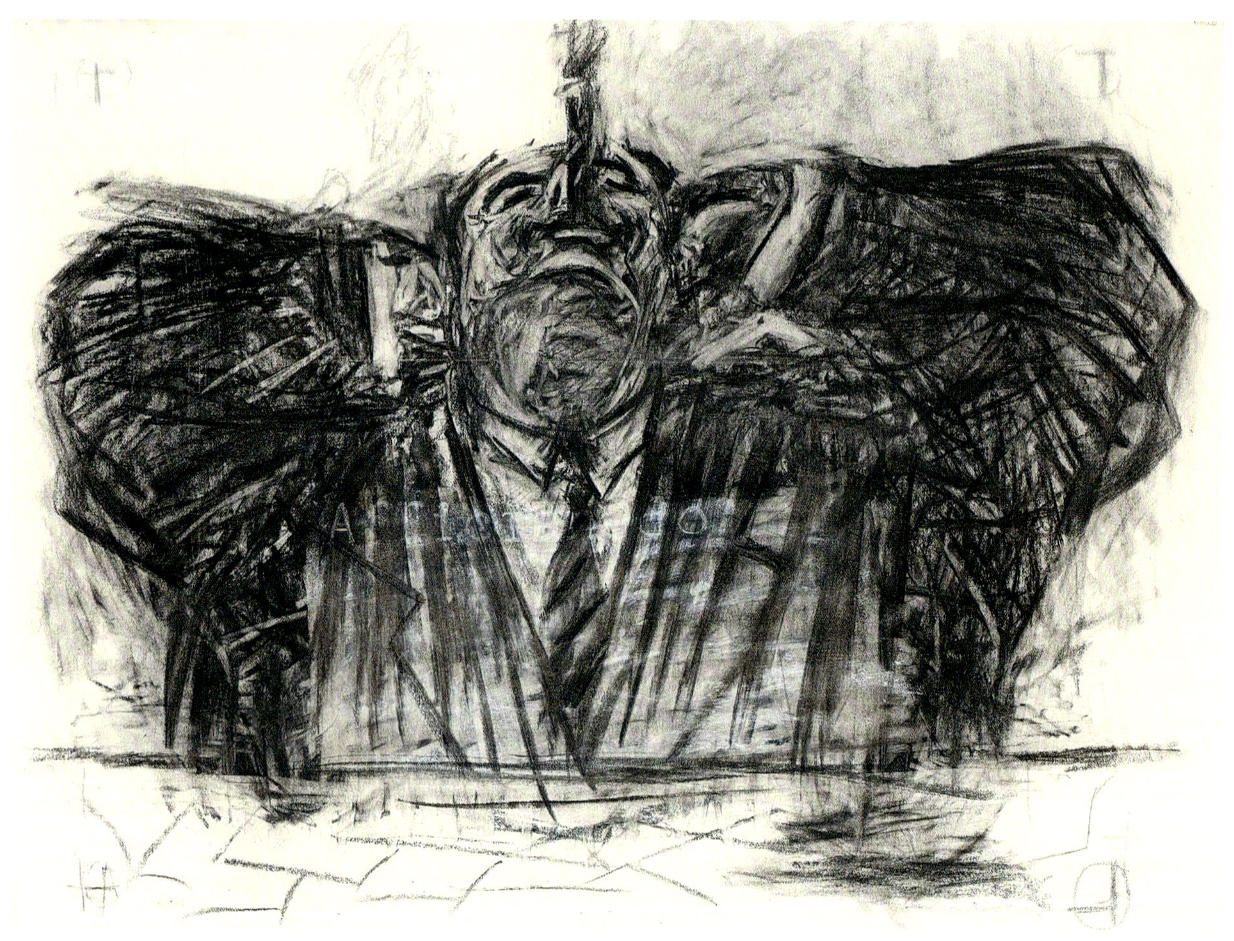

58
Drawing for the film *Johannesburg, 2nd Greatest City after Paris* [Soho with Cigar], 1989
Charcoal on paper
39 2/5 x 51 1/5 in. (100 x 130 cm)
Collection of the artist, courtesy Marian Goodman Gallery, New York, and Goodman Gallery, Johannesburg

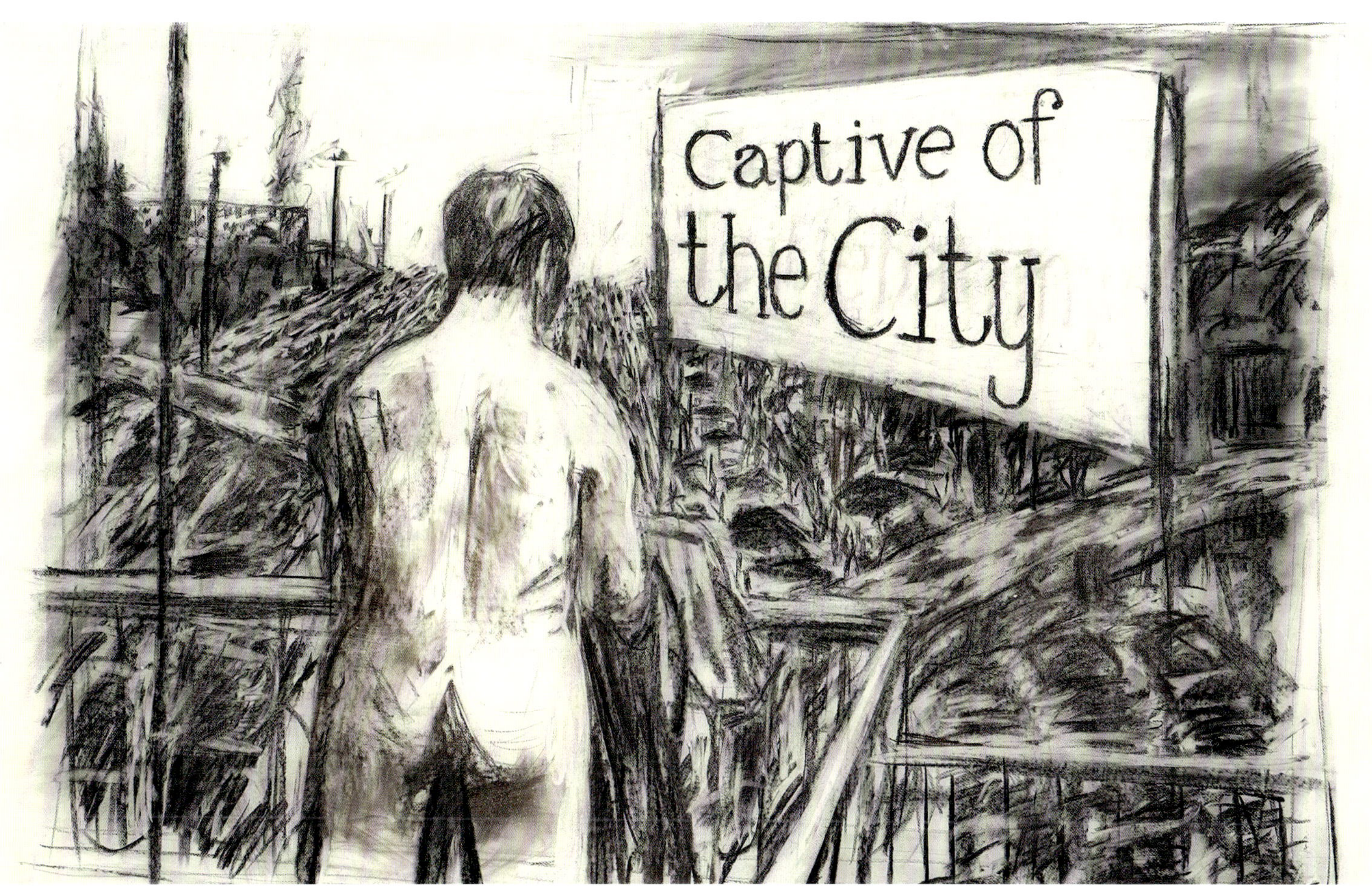

59

Drawing for the film *Johannesburg, 2nd Greatest City after Paris* [Captive of the City], 1989

Charcoal on paper

37 4/5 x 59 2/5 in. (96 x 151 cm)

Collection of the artist, courtesy Marian Goodman Gallery, New York, and Goodman Gallery, Johannesburg

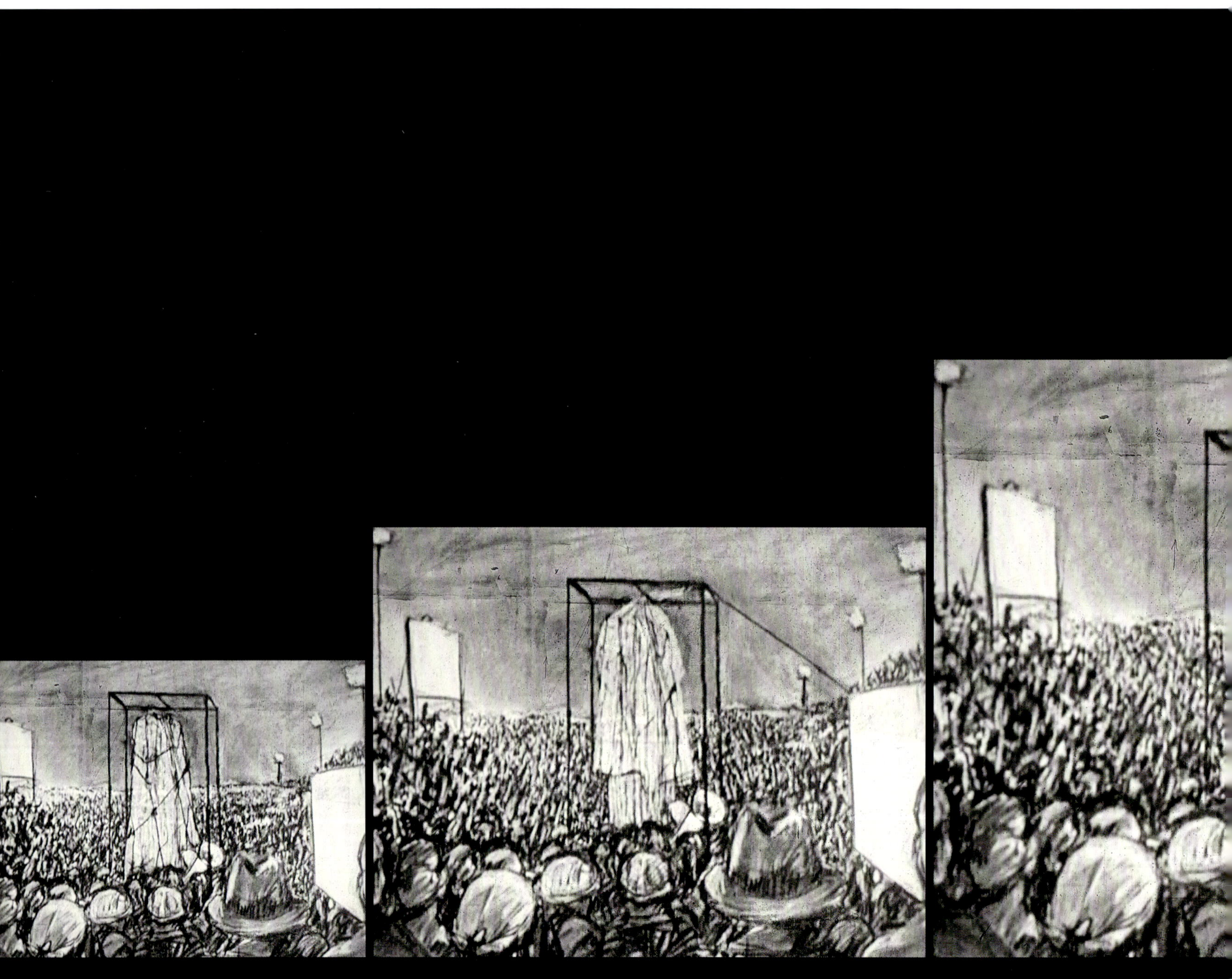

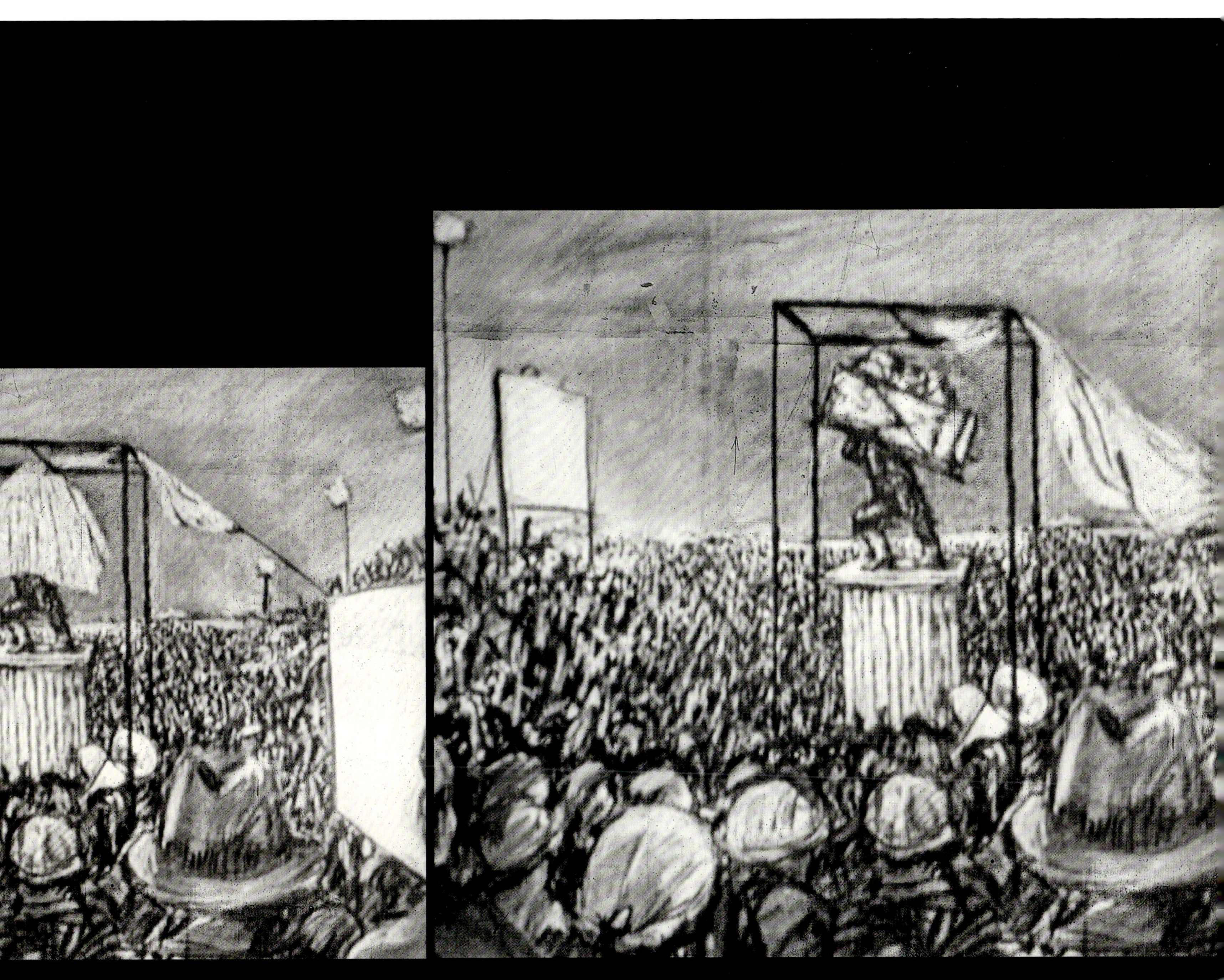

60–64
***Monument*, 1990**
16mm animated film transferred to video, 3:11 min.
Collection of the artist, courtesy Marian Goodman Gallery, New York, and Goodman Gallery, Johannesburg

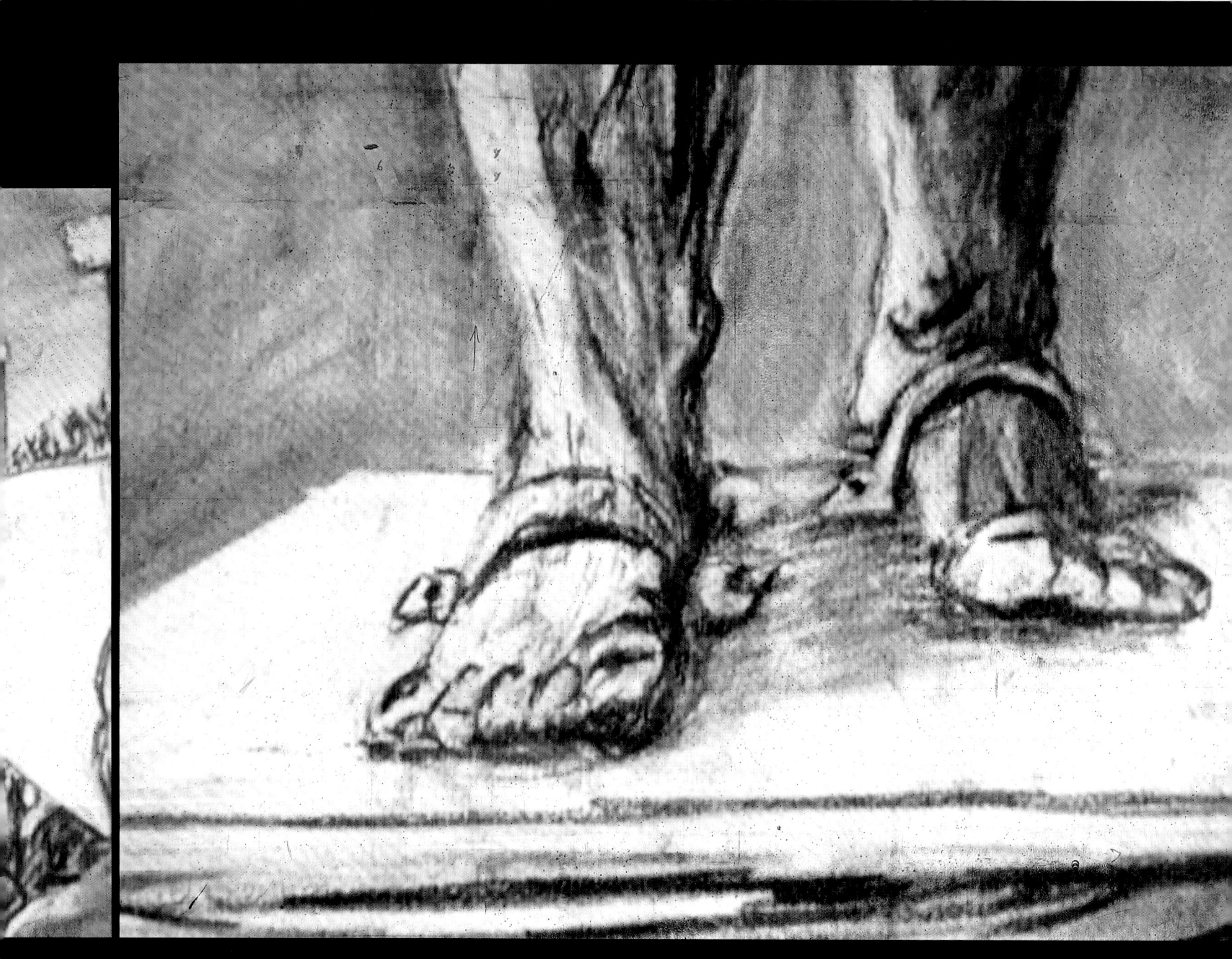

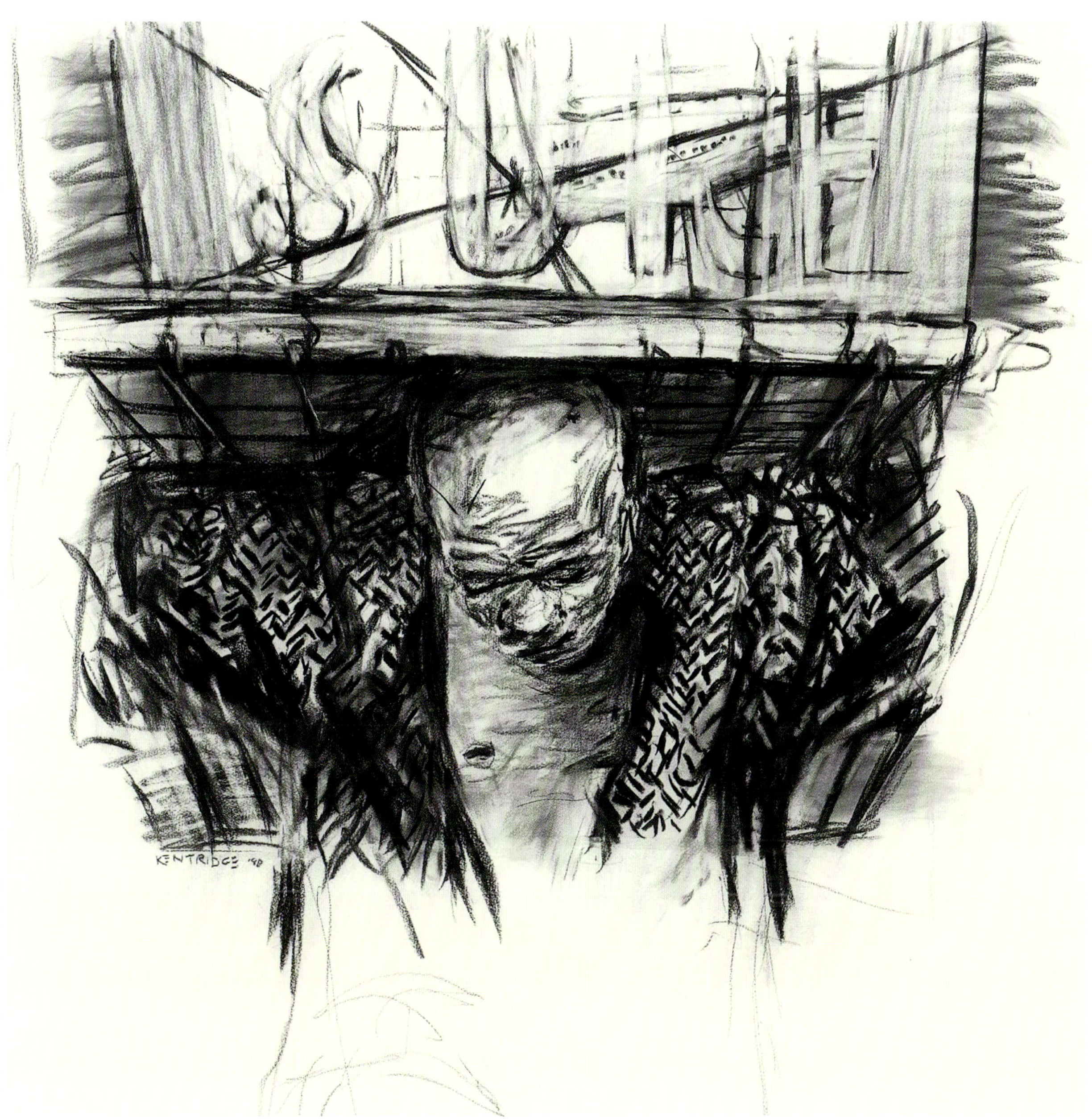

65

Drawing for the film *Monument*
[Harry—Close-up of Head and Load], 1990
Charcoal on paper
59 x 47 1/4 in. (150 x 120 cm)
Collection of the artist, courtesy Marian Goodman Gallery, New York, and Goodman Gallery, Johannesburg

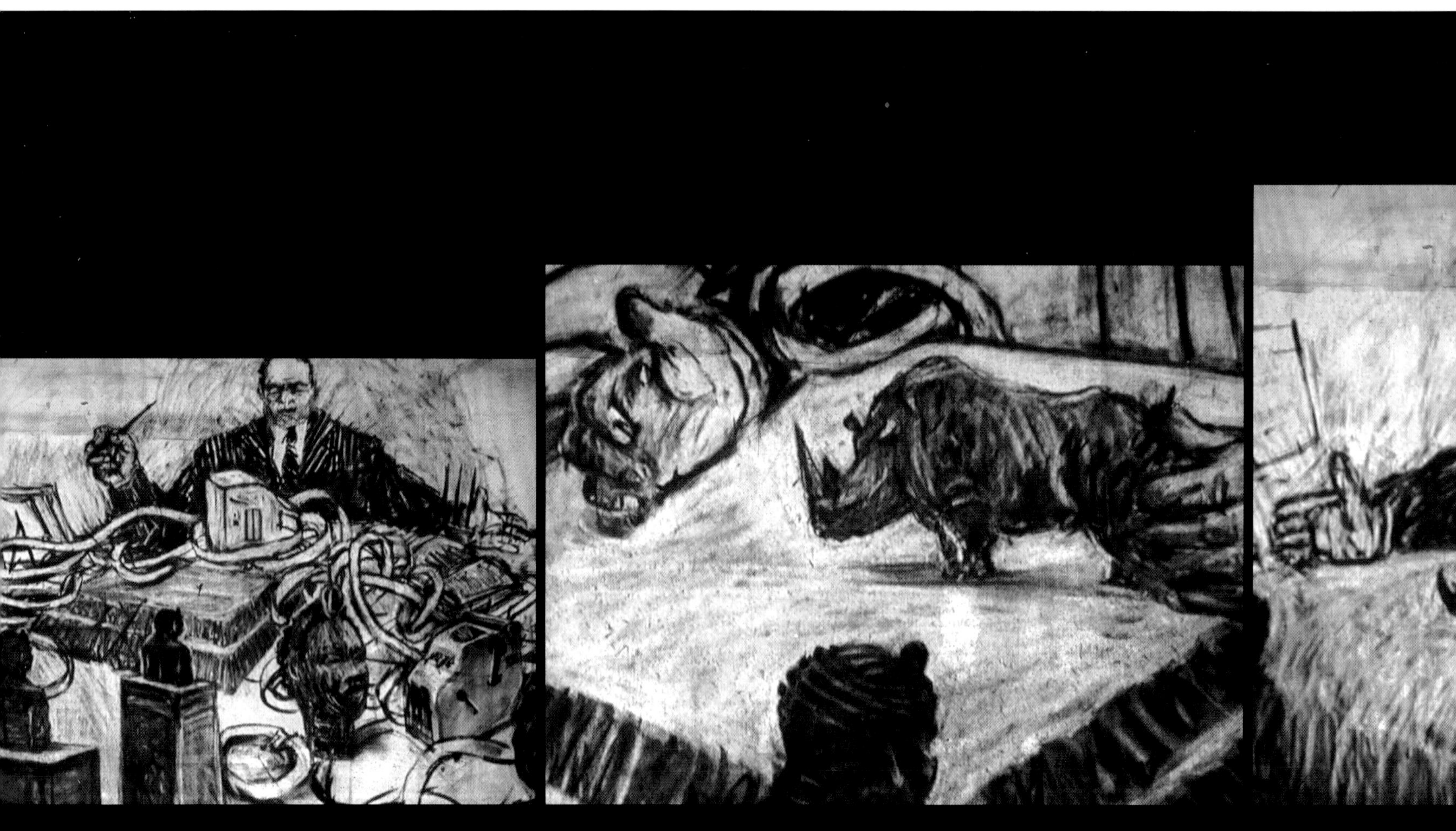

66–69
***Mine*, 1991**
16mm animated film transferred to video, 5:50 min.
Collection of the artist, courtesy Marian Goodman Gallery, New York, and Goodman Gallery, Johannesburg

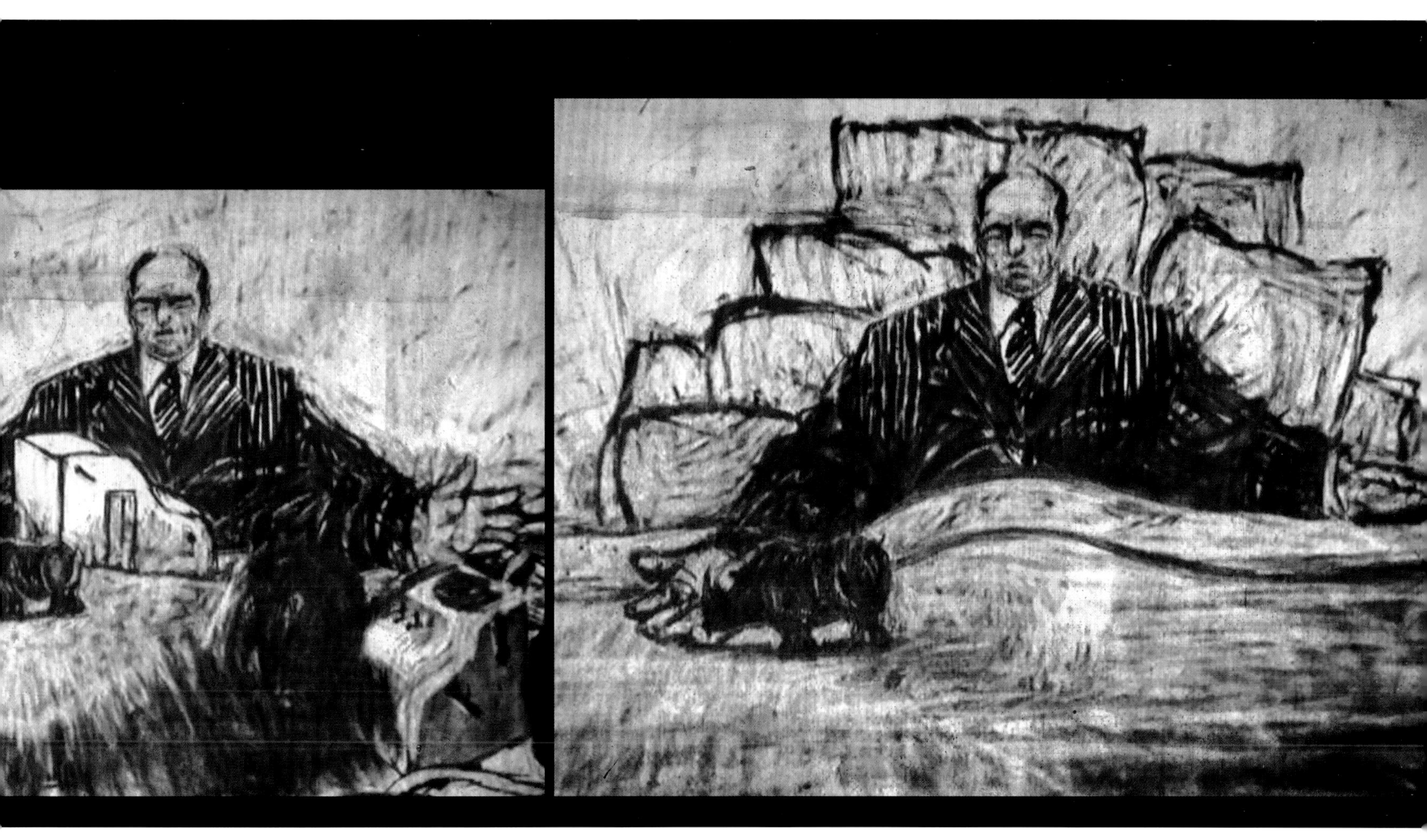

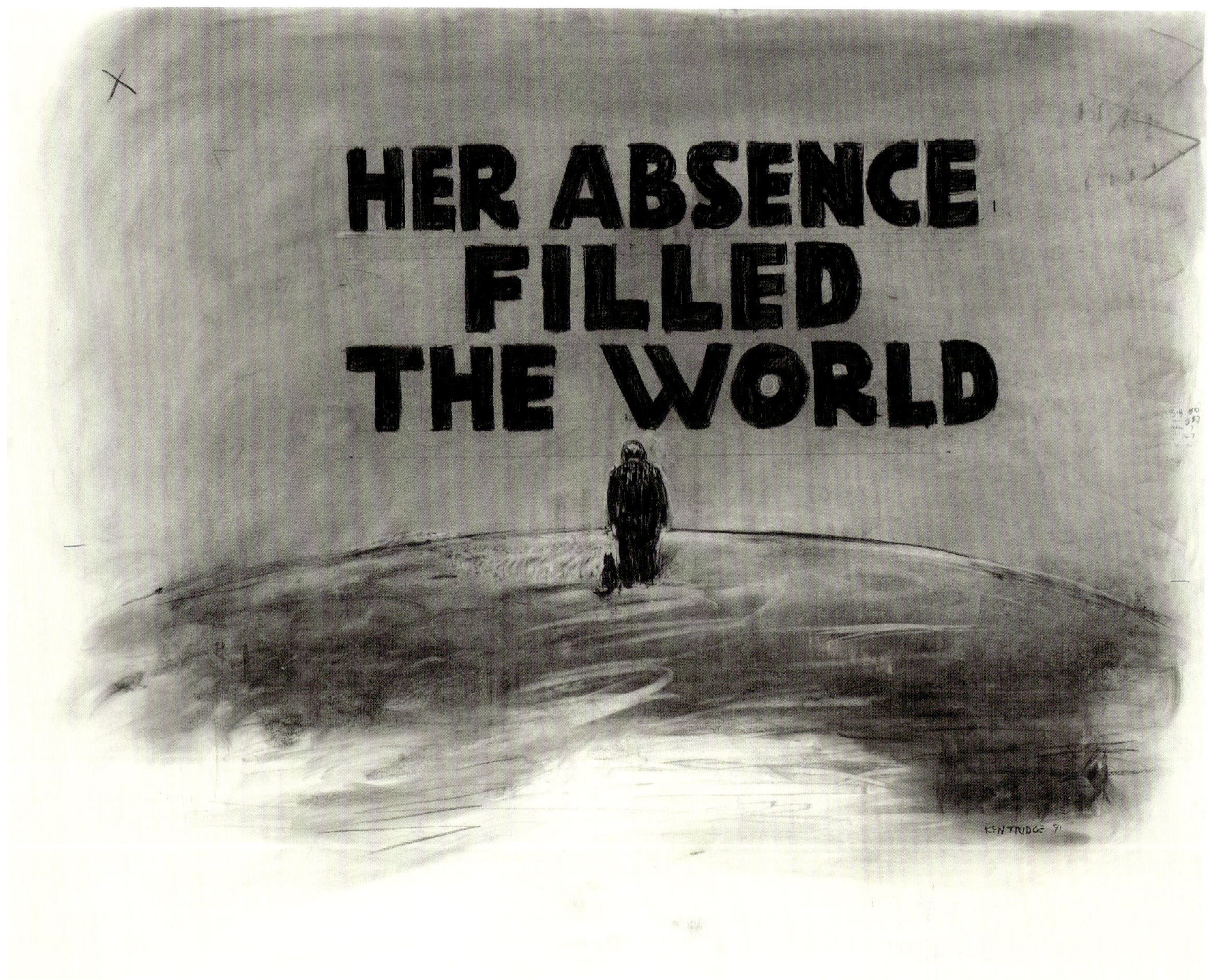

70
Drawing for the film *Sobriety, Obesity & Growing Old* [Her Absence Filled the World], 1991
Charcoal and pastel on paper
47 1/4 x 59 in. (120 x 150 cm)
Collection of the artist, courtesy Marian Goodman Gallery, New York, and Goodman Gallery, Johannesburg

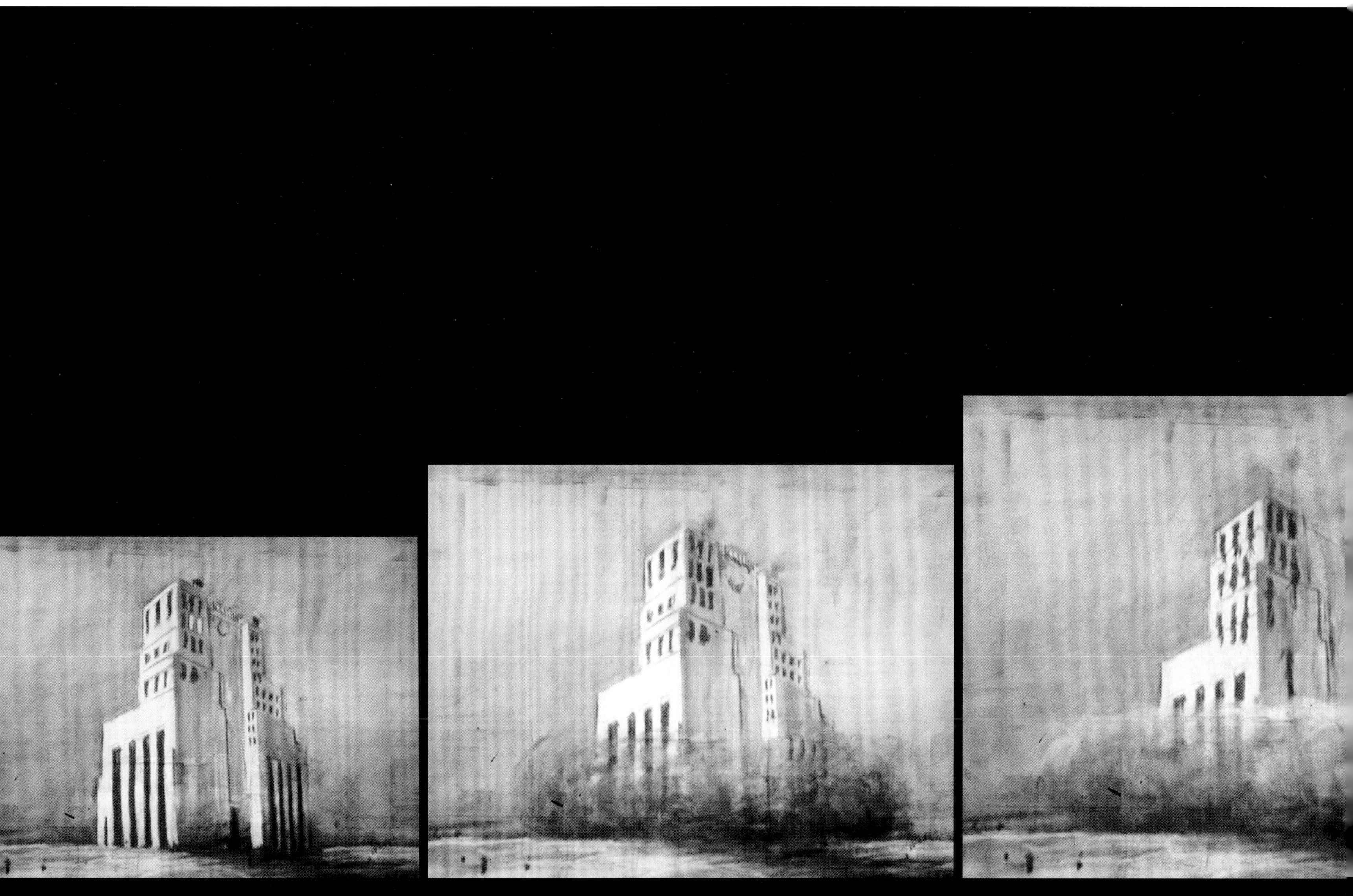

71–76
***Sobriety, Obesity & Growing Old*, 1991**
16mm animated film transferred to video, 8:22 min.
Collection of the artist, courtesy Marian Goodman Gallery, New York, and Goodman Gallery, Johannesburg

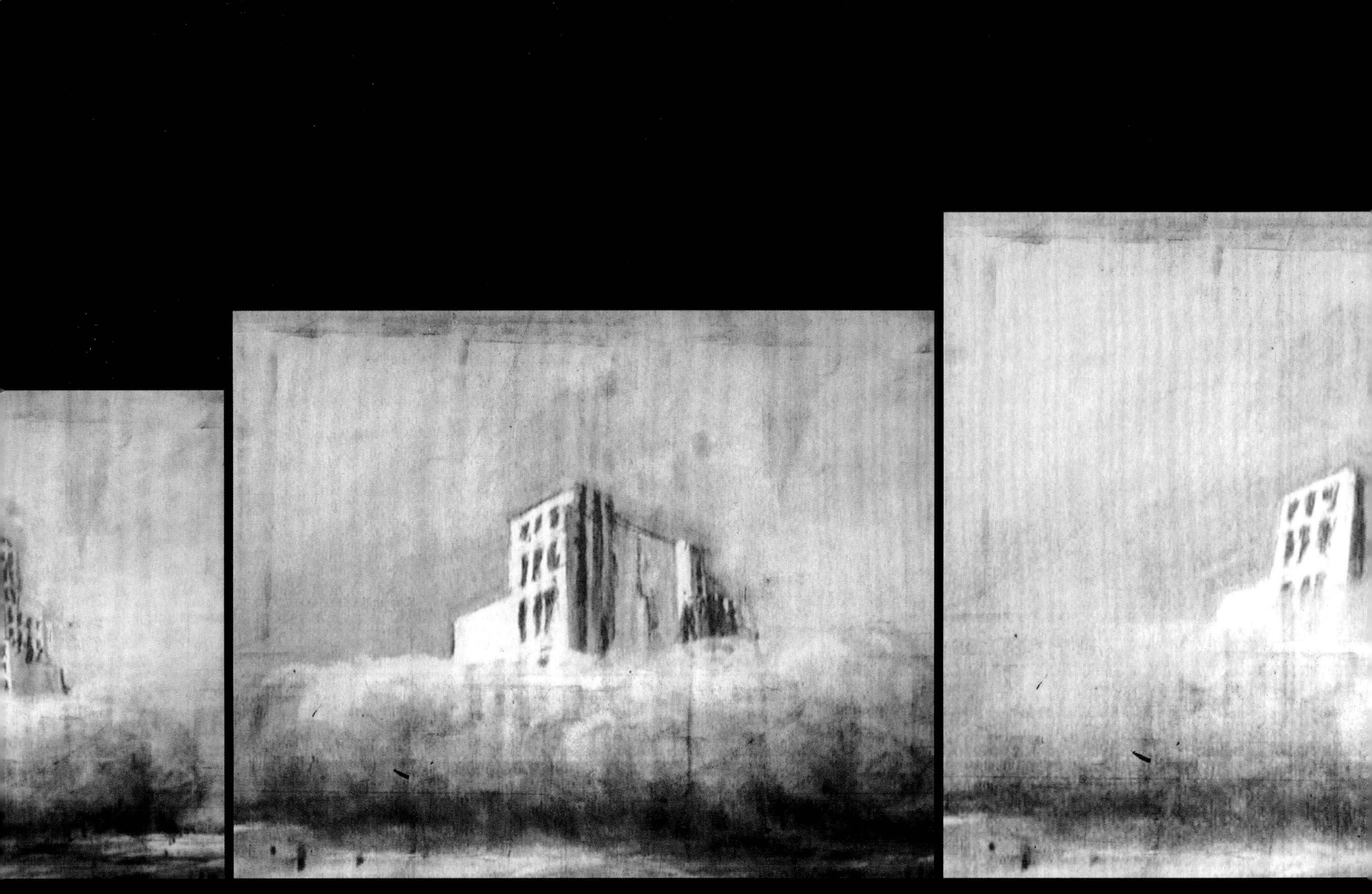

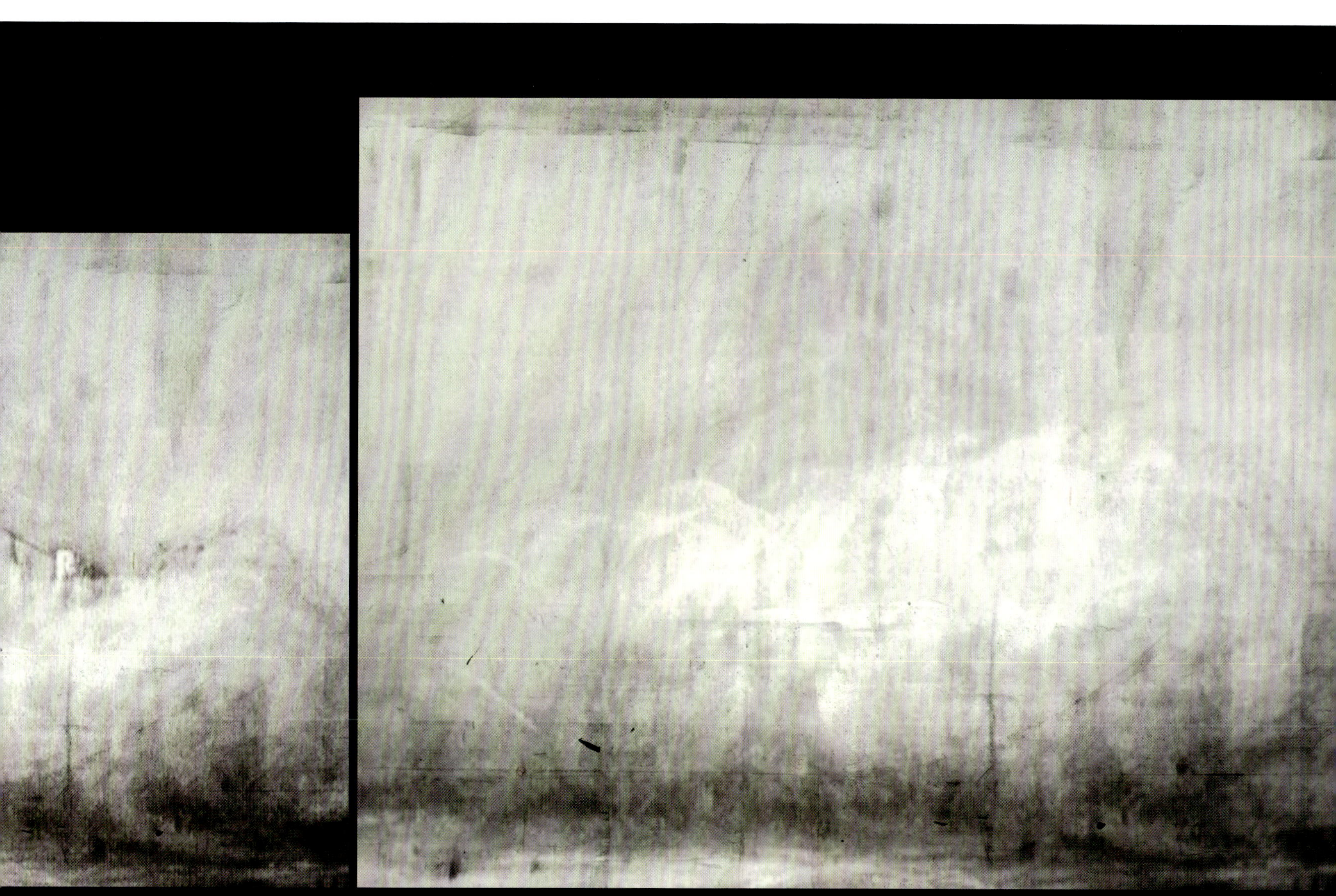

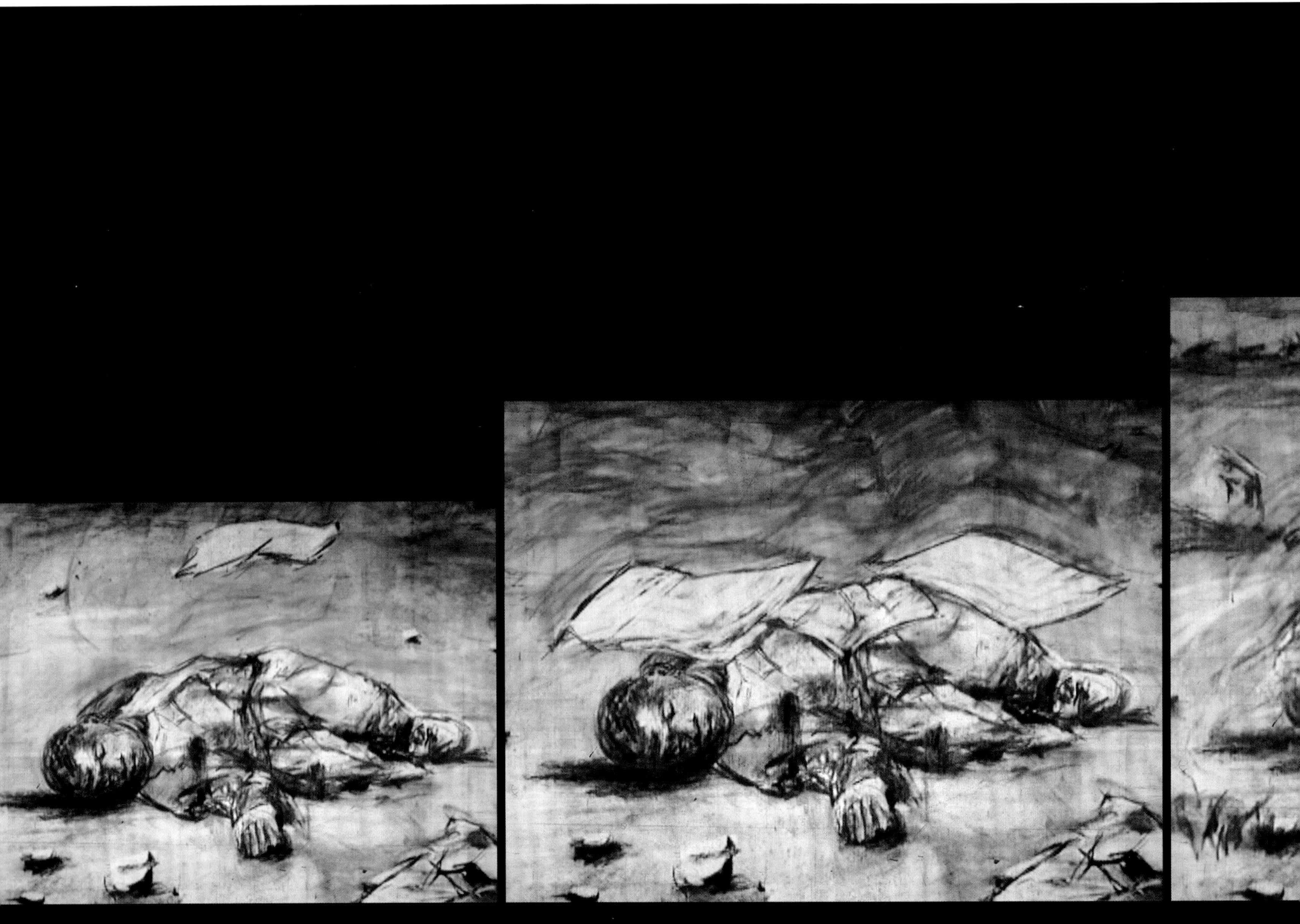

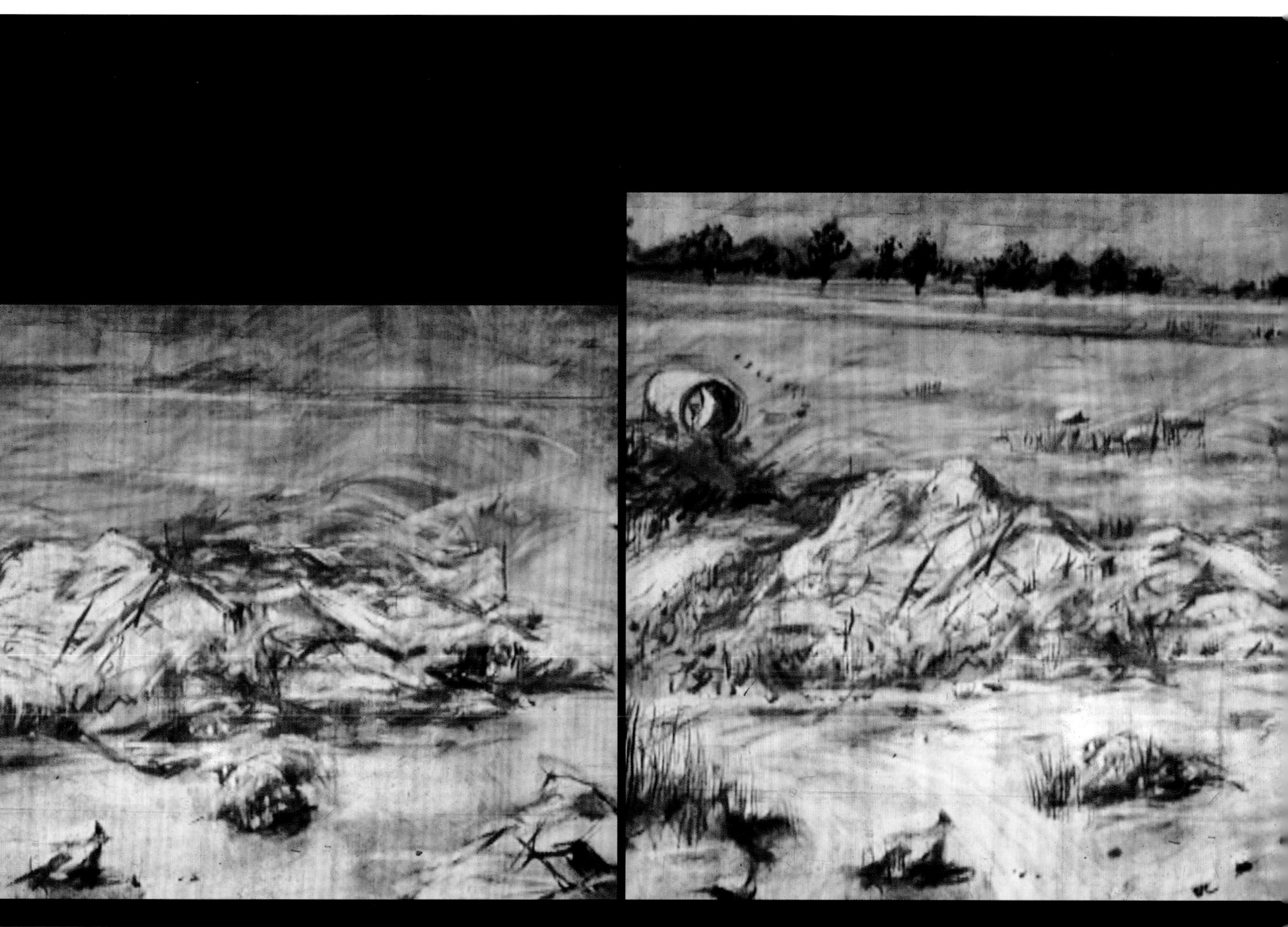

77–81
***Felix in Exile*, 1994**
35mm animated film transferred to video, 8:43 min.
Collection of the artist, courtesy Marian Goodman Gallery, New York, and Goodman Gallery, Johannesburg

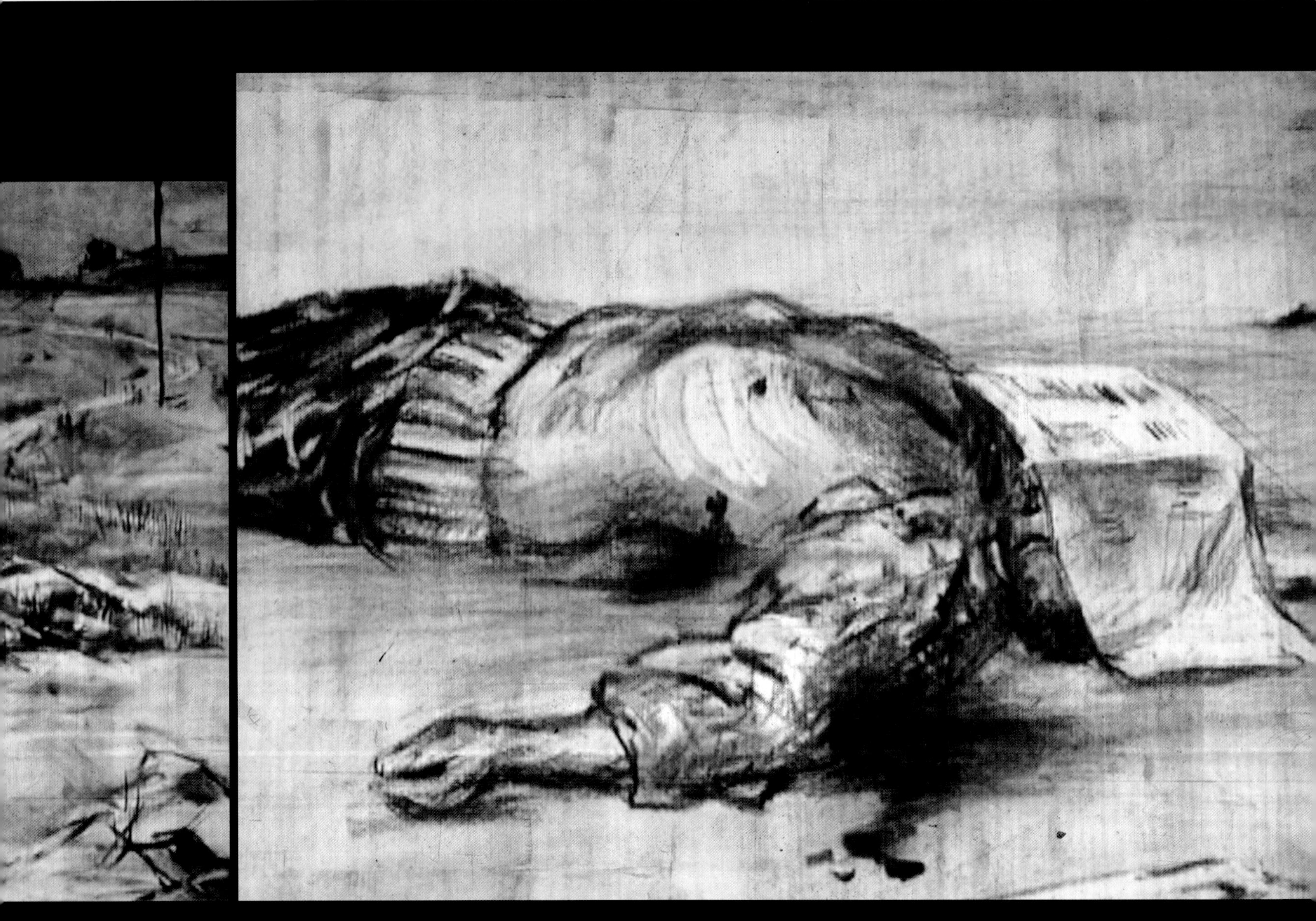

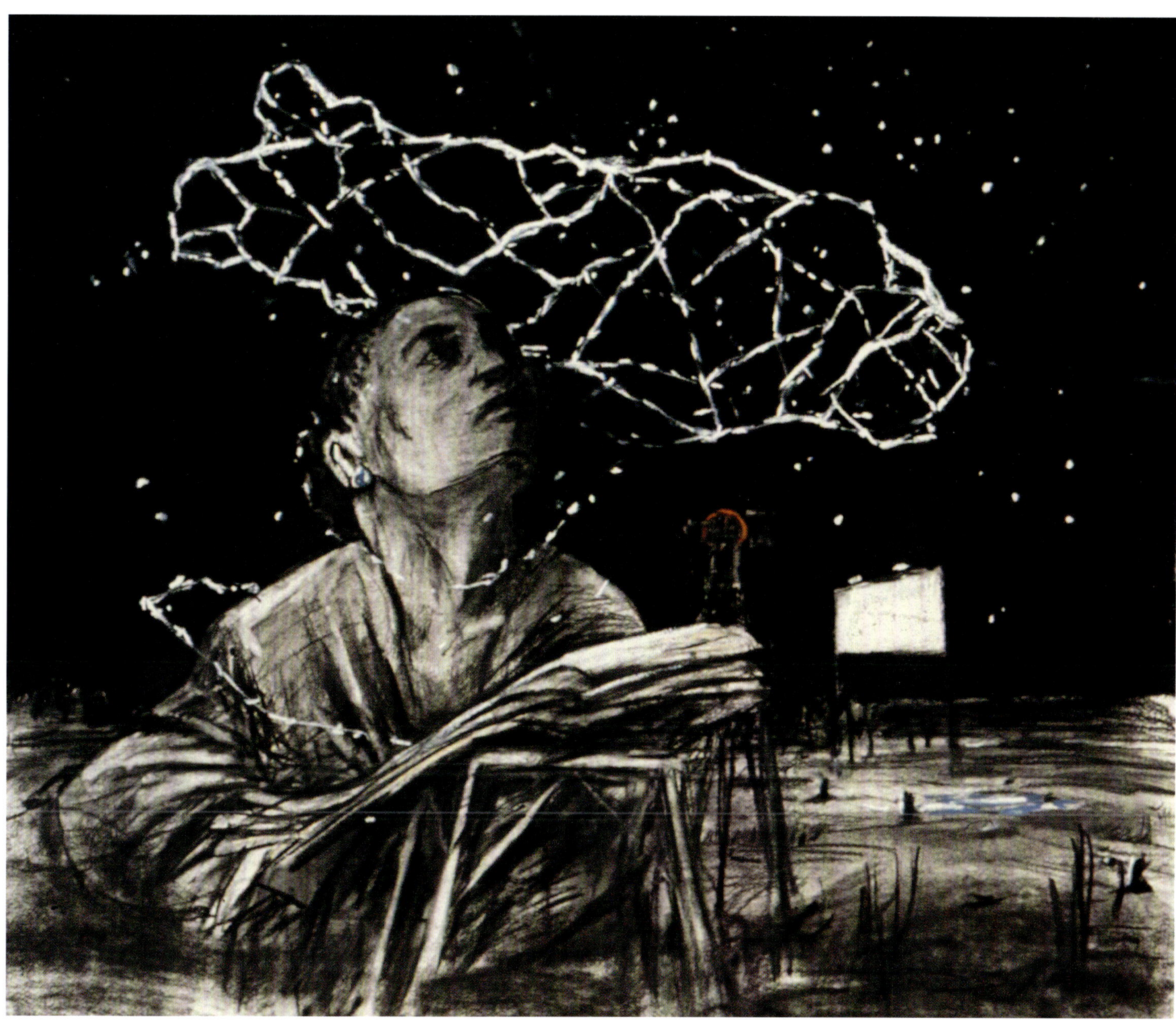

82
Drawing for the film *Felix in Exile* [Constellation], 1994
Charcoal and pastel on paper
31 1/2 x 47 1/4 in. (80 x 120 cm)
Private collection, Johannesburg

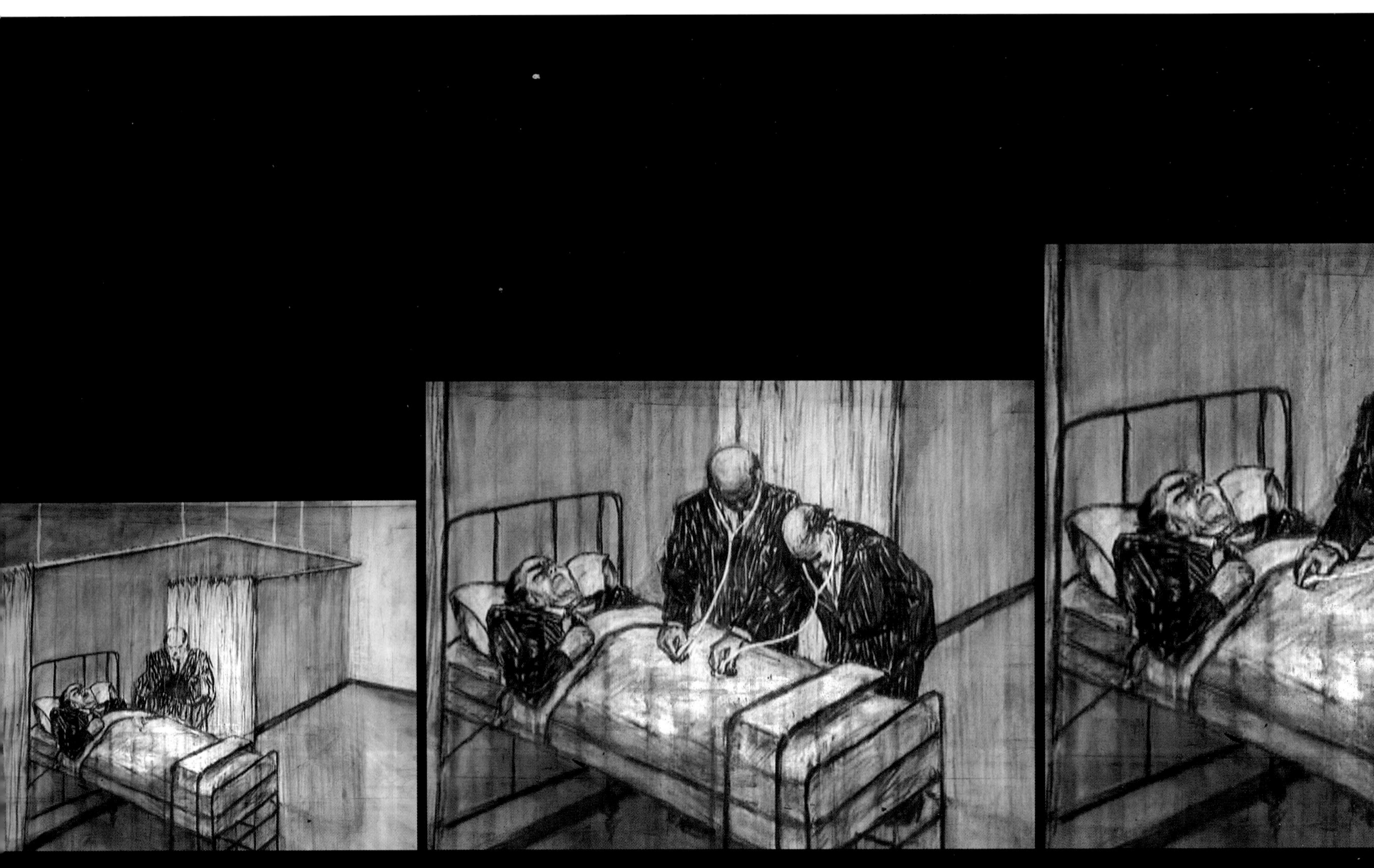

83–86
***History of the Main Complaint*, 1996**
35mm animated film transferred to video, 5:50 min.
Collection of the artist, courtesy Marian Goodman Gallery, New York, and Goodman Gallery, Johannesburg

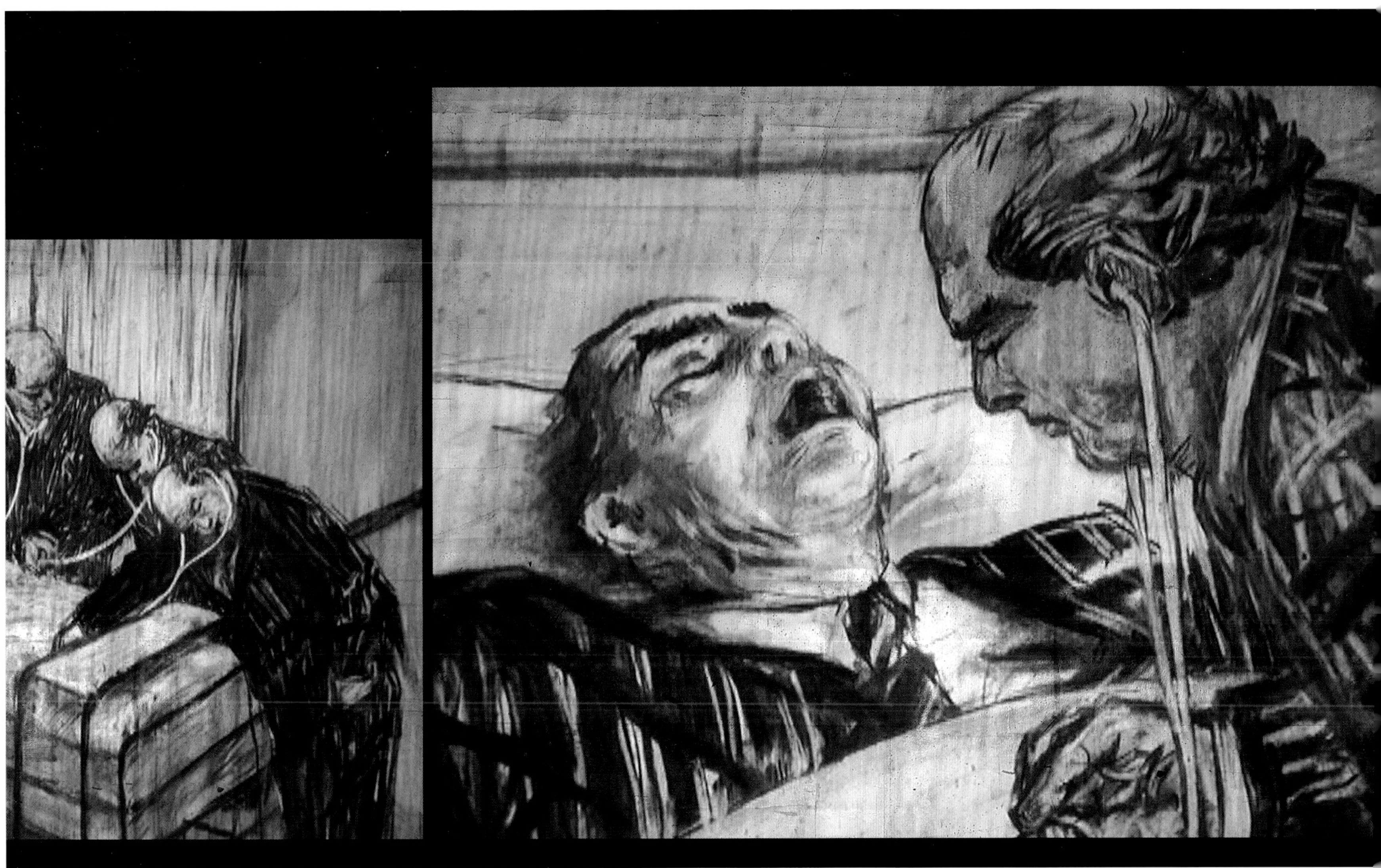

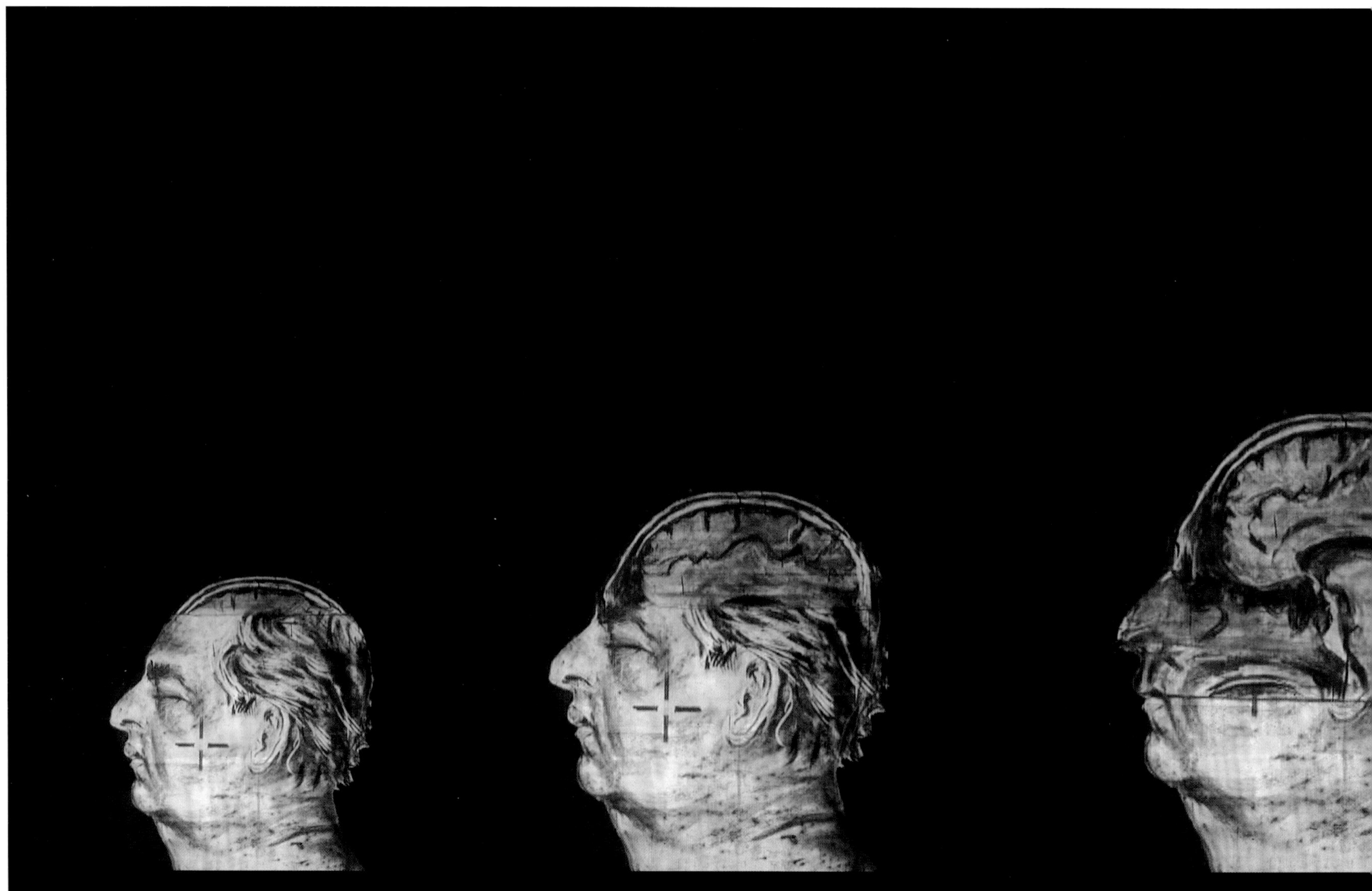

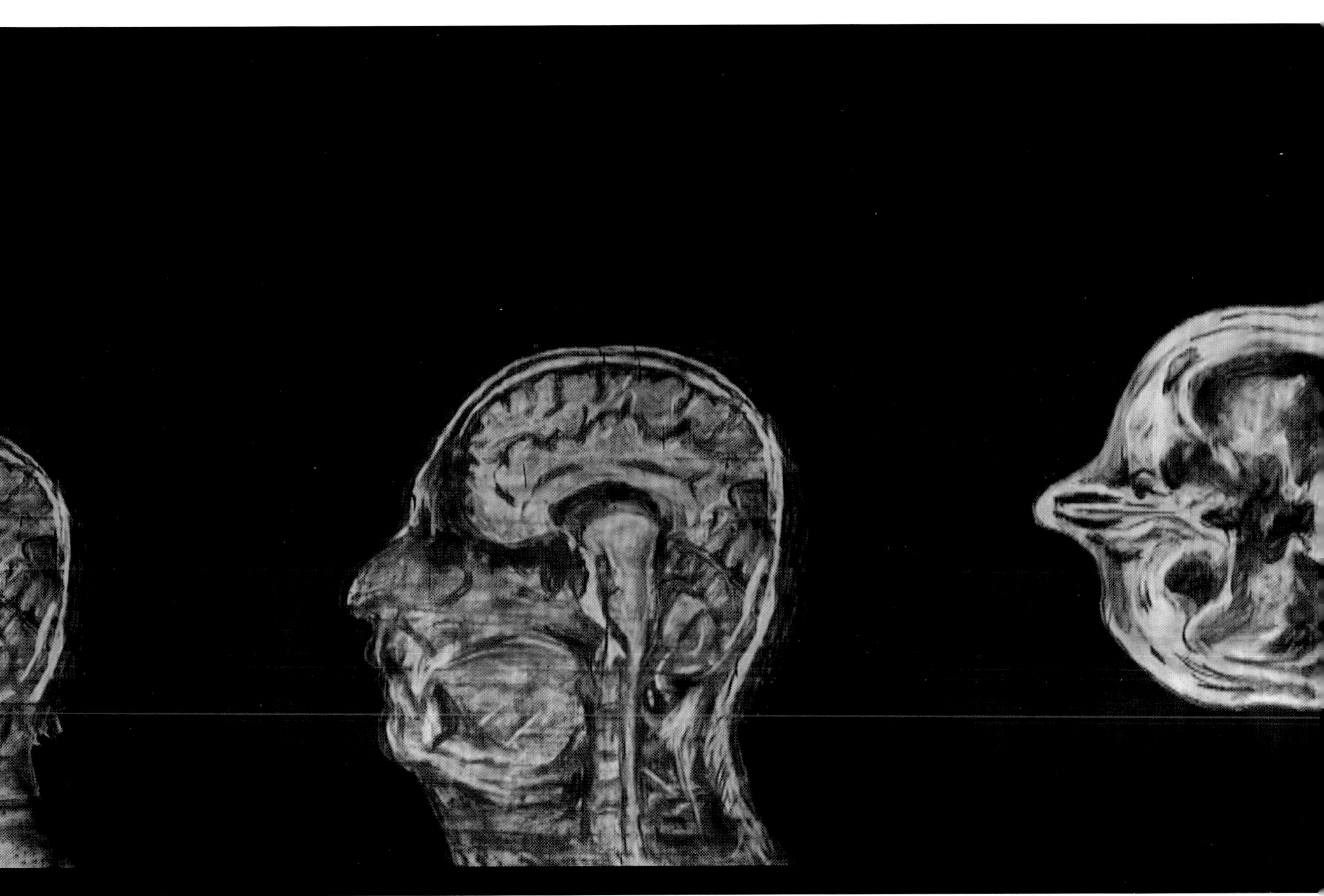

89–94
***WEIGHING...and WANTING*, 1998**
35mm animated film transferred to video, 6:20 min.
Collection of the artist, courtesy Marian Goodman Gallery, New York, and Goodman Gallery, Johannesburg

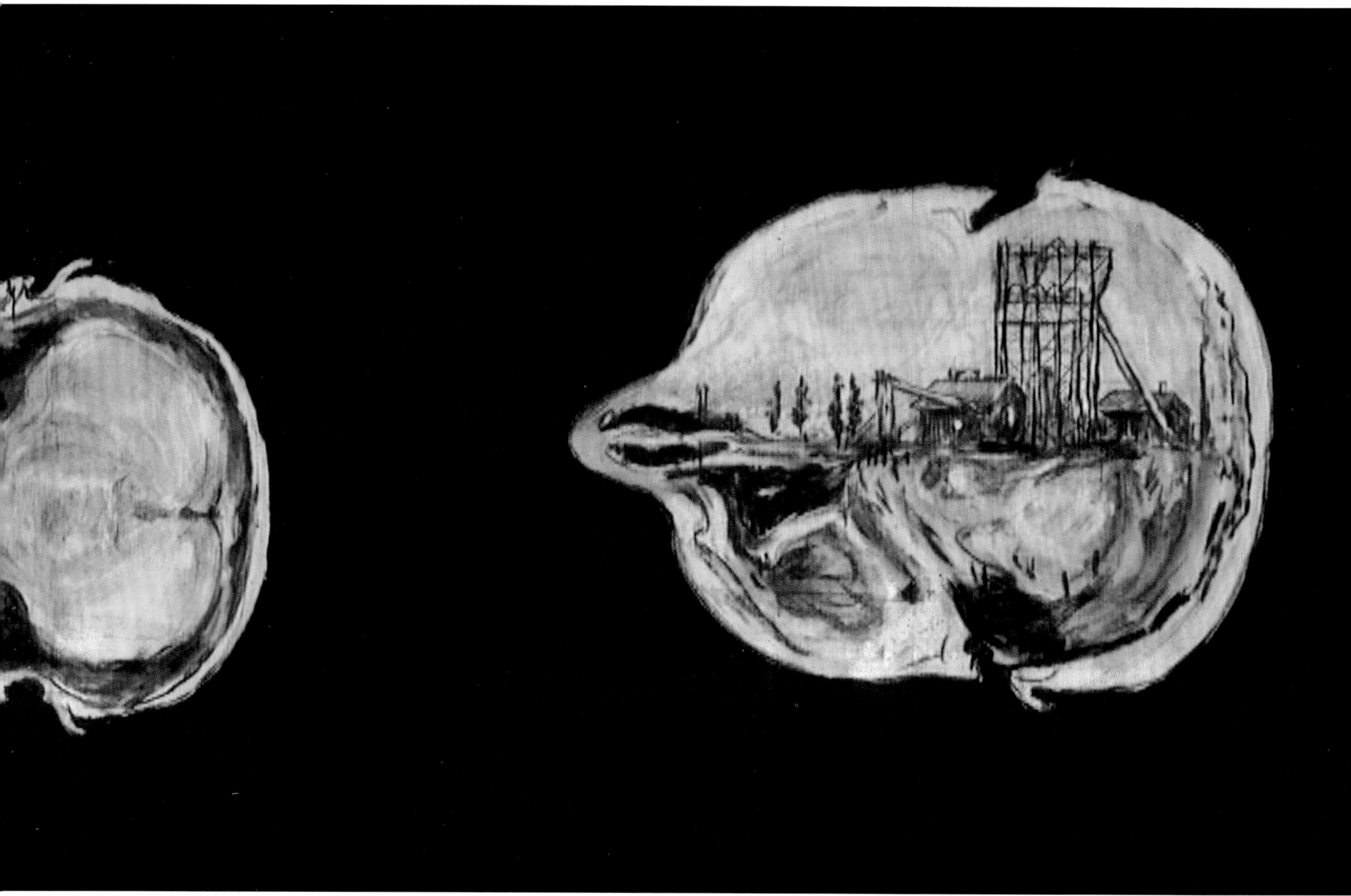

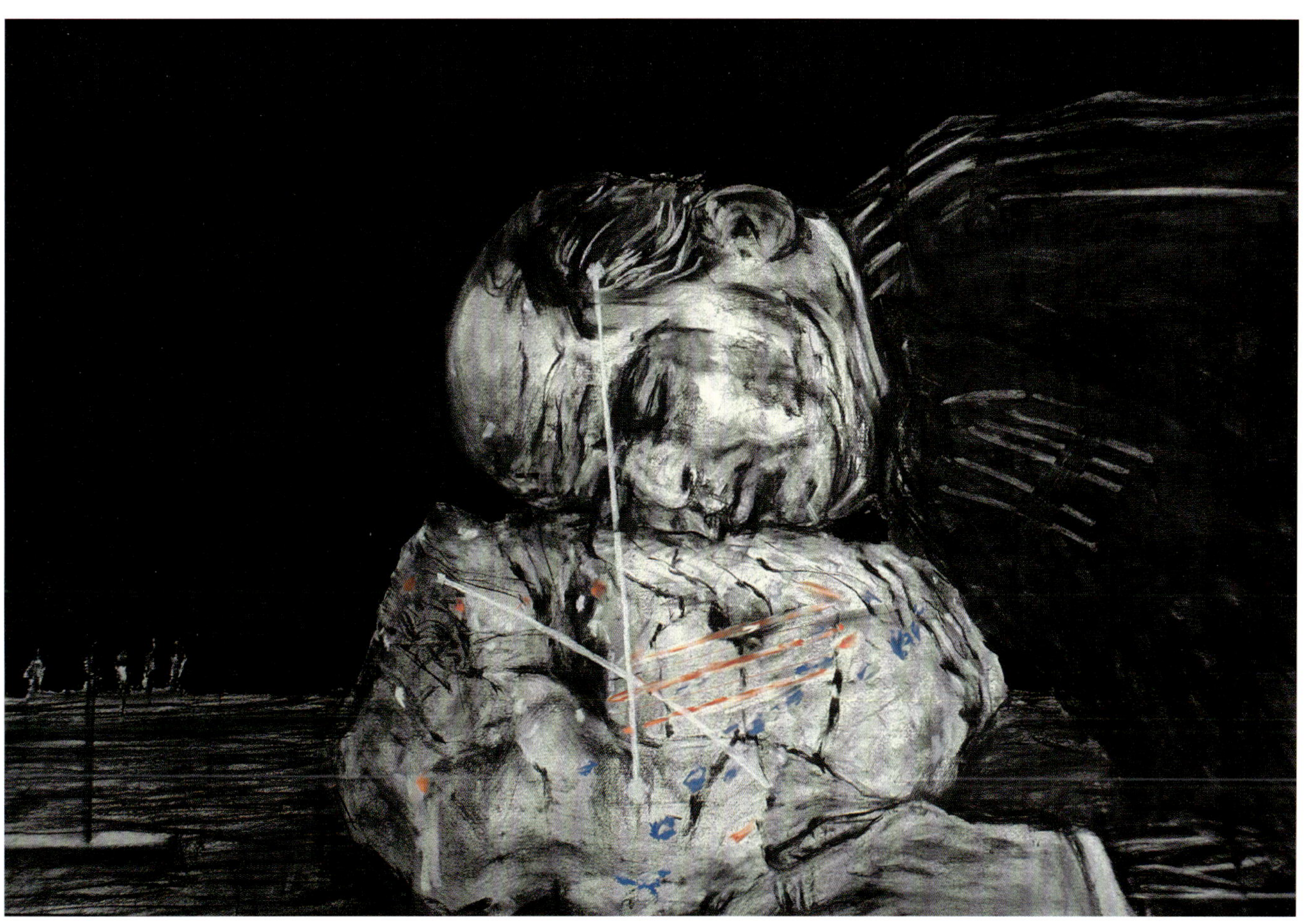

95
Drawing for the film *WEIGHING...and WANTING* [Soho with Head on Rock], 1997
Charcoal, pastel, and gouache on paper
48 1/2 x 63 in. (123.2 x 160 cm)
Museum of Contemporary Art, San Diego, museum purchase

96 (FOLLOWING PAGES)
Drawing for the film *WEIGHING...and WANTING* [Industrial Landscape], 1997
Charcoal on paper
48 1/4 x 63 in. (122.6 x 160 cm)
Museum of Contemporary Art, San Diego, museum purchase

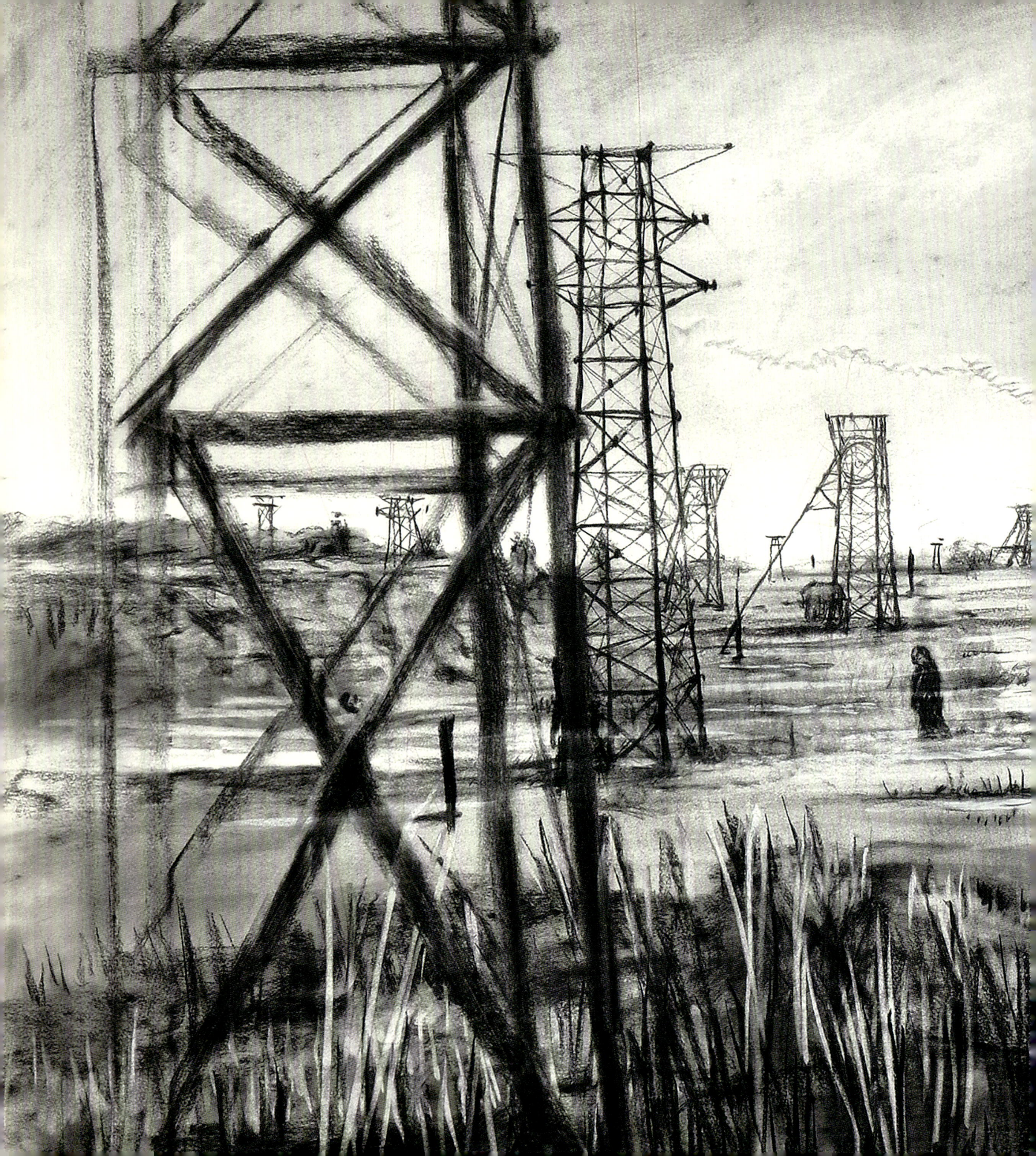

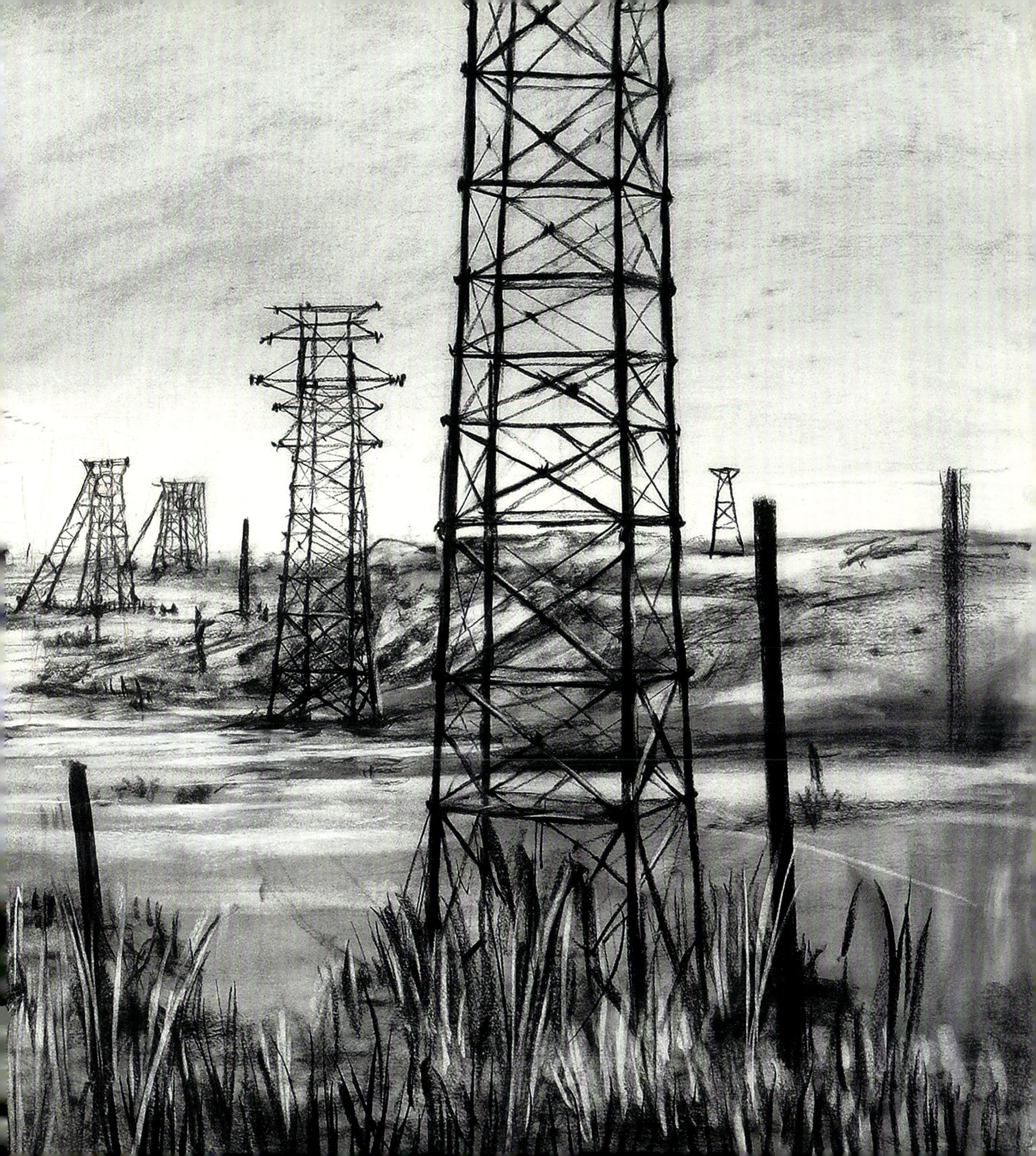

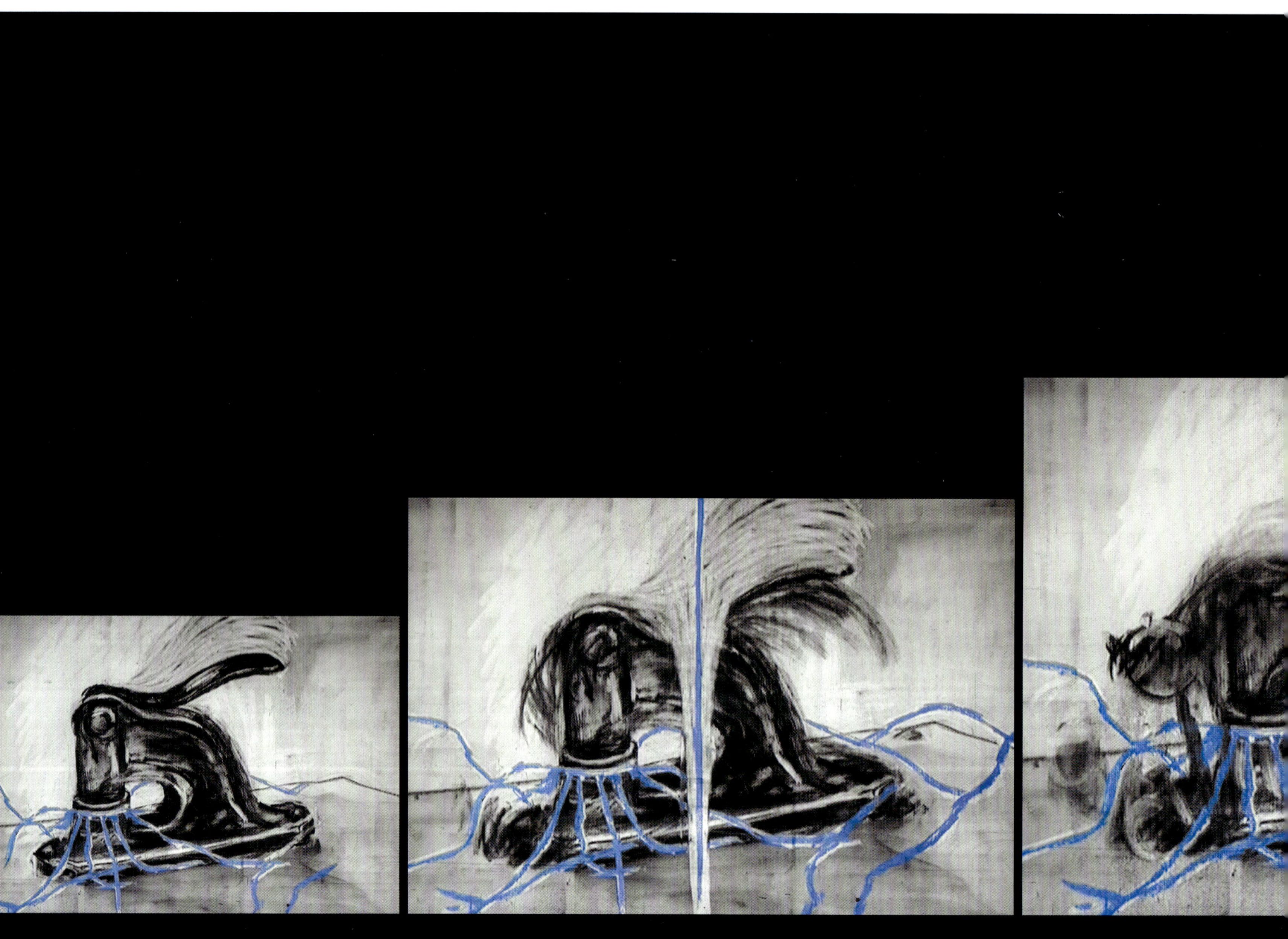

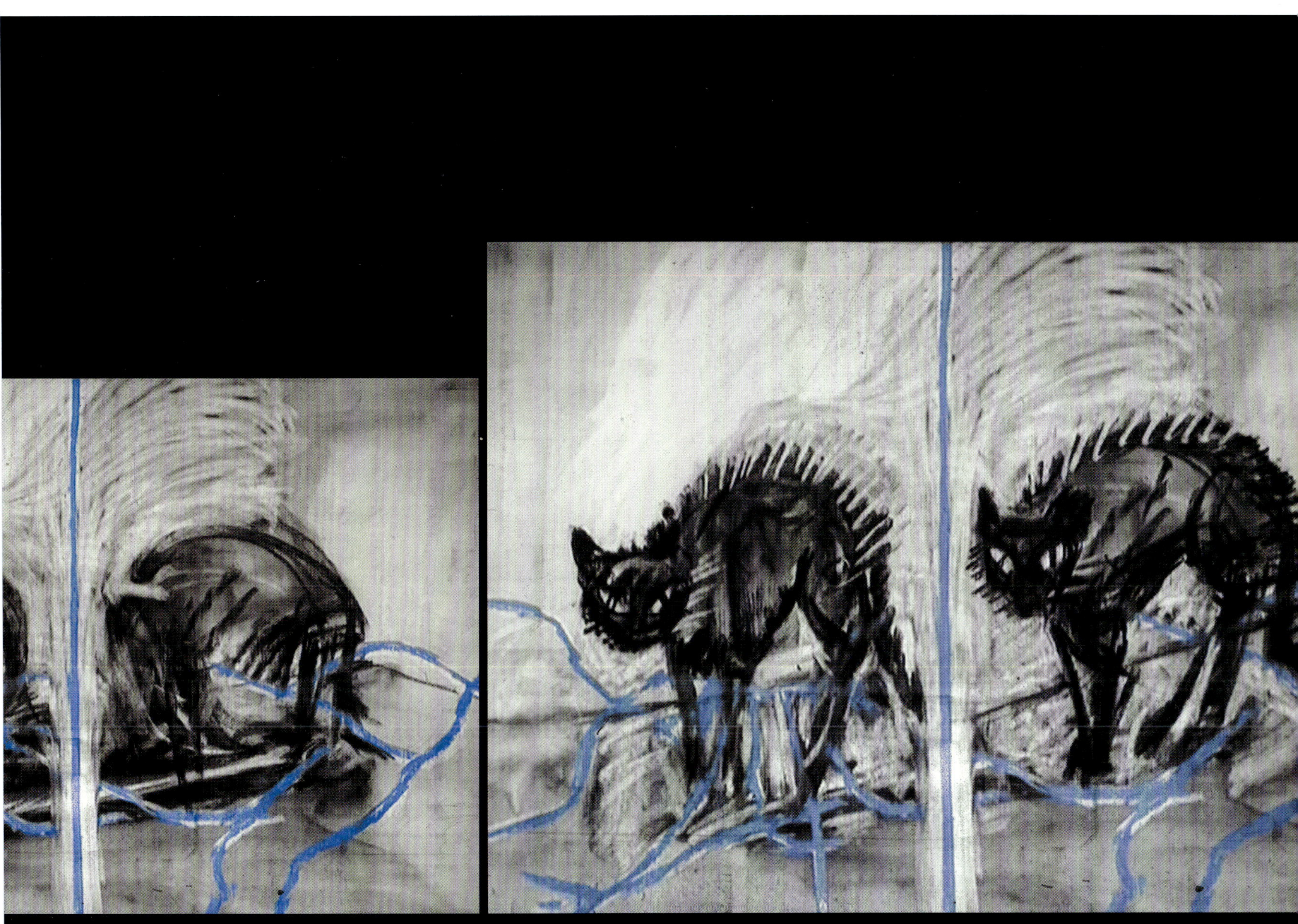

97–101
***Stereoscope*, 1999**
35mm animated film transferred to video, 8:22 min.
Collection of the artist, courtesy Marian Goodman Gallery, New York, and Goodman Gallery, Johannesburg

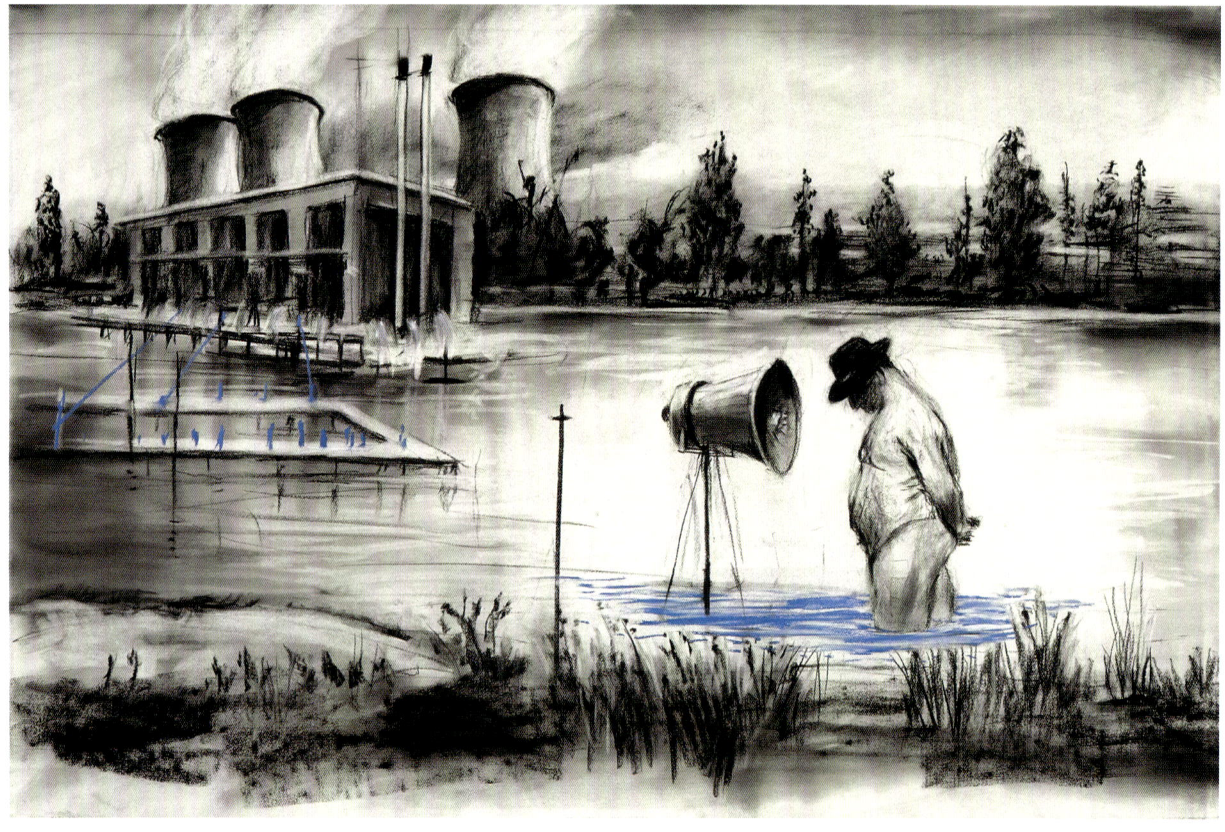

103
Drawing for the film *Stereoscope* [Felix in Pool with Megaphone], 1998–99
Charcoal and pastel on paper
31 7/16 x 48 3/8 in. (79.9 x 122.9 cm)
Hirshhorn Museum and Sculpture Garden, Smithsonian Institution, Washington, D.C., Joseph H. Hirshhorn Purchase Fund, 1999

104
Drawing for the film *Stereoscope* [Felix Crying], 1998–99
Charcoal, pastel, and colored pencil on paper
47 1/4 x 63 in. (120 x 160 cm)
The Museum of Modern Art, New York, gift of The Junior Associates of the Museum of Modern Art, with special contributions from Anonymous, Scott J. Lorinsky, Yasufumi Nakamura, and the Wider Foundation

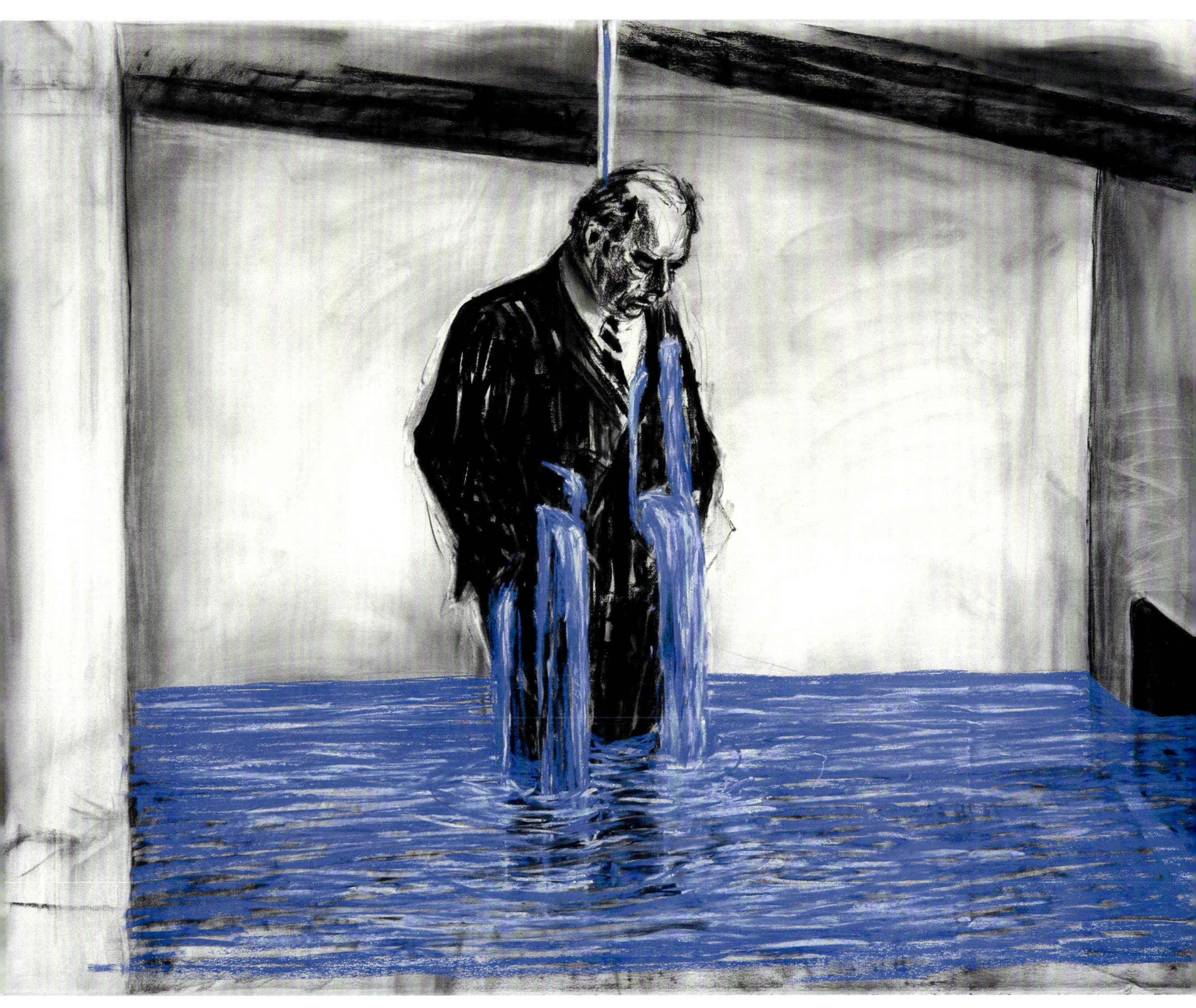

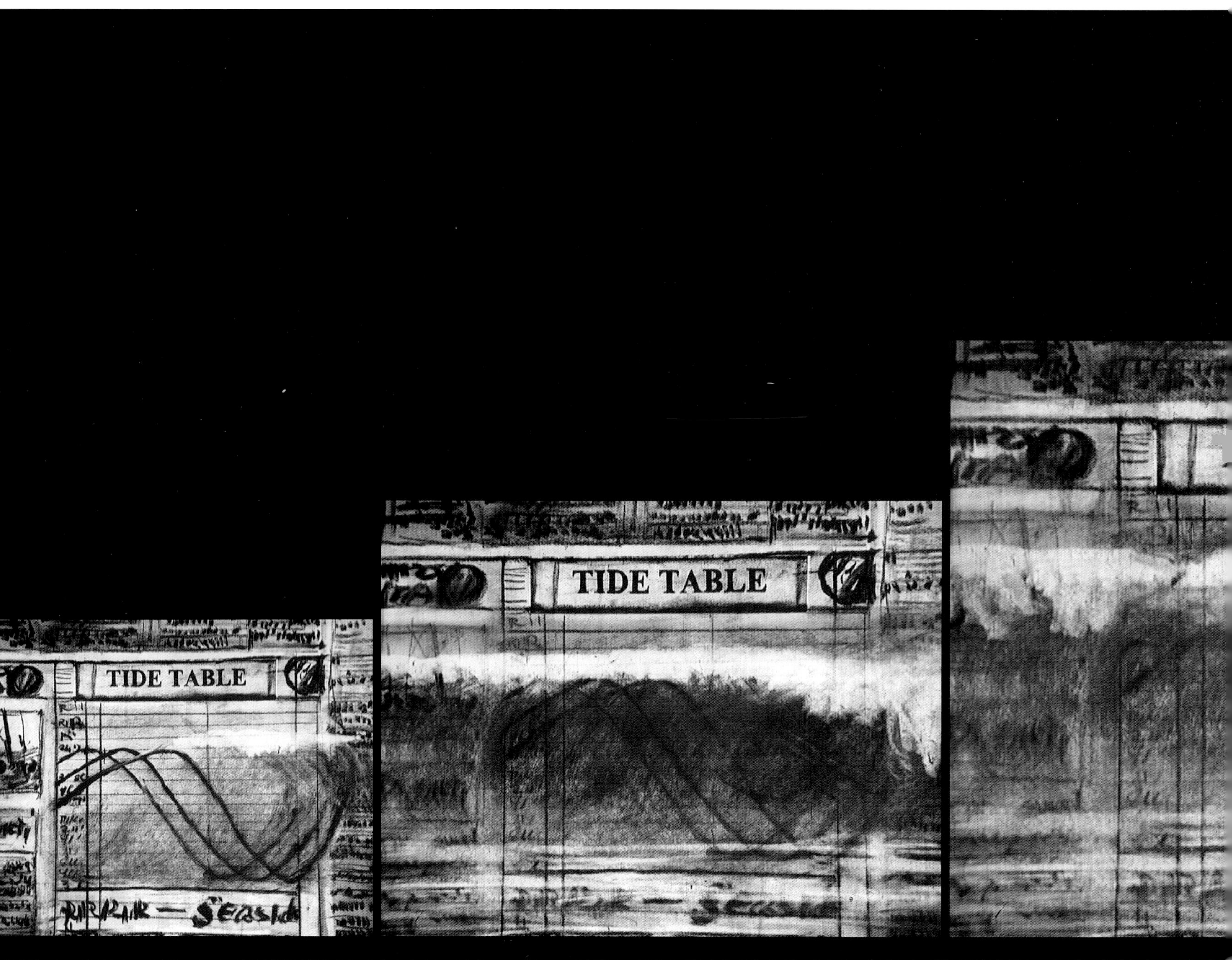
TIDE TABLE
TIDE TABLE

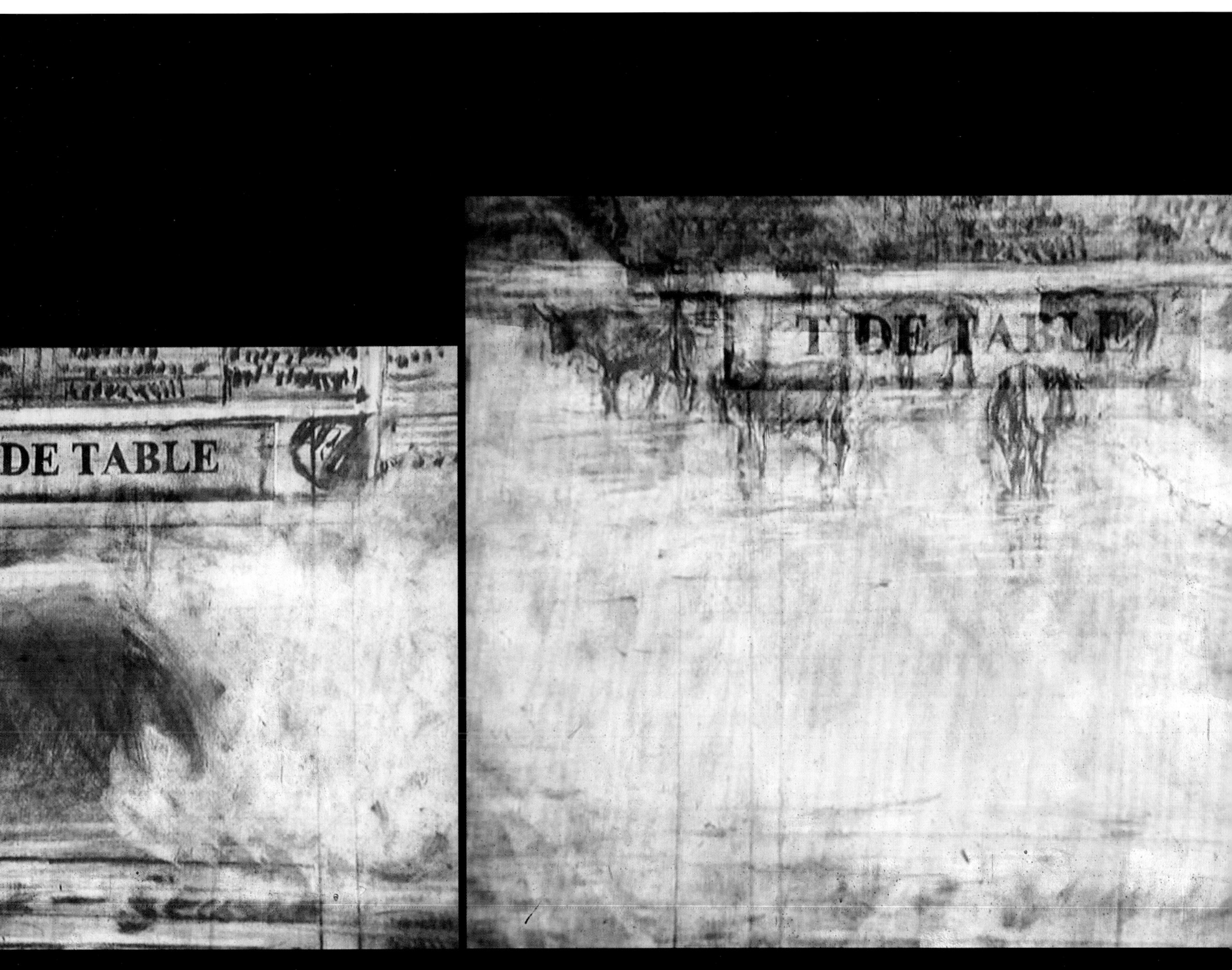

105–9
***Tide Table*, 2003**
35mm animated film transferred to video, 8:50 min.
Collection of the artist, courtesy Marian Goodman Gallery, New York, and Goodman Gallery, Johannesburg

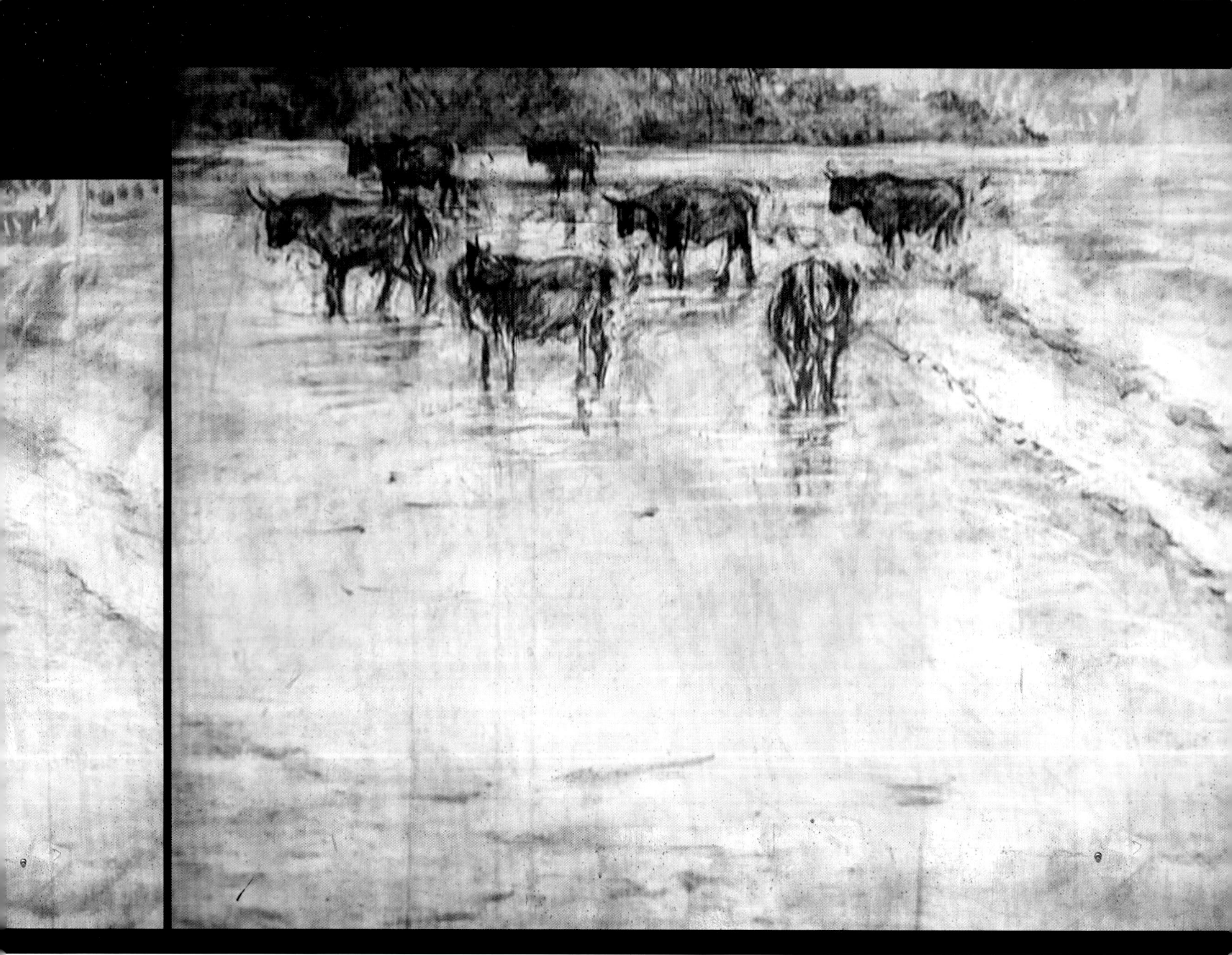

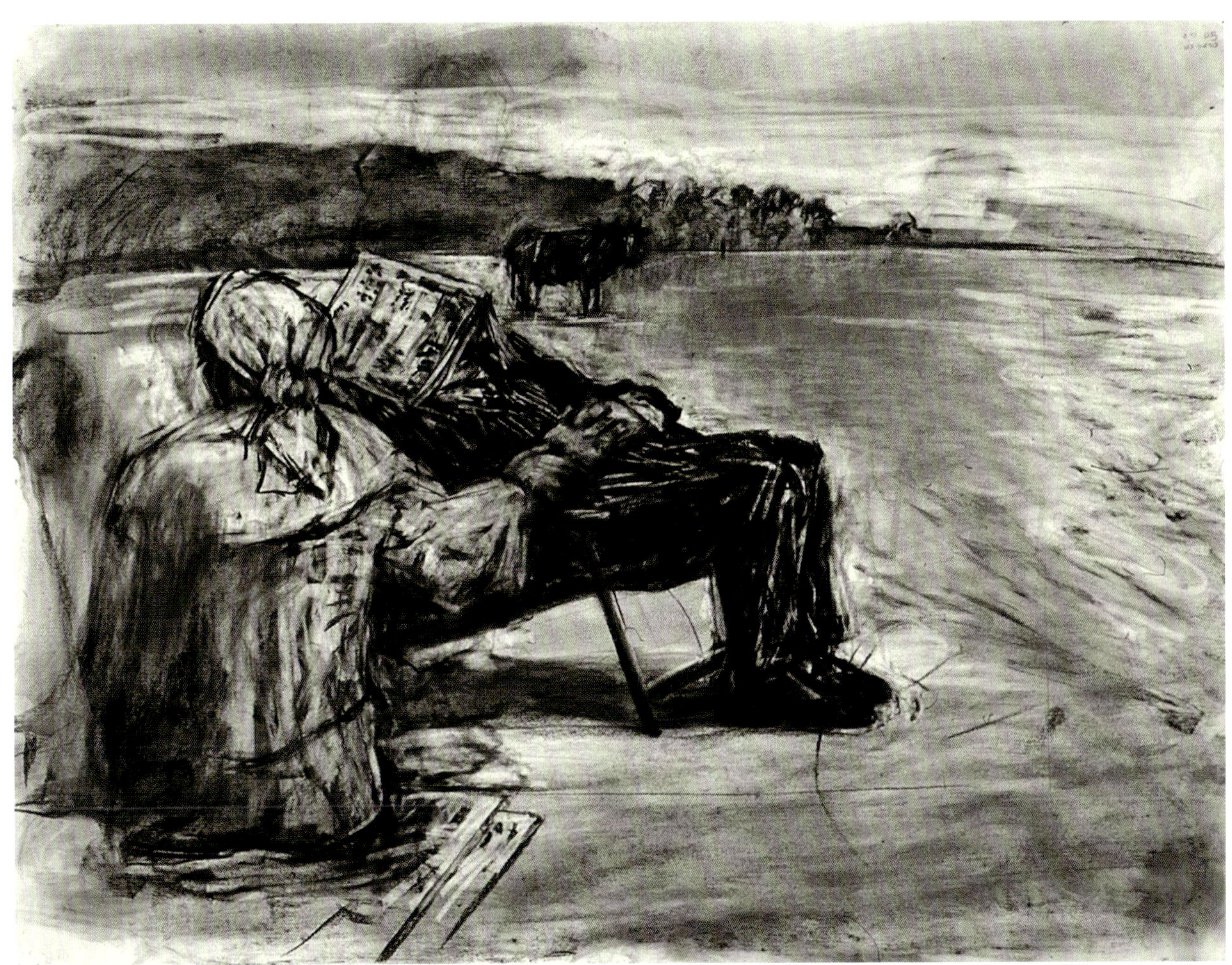

110
Drawing for the film *Tide Table* [Soho Sleeping], 2003
Charcoal on paper
47 1/4 x 63 in. (120 x 160 cm)
Courtesy the artist and Marian Goodman Gallery, New York

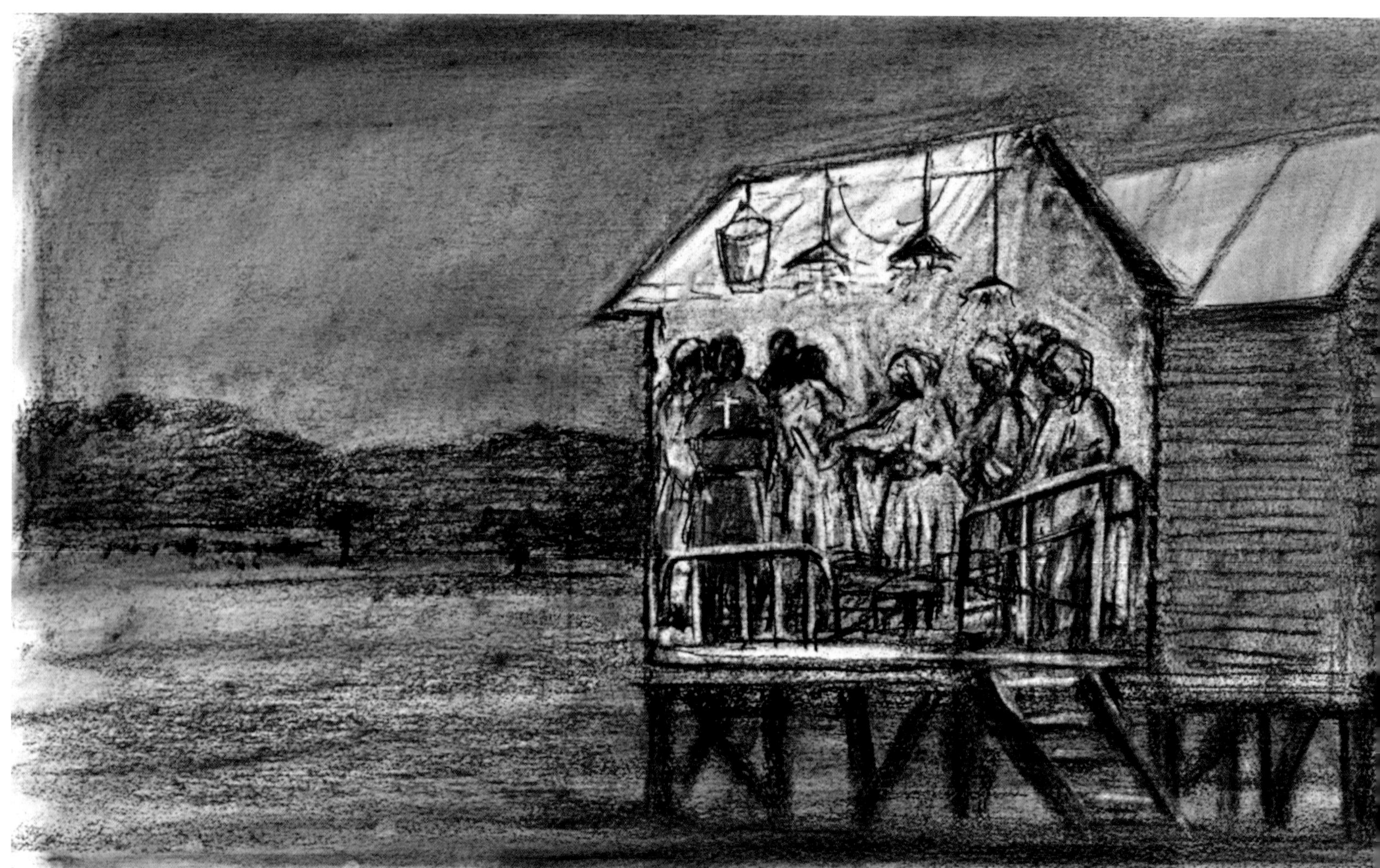

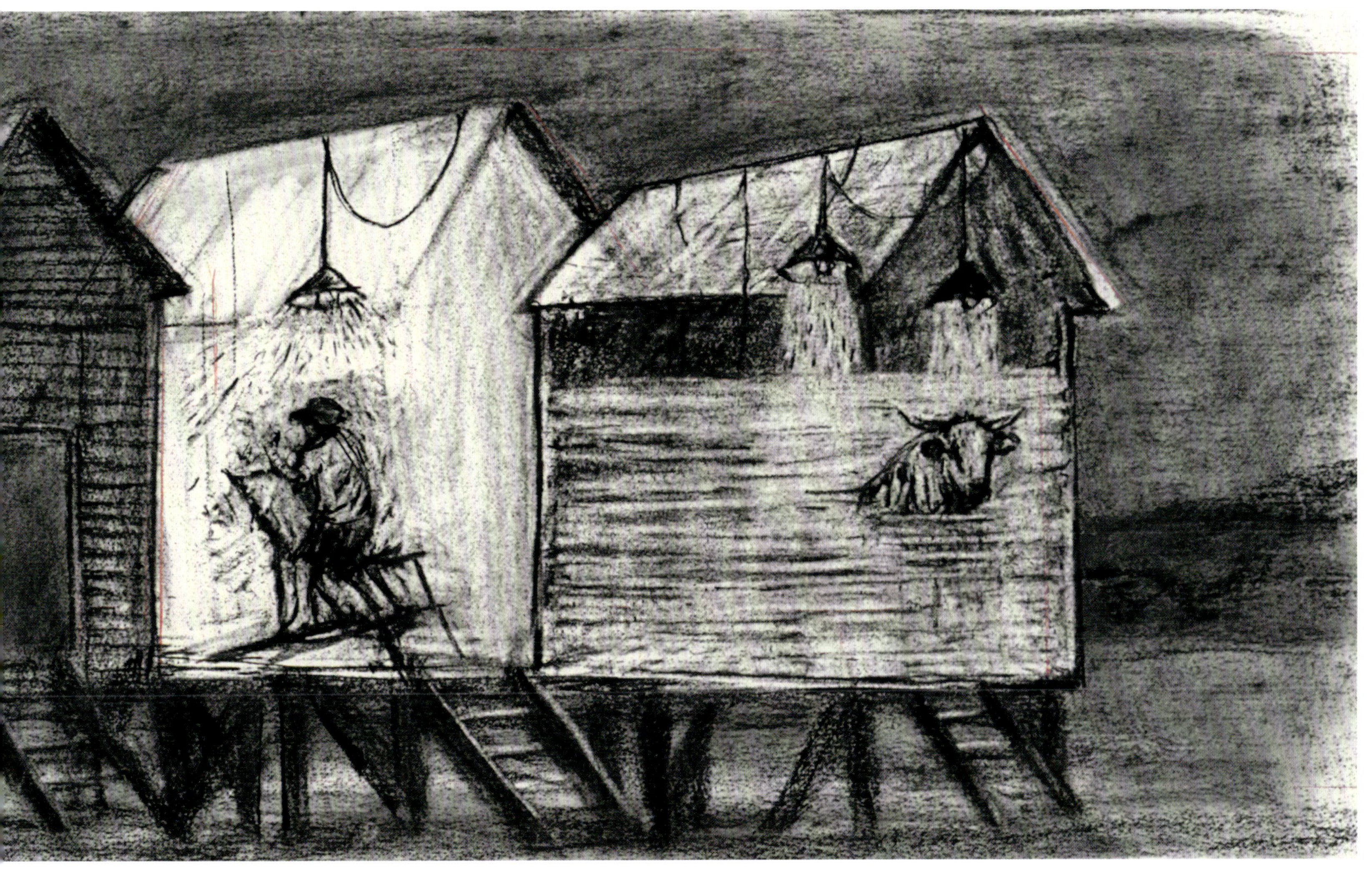

111
Drawing for the film *Tide Table* [Huts Interior], 2003
Charcoal on paper
25 x 66 in. (63.5 x 167.6 cm)
Collection of Brenda Potter and Michael Sandler

ON TEARS AND TEARING

THE ART OF WILLIAM KENTRIDGE

Carolyn Christov-Bakargiev

It is self-evident that nothing concerning art is self-evident anymore, not its inner life, not its relation to the world, not even its right to exist.

—THEODOR W. ADORNO[1]

William Kentridge proposes a way of seeing art and life as a continuous process of change rather than as a controlled world of certainties. He constantly questions the impact of artistic practice on today's world and has investigated how our identities are shaped through shifting ideas of history and place, looking at how we construct our histories and what we do with them. His is an elegiac art that explores the possibilities of poetry in contemporary society: it speaks through tears, those pouring out of Soho's pockets and flooding the room in the 1999 film *Stereoscope*.[2] Yet it also provides a raw, vicious, and satirical commentary on that society: it speaks through tearing—the torn black paper of a procession of the dispossessed.

Kentridge's practice explores how perception and experience are transformed into knowledge; the nature of emotions and memory; the relationships between desire, ethics, and responsibility; and the shaping and shifting of subjective identities. His work addresses issues of agency and inaction, public and private, subjugation and emancipation. Though rooted in his native South Africa, a country once divided by apartheid and still wracked by violence even in this postrevolutionary age, his art relates broadly to contemporary life in many parts of the world. His most recent projects turn to the Russian avant-garde, specifically its relations to political and social change and the collapse of its revolutionary ideals, perhaps as an indirect way to reflect on the possibility of reimagining or reactualizing hope and agency in our own time.

1. Theodor W. Adorno, *Aesthetic Theory,* trans. Robert Hullot-Kentor (Minneapolis: University of Minnesota Press, 1997), 1.

2. In 1997 I asked Kentridge to comment on Adorno's assertion of 1949 that, after Auschwitz, it would be barbaric to write poetry. He replied: "Alas there is lyric poetry. 'Alas,' because of the dulling of sensibilities we must have in order to make that writing or reading possible. But of course, also, thank goodness that such poetry can still be read. The dulling of memory is both a failure and a blessing." Kentridge often uses the word *dulling* to indicate a state of insensibility toward what should, or could, be intensely and authentically experienced. His creative impulse stems from exploring the effects of that dulling. Just as Kentridge sees dulling as a two-sided coin, he perceives the world of drawing as a double-edged practice. It comprises intentionality and chance, making marks and erasing them, revealing how vision is constructed while encouraging the loss of oneself in the fiction he stages.

3. *Ubu and the Truth Commission* was made with Handspring Puppet Company, with whom Kentridge has collaborated on theatrical projects since 1992.

4. *Sleeping on Glass*, an installation involving a bureau, a mirror, and a film comprising animated drawings, shadow figures, and live-action footage, represents moments of restless slumber and the apparently illogical world of dreams, where the sleeper is caught between desire and fear, obsession and repetition. In the first part of the film a woman sleeps while the camera turns to a view of Soho (or perhaps Felix, or is it a self-portrait of the artist?) sleeping on a rock. In the second part a figure made of torn black paper cycles round and round in an endless loop. Characters such as Nandi and Harry from *9 Drawings for Projection* appear, suggesting Johannesburg and its troubles, along with ominous images of cranes with hooks and shrouded, wraithlike figures waving flags. In the final moments everything returns to the melancholy calm of the beginning.

5. These also developed out of Kentridge's earlier interest in precinematic devices such as phenakistoscopes, shadow plays, anamorphosis, stereoscopes, and other optical devices or phenomena that appear to be obsolete today.

6. This was arguably the twentieth century's first attempt at genocide: starvation and poisoning of wells in the Namib Desert led to the death of 70 percent of the Bantu peoples. Interestingly, the German government apologized in 2004, shortly before Kentridge made *Black Box*.

Generally speaking, though he has throughout his career moved between film, drawing, theater, and opera, his primary activity remains drawing—and he sometimes conceives his theater and film-based work as an expanded form of drawing. And yet, even within this broader view of his output, Kentridge tends to proceed in phases, both thematically and technically. Indeed, except for the Soho Eckstein films, the stories of which are uniquely his own, he generally enjoys working in a reactive and interpretative/conversational mode rather than in the more active role of initiator of narratives. He has thus produced bodies of work that develop over time and react to cultural practitioners of the past. For example, Johann Wolfgang von Goethe's tragic play *Faust* (1806–32) and Francisco de Goya's early-nineteenth-century etchings *The Disasters of War* both lie behind Kentridge's early work on colonialism and the Enlightenment, including his play *Faustus in Africa!* (1995), while Alfred Jarry's play *Ubu Roi*, first performed in 1896, was the source of a number of Kentridge projects, notably the play *Ubu and the Truth Commission* (1996) and the film *Shadow Procession* (1999).[3] His 1998 production of Claudio Monteverdi's *Il ritorno d'Ulisse in patria* (1640) was Kentridge's first experience in directing an opera, but Monteverdi's music and his frail and vulnerable Ulysses on the beach had previously been important for the development of the 1996 animation *History of the Main Complaint* as well as *Sleeping on Glass* (1999), which used erotic madrigals by the same composer.[4] In 2001 the Italian novelist Italo Svevo's 1923 novel *Confessions of Zeno* inspired a large body of work in which Kentridge explored, against the backdrop of the First World War, both the figure of Svevo himself and his main character Zeno—an example of the crisis of the modern self, aware of his weaknesses yet unable to influence the course of his own life, let alone that of history. The French experimental filmmaker, actor, and producer Georges Méliès's early magical feats on film prompted a number of works begun in 2003.[5] Later, Mozart's *The Magic Flute* (1791) was the source of another body of work, beginning with the 2003 projection on blackboard *Learning the Flute*, followed by the direction of the opera in early 2005, and concluding later that year with *Black Box/Chambre Noire*, a sculptural installation with automatons and projections. *Black Box* worked as a metaphor both for what goes on in the artist's studio and for the mechanisms of the mind, set against a backdrop exploring the dark sides of the Enlightenment and German colonialism through references to the 1904–6 Herero and Namaqua massacres in German South-West Africa (today's Namibia).[6]

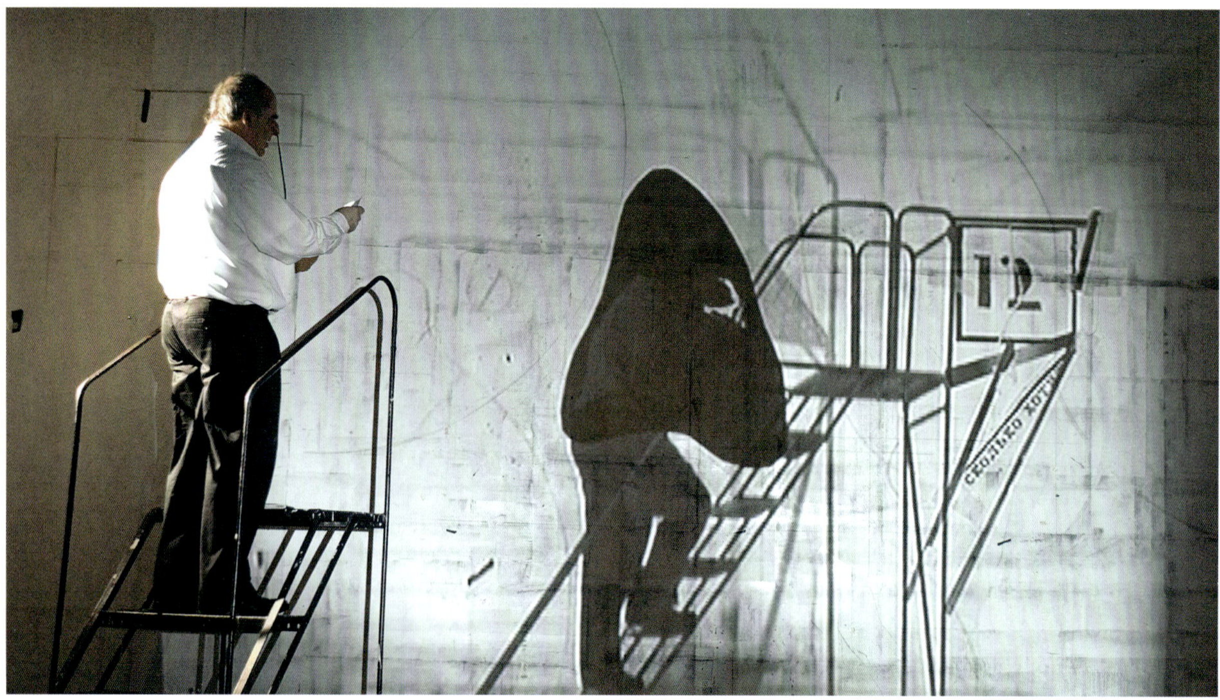

FIG. 17 Kentridge performing ***I am not me, the horse is not mine*** (2008) at the Biennale of Sydney, 2008

In 2007, in anticipation of staging Dmitri Shostakovich's late 1920s opera *The Nose*, Kentridge began to think about the Nikolai Gogol short story upon which the opera was based. Again, an entire body of preliminary works in drawing, film, and performance are spinning out from this source. Through the metaphor of *The Nose*, Kentridge has created both a lecture/performance (figs. 13, 17, 42) and a grand, open-ended installation that the audience enters into, as if it were inside *Black Box* again, while the Nose, a "phantom limb" disconnected and gone mad, goes off to live its own megalomaniacal life. Published in 1836, the Gogol story describes a Saint Petersburg official named Kovalyov who finds his nose missing one morning. When he locates and confronts it, the Nose—having acquired a higher rank than its owner—refuses to return to his face. A police officer returns the Nose, caught while attempting to flee the city, to Kovalyov. Yet even with the aid of a doctor, it cannot be reattached. One morning Kovalyov wakes up and his nose is inexplicably back on his face.

This new body of work represents a dynamic and intuitive investigation of the twentieth-century mind. We may all agree that the twentieth century is "over," just as the racist political system called apartheid was "over" when the African National Congress won the South African elections of 1994, and yet that century, still so close in time, has been utterly and completely denied. We condemned as horrors Stalin and Hitler, the Holocaust and the nuclear bombs over Nagasaki and Hiroshima, revolution, modernism, and Freud without ever having worked through what actually was—there has been no Trauerarbeit, no process of true mourning for a century that also provided some of the greatest revolutionary ideals and celebration of life. By contrast, we sometimes seem to wander like orphans in our own time, in a "projectless," seemingly aimless universe determined by statistics, unable to act with any sense of agency, unable to imagine what the twenty-first century might become, other than a society of pointless spectacle and financial speculation. As always for Kentridge, this denial stimulates an outward impulse to understand the world at large as well as an inner search into the self (or selves) as it appears and disappears, endlessly torn apart and recomposed. In his reflections on the twentieth century, he attempts to unravel the meanings and motivations behind the political and artistic impulses to revolt and to be "avant-garde" that characterized the age at its inception, including the individual's drive to self-abnegate for the good of the collective cause. Rather than simply judging the century, Kentridge foregrounds inquiry itself as a set of detached fragments that are never fully composed. He also engages in forms of self-reflection, looking back at his own past with both relief and nostalgia.

With a similar retrospective gaze, yet from a different perspective, the French philosopher Alain Badiou has also engaged in an attempt to understand the twentieth century: "My aim is not to rehabilitate the century," he writes, "but only to think it, to show how it is thinkable."[7] He describes it as a time when politics turned to tragedy[8] and when the possibility of mankind's change was contingent on the destruction of an older version of humanity—implying that man is a material to be shaped, torn apart, and recomposed differently. He identifies the twentieth century as a time in which the ideas of the previous century were set into practice, opposing the paradigm of organicism to the notion of individual wisdom, to the point that the individual could be sacrificed when the categories being discussed exceeded singularity. At the same time, whereas the nineteenth century adhered to the notion that history just somehow inevitably progressed (Hegel and Marx), the twentieth century was obsessed with the idea that each person could potentially make history, changing its course (Lenin). It was also traversed by a passion for the real, a celebration that can be seen in art in the long trajectory toward removing the divide between art and reality (from the readymade and collage onward), and in politics in the realization of elements that had once belonged to the realm of possibility, ideas, and ideology. There was thus a great tension between the lack of singularity and the heroic nature of individual realization. Badiou asserts that the century ended around 1980 with what he calls a second restoration: "The century would thereby express the victory of the economy, in all senses of the term: the victory of Capital, economizing on the unreasonable passions of thought.... Today's intellectual hegemony, encapsulated in the slogan 'there is no alternative'...is really just a promotion of a *politics with no alternative, a politique unique*."[9] The difficulty of rejecting what Badiou would term the "economic appropriation of technics" without celebrating the agency of the will to change of the twentieth century is what Kentridge currently faces in his art—which ultimately explores the potential of not-understanding the world as a constructive space for knowledge. In many ways, his project to not-understand the twentieth century through artwork is a way of keeping open and alive the intellectual sphere itself, today regarded with suspicion as potentially reviving the demons of the last century.

The question of Shostakovich's opera and its relation to Gogol is thus key to understanding Kentridge's *Nose* projects. His work reflects on the twentieth century by looking at how that century dealt ambivalently with the previous one. In Badiou's words:

> We could say that the meaning of the twentieth century is determined by the way one thinks through its connection to the nineteenth.... Ideal finality: the twentieth century fulfills the promises of the nineteenth. What the nineteenth century conceived, the twentieth century realizes, for instance the Revolution, as it was dreamt by the Utopians and the first Marxists.... Negative discontinuity: the twentieth century renounces everything that the nineteenth century (the golden age) promised.[10]

7. Alain Badiou, *The Century* (Cambridge: Polity Press, 2007), 6.

8. Notes Badiou: "The century is the site of apocalyptic events—events so ghastly the only category capable of reckoning with the century's unity is that of the crime: the crimes of Stalinist Communism and the crimes of Nazism. At the heart of the century lies the Crime which provides the paragon for all the others; the destruction of the European Jews. This century is an accursed century." Ibid., 2.

9. Ibid., 3–4.

10. Ibid., 19.

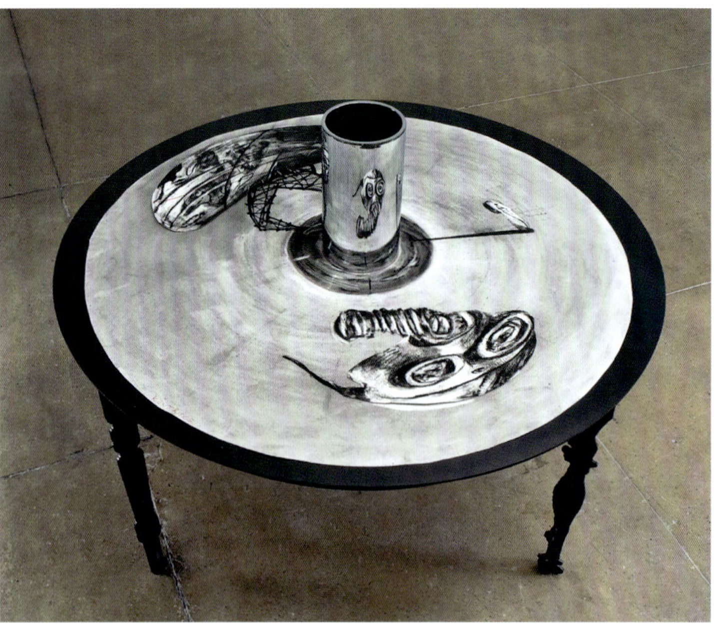

FIG. 18 William Kentridge
***What Will Come (has already come)*, 2007**
Steel table, cylindrical steel mirror, and 35mm animated film transferred to video, 8:40 min.
41 1/4 x 48 x 48 in. (104.7 x 121.9 x 121.9 cm)
Norton Museum of Art, purchase, acquired through the generosity of the Contemporary and Modern Art Council and the R. H. Norton Trust, 2008

One of the enigmas of the twentieth century is the passage from the extraordinary creativity and inventiveness of Europe in its early years to the terrible economic depression and totalitarian regimes of the 1930s and 1940s. Yet this enigma may also be seen as a continuity if our point of view shifts to a broader one that acknowledges the tragedies and crimes Europe perpetrated from the late nineteenth century through 1914, for example in Africa. As Badiou points out:

> After two or three centuries of the deportation of human meat for the purpose of slavery, conquest managed to turn Africa into the horrific obverse of European, capitalist, democratic splendor. And this continues to our very day. In the dark fury of the thirties, in the indifference to death, there is something that certainly originates in the Great War and the trenches, but also something that comes—as a sort of infernal return—from the colonies, from the way that the differences within humanity were envisaged down there.[11]

It is this connection between the history of Europe and its relations to Africa that Kentridge reveals in works such as *Zeno Writing* (2001) and the anamorphic projection *What Will Come (has already come)* (2007; fig. 18, pls. 170–72). The latter film is based on anamorphic drawings, which are projected onto a round table and reflected in a mirrored cylinder that corrects the distorted forms. As its title suggests, it refers to history's cyclical nature. The images pictured in this merry-go-round range from familiar carousel animals such as horses to camels, tanks, and airplanes. The fairground ride thus evoked is that of Italy's aggression in Ethiopia in the 1930s, also suggested by a soundtrack that includes carnival sounds, Shostakovich, Ethiopian and Eritrean music, and "Faccetta Nera," a period Italian song associated with Fascism. The heart of the film is the double image: the distorted, "real" image that is projected and the corrected, "imagined" image that is reflected in the mirror. It is the task of the viewer to see the images and understand how meaning is constructed from both.

11. Ibid., 8.

Kentridge welcomes imperfection, failures, shadows, oblique glances rather than direct views, provisional moments of beauty rather than attempts at grand accomplishments. His interests are broad, and the techniques he employs have varied widely from charcoal on paper to shadow puppetry, from torn paper figures to traditional tapestries and bronze sculptures, from live-action film to animations based on trails left by ants crawling over sugar poured on paper. Yet for all this variety and openness to experimentation, he does not value innovative practice per se, nor art historical breakthroughs in style, medium, or technique, preferring instead the realm of obsolescence.[12] In sum, he defects from rather than enlists in the vanguard.

This "responsible" attempt to keep certainty at bay implies a negative dialectic, and also a suspicion of the possibility of a direct, positive communication of meaning. For the philosopher Theodor Adorno, that which is immediately (and unmediatedly) understandable is essentially false, and the truth of artworks lies in their ability to avoid it:

> The truth of discursive knowledge is unshrouded, and thus discursive knowledge does not have it; the knowledge that is art, has truth, but as something incommensurable with art.... The enigma of artworks is their fracturedness.... [Art] achieves meaning by forming its emphatic absence of meaning.[13]

The politics of art thus lie in the awareness and consequences of the fact that the direct embodiment of meaning opens the way for the culture industry to absorb art as yet another object of production and consumption, making it a space of closure rather than emancipation. Kentridge's sense of the political is similar, and also by necessity indirect. "I am interested in a political art," he has stated, "that is to say an art of ambiguity, contradiction, uncompleted gestures and uncertain endings."[14]

12. Obsolescence operates on various levels in his work. "Kentridge draws upon a European legacy of oppositional art from Goya to Hogarth to Beckmann, but...his work is oddly out of sync with current trends in Europe. Though he uses the prevailing technology of video projection, for example, the drawings that form the basis of his animated films retain a more old-fashioned appearance....A sense of belonging to a cultural 'periphery' of Europe, and therefore of *geographic* distance from a 'centre,' is translated into the visual imagery of objects that represent a *historical* distance from today's accoutrements....The simultaneous presence in the work of CAT scan machines and other examples of modern equipment, however, indicates the way in which experience is layered: the computer exists side-by-side with the old-fashioned telephone....The drawing style adopted by Kentridge is also reminiscent of early 20th-century oppositional vanguard art like Berlin Dada and German Expressionism. These drawings are combined with the contemporary techniques of video-projection and installation on the one hand, and music and captions recalling the distant age of silent movies on the other." Carolyn Christov-Bakargiev, *William Kentridge* (Brussels: Société des Expositions du Palais des Beaux Arts / Vereniging voor Tentoonstellingen van het Paleis voor Schone Kunsten, 1998), 9–11 (hereafter cited as Christov-Bakargiev, *William Kentridge* [1998]).

13. Adorno, *Aesthetic Theory*, 126–27.

14. Quoted in Christov-Bakargiev, *William Kentridge* (1998), 14.

In celebrating the leftover, the shadow, the trace, the discarded, the unproductive, the doubt, the unresolved, the uncertain, the "dirty" smudge rather than monochromatic white, "poor animation" rather than pristine, high-tech digital effects, Kentridge's art is certainly a statement against modernism's search for purity and purification—for the absolute essence of art. However, modernism was never only about that objective. The obverse side of the coin was the avant-garde attempt to bridge art and life, to locate a hybrid space where reality and the symbolic could coincide. This is the modernism of the Dadaists, the Surrealists, and the collage. It is the modernist quest for the truth of the artistic act itself, which is part of reality. An artwork can be accepted as truthful (and its fictitious and symbolic nature can be accepted as meaningful) only if it plays out the gap between this symbolic nature and the reality of its existence as a fiction—only if it is embodied in the reality and authenticity of the medium thanks to which and through which it exists. A painting is paint on a canvas first and foremost, a drawing is charcoal on a piece of paper, a projection is light moving through a device and onto a physical reality that operates as a screen. For Kentridge, as for the modernists of the early twentieth century, it is vital that the process of making art be rendered visible. This is characteristic of even his earliest work: he would erase and draw until the rough paper surface was consumed by tactility, revealing the process of thought and feeling. It is also true of more recent projects that investigate artistic practice in the studio, such as *7 Fragments for Georges Méliès* (2003), insofar as he openly declares that the perfection of form and seamless representation are illusions achieved through simple film-editing techniques. And it is certainly true of works such as *Black Box*, in which the studio and its apparatus, mechanics, and image-making devices collapse together to become the subject and content of the work. In many ways this recalls the distancing technique of Brechtian theater, set up to reveal the real. "What is this 'distancing' that Brecht turned into a maxim for the actor's performance?" Badiou asks. "It is the display—within the play—of the gap between the play and the real.... Representation is a symptom (to be read or deciphered) of a real that it subjectively localizes in the guise of misrecognition.... Distancing—conceived as the way that semblance works out its proper distance from the real—can be taken as an axiom of the century's art, and of 'avant-garde' art especially."[15]

15. Badiou, *The Century*, 48–49.

Underlying all of Kentridge's work is his suspicion of the production of visual imagery and the mechanisms by which such production is achieved: the photographic and projection apparatus and machinery that both record and reveal images while interrupting their freedom to disappear, the tools of art yet also the tools of the culture industry and its power to control and limit contemporary experience.

Another way of understanding Kentridge's work is by looking at how his practice has developed over the years through the adoption of, and experimentation with, a series of successive yet overlapping techniques, each mutually related and also linked to broader philosophical and psychoanalytical questions, and each embodying elementary antiproductive and negative gestures.

Adopting a typically anti-Enlightenment stance based on skepticism and self-doubt, Kentridge based a first wave of two-dimensional work on the erasure of drawings, most poignantly noticeable in his *9 Drawings for Projection*, begun in 1988. A second wave, which began in 1995 with works referencing the shadowy antihero Ubu, explored the negative and positive aspects of objects through shadows. A third wave, stemming from that work and specifically from *Shadow Procession*, has been and still is based on the act of tearing—destroying images by tearing them into fragments, then recomposing them into new, provisional configurations by filming successive moments of collage. Not by chance, this latest attention to tearing goes hand in hand with the artist's exploration of forms of agency that can be found in the impulse toward aesthetic and social change—in the tearing of language from humanity and the upending of any stable notion of truth that occurred in the late nineteenth century and much of the twentieth (the focus of recent work based on *The Nose*).

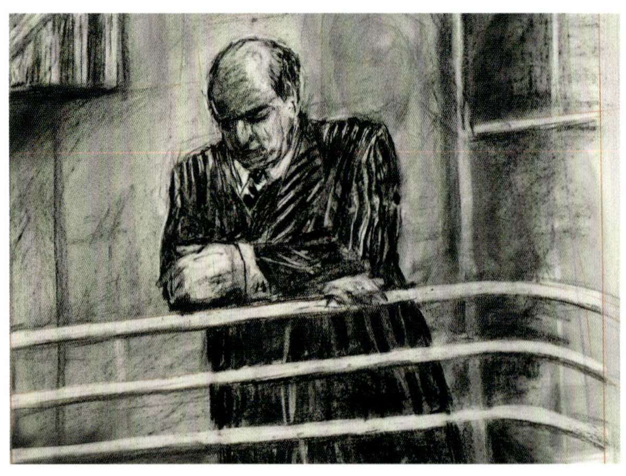

FIG. 19 William Kentridge
Drawing for the film *Tide Table* [Soho on Balcony], 2003
Charcoal on paper
32 x 48 in. (81.3 x 121.9 cm)
San Francisco Museum of Modern Art, Accessions Committee Fund purchase: gift of Jean and James E. Douglas Jr., Doris and Donald Fisher, Patricia and Raoul Kennedy, Elaine McKeon, and Judy Webb

ERASURE

Over the years, numerous essays on Kentridge's work, as well as his own lectures and interviews, have pointed out that his technique of erasure engenders a time-based, open form of process drawing. This openness to change, and its implied belief in the nonfiniteness of language, is an aesthetic position that is based on a political perspective—a refusal of all authoritative and authoritarian types of discourse embedded in most forms of communication, from advertising to politics. The process of facture remains visible, making the viewer conscious of the spatial and temporal disjunctures of the drawing rather than creating an illusion of fluidity. And, because erasure is necessarily imperfect, traces of the preceding stages of each drawing can still be seen. These smudges and shadows reflect the way in which events are layered in real life—how the past affects the present through memory.

This technique of consecutive erasure and drawing is not a novelty in the field of animation, having been variously adopted in the early history of the medium. But the way in which Kentridge uses it—as a metaphor for a new, flexible paradigm of radical thought based on indirect gazes, shadows, and continuously "falling short," grounded in duality and ambivalence—is particularly topical today. He uses erasure as a metaphor for the loss of historical memory—the incomplete amnesia with which society confronts injustice, racism, and brutality. Yet erasure also questions the notion that any definitive statement is ever possible; it denies the value of complete or binary theories of politics and social relations (or of any finished artwork). Kentridge's device allows for the emergence of a palimpsest—a synchronic image that contains its own diachronic denial through a layering of traces of earlier, erased drawings (see fig. 19).

The art historian Rosalind Krauss has suggested that Kentridge deliberately pulls his work back to a prefilmic moment. She points out that Kentridge, when talking or writing about his art, avoids directly expressing outrage over apartheid, thus shifting our attention away from content and toward his creative process.[16] He never denounces injustice head-on, as if suspicious of the ways in which historical memory is transformed into spectacle. He expands the field of improvisation by moving back and forth from the paper to the camera as he records the evolving drawing one frame at a time. During the time and space of this "dance," free associations occur that ultimately determine the open narrative and the meaning of the artwork. His work emerges not out of a wish to achieve motion, to "animate," comments Krauss, but rather through the impulse to interrupt the flow of film, to reach back from filmic animation to a form of palimpsest, "dragging against the flow of film."[17] The technological universe has by now so infected our bodily and graphic experiences, our subjectivity, that Kentridge's recourse to the palimpsest becomes a way of avoiding the spectacularization of memory. His work thus focuses on the recrudescence of the hand-drawn in an age when popular culture is profoundly engaged with the digital.

16. In one essay, however, Kentridge does address "the immovable rock of apartheid": "To escape this rock is the job of the artist. These two constitute the tyranny of our history. And escape is necessary, for as I stated, the rock is possessive, and inimical to good work. I am not saying that apartheid, or indeed, redemption are not worthy of representation, description or exploration, I am saying that the scale and weight with which this rock presents itself is inimical to that task." Kentridge, "Dear Diary: Suburban Allegories and Other Infections" (1990), in Christov-Bakargiev, *William Kentridge* (1998), 75.

17. Rosalind Krauss, "'The Rock': William Kentridge's Drawings for Projection," *October* 92 (Spring 2000): 10.

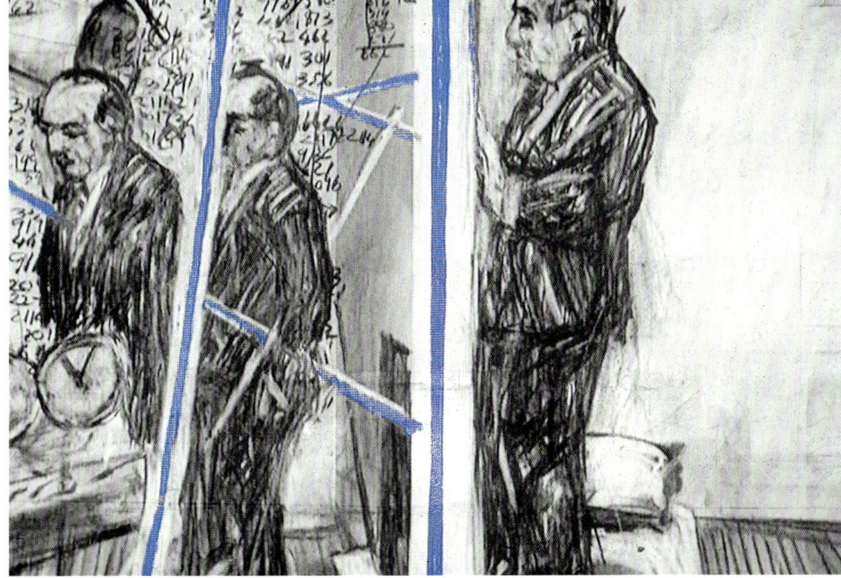

FIG. 20 William Kentridge
***Stereoscope*, 1999**
35mm animated film transferred to video, 8:22 min.
Collection of the artist, courtesy Marian Goodman Gallery, New York, and Goodman Gallery, Johannesburg

Kentridge's *9 Drawings for Projection*, begun in 1989 with *Johannesburg, 2nd Greatest City after Paris* (pls. 52–56), are made using charcoal and erasure. They revolve around the double and opposing parts of the self embodied by the "productive" Soho Eckstein, a property developer, and the "nonproductive" Felix Teitlebaum, an artist and a lover. Two films in particular, *Sobriety, Obesity & Growing Old* and *Stereoscope*, represent a sustained inquiry into this splitting of personality.[18]

Sobriety, Obesity & Growing Old (1991; pls. 71–76) depicts the collapse of Soho's empire (or, rather, Soho collapsing his empire), which is represented as a modern city of skyscrapers that recalls Johannesburg in the 1950s. Returning to the theme of Felix's relationship with Mrs. Eckstein (introduced in *Johannesburg, 2nd Greatest City after Paris*), *Sobriety* tells the story of Soho's loss of his wife, who leaves his world of architecture and rationality for Felix's open landscape of megaphones, loudspeakers, and emotion. Soho sits in his office and watches the couple making love on the screen of a picture frame. Under the pressure of Felix and Mrs. Eckstein's passion (represented by water), crushed by the weight of Soho's loss and solitude, the buildings of Johannesburg literally melt and crumble—they are erased.[19]

Stereoscope (fig. 20, pls. 97–101), made in 1999, marks the beginning of Kentridge's particular interest in stereoscopic vision—both its mechanisms and the notion of a self literally divided, unable to synthesize the two views from the right and left eyes. The film again represents the pinstriped and solitary Soho, this time attempting to cope with the immensity of the horror he perceives around him while "finding a line between choosing a more solitary life or being promiscuously social."[20] Unable to focus on his papers, Soho listens to the outside world, holding his head in his hands as the noise of protests, beatings, shootings, and explosions invades the protected and enclosed universe of his office and home. He must negotiate his sense of powerlessness and isolation from the collective, his sense of participation in yet isolation from history. Blue lines rush across the scenes, finally retreating and falling—perhaps a visualization of our growing world of global networks and communications, overloaded and collapsing. Soho's mind bursts into two as he doubles up and becomes divided even from himself—unable to achieve the stereoscopic vision by which we normally see three-dimensionally because our mind fuses together two separate images, one from each of our eyes. The image onscreen becomes that of a room divided in two: one room becomes more and more empty while the other is increasingly crowded, eventually overwhelmingly so, as blue water runs down from Soho's pockets like a flood of tears from his heart.

Stereoscopic vision allows us to see the world as unitary. *Stereoscope*, however, presents the reverse, describing selves that divide and fall out of sync. The film highlights our negotiation between different selves. It posits no single meaning, each element containing its own opposite, yet themes and images recur.

18. This theme—already present in the erasure-based works on the level of content and narrative—would reemerge in later works as the relationship between objects and their shadows, the negative and the positive of film and photography. More recently, splitting has developed into a fascination for the experience of tearing and fragmenting filmic installations, suggesting an ongoing sense of ambivalence and the impossibility of any positive dialectic.

19. This could be a direct reflection of events in South Africa at the time: opposition to the apartheid regime, demonstrations and marches, followed by the lifting of the ban on political organizations (1990) and the relaxation of most of the State of Emergency regulations and restrictions (1991).

20. Kentridge, conversation with the author, 2008.

SHADOWS

We know very little about the birth of painting, said Pliny the Elder in his *Natural History* (xxxv, 14). One thing, however, is certain: it was born the first time the human shadow was circumscribed by lines. It is of unquestionable significance that the birth of Western artistic representation was 'in the negative'. When painting first emerged, it was part of the absence/presence theme (absence of the body; presence of its projection). The history of art is interspersed with the dialectic of this relationship.

—VICTOR I. STOICHITA, 1997[21]

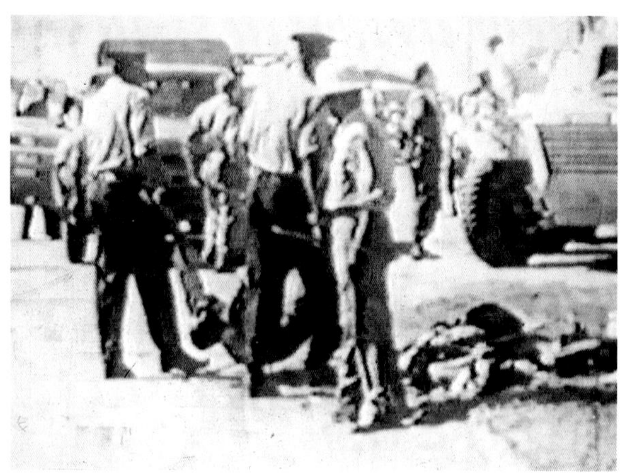

FIG. 21 William Kentridge
***Ubu Tells the Truth*, 1997**
35mm animated film with documentary photographs and 16mm archival film transferred to video, 8 min.
Collection of the artist, courtesy Marian Goodman Gallery, New York, and Goodman Gallery, Johannesburg

When he made *Stereoscope*, Kentridge was already deeply involved in his shadow-based works, looking at reality obliquely, in a reversal of Plato's notion of the need to search for knowledge directly. In Kentridge's world, shadows are praised.[22] Erasing drawings made their traces the focus of the artist's attention. The negative space of the trace, which indicates meaning through absence, soon triggered in Kentridge a fascination for exploring shadows as the negative of objects or people—the voids rather than the things themselves. Kentridge's belief in uncertainty as a source of knowledge is reflected in his interest in shadow vision as opposed to direct vision: shadows imply an indirect gaze and suggest that it may be better, at times, to look aslant.

Shadows and their distortions figure prominently in Kentridge's recent installation *I am not me, the horse is not mine* (2008), yet his use of shadows began around 1996 with the first of a series of projects inspired by Albert Jarry's 1896 play *Ubu Roi*.[23] The universe of shadows, shadow puppetry, and shadow projections began to capture his interest.

Jarry wrote *Ubu Roi* as a satirical and grotesque expression of the way in which arbitrary power engenders madness. He achieved this through the portrayal of a ridiculous but devastating despot who is also a licentious libertine, an emblem of clumsy and brutal deeds done in the service of a calculating state. Jarry countered this arbitrary power with what he called "pataphysics," or the science of imaginary solutions, unmasking its absurdity through farce—an approach that led to a new genre, the Theater of the Absurd. From a South African perspective, Ubu was a particularly powerful metaphor for the insane policy of apartheid, which was presented by the state as a rational system.

In 1996 the artist Robert Hodgins, with whom Kentridge has often collaborated, suggested a group show of prints on the theme of Ubu. In response, Kentridge developed a portfolio of etchings in which he layered chalk representations of Jarry's cartoon-like line drawings of Ubu with his own contrasting tonal drawings of a naked man (stemming from photographs of himself in the studio). The result was a series of outrageous images entitled *Ubu Tells the Truth* (pls. 112–19). The project not only represented a further exploration of Kentridge's familiar theme of the coexistence of disjunctive selves within a single person, but also implied that Ubu was an endemic part of any individual. By grappling with the Ubu within oneself—as Soho did in the erasure-based films—the despotic tendencies he represents might perhaps be controlled and contained within the individual, and by implication within society.

21. Victor I. Stoichita, *A Short History of the Shadow* (London: Reaktion Books, 1997), 7.

22. See Kentridge's references to Plato's Allegory of the Cave in his 2001 lecture and essay "In Praise of Shadows," in *William Kentridge*, ed. Carolyn Christov-Bakargiev (Rivoli, Italy: Castello di Rivoli; Milan: Skira Editore, 2004), 151–61 (hereafter cited as Christov-Bakargiev, *William Kentridge* [2004]).

23. In 1975 Kentridge had performed the role of Captain McNure in a Junction Avenue Theatre Company production of *Ubu Rex*, an adaptation of Jarry's play.

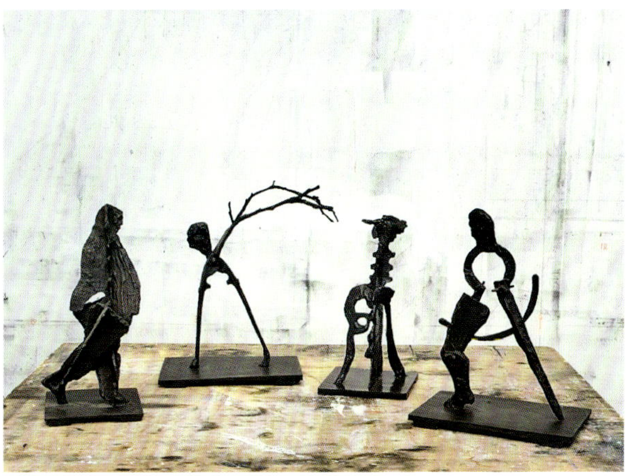

FIG. 22 William Kentridge
***Promenade II*, 2002**
Bronze
14 3/4 x 10 5/16 x 6 3/4 in. (37.5 x 26.2 x 17 cm)
Collection of the artist, courtesy Marian Goodman Gallery, New York, and Goodman Gallery, Johannesburg

The initial suite of etchings evolved into the film *Ubu Tells the Truth* (1997; figs. 10–11, 21, pls. 120–29) and *Ubu and the Truth Commission*, a theatrical work that explored the personal tales of atrocity related by witnesses to the South African Truth and Reconciliation Commission, as well as the confessions of perpetrators, as symbols of the larger national narrative of reconciliation in the mid-1990s. In *Ubu Tells the Truth*, burlesque is constantly contrasted with factual material. Kentridge collages together drawings, paper cutouts, archival photographs, and found film: from images of police with whips, lashing into a running crowd in Durban's Cato Manor neighborhood in 1960 or storming a group of students at the University of the Witwatersrand during the State of Emergency in 1985, to footage of the Soweto uprising of 1976. Importantly, he represents Ubu as a dark shadow moving clumsily and violently behind a backlit screen, a technique Kentridge would develop further in other shadow-based works.

As his interest in shadows and negativity increased, Kentridge began to cast shadows of objects in animations such as *Shadow Procession* (pls. 135–43) and in bronze sculptures that paradoxically seem to give them substance (*Promenade II* [2002; fig. 22]), and to create processions of shadows made of torn black paper.[24] For *Shadow Procession* he filmed the silhouettes of scissors, compasses, coffeepots, and figures made of torn pieces of paper. An enormous Ubu with oversize hands and a bloated belly cracks his whip, followed by a string of emaciated shadow figures that shuffle across the screen. The music changes to choral singing as the figures rise up and walk slowly, painfully, to the sounds of a march made from recordings of South African political rallies in the 1990s.

In early 1999, grappling with how to give substance to what goes on in the mind as well as the immateriality of shadows, the artist began to create a new series of works that involved the projection of images onto three-dimensional objects. *Sleeping on Glass* and *Medicine Chest* (2001) are both projections on mirrors. *Learning the Flute* (pls. 149–50), a projection on a blackboard, was the first work to stem from Mozart's opera *The Magic Flute*. This was followed by the miniature theater projections of *Preparing the Flute* (2005; pls. 151–54) and *Black Box* (fig. 29, pls. 163–69), and more recently by the anamorphic projection *What Will Come*.

24. See Jane Taylor, "The Shadow of a Doubt: William Kentridge's Bronze Age," in Christov-Bakargiev, *William Kentridge* (2004), 50–57.

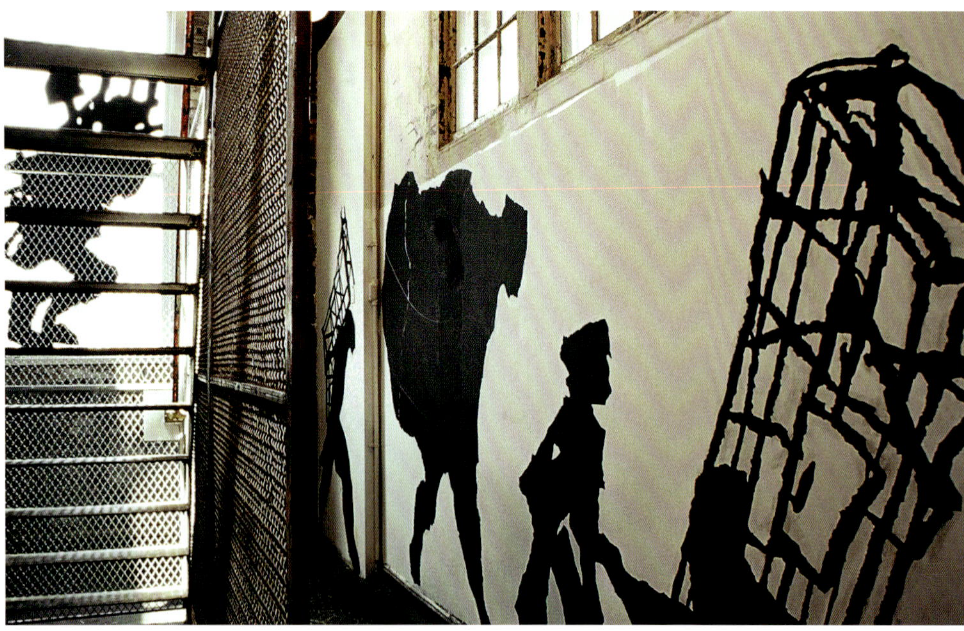

FIG. 23 William Kentridge
***Stair Procession*, 2000**
Torn paper, tape, and glue
Dimensions variable
Courtesy the artist

TEARING

In 2000 Kentridge tore up large pieces of black photographic backdrop paper and glued the fragments onto the walls of a stairwell to create *Stair Procession* (fig. 23), a filmic procession of characters marching up or down the stairs. The graphic impact of the project is characteristic of Kentridge's draftsmanship, which has always been admired for its simplicity and immediacy. In an attempt to reduce intentionality and control even more than it already had been in his signature erasure-based drawings, he began to explore other techniques, looking at the chance encounter between the gesture of tearing and the semirandom shapes it produced. He tears black paper to explore how little an artist must do to create shapes that viewers read as figures—how few shapes can ever really be abstract. He also paints figures and tears up the images only to collage them back together in similar—yet different—configurations.

Tearing also informs the way Kentridge makes installations out of projections, part of an ongoing research into the machinery of photography, film, and video production and the mechanisms of perception. Indeed, since late 2003, when he created *7 Fragments for Georges Méliès* (figs. 44–46, 53–55, pls. 8–27), he has also torn apart the notion of a finished film and reversed the process of editing—he tends to edit fragments of film apart rather than joining them together in a coherent, linear projection. *7 Fragments* and *Journey to the Moon* (2003; pls. 28–47) are homages to the French filmmaker, actor, and producer Méliès, who experimented with the magical possibilities of the nascent technology of film in the late nineteenth century and first decade of the twentieth century. In works such as *Le locataire diabolique* (The Diabolical Renter, 1909), simple substitutions, changes of scale, and other tricks performed between the filming of successive frames enabled Méliès to perform impossible feats such as fitting an entire apartment into a suitcase.

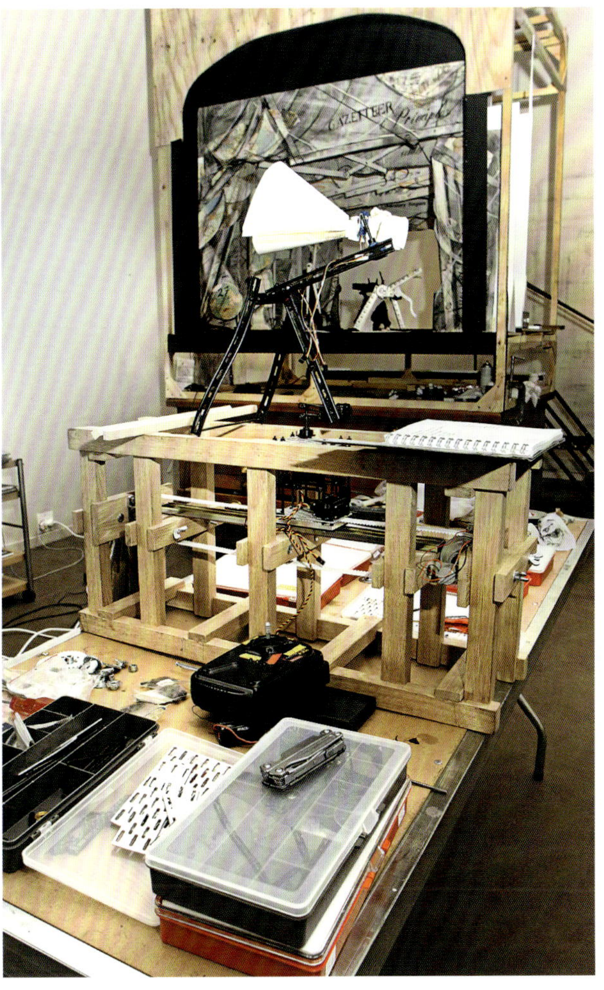

FIG. 24 View of Kentridge's studio during the making of ***Black Box/ Chambre Noire*** (2005)

When one looks at photographs of Kentridge's studio during the making of *Black Box* or *Preparing the Flute,* one sees a mise en abyme where microcosm and macrocosm are joined and mirrored: the studio, with its clutter of tools, tables, chairs, wires, cameras, coffeepots, torn paper, and drawings, looks much like the space being created within those miniature theater boxes. What is represented is metaphorically identical with the space where the representation is created, thus suggesting a relation between inner and outer worlds—the artist's studio and the space beyond the studio with its social responsibilities. That relationship was also at the heart of the *Méliès* fragments insofar as they investigated the legitimacy of artistic practice in the studio, detached from the outside world, and how that practice might ultimately impact the world at large.[25]

By tearing images apart and putting them back together in provisional and fragmented ways, Kentridge foregrounds the manual and simple means through which strange effects can be achieved. The artist's studio is revealed as a place where the miraculous can come about through use of the most common, everyday elements, suggesting by extension the empowerment of the viewer. This goes hand in hand with a form of artistic agency wherein machines and mechanical devices are no longer viewed as inherently violent, as they were in his earlier works. In films such as *Johannesburg, 2nd Greatest City after Paris,* Soho's self-reflexive business concerns were represented by calculators, typewriters, and telephones. Cameras on tripods were machine guns whose aggression could only be deflected through art. Since working on the mechanics of visual perception and precinematic devices, however, Kentridge has embarked on a journey to disenfranchise mechanics, no longer presenting them only as dehumanizing instruments of control but also as tools for experimenting with the manipulation and expansion of vision.

25. The same relation between inside and outside space was present in earlier works such as *Felix in Exile* (1994), in which the "black box" was a suitcase full of drawings that flew out and covered the walls of the lonely hotel room where Felix waited and yearned—itself a box filled with drawings (see fig. 6).

The works resulting from Kentridge's current interest in Gogol's *The Nose* and the Shostakovich opera constitute a significant chapter in his exploration of tearing. *I am not me, the horse is not mine*—the installation of eight video fragments that premiered in June 2008 in the abandoned warehouse of a twentieth-century military shipyard in Sydney's harbor[26]—recalls the experience of the *Méliès* fragments: that of being inside the artist's mind. It is a form of inverted Cubism where one is inside the object rather than trying to understand it from the outside. We are simultaneously inside the studio and inside a condition where points of view shift and it becomes impossible to see all that is going on at once, let alone edit all the fragments into one continuous, seamless image.

Kentridge's title, which paraphrases a traditional Russian colloquialism used to reject culpability, adroitly yet indirectly suggests that our culture, at the beginning of the twenty-first century, is in a state of historical and psychological denial. "*I am not me, the horse is not mine*," the artist has stated, "takes the short story, its earlier history and its possible future histories as the basis for looking at the formal inventiveness of the different strains of Russian modernism, and at the calamitous end of the Russian avant-garde."[27] Indeed, Gogol's *The Nose*, itself inspired by Laurence Sterne's *Tristram Shandy* (1759), inspired in its turn by Miguel de Cervantes's *Don Quixote* (1605), uses the absurd and the fantastic as narrative devices. These were rare at the time but prefigured much early-twentieth-century modernist writing. Read in reverse, *Nos*, the Russian title of Gogol's story, is *Son*, the Russian word for "dream"—a nuance that Gogol may have used intentionally to suggest that the entire tale could be a dream. Gogol's absurd story anticipated Surrealism, but what actually occurred in Soviet Russia during the late 1920s and 1930s was the surreal come true: avant-garde art was banned, modernism was crushed, and many members of the Communist party were killed during the Stalinist purges. Shostakovich's opera was written after the great revolutionary period of the early twentieth century, in a society already under the pressures of Soviet government-imposed standards. Gogol's allegory of power and identity may have allowed Shostakovich an indirect narrative through which to expose the absurdity of his time—a revolution gone mad, detached from its initial ideals and from the body of society.

26. *I am not me, the horse is not mine* premiered on the occasion of the 16th Biennale of Sydney, *Revolutions—Forms That Turn*, on view June 18 through September 7, 2008.

27. Kentridge, conversation with the author, 2008.

Kentridge's installation and the lecture/performance of the same title refer to those modernist and revolutionary impulses and include visual references to the constructivist language of El Lissitzky, shadows, and torn paper as well as archival film material from the Soviet Union of the 1920s and 1930s. Looking at the period prior to the division of politics from engaged avant-garde art, when both were still joined by "a sense of openness, of possibility, or forming something new—of agency," he creates an "elegy for the formal artistic language crushed in the 1930s and for the possibilities of human transformation."[28]

The installation comprises eight fragments in total. *His Majesty the Nose* (pls. 197–201) begins with a view of a ladder in an empty studio. The Nose figure begins to climb up the ladder, then collapses into fragments of torn black paper. Over and over he tries to climb the ladder, each time toppling down like an abstract collage of bits of banners, globes, and texts—a modernist poem in motion or a vision of language collapsing. Metaphorically, the fragment depicts megalomania, climbing in power, and endlessly being crushed by ambition. In another fragment, *The Horse Is Not Mine* (pls. 182–91), pieces of torn paper fall into place in the shape of a horse; the Nose acquires a steed in his rise up the social ladder. In *Prayers of Apology* (pls. 202–8), based on transcripts from the plenum of the Central Committee of the Soviet Communist party, a series of words appear on the screen. They are excerpts of tense exchanges between Nikolai Bukharin and committee members in which Bukharin's self-defense collapses linguistically; he is met by accusations such as "You practiced too much duplicity!" and roars of laughter. A lieutenant of Lenin and an early member of the Communist party as well as one of its leading theoreticians, Bukharin became part of the Central Committee in 1918. His story expresses the self-destruction of the Bolshevik party—he remained loyal throughout the purges that began in 1929 and was therefore unable to resist accusations when his own time came. For Kentridge, "The tragedy of his situation resides in the impossibility of reconciling his need to believe in the party and the cause to which he had given all his life, and the new world of illogic, of line, or strategy which he had embraced for the sake of his party."[29] *Prayers of Apology* reveals the inversion of logic that occurs when language is severed from truth in the theatricality of the staged trial. When Bukharin ultimately says, "It is very difficult for me to die," Stalin replies, "And it's easy for us to go on living?"

28. Ibid.

29. Ibid.

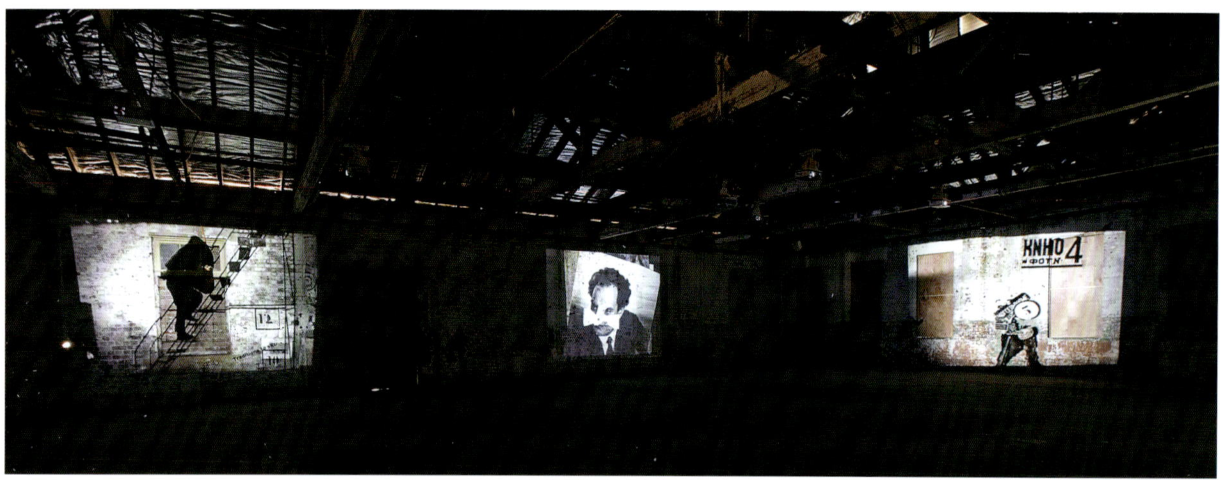

FIGS. 25–26 William Kentridge
***I am not me, the horse is not mine*, 2008**
DVCAM and HDV transferred to video, 6:01 min.
Collection of the artist, courtesy Marian Goodman Gallery, New York, and Goodman Gallery, Johannesburg

A Lifetime of Enthusiasm (pls. 174–81) is a procession piece that explores the construction of enthusiasm and energy expressed during the years of the revolution through marches and public speeches. A man walks across the stage with a red banner that rips and yet is still brandished about. He is followed by a parade of characters that includes the Nose, a black suprematist circle, puppets, automatons, a horse made of torn pieces of paper, Tatlin's tower, megaphones, and other apparatuses of communication. Stalin appears carrying a flag, as do words: "We also let blood," "This is about war," "War is about." Kentridge seems to suggest that we cannot appreciate avant-garde impulses in art without also understanding the avant-garde's belief and hope in the transformation of humanity, misjudgments notwithstanding. In *Country Dances I (Shadow)* (pls. 223–29) we see shadows of Africans improvising Russian folk dances. Filmed against a brightly lit backdrop, the figures are stretched and made gigantic by the shifting light. *Country Dances II (Paper)* (pls. 235–39) replaces the shadow figures of *Country Dances I* with forms composed of torn fragments of paper and texts taken mainly from a Russian encyclopedia. It celebrates the energy and possibilities of modernist collage while also exploring the process of abstraction and increasing misunderstanding. Kentridge's method repeats on a technical level the schism between truth and language in the postrevolutionary purges.

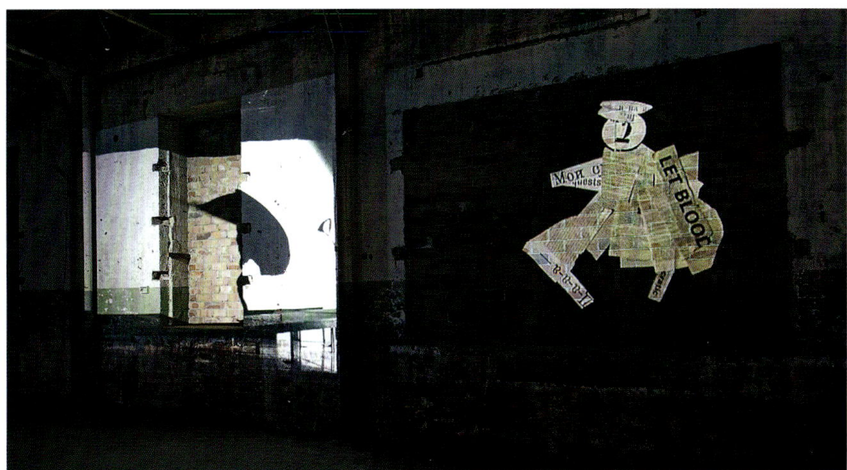

The trials that Kentridge references in these fragments have also been addressed by Badiou, who frames them in terms of the relationship between theater and reality in twentieth-century culture:

That Ridiculous Blank Space Again (A One-Minute Love Story) (pls. 209–18) is about the cruelty, absurdity, and lack of logic in human behavior and relations, and also addresses the underside of political and aesthetic utopias. It visually represents a short story by Daniil Kharms, a Russian writer who died of starvation in a Leningrad prison in 1941. In this simple animation, Kentridge creates two modernist-looking collages made of pieces of paper that are not glued together, which he shapes and reshapes to construct the simple narrative: they meet and part, one returns and beats the other, they come back together morphed into one, and finally one drags the other offscreen. Finally, in *Commissariat for Enlightenment* (pls. 192–96), Russian futurist triangles and circles fall onto the stage of the projected image. The artist washes his hands with water from a bucket, then attempts to form the figure of a horse out of torn bits of paper, but the composition escapes him. All the while recur elements of early archival photographs, excerpts from films of Stalinist celebrations, images of the Nose diving into a swimming pool, and scenes of Shostakovich playing the piano.

> It is precisely the energy of the real that presents itself as a mask.... After all, in these trials it is purely and simply a matter of killing people, of liquidating a significant part of the communist establishment.... Why stage trials in which predesignated and most often resigned victims will be forced to recount utterly far-fetched things? Who would ever believe that throughout their whole lives people like Zinoviev and Bukharin were Japanese spies, Hitler's puppets, hirelings of the counter-revolution, and so forth? What is the point of this gigantic sham?... It is... difficult to establish the necessity of these trials, especially since a large number of high-ranking officials, particularly among the military, were eliminated in the basements of the secret service without the slightest public performance. For these trials are pure theatrical fictions. The accused themselves, who had been carefully prepared, by torture if necessary, had to conform to a role whose performance had been rehearsed and pretty much scripted in the punitive corridors of the regime.[30]

30. Badiou, *The Century*, 50–52.

In many ways, the theatricality of the violence implied in *I am not me, the horse is not mine* is directly descended from Kentridge's portrayal of the grotesque tyrant Ubu. Torn from its body, the Nose moves through the world ambitiously yet obtusely, unable to scale a ladder or achieve true autonomy. In the *Méliès* fragments, the question of the relationship between artistic experimentation (the avant-garde) and the outside world remains open, as does the question of artistic and intellectual responsibility in society. These are unresolved dilemmas in the *Nose* projects as well, though Kentridge addresses them head-on by referring to the moment par excellence when revolutionary art was supposed to be one with art for the revolution. On one level, Kentridge looks at how language was disjointed from reality and truth in the twentieth century, how the power of words to name things decomposed with the rise of advertising and facile journalism in the West, and how ideological commitment to a collective cause appeared more important than singular truth under totalitarian regimes. On another level, since history repeats itself, he is also speaking of today and our current state of denial. Indeed, the obsession with the detached Nose suggests the loss of a part of ourselves. It suggests a modernity torn apart, or the tearing of language's ability to symbolize and re-present the real. It even questions the coherence of the body in the digital age and the current culture industry, characterized still as a society of spectacle but also as a state of unreal economic relations, where finance has been disconnected from production and from any substantial articulation or satisfaction of desire or need.

Denial involves both one's inability to recognize oneself, and thus accept that one shares forms of culpability or responsibility for one's own actions, and a refusal to admit that one has taken part in actions (modernity's revolutions) now commonly believed to have been wrong. Denial thus constitutes a form of detachment: an "I" torn from "me" (the engaged subject riven from awareness of the objective or accusative case, or the internal recognition of being an actor in events). This "tear" exists on the level of language—the language used at the Soviet meetings, for example, was theatrically detached from the reality of human lives that were affected by its consequences (and is somehow strangely parallel to the discrepancy between language and truth in political speech today, both on the internet and in daily life). The phantom limb, violently torn from the body, is painful. And yet, recent studies show that therapy based on the use of projected or mirror images of the remaining limb can eliminate the pain.[31] Similarly, Kentridge seems to suggest that by reengaging and reliving the avant-garde impulse, by reactualizing its enthusiasm, we can transform the pain of denial into something new, albeit provisional. Recognizing detachment and denial as a tear is therefore necessary to psychological and cultural healing. The Nose, torn from its body, does not recognize the whole from which it came because it does not accept that it has been separated from it. Today, at the beginning of the twenty-first century, we do not always recognize that postmodern culture was torn away from the twentieth century: we have not fully assessed the body we are still part of. Bukharin, just before dying, wrote to Stalin to ask if he really believed all that Bukharin had been accused of ("Finally I need to know. Did you really believe what was said?"). A chasm, a tear, a rip, a fissure in the seamless detachment of language from reality, disrupting the theater of the trials, occurred briefly and suddenly.

31. I am indebted to the ideas of the neuroscientist Angela Sirigu, who has performed fascinating work on the experience of phantom limbs.

Experiencing the first *Nose* installation in Sydney, I saw a theater without theater, one characterized by shadows, sound, and the fragmentation of the linearity of narrative through which, and only indirectly, reality can appear. Projected directly onto the rough brick walls of an old building, the images broke through the distinction between stage and audience, appearing with even more immateriality than they would have had they been projected onto screens. The fragments became signs of the fragmentation of the revolutionary impulse. They appeared naked and collapsed into terror. They suggested a great injustice caused by stupidity, or perhaps without any cause: the human folly that wasted the revolution, transforming it into totalitarianism, as if human stupidity were somehow inevitable.

Once again I remembered Adorno's "negativity" and his views on art and society:

> The sea of the formerly inconceivable, on which around 1910 revolutionary art movements set out, did not bestow the promised happiness of adventure. Instead, the process that was unleashed consumed the categories in the name of that for which it was undertaken.... For absolute freedom in art, always limited to a particular, comes into contradiction with the perennial unfreedom of the whole. In it the place of art became uncertain. The autonomy it achieved, after having freed itself from cultic function and its images, was nourished by the idea of humanity. As society became ever less a human one, this autonomy was shattered. Drawn from the ideal of humanity, art's constituent elements withered by art's own law of movement. Yet art's autonomy remains irrevocable. All efforts to restore art by giving it a social function—of which art is itself uncertain and by which it expresses its own uncertainty—are doomed.... Art must turn against itself, in opposition to its own concept, and thus become uncertain of itself right into its innermost fiber.[32]

Despite the apparent negativity of such an argument, one senses in both Adorno of the late 1960s and Kentridge today a sympathy for the energy, hope, and enthusiasm of the revolutionary moment, and an awareness that although the autonomy of art and artistic practice is inevitable, it is contingent always on the outside world and on an active form of outrage.

We end with a quote and a tear: "The basic levels of experience that motivate art are related to those of the objective world from which they recoil."[33]

32. Adorno, *Aesthetic Theory*, 1–2.

33. Ibid., 6.

3

OCCASIONAL & RESIDUAL HOPE

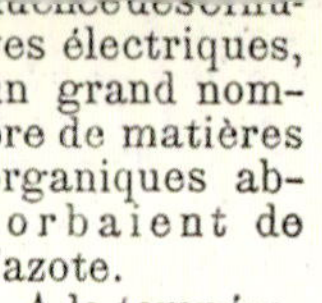
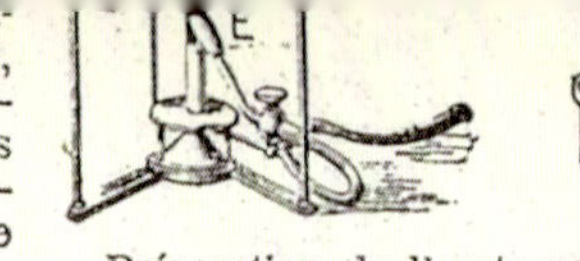
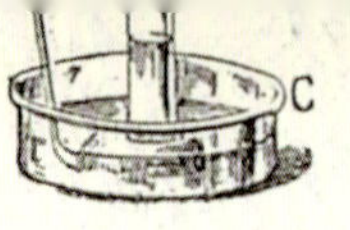
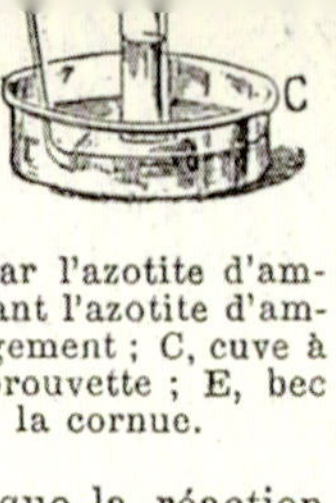
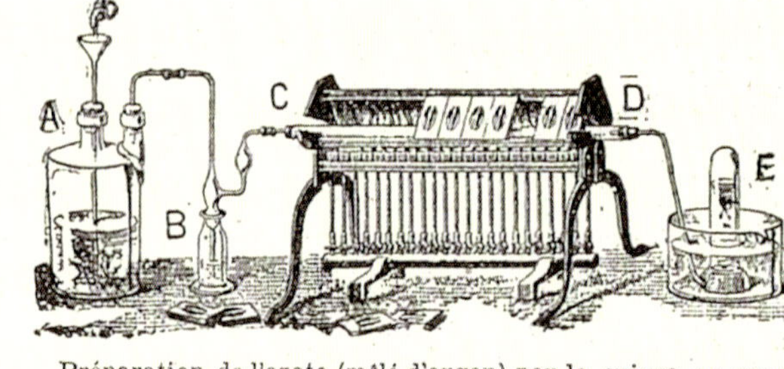
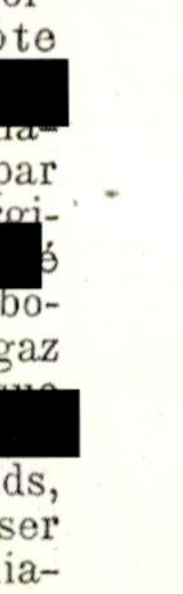

UBU & THE PROCESSION

Shadow Procession was made in two sections, each for a specific event. The first part to be made (the last section of the film) was conceived to be projected onto the front wall of a museum on the opening evening of an exhibition in Barcelona. Because I anticipated it being shown only once, it was made at speed and with openness to what it would become (it would only be seen once, so it didn't matter if it was very thin). All three of my children joined in making some of the puppets—the action man and other toys of my son were purloined, fish paste was spread on the table to entice the new family cat to parade.

The second part of the film was made several months later for the Istanbul Biennial, where it was to be shown in the Yerebatan Sarnici, a sixth-century underground water cistern. It was not completed in the two-day rush of the first part (the biennial would be on for three months, not one evening), but it was still made with the sense that it was a fragment (the procession reaches no destination). The technique of working with jointed paper figures came from shadow puppets I had been introduced to in theater work with Handspring Puppet Company. Whereas in the theater pieces they had been figures at the margins, glimpsed between scenes, here they had to hold their own.

This transition from what is marginal, or at best occasional, to being the heart of the matter was the surprise and the pleasure of making the film. There was meant to be a third section to the film (the intermezzo of the Ubu shadow is just that: a connection, not a resolution). But I could not find it, not formally but intentionally. I could not find a destination, neither a utopia nor a killing field. The fact of transition of movement was essential. Any definite destination felt tendentious. The music for the film was going to have been a song sung at funerals, but in the end the up-tempo "What a Friend We Have in Jesus" was the music that worked. That made a space for agency or hope in the march.

The figures in the procession and in *Ubu Tells the Truth* have a deliberate crudeness (the result of tearing rather than cutting). The figures need an active recognition by the viewer (and when making them I am a viewer). The viewer has to take very crude figures and imbue them with specificity. This is both active and involuntary. You know you are looking at crude, torn shapes but you cannot help seeing into them—a particular limp, a load on a head rather than a random shape.

The *Ubu* film is a residue of the theater piece *Ubu and the Truth Commission*. All the material in the film was used as back-projection in the play, and many of the images were there to clarify or amplify specific moments of the play. The edited film came at the end or almost the end of the process of making and performing the piece. But the *Ubu* project as a whole started with a series of etchings. These etchings were the basis for the visual language of the play (simple blackboard drawings over the thumbprint, soft-ground fleshiness of Ubu in the prints became the projected white lines behind the flesh of the actor in the play). The combination of Jarry's grotesquerie and the sober archival testimony of witnesses for the Truth and Reconciliation Commission (which formed the text of the play) needed a visual equivalent. This became a mix of simple animation and archival film footage. This jump, demanded by the needs of the play, was a formal move I doubt I would have made if I had simply been making a film.

In terms of images *Shadow Procession* and *Ubu Tells the Truth* move out of the studio into a raucous public space. In both cases it required something outside of the films—the occasion of an exhibition opening or a theater piece—for the films to find their language. **WK**

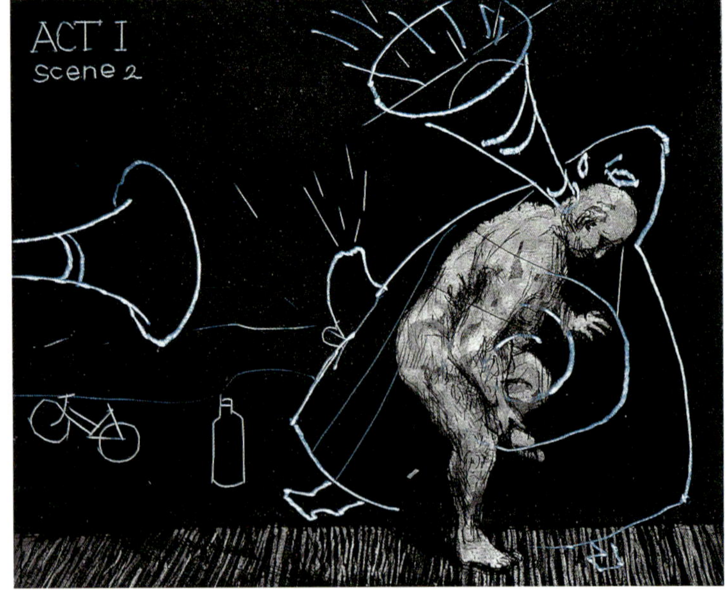

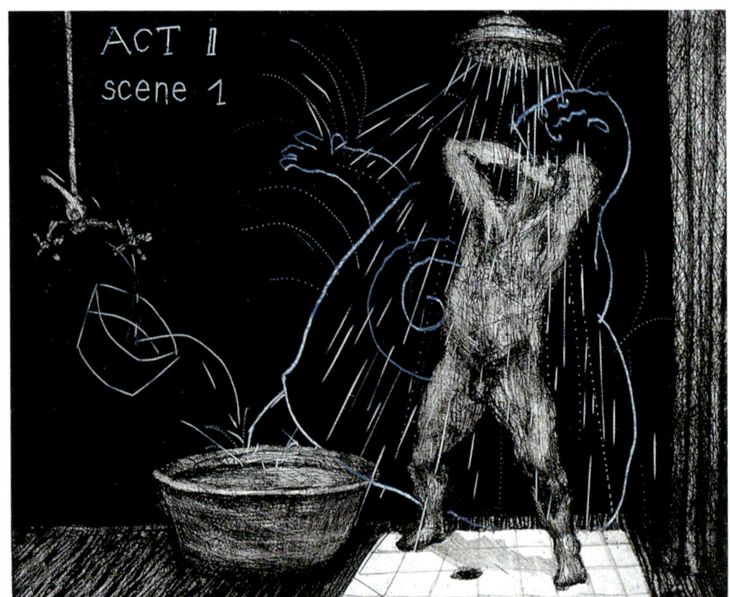

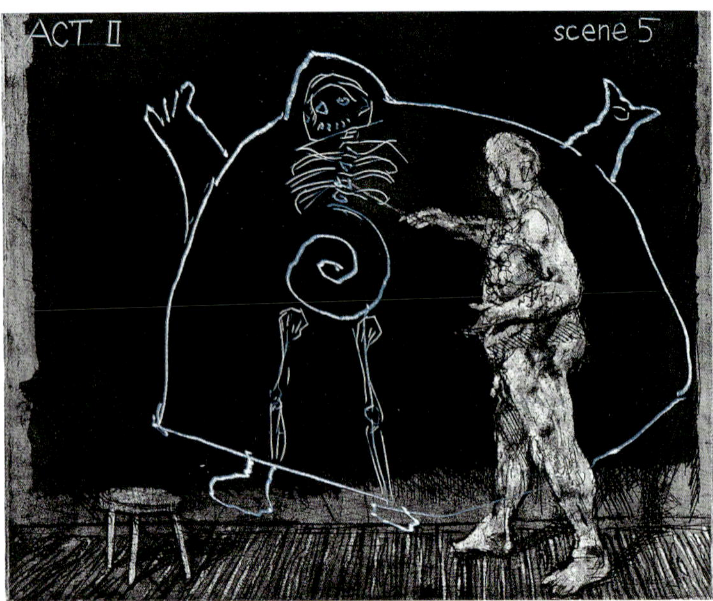

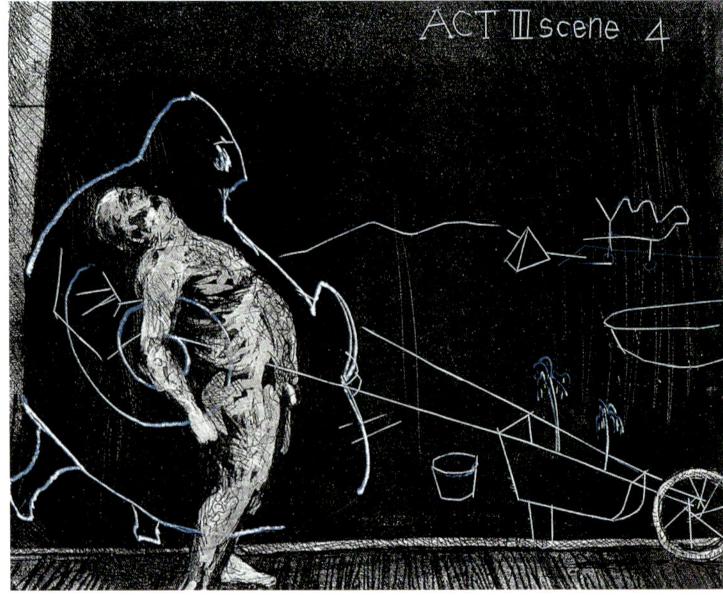

112
***Ubu Tells the Truth: Act I, Scene 2*, 1996**
Hardground, softground, aquatint, drypoint, and engraving, ed. 44/50
10 x 12 in. (25 x 30.5 cm)
Collection of the artist, courtesy Marian Goodman Gallery, New York, and Goodman Gallery, Johannesburg

113
***Ubu Tells the Truth: Act II, Scene 1*, 1996**
Hardground, softground, aquatint, drypoint, and engraving, ed. 44/50
10 x 12 in. (25 x 30.5 cm)
Collection of the artist, courtesy Marian Goodman Gallery, New York, and Goodman Gallery, Johannesburg

114
***Ubu Tells the Truth: Act II, Scene 5*, 1996**
Hardground, softground, aquatint, drypoint, and engraving, ed. 44/50
10 x 12 in. (25 x 30.5 cm)
Collection of the artist, courtesy Marian Goodman Gallery, New York, and Goodman Gallery, Johannesburg

115
***Ubu Tells the Truth: Act III, Scene 4*, 1996**
Hardground, softground, aquatint, drypoint, and engraving, ed. 44/50
10 x 12 in. (25 x 30.5 cm)
Collection of the artist, courtesy Marian Goodman Gallery, New York, and Goodman Gallery, Johannesburg

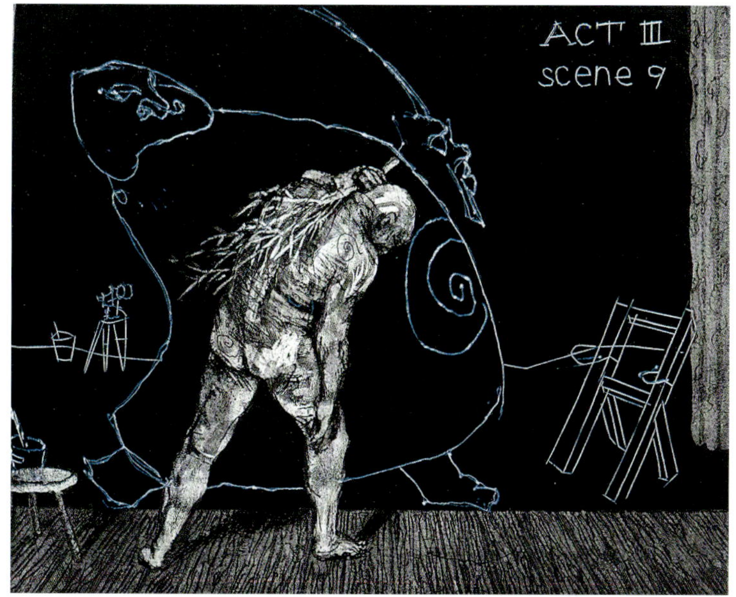

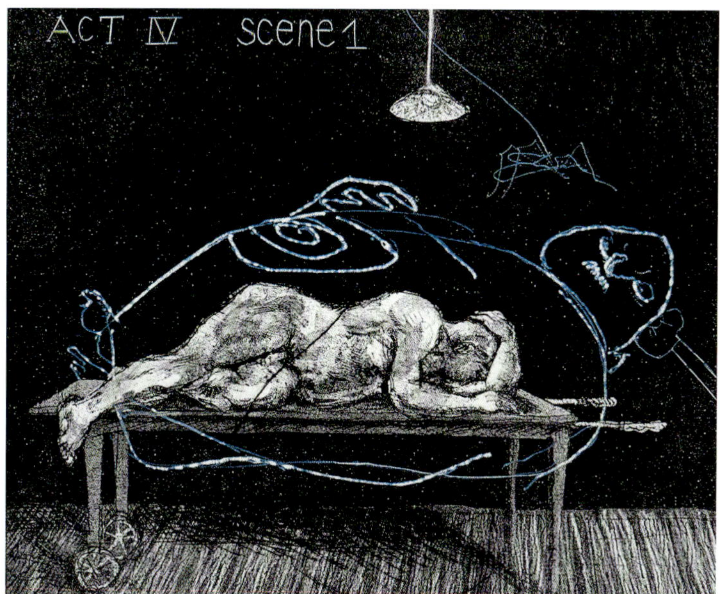

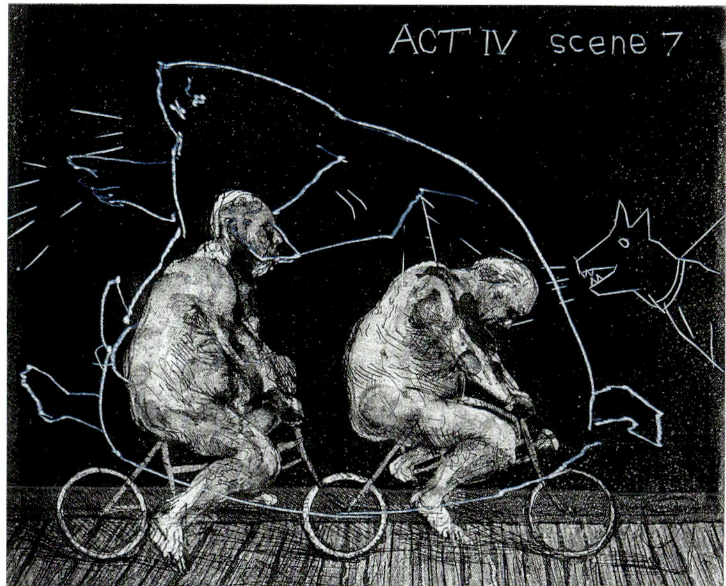

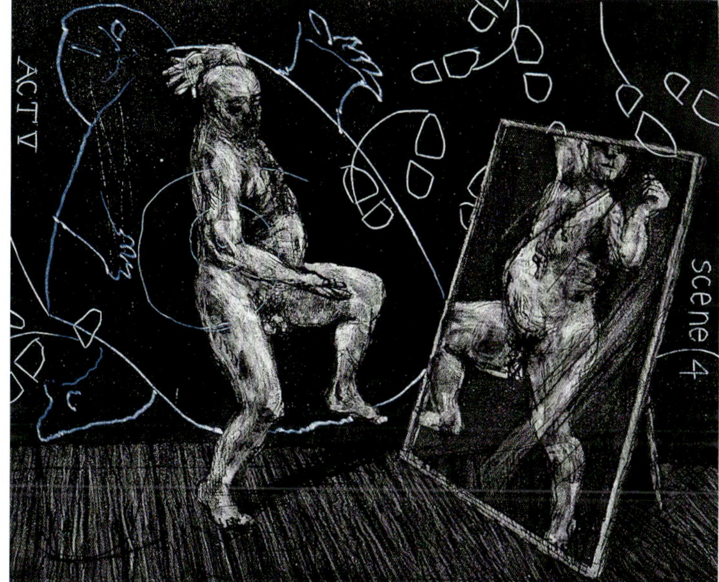

116
***Ubu Tells the Truth: Act III, Scene 9*, 1996**
Hardground, softground, aquatint, drypoint, and engraving, ed. 44/50
10 x 12 in. (25 x 30.5 cm)
Collection of the artist, courtesy Marian Goodman Gallery, New York, and Goodman Gallery, Johannesburg

117
***Ubu Tells the Truth: Act IV, Scene 1*, 1996**
Hardground, softground, aquatint, drypoint, and engraving, ed. 44/50
10 x 12 in. (25 x 30.5 cm)
Collection of the artist, courtesy Marian Goodman Gallery, New York, and Goodman Gallery, Johannesburg

118
***Ubu Tells the Truth: Act IV, Scene 7*, 1996**
Hardground, softground, aquatint, drypoint, and engraving, ed. 44/50
10 x 12 in. (25 x 30.5 cm)
Collection of the artist, courtesy Marian Goodman Gallery, New York, and Goodman Gallery, Johannesburg

119
***Ubu Tells the Truth: Act V, Scene 4*, 1996**
Hardground, softground, aquatint, drypoint, and engraving, ed. 44/50
10 x 12 in. (25 x 30.5 cm)
Collection of the artist, courtesy Marian Goodman Gallery, New York, and Goodman Gallery, Johannesburg

120–29
***Ubu Tells the Truth*, 1997**
35mm animated film with documentary photographs and 16mm archival film transferred to video, 8 min.
Collection of the artist, courtesy Marian Goodman Gallery, New York, and Goodman Gallery, Johannesburg

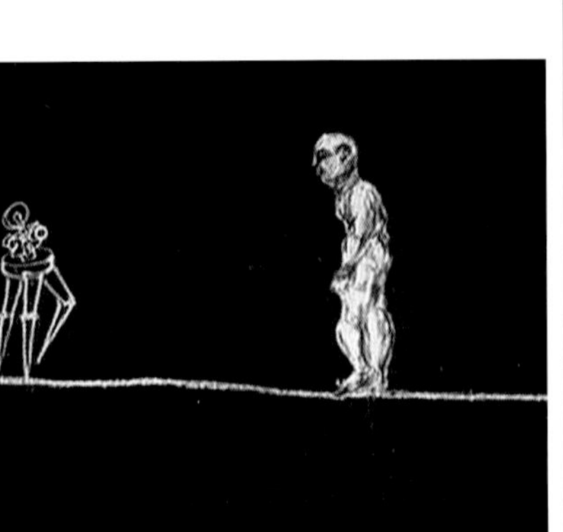
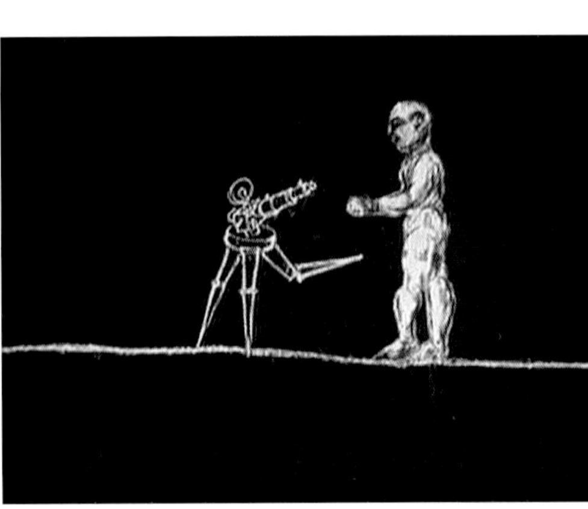
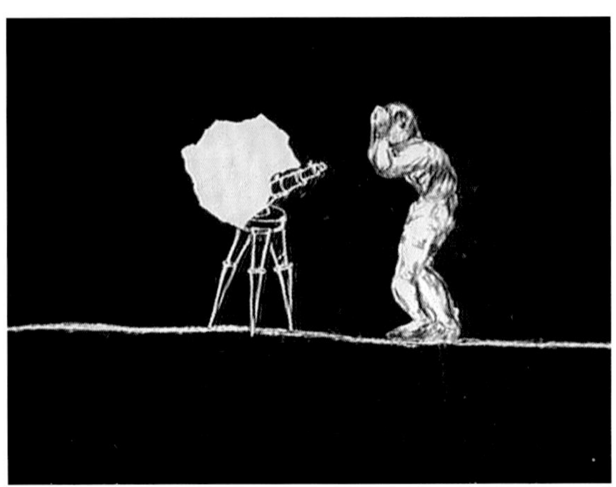
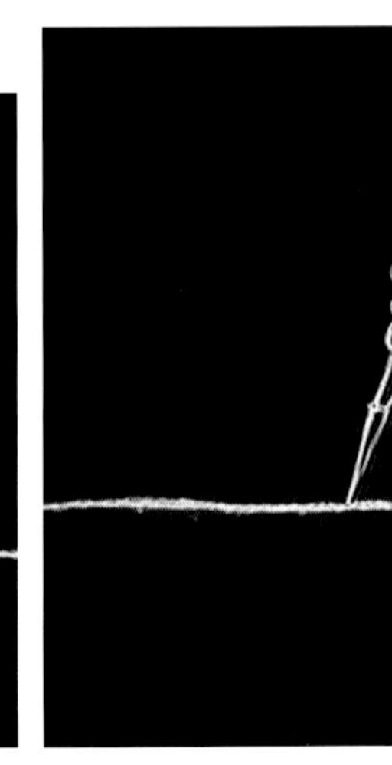
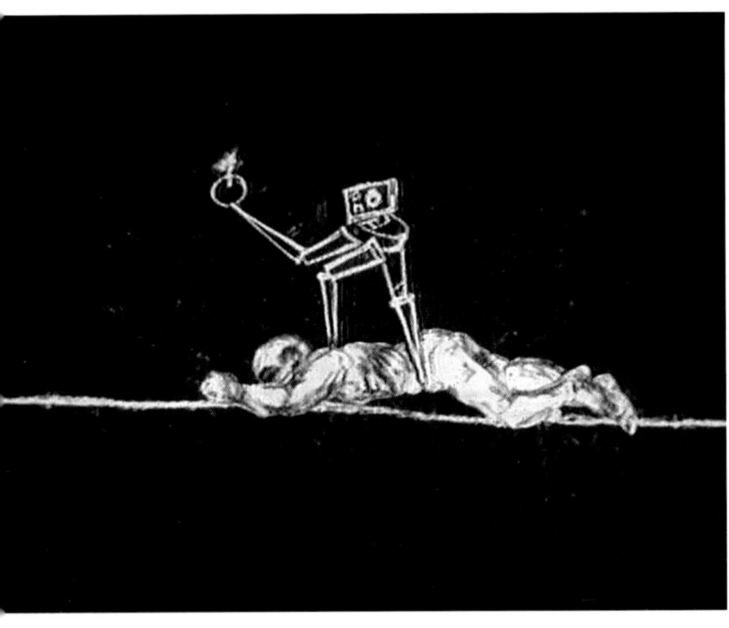
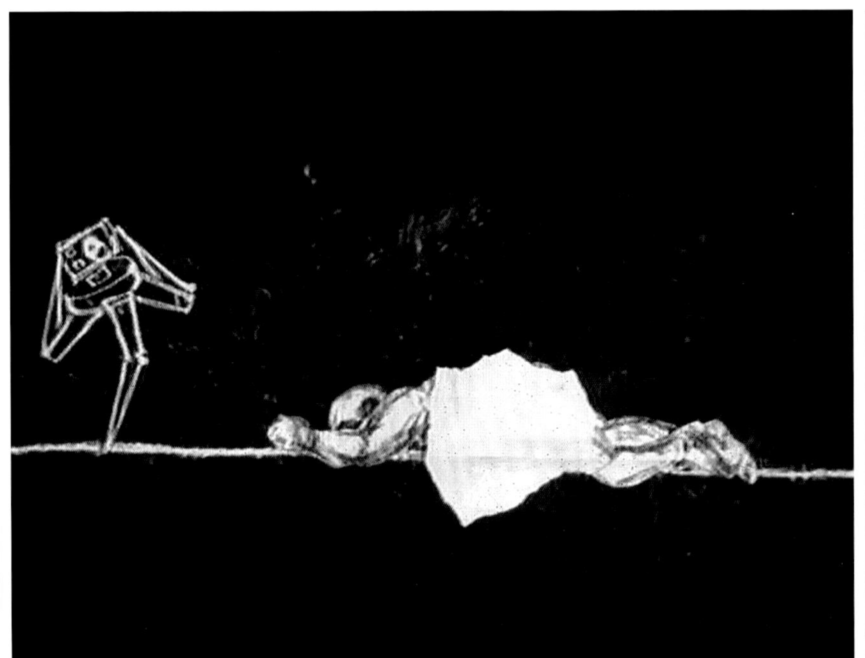
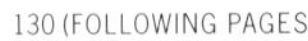

130 (FOLLOWING PAGES)
***Ubu Drawing (Sleeper)*, 1997**
Charcoal, gouache, pastel, and dry pigment on paper
42 1/2 x 84 3/5 in. (108 x 215 cm)
Collection of Jimmy and Becky Mayer

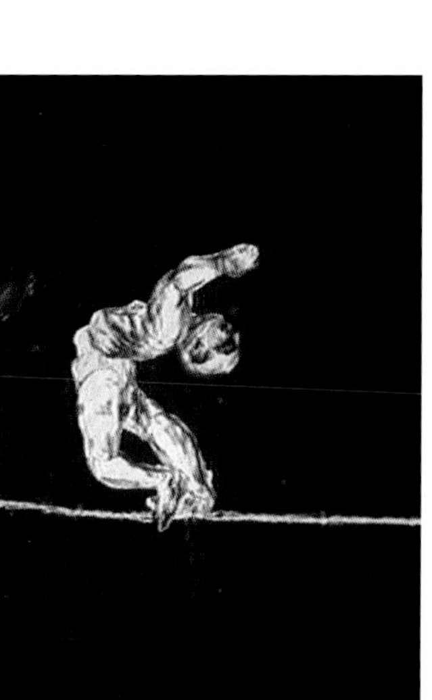

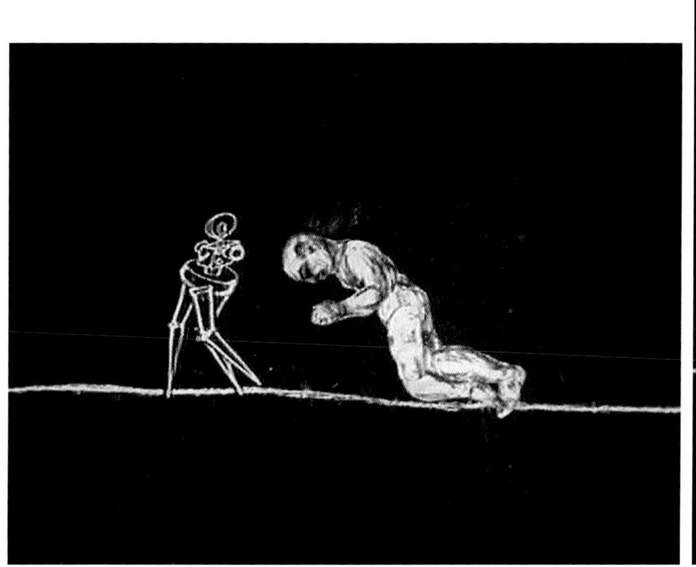

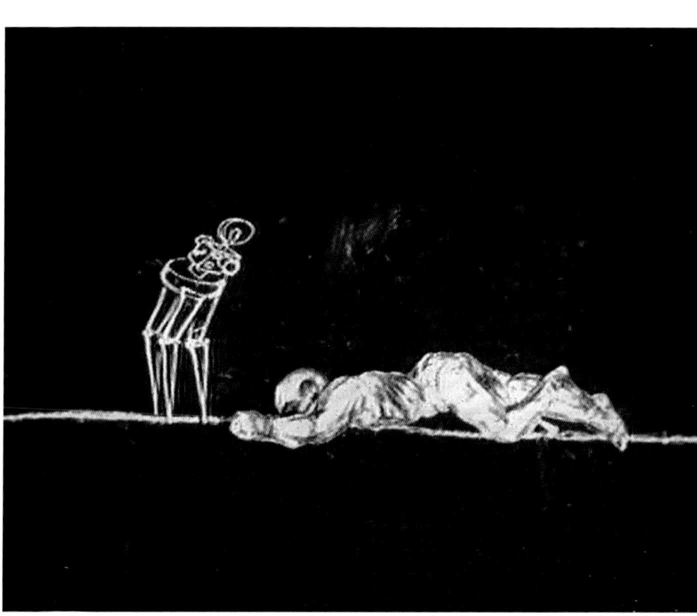

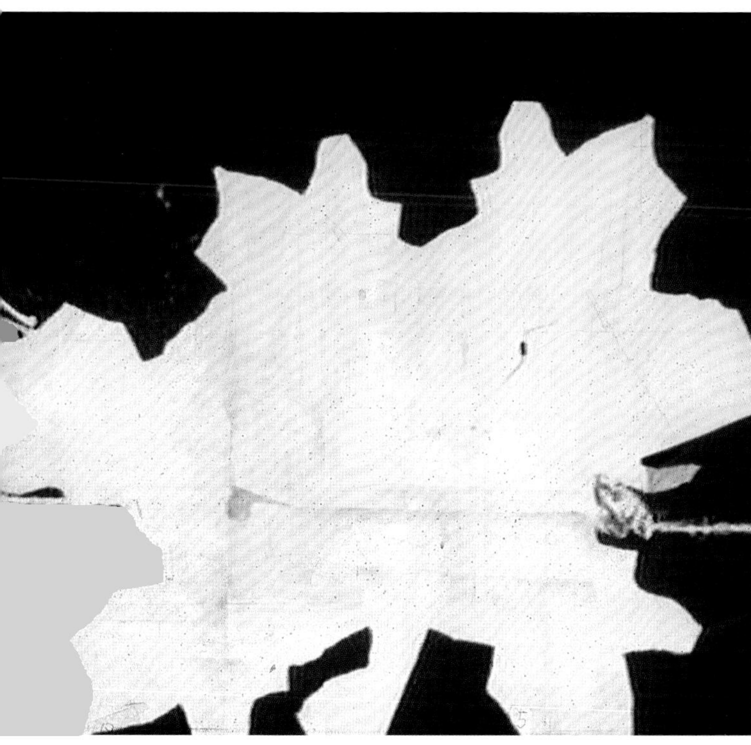

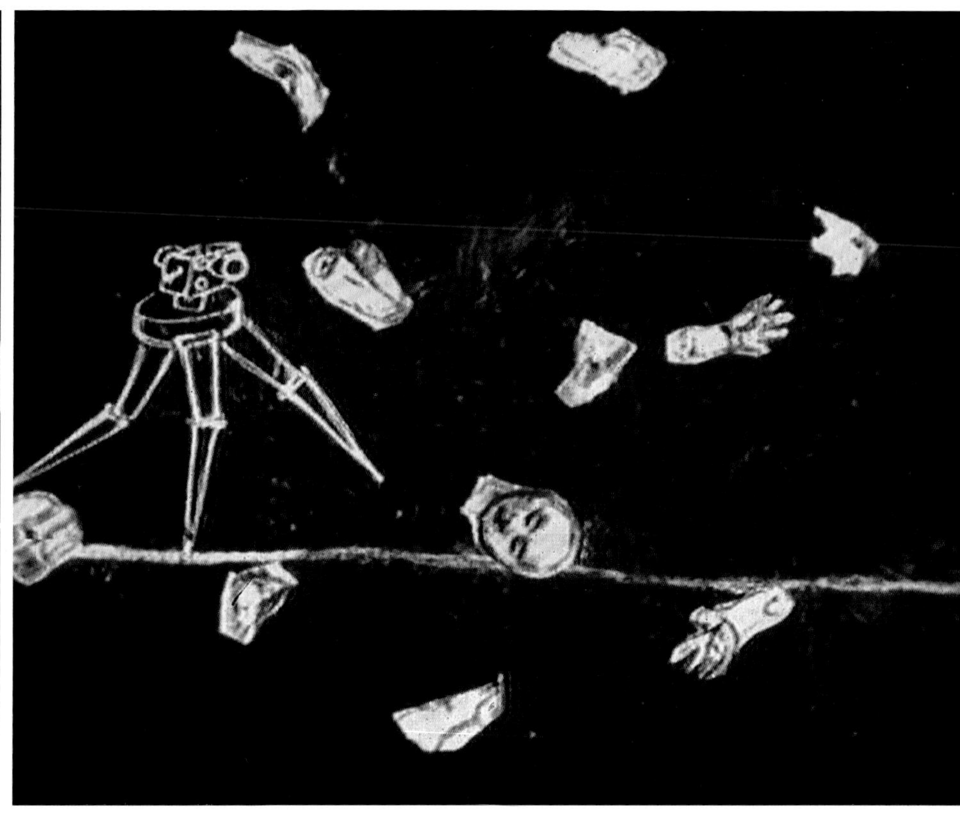

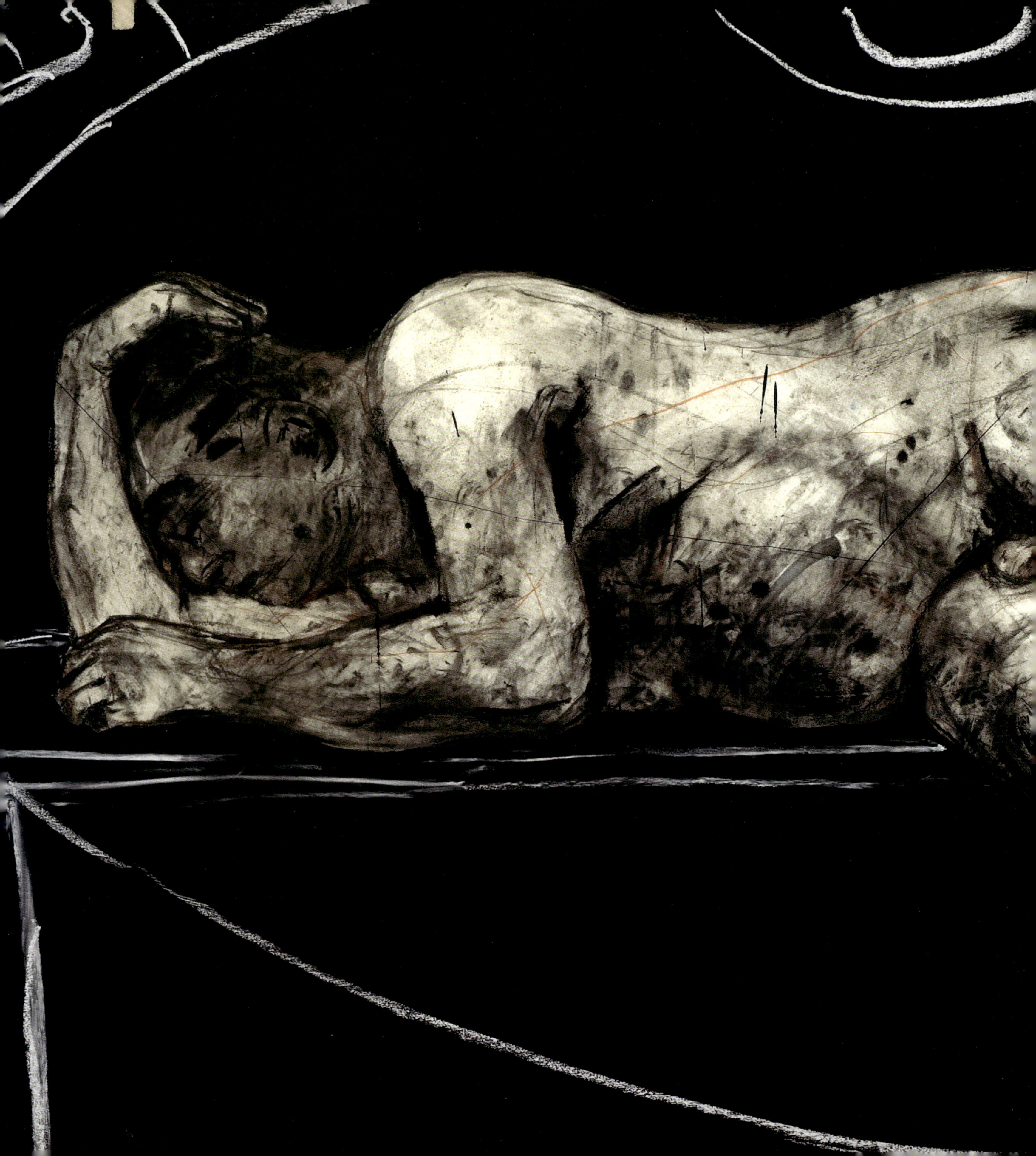

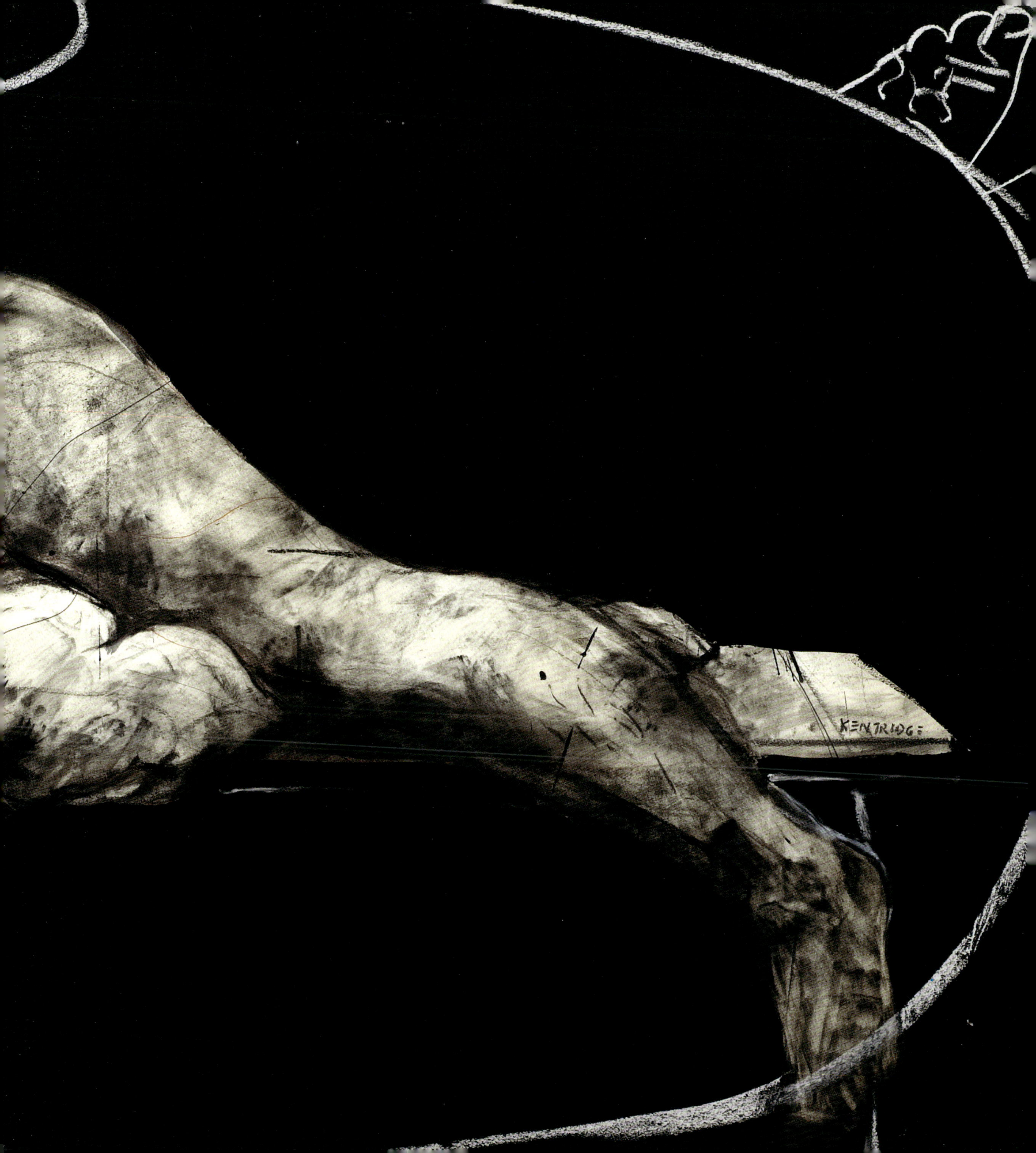
KENTRIDGE

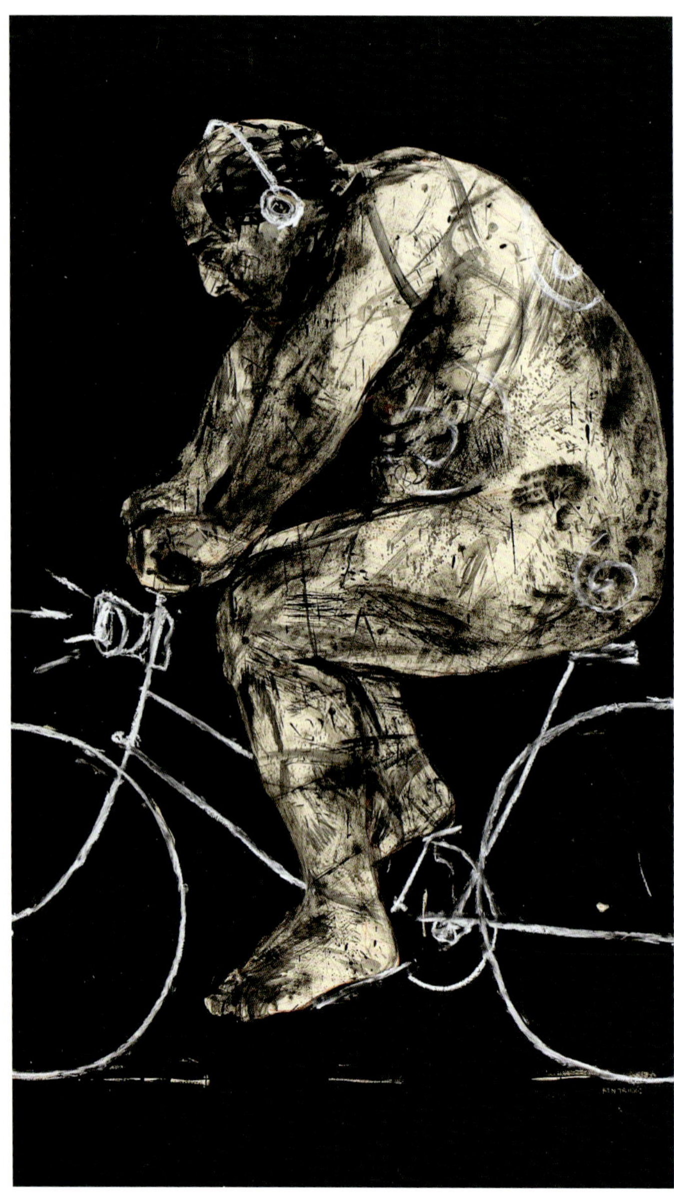

131
***Ubu Drawing (Bicycle)*, 1997**
Charcoal, gouache, pastel, and dry pigment on paper
63 1/3 x 43 1/2 in. (177 x 106 cm)
Collection of Kenneth and Sherry Endelson, Boca Raton, Florida

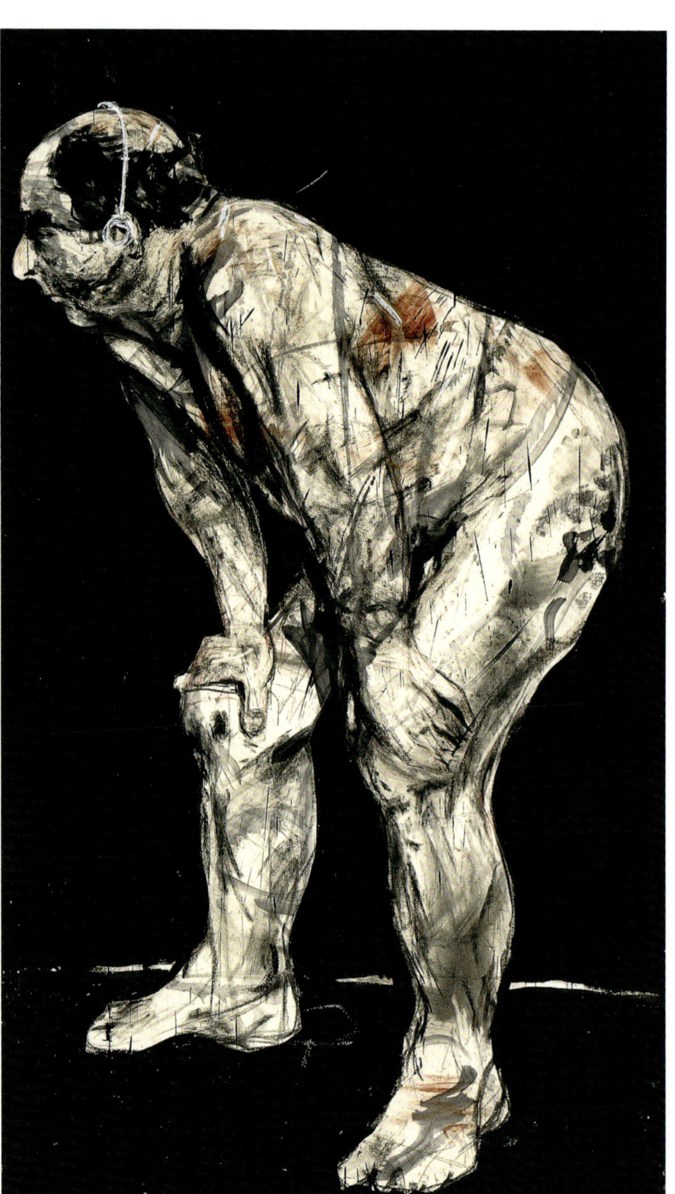

132
***Ubu Drawing (Listening Man)*, 1998**
Gouache, charcoal, dry pigment, and pastel on paper
75 1/2 x 42 1/2 in. (192 x 108 cm)
Collection of Donna and Howard Stone

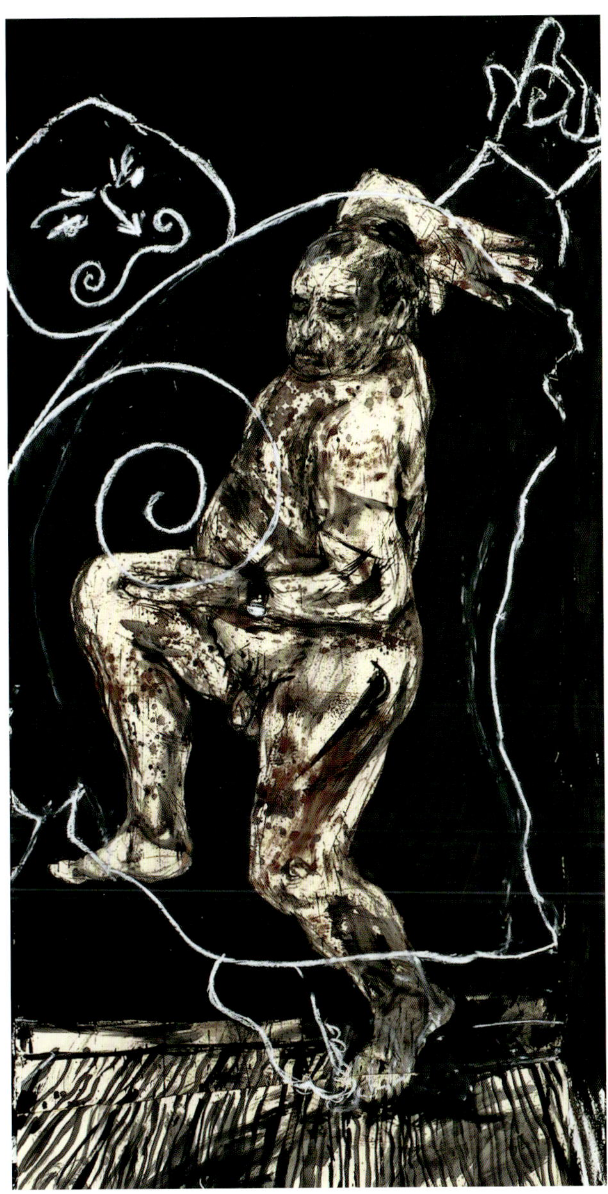

133
***Ubu Drawing (Dancing Man)*, 1998**
Gouache, charcoal, dry pigment, and pastel on paper
93 x 48 1/2 in. (236.2 x 123.2 cm)
Collection of Aaron and Barbara Levine

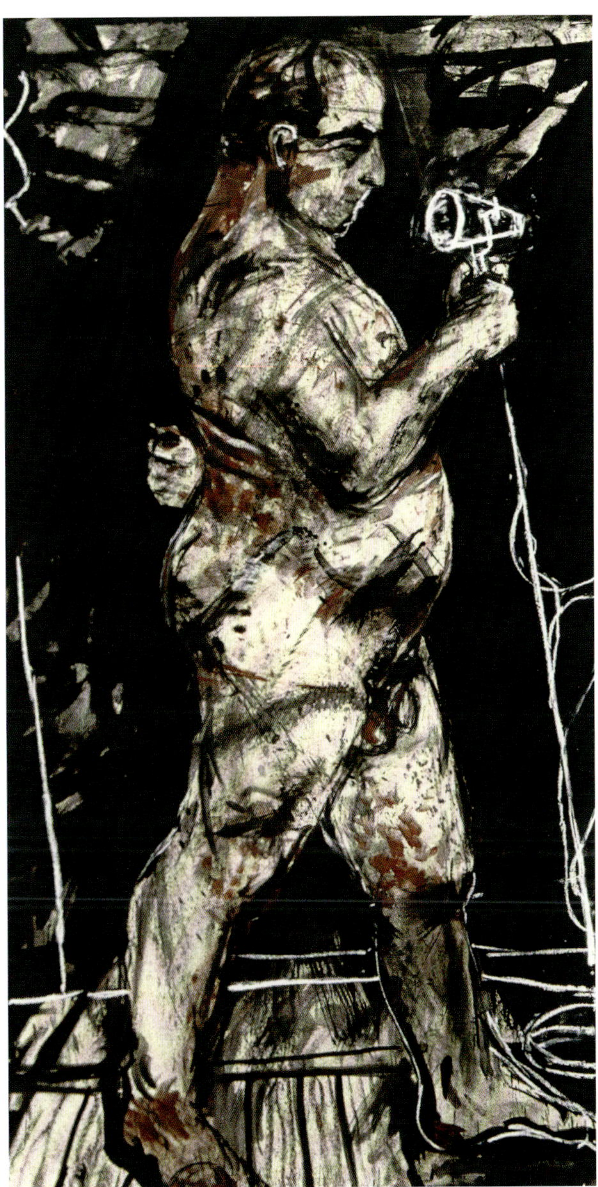

134
***Ubu Drawing (Man with Microphone)*, 1998**
Gouache, charcoal, dry pigment, and pastel on paper
100 x 42 1/2 in. (255 x 108 cm)
Collection unknown

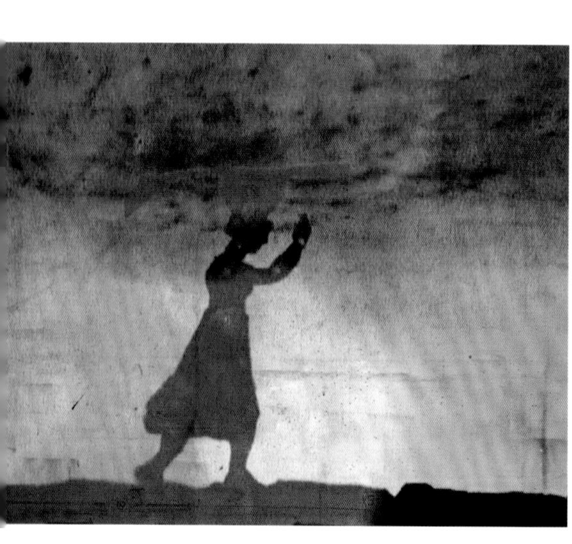

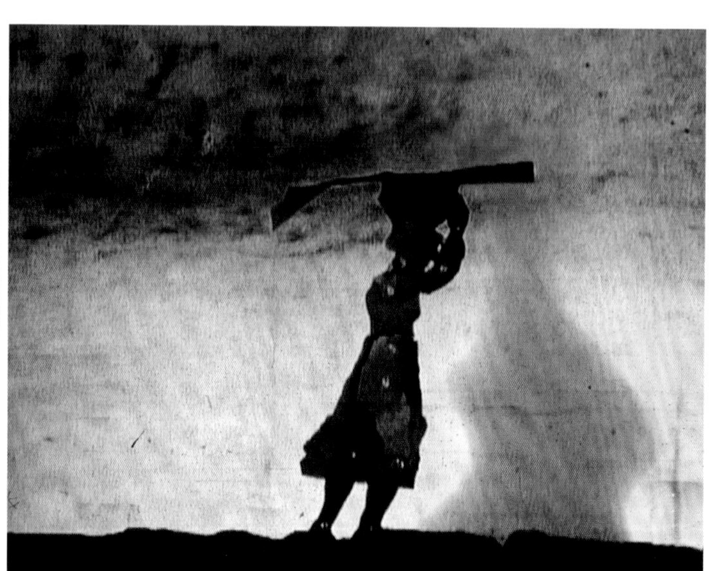

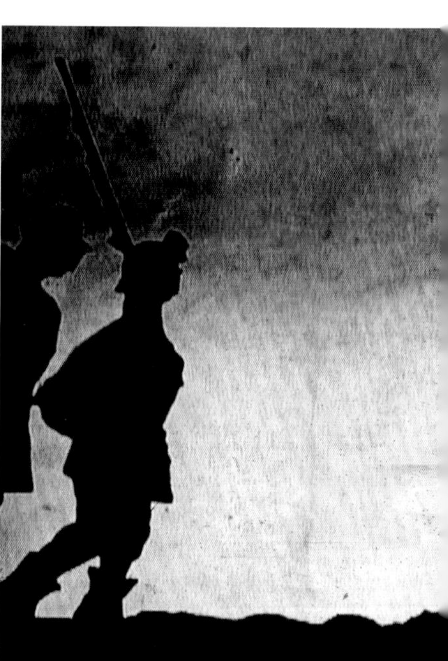

135–43 (THESE AND FOLLOWING PAGES)
***Shadow Procession*, 1999**
35mm animated film transferred to video, 7 min.
Collection of the artist, courtesy Marian Goodman Gallery, New York, and Goodman Gallery, Johannesburg

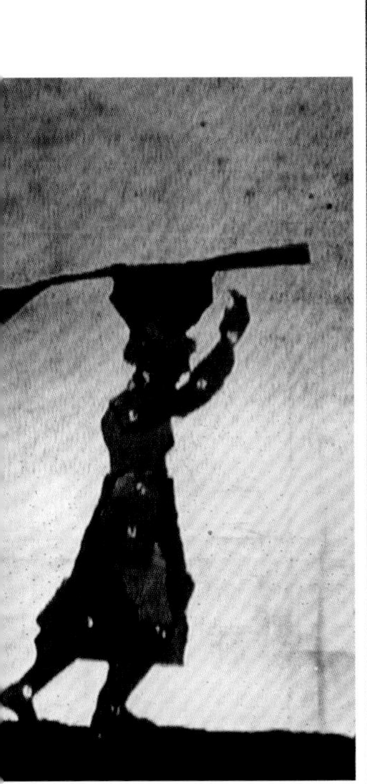
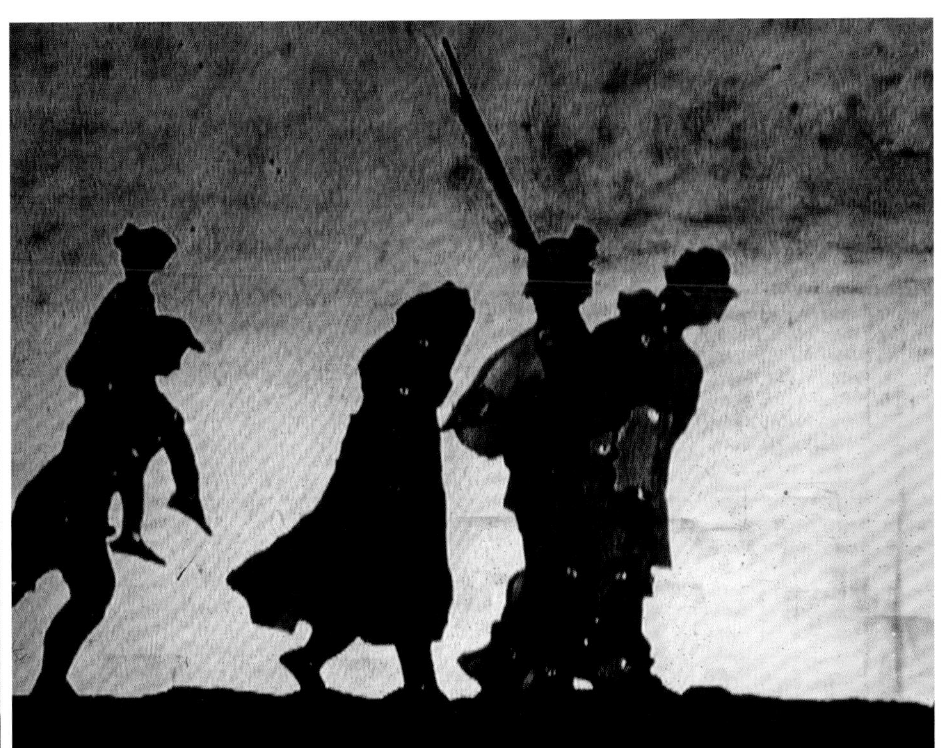
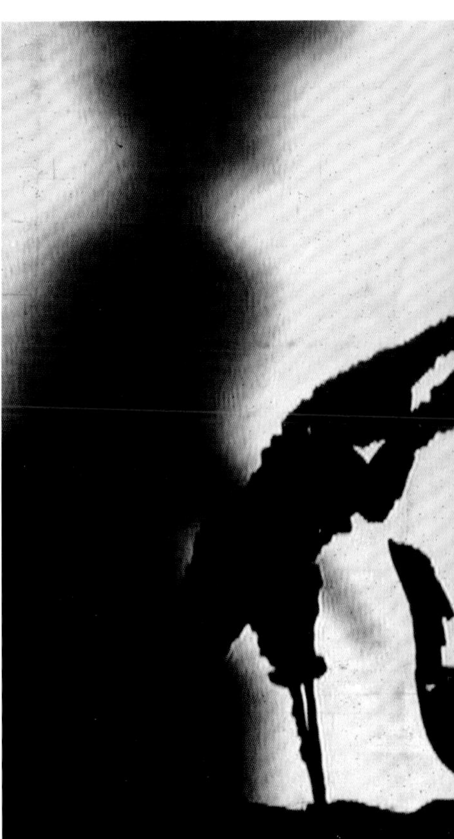

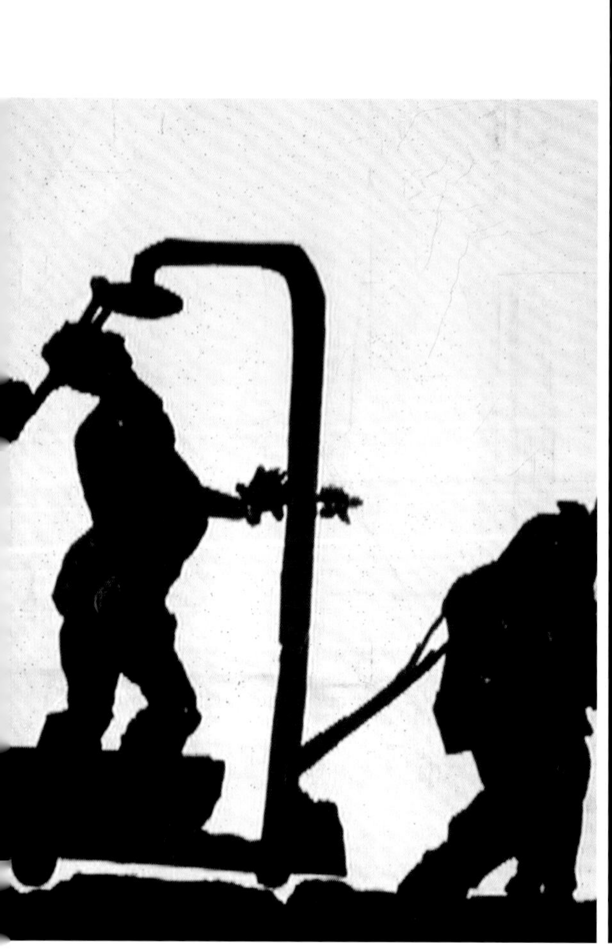

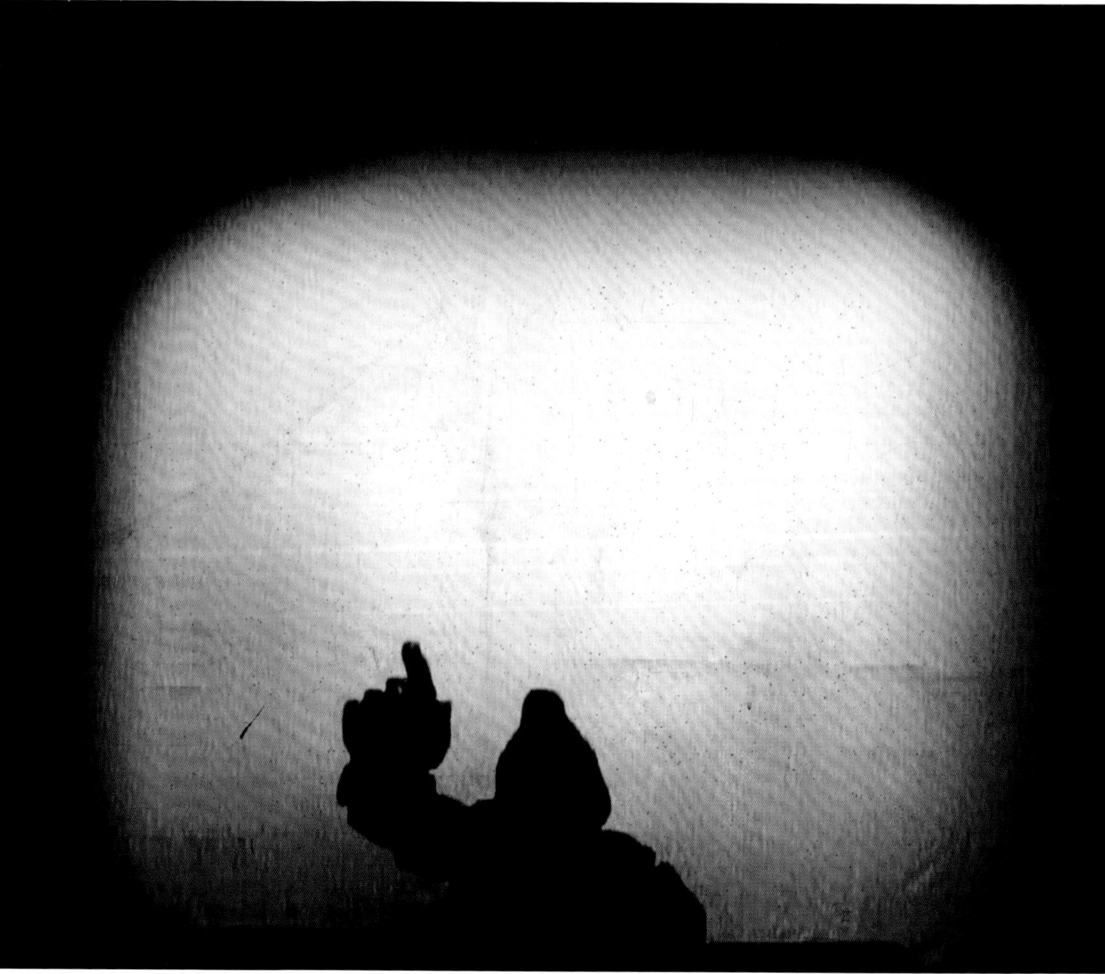

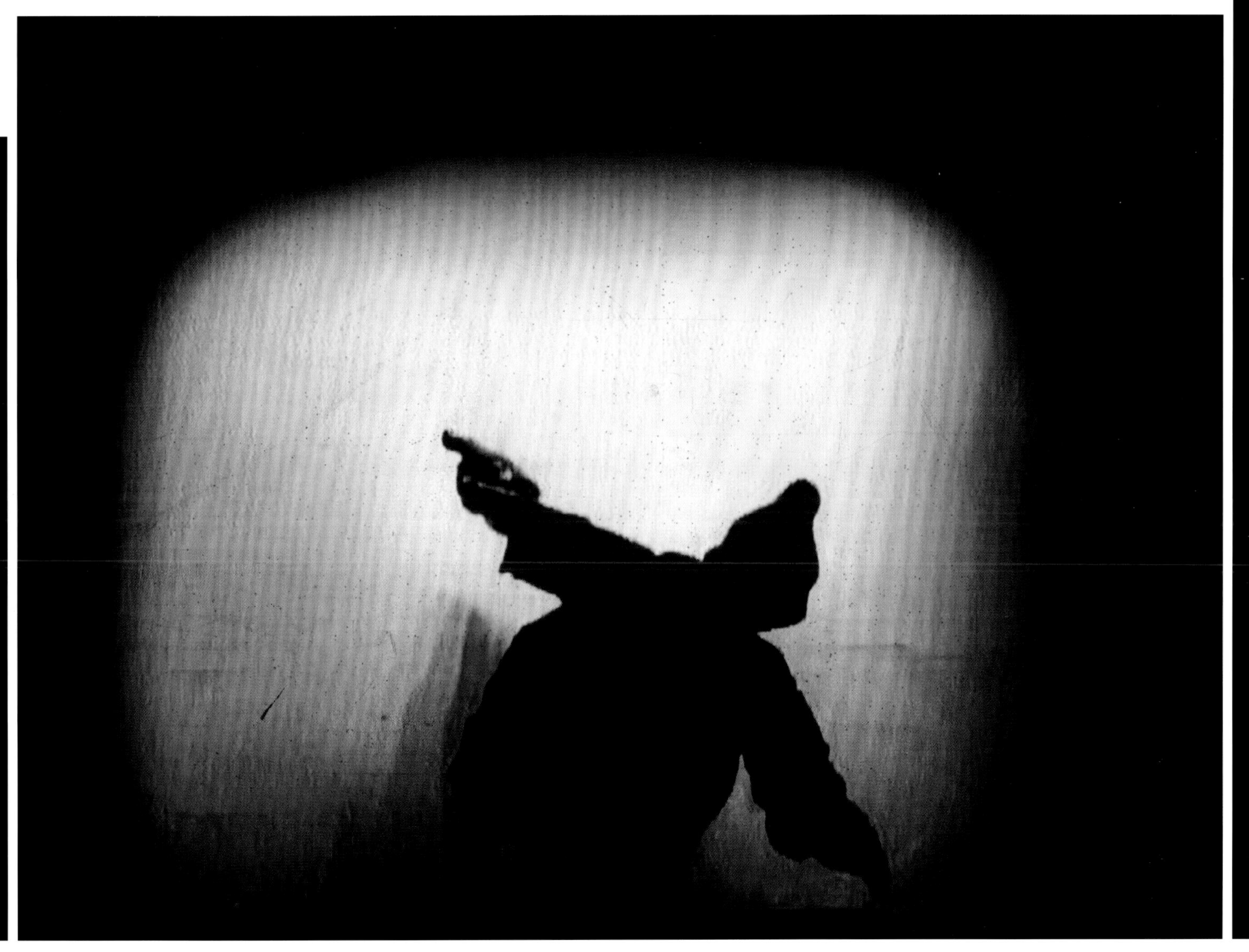

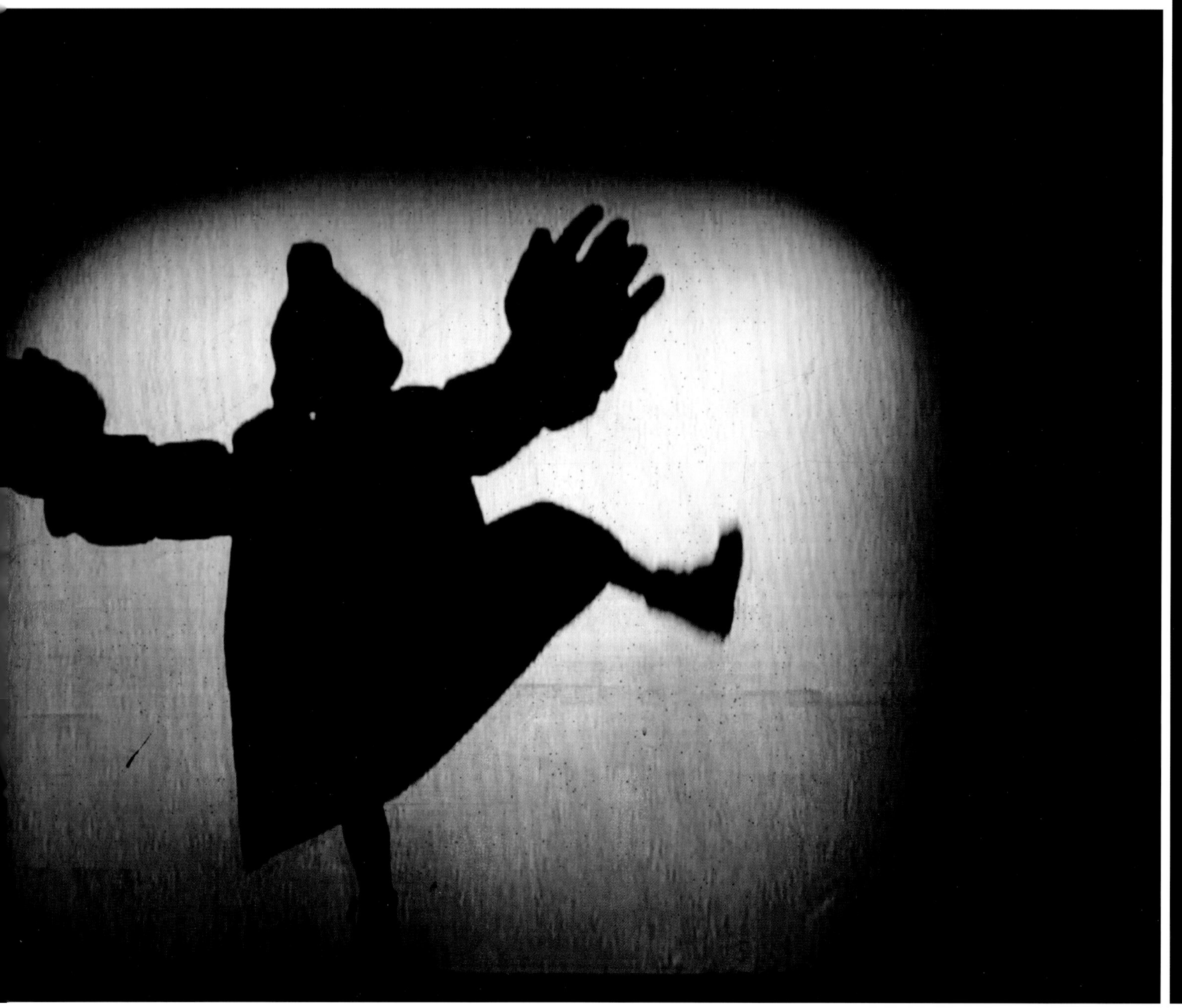

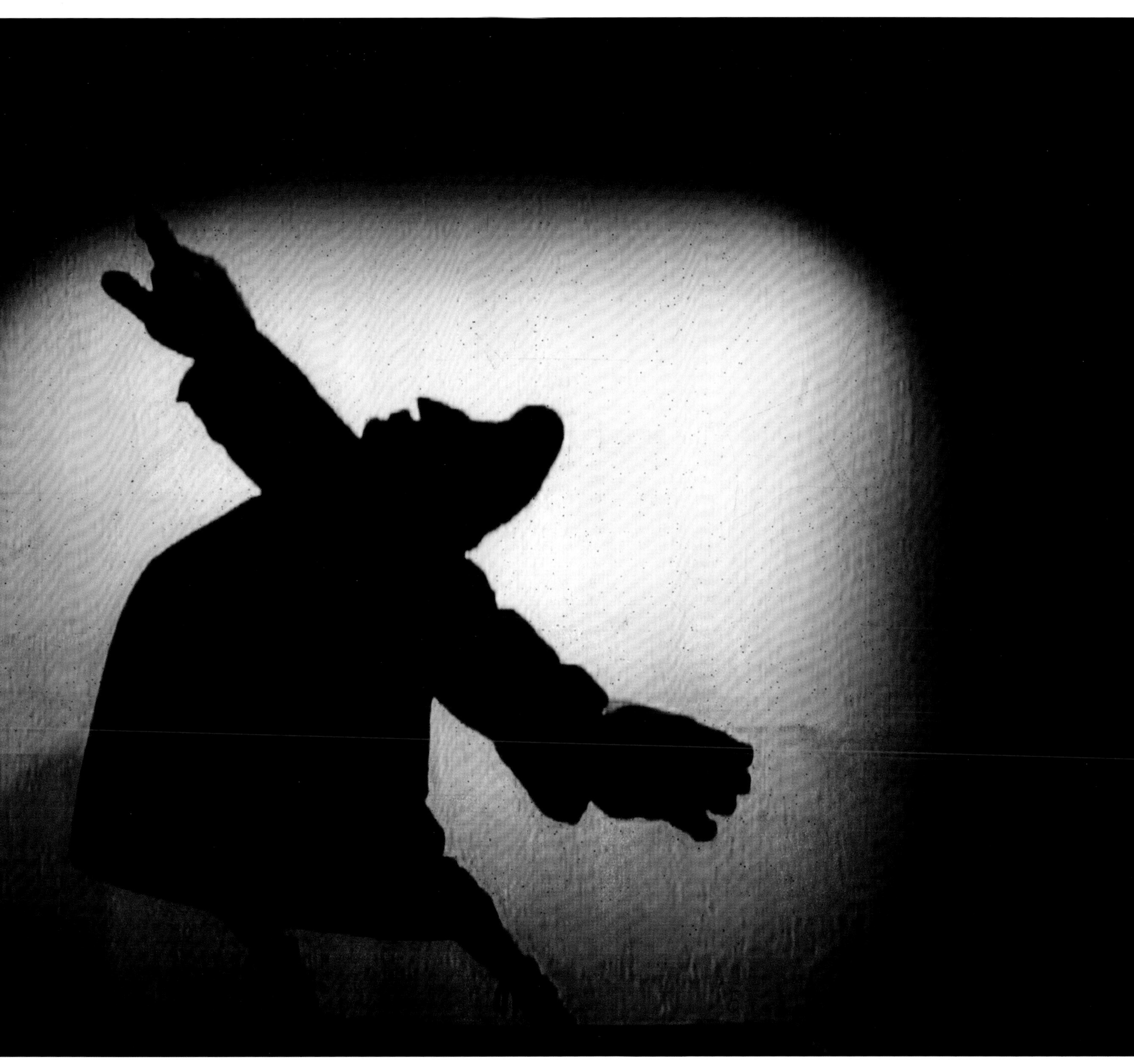

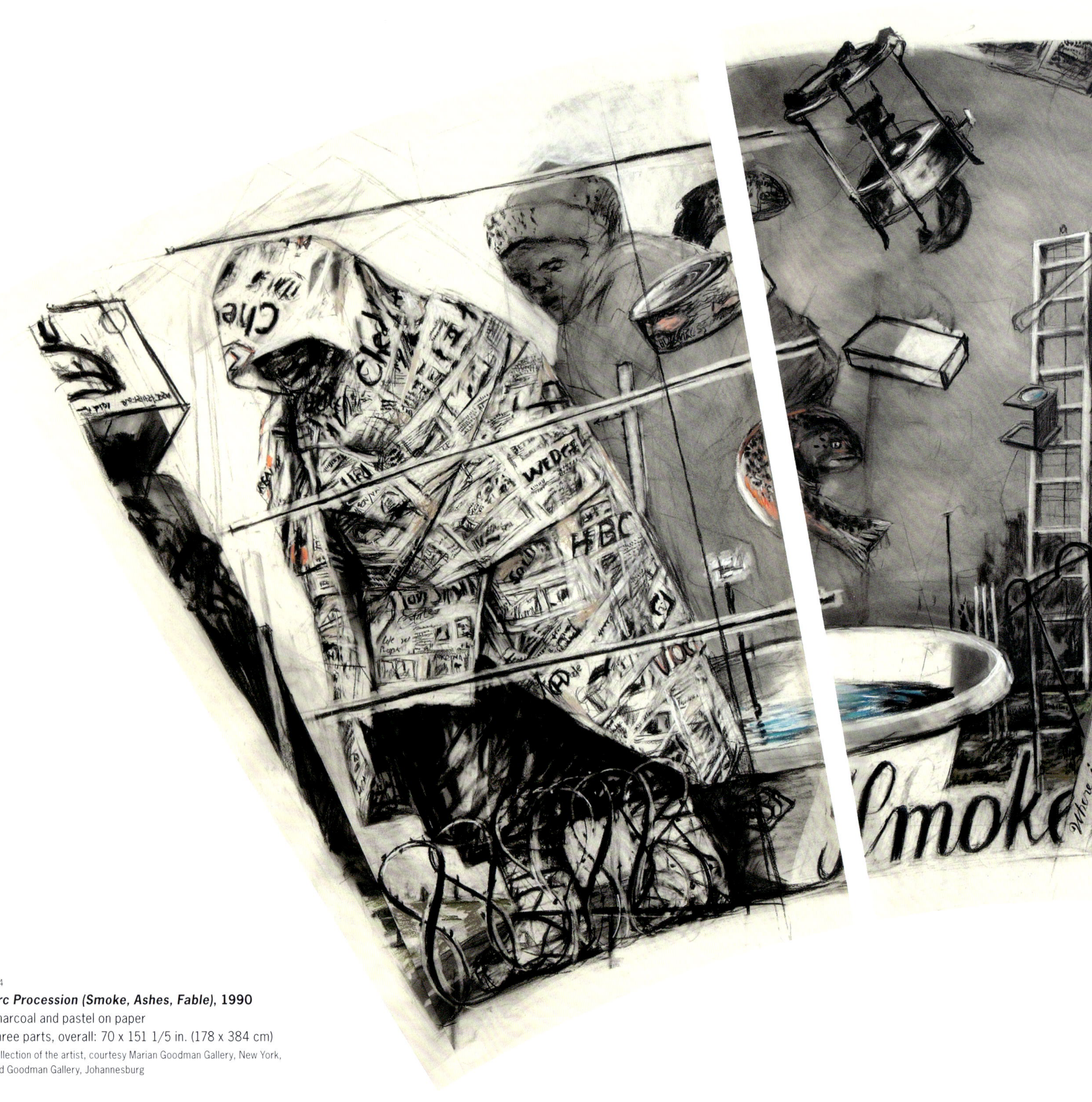

144
***Arc Procession (Smoke, Ashes, Fable)*, 1990**
Charcoal and pastel on paper
Three parts, overall: 70 x 151 1/5 in. (178 x 384 cm)
Collection of the artist, courtesy Marian Goodman Gallery, New York, and Goodman Gallery, Johannesburg

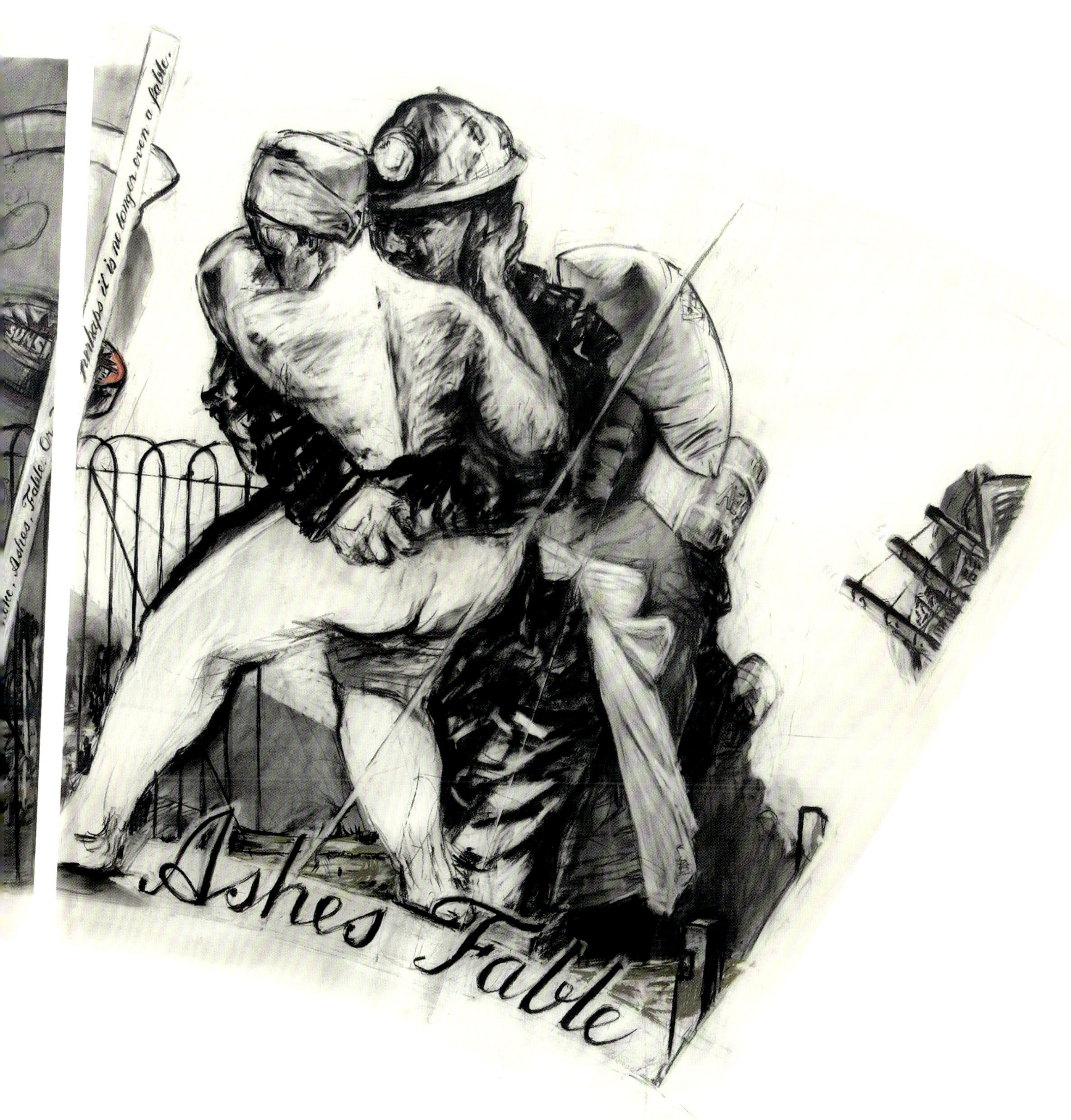
perhaps it is no longer even a fable.
Ashes, Fable.
Ashes Fable

145 (TOP)
***Procession on Anatomy of Vertebrates*, 2000**
Charcoal on book pages
11 x 70 in. (27.9 x 177.8 cm)
Collection of Brenda Potter and Michael Sandler

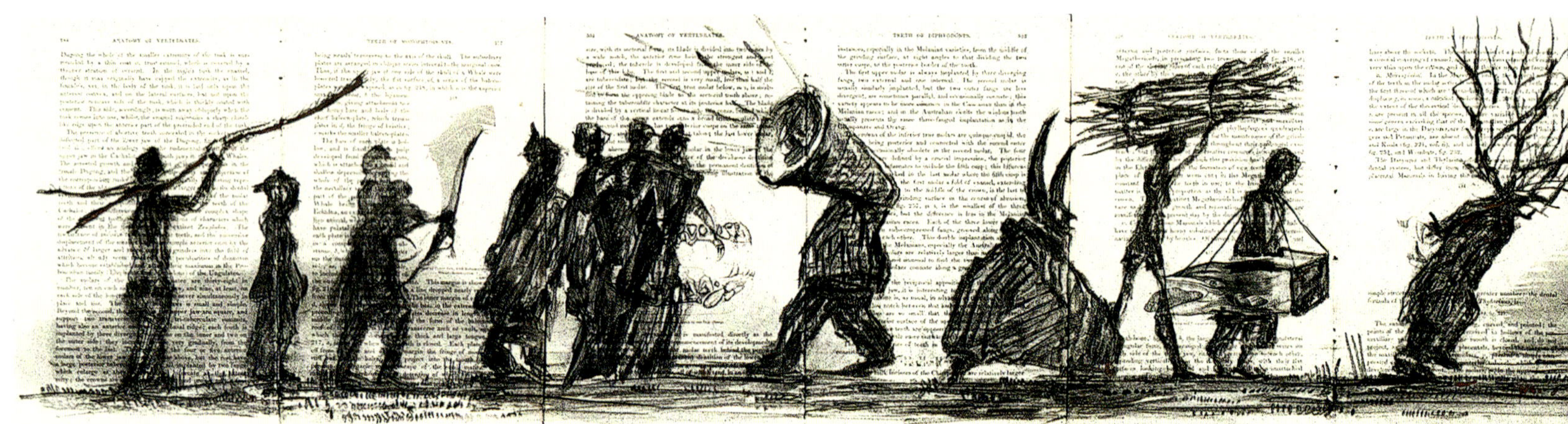

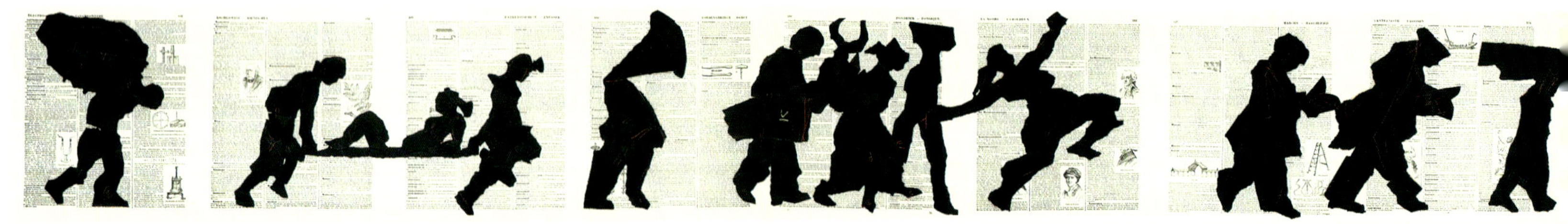

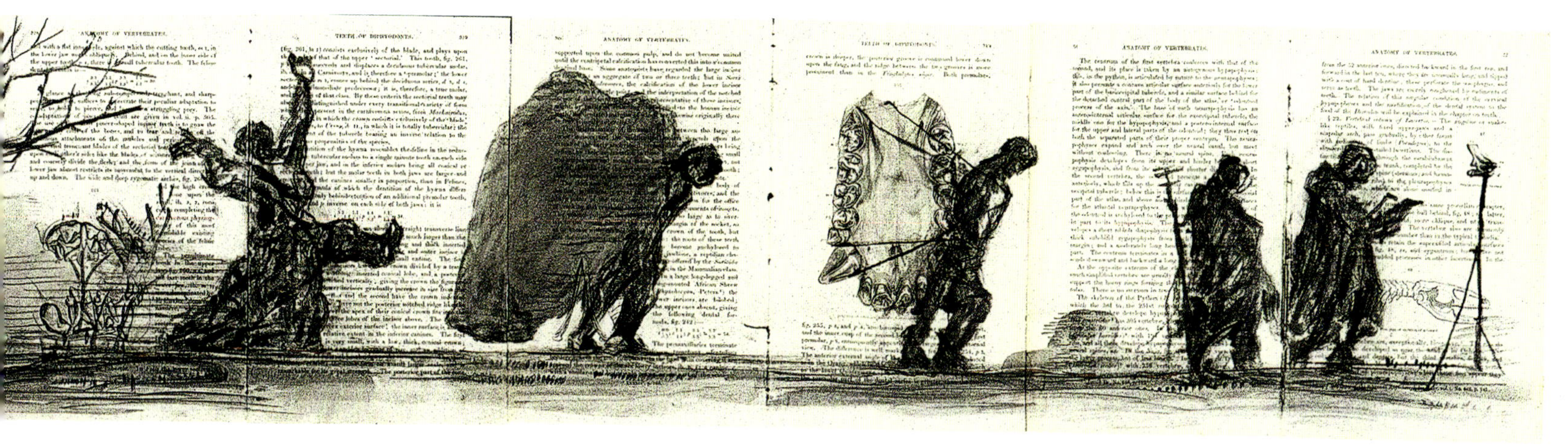

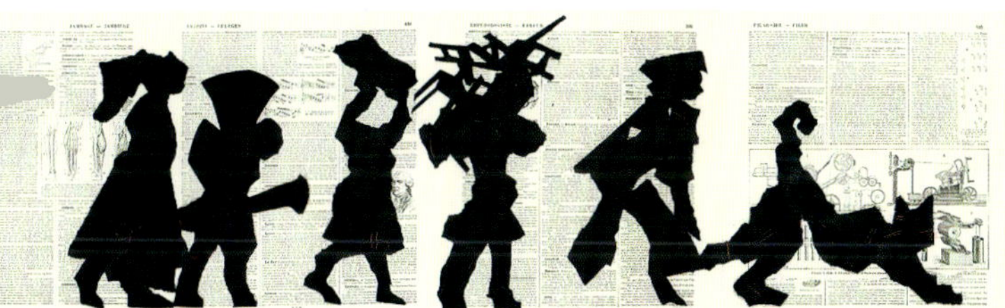

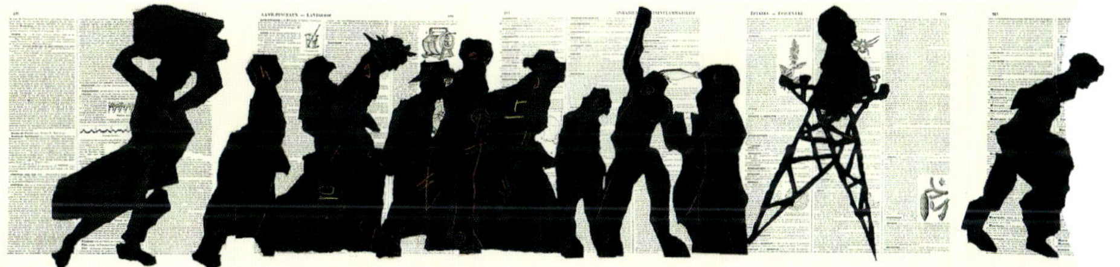

146–47 (BOTTOM AND FOLLOWING PAGES)

***Portage*, 2000**

Collage on book pages

Eighteen panels, each: 10 4/5 x 9 1/4 in. (27.5 x 23.5 cm); 10 4/5 x 168 1/8 in. (27.5 x 427 cm) overall

Collection of the artist, courtesy Marian Goodman Gallery, New York, and Goodman Gallery, Johannesburg

curies immolait une vache pleine en l'honneur de Tellus, la terre fertile, et les pontifes offraient au Capitole un sacrifice au nom du peuple tout entier.)

FORDINGBRIDGE, comm. d'Angleterre (comté de Hants), sur le fleuve côtier Avon ; 3.191 hab. Toiles.

FORDINGTON, comm. d'Angleterre (comté de Dorset), sur le fleuve côtier Frome ; 3.275 hab.

FORDON, ville d'Allemagne (Prusse [prov. de Posen]), sur la Vistule, en aval du confluent de la Brahe ; 2.348 hab. Commerce de grains.

FORDOUN, comm. d'Ecosse (comté de Kincardine), le Strathmore, au pied des Grampians ; 2.115 hab. à bâtir. Sources minérales.

FORDUN (John), annaliste écossais, mort Prêtre ou chanoine à Aberdeen, Fordu chargé, après la destruction des archives Edouard Ier, de rechercher les docum l'histoire de son pays : ses voyages de ceraient entre 1363 et 1384. Il dut m année où s'arrêtent ses annales : *Ch Gesta annalia*, que Walter Bower le *Scotichronicon* ; d'après Bo l'auteur des livres I à V et d du livre VI, mais Bowe dans l'œuvre de son pré

FORDYCE, comm. golfe de Murray ; 4

FORDYCE (Da en 1711, mort deen et laissa et de morale : *the Elements o*

FORDYCE (Ja cédent, né à Al devint pasteur acquit une grand *women* (1765) ; également un v

FORDYCE (G en 1736, mort e sur la températ la digestion. Il f *tions sur la fièvre aliments* (1791-1802

FOREIGN-OFFIC *bureau étranger*), m direction de la il es

Forms de la Suisse

FORELAND (No comté de Kent), d'un phare impor

FORELLE La forelle

FOREN 7.538 hab.

FORER *une clef, un*

FORERIE forage des ca

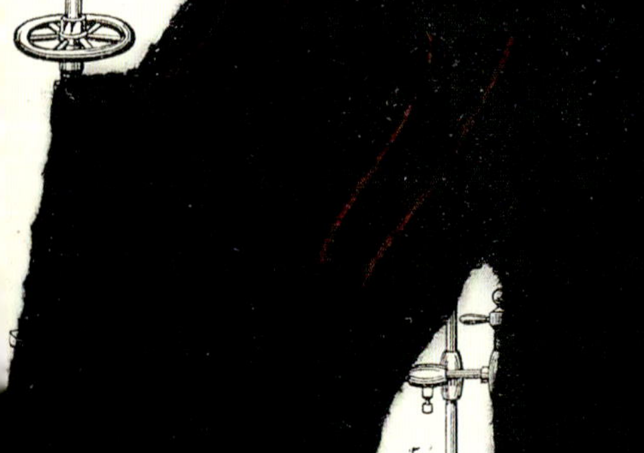

: 1. A engrenage ; 2. Mo nne tournante ; 5. Pour éta Vilebrequin à cliquet po

à la main, qu'emploi trous dans le fer. (Il s dits « foreries portativ

Fo Fore — tants **Fo** tas

personne née dans le — *Les* FORÉSIENS. rez où à ses habi-

chaux, de po- la stilbite.

d. et à 28 kil. de la Selle ;

Dr. coutum. Péage exigé s à travers payer cha-

, forêt, et Angleterre,

forest-bed nombreux vers mam- u'on y ren- encore en à-dire à la

alien, connu de Philippe d , né à Soldio en 1464, mort à Bergame en 1520 il entra dans l'ordre des ermites de Saint-Augu ont il devint prieur. Il fonda plusieurs bibliothèques et se livra à des travaux historiques.

FORESTI (E.-Felice), patriote italien, né près de Ferrare vers 1793, mort à Gênes en 1858. Il conspira contre la domination autrichienne et, arrêté en même temps que Silvio Pellico, Gonfalonieri, Maroncelli et d'autres patriotes, fut incarcéré à Venise (1819). Après deux ans d'une captivité des plus cruelles, il fut condamné à mort, peine immédiatement commuée en vingt ans de détention, qu'il subit avec ses compagnons, d'abord dans l'île Saint-Michel, puis au Spielberg. A son avènement au trône, mpereur Ferdinand commua leur peine en celle de l'exil mérique (1835). Foresti devint professeur de langue littérature italiennes au collège de Columbia, et une *Chrestomathie italienne* (1847). Plus tard il fut consul des Etats-Unis à Gênes, où il mourut.

ntaisies pour cet instrument, et un ouvrage *graphie des instruments à six pistons et à tubes études pratiques et théoriques pour le nouveau Adolphe Sax.*

(Henri), général vendéen, né à La Pomme- 1775, mort à Londres en 1806. Quand éclata ndée, il commanda une division, et se dis- Montreuil, à Saumur. Après les revers Loire, Forestier organisa les bandes ient tenir tête à Hoche. Il était lieute- doudal, quand la pacification de la res. De 1799 à 1801, il reparut en amnistie, fut dénoncé et condamné il put se cacher, atteignit la fron- l'Angleterre.

Joseph), dit **Le Forestier**, peintre à Saint-Domingue en 1790, mort à il exposa un *Ecce Homo* d'un grand n *Jésus-Christ guérissant un possédé*. *Vocation de saint Front* (1831) ; *le Sa-* (1835) ; *les Funérailles de Guillaume le Conquérant*. Après 1850, Forestier produisit peu. Il avait en 1849, aux côtés du colonel Guinard, l'ami de Cavaignac.

stier (PAUL), pièce en quatre actes et en vers, par ugier (Théâtre-Français, 1868). — Paul Forestier, eintre, a pour maîtresse Léa de Flers, femme sé- Son père, Michel, persuade à Léa, sinon de rompre, moins de s'éloigner quelque temps pour éprouver r de Paul. Celui-ci, croyant à une trahison, se laisse r par dépit ; et, de son côté, Léa, à l'heure même où sait que le jeune homme entre dans la chambre nup- e, tombe aux bras d'un bon garçon, de Beaubourg, fort nné de l'aubaine. Mais bientôt Paul apprend tout de la uche même de sa maîtresse. « Ton crime est le mien », ui dit-il ; et, entraîné par une passion irrésistible, il s'apprête à quitter sa femme, à partir en compagnie de Léa. Ce serait assurément le dénouement logique de la pièce, le seul qui s'accorde avec les données. Augier a voulu que la jeune femme de Paul cherchât un refuge dans le suicide, qu'elle écrivît, avant de se donner la mort, une lettre tout à fait touchante : que cette lettre, tombée dans les mains du mari coupable, le fît renoncer à son projet de fuite et trouver le bonheur près du foyer conjugal. *Paul Forestier* eut un grand succès. Cette comédie mérite de rands éloges pour ce qu'elle a de franc, de vigoureux, de ement pathétique.

RESTIÈRE (*rè-sti*) n. f. Genre d'oléacées, comprenant huit arbustes américains caractérisés par des fleurs mes, dioïques, petites et peu éclatantes, groupées erses façons.

FORESTIÈRES (LES VILLES). Nom donné autrefois à plusieurs villes sur le Rhin, dans le cercle allemand de Souabe, aux abords de la Forêt-Noire, telles que Lauffenbourg, Rheinfelden, à la Suisse ; Seckingen, Ensisheim et Waldshutt, au grand-duché de Bade. De nos jours, la même dénomination désigne les quatre villes suisses de Lucerne, Altdorf, Stanz et Schwytz, situées dans la partie montagneuse et boisée du pays.

FOREST-LEZ-BRUXELLES, comm. de Belgique (prov. de Brabant), arrond. de Bruxelles, sur la Sensee, affluent du Rupel ; 12.500 hab. Fabrique d'indiennes.

FOREST-MARBLE (*rèst'-marbl'* — de l'angl. *forest*, forêt, et *marble*, marbre) n. m. Calcaire coquiller compact appartenant à la formation dite « argile de Bradford », et qui a été autrefois exploité comme marbre dans la forêt de Whichwood. (Le forest-marble appartient à la partie supérieure de l'étage bathonien, qui constitue lui-même la partie supérieure du jurassique moyen.)

FORET (*rè* — rad. *forer*) n. m. Instrument en acier, employé pour percer de petits trous dans les métaux de faible épaisseur. (Le plus souvent commandé à la main à l'aide

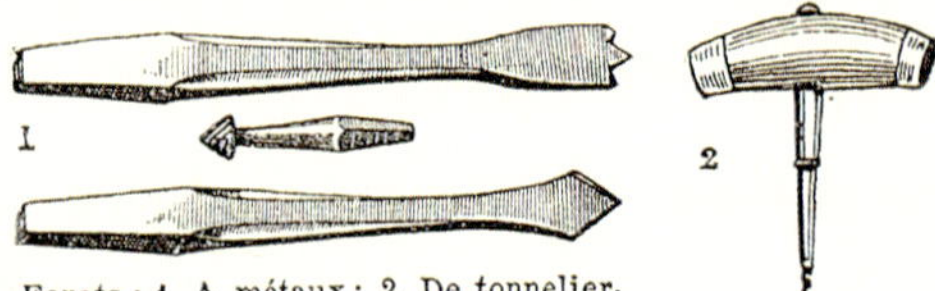

Forets : 1. A métaux ; 2. De tonnelier.

d'un archet ou d'un vilebrequin, il sert quelquefois d'outil dans les machines à percer.) ‖ Petit instrument de fer, avec lequel on perce un tonneau. ‖ Sorte de tire-bouchon sans vis, qui fait quelquefois partie d'un couteau de poche.

FORÊT (*rè* — ancienn. *forest* ; du bas lat. *forestis* [s.-entend. *sylva*], de *foris*, dehors ; proprem., *bois du dehors*, par oppos. aux parcs enclos de murs) n. f. Grande étendue de terrain plantée de bois ; ensemble des grands arbres qui occupent, qui couvrent cette étendue. ‖ *Forêt vierge*, Vaste forêt existant de temps immémorial et n'a jamais été soumise à une exploi ation réguliè

— Par anal. Réunion d'objets massés en *Une* FORÊT *de mâts, de cheveux*.

— *Eaux et forêts*, Administrat et les sont exclues des rég végétation ne peut guè et il lui faut, d'autre part régulière d'humidité pour circulation de sa sève ; par là des régions à courte saiso nairement sec.

Les régions forestières pa jourd'hui par les progrès du donc dans les régions tempérées plus abondamment et le plus rég Europe, tous les pays atteints niques, et particulièrement le teau schisteux rhénan, où s'éte de l'Ardenne, les plateaux de l'Alle Noire, Franconie, Thuringe), dans lande, la Russie au nord du 55e para septentrionale. Dans ces forêts apparaisse selon l'ordre de croissance et de durée des températures de la saison chaude, le pin et le bouleau, le chêne et le hêtre. Da le nouveau monde, une zone forestière correspondan existe au Canada et au nord des prairies du Far-West.

Peu nombreuses dans le domaine méditerranée climat sec, et reléguées au flanc arrosé des montag les forêts reparaissent, au delà des déserts subtropica alimentées par les régulières et abondantes pluies *équatoriales*. Elles sont composées surtout de lauri de guttifères, de palmiers, et encombrées d'une vé étonnamment luxuriante de lianes épiphytes. C *forêts vierges*, qui couvrent, en Afrique, à peu pr surface du bassin congolais (forêt équatoriale a mée par ses deux principaux explorateurs, E. Foa), en même temps qu'une longue et côtière au nord du golfe de Guinée, et, dans Sud, le large et humide bassin de l'Amazo deira, désignées dans la langue du pays pa

— Sylvic. Outre que la *forêt* met en duits (bois d'œuvre, bois de chauffag tannage des cuirs, liège, fruits, essenc etc.), des terres souvent pauvres, elle considérable et bienfaisante, au point dont elle diminue la sécheresse, et du qu'elle régularise. Dans les pays de mont vient la formation des torrents et leurs dév les plaines, elle constitue un obstacle na violence des vents et forme un rideau prote cultures des terres voisines. Pour ces diverse gouvernements, dans aucun pays civilisé, ne se sent complètement de l'exploitation des forêts. E une grande partie du domaine boisé (environ le est la propriété de l'Etat, et une plus grande partie (un pe plus du tiers) se trouve administrée par ses agents spéciaux. Malgré des défrichements qui furent exagérés, et

Fam. Malgré : Malade qui FOND à vue d'œil. ‖ Disparaître rapidement : *L'argent* FOND *entre les mains.*
— Par exagér. *Fondre en larmes, Fondre en pleurs,* ser des larmes abondantes
— S'abîmer, s'effo
... Tel,
Fond ... es brisées,
BOILEAU.
-- Tomb ... FOND *sur*
navire. ‖ ... gé avec
gueur ... *milieu de la*
volaille
— Lo ... c une mau-
vaise a ... donner.
Fond
... sseur, Système
à produire des
‖ Tissu produit
de convention pour le
rd et l'Angoumois, et vala
p chargé de sirop.
e liquéfier, passer à
r par des nuances
fférentes. ‖ Dispara
dre en eau. Se dit
er, solidifier,
. Ne
bo
z, fons, et
érée comme
sur lequel on
on FONDS. ‖ *Biens-fonds,*
FONDS. ‖ *Fonds servant,*
‖ *Fonds dominant,* Celui
établie. ‖ *Le fonds et le*
r opposition à USUFRUIT ;
ET : *Mangez vos* REVENUS,
Mettre, Placer son argent,
n argent, ses biens, moyen-
êter à fonds perdu, Prêter
ital dont quelqu'un dispose
le entreprise : *La moindre*
dérables.
Être en FONDS. ‖ *Les fonds*
s d'argent.
Ressource, objet exploitable : *C'est le* FONDS
oins. (La Font.) ‖ Matière, objet qui sert à
res : *Les végétaux paraissent être le premier*
immeubles (sol et constructions), mais
mobiliers, argent comptant, valeurs de
créances.
est l'ensemble des biens que la femme
dot et qui sont régis par des règle
t pour but d'en assurer la conservation
s de la dissolution du mariage (C. civ.
comprend sous cette désignation, non
mises en commun par les associés
social, mais encore la plus-value de
es les acquisitions faites à un titr
té.
te expression embrasse les diffé
et passifs, dont se compose un
t, dans un acte de liquidation de su
ue les *fonds* ou capitaux
t produits naturels, échus
tage.
Fonds servant. On n
profit duquel un
celui qui est assu
oits et obligation
ntés pa
t, le
nat
ent,
ant un endr
r l'exer ... s droits, et celui-ci
user. En outre, il a toujours la faculté de s
de son obligation en abandonnant la propriété du fonds

getti ou de la partie d ... nds qui doit la servitude.
son côté, le propriétai ... fonds dominant doit s'ab-
enir de tout acte qui po ... aggraver la condition du
nds servant.
Fonds perdu. C'est le n ... é au capital aliéné sans
etour auquel on a substitu ... ice d'une rente viagère.
a rente viagère, contrai ... ce qui se passe pour
rentes perpétuelles, n ... te pas de créance d'un
l ; elle est constitu ... perdu : elle n'est donc
créance d'arréra ... tituent le principal, le
être entier ... ère ; elle s'acquitte et
le créanci ... oit ces
ui en resta ... à la
de laque
tièrem
ncie
t d'essence
e capit ... urni par le créancie
sse le ... er (C. civ., art. 1909
le co ... Le *fonds de commer*
juri ... mposée des éléments
le *matériel d'explo*
premières, le *dro*
fonds est exploi
ité, *jus univer*
rc ... st ind
comm ... *nds*
fonds d ... par le
Fon ... préle-
vée ... ribua-
bles ... pôts
et a ... fec-
ti ... de
a ba
s de
es fonds publics est i ... cote éta-
e par les agents de change ; su ... à côté des
fonds d'État ou des villes, sont adm ... urveillance
de l'administration, d'autres vale ... offrant des
garanties de stabilité. La hausse ... des fonds
publics peut résulter de causes f ... ge, fausses
uvelles, etc.), ou de causes n ... ue l'amé-
ration ou l'affaiblissement d ... ou enfin
de causes accidentelles (la guerre, ... ions).

FONDUE (*dû* — ... tain de *fondre*) n. f. E
tremets tiré de la
donne ainsi la rece
prenez des œufs, un
fortement et mettez-le
de leur poids de froma
de leur poids de beur
pendant que ce mélang
épaississe, tout en deme
ez fortement. Serv
OUK n. m. Num
Turquie, qui porta
environ 9 fr. 58 c. ‖ Or
ou **FONDULUS** (*lu*
mes, famille des cy
formes cylindriqu
ombreuses esp
d'Amérique.
es États-Uni
-Baptiste Bo
eaux en 1766,
des chefs de la
ce départeme
vec son b
propos
tous les Bourbons,
en la personne d'H
15 avril, il prit la d
arisiennes deman
r la liste de pr
use de ses a
par Aman
s girond
NFRÈDE
à Bordeau
ribune, feu
eurs procès,
s lequel il com
on. Après la ré
eau gouverneme
journaux.
FONG n. m. Sa
reurs de la Chin
grands prêtres d
protection et le
du ciel) et des d
FONGE (*fo*
employé, da
gner le bo
FONGI
vant
qu'un
par e
FO
ter ... onditi
l'us ... restitu
nat
at. *fung*
habite
lant des
nt les lar
ICOLIDÉS.
m. pl. Famille
des tipules te
bolitophila,
COLIDÉ.
. pl. Famille d'ant
des polypiers co
Les fongidés se sub
hoserinés. Leurs no
t dans les mers chau
— *Un* FONGIDÉ.
FUNGIA (*fon-ji*) n. f. Gen
tribu des *fonginés,* comprena
scoïdes, ressemblant à des ch
s *fongies* sont ainsi nommées pa
fait un chapeau de champign
privé de son pédoncule. On
es, répandues en diverses me
discus (Pacifique), etc.
E (*ji* — du lat. *fungus,* champig
nat. Qui a la forme d'un champ
lles fongiformes, Papilles de se
bords de la langue.
n. f. Substance chimique, ext
cellulaires des cham
ellulose de D
, formée en
FONGINÉS ou **FO** ... (*ji*) n. m. pl. Tribu d
zoaires, famille des *fongidés,* comprenant les genre
ehrenbergie, halomitre, herpétolithie, etc. — *Un* F
OU FUNGINÉ.
FONGIQUE (*jik'* — rad. *fungus*) adj. De la natu
champignons, ou qui ressemble aux champignons
tation FONGIQUE. *Production* FONGIQUE.

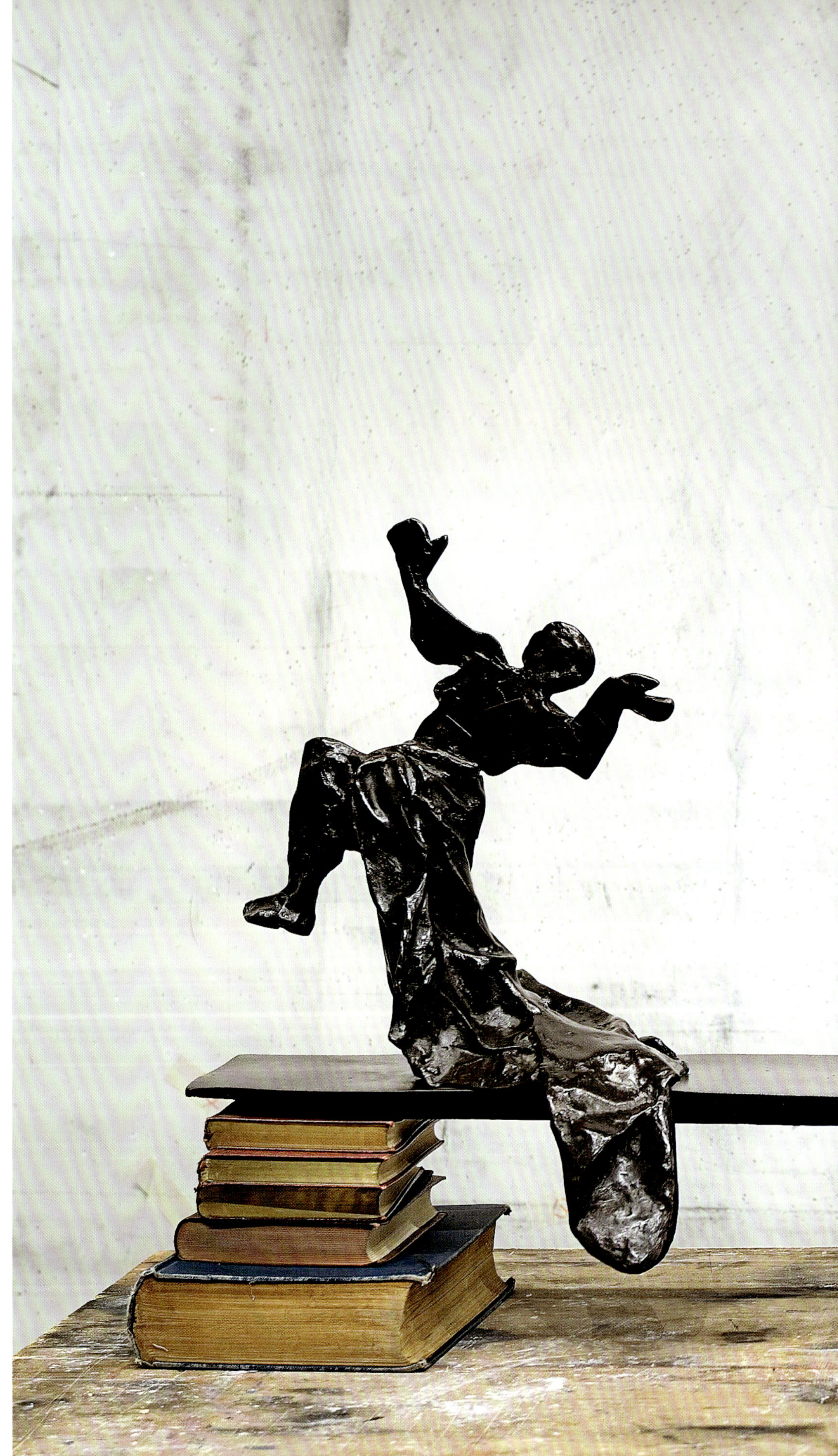

148
***Bridge*, 2001**
Bronze and books
23 5/8 x 36 3/4 x 7 1/2 in. (60 x 93.2 x 19 cm)
Collection of the artist, courtesy Marian Goodman Gallery, New York, and Goodman Gallery, Johannesburg

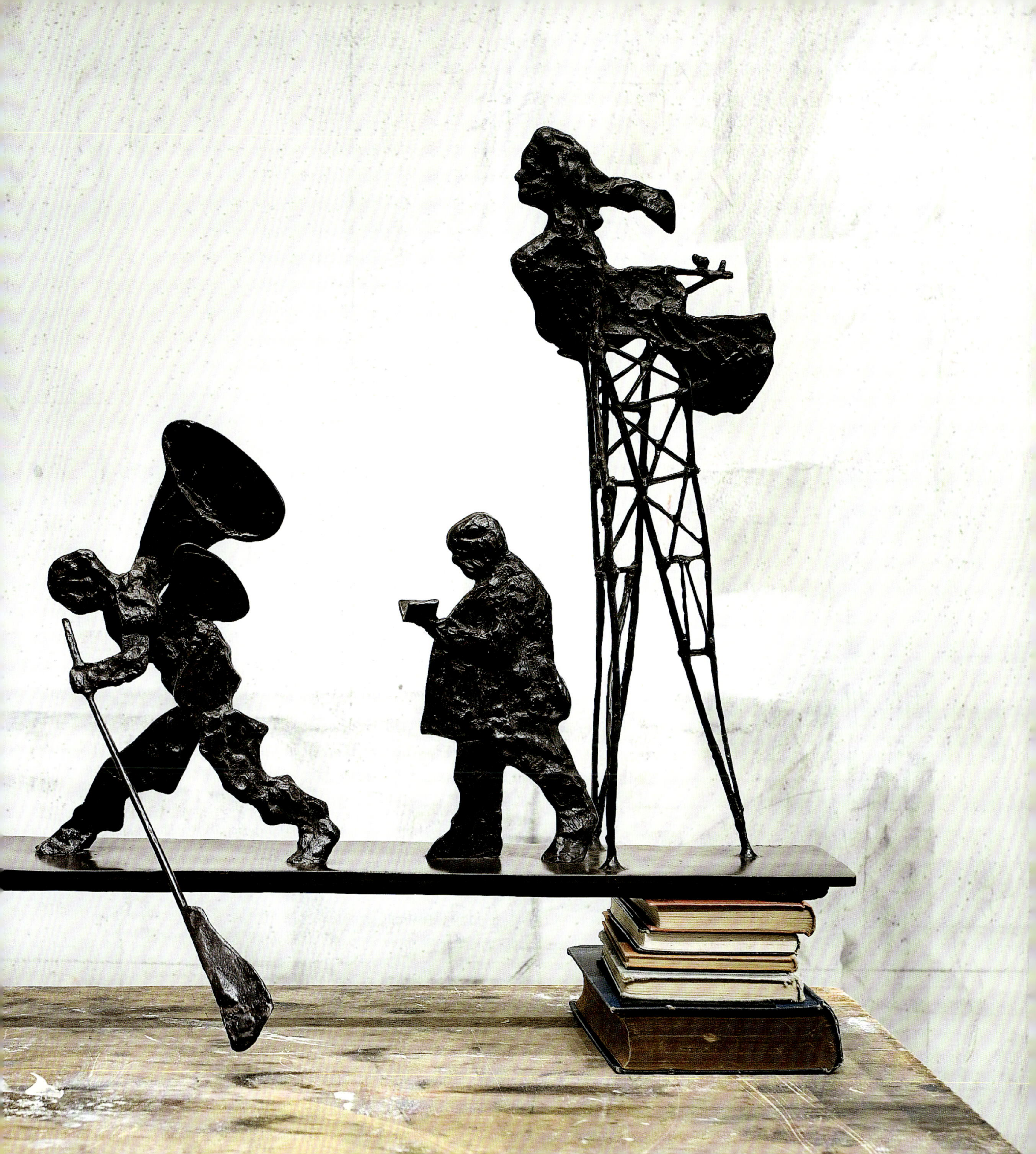

WALKING AND LOOKING
TECHNOLOGY AND AGENCY IN WILLIAM KENTRIDGE'S FILM WORK

Rudolf Frieling

William Kentridge's charcoal drawings have received much critical attention as the most prominent aspect of an oeuvre that also spans film, installation, sculpture, and theatrical works. Adding to that perception, Kentridge has underlined time and again that his work is driven by manual labor and that, as a consequence, he has "avoided the siren calls of high-tech digital animation," opting instead for obsolete film techniques that provide a "safe haven" from the pitfalls of an aesthetic built on digital effects.[1] His emotional relation to technology is linked to images of tangible objects, perhaps most acutely embodied in his loving depictions of an old black Bakelite telephone that he remembers from his childhood. For the critic Walter Benjamin, objects could become signifiers of civilization processes; he wrote a whole text about the magical yet terrifying intrusion of the telephone into the bourgeois interior, pointing out that it is precisely the distance of an instrument or the obsolescence of a technology that allows one to access long-repressed memories of childhood. Whether representing a toy that magically moves or a telephone that bridges unimaginable distances, Kentridge's cinematic work is about tapping into the unfulfilled promise of these now-distant echoes of illusion and direct engagement.

This essay will not reiterate the analysis of Kentridge's films based on his technique of drawing, erasure, and collage but rather will investigate the ways in which he encourages agency on the part of the viewer. His moving images exemplify an aesthetic of spatial relations that is deeply linked to the dynamic position of an artist who asks the viewer to become his accomplice. It is as much an argument about the failed utopia of new technologies as about the pleasure and playful engagement of time-based art. From this perspective, Kentridge emerges as an artist who not only draws for projection but also questions the very foundation of what it means to produce and perceive moving images.

1. William Kentridge, "Some Thoughts on Obsolescence," in "Artist Questionnaire: 21 Responses," ed. George Baker, *October* 100 (Spring 2002): 17. He did try using computer-generated images once, in the film *Easing the Passing (of the Hours)*, a 1992 collaboration with Deborah Bell and Robert Hodgins, but digital tools and the digital aesthetic proved an ill match for his working process.

DEPARTING FROM CINEMA

The beginnings of Kentridge's career as a filmmaker are still relatively unexplored. Even prior to *9 Drawings for Projection*, a series that started in 1989 with *Johannesburg, 2nd Greatest City after Paris* (pls. 52–56), he had a longstanding interest in animation techniques—a fascination that goes back to the flip book he produced at the age of fourteen and his experiments with animation and drawing on celluloid at age eighteen. Dissatisfied with the idea of concentrating on one artistic discipline, he explored film, the stage, and the fine arts simultaneously for some time. He eventually abandoned the goal of commercial filmmaking, realizing that producing feature-length films and directing crews of specialists—"jumping through producers' hoops"[2]—were not for him. It was his refusal to play the game of fund-raising, negotiating, and compromising as well as his increasing frustration with his job as a television art director that led him back to the studio. There he began to "indulge" the old technique of stop-motion animation, to which he had been introduced by a friend who filmed him at work on a theatrical backdrop. Kentridge realized his first stop-motion film in charcoal in 1989 and pursued that approach for more than a decade.[3] Seeing movement emerge out of what had been static "didn't feel like a change of direction," he states. "Rather a separate activity I allowed myself, parallel to drawing. But not to be taken seriously."[4]

Kentridge was relieved to be able to control every aspect of his production personally, without being pressed by timetables, schedules, or a waiting crew—a fact so essential that to this day he cannot even work with an assistant at the camera. He found it an indispensable freedom to be able to explore a scene that unfolded out of a first drawn line or visual idea while resisting the temptations of a traditional cinematic plot. Suddenly he had all the time in the world to make a film, and the as yet unknown narrative would come to him in due course. He could wait for things to take shape and suggest the direction of movement. No script was necessary—in fact, the unscripted nature of his films was probably at the heart of their success with the public from the very beginning. Kentridge's vision emerged through an unpredictable sequence of landscapes, cityscapes, and actions within these settings. "*Johannesburg* was very much the first attempt at finding a language, trying to discover what animation did," he says. "The fact that one can make a crowd move across a sheet of paper, that was the miracle."[5]

2. Ibid.

3. Kentridge has always used a combination of film and video formats. Since his original work stems from the stop-motion film camera, I refer to all his moving-image productions as films, even if they are eventually presented as video installations.

4. Kentridge, email to the author, October 11, 2008.

5. Kentridge in a 1999 interview with Lilian Tone, "William Kentridge: *Stereoscope*," http://home.att.net/~artarchives/tonekentridge.html. Unless otherwise noted, all URLs cited in this essay were accessed October 19, 2008.

Historically, the technique of animation is based on series of individual drawings that were popularized in the twentieth century through mass-media reproduction in comic books or newspapers. There is probably no other representational form that speaks more to the powers of childhood imagination than the cartoon. These visual abbreviations—whether Donald Duck comics or Japanese manga—are schematic exercises in the perception of moving images. It is precisely the leap from one frame to another that activates the process of reading them as an experience of continuous narrative progression. It also introduces the notion of the cinematic jump cut—our interior apparatus of perception knows how to make sense of a film despite its status as a series of disjointed fragments. In fact, the very technology of film as a succession of still photographs relies upon the brain's capacity to perceive a linear progression as a continuity. If the animated cartoon is the realization of phantasmagoric plasticity, the drawn cartoon uses a stock repertoire of scenes, gestures, characters, and styles with an economy of means that presupposes the viewer's willingness to cooperate. Given an opening scene, the reader is able to recognize the tone and setting of a narrative and fill in the gaps between individual frames. An action scene can be condensed in a single image: a speeding body uttering some unintelligible sound. Comic strips and animated cartoons tend to work with a reduced set of characters and symbolic actions with which the public is highly familiar. Relying on an abbreviated, low-resolution visual language, they are universal indexes of a kind of visual Esperanto—a term that the media critic Lev Manovich has used to describe the promise of the cinema in the early twentieth century.[6]

In Kentridge's *9 Drawings for Projection* we encounter a similarly reduced set of characters (specifically Felix Teitlebaum, Soho Eckstein, and Mrs. Eckstein), but the visuals do not prefigure the narrative. A Kentridge charcoal animation may evince a specific aesthetic and atmosphere, but the actions that unfold within one drawing or between two consecutive drawings are twists and turns that the director did not foresee when he embarked on his journey. More than once Kentridge has commented that he needs to find the image as it suggests itself. Drawing a line across the paper is a manual action in time that will eventually indicate to what end it has been made. The line is thus a means to go elsewhere, supported by a trust in the hand that draws or erases and in the movement that is thus revealed but not yet realized. Although Kentridge would reject the term *poetic* to describe his work, his working method invokes a poetics of transformation (consider, for instance, the metamorphosis of an espresso pot into a rocket in the 2003 film *Journey to the Moon*). The viewer is often taken by surprise, lured by the fluidity of his transitions: Just how did he get from A to B? Did we see this coming?

6. Lev Manovich, *The Language of New Media* (Cambridge, MA: MIT Press, 2001), xv.

Kentridge's point of departure is usually a visual idea, an image without a narrative. Since there is no script, the transition between one finished scene and the following sequence is undefined and open, requiring inventive leaps that are guided by the continuity of the drawing hand. The art historian Rosalind Krauss calls it a "technique of extreme parsimony and of endless round-trips"[7]—a method of subtraction rather than addition. In traditional animation, drawings on single transparent sheets are placed on top of one another, much like a flip book, in order to achieve the seamless transitions that render the narrative fluent and continuous. Rather than relying on montage and cuts, Kentridge's films fascinate by virtue of their continuous narrative space. Unlike traditional animation, though, the plasticity of his transformations is not seamless. His hand wanders back and forth, drawing and erasing as we watch. Although we witness this process, we are still transported into the realm of illusion—an effect totally unforeseen by Kentridge when he did his first charcoal animation, which he considered imperfect precisely because he could not get rid of the traces.

The blank space between two frames requires the active engagement of the viewer in the process of making sense. When the gap is minimal, the activity is hardly felt and the animation is smooth; when the gap is wide open, the lack of coherence manifests as an open question. Kentridge's poetics operate through contexts or situations with various degrees of contingency, a quality that can be traced back to two early animations from the 1980s. Notes Kentridge: "Both worked on the principle of whoever came into the studio or gallery would be in the film. So there are friends, beggars, my daughter, and my wife in *Vetkoek/Fête Galante* and schoolkids, other visitors, friends, and students in *Exhibition*. Both improvised in the moment."[8] The visitor is thus literally as well as figuratively drawn into an openly structured narrative, one that can start in the middle and may have no resolution yet has a distinct logic of its own—which comes, as Kentridge maintains, "from the needs of the medium and the manual process."[9] Both were drawn in response to the declared state of emergency in South Africa, and their very openness represented a stance of resistance to the politics of separation. *Vetkoek/Fête Galante* (1985) is the first film in which he used the technique of stop-motion animation. Here, as in the 1987 film *Exhibition,* he stages a process of collaboration that addresses not only the notion of resistance but also that of pleasure. In *Vetkoek* we see the artist's wife, Anne, write the words *persistence of pleasure* before he steps up to erase them—a movement and its countermove, a step forward and a step back, a moment of pleasure and its loss.[10] From here to his most recent projections, we follow the trajectory of a visual language that is deeply embedded in a dialectical to-and-fro. Whether a looped procession or a spiraling newsreel, these circular processes seem linear as they move across the screen.

7. Rosalind Krauss, "'The Rock': William Kentridge's Drawings for Projection," *October* 92 (Spring 2000): 6.

8. Kentridge, email to the author, October 11, 2008.

9. William Kentridge and Angela Breidbach, *William Kentridge: Thinking Aloud; Conversations with Angela Breidbach,* Kunstwissenschaftliche Bibliothek, vol. 28, ed. Christian Posthofen (Cologne: Walther König, 2006), 112.

10. The film may be viewed on the DVD that accompanies this catalogue.

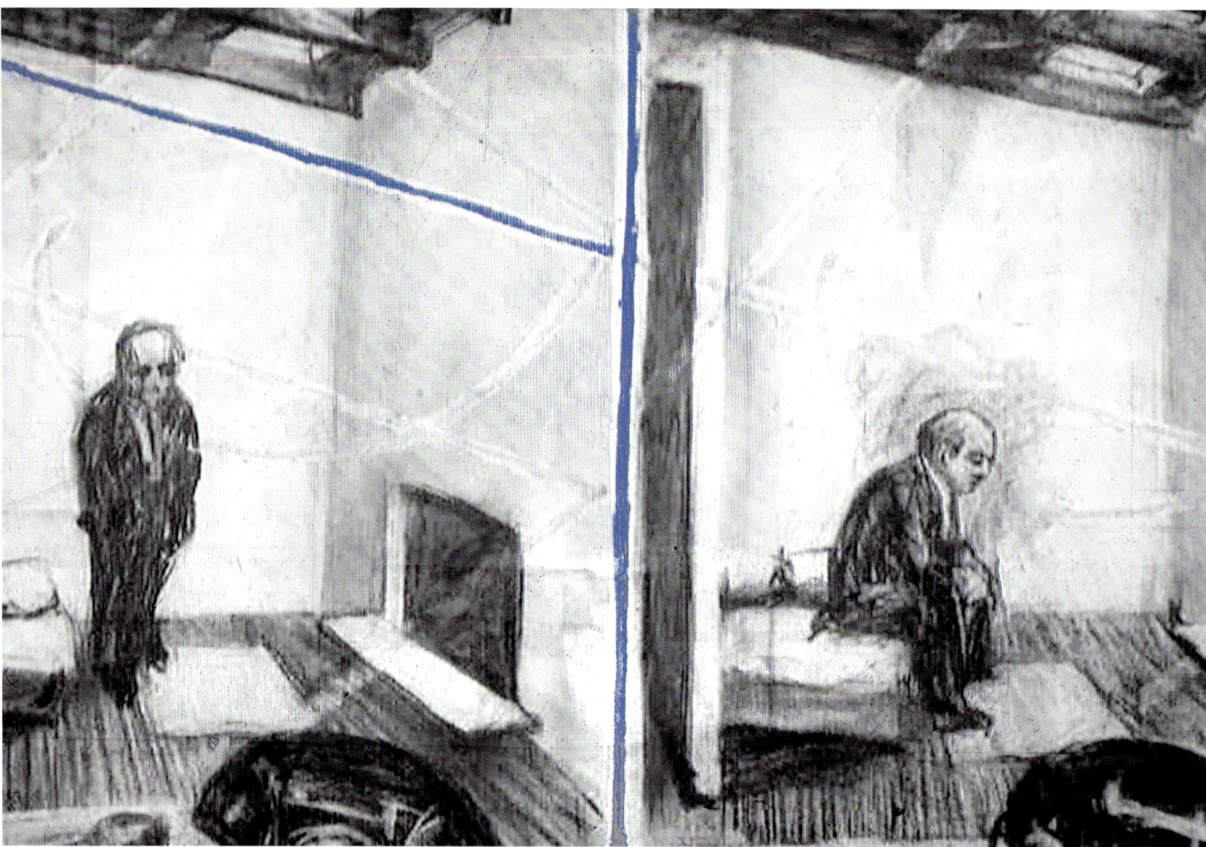

FIG. 27 William Kentridge
***Stereoscope*, 1999**
35mm animated film transferred to video, 8:22 min.
Collection of the artist, courtesy Marian Goodman Gallery, New York, and Goodman Gallery, Johannesburg

Much attention has been given to the political and postcolonial themes of Kentridge's work, which are closely linked with his interest in the agency of the viewer. The perceptual process has also been discussed at length, particularly in his informative conversations with Angela Breidbach. What has not yet been taken into consideration, however, is the notion of Kentridge as an installation artist, one who produces an expanded cinema space for exploration by the viewer. After *Vetkoek* and *Exhibition,* his filmic representations have tended to visually exclude the viewer, preserving the illusion of the theatrical fourth wall as a structuring principle. One notable exception is the moment in *History of the Main Complaint* (1996) when Soho's (or is it Kentridge's?) eyes look out at us from the rearview mirror of a car (see fig. 48). This direct gaze at the camera, forbidden in the realm of illusionistic practice, acknowledges that someone must be looking, positioned at the other side of the screen.[11] But the moment passes, and, as with most of Kentridge's early animations, the viewer ultimately follows the characters and narratives as in any traditional film, transformed by the sheer magic of seeing a "crowd move across a sheet of paper." In cinema, as in theater, the viewer consciously and gladly becomes the accomplice of the magician.

The cinematic process of viewer identification with the perspective of the camera initially led Kentridge to a set of presentations that all favored the cinematic frame of theatrical projection or the small

11. In Walter Benjamin's thesis on history, the rear view is a moment of recognition of the catastrophic past that will be the future: "There is a painting by Klee called *Angelus Novus.* It shows an angel who seems about to move away from something he stares at. His eyes are wide, his mouth is open, his wings are spread. This is how the angel of history must look. His face is turned toward the past. Where a chain of events appears before *us, he* sees one single catastrophe, which keeps piling wreckage upon wreckage and hurls it at his feet. The angel would like to stay, awaken the dead, and make whole what has been smashed. But a storm is blowing from Paradise and has got caught in his wings; it is so strong that the angel can no longer close them. This storm drives him irresistibly into the future to which his back is turned, while the pile of debris before him grows toward the sky. What we call progress is *this* storm." Walter Benjamin, "On the Concept of History" (1940), in *Selected Writings,* vol. 4, trans. Harry Zohn (Cambridge, MA: Harvard University Press, 2003), 392–93.

screen of its little brother, the video monitor. He used monitors almost exclusively in exhibition and festival settings until the mid-1990s, when he switched to the larger scale of the projected image. In 1997 a projection of *History of the Main Complaint* at *Documenta X* introduced Kentridge to an international audience; it was the move away from the small monitor that made his work accessible to the larger public. In fact, Kentridge's animations are a rare case of a hugely popular displacement of animation from the cinema to the gallery. At the time, the strangely timeless character of his technique was matched by a growing sense of film as increasingly obsolete. *Documenta X* not only featured more video projections than any previous edition, it was also the first large international exhibition to include internet-based works. The success of the presentation inspired Kentridge to explore more installation options, both technologically and conceptually. His imagery eventually changed as well, but what impacted him first was the notion of expanding on traditional representational form and scale.

Stereoscope (1999; figs. 20, 27, pls. 97–101) is among the last of Kentridge's charcoal animations. Despite the artist's claim that he is bad at scripted narratives, this genre of his practice is defined by a continuity of narrative as it is "written" by the hand in motion—by the folding and unfolding of the drawn line. Incorporating traces of drawing and erasure, it is an aesthetic that takes for granted the illusionistic technologies of cinematic representation. Many writers have noted a deeply antitechnological stance in Kentridge's work, citing cameras on tripods that become machine guns and central characters caught in environments dominated by communication and imaging devices. Gradually, however, Kentridge began to develop an interest in apparatuses and their relation to the representation of his films in space. Carolyn Christov-Bakargiev speaks of the artist's "journey to disenfranchise mechanics, no longer presenting them as dehumanizing instruments of control but rather as challenging devices to expand vision and open up complex visual thoughts through playful experimentation."[12]

12. Carolyn Christov-Bakargiev, "On Defectibility as a Resource: William Kentridge's Art of Imperfection, Lack, and Falling Short," in *William Kentridge*, ed. Carolyn Christov-Bakargiev (Rivoli, Italy: Castello di Rivoli; Milan: Skira Editore, 2004), 37.

Since the late 1990s his work has become much more ubiquitous and multifaceted in its representational formats. *Stereoscope*, though still a linear film, is emblematic of the shift toward a fundamental questioning of representation in its simplest form. The narrative and the character of Soho are doubled and placed in a set of parallel spatial frames. Notes Kentridge: "In *Stereoscope*, the question of living in a full room and an empty room was going to be the starting point. It became the entire film."[13] The basic dichotomy of split screens plays out without actually requiring the audience to watch the film through stereo viewers. Kentridge proffers a narrative that shifts from left to right, introducing a split frame in which two dramatic sets appear at the same time. Eschewing the elaborate efforts of virtual-reality engineers and the movie industry to create immersive environments (from the 3-D CinemaScope productions of the 1950s to contemporary IMAX theaters), Kentridge engages his viewers by dismantling the very basis of illusionistic representation. As one author describes it, "The artist employs a reversed maneuver, where the use of a split screen device can be seen to dismember three-dimensional reality into complementary but unsynchronized realities."[14]

13. Cheryl Kaplan, "Inside the Black Box: William Kentridge in an Interview," *db-artmag* (July 2005), http://www.db-artmag.de//2005/7/e/1/383.php.

14. Tone, "William Kentridge."

Technically speaking, they are actually not unsynchronized; we always see the two sets fixed within the same film frame. And in terms of figural representation, by juxtaposing two images on the same plane Kentridge continues to stress the similarity rather than disparity of two animated drawings. This indicates that he was not actually interested in exploiting the technique of stereoscopy but rather in exploring two related and parallel spaces. Still, the title of this film does confront the viewer with the idea of stereoscopy, which might lead one to imagine a device that could render Kentridge's imagery three-dimensional. This suggests a notable and even violent disruption of perception, even if only imagined. When stereoscopic moving images do not account for the slight displacement of perspective between our left and right eyes, it results in utter confusion for the brain—we see only a blurred superimposition of two shaky images that never fully come together. The implied question is thus how much two synchronized images can differ yet still make sense perceptually. What is the persistence of vision as we watch a single disjointed figure? What is the limit of the image? And what is the balance between two different states of aggregates of a single unit? Interestingly, after making *Stereoscope* Kentridge began to turn his attention to precisely these matters of perception.

Historically, the locus of a stereoscopic image was tied to an apparatus that addressed the individual viewer's pair of eyes. It was inside the viewing device that the three-dimensional picture materialized. The image thus had a fixed position vis-à-vis the viewer, and only by excluding the competing reality of peripheral vision could it take shape. The three-dimensional effect was caged by the picture's technical disposition. Freeing it from such physical constraint has been a constant drive in artistic production since the baroque period.[15] Within the context of cinematic discourse, this motivation has been mirrored by the longtime conflict between the cinematic apparatus as a recording device versus a production device: consider, for example, the documentary cinema of the Lumière brothers, in which the camera moves in order to capture dynamic reality, as compared to the phantasmagoric films of Georges Méliès, who created movement by animating a mise-en-scène in front of a static camera. In *7 Fragments for Georges Méliès* (2003; figs. 44–46, 53–55, pls. 8–27), Kentridge used for the first time what was to become the second important signature of his film production: a combination of live action and stop motion. He started by shooting footage with a 16mm camera at twenty-four frames per second, then projected and refilmed this footage with a 35mm animation camera at one frame per second, and finally edited and transferred it to video for viewing. It is notable that *7 Fragments* has not only appeared in galleries as a large-scale installation but has also been staged in public settings; in 2007, for instance, the work was projected onto the windows of the art gallery at the University of Brighton, England. Fully exploring the potential of projections to incorporate and appropriate all kinds of surfaces has become an important strategy for Kentridge. It is a trajectory that started as early as 1995, when he drove a truck with a film projector through the streets of Johannesburg, turning exterior walls into screens for the project *Memory and Geography*.[16] He was keen to break out of the box of the video monitor and the gallery—containers that did not seem able to accommodate an expanded cinematic practice.

15. Consider the long debate within the arts regarding media technologies—whether they should be openly incorporated into the representation or hidden in favor of spatial illusion.

16. The project was a collaboration with the artist Doris Bloom for *Africus*, the 1st Johannesburg Biennale. A later example is Kentridge's 2001 installation of *Shadow Procession* (1999) in New York's Times Square (fig. 16).

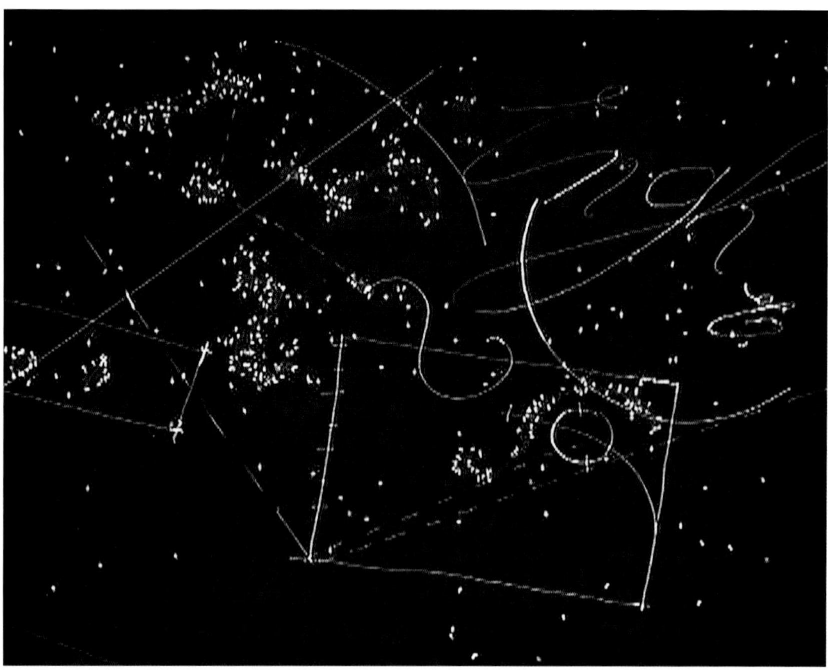

FIG. 28 William Kentridge
***Day for Night*, 2003**
16mm film transferred to video, 6:32 min.
Collection of the artist, courtesy Marian Goodman Gallery, New York, and Goodman Gallery, Johannesburg

"If the seven earlier fragments are about wandering around the studio waiting for something to happen," says Kentridge, "*Journey to the Moon* was an attempt to escape."[17] The locus of production—the artist's studio—becomes a site of limitation and routine. The film (pls. 28–47) reveals Kentridge incorporating live action into the animation, and it also draws on fresh subject matter from the outside world (one segment, for example, stars ants that he controlled with trails of sugar). This experimentation with live-action cinema represents a direct address of the audience, asking viewers, in Kentridge's words, "to make an elision between the actor and the screen."[18]

Within the history of cinema there is a long modernist tradition of reflection upon the film production process. With *Day for Night* (2003; fig. 28), which is invariably projected in the same space as *7 Fragments* and *Journey to the Moon*, Kentridge aligned himself with that tradition, paying homage to François Truffaut's seminal film *La nuit américaine* (Day for Night, 1973), whose title refers to the old cinematographer's trick of using camera filters to simulate a night atmosphere during daylight shoots.[19] In Kentridge's *Day for Night* this is achieved with a simple reversal from positive to negative, which turns the army of black ants, busy devouring traces of sugar, into a constantly shifting constellation of stars in the night sky. Although Kentridge had used multiple projections before (on a smaller scale), this nine-channel projection did something new, presenting a film in conjunction with outtakes, extra scenes, and related material. The installation is a spatial representation of the artist's process rather than a projection of a finished work. The large projection of *Journey to the Moon* identifies that film as the master narrative, but this is accompanied by a peripheral vision of the master himself, allowing the viewer to walk freely between these parallel and juxtaposed visions. Walking between the plane of the drawing and the lens of the camera has always been Kentridge's way of finding form. With *7 Fragments,* walking between the projected images also became part of the viewer's configuration of perception.

17. William Kentridge, "'Journey to the Moon' and '7 Fragments for Georges Méliès' Including 'Day for Night'" (2003), in Christov-Bakargiev, *William Kentridge*, 193.

18. Ibid.

19. See also Federico Fellini's *8 1/2* (1963) or Jean-Luc Godard's *Le mépris* (1964).

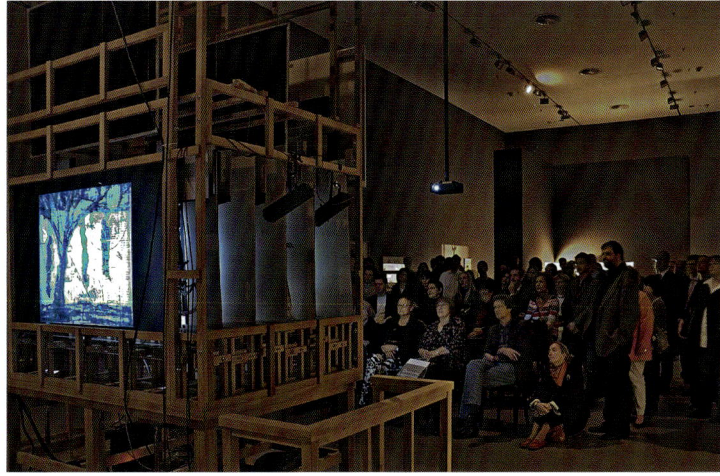

FIG. 29 William Kentridge
***Black Box/Chambre Noire*, 2005**
Model theater with drawings (charcoal on paper), mechanical puppets, and 35mm animated film transferred to video, 22 min.
141 3/4 x 78 3/4 x 55 in. (360 x 200 x 139.7 cm)
Commissioned by Deutsche Bank AG in consultation with the Solomon R. Guggenheim Foundation for the Deutsche Guggenheim, Berlin

INVESTIGATING PRECINEMATIC TECHNOLOGY

The films in general are drawings in four dimensions.
—WILLIAM KENTRIDGE, 2005[20]

Kentridge's trajectory of the last ten years, from *Stereoscope* to recent large-scale projection installations, has increasingly tended toward the direct activation of the viewer as the artist's fellow traveler. This is mirrored by his embrace of collaboration in the making of his films. At times he literally leaves the studio, seeking out the present tense of the theatrical stage as a site of collaborative imagination. He has been involved with the theater since before he began making films; he returned to this context in the 1990s with *Woyzeck on the Highveld* (1992) and *Faustus in Africa!* (1995). Kentridge's ongoing collaboration with theatrical companies, particularly Handspring Puppet Company of Johannesburg (with whom he staged a production of the Monteverdi opera *Il ritorno d'Ulisse in patria* in 1998), has led him to investigate the creation of maquettes and models that simulate theatrical effects on a small scale. Like the artist Janet Cardiff, who has used the cinema context as a stage for narratives that address and include the viewer, Kentridge has produced two works—*Preparing the Flute* (2005; pls. 151–54) and *Black Box/Chambre Noire* (2005; fig. 29, pls. 163–69)—that represent research into precinematic machines of illusion and perspective as a means of creating a linear yet multilayered space for vision. "*Black Box* references the black box of the theater, a space for experimenting, the chambre noire—the space between the lens and the camera's eyepiece," he says. "Formally, the *Black Box* has something to do with vaudeville, which, in the 1890s, provided one of the transitions to movies."[21] The theatrical stage is brought to life by the skill and conviction of the performers and the willingness of the audience to suspend disbelief, supported by an architecture that, like cinema, presumes an ideal viewing perspective. Whereas cinematic illusion rests upon the viewer's identification with the camera and the projection beam, Kentridge's theatrical creations—whether produced in actual theaters or in miniature—confront the viewer with multidimensional layers of live action and rear projection.

20. Kaplan, "Inside the Black Box."

21. Kentridge continues: "The six characters are a Megaphone man who's the narrator; a transparent Herero woman defined by the head-dress: she's actually a spring with a piece of transparent gauze on her head. A mechanical running man: a cut-out piece of paper that runs; a pair of dividers, that's the measuring arm, measuring skulls and geography; an exploding skull that makes a brief appearance; and a second Herero woman based on a German postal scale from 1905, a scale for weighing letters." Ibid.

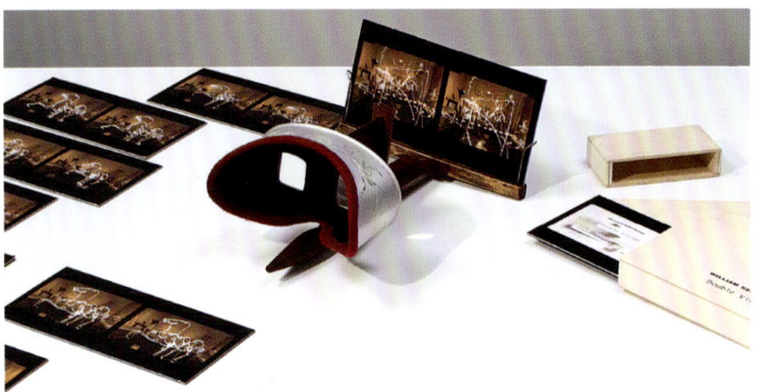

FIG. 30 William Kentridge
***Double Vision*, 2007**
Stereoscopic cards and viewer, ed. of 25
Eight cards, each: 3 1/2 x 7 in. (8.8 x 17.8 cm);
viewer: 1 1/3 x 7 1/4 x 7 1/2 in. (3.3 x 18.5 x 19 cm)
Collection of the artist, courtesy Marian Goodman Gallery, New York

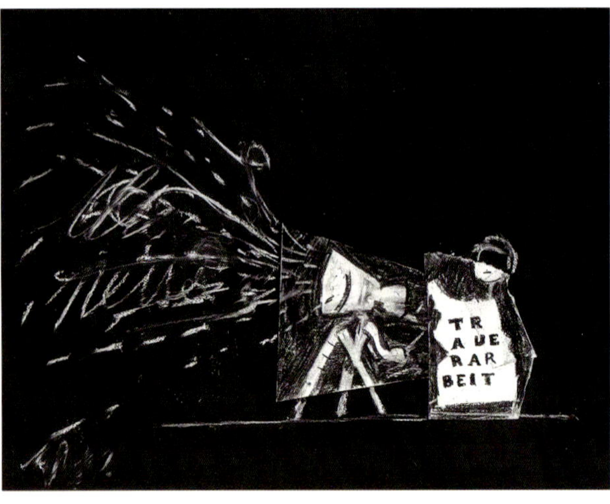

FIG. 31 William Kentridge
Drawing for the installation *Black Box/Chambre Noire* [Trauerarbeit], 2005
Charcoal and collage on paper
19 3/4 x 25 2/5 in. (50 x 64.5 cm)
Commissioned by Deutsche Bank AG in consultation with the Solomon R. Guggenheim Foundation for the Deutsche Guggenheim, Berlin

As Angela Breidbach observes, objects project themselves onto the eye of the viewer, who becomes the recipient of visual impulses. On Kentridge's stage, the various layers—the projections, live actors, and puppets or mechanized objects—must be actively combined into a coherent picture. This works only when the viewer is generously taking part in the creation of a unified time and space. Far removed from the Brechtian notion of alienation effects, Kentridge's art thrives on the gaps between each layer of representation and performance. This indicates a certain resistance on Kentridge's part to being categorized as either a fine artist, filmmaker, or art director, but it is above all an exercise in the pleasure of complexity.

Traditional theatrical and cinematic spaces share a fundamental principle with optical apparatuses: they predetermine a master perspective, fixing the physical position of the viewer. In the most extreme form there is a designated spot to place one's eyes and nose—a fact exploited by Kentridge in his 2008 exhibition at Marian Goodman Gallery, New York, which included a number of works to be examined through stereoscopic viewers (see fig. 30). Stereoscopic and telescopic devices establish a clear distinction between an object and its visual representation through a mechanical setup. To look through a lens or into a machine is to see a world invisible to the naked eye. The mechanism eliminates any contingencies of peripheral perception, liberating a new and intimate vision. Consider, for example, Kentridge's conception, for *Black Box*, of a "Trauerarbeit machine on stage [that] could turn, and things would come out of it" (see fig. 31).[22] Through the means of theatrical technology, he reviews and reformulates Freud's concept of Trauerarbeit, the activity of mourning the loss of a loved one—an endless work of projection and repression, loss and memory.

22. Ibid.

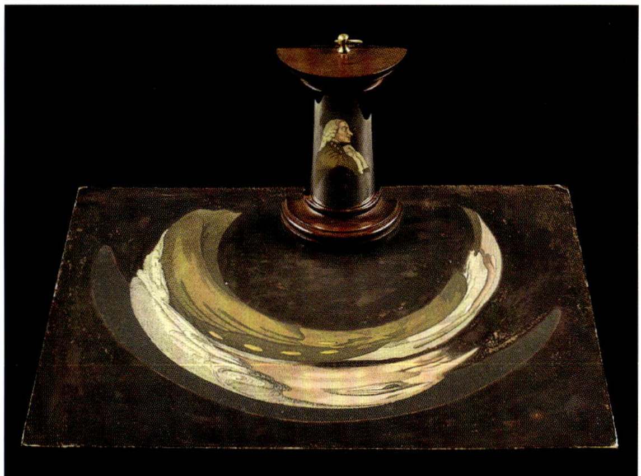

FIG. 32 William Hogarth
***Zoomorphosis* (detail), ca. 1750**
Etchings mounted on oak, mirrored cylinder, and mahogany case
Seven etchings, each: 8 1/3 x 11 1/5 in. (21.2 x 28.5 cm);
cylinder: 4 1/2 x 2 5/8 x 1 2/5 in. (11.4 x 6.9 x 3.5 cm);
case: 14 5/8 x 9 5/8 x 5 1/8 in. (37.4 x 24.5 x 13 cm)
Research Library, the Getty Research Institute, Los Angeles

The technology of anamorphism complicates the referential relationship between an object and its representation, as it requires the viewer to find the precise angle and position at which the distorted image is resolved.[23] Kentridge took the tradition of anamorphic vision one crucial step further with his film *What Will Come (has already come)* (2007; fig. 18, pls. 170–72). He made the animation's drawings while looking at the surface of a cylindrical mirror—a process that alludes, perhaps, to another precinematic trope: the crystal ball that reveals past or future events. The film—the first of its kind—approaches the dream of three-dimensional cinema in a simple, analog way, acknowledging important artistic precedents in anamorphic drawing and historical contexts of entertainment (see fig. 32). The viewer looks down on a round table with a mirrored cylinder at its center. A continuous array of scenes spin around the table and take shape as they are reflected by the curved surface. The content is inherently intertwined with the technical display: it is a toy that morphs visual pleasure (the viewer's expectation of entertainment, enhanced by the soundtrack) and postcolonial guilt (the history of Ethiopia's suffering under Fascist occupation). Interestingly, Kentridge has described *Black Box* in similar terms: "A black box miniature theater is an optical toy that is a forerunner of cinema. Instead of having actors on stage, it's about seeing a child's miniature toy theater and its machinery moving."[24] Through projects such as these, he posits truth via dynamic representations of past events, giving his moving images an object status that allows the viewer to negotiate a position of proximity or distance. In some ways, the experience of *What Will Come* is similar to that of looking at a stereo view: we need to come close in order to be able to see what is offered.

Ultimately, however, the artist's mechanical devices reconnect us with a lost utopia of moving images at a moment when the film medium is on the verge of becoming obsolete. In this respect they invoke the distinction between a human actor and a puppet, a representational gap that enables us to grasp a repressed truth—memory compared to reality at a moment when an object is truly lost and cannot be found again. These precinematic devices cannot become formative touchstones for the children of our time; they are remnants of a past that has been irretrievably lost. But as grown-ups we can recognize a dream buried or deferred—a dream of looking at truthful representations. It is the recognition of that dream that fascinates the viewer. The impact of *What Will Come* depends on our active participation: only by walking, by deliberately shifting perspectives, can we make Kentridge's merry newsreel of nightmarish dreams come into focus. This adds an inherent sense of nonclosure to complexity. The work becomes a Trauerarbeit that, as Freud stated, will never come to an end.

23. Baroque spaces are full of anamorphic and other illusionistic devices, intended to encourage aristocratic viewers to explore the sites and to surprise them with unforeseen vistas. The mutual understanding between artist and viewer was that such representations did not necessarily serve a symbolic function but rather referred to a fantasy world of boundless forms and visions.

24. Kaplan, "Inside the Black Box."

POSTCINEMATIC CINEMA: FILM AS AGENCY

The hope is that... the arcane process of obsessively walking between the camera and the drawing-board will pull to the surface, intimations of the interior.

—WILLIAM KENTRIDGE, 1998[25]

What seems to resist coming to the surface needs to be circumscribed, intrigued. It eludes intention or planned execution. To engage in this dance again and again is, as Kentridge observes, an obsession that is rewarded by unforeseen findings. In the 1805 essay "On the Gradual Construction of Thoughts Whilst Speaking," the German writer Heinrich von Kleist speculated about the processual nature of finding the right form to express an idea. The beginning, according to Kleist, is a simple trust that the right words—or, in Kentridge's context, the right forms—will emerge as one speaks. For Kentridge, it all begins with his process of pacing back and forth between the drawing and the camera or, even earlier, as he prepares his materials in the studio. For the viewer of his multichannel installations, it involves a trust that by walking the space—by taking in various perspectives, focusing on a single projection, abandoning a certain narrative, and returning to other fragments—one will find a rhythm of spatial collage that reveals the coherence of a method and its materials.

There is an important precedent in Kentridge's oeuvre for this strategy of active involvement of the viewer. *Overvloed* (1999; fig. 33), a temporary projection in Amsterdam, posed a direct physical challenge to its audience. The procession-themed work was designed to be projected onto the vaulted ceiling of the baroque Koninklijk Paleis, blending with an existing fresco and presenting a series of inverted East African and Dutch sayings from the Dutch Golden Era. Viewers were given rectangular handheld mirrors with which to correct the reversed text and catch glimpses of the projection without getting stiff necks (see fig. 34).

25. Quoted in Rosalind Krauss, "'The Rock,'" 13.

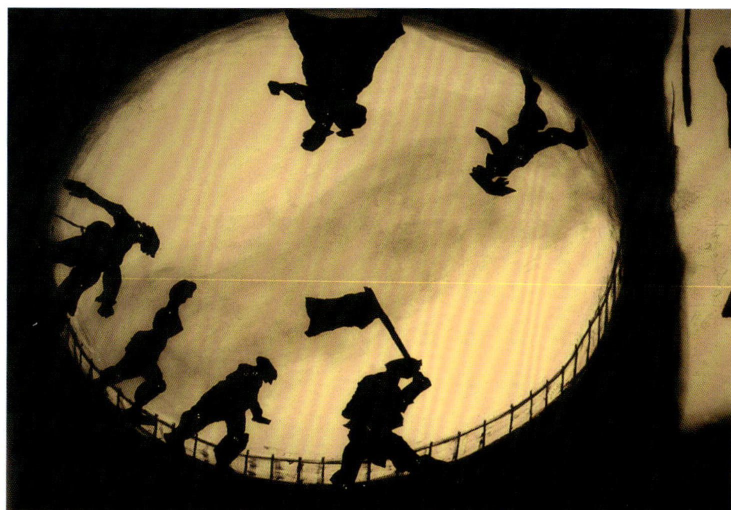

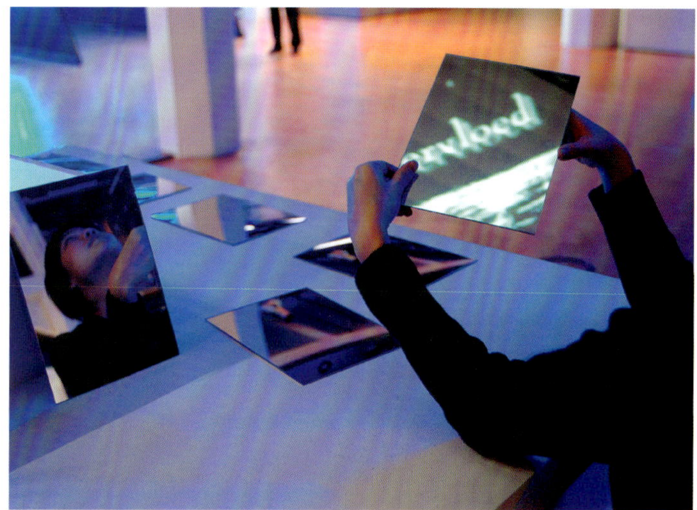

FIGS. 33–34 William Kentridge
***Overvloed*, 1999**
35mm animated film transferred to video, 6 min.
Collection of the artist, courtesy Marian Goodman Gallery, New York, and Goodman Gallery, Johannesburg

The projection introduced an interactive component new to Kentridge's work, emphasizing the process of looking while recognizing that each individual would catch a different reflection. Images were bound to be fragmented and even further distanced in the mirrors. In the theater, an onstage mirror is one of the most common devices used to incorporate the audience into a scene. In Amsterdam, the mirrors in the viewers' hands redirected the gaze to a small slice of the larger projection. It took a while to figure out how to use the device and explore various viewpoints by moving about in space. In stark contrast to the revolutionary camera eye of the Russian filmmaker Dziga Vertov, which introduced audiences to a multiplicity of shifting perspectives but ultimately immobilized spectators in their seats, Kentridge's static camera not only set pictures in motion but also the viewer.

Vertov is the cinematic pioneer who has been associated most prominently with the revolution of cinematic perception. His seminal *Man with a Movie Camera* (1928) has come to represent what Vertov himself called the kino-eye: a practice of dynamic documentation of reality in the form of fast-paced newsreel footage. His equally influential counterpart, Sergei Eisenstein, was the first to have married projection and theatrical space in his 1921 production of Alexander Ostrovsky's play *Enough Simplicity in Every Sage,* also known as *The Sage*. Kentridge is obviously deeply indebted to these exponents of the Russian avant-garde and to their impact on our memory of a lost revolutionary utopia. His most recent installation, *I am not me, the horse is not mine* (2008; figs. 25–26, 35, pls. 174–239) reconnects with the Russian aesthetic of constructivism and montage, as well as its pathos, by combining eight projections of varying scale in a single space. The work revisits the language of the avant-garde both visually and textually, with fragments and loops that circle around the loss of revolutionary ideals. The installation's title alludes to the disillusionment of the avant-garde in the wake of the Soviet Central Committee accusations that culminated in the trials of 1937—an irrational turn of events that no one has been able to explain historically.[26]

Significantly, one of the film fragments in *I am not me,* titled *Commissariat for Enlightenment* (pls. 192–96), includes archival footage and a few seconds of Vertov's *Man with a Movie Camera*. "The intrigue is not to separate the brilliance of filmmaking from the ideology," says Kentridge, "but to understand how the film was dependent on the strength of the beliefs."[27] To this end, the title sequence of each fragment is built upon the idea of the cinematic newsreel, transporting us to places all over the world at a time when television had not yet reached out to every household. Vertov's cinema was produced and screened on the road, but today the museum has become the cultural space in which these distant memories resurface as a promise with universal appeal. There is no narrator, though, implying the loss of belief in an authoritative voice. What dominates the space of the installation instead is the carnival and march music that accompanies the endless procession of revolutionaries.

Another fragment, *A Lifetime of Enthusiasm* (pls. 174–81), represents "that part of the enthusiasm that could not be extinguished even as, from the 1920s on, the cost, the casuistry and terror of that enthusiasm became clearer."[28] It is a careful mise-en-scène of projected and live-action figures on a ramp, endlessly marching toward the glory of a better society: the revolution as a gay parade. None of us has actually seen Tatlin's famous *Monument to the Third International* (1920), but we would recognize even the mere silhouette of this avant-garde icon. We turn around, move about from screen to screen, and wonder where we fit in. What is the viewer's position in Kentridge's expanded cinema?

26. Ironically, the radical revolution of artistic practice proposed by Vertov and Eisenstein, among others, was ultimately challenged by the traditions of Russian folk culture, upheld as a true representation of the people precisely because it was an art that did not need an avant-garde.

27. William Kentridge, "Commissariat for Enlightenment," in *William Kentridge: I Am Not Me, the Horse Is Not Mine,* by William Kentridge et al. (Johannesburg and Cape Town: Goodman Gallery Editions, 2008), 41.

28. William Kentridge, "A Lifetime of Enthusiasm," in ibid., 23.

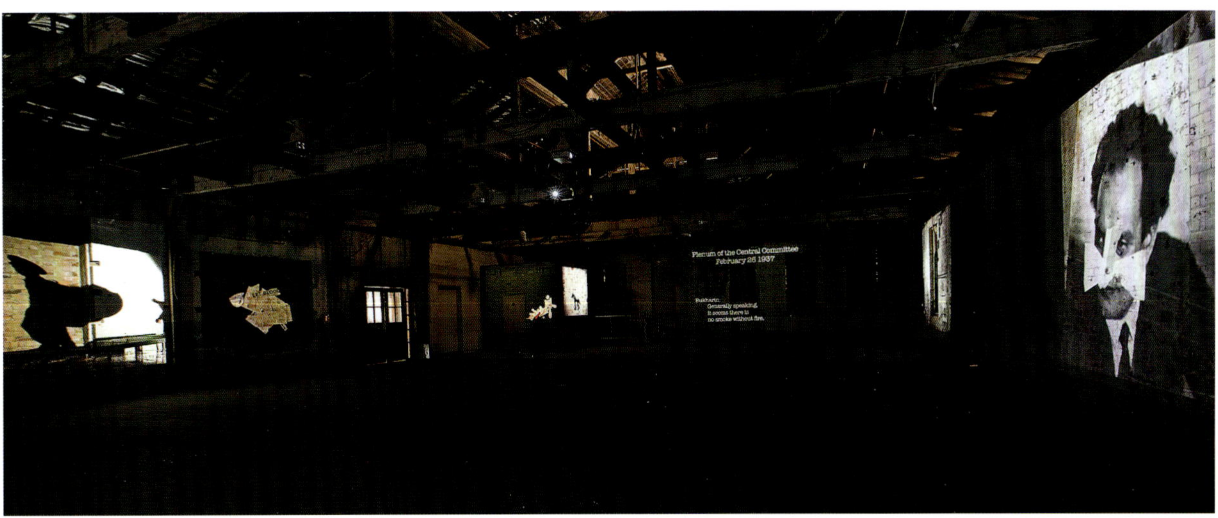

FIG. 35 William Kentridge
***I am not me, the horse is not mine,* 2008**
DVCAM and HDV transferred to video, 6:01 min.
Collection of the artist, courtesy Marian Goodman Gallery, New York, and Goodman Gallery, Johannesburg

For a 2008 exhibition entitled *William Kentridge: Everyone Their Own Projector* at Marian Goodman Gallery, Paris, the artist presented works drawn on or collaged from the pages of old encyclopedias and art history books, appropriating knowledge that has long been overcome by more recent definitions and concepts.[29] The artist's reuse of these clippings and cutouts emphasized that the fragments have lost their context of belief, becoming icons of lost systems of knowledge. Kentridge and Breidbach have pointed to the scientific notion that objects project their images onto our retinas through varying degrees of refracted light. The human eye hence emerges as a hybrid that sees and is seen at the same time. As a consequence, we project our own experience onto life and construct our world out of fragments of perception, building upon icons, memories, and visual and acoustic traces that evoke the original context and the loss of it at the same time. We move through space in search of a master perspective that has been lost once and for all. It is an archaeology on the fly, moving the viewer to actively construct a world out of fragmented memories. Entangled in this continuous work of mental reassessment, we can only wish that we were always in the state of mesmerized excitement provoked by Kentridge's work in two, three, or four dimensions.

Spending time in spaces such as *7 Fragments for Georges Méliès* or *I am not me, the horse is not mine* allows us to experience the movement of forms cut loose, a dance of joyful anarchy on the brink of perception that requires the active participation of the viewer. This kind of anarchy, which is entirely in the spirit of a trickster like Méliès, can be oblivious to its sometimes disastrous collateral damages—what Max Horkheimer and Theodor Adorno termed the dialectic of enlightenment, when enlightenment is turned into myth and technology is not in the service of man but rather a weapon that destroys human relations. Coming out of a Kentridge installation, however, we cannot help but be affected by his exuberance and enthusiasm. The artist has not stopped taking his obsessive, solitary walks between the camera and the drawing in his studio, but he is seeking more and more the company of collaborators to walk with him. And this is where we come in.

29. Kentridge has selected similar pages—torn from encyclopedias, maps, and other found objects—for the pages that open each of the present catalogue's plate sections.

4

SARASTRO & THE MASTER'S VOICE

THE MAGIC FLUTE

Sarastro, the high priest in Mozart's *The Magic Flute*, guides the hero of the opera in his journey toward wisdom. As a symbol of the Enlightenment, Sarastro combines all knowledge with all power. In the 218 years since Mozart wrote the opera, we have come to realize what a toxic mixture this is: the combination of certainty (because with knowledge or wisdom comes also the certainty of that wisdom) and the right to a monopoly of violence.

The opera production and *Learning the Flute* and *Preparing the Flute* look at the Enlightenment in its optimistic phase. *Black Box/Chambre Noire* examines one of its calamitous trajectories.

Learning the Flute, which started the whole *Flute* project, was made to find the visual language for the opera. The form, the blackboard, was the given; the photographic positive and negative of black drawing on white paper, reversed to produce white chalk drawings on the blackboard, was the discovery. This shifting from positive to negative and back again gave me the photographic language and the theme of the subsequent work, but it also became a way of thinking of darkness and light, of the Queen of the Night and Sarastro, priest of the sun.

Preparing the Flute and *Black Box* both use miniature theaters. The first was made as a model with which to prepare the production: slightly larger than the usual maquette of a theater used in set design, but of a size large enough to see and test the projections that were central to the production. After the production was finished, I wanted to go back to the miniature scale of the model—to get away from the craziness of the full-scale production, with its many singers, musicians, technicians, and administrators, all of whom had their own needs and pressures, and return to the calm of a studio. I also wanted to look at themes that had emerged while working on the opera that I had not been able to examine in the opera itself.

While the tabletop size of the two miniature theaters is many times smaller than a real theater, they are also in shape similar to but several times larger than a box camera. One of the associations of *Black Box* is the *chambre noire*: the inside of a camera, the space between the lens and the eyepiece or film plane. The space where the light is inverted, captured. One image is separated and held through the strange optical, mechanical, chemical photographic process. The stage has become a camera, the images shown or played out like photographs of the world outside the camera (or theater).

In Mozart's opera there are hints at the dangers and limitations of Sarastro and his certainties. In *Black Box* I wanted to look at the political unconscious of *The Magic Flute*—at the damages of colonialism, which described its predations to itself as bringing enlightenment to the Dark Continent. Specifically, *Black Box* looks at the colonial war of 1904 in what was then German South-West Africa and at the genocide of the Hereros.

Philip Miller took many of the musical themes of Mozart's opera and refigured them. He recast Sarastro's reassuring singing (which George Bernard Shaw described as the voice of God) as a military brass march. He also used different fragments of Herero music from Namibia. I also worked with Jonas Lundquist, a genius of mechanical skill who made the mechanical characters of *Black Box*. It is not a sequel to *The Magic Flute*; rather, it is a sort of health warning to accompany it.

In Mozart's opera music is enough to tame the wildest beasts, and a rhinoceros becomes a pet that dances on cue. Nature is benevolently calmed by music. In *Black Box* that rhinoceros, now captured on archival film, is hunted down (the destructive force of the same culture). These two moments of that distressing dialectic are the bookends of the project. **WK**

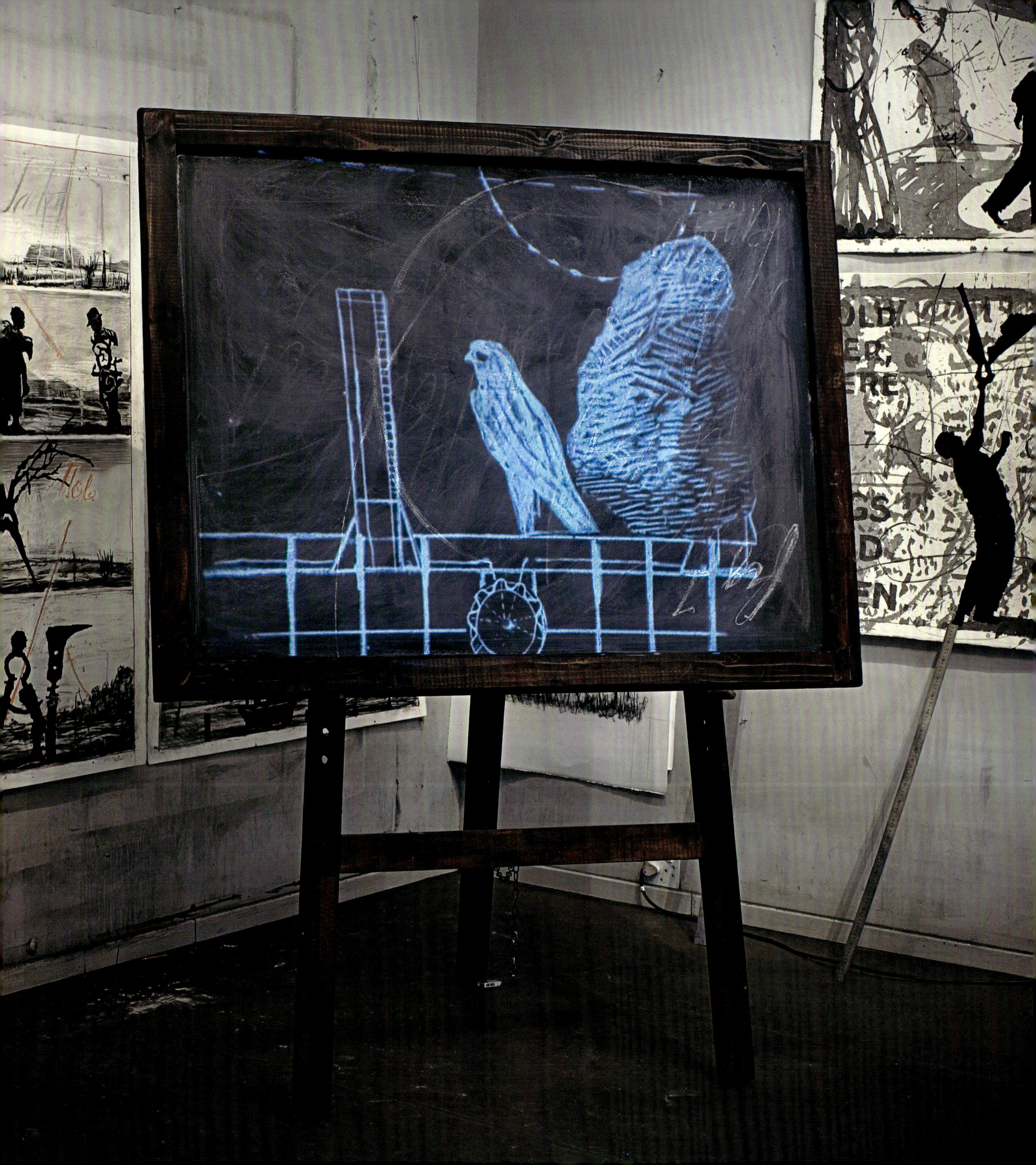

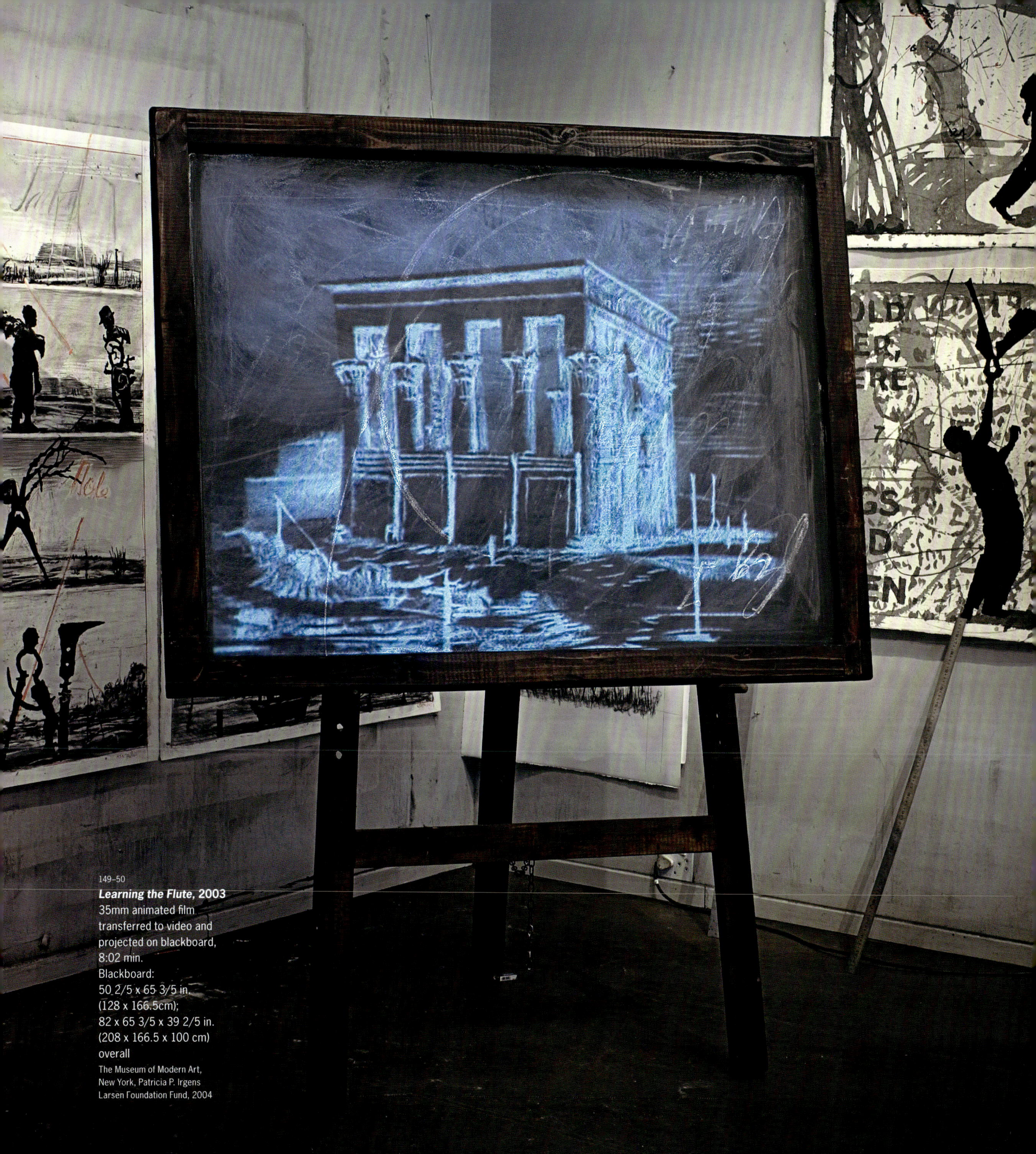

149–50
***Learning the Flute*, 2003**
35mm animated film
transferred to video and
projected on blackboard,
8:02 min.
Blackboard:
50 2/5 x 65 3/5 in.
(128 x 166.5cm);
82 x 65 3/5 x 39 2/5 in.
(208 x 166.5 x 100 cm)
overall
The Museum of Modern Art,
New York, Patricia P. Irgens
Larsen Foundation Fund, 2004

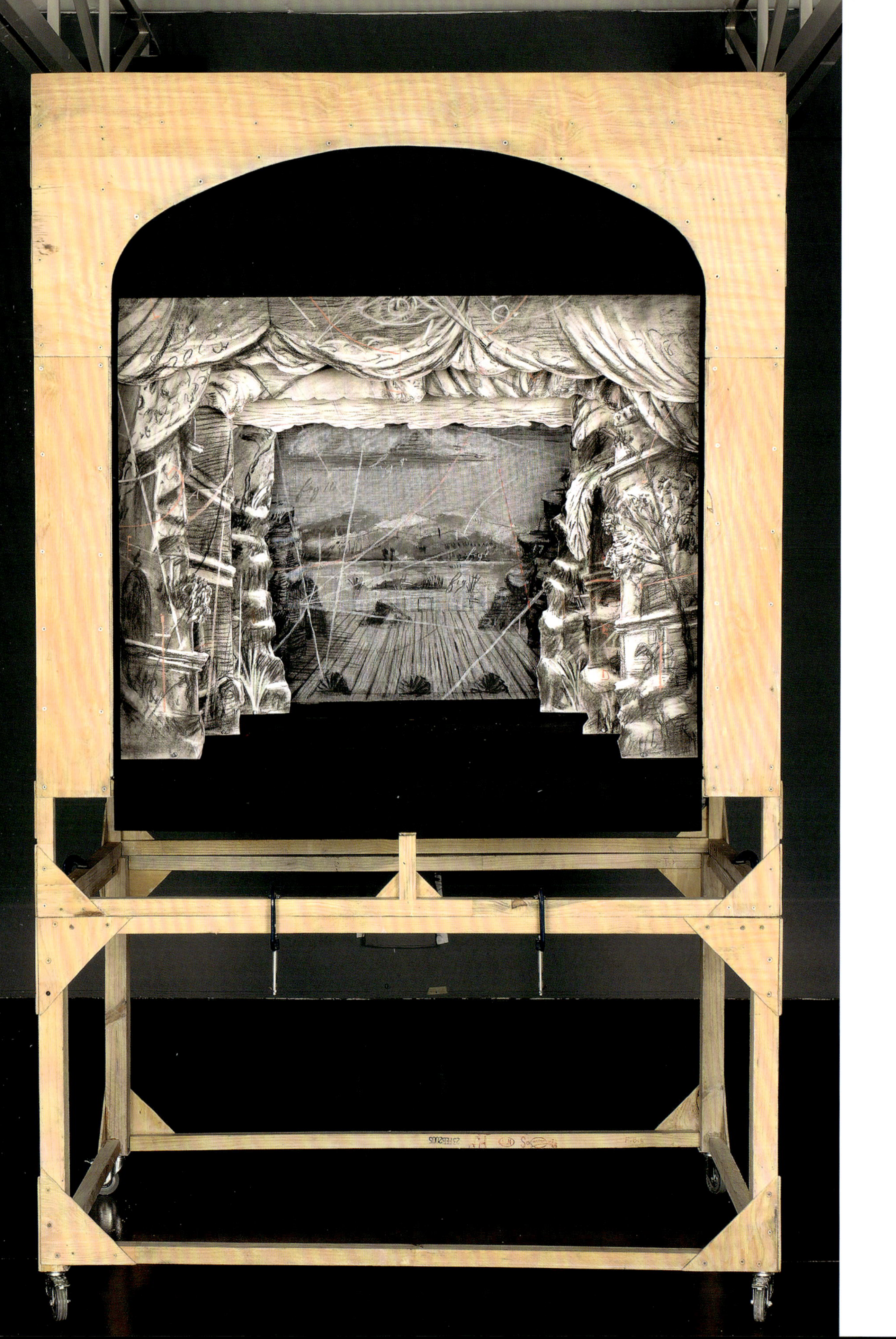

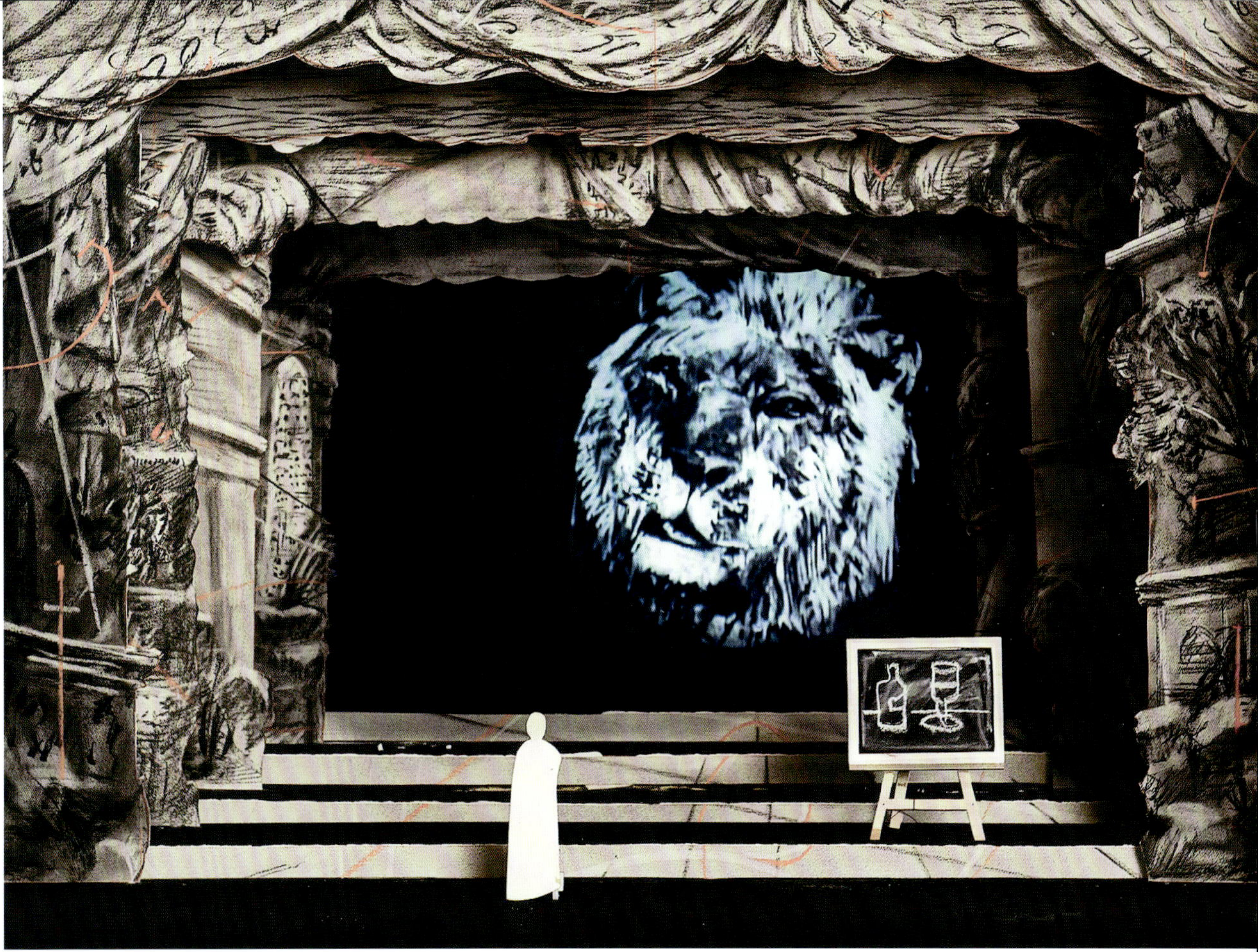

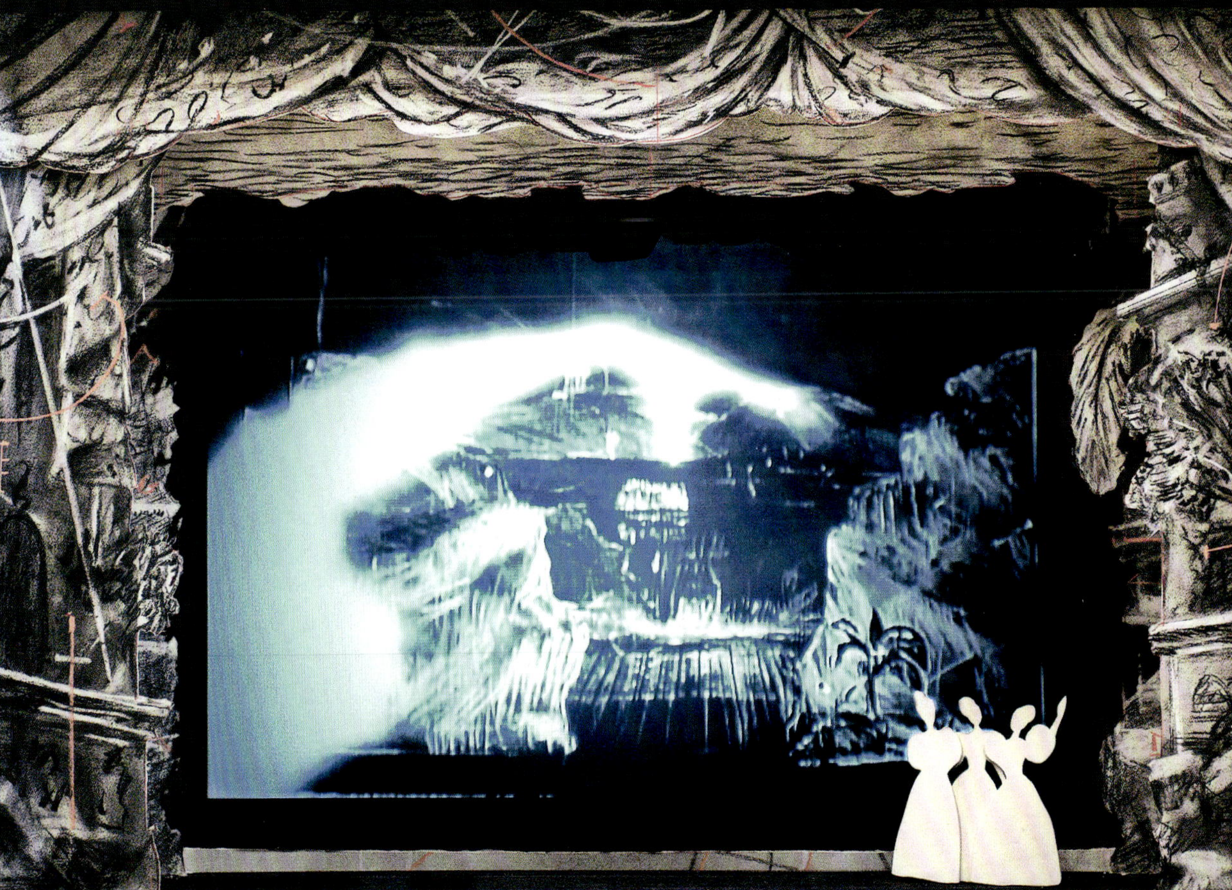

151–54 (THESE AND FOLLOWING PAGES)

***Preparing the Flute*, 2005**

Model theater with drawings (charcoal, pastel, and colored pencil on paper) and 35mm animated film transferred to video, 21:06 min.
95 x 44 x 60 1/2 in.
(241.3 x 111.8 x 153.7 cm)

San Francisco Museum of Modern Art, fractional and promised gift of Doris and Donald Fisher

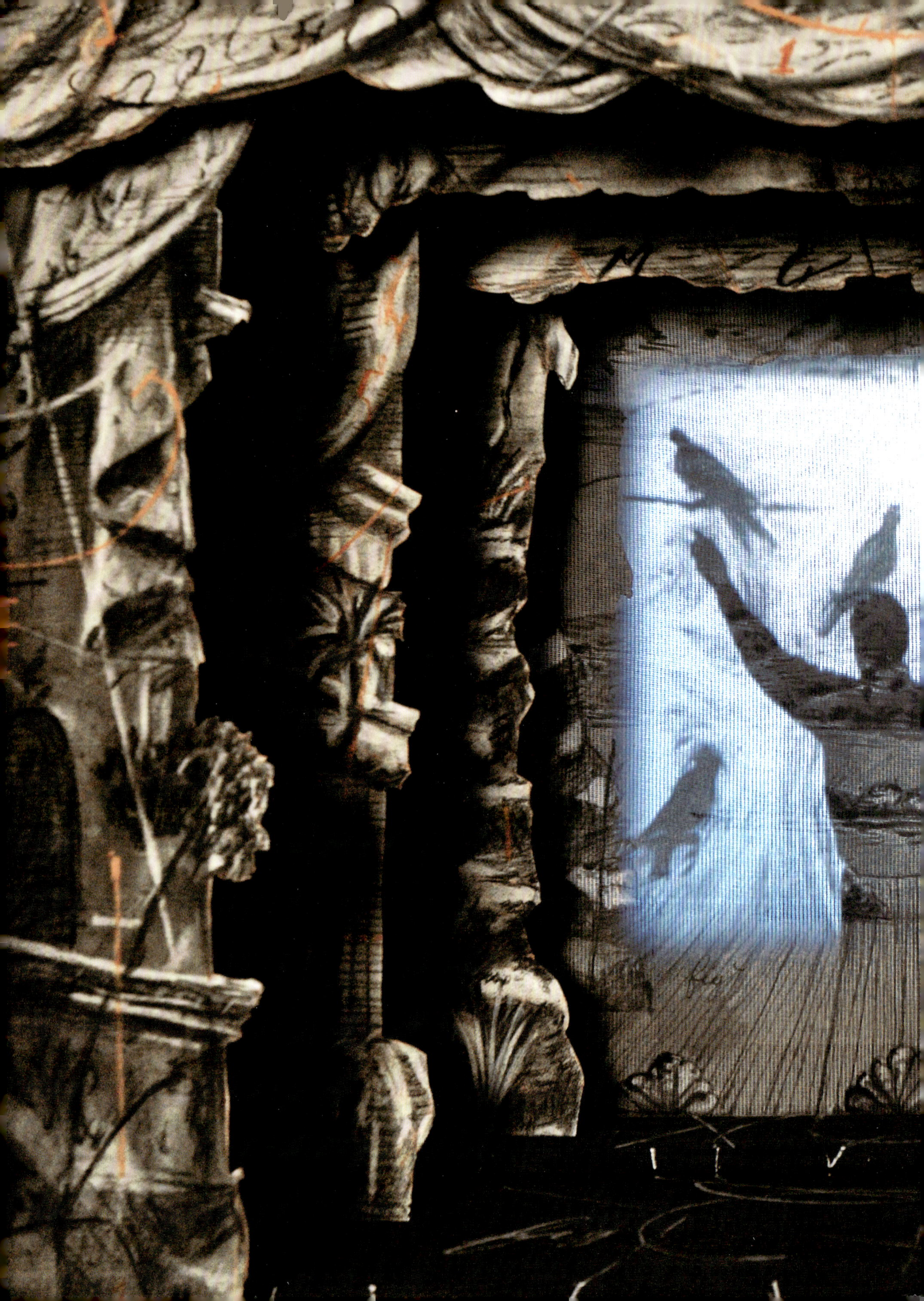

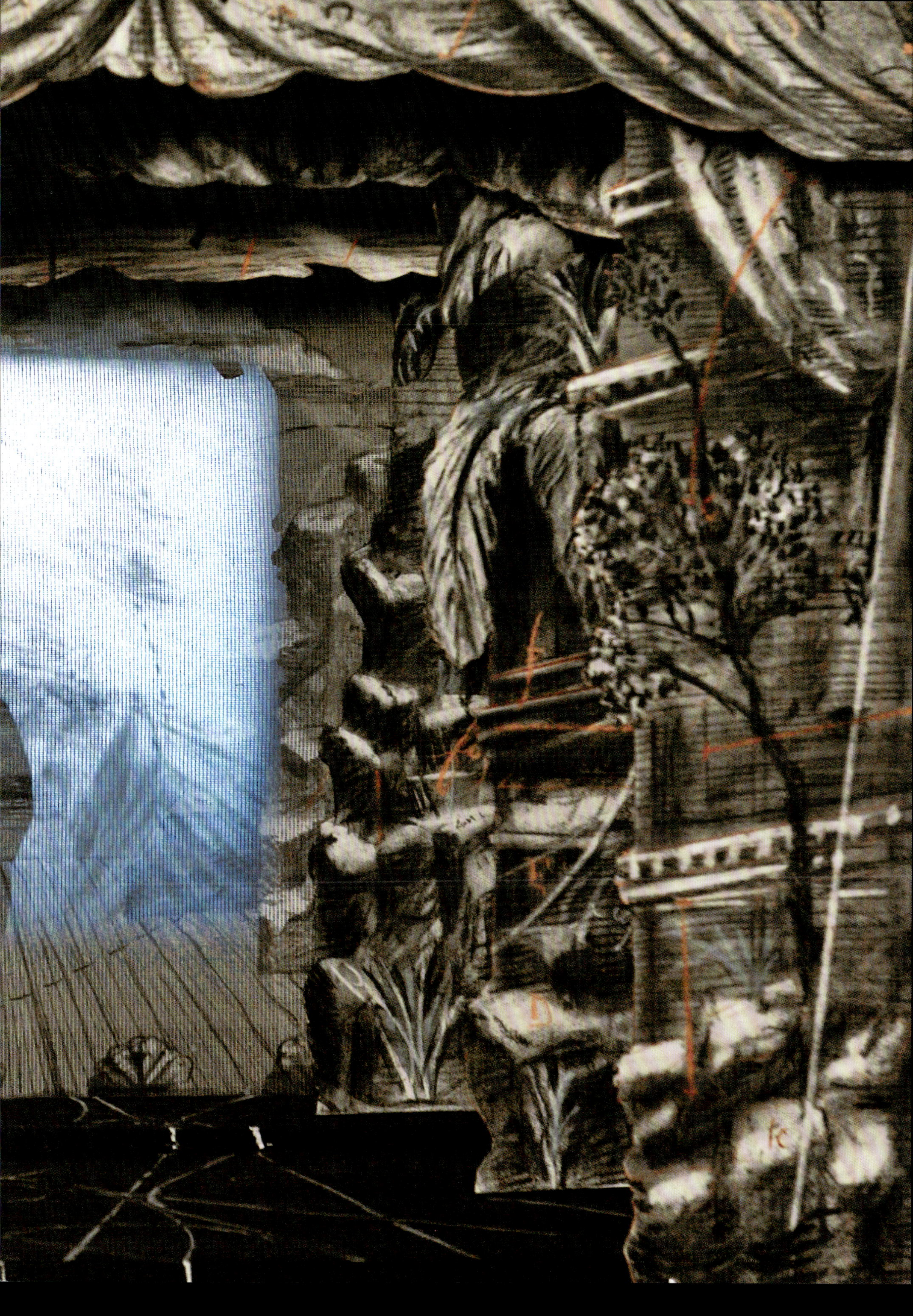

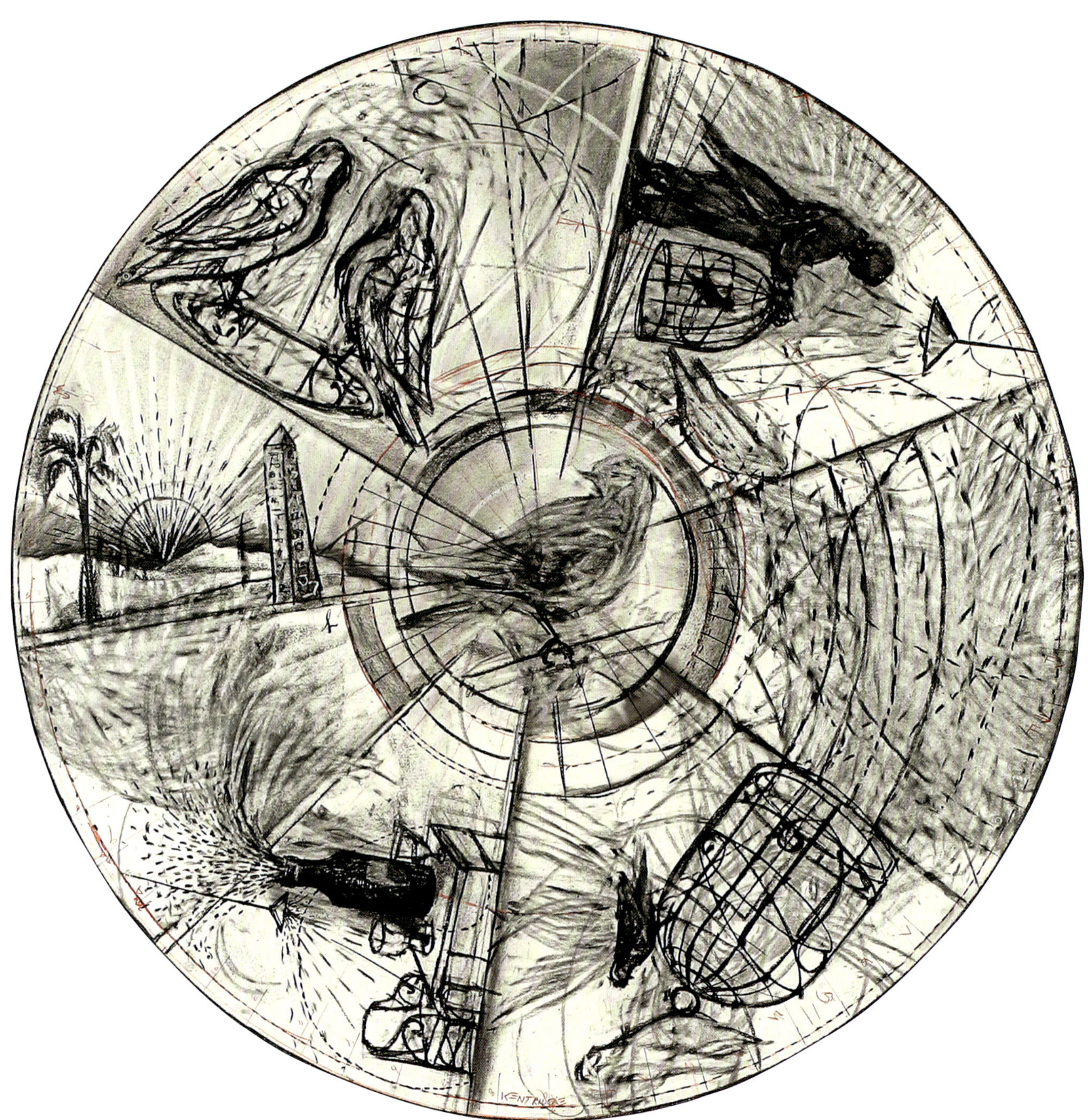

155
Drawing for the opera *The Magic Flute*, 2004–5
Charcoal and colored pencil on paper
48 x 48 in. (121.9 x 121.9 cm)
Collection of Brenda Potter and Michael Sandler

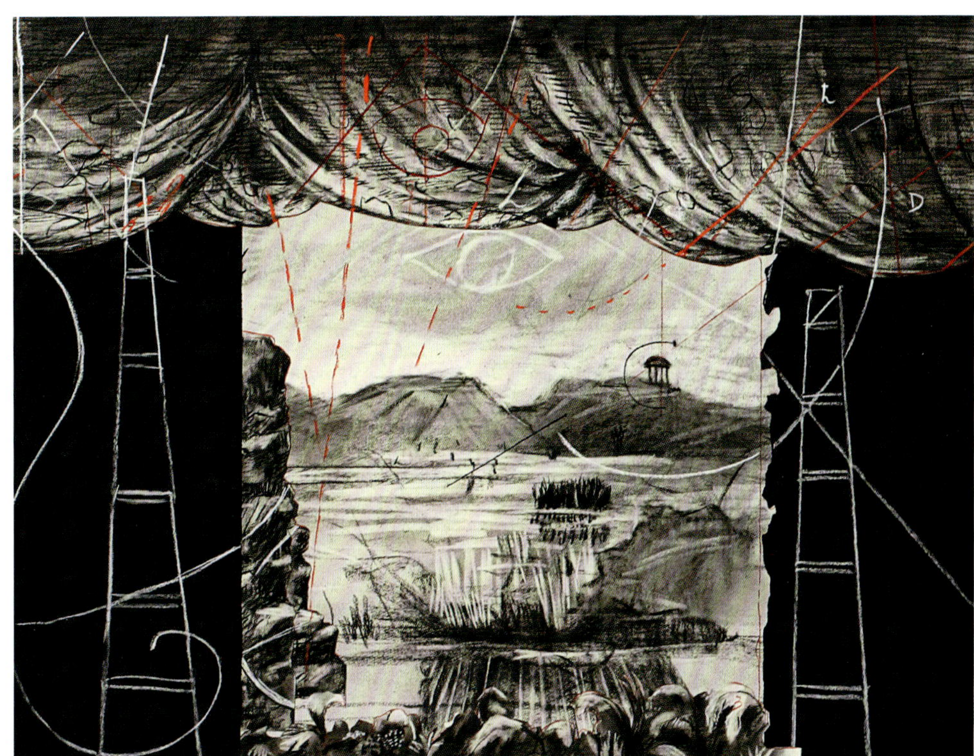

156
Drawing for the opera *The Magic Flute*, 2004–5
Charcoal, pastel, colored pencil, and collage on paper
39 2/5 x 51 1/5 in. (100 x 130 cm)
Collection of Joel and Anne Ehrenkranz, New York

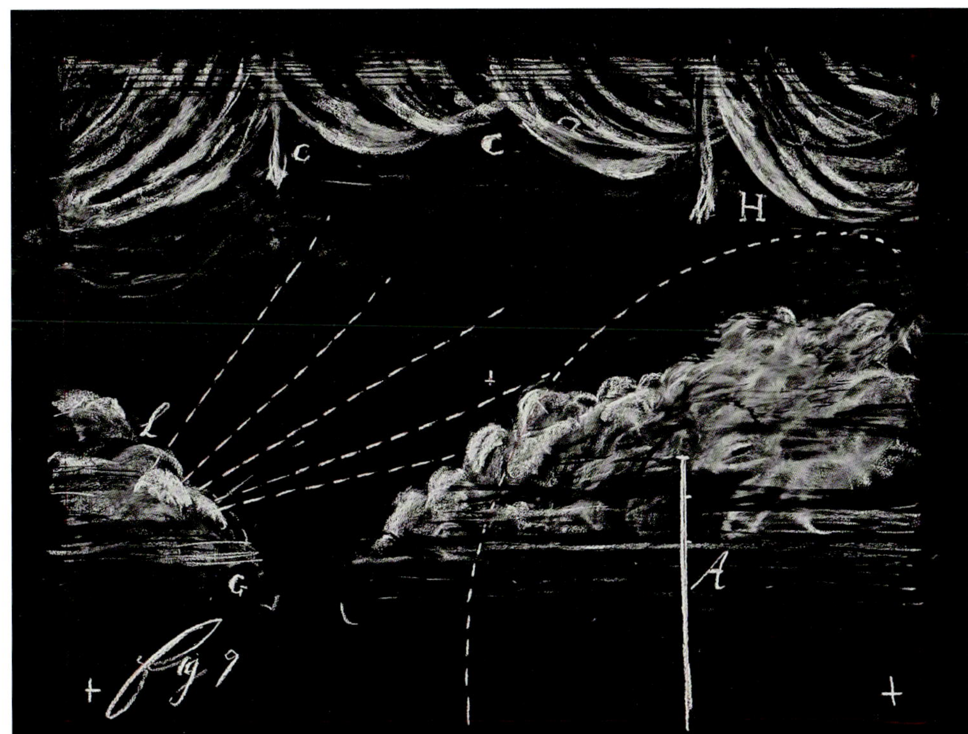

157
Drawing for the opera *The Magic Flute*, 2004–5
Pastel on paper
29 7/8 x 44 1/4 in (75.9 x 112.4 cm)
Courtesy Marian Goodman Gallery, New York

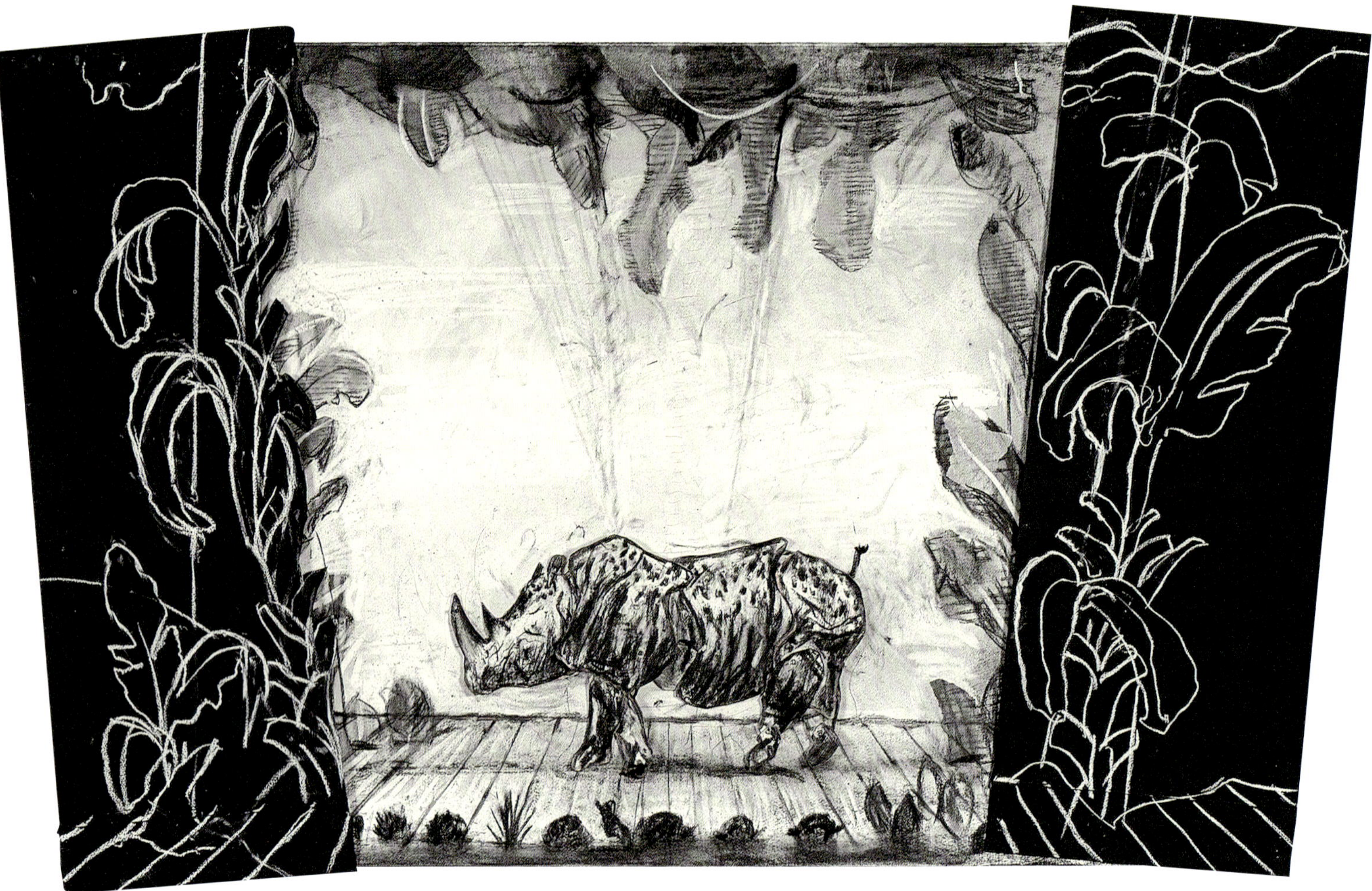

158
Drawing for the opera *The Magic Flute* [Rhino on Stage], 2004–5
Charcoal, pastel, colored pencil, and collage on paper
32 5/8 x 52 1/2 in. (83 x 133.5 cm)
Private collection, New York

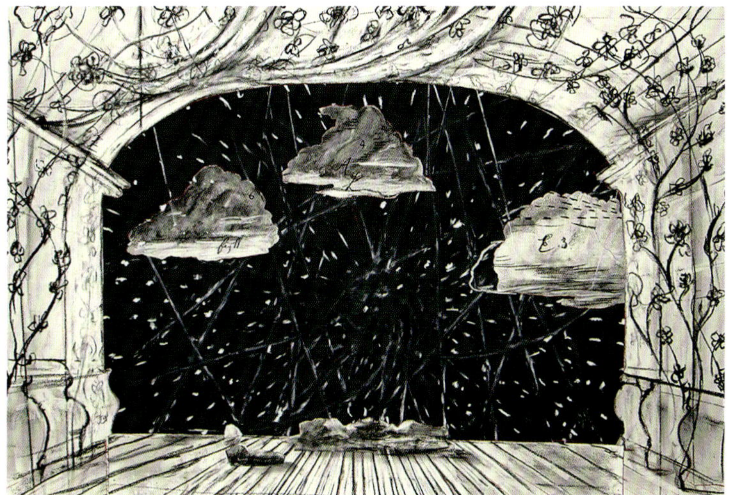

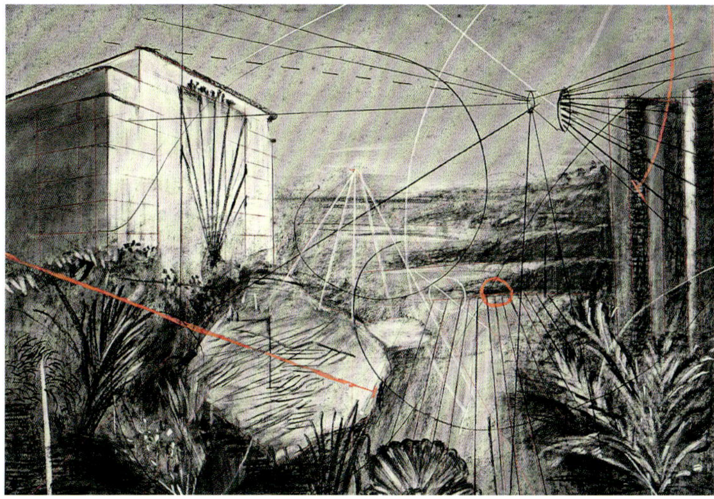

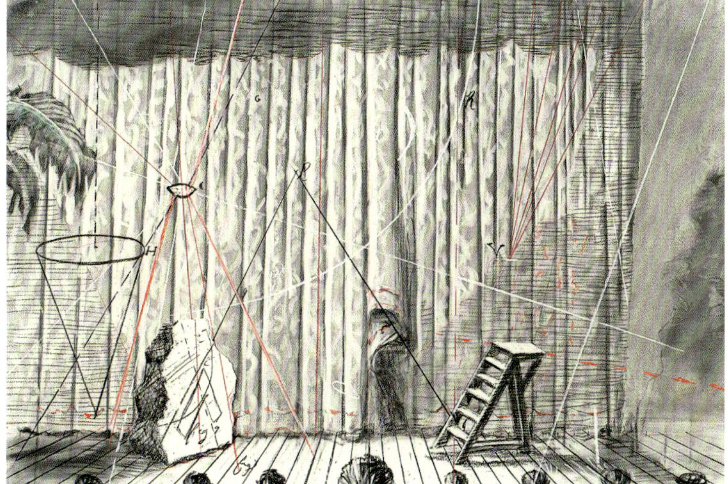

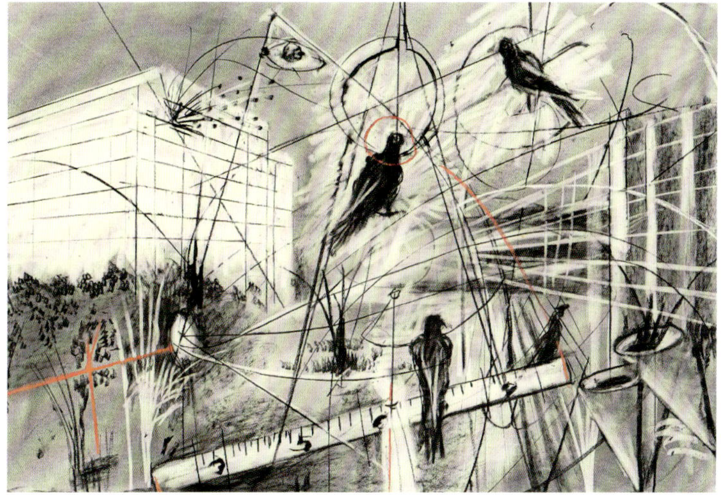

159
Drawing for the opera *The Magic Flute*, 2004–5
Charcoal, pastel, colored pencil, and collage on paper
31 1/2 x 47 1/4 in. (80 x 120 cm)
Private collection, Ross, California

160
Drawing for the installation *Preparing the Flute*, 2004–5
Charcoal, pastel, and colored pencil on paper
31 3/4 x 47 5/8 in. (80 x 120 cm)
Courtesy the artist and Marian Goodman Gallery, New York

161
Drawing for the opera *The Magic Flute*, 2004–5
Charcoal, pastel, and colored pencil on paper
46 1/2 x 63 in. (118.1 x 160 cm)
Collection of Joan and Richard Barovick

162
Drawing for the opera *The Magic Flute*, 2004–5
Charcoal, pastel, and colored pencil on paper
47 1/4 x 63 in. (120 x 160 cm)
Courtesy the artist and Marian Goodman Gallery, New York

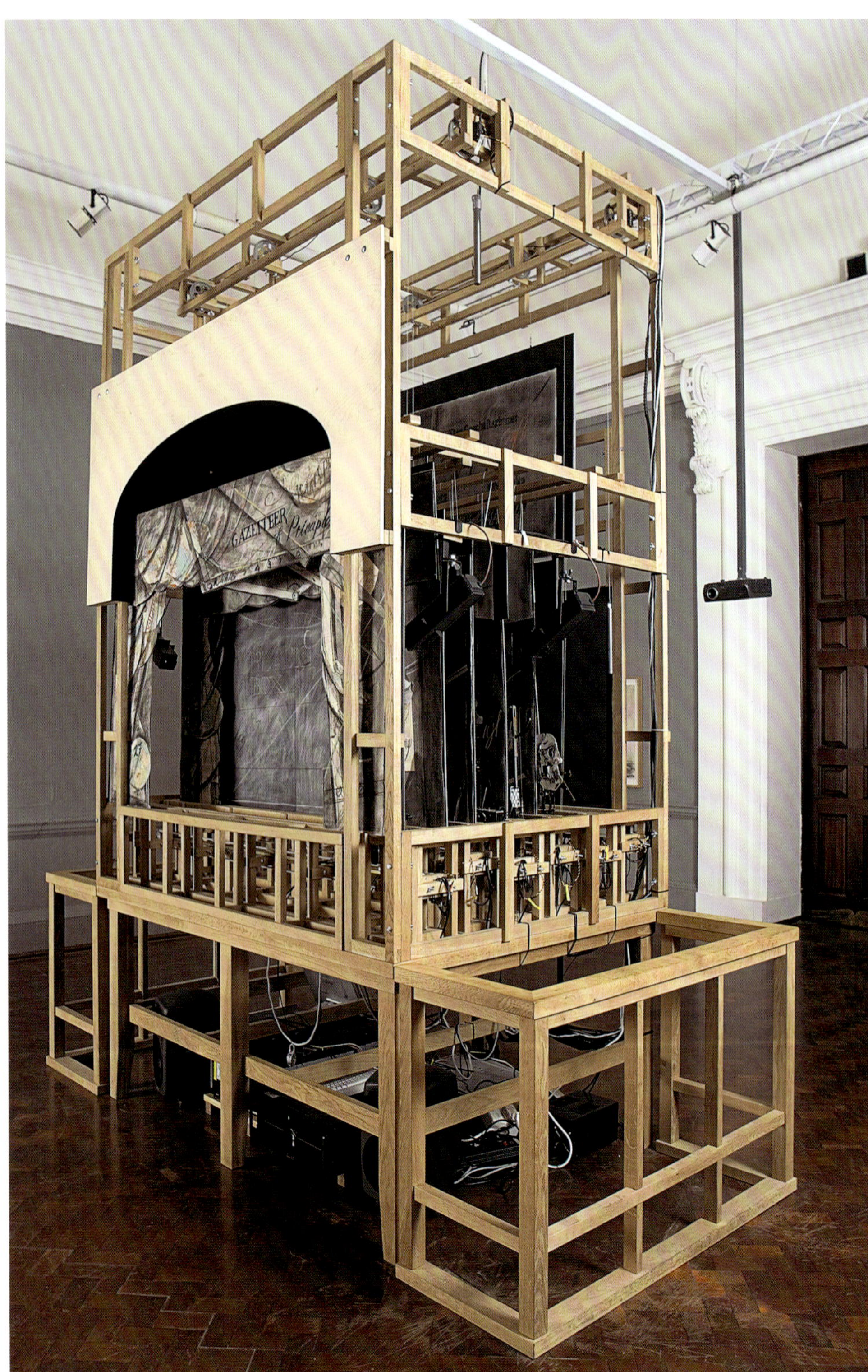

163–69 (THESE AND FOLLOWING PAGES)

Black Box/Chambre Noire, 2005

Model theater with drawings (charcoal on paper), mechanical puppets, and 35mm animated film transferred to video, 22 min.

141 3/4 x 78 3/4 x 55 in. (360 x 200 x 139.7 cm)

Commissioned by Deutsche Bank AG in consultation with the Solomon R. Guggenheim Foundation for the Deutsche Guggenheim, Berlin

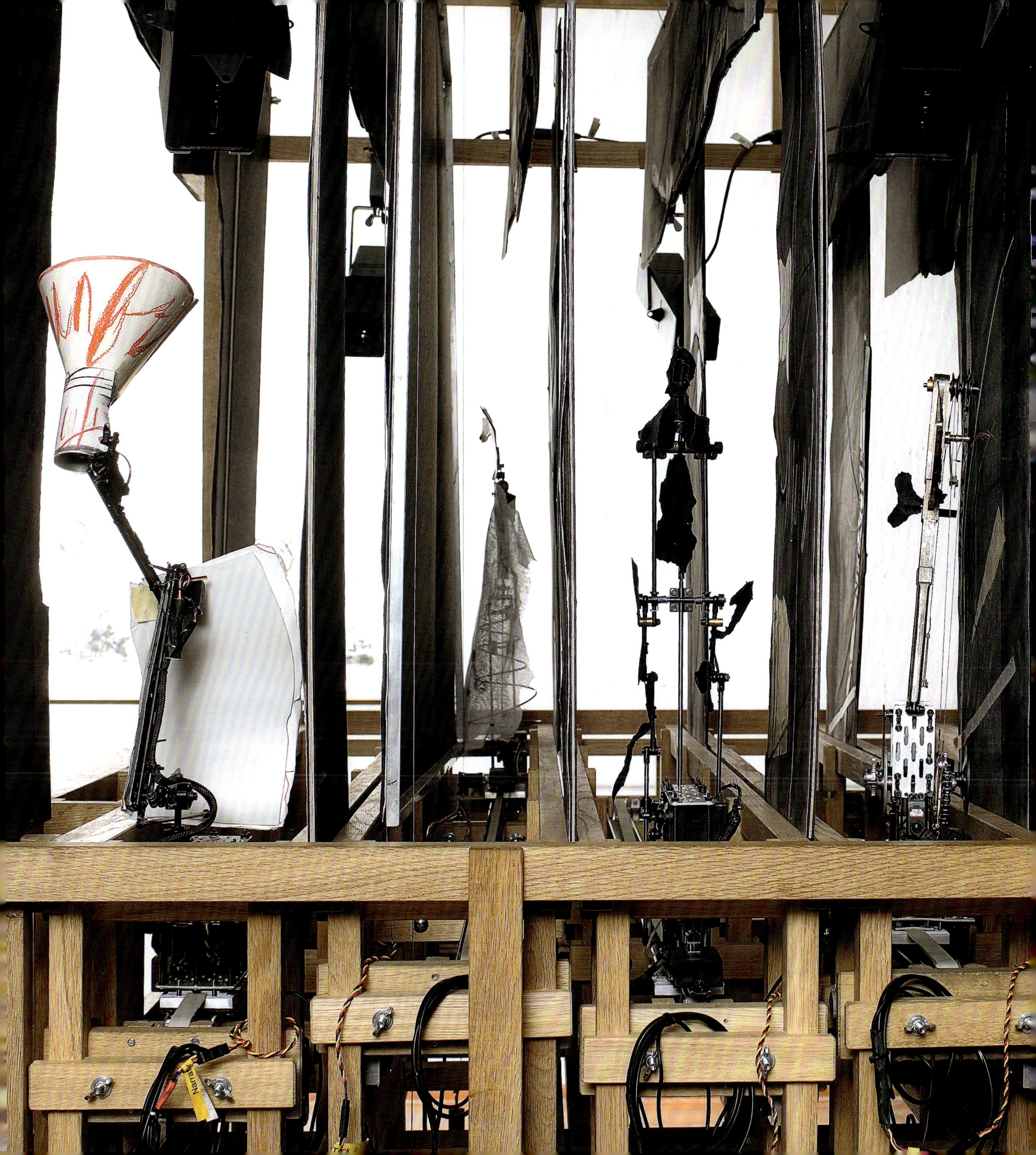

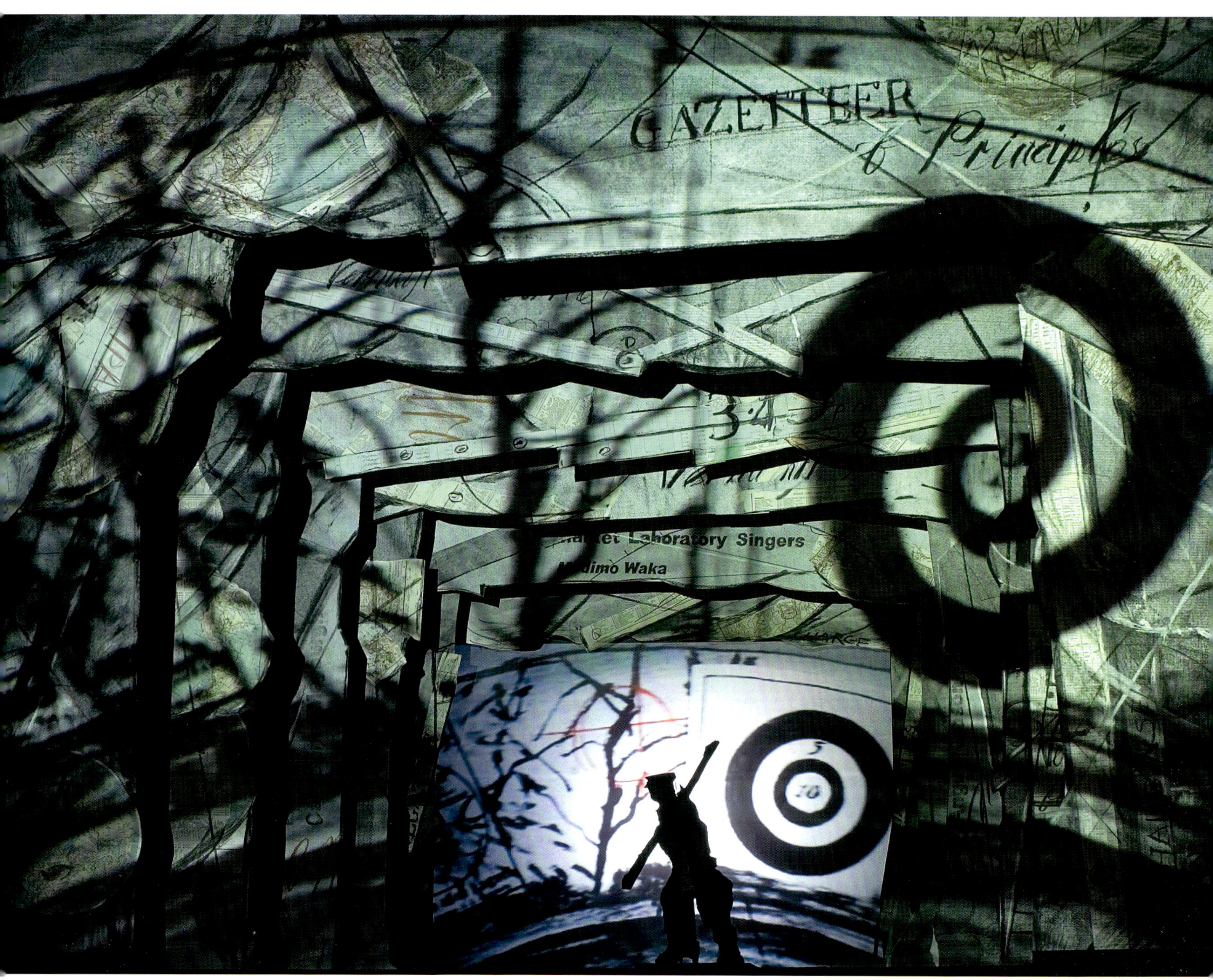
GAZETTEER
Laboratory Singers
10

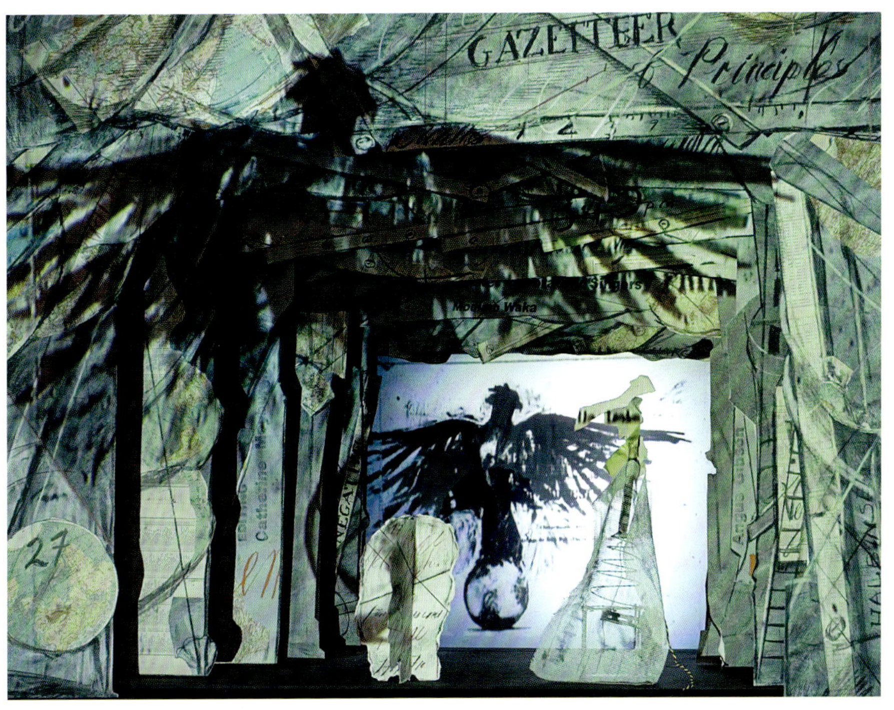
GAZETTEER
Principles
27

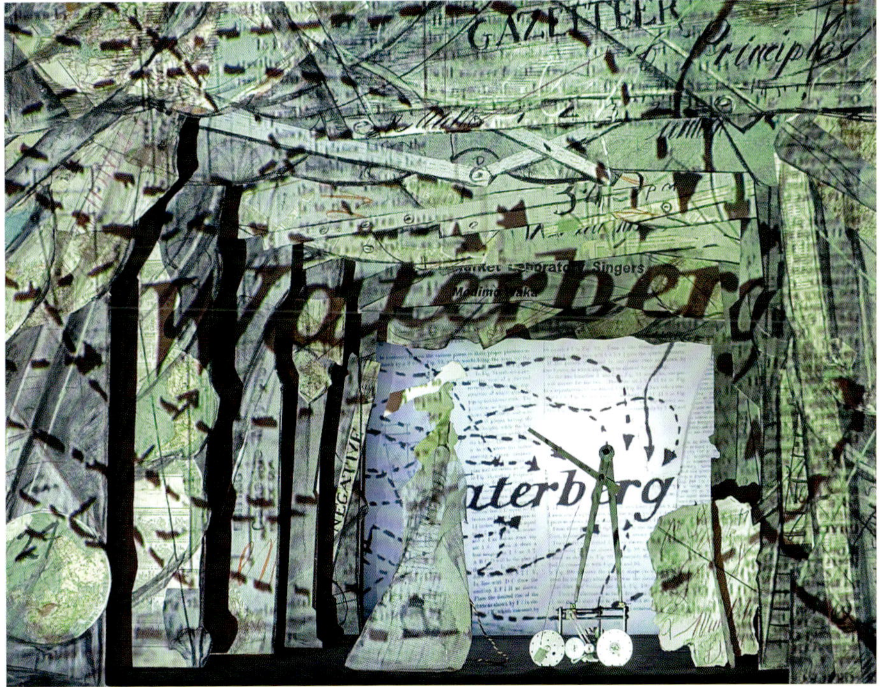
GAZETTEER
Principles
aterberg

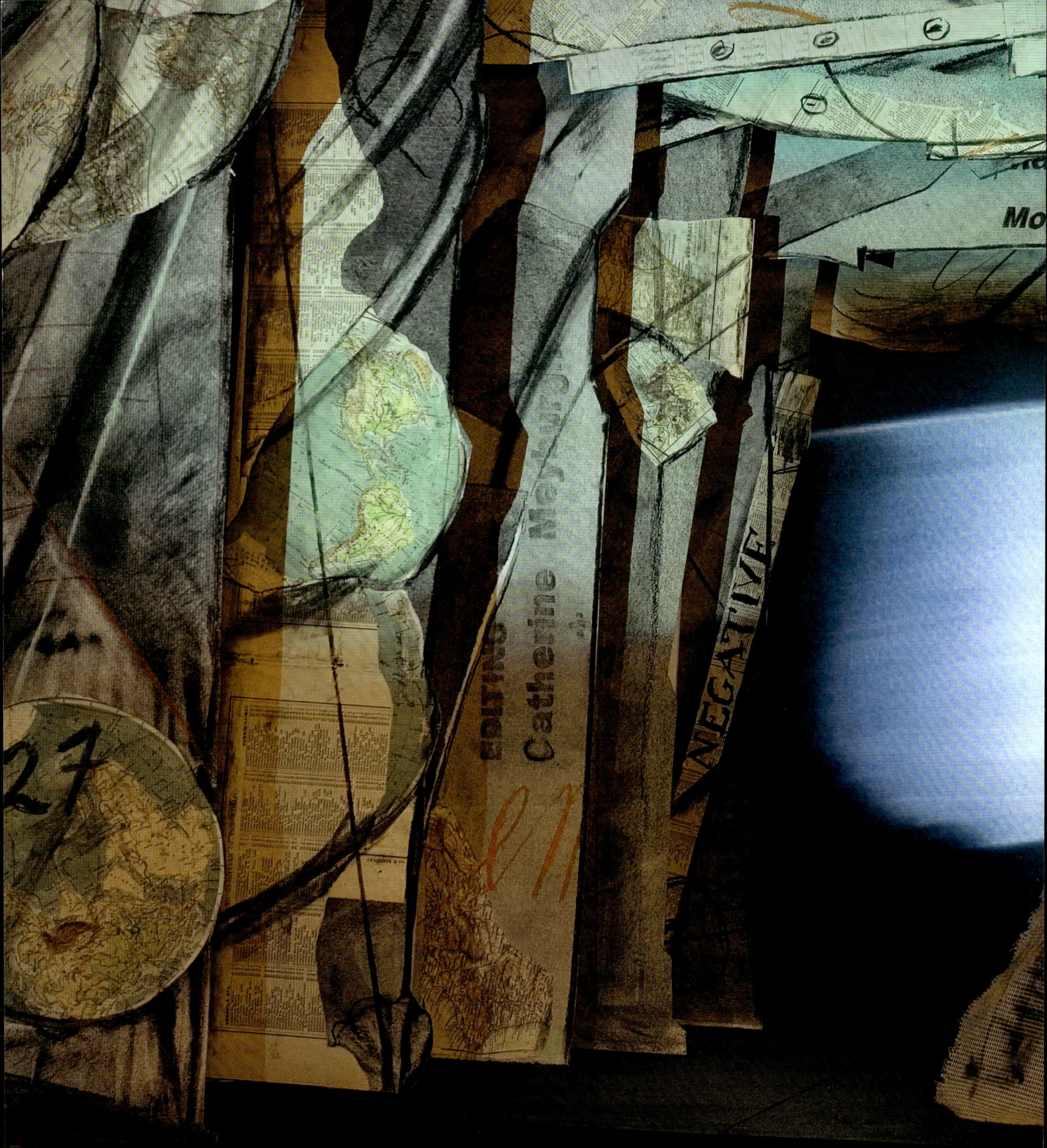
EDITING
Catherine
NEGATIVE
27

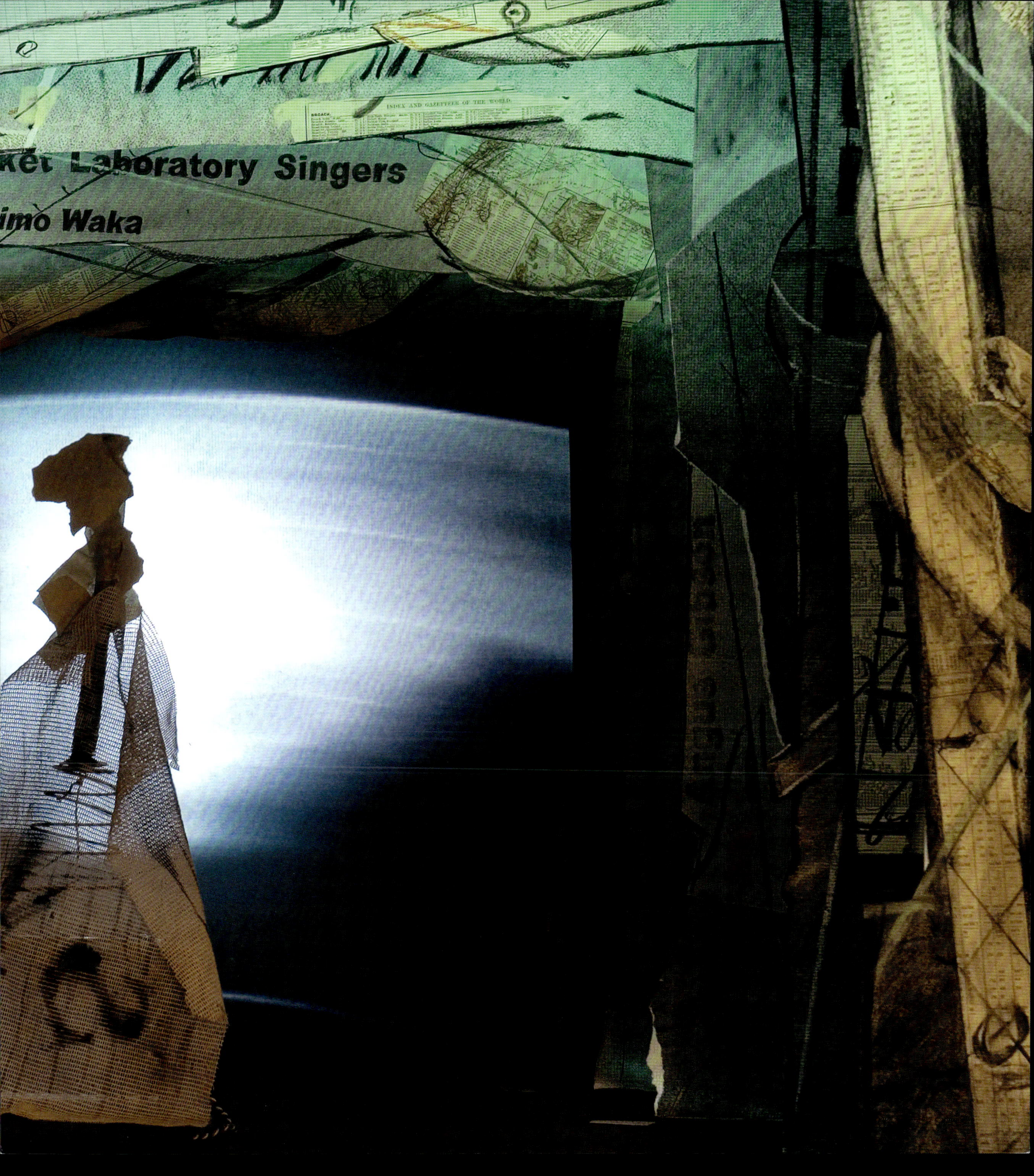
Laboratory Singers
imo Waka

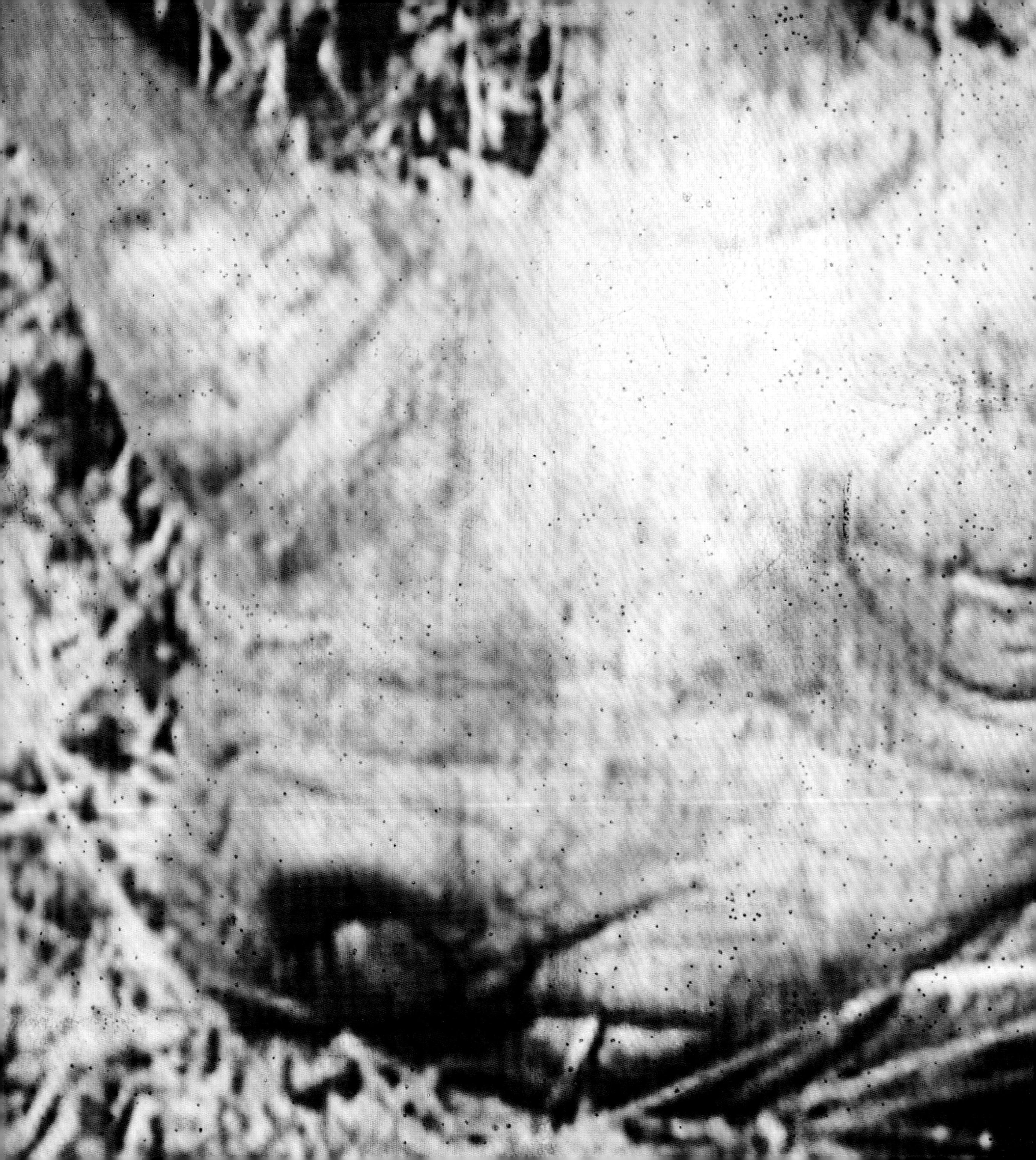

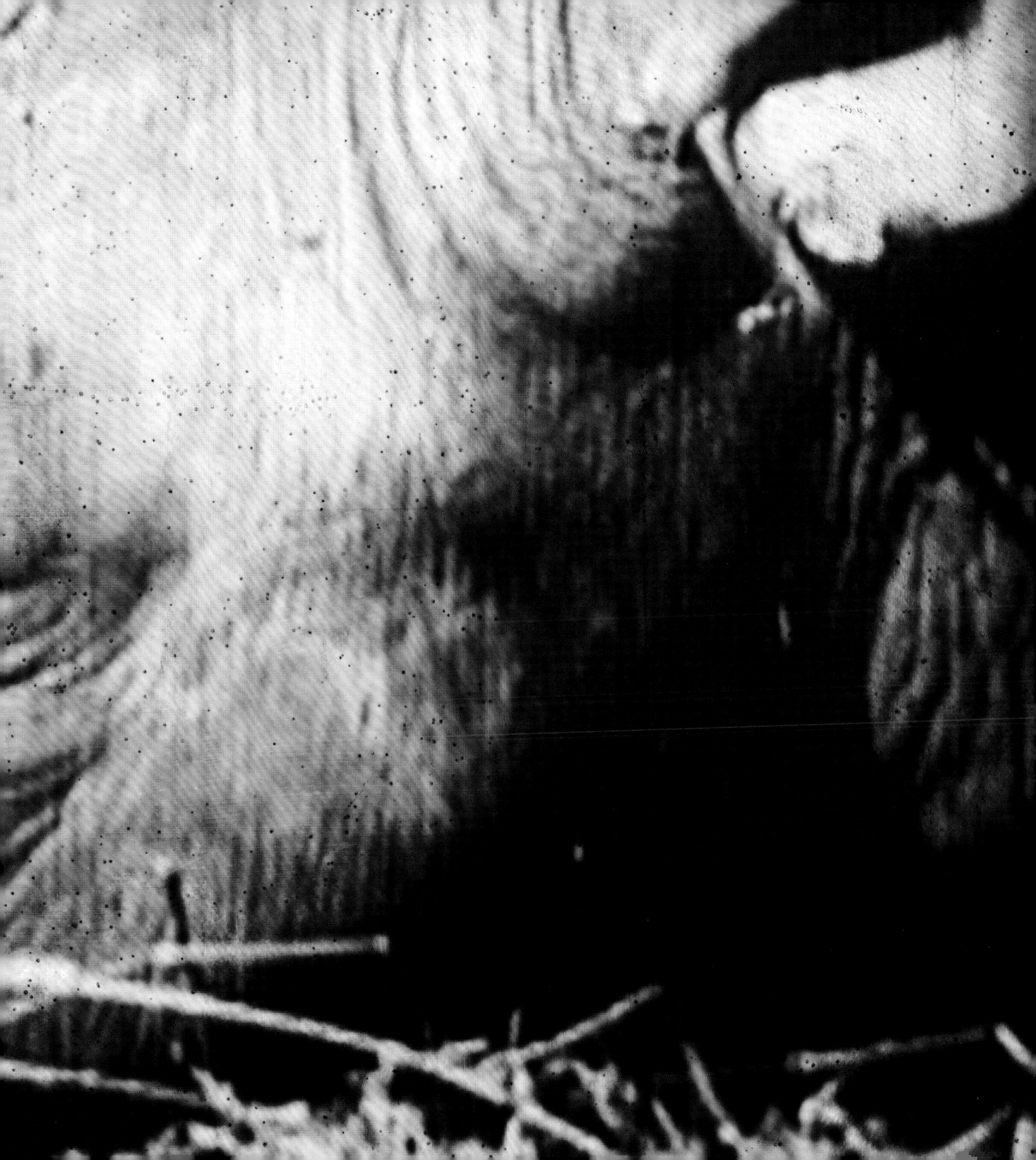

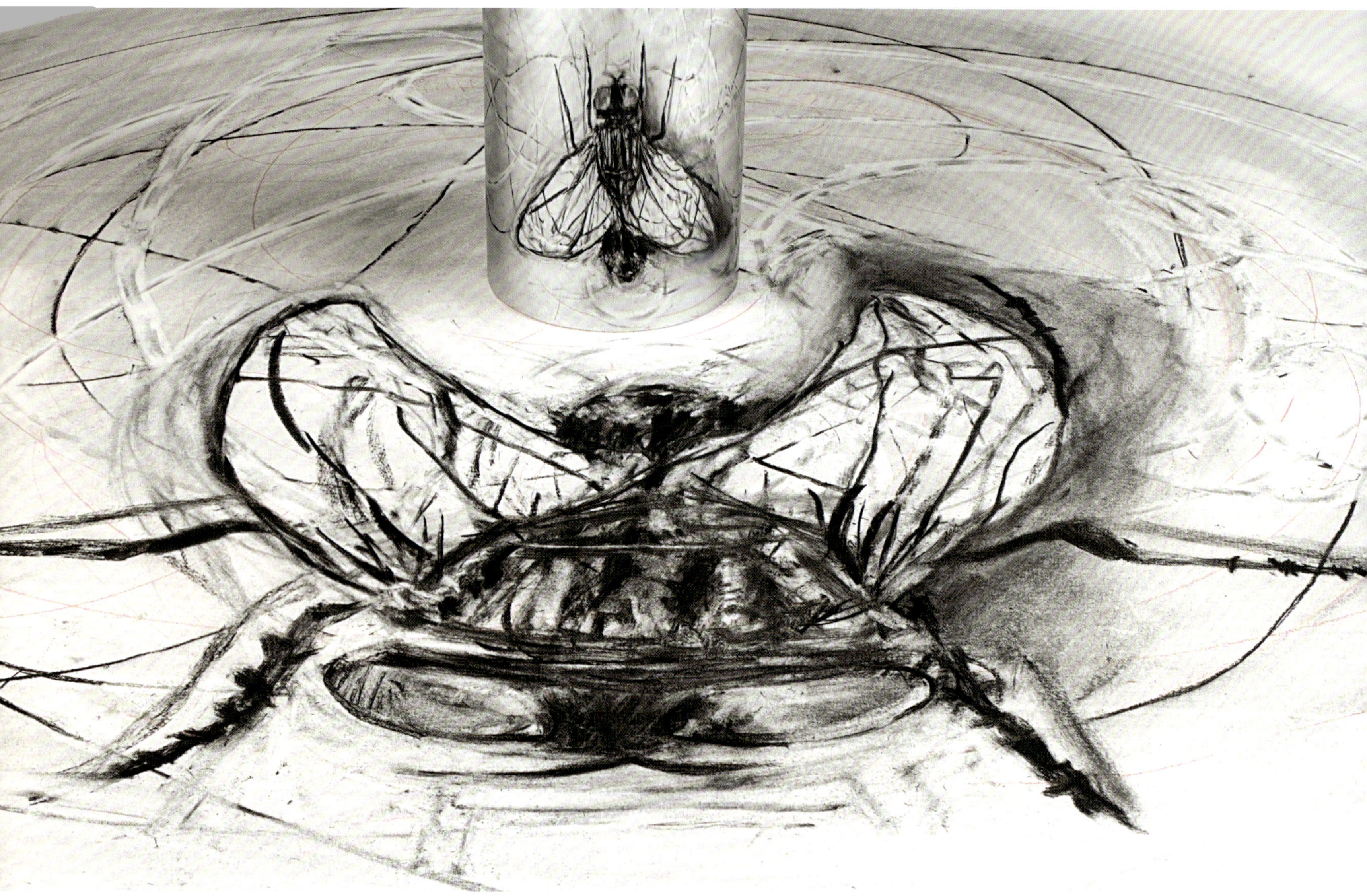

170–72 (THESE PAGES AND FOLLOWING)

***What Will Come (has already come)*, 2007**

Steel table, cylindrical steel mirror, and 35mm animated film transferred to video, 8:40 min.

41 1/4 x 48 x 48 in. (104.7 x 121.9 x 121.9 cm)

Norton Museum of Art, purchase, acquired through the generosity of the Contemporary and Modern Art Council and the R. H. Norton Trust, 2008

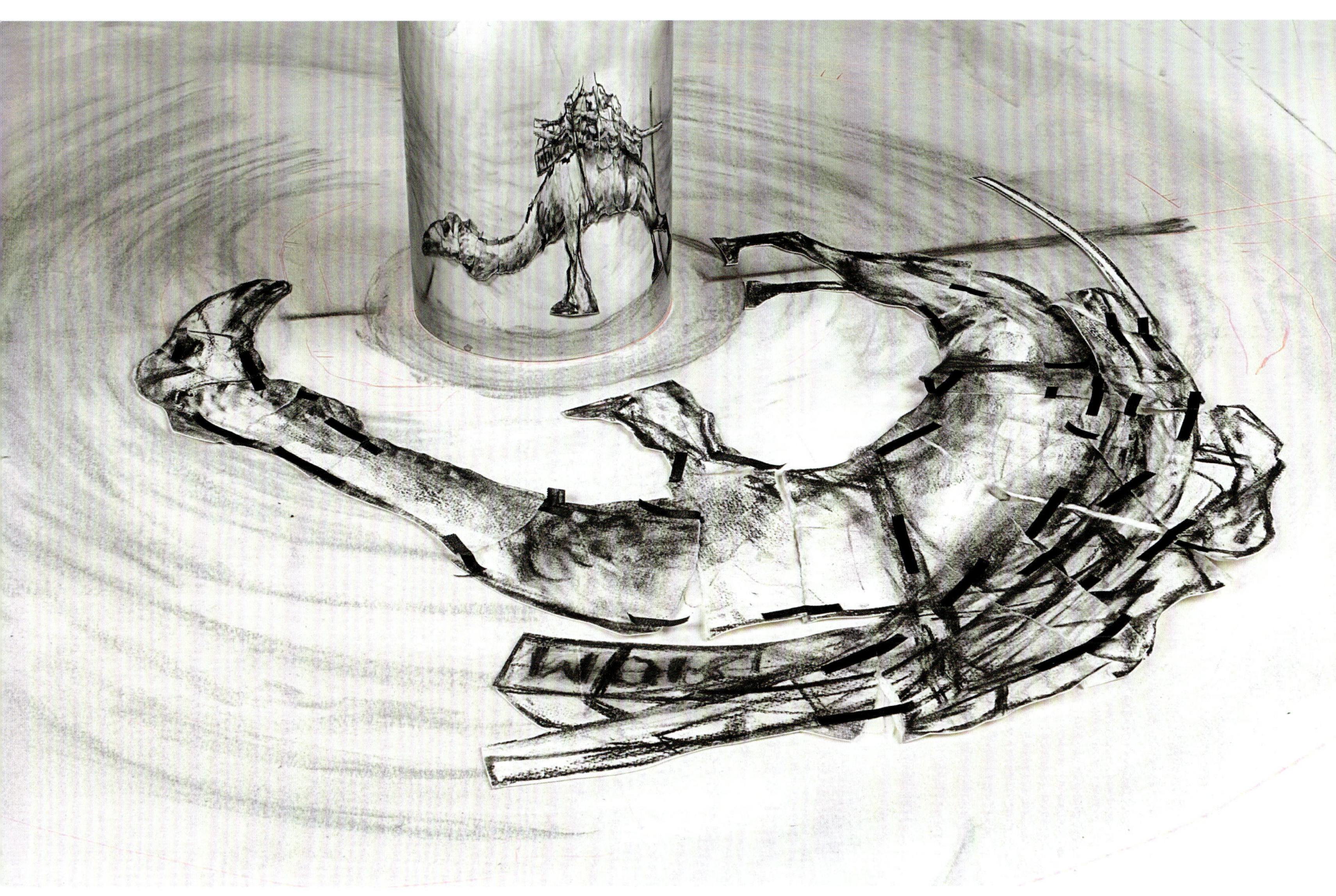

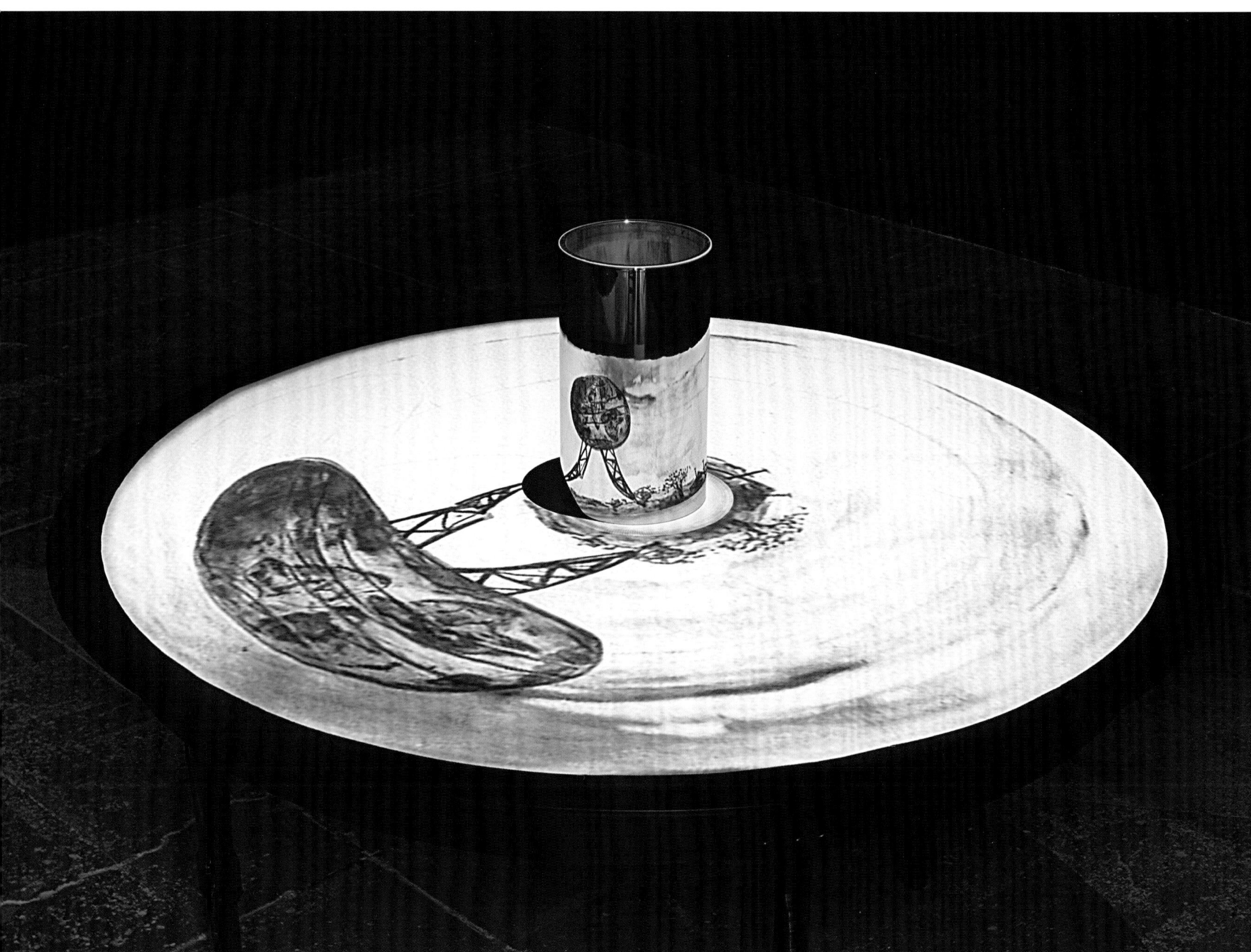

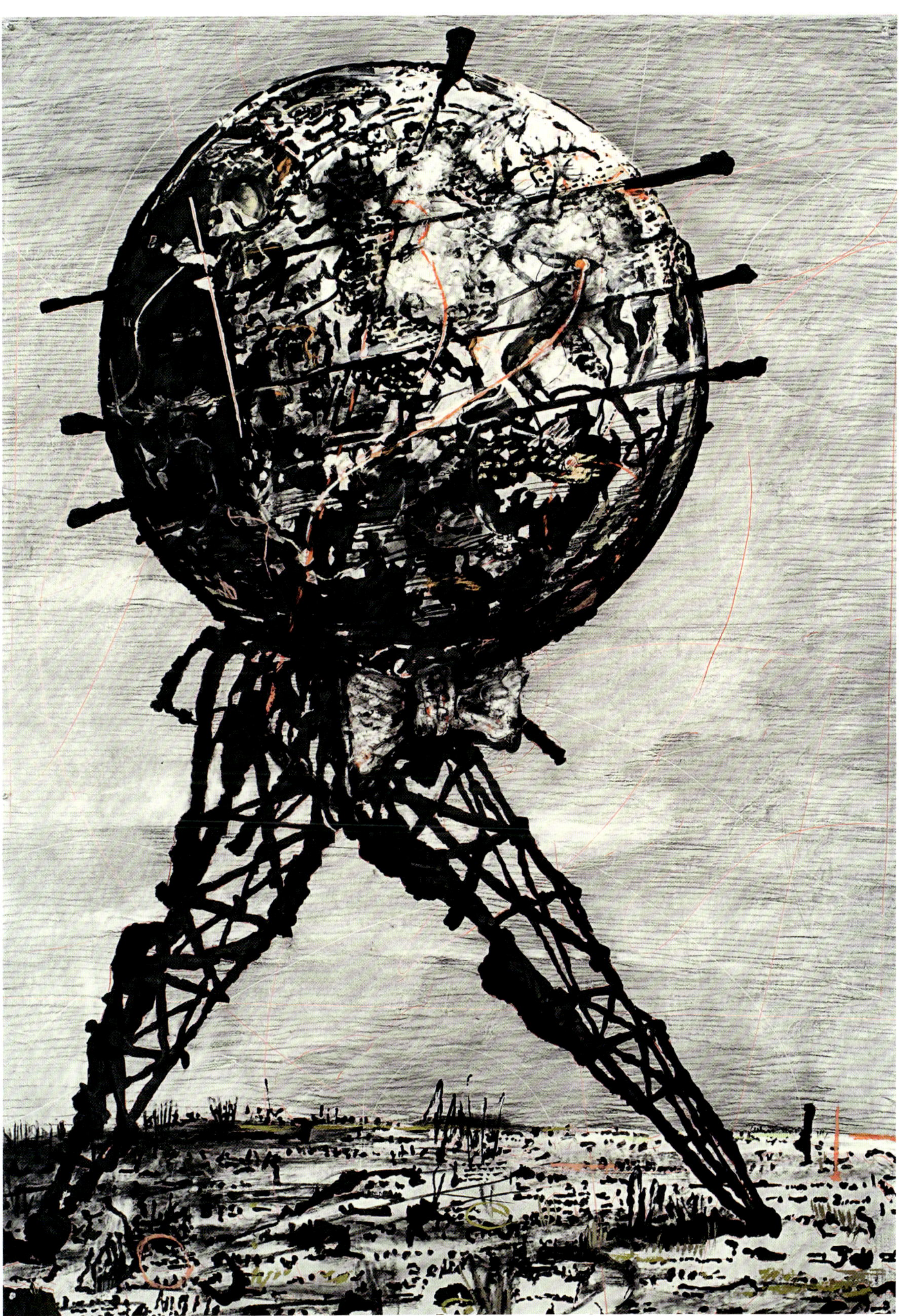

173
Drawing for *Il Sole 24 Ore* [World Walking], 2007
Charcoal, gouache, pastel, and colored pencil on paper
84 x 59 in. (213.5 x 150 cm)
Collection of Doris and Donald Fisher

WALKING THE LINE
DRAWING, PRINTMAKING, AND PERFORMANCE IN THE WORK OF WILLIAM KENTRIDGE

Cornelia H. Butler, Judith B. Hecker,
and Klaus Biesenbach

All fact is an abstraction of something that is inherently moving and changing. There is a sense in which animation deeply connects to my sense of the world as provisional. Whatever is there is liable to change. Certainties can disappear. Emotions felt so unbelievably strongly don't necessarily endure: they shift and change.
—WILLIAM KENTRIDGE, 2008[1]

Drawing, like painting, is today discussed in terms of its rise and fall, its ebbs and flows, the eccentricities of its reception and market. Those of us who nurture its history and discourse speak with reverence about the intimate world we access through the attenuated vision and slowed attention it demands. The recent return of drawing to the forefront of contemporary art practice began in the early 1990s, when the appeal of its immediacy, its undervalued status, and its potential to communicate meaning and subjectivities in a newly globalized world were widely recognized as emblematic of startling innovation in an expanded field. William Kentridge's films—drawings that unfold over time and through prolonged engagement—are emblematic of a moment when our visual world expanded through the representation of the narratives of geopolitics.

If drawing is associated with a kind of authenticity and an almost kinesthetic channeling of an artist's consciousness, Kentridge's process represents a hybrid methodology that is a sign of its time both in its effusive expression of drawing as process and its proposal of a performative, politicized subject for drawing.[2] His work is structured around narrative and yet functions formally as a visual record of the activity of drawing. It is both subject and verb, performance and performed. The peculiar and unforgettable encounter with the artist's films resonates because of this duality and because of the way in which the films record the history of line as it moves across the page. The medium of drawing can be said to have its own tension and interior logic, its modern history characterized by the pendular shift between form and image, the line becoming abstracted and independent of representation. The animated conflation of the two is at the core of Kentridge's production; it is what gives his project of film, drawing, performance, and stage design its power and uniqueness.

1. Quoted in Sally O'Reilly, "Ways of Seeing," *Art Review* 21 (April 2008): 77.

2. Laura Hoptman discusses Franz Ackermann's notion of the emancipation of drawing in her summary of the emergence of drawing as a primary medium in the 1990s. See Hoptman, "The Emancipation of Drawing," in *Drawing Now: Eight Propositions* (New York: Museum of Modern Art, 2002), 167.

Kentridge's films and drawings came to Western audiences at a moment when South Africa's terrible racial history was hurtling toward apartheid's dramatic dissolution. The artist's choice to remain in his homeland coincided with a nascent discussion in the arts concerning the local versus the global and the relative merits of subject matter and forms that could be understood as indigenous or vernacular. What was remarkable about encountering the artist's work in the 1990s was the way in which the screen of the film seemed to map a space of embodied consciousness—the drawings and story unfolding through the process of their own making. The viewer, sensing something familiar, intimate, and even romantic in the character of the artist, is simultaneously disturbed by a deeply unsettling pattern of violence and suffering invented and perpetuated by one's fellow human beings. This rupture of consciousness and perturbation of conscience are at the heart of what Kentridge communicates in his work, the provisional world he describes and captures through the performative line or the exteriorization of emotions and human subjects through the act and accretion of drawing.

The hand of the artist is animated by the line that creates form through a process of revision. The additive process of drawing is turned on its head and what we see is a kind of accumulation in reverse. The drawings on which the films are based are literally erased and reworked between frames; the protagonists are embodied through erasure and negation. As a representation of the process of making, of the consciousness of making, Kentridge's line enacts both the historical rupture and revision that the artist and his country have undergone over time. In *Felix in Exile* (1994; pls. 77–81), the character of Felix Teitlebaum wanders through what seems to be the wasteland of a landscape scarred by death, violence, and sorrow. It is a touching, fragile narrative of the daily life of the everyman.

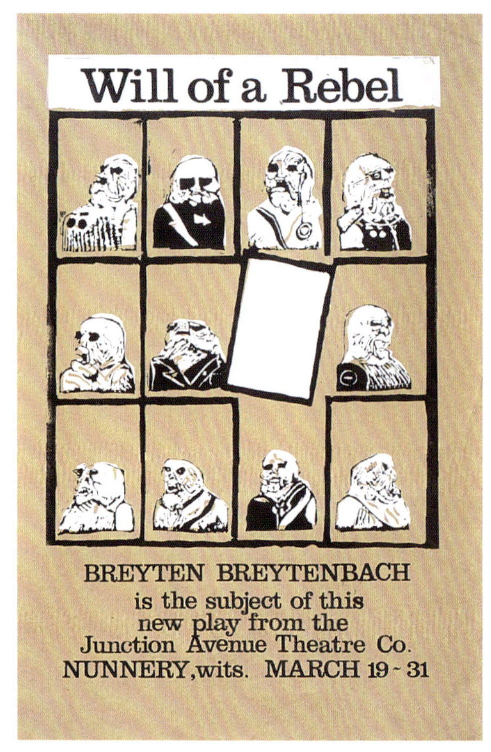

FIG. 36 William Kentridge
***Will of a Rebel*, 1979**
Silkscreen
23 1/4 x 14 3/4 in. (59 x 39.5 cm)
Collection of the artist, courtesy Marian Goodman Gallery, New York, and Goodman Gallery, Johannesburg

PERFORMANCE INTO/OUT OF PRINTMAKING

Performance and printmaking have steadily—and sometimes radically—commingled in Kentridge's work, from his early student days to his most recent operatic productions. In the 1970s, as a founding member of the politically engaged Junction Avenue Theatre Company in Johannesburg, Kentridge was the troupe's principal poster designer; he also designed sets and ultimately both acted in and directed plays. The posters he created in the small print workshop attached to the theater reveal an artist experimenting with motifs from plays and his own developing style, using the straightforward, bold designs that are an outgrowth of silkscreen printing (see fig. 36). This early engagement with theater not only provided a formative opportunity for hands-on activity with printmaking; the theater itself provided fodder for Kentridge's musings on the subjects of performance, space, and audience in other work produced during the period.

Kentridge's first one-person exhibition in 1979 comprised a series of thirty monotypes, entitled *Pit*, that evoke the dark, dramatic space of the theater through their exaggerated verticality, heavy inking, and cropped staging (see pl. 1). In these prints, the performers or models enact simple activities, sometimes disengaged from one another (sipping tea, sunning, swimming) and at other times interacting (modeling for an artist). Several scenes are dreamlike: a woman looking at art while holding a man on a leash, a woman holding a gun while a man reads a book. The audience is sometimes absent, but is often present as a voyeuristic yet faceless array of people overlooking an open-air balcony or gazing through overhead windows. The pitlike atmosphere of the stage derives from the steep walls and the pervasive darkness, which results from the monotype technique itself. Kentridge created these prints by covering a Plexiglas plate entirely in black ink, and then making fine marks by removing areas of ink with his fingertips, tissue paper, cotton balls, and matchsticks[3]; these marks show as light areas when printed on paper. The results are sinister and otherworldly.

3. See Susan Stewart, *William Kentridge: Prints* (Johannesburg: David Krut; Grinnell, IA: Faulconer Gallery, 2006), 24.

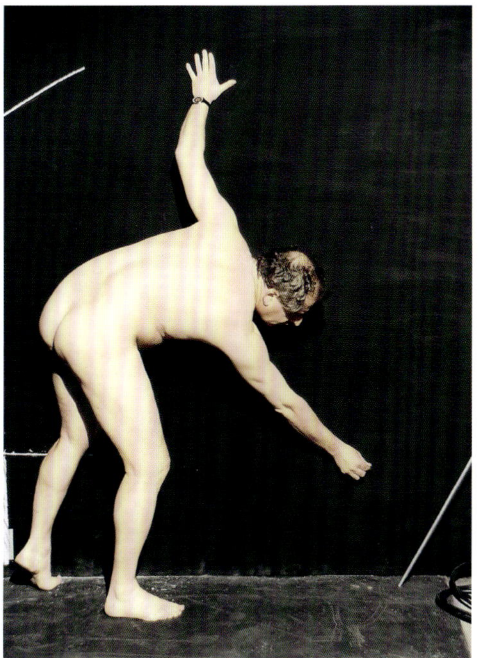

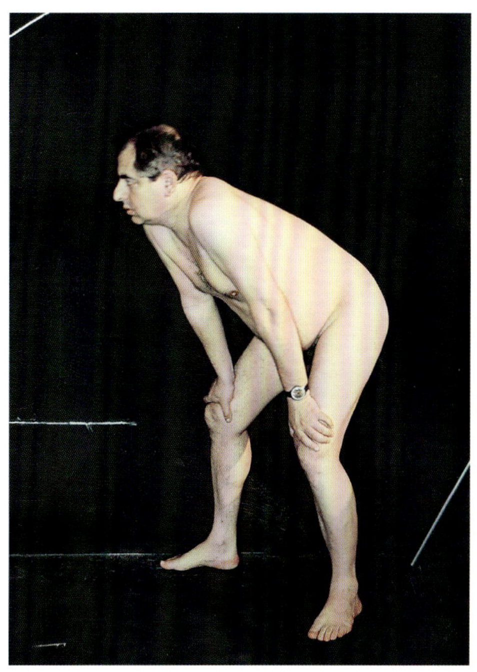

FIGS. 37–38 Kentridge's source photographs for ***Ubu Tells the Truth*** (1996)

Whereas the monotypes established Kentridge's interest in envisioning, in two dimensions, the space of the theater and the interaction of performer and audience, a 1996 portfolio of etchings on the subject of Ubu represents an unusual moment when the artist's prints themselves generated a full-scale theatrical production. Kentridge's earliest involvement with the subject of Ubu was as an actor in the Junction Avenue company's 1975 staging of *Ubu Rex,* an adaptation of the French dramatist Alfred Jarry's 1896 *Ubu Roi*. Years later, on the centenary of Jarry's production, Kentridge revisited the subject through the format of the print portfolio. Jarry's play, a satirical expression of the life of a brutal despot, became a potent metaphor for the barbaric system of apartheid in South Africa.

The set of eight etchings, titled *Ubu Tells the Truth* (pls. 112–19), is among Kentridge's most technically rich and thematically potent print projects. The prints comprise layered impressions of two different plates that combine to produce the illusion of two realities. The cartoonlike white chalkboard line of Ubu's world derives from an engraved plate; this image is printed over a more textured human counterpart created using etching (including fingerprints), aquatint, and drypoint. As the human figure showers, draws, sleeps, scratches, dances, and bicycles, the rotund Ubu mimics these actions in his own exaggerated, grotesque way. It is relevant to note that Kentridge based the human figure in these etchings on photographs he took of himself performing against a black backdrop in the studio (see figs. 37–38): "I decided I might as well enact those poses myself. I placed the camera, with a self-timer, on one side of the studio, and I performed Ubu in front of the blackboard."[4] The use of performance in the process of making the prints underscores the merging of media so characteristic of Kentridge's work; it also elucidates his apt choice of the print portfolio, with its traditionally serial format, as the medium for conveying this action-based, narrative subject.

4. Carolyn Christov-Bakargiev, "Interview," in *William Kentridge*, by Dan Cameron, Carolyn Christov-Bakargiev, and J. M. Coetzee (London: Phaidon, 1999), 31.

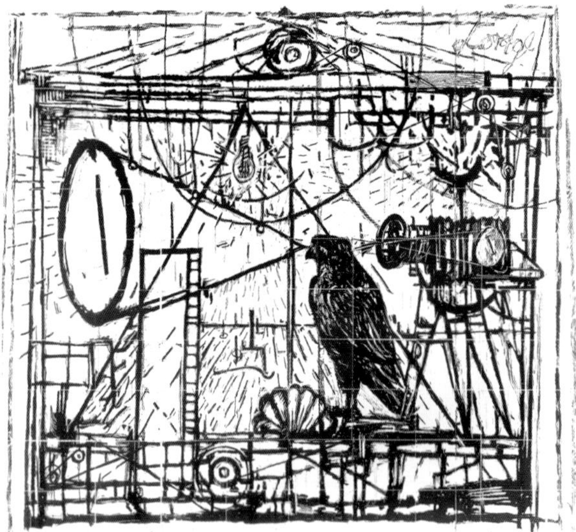

FIG. 39 William Kentridge
***Learning the Flute*, 2004**
Letterpress, ed. of 18
110 7/8 x 139 5/8 in. (281.6 x 354.6 cm)
Collection of the artist, courtesy Marian Goodman Gallery, New York, and Goodman Gallery, Johannesburg

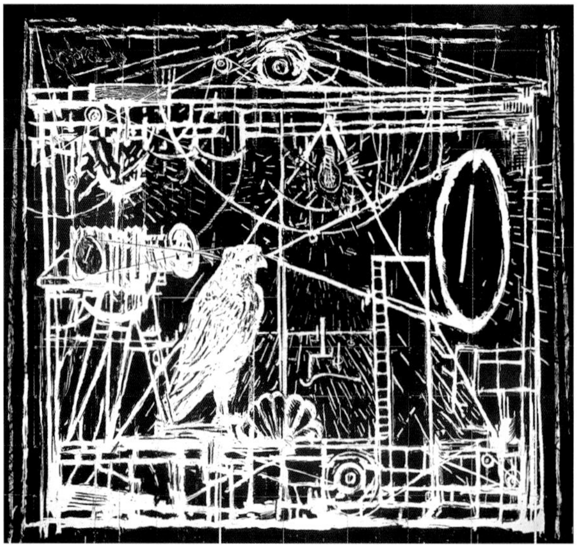

FIG. 40 William Kentridge
***Learning the Flute (Reverse)*, 2004**
Photolithograph, ed. of 18
110 7/8 x 139 5/8 in. (281.6 x 354.6 cm)
Collection of the artist, courtesy Marian Goodman Gallery, New York, and Goodman Gallery, Johannesburg

In the footsteps of his *Ubu* etchings, Kentridge produced the play *Ubu and the Truth Commission* (1996), a collaboration with Handspring Puppet Company and the writer Jane Taylor. He also created the animated film *Ubu Tells the Truth* (1997; figs. 10–11, 21, pls. 120–29) and a series of related drawings (1997–98; pls. 130–34). Kentridge's most direct statement on the atrocities of apartheid, the *Ubu and the Truth Commission* play explores personal stories of apartheid-era violence and victimization made public during Truth and Reconciliation Commission hearings. Visual motifs from the prints and their themes of interrogation, flagellation, shame, and guilt became the jumping-off points for the play.[5] Kentridge notes that the idea of combining an actor onstage with a schematic white-line projection on a screen behind the actor stemmed directly from the overlapping figures in the *Ubu* prints.[6] Significantly, although discussions of a theatrical performance were not initiated until after the etchings were completed, the artist inscribed each print with fictitious act and scene numbers, seen in the corners or at the edges of each composition.

A more recent instance of prints and performance mutually informing and inspiring one another came as Kentridge developed his 2005 production of Mozart's opera *The Magic Flute*. During this time he created a large body of preparatory work that included an outpouring of prints along with drawings, films, and a miniature theater (see pls. 149–62). In these projects Kentridge explored the opera's themes of lightness and darkness, as embodied by the Queen of the Night (associated with obscurity and the moon) and her antagonist Sarastro (associated with insight and the sun). As he began to experiment with the opposition of black-and-white imagery in his work, Kentridge seized upon printmaking's inherent qualities of reversal and variation to create a massive multipart edition entitled *Learning the Flute* (2004; figs. 39–40). For the project Kentridge made a nine-foot black ink drawing on clear acetate and then worked with a master printer to produce two prints that mirror each other in composition and coloration. Both prints were executed with black ink, but in the second one not only is the image mirrored, the inking is also reversed: areas of white, uninked paper in the first print become areas of black ink, while the black areas in the first print become

5. See Rory Doepel, *Ubu: ±101* (Johannesburg: French Institute of South Africa/University of the Witwatersrand, 1997), for background on the genesis of the *Ubu* work and a more detailed discussion of the prints and performance.

6. See Stewart, *William Kentridge: Prints*, 60.

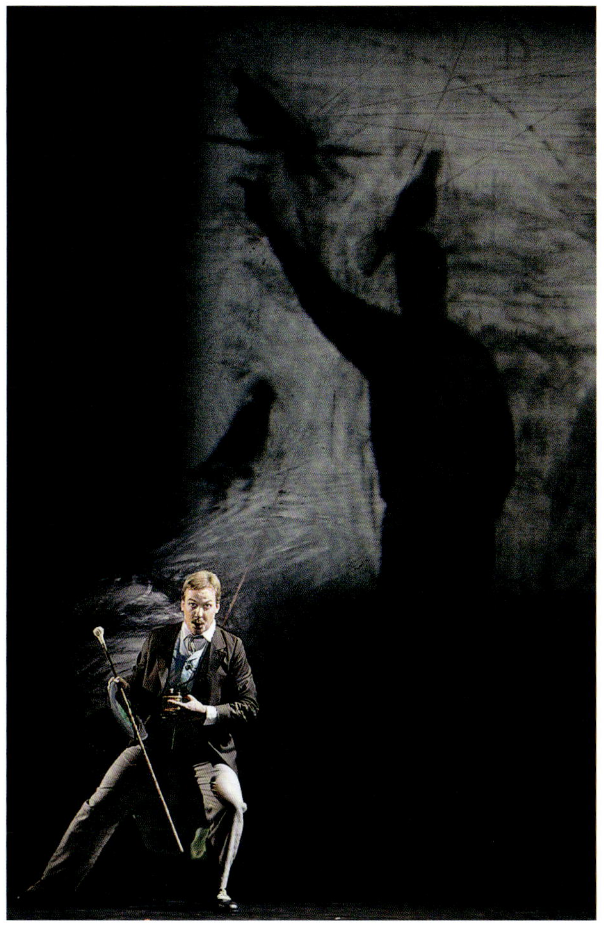

FIG. 41 A scene from Kentridge's staging of the opera ***The Magic Flute*** (2005) at La Monnaie/De Munt, Brussels, 2005

white paper. Making matters more multifaceted, Kentridge chose to print half of the prints on unbound pages from a 1950 edition of *Chambers's Encyclopaedia* and half on plain white sheets of paper cut to the size of the unbound encyclopedia pages. A complex and laborious technical feat of printmaking, the project is also thematically intricate. Images of pyramids, temples, falcons, and the like—motifs from Kentridge's *The Magic Flute* and from encyclopedias—underscore the sense of history bound to the opera. Kentridge's exploitation of positive and negative imagery and coloration, meanwhile, speaks directly to the themes of light and darkness at the opera's philosophical core.

From his earliest projects, Kentridge has consistently inserted his likeness into his work—his body as an actual model for work or his life as an indirect point of reference. Considering that he began his career in part as a stage actor, it is logical to think that he would, at some later point, reassert himself onstage. In his background projection for the opera *The Magic Flute,* we see the artist's moving silhouette—just a step removed from live performance itself (see fig. 41). It is fitting that Kentridge turned to printmaking to continue investigating this coupling of performance and creation. In 2006 he created a portfolio of ten prints entitled *Bird Catching* and based on *The Magic Flute* opera. Here we see Kentridge standing onstage, drawing, interacting with birds, and morphing into a torn paper collage. This merging of Kentridge's roles as artist, performer, and subject remains at the forefront of his practice, revealing the artist as actor coming full circle.

THE PERFORMING/ MOVING IMAGE

In the spring of 2008 Kentridge was busy rehearsing a performance that would debut at the Biennale of Sydney a few months later. The artist had filmed himself drawing on the main wall of his workspace, then projected this video onto the very same wall. During the rehearsal he walked across his studio and stood in front of the wall, beside the projected image of himself—the artist himself interacting with the filmic self represented by the moving image. The end product of superimposed, multiplied images was meant to be realized in front of a live audience.

During the actual performance in Sydney, titled *I am not me, the horse is not mine* (figs. 13, 17, 42), viewers could see up to four different Kentridges—three prerecorded projections and one live—gesturing, acting, and lecturing. As Kentridge intends to perform this piece regularly in the future, it will become a sort of portrait of Dorian Gray—Kentridge, the aging live actor, appearing alongside his projected younger self. The body of the performer of course casts a shadow over the projected image, a phenomenon that had already occurred when Kentridge acted for the camera to create the first layers of the portraits. According to the artist:

> A shadow is superficially like a silhouette, a dark two-dimensional trace of a being, its movements directly connected to the movements of the dancer. But there is a big shift. A shadow is a silhouette with *attitude*. As the light source is moved in relation to the subject, the shadow changes. It is still of course directly connected to its source, but elongations and compressions occur.[7]

The shadow assumes a life of its own by taking on properties independent of the performer. In the film *Shadow Procession* (1999; pls. 135–43), the silhouettes of torn paper forms march toward an unknown destination. When the work is presented, the viewer's own physical presence casts a shadow onto the projected image, instantly becoming a moving, active part of the parade. The layers Kentridge describes—"a dance, a shadow of a dance... a shadow of the shadow of the dance"[8]—are conflated.

A much younger Kentridge appears in his first stop-motion animation, *Vetkoek/Fête Galante* (1985), in which he follows a blank surface through the process of his self-proclaimed "poor-man's animation," using charcoal drawings, collages, and live actors.[9] The white background undergoes many changes, drawings, tears, and layerings as the setting for "The Battle of Yes and No"—a parable in which the two become one. Drawing for stop-motion animation is always an intense process, but the performative act of turning the page (or, to be more precise, *changing* the page—erasing and adding to the image that will be photographed) is normally left out. Instead of excluding from the viewer's gaze the act of manipulating the image, Kentridge reveals the before and after of the shot, showing himself and his fellow actors working on the moving image. In another early film, *Exhibition* (1987), the phrase "opening the exhibition" precedes a series of drawings presented in a slide-show format. Kentridge performs the role of the artist in a scene captioned "the artist explains his work" (later we discover that "his explanation was not accepted"). In a telling interval the phrase "this too will pass" is written and then erased a moment later.

7. William Kentridge, "Country Dances I (Shadow)/Country Dances II (Paper)," in *William Kentridge: I Am Not Me, the Horse Is Not Mine*, by William Kentridge et al. (Johannesburg and Cape Town: Goodman Gallery Editions, 2008), 29.

8. Ibid.

9. The film may be viewed on the DVD that accompanies this catalogue.

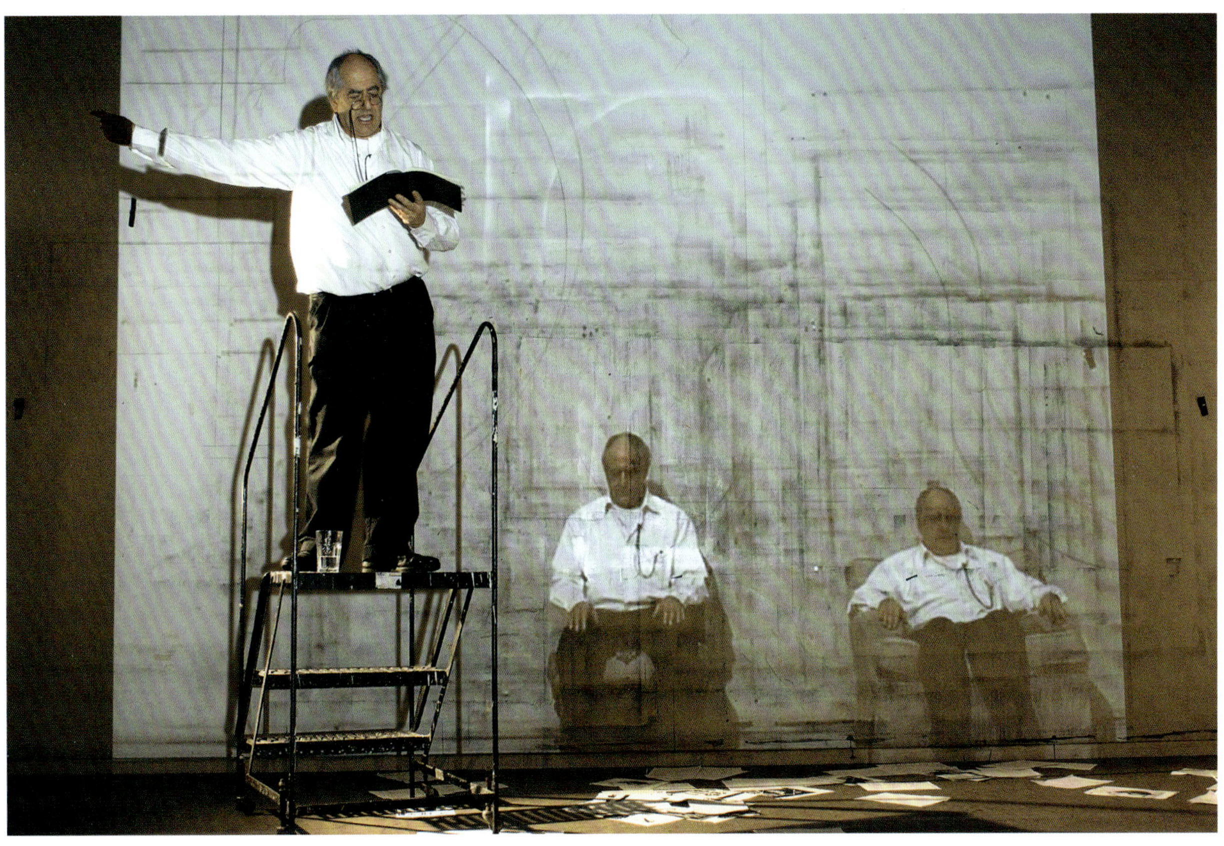

FIG. 42 Kentridge performing ***I am not me, the horse is not mine*** (2008) at the Biennale of Sydney, 2008

In 2003 Kentridge depicted himself in a suite of seven short films entitled *7 Fragments for Georges Méliès* (2003; figs. 44–46, 53–55, pls. 8–27). The French filmmaker Méliès pioneered the use of effects such as stop-motion and time-lapse photography, dissolves, and hand-painted color to transform reality via film. Rather than recording the "real," he constructed backdrops in his studio and staged the acting in front of them. In his homage to Méliès, Kentridge uses drawing, sculpture, animation, and film to portray himself as the main protagonist in a series of studies of life in the studio. In one fragment the artist emerges from a charcoal drawing; the film is reversed, creating the illusion that he is repairing a torn self-portrait. Once the drawing has been put back together, he exits the studio before emerging from the drawn image again. In the context of contemporary art, the motif of the artist in the atelier calls to mind the early videos and films of Bruce Nauman, whose musings and repetitive exercises in the studio have become seminal images of performative experimentation. Kentridge referenced Nauman directly in a 2005 interview: "There's one narrative film that's a version of [Méliès's] famous journey to the moon. It comes out of the lecture I did at Dia on Bruce Nauman, out of looking at Nauman's early films where he is walking round and round his studio.... There's obviously a similarity to Méliès in his studio as seen against his painted backdrops."[10] Whereas Nauman stomps about the studio as though waiting for an idea to come to him, making the creative process the subject of the work, Kentridge shows himself drawing, acting, and moving, portraying the act of art making as a performative process that both passes and visualizes time.

10. Cheryl Kaplan, "The Time-Image," *PAJ: A Journal of Performance Art* 27, no. 80 (May 2005): 37.

Kentridge studied mime and acting at the École Jacques Lecoq in Paris in the early 1980s; his acting credits include a variety of productions at theaters in Johannesburg. He has said that he knew right away that he did not have the skills to make it as an actor: "I knew very early on I would never be a performer."[11] But he has also conceded to learning much more about what it is to make a work of art from his time studying the theater than from any of his fine arts training. It is significant that the recurring characters of Felix, the romantic, contemplative artist and existentialist, and Soho, the rapacious businessman, can be read as surrogates for Kentridge himself; they resemble him physically and allegorically live out aspects of his biography, enacting or reperforming events from his own lifetime, memories, and dreams. In a sense, Kentridge is performing through these ambiguously constructed avatars; he uses his self-portrait over and over again. Other protagonists bear striking similarities to individuals that are close to him in real life.

In the space between writing, drawing, and daily experience are the puppets that Kentridge has repeatedly made use of in his artistic practice. He elaborates, "I've learned a huge amount from theatre. I came to the puppets with a lot of that thinking."[12] The puppets, created by a company with which Kentridge has often collaborated, operate in a space between live performance and an imagined sequence of drawing. A puppet is one step removed from an actor—a three-dimensional drawing set in motion. In the work that is developing out of his staging of Dmitri Shostakovich's opera *The Nose,* scheduled to premiere at the Metropolitan Opera, New York, in 2010, the character of the Nose is represented as a puppet and with a mask, functioning both as subject and prop.

Kentridge has pointed out that opera has a unique capacity to slow time; a performer might hold a single note or sing about one instant for many minutes.[13] Presented in a conventionally theatrical environment, many of his recent endeavors have adapted the operatic form—consider, for instance, his interpretation of Claudio Monteverdi's opera *Il ritorno d'Ulisse in patria* (1998; fig. 43) and *Zeno at 4 A.M.* (2001), productions that combine actors, musicians, puppets, and projections of moving images (a kind of theater within a theater). Most recently, in 2005, he took on a large-scale production of Mozart's *The Magic Flute.* Kentridge has managed to transfer the slowness and duration of these epic productions to works intended for the gallery environment, where a shorter attention span is generally demanded of the viewer. His multilayered animations, as time-based narratives and as products of a laborious production process, expand a moment in time before it is essentially over.

11. Ibid., 33.
12. Ibid., 34.
13. See ibid., 44.

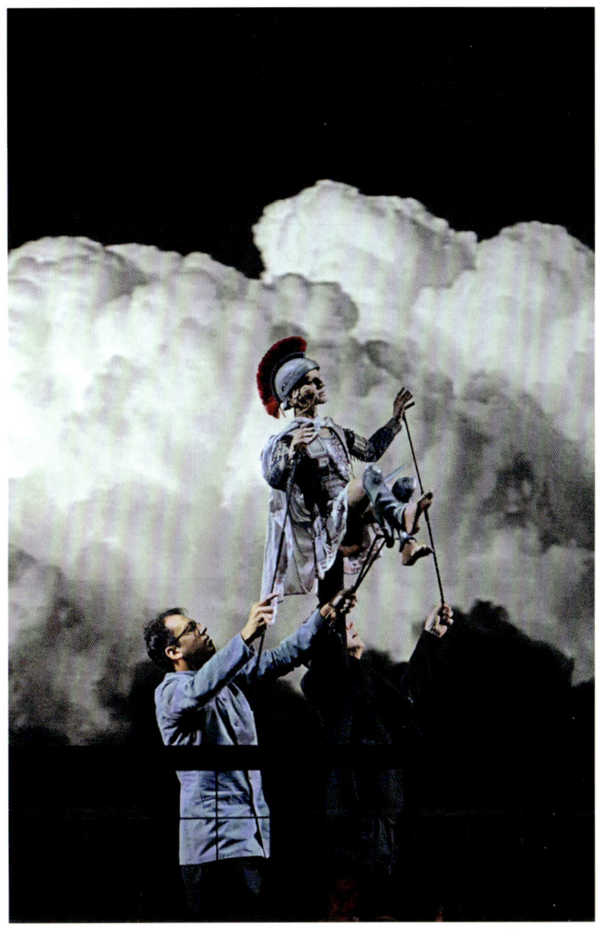

FIG. 43 A scene from Kentridge's staging of the opera ***Il Ritorno d'Ulisse*** (1998) at Teatro La Fenice, Venice, Italy, 2008

For Jacques Derrida, "The act of writing...is precisely the production of traces."[14] Even as we write, we erase. Applying the same idea to performance, the farther along we are in the act, the closer we are to the end. There is an intrinsic (sad, ironic) mortality in performance—as it grows and swells it moves closer and closer to extinction. Kentridge conveys the passage of time in many of his animations through the technique of erasure. He draws a key frame, erases certain areas, and redraws them to create the next frame, thereby signaling the impression of movement. He leaves visible the traces or shadows of what has been erased—physical remnants of past actions and vestiges of his process. As Kentridge points out, "The activity of drawing is a way of trying to understand who we are or how we operate in the world.... [It] is a slow motion version of thought."[15]

A successful performance is often described as timeless. Kentridge's directorial ability to suggest vastness in a finite moment similarly liberates his films, theatrical productions, and kinetic sculptural works from the constraints of time. Even an illusory construction such as *What Will Come (has already come)* (2007; fig. 18, pls. 170–72), in which a mirrored cylinder at the center of projected anamorphic images deciphers and completes the distorted visual information, is cyclical and seemingly endless. Each time a rotation is made the content changes, but the beginning and end are conflated, making the work essentially timeless.

In his performance *I am not me, the horse is not mine,* Kentridge simultaneously functions as the author and as a performer interpreting the instructions of the other Kentridge (the director). These are precisely the kind of complexly layered roles that are interwoven in the artist's operas and other theatrical productions. In *The Magic Flute* the musical instrument is a magical tool, the means through which art can make an impact on the world. Kentridge's own tools, whether charcoal, pastel, or pencil, are just as magical, creating and leaving traces that stay alive long after the performance has ended. As in Méliès's *Le voyage dans la lune* (A Trip to the Moon, 1902), Kentridge's world is a collage of painted and drawn backgrounds, of models and puppets, but he himself is ultimately the most real player in it.

14. Mieke Bal and Norman Bryson, "Semiotics and Art History," *The Art Bulletin* 73, no. 2 (June 1991): 190.

15. Quoted in Arthur C. Danto, "Drawing for Projection," *The Nation* 273, no. 3 (July 16, 2001): 43.

5

LEARNING FROM THE ABSURD

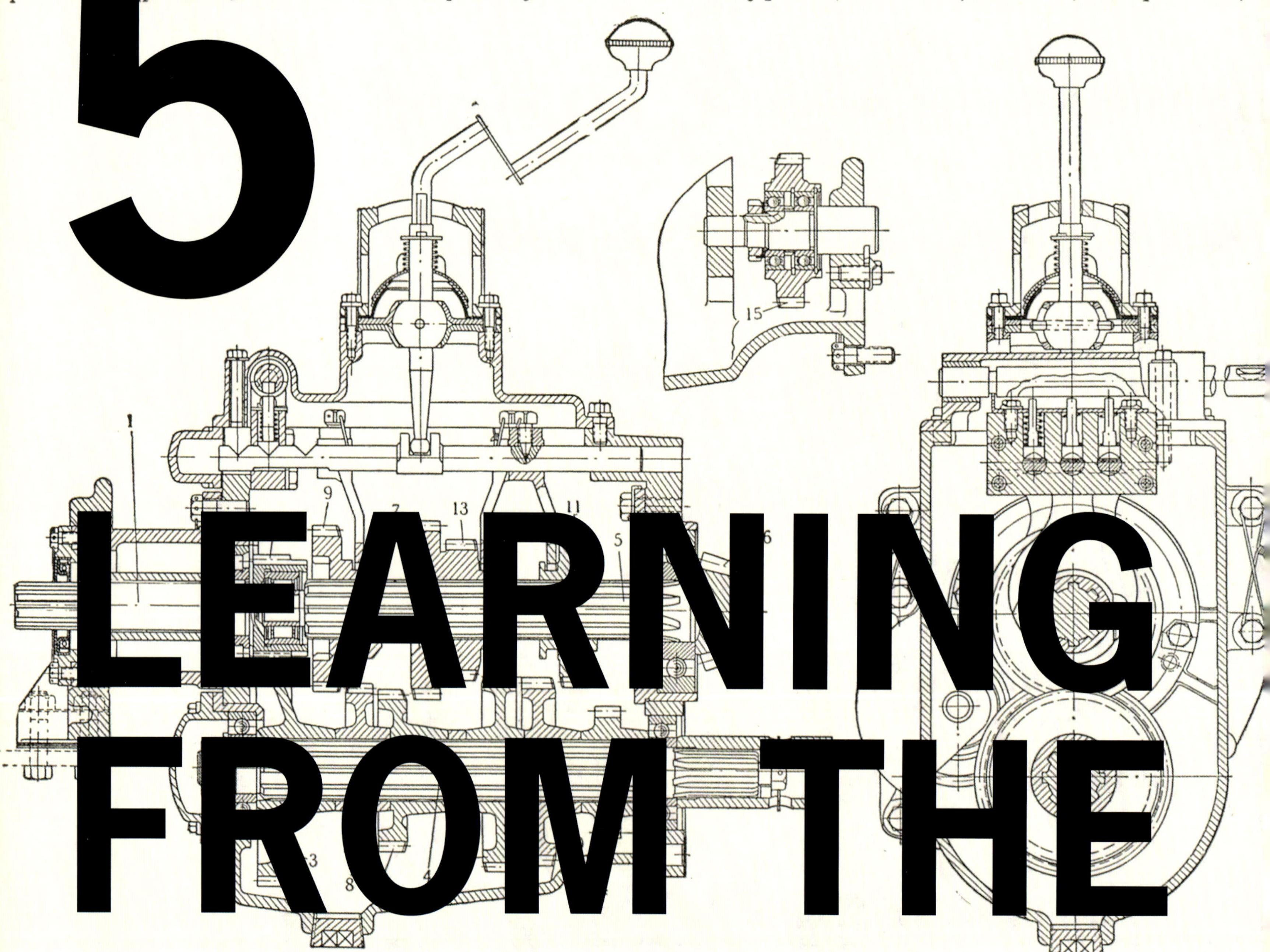

THE NOSE

A man wakes one morning and finds his nose gone. He attempts to track it down through the streets of his city, going to the police, placing newspaper advertisements for its return, seeking medical advice. When he does meet his nose (in a cathedral) he realizes to his dismay that his nose is of a higher rank than he is. His own nose will not speak to him. When his nose is arrested (trying to leave the city in disguise), it still will not rejoin his face. But one morning he wakes and the nose is back in place.

This is the substance of the short story "The Nose," published by Nikolai Gogol in 1836. His story had as one of its roots a section of Laurence Sterne's 1759 novel *Tristram Shandy*, which includes an episode of a man who loses his nose. Sterne in turn had an antecedent in Miguel de Cervantes's *Don Quixote*, published in 1605. There is a strand of sober absurdism that runs through all three authors, who use the impossible and fantastic as a central narrative device. It is a strand that comes from the edges to the center of the stage in twentieth-century modernism. This trajectory of the absurd exploded into twentieth-century Russian modernism in 1930, when Gogol's short story was turned into an opera by Dimitri Shostakovich. (The opera was a popular success but was suppressed shortly after its opening.)

I am not me, the horse is not mine takes Gogol's short story, its literary forebears, and its possible future histories as the basis for looking at the formal inventiveness of the different strains of Russian modernism, and also at the calamitous end of the Russian avant-garde.

The work for the eight projections was done as preparation for a production of Shostakovich's opera. It is initially about a nose on the loose, or a nose with locomotion (in most cases a paper nose superimposed on top of a filmed body). But I was also looking at old film material from the Soviet Union in the 1920s and 1930s. A workshop with student actors in Johannesburg furnished many of the silhouettes used. On top of projections of these human figures I added or interposed paper cutouts, trying to find a link between the constructivist language of El Lissitzky and the earthy vocabulary of the Russian filmmakers and writers such as Maxim Gorky. These were languages that at the time were very different, even antithetical, but that in hindsight are joined by a sense of openness, of possibility, of forming something new—of agency. As if the upheavals of the 1917 revolution could provide an energy for new images, words, language. At the time it seemed the paths could run parallel, but now we know that even in 1918 Lenin was looking for "reliable antifuturists," and that the red wedge that would defeat the white circle would soon be swept away, too.

I am not me, the horse is not mine is an elegy (perhaps loud for an elegy) both for the formal artistic language that was crushed in the 1930s and for the possibilities of human transformation that so many hoped for and believed in during the revolution.

There is a transcript of some meetings of the plenum of the Central Committee of the Communist Party of the Soviet Union in which Nikolai Bukharin, a close lieutenant of Lenin, is fighting for his political and physical life. The title of the projections comes from these transcripts. It is a Russian peasant saying used to deny all guilt. It is not what the owner of the nose would say of his nose, but it is what his nose would say of him.

There is a dark comedy in the failure of Bukharin's language to work any more—and in the laughter provoked by his most passionate pleas. The most grotesque absurdism only approaches this theater. Only the absurd—the rupturing of expected causes and results, the rupturing of expected order in the world—seems able to depict this reality. **WK**

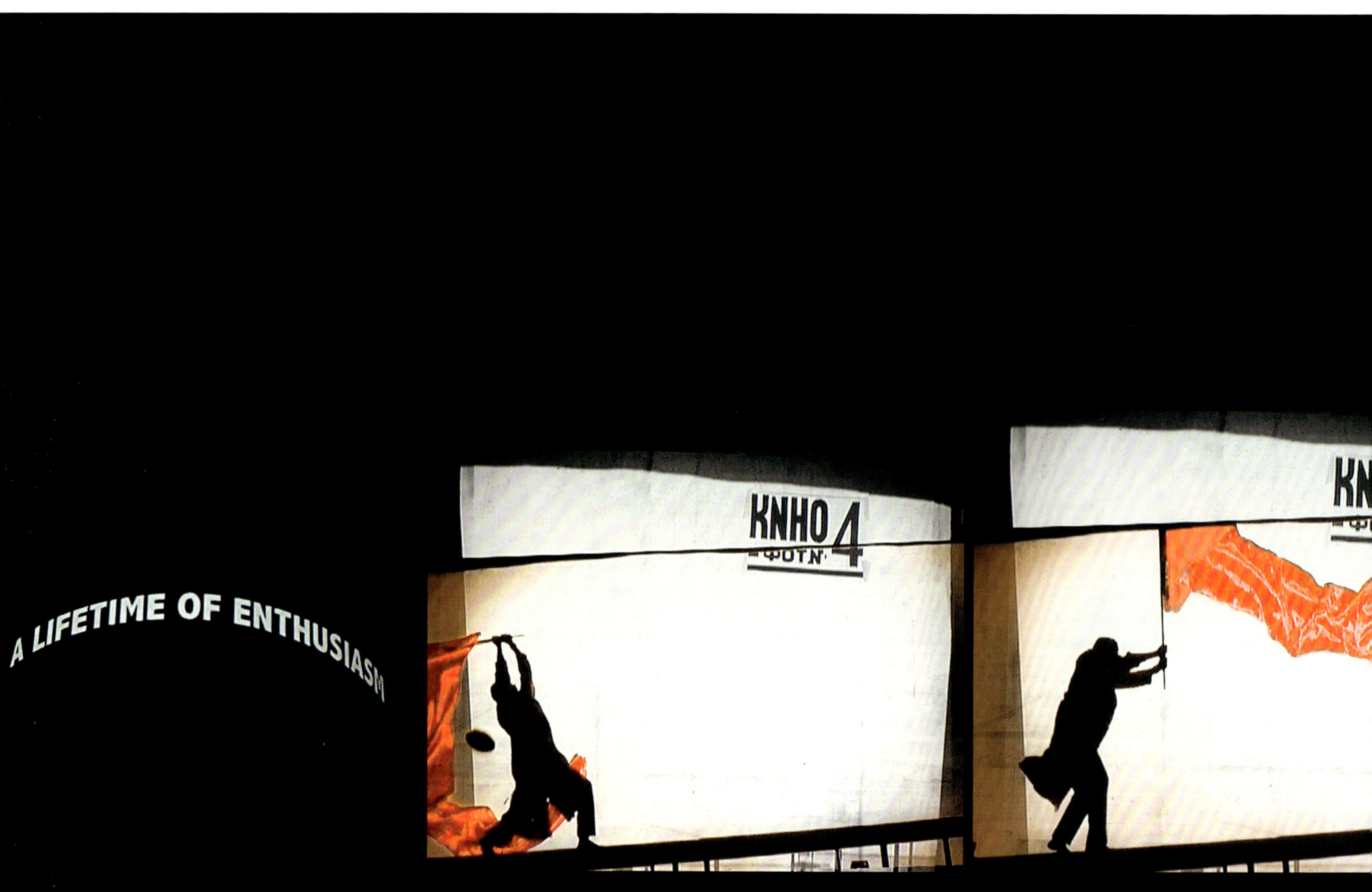
A LIFETIME OF ENTHUSIASM
KNHO 4

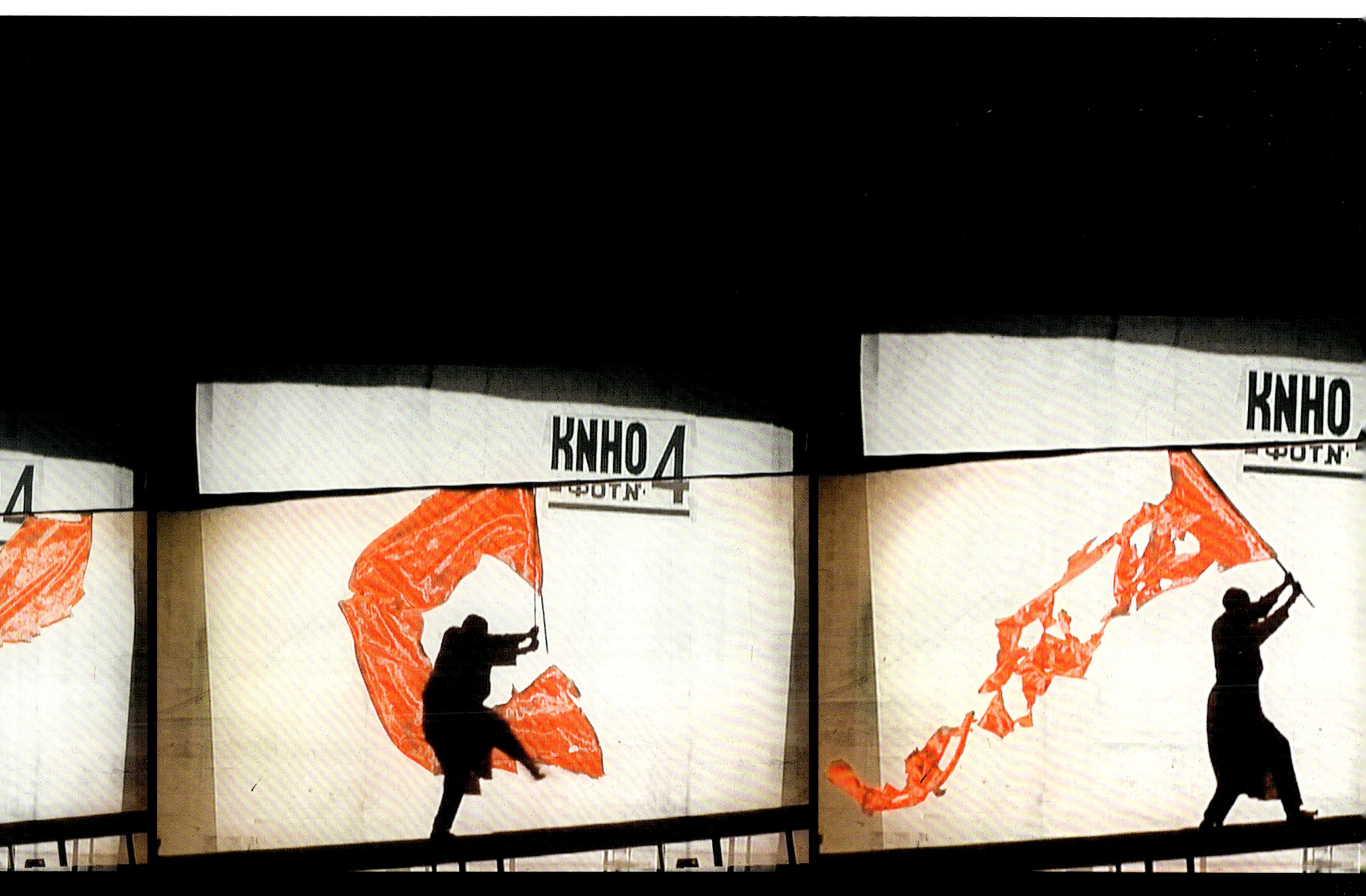

174–81 (THESE AND FOLLOWING PAGES)

***A Lifetime of Enthusiasm*, from *I am not me, the horse is not mine*, 2008**

DVCAM and HDV transferred to video, 6:01 min.

Collection of the artist, courtesy Marian Goodman Gallery, New York, and Goodman Gallery, Johannesburg

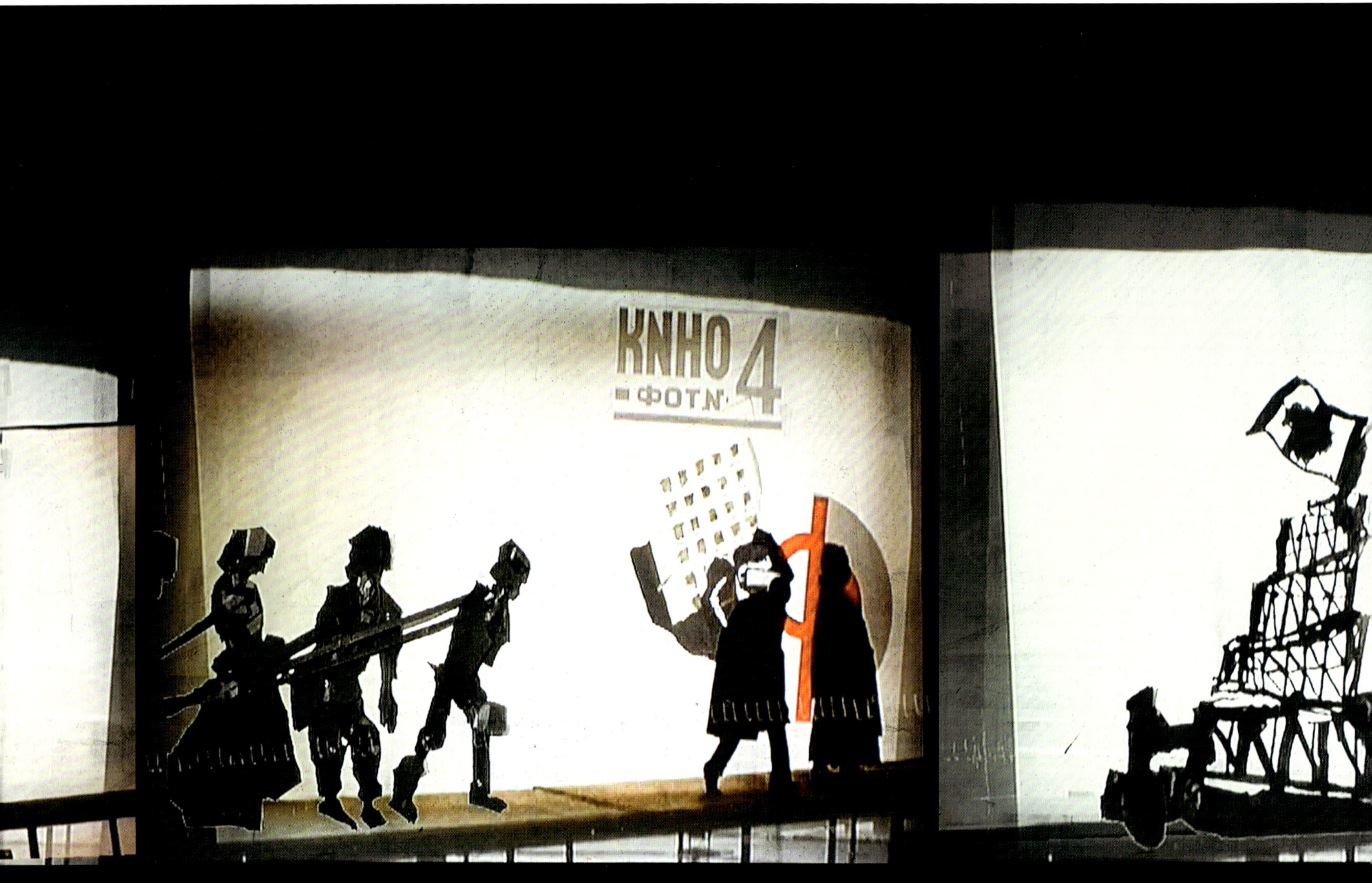
KNHO 4
ФОТN

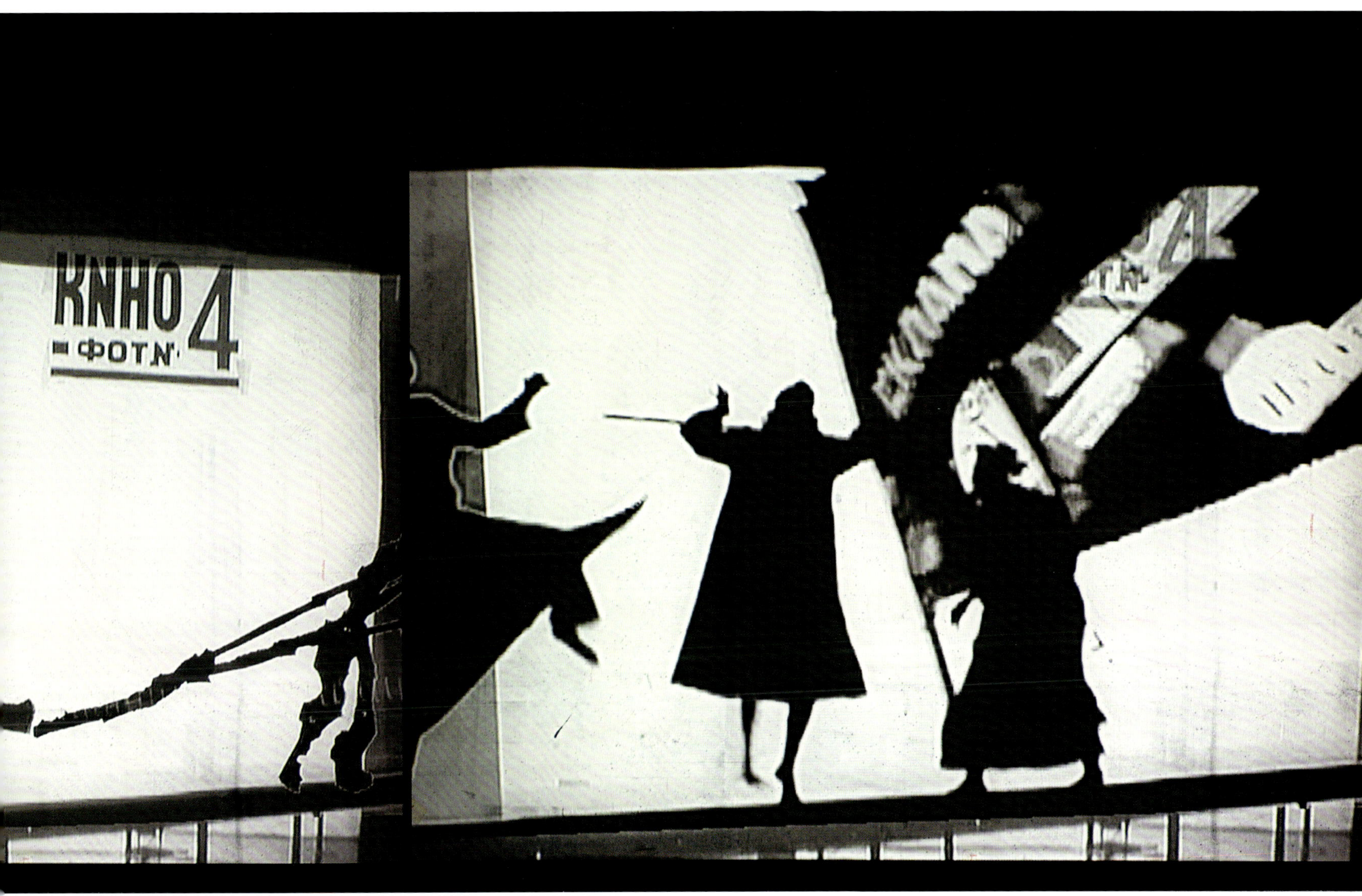
КИНО
ФОТИ
4

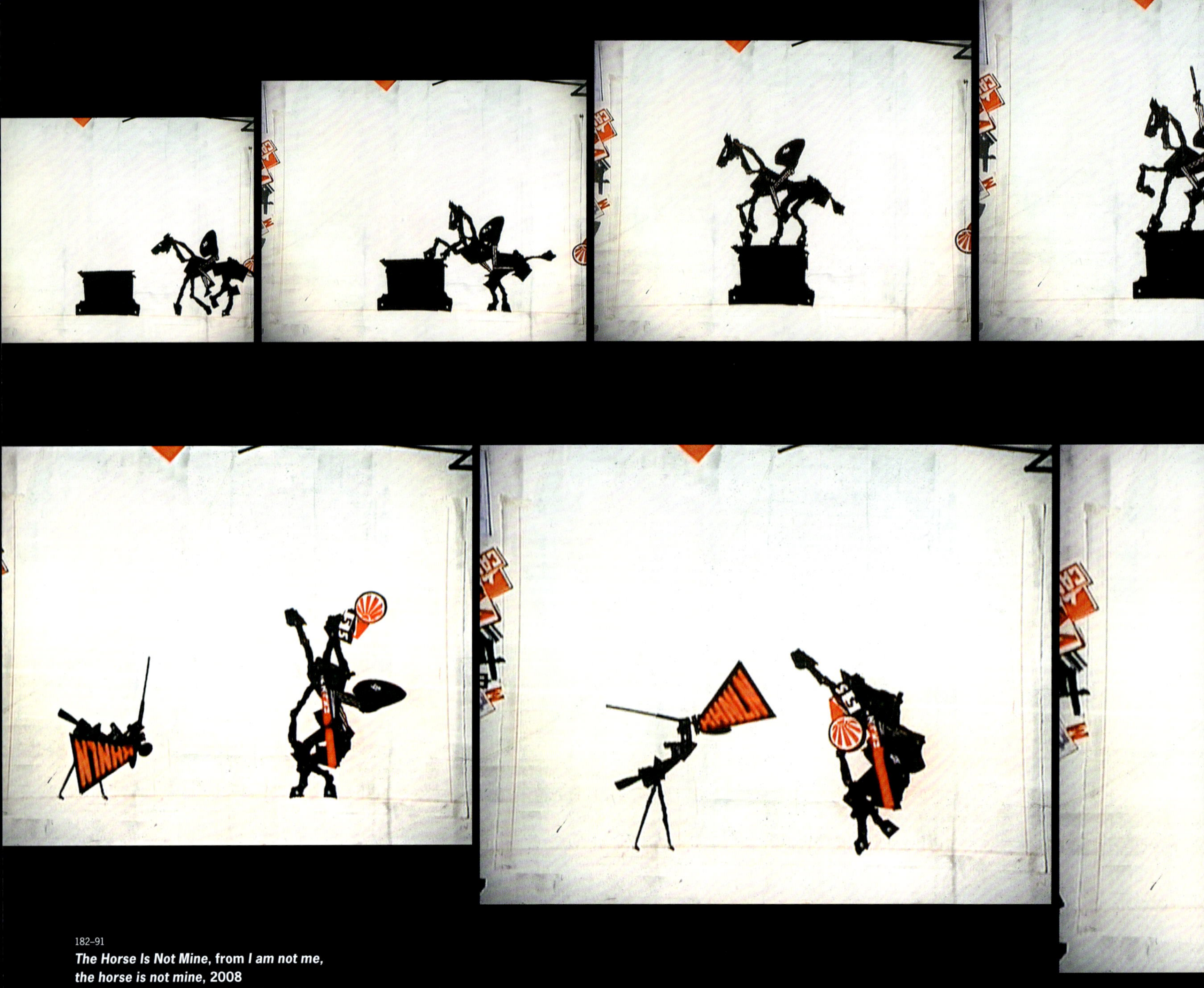

182–91
***The Horse Is Not Mine*, from *I am not me, the horse is not mine*, 2008**
DVCAM and HDV transferred to video, 6:01 min.

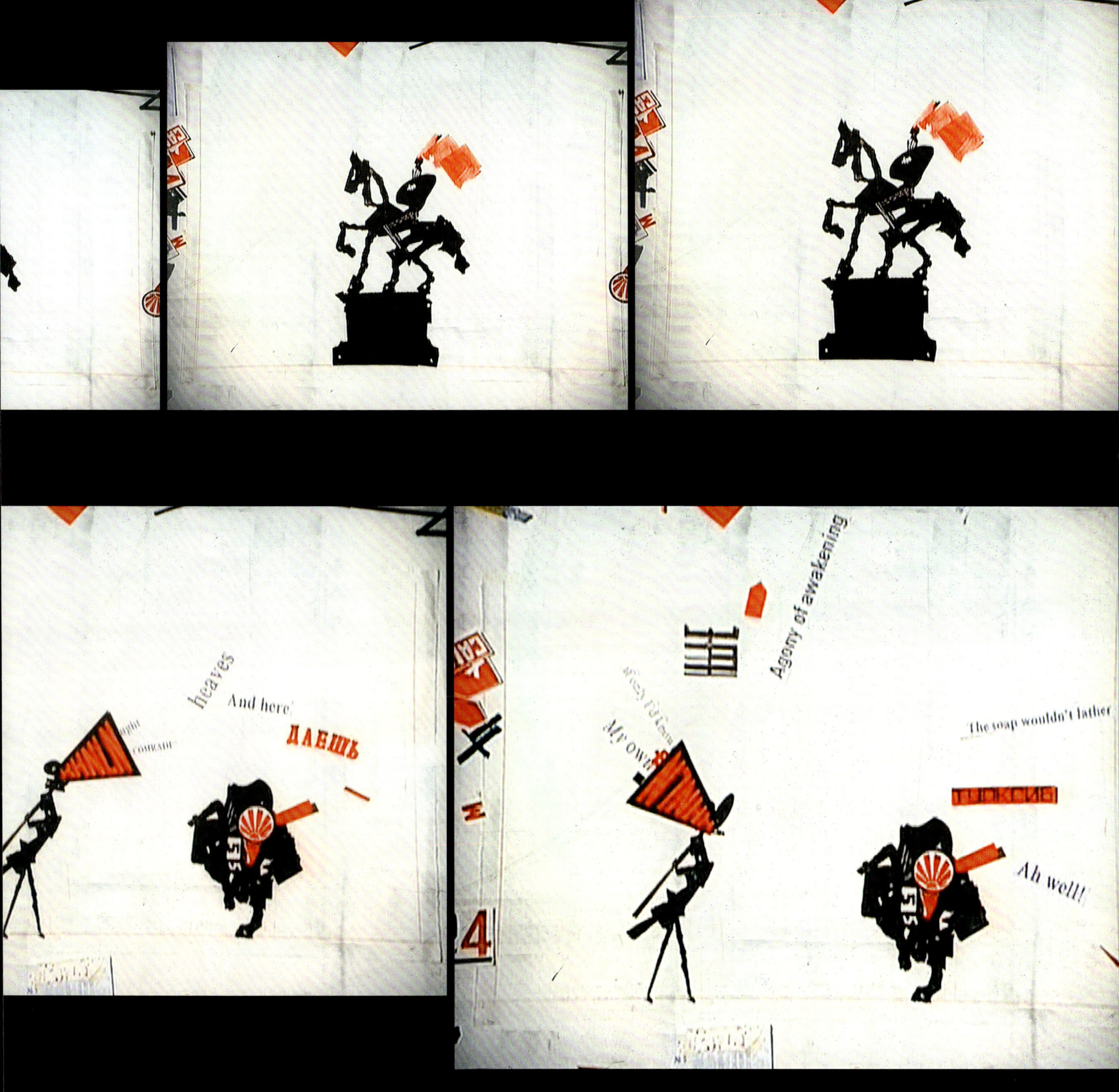
heaves
And here!
ДАЕШЬ
Agony of awakening
The soap wouldn't lather
Ah well!

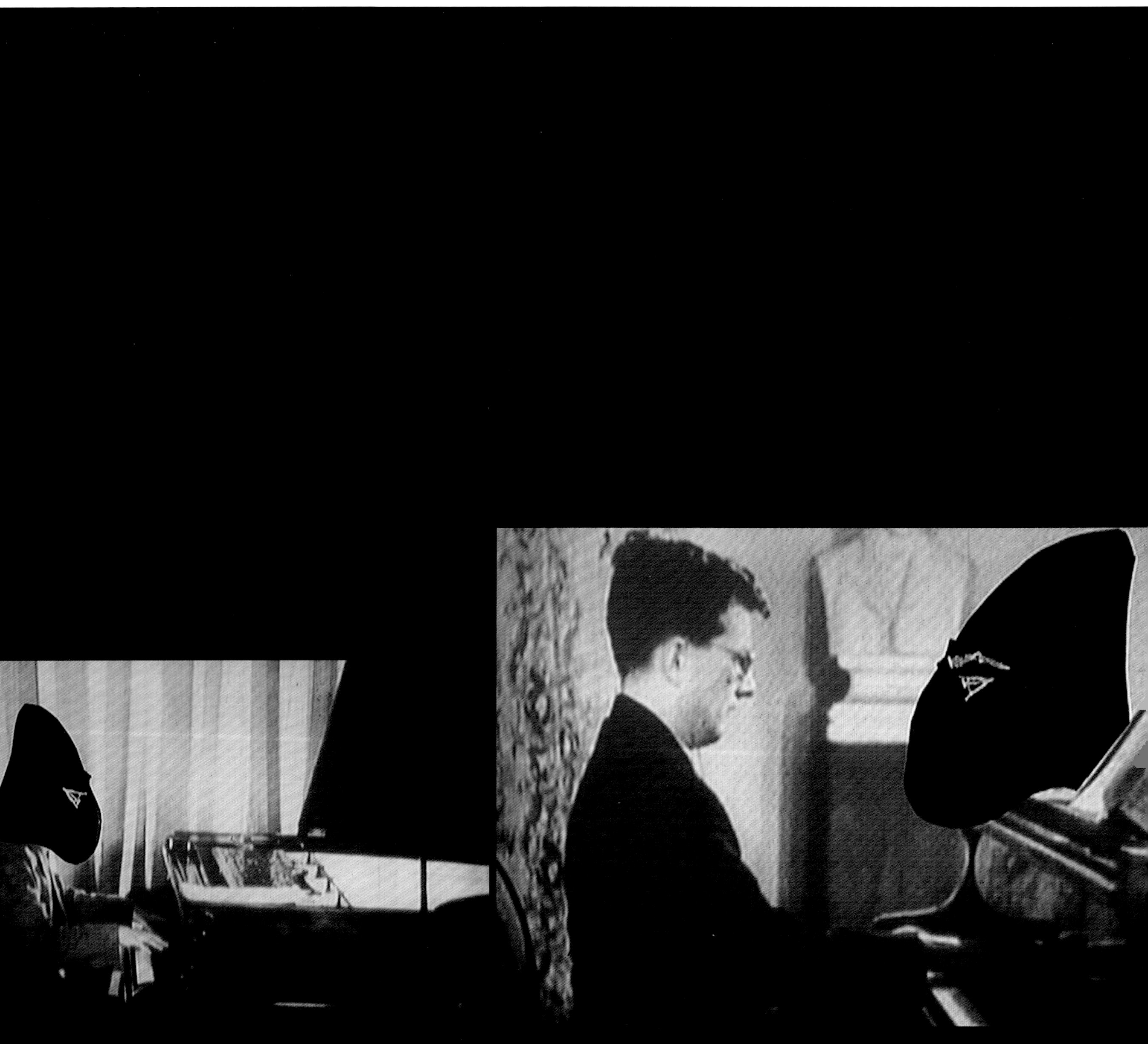

192–96 (THESE AND FOLLOWING PAGES)
***Commissariat for Enlightenment*, from *I am not me, the horse is not mine*, 2008**
DVCAM and HDV transferred to video, 6:01 min.
Collection of the artist, courtesy Marian Goodman Gallery, New York, and Goodman Gallery, Johannesburg

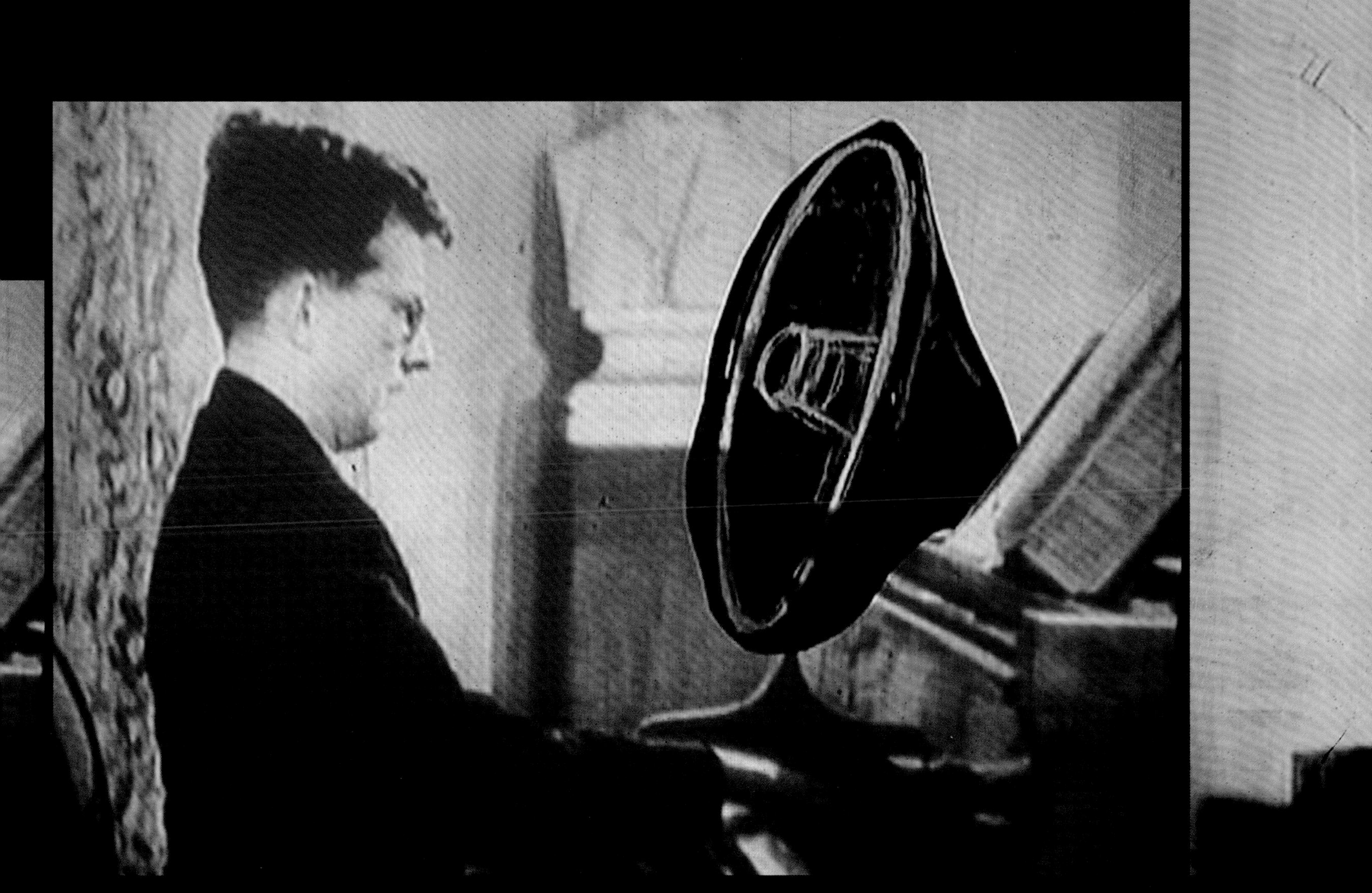

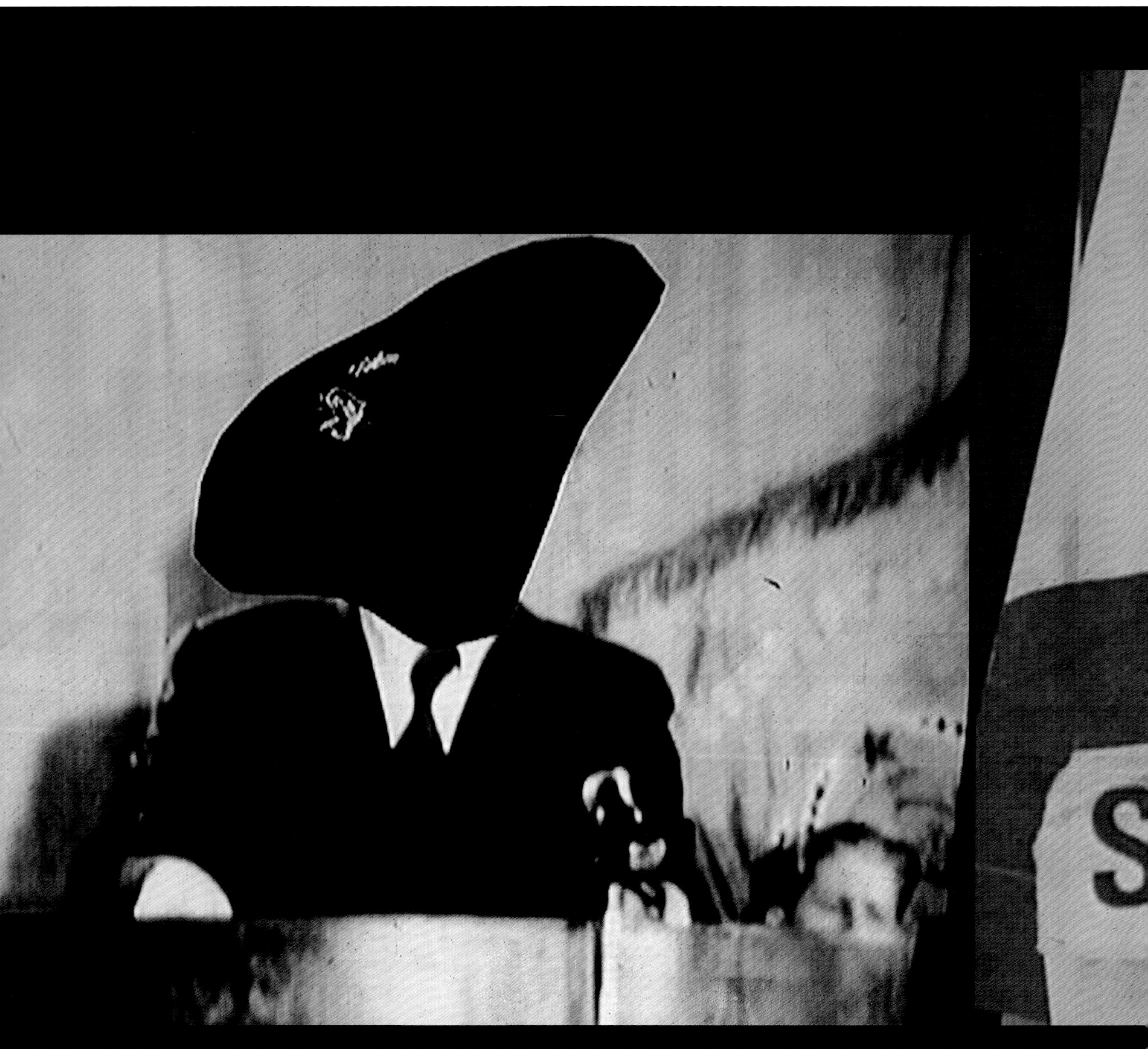

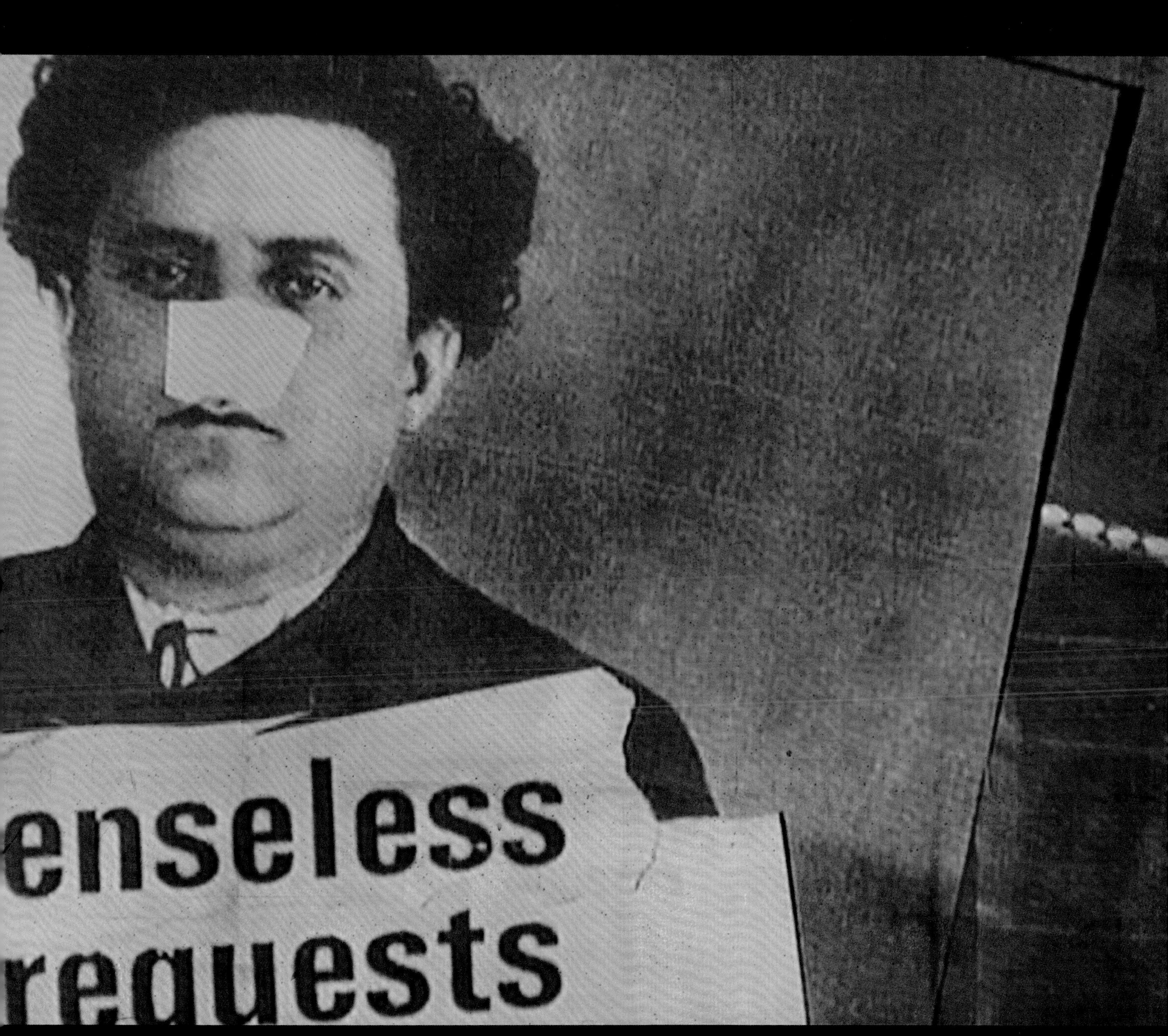
enseless
requests

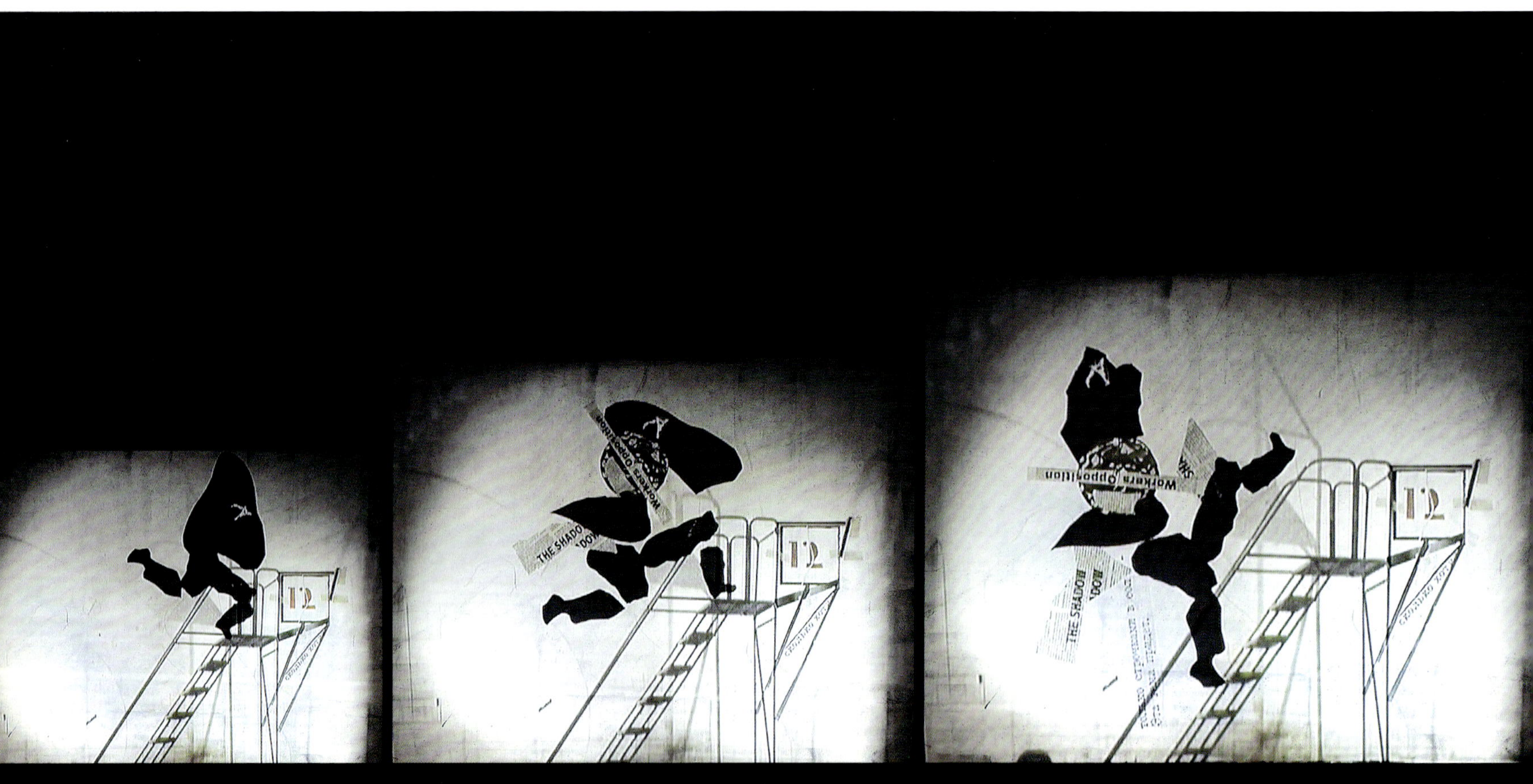

197–201
***His Majesty the Nose*, from *I am not me, the horse is not mine*, 2008**
DVCAM and HDV transferred to video, 6:01 min.
Collection of the artist, courtesy Marian Goodman Gallery, New York, and Goodman Gallery, Johannesburg

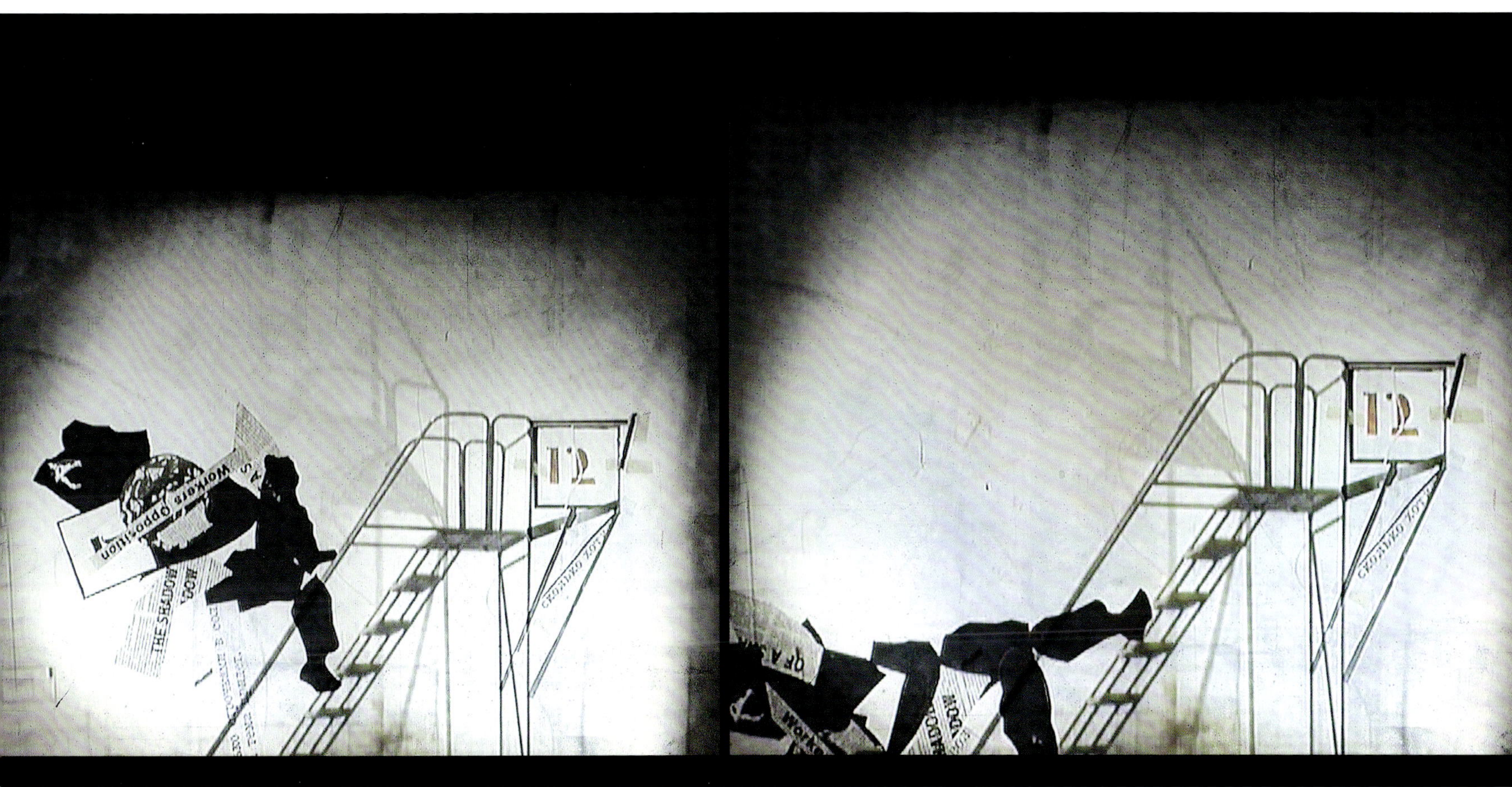
Workers Opposition
THE SHADOW
12
12

Plenum of the Central Committee
February 26 1937

Plenum of the Central Committee
February 26 1937

Comrade Bukharin:
In conclusion,
I feel compelled to recall
a certain ditty

Plenum of the Central Committee
February 26 1937

Comrade Bukharin:
which was published in
its time in the now
defunct Russian Gazette.

Plenum of the Central Committee
February 26 1937

Comrade Bukharin:
"They may beat me,
they may beat me senseless,
they may beat me to a pulp,

202–8
***Prayers of Apology*, from *I am not me, the horse is not mine*, 2008**
DVCAM and HDV transferred to video, 6:01 min.
Collection of the artist, courtesy Marian Goodman Gallery, New York, and Goodman Gallery, Johannesburg

Plenum of the Central Committee
February 26 1937

Comrade Bukharin:
but nobody is gonna
kill this kid,

Plenum of the Central Committee
February 26 1937

Comrade Bukharin:
not with a stick,
not with a bat,
or with a stone."

Plenum of the Central Committee
February 26 1937

But I cannot say,
that nobody will kill me.

209–18

***That Ridiculous Blank Space Again* (*A One-Minute Love Story*), from *I am not me, the horse is not mine*, 2008**

DVCAM and HDV transferred to video, 6:01 min.

Collection of the artist, courtesy Marian Goodman Gallery, New York, and Goodman Gallery, Johannesburg

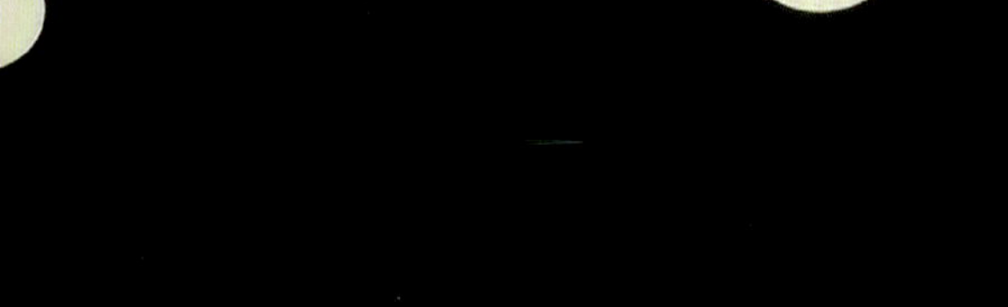

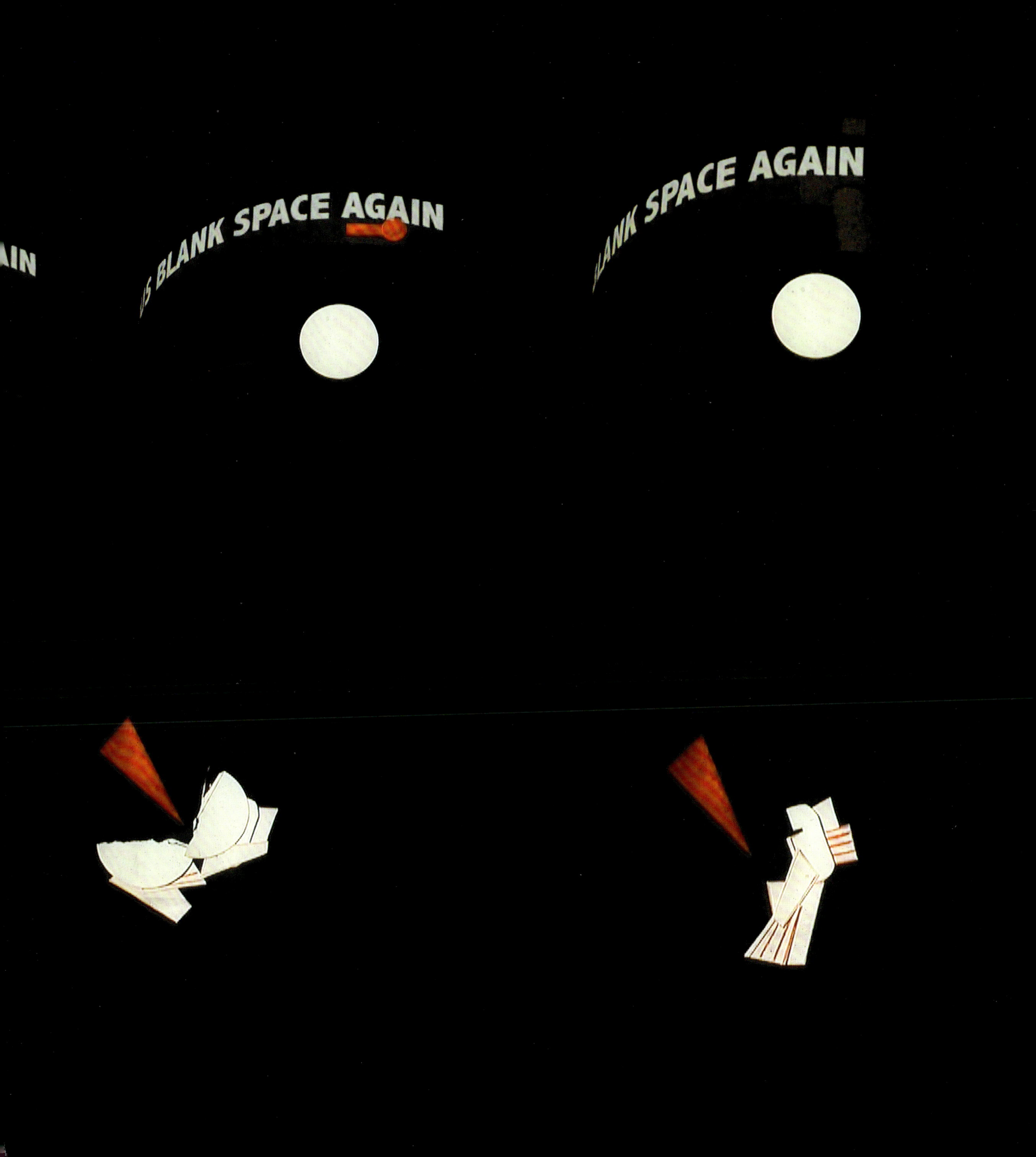

BLANK SPACE AGAIN

BLANK SPACE AGAIN

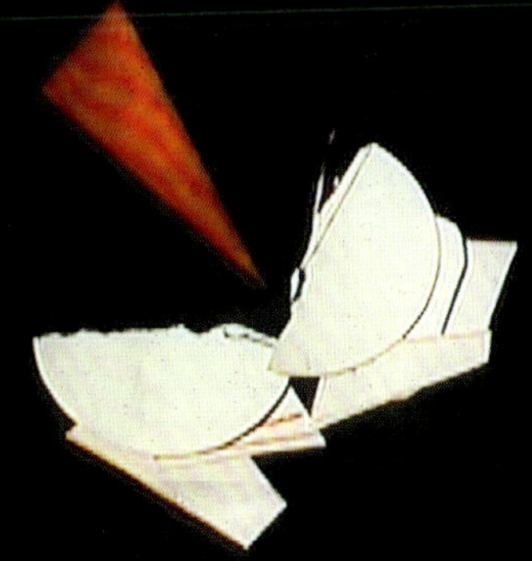

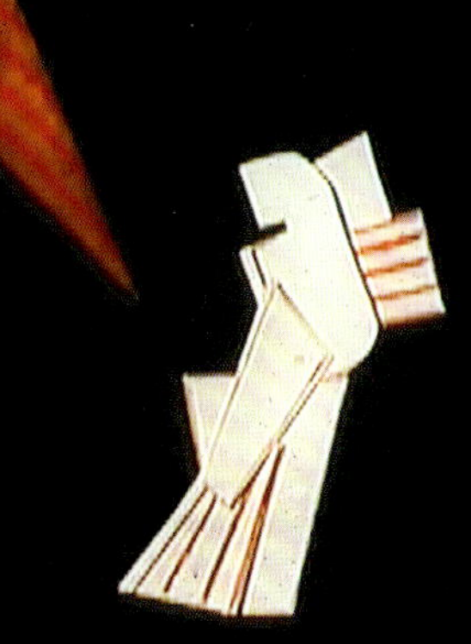

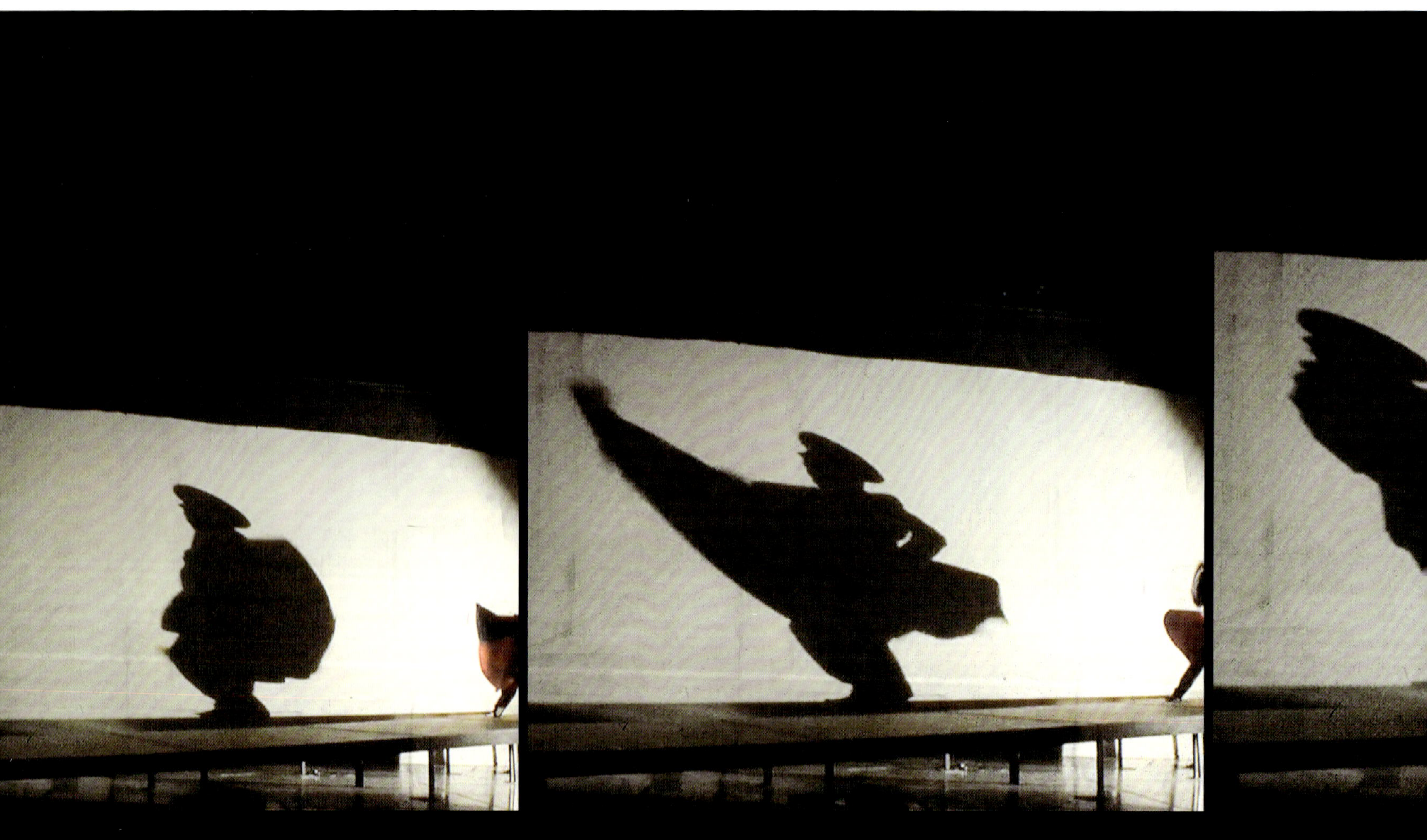

219–22
***Country Dances I (Shadow)*, from *I am not me, the horse is not mine*, 2008**
DVCAM and HDV transferred to video, 6:01 min.
Collection of the artist, courtesy Marian Goodman Gallery, New York, and Goodman Gallery, Johannesburg

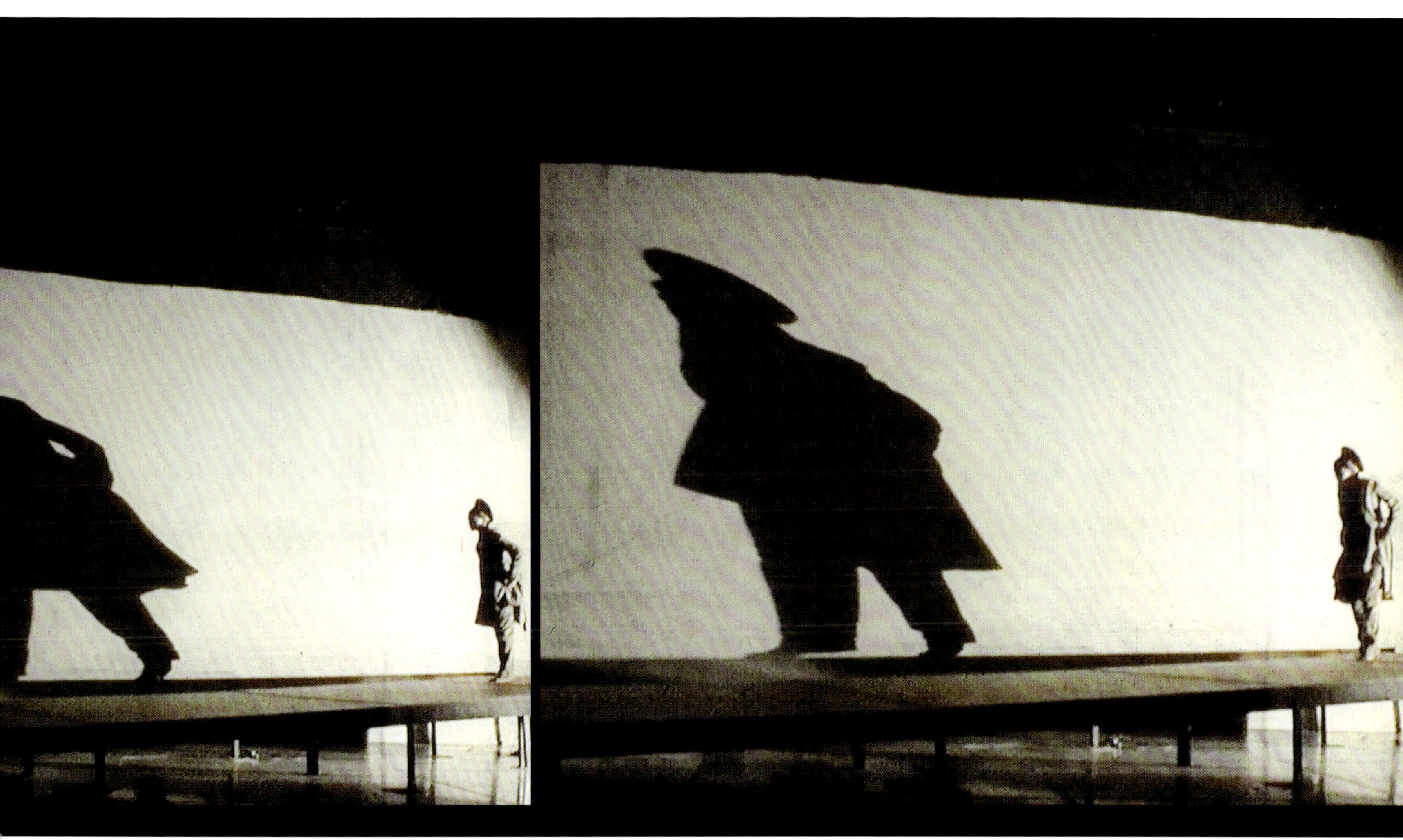

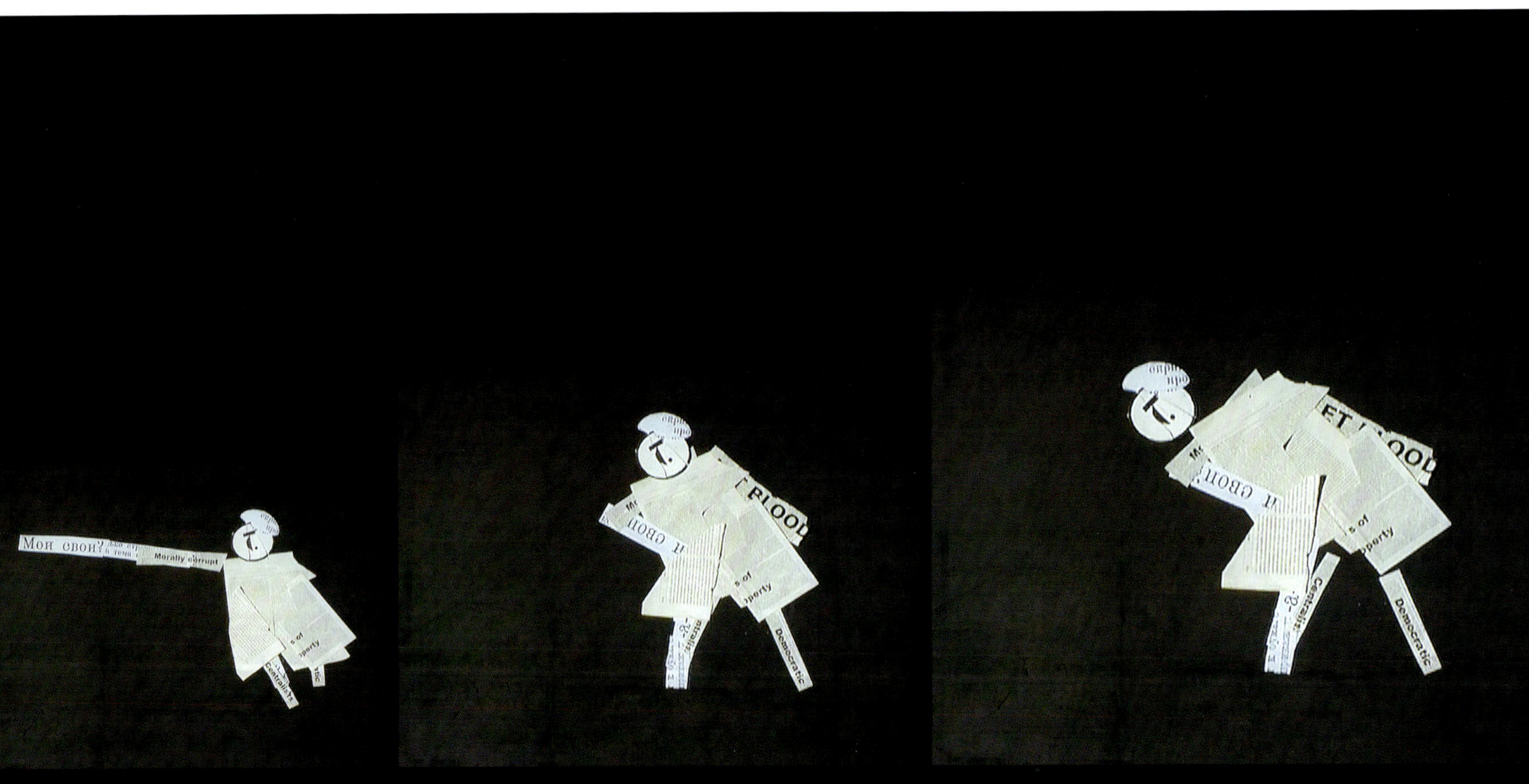
Мои свои?
Morally corrupt
Democratic
Democratic
Centralist

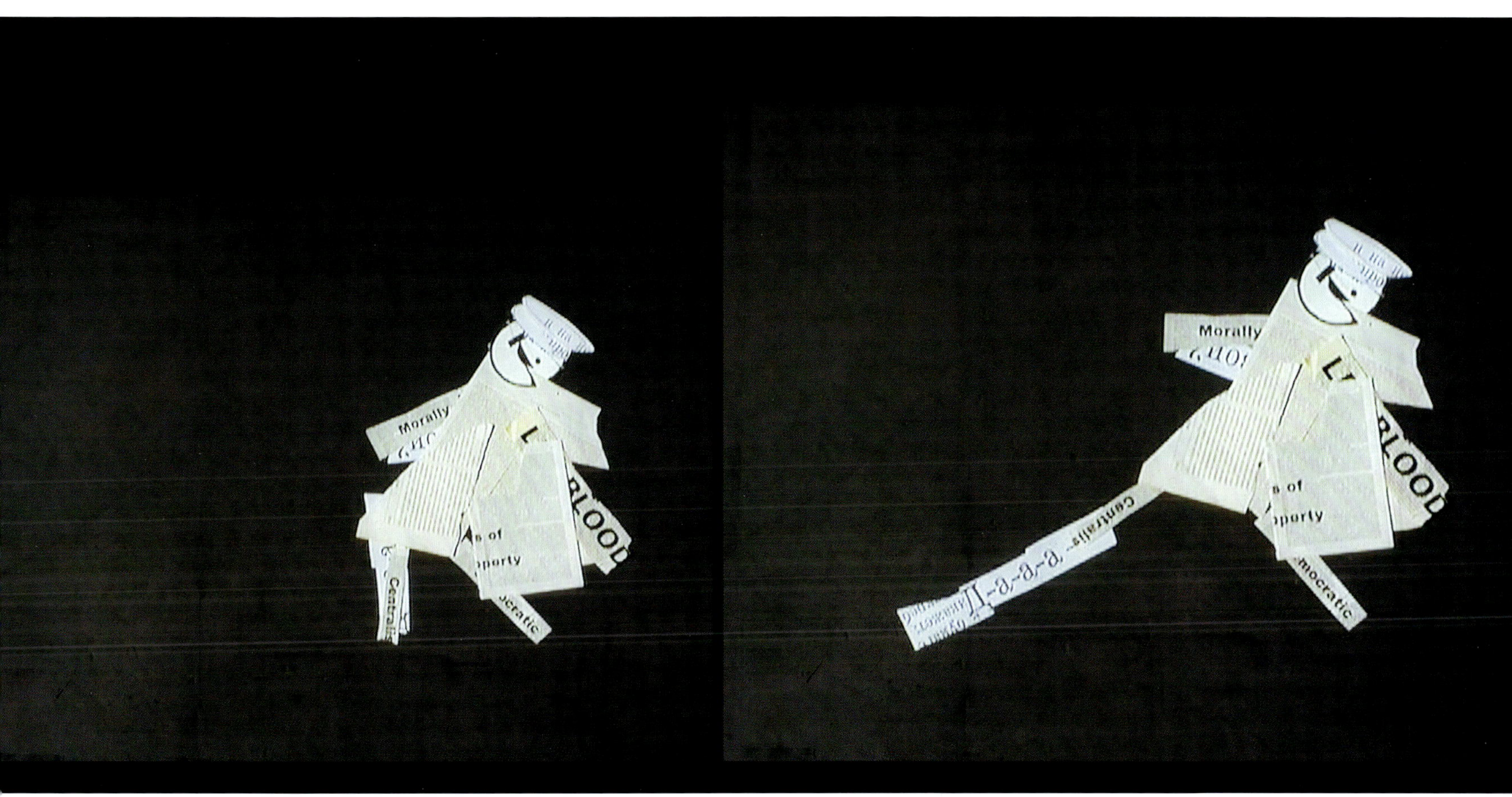

223–39 (THESE AND FOLLOWING PAGES)

***Country Dances II (Paper)*, from *I am not me, the horse is not mine*, 2008**

DVCAM and HDV transferred to video, 6:01 min.

Collection of the artist, courtesy Marian Goodman Gallery, New York, and Goodman Gallery, Johannesburg

VEXATION UPON VEXATION

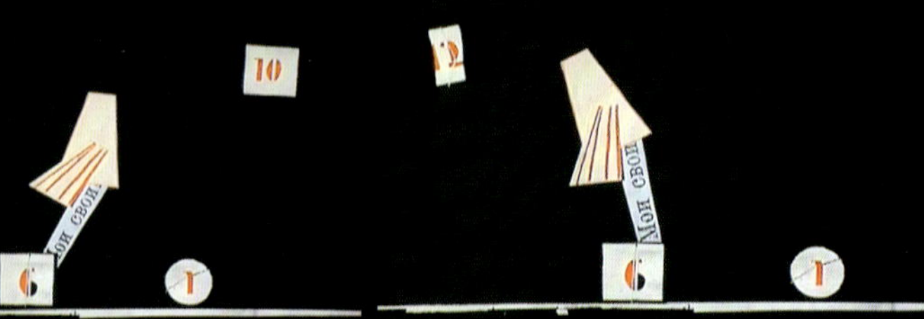

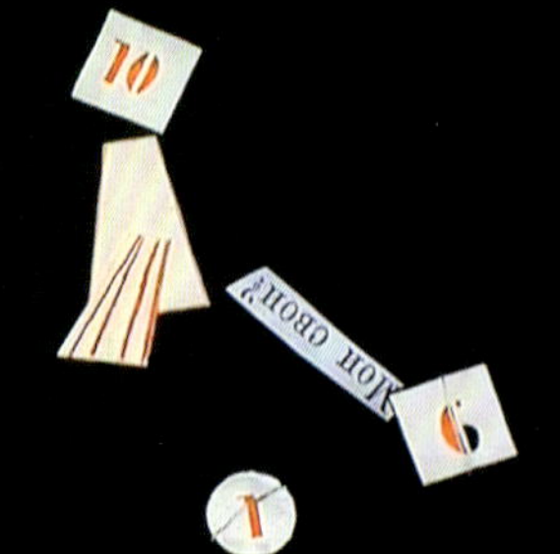

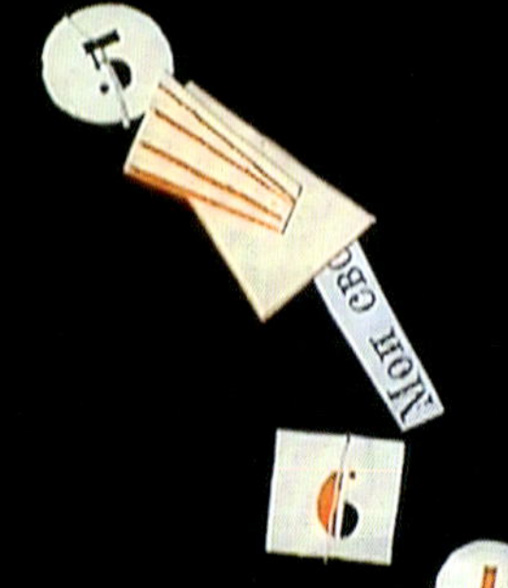

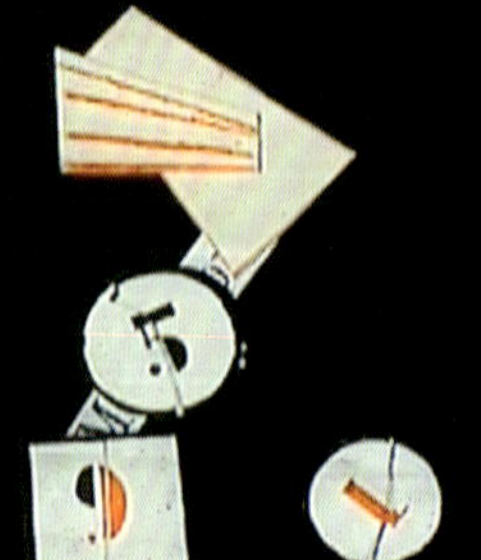

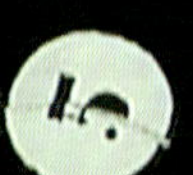

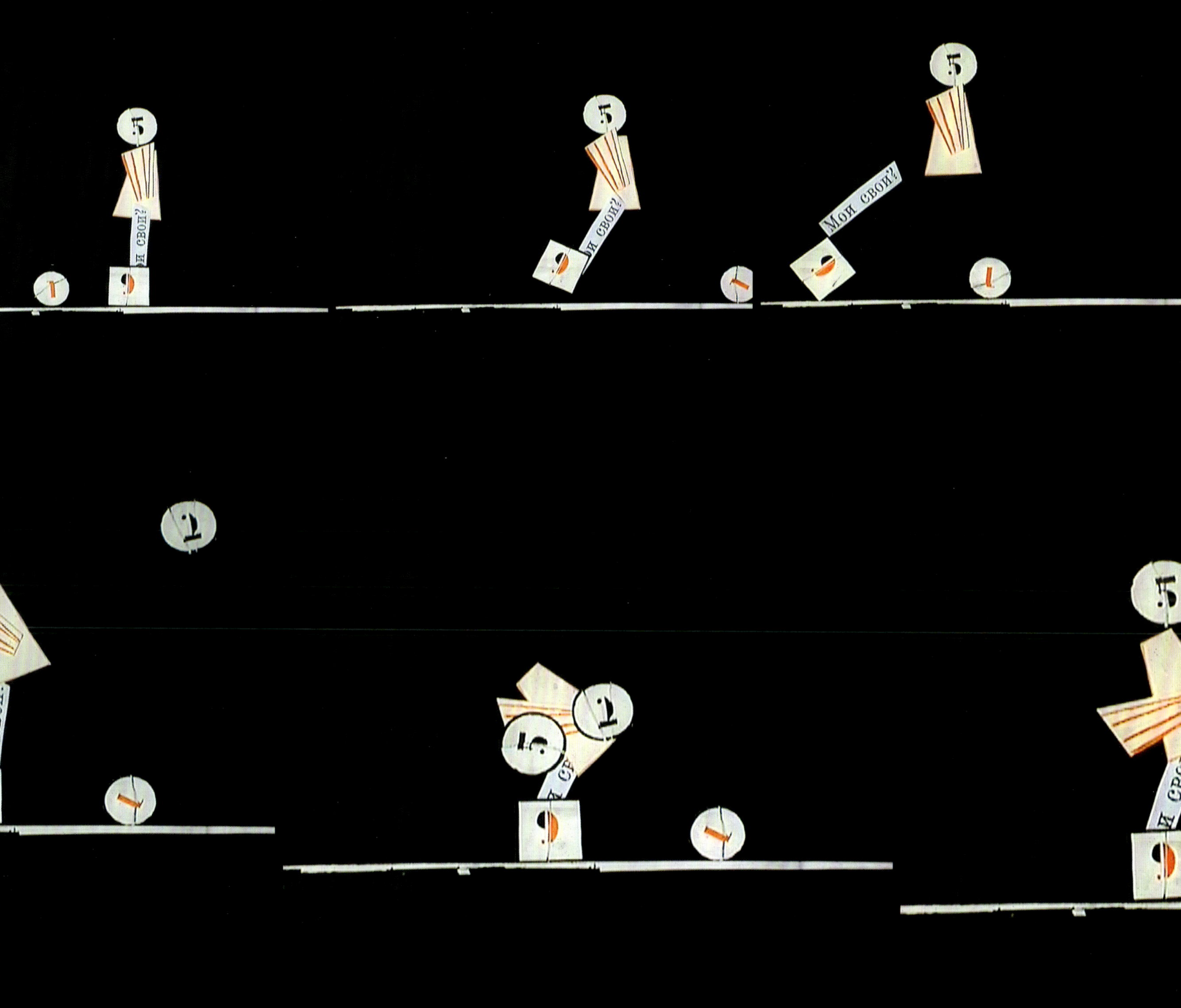
Мои свои?

DOUBLE LINES
A "STEREO" INTERVIEW ABOUT DRAWING WITH WILLIAM KENTRIDGE

Michael Auping

Usually when you address the role of an artist's drawing practice, you are comforted by the thought of having chosen a neat and relatively confined aspect of a much larger body of work: a side topic with relatively precise boundaries. That is not the case with William Kentridge. Drawing is not simply a discrete part of the whole in Kentridge's art. It insinuates itself into the way he thinks and certainly into how he constructs images. Drawing, in other words, is not a secondary medium to this artist, and his relationship to it is anything but fixed. Talking with Kentridge, you get the sense that facing a sheet of paper with a graphite pencil or a piece of charcoal in hand is not a preliminary activity but a primary one. It is the place where he is perhaps the most critical of himself and his art.

He has been drawing since he was a self-conscious young student taking art lessons alongside his mother, and he has over time developed a unique understanding of drawing and its history. At the same time, he wears this knowledge unpretentiously and markedly downplays his own talents as a draftsman. Kentridge does not claim to possess any special key to how drawing works. Rather, he works his way through it in the process of creating installations and films. For Kentridge, drawing involves a foundational struggle to communicate through images, a mode that requires continual adjustment, correction, and newly formed recognitions. In many ways Kentridge is an old-fashioned existentialist, constantly reflecting on and doubting what presents itself as beauty or truth. His stark, graphic world of black and white—with rare but pointed touches of blue and red—vibrates with the transfiguring distortions of thought.

This dialectical energy is especially apparent in Kentridge's films, which constitute a special hybrid of drawing and animation. Staring into the restless graphic markings that make up each film, it is natural to wonder whether we are seeing a film that looks more like a drawing or a drawing that aspires to be a film. Kentridge's process supports both scenarios. Rather than starting with a storyboard and producing scores of individual drawings to illustrate an already conceived narrative, as is typically the case with an animated film, Kentridge employs a few large sheets of paper that he works and reworks into a film story. In the simplest of terms, Kentridge pins a sheet of paper to the wall and starts to draw; he stops spontaneously at different points in the drawing's development and steps back to a camera to record that moment as a single frame. He then returns to the sheet of paper and continues drawing, repeating this back-and-forth process—occasionally pinning up a new sheet of paper—until the drawing or image-story has exhausted itself.

The magic of animated images lies to a considerable extent in their clean, mechanical fluidity. We are not meant to know or care that they have been made by human hands, but instead to believe that they have somehow been conjured from the projection machine. Kentridge's animations engage a different kind of magic, not so much a sleight of hand as what the artist calls "stone-age filmmaking." We feel the presence of hands working and forming throughout. In some cases we actually see the artist's hands in the process of drawing the film. Even when we do not, Kentridge's energetic hands seem ever-present as marks appear, develop, are erased, and are reconfigured. I imagine Kentridge's films as continuous loops of ideas. Like graffiti on city walls, the imagery is constantly invented, displaced, and reinvented.

A Kentridge film is in fact a drawing in process: an extension of the sheets of paper he pins up around his studio. These sheets of paper—like cells that create a larger body—are not forgotten or set aside at the commencement of something more formal, such as a painting or a sculpture. That the artist often prefers to show his drawings inside miniature theaters—the lights coming on between films to illuminate the drawings—indicates the centrality that Kentridge gives to the medium. In a sense, the drawings are the main characters in the story, characters that literally morph into other forms and identities. One might argue that drawing sets those second lives in motion. For Kentridge, drawing, as well as art in its broadest sense, is not about setting something in place, establishing static symbols or definitions. His drawings—whether large single sheets activated by energetic charcoal marks, part of an animated film, or embedded into installations and magnified with stereoscopic devices—are fundamental models of how making and seeing can ramble into meaning.

In the following interview, recorded in New York on January 16, 2008, Kentridge describes his longtime engagement with drawing. It is not, however, a standard interview. Every interview has its own process, but most generally involve an original recording followed by changes, additions, and deletions to the transcript—a polishing-up, as it were. This is not Kentridge's approach. He is not a polisher. He is a questioner. Reflecting the dialectical character of Kentridge's art, the interview takes the form of a self-argument. His first response to the transcript was "I don't recognize myself." As with his alter egos Felix and Soho, Kentridge in essence doubles himself in this interview by not only answering my original questions but also questioning his own answers. In some cases his second response seems "louder," perhaps bolder, than the original answer, putting his first thoughts, erudite but perhaps too polite, in their place. To argue with oneself, at times seeming to contradict oneself, might seem self-defeating, but it is in fact a critical means to the kind of realism art can create. Kentridge's process, and the art that results from it, reconsiders the foundational contradictions that are at the heart of philosophical aesthetics. As one contemporary theorist has pointed out, it is the artist who is always at the forefront of recognizing the dilemma: "To struggle with contradiction is by that very act to be at one with the world, which has, so to speak, the same problems as ourselves. If the essence of reality is contradiction, then to be self-divided is to be rooted in the real."[1] This doubling of Kentridge's voice and shifting of viewpoints within a single interview parallels in linguistic terms the effects of his stereoptic drawings, in which multiple viewpoints are combined to create a fuller, more dimensional picture of a subject.

1. Terry Eagleton, *The Ideology of the Aesthetic* (Oxford: Basil Blackwell Ltd, 1990), 125.

MICHAEL AUPING When did your career in drawing begin—I mean fundamentally, even remedially?

WILLIAM KENTRIDGE Well, my mother's story is that I was drawing from when I was three. I suppose I drew as children do. It's difficult to know when I began to take it seriously. I went to children's art lessons from the time I was about eight. I seemed to take to drawing more than other media. When I was about fourteen, I started joining my mother in evening life-drawing classes at an art school in Johannesburg. That was a turning point because as an adolescent you begin to make some important decisions with regard to what art is.

Decisions? There are no decisions. We knew the artist who taught the classes. My mother went to the lessons. It seemed an adult thing to do—to draw naked women. Not the drawing itself, but to be in the presence of a naked stranger and keep an urbanity. To look but not to stare. To turn adolescent tumescence into talk of shape, tone, and line.

You either stop doodling around, drawing airplanes and the sort, or you don't. I remember wanting very badly to move to the next step.

I don't remember this at all. I was conscious though of being at an impasse at the children's art class I still went to at the age of fifteen. There was something somewhat shameful about still being there at that age, like being forced to wear short trousers while everyone else was in jeans. There was a house style to the art school, halfway between children's drawings and curio art Synthetic Cubism. Thick black outlines and bright colors. I knew that this was not what someone my age should be doing.

Then when I finished high school I went to the Johannesburg Art Foundation. I continued to draw, but I also did some painting.

MA When did you begin to think of drawing as an end in itself—as something you could build a career around?

WK That was a slower process that involved some confidence building. When you are a student, of course, there is this innate sense that real artists use paint and canvas. It was fine to be drawing, but at some point you needed to graduate to oils. I remember as a child saying, "When will I be able to use oil paint?" Then for my bar mitzvah one of my uncles gave me a set of oil paints. I tried to be very careful and attempt some still lifes, but I really didn't have a clue as to how to use the medium. That was disconcerting because when I was in art school it was really brought home to me that drawing should be thought of as a secondary activity. It was something you practiced, like musical scales, rather than the final expression. Painting was the real thing.

MA So you stuck with drawing out of stubbornness or desperation?

WK Probably both. But there were some things that brought me round to understanding drawing in a more profound way. One of those things was etching. I did quite a lot of etching early in my career. It gave me a deeper knowledge of drawing.

What is this deeper knowledge pretension? It did no such thing. It gave me, him, you an excuse not to use color. To have a medium that is legitimately monochromatic. To rescue me from being stuck in the colored mud of my oil paint.

I learned a good deal about line making. Printmakers tend to look more closely at how drawing is done. They think of it as a special knowledge, which in many ways it is.

I don't know what this means. Except that the plate is closer to your nose than a sheet of paper. That if you are not careful, you draw with your knuckles and not your whole arm. In fact, I think the opposite is true. You know less about line making and have to trust other faculties. You know less because you usually cannot see the intensity of the line. This is revealed only when the plate is printed and is a result of the ink, the pressure, the acid. One of the pleasures of printmaking is drawing blind.

It slowed the drawing process down and from that standpoint I was watching myself draw in a more conscious way. I also became more conscious of tonal activity, shadows, how texture could activate a surface. I liked the process of scratching and digging into a material or a plate to make a line. I think printmaking in general made me aware of just how physical drawing could be. I've always enjoyed the physicality of drawing. My more mature drawing came out of my earlier activity in etching. I was able to take what I learned and expand the scale, and feel more accomplished as a draftsman.

My more mature drawing? I am still waiting for this. As for being more accomplished as a draftsman, I have become less accomplished. But maybe more adept at using the crassness of my lines.

I also studied a lot of graphic art at that time, and I saw that major artists—from Francisco de Goya to William Hogarth—had engaged drawing and printmaking as singularly important and valid media. They employed what many people think of as intimate and supplementary media to make significant statements, not just formally but socially and politically.

MA Do you think that drawing as a medium might lend itself to political statement, maybe more than other media?

WK I'm not sure about that, but the role of drawing historically in different political contexts is something I have thought a lot about. Every artist is a political artist on some level. If you make an abstract painting, it is in effect a political statement. In South Africa you cannot really escape thinking about political realities. I do think drawing and printmaking reflect their historical context as much as painting and sculpture. It's interesting to think about the difference between Northern European Lutheran engraving and Southern European Catholic etching. The serigraph corresponds to the Cold War. And digital prints and Photoshop correspond to an era of smart bombs, when no one is responsible for anything because everything can be continually shifted and changed.

This is a bit crass. You can find a politics in all art certainly, in how it relates to power relations in society. How it engages or refuses to engage with the politics around it. Abstract painting is not a political statement in itself: the world of power is passing, the world of the spirit is paramount. There is obviously a strong polemic (aesthetic polemic in Robert Motherwell's black-and-white paintings for the Spanish Republic).

In South Africa in the 1970s there was quite a strong body of black artists working figuratively in drawing and linocut. I was particularly aware of the artist Dumile Feni. I remember he stayed at the house of Bill Ainsley, who was my teacher, and I saw his work there. He did fantastic large-scale figurative drawings—some of the drawings he did before he came to America are astonishingly powerful. Seeing that work was very important for me in being able to see drawing as a legitimate activity, an activity that in its own way is equal to painting, and as a medium that could make a statement about the world, personally or politically.

In South Africa there were also abstract painters who were very committed to transformation. Their insistence on maintaining the practice of American Color Field painting was a challenge and a goad to the notion of easy political art. I felt at sea, uncertain of the direction or purpose of any mark, thrown back onto questions of taste rather than necessity.

MA Drawing also seems more accessible than painting, just in terms of material.

WK That's true. If you have little money, drawing materials are not that difficult to come by. Drawing does not in most cases require special tools. In South Africa that matters in some fundamental ways. There is a democracy to drawing, and a certain kind of work ethic. One of the things that attracts me to drawing, and that in some way relates to its politics, is that it is a demonstration of agency. There is something about the act of drawing that reflects a process of labor. You have a sense of work, at least for me.

There is no work ethic. Or that is not what I am interested in. It is the appearance of work, making visible the hours on the paper. In an era in which the human labor in everything was clear, there was something utopian in making art appear effortless or at least miraculous. Now that we take the impossible for granted—digital animation, Photoshop (the invisible workings of a computer compared to the very visible and audible mechanics of a typewriter)—there seems a place for showing physical process. (And through this mental process; this is not clear, but some impulse in this direction sits in my guts—not that they are to be trusted either.)

Everyone who draws has a distinct personality to their lines and their images. You are aware that a specific, though not always perfect, hand has made this image. An Ingres drawing might be an exception. They often look like they were not done by human hands but by some divine skill. The making of a painting is work also, but you often get the impression that a painting somehow arrives by magic. I don't feel that way with drawing. In South Africa the element of work or labor, even in the arts, is important. The conceptualization of art that America is so comfortable with is not a foreign thing in South Africa, but it doesn't translate with the same ease. Effort in the form of basic human skills—well, there is something to be said for that, the agency of labor.

To glide above that, working only the realm of the conceptual, using hired hands to do the actual labor has been tainted here, or made impossible by the image of the white overseer in his shorts in the shade, watching a gang of laborers doing the work. Not to say that this is necessarily an accurate image, and even though labor is less visible in Western Europe and North America, I do understand it is still there—but the image and its shame are more present here.

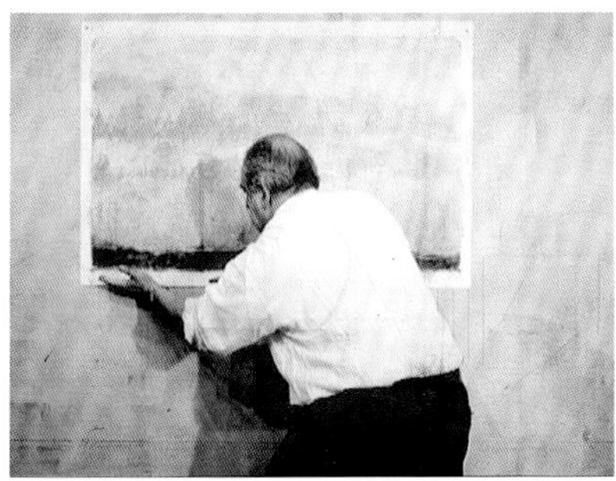

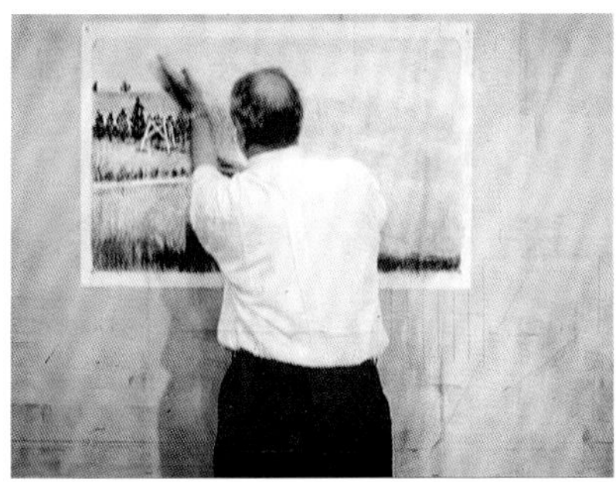

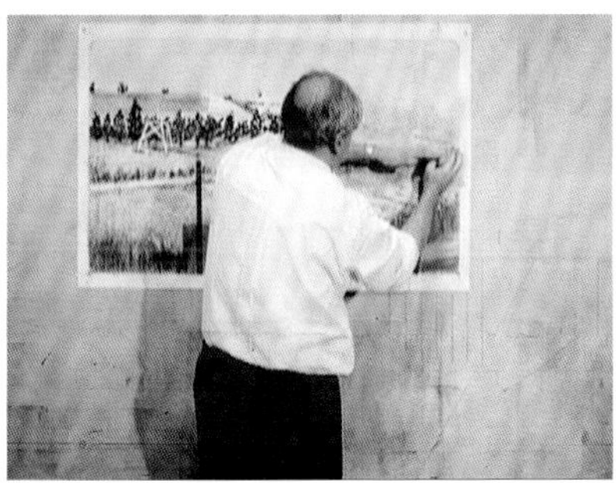

FIGS. 44–46
William Kentridge
Moveable Assets, from 7 Fragments for Georges Méliès, 2003
35mm animated film transferred to video, 2:40 min.
Collection of the artist, courtesy Marian Goodman Gallery, New York, and Goodman Gallery, Johannesburg

MA Almost all of your drawings are done with charcoal, aren't they?

WK Yes, for some years now. When I think back to my first art lessons as a child, I remember being given a piece of charcoal. I had never used charcoal before and I remember thinking that it was an amazing material. It was not a pencil. It was much more special, more serious than a pencil.

No such memory!

It could be as messy as painting, but it wasn't painting. With a pencil or charcoal, I felt more connected to the sheet than with a paintbrush. For some reason, early in my career I stayed with pencil and some india ink. It wasn't until about 1984 that I reengaged with charcoal. It feels comfortable for how I work and the feeling I want to get when I'm drawing.

This is wrong. It's not about the feeling I want to get. It's that the surfaces and tone that charcoal makes in themselves make the activity prosper. The material provides the context for the work to happen. No, *context* is too clinical; it provides the comfort for the work to happen.

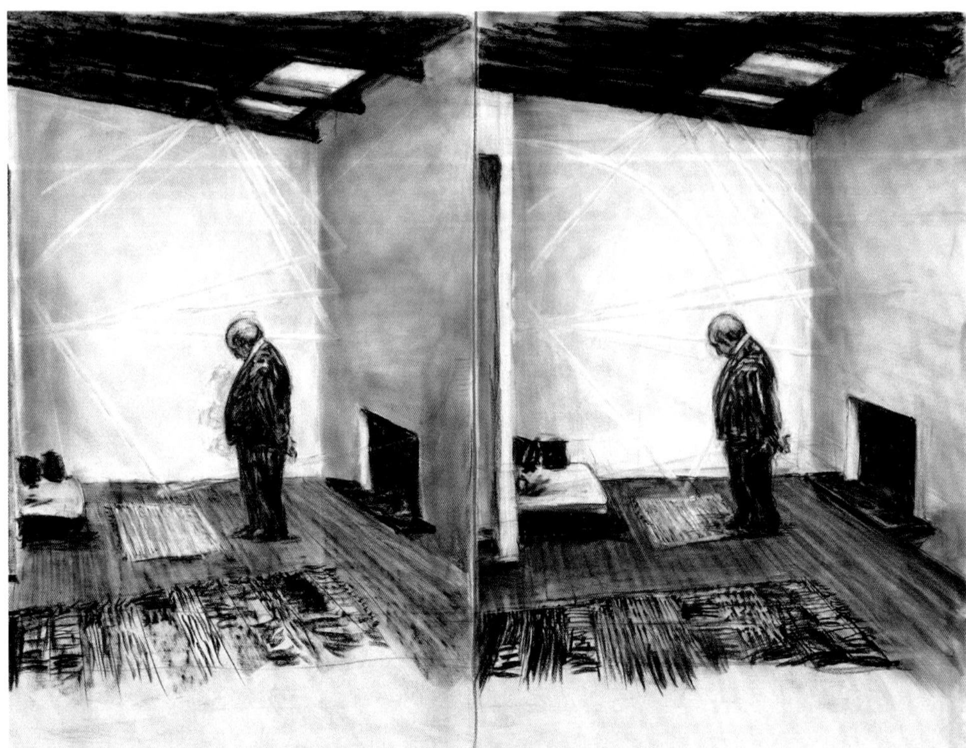

FIG. 47
William Kentridge
Drawing for the film *Stereoscope*, 1999
Charcoal and pastel on paper
47 1/4 x 63 in.
(120 x 160 cm)
Collection of Gaby Linscheid

MA Do you think that might be because charcoal seems somehow more painterly?

WK There might be an analogy there. If you have worked with charcoal you know that it can be a rich medium. One of the challenges for me was how does one deal with large tonal areas, more in terms of atmosphere than materiality, which is how I think of painterliness. I don't like to start with a completely white sheet. The backgrounds carry some of the content in terms of atmosphere. I like to start my drawings with a tone, and with charcoal I can modulate this by adding bits of charcoal and erasing. I'm not sure it is painterly, but it does allow me to have a kind of palette. It gives the drawing a further dimension beyond a line on a white page. It's another way of bringing a drawing to life, giving it some visual texture and even a sense of movement. If you are enormously patient, you can do this with pencil and cross-hatching. With charcoal, however, you can make a thick, rich black line and you give it a wipe with a piece of chamois leather and it's slightly erased but spread around the surface. I also like charcoal because of the indeterminacy of the point. I use a fairly heavy piece of charcoal, about one and a half inches in diameter. It's like holding a small object rather than a long, thin point, and you have to trust that your hand, wrist, and arm can guide the edges of it as you draw. The crudeness of it is important for me. It's like a primitive technology, an extremely fundamental and ancient way of marking. It is not facile. It encourages drawing from the shoulder rather than the knuckles. It's not about minute motor control.

It's about more than control. It is about the source of an image. There is a way of drawing something carefully, checking angles, measuring thumb against pencil, arm outstretched, the grammar of drawing lessons; and a way of working faster, almost blind, trusting habit and training. So that somewhere between the paper, arm, and point an image will emerge that can be recognized even if not known in advance. I am very bad at rendering a specific image. The more I try to analyze and copy a face, the farther it gets away from any likeness. (I must confess to standing and watching pavement portraitists and wondering at how the best of them get such accuracy.)

I work on relatively large sheets of paper, and with charcoal I can cover a greater distance as I'm making the image. At the same time, it dictates that I stand a little farther away from the paper. It's a different kind of mark making than you normally associate with drawing. I also like the fact that the charcoal is actually a piece of burnt tree. It suits South Africa.

MA You are speaking of the landscape? I did want to ask you about your depictions of landscape. They are pretty bleak, as if there had been a fire. I always assumed that was a comment about the history and politics of South Africa, sort of after the deluge.

WK I know what you mean, but there is a more literal reference. In the area around Johannesburg you have very dry winters. The ground gets terribly dry, and you have fires and everything goes black. You find yourself in a landscape that is literally made out of charcoal. You could take a large sheet of paper and rub it around and do a frottage of the South African landscape. You also have a very harsh light, and with the absence of color it is a scene that becomes very bleached, desolate looking.

MA How do you generally begin one of your drawings?

WK Some are more narrative than others. They often begin as a single image: some nagging vision from my past, or something I get fixed on in my studio, or something from the newspaper that has caught my eye that is odd or troubling. Sometimes to explain something to myself I need to draw it.

I think, more accurately, the first decision is whether I am making a film or not. Is there a camera lurking? And this can be provoked by a sentence as well as an image. The phrase of the philosopher Emmanuel Levinas, *le visage d'autrui* ("the face of another"), is enough to set in chain a series of images of possible drawings, the kernel of a new film. (Next Soho Eckstein film? Perhaps.) The drawing itself is not necessarily narrative. Perhaps this is the difference—a drawing done with the knowledge that it will be in service to the images before and behind it. The drawing itself changes with this expectation. Drawing verb and noun here.

MA Speaking of the newspaper—I don't want to suggest that you make political cartoons, but have they ever been a source of inspiration? Or do you not relate to that kind of political content?

WK They have certainly had an effect on me, particularly in the historical sense. Political cartoons have a great tradition of draftsmanship, from Thomas Rowlandson to Honoré Daumier (George Grosz as well—although he did not do cartoons, he was certainly a great draftsman and had a keen eye for the political). I see political cartoons as having a wide range of types. They can be of a very high quality with a complex set of relationships or they can be very generic.

I actually did some political cartooning. There was a South African newspaper that started in the mid-1980s called the *Weekly Mail* [now the *Mail & Guardian*]. For their first six issues they asked me to do some cartoons. After six issues, I said that I didn't think it was working for me and they said they didn't think it was working for them. We were both enormously relieved to be able to withdraw without damaging each other.

MA Why wasn't it working for you?

WK It wasn't working because the process started the wrong way around. You had to work out precisely what you wanted to say first, and then push the drawing to say that. It was really about trying to illustrate an idea. The idea would always take pride of place. It would be a matter of making decisions about what was going on that day, deciding quickly what it meant, and then illustrating your statement about it. I didn't think in a place like South Africa at that time, given the intense politics of that time, that things could be summed up in the immediacy of a deadline.

This is only half the question. It has as much to do with nib and ink, with economy of line, with the impossibility of successive erasure, of doing a drawing twice, once in pencil, then inking it in. Of drawing through the knuckles. The drawing felt artificial. The instrumentalism of analysis I could live with; the discomfort of the pen defeated me.

More importantly, it's just not the way I work things through in my art. My work engages social and political conditions but it comes about gradually, always through drawing. I may start out with something political on my mind, and then it ends up about an empty chair in my studio. Or just the opposite. It is a different kind of truth, if you will. It would have to be a unique newspaper that could allow things to meander between the psychological and the political in that way. Newspapers like to appear to be without contradictions, accidents, or doubt. A political cartoon has to be unambiguous and clear. My drawings are usually neither. My drawings certainly have a political view, but it is also a very personal one.

A political view? This is an easy generalization. A drawing of a fragmented horse (a silhouette dispersed across a page) with the caption "I am not me, the horse is not mine" has a political reference to the Russian peasant phrase denying guilt, but I came across it in the defense of a Soviet Politburo member who was purged in the 1930s. So one can ascribe a politics to the context itself—fragmentation and reconstruction. The resistance of the world to its reascription. These associations may be there, but to characterize them as a "view"?

MA I was thinking the other day that if Felix made art he would draw. He would not be a painter.

WK No, he wouldn't. I can't imagine Felix as a painter. I can imagine Soho as a painter: like Winston Churchill, putting up an easel at the beach and painting seascapes. It would be interesting to do a show of drawings by Felix and paintings by Soho. As we talk, it makes me wonder what are the paintings that Soho does and what drawings would Felix do. I guess I'll have to do them.

In truth, Felix has been absent for many years. He last appeared in *Felix in Exile* fourteen years ago. The last four films—*History of the Main Complaint, WEIGHING...and WANTING, Stereoscope*, and *Tide Table*—have featured only Soho. When I made the sad realization that Felix and Soho had both become a split, displaced self-portrait, it became difficult to get to Felix. The loss of lack of knowledge is the sadness.

MA It seems to me that Felix is in a constant state of redefining his thoughts and feelings. So he would always be redrawing himself. Also, rightly or wrongly, I associate Felix with you, the artist.

WK Well, of course, I do identify with Felix. But a certain part of me also identifies with Soho. They both seem to encompass the good and bad qualities that make us human: self-protection, generosity, closeness, ambition, greed, confidence, anxiety, all those things. Those two characters are both part of one brain trying to figure out its relation to the world. They were drawn essentially as a demonstration of thinking. You start with a scratch and a line and a muddle and you try to find clarity.

MA Are you talking about the clarity of a specific idea or a formal compositional clarity—an image that is simply interesting to look at?

WK That's always a question one has in making an artwork. I often find that if I start drawing, and find a certain formal clarity in that drawing, then the content, sometimes in the form of a story, will come along. Drawing, at least for me, is always turning a corner, and I can't always see what's around that corner. In a sense, you just keep drawing.

In the *hope* that it will turn a corner, and reveal something I cannot see at the beginning.

Just in the simple act of adjusting, an outline or an image can become something very different, and all of a sudden the plot thickens. In that sense, drawing is a way of processing. I don't seem to be able to do that with painting. I can draw and adjust and erase and that usually develops into a type of narrative. The process of thinking and adjusting while painting is so much slower for me. I'm sure there are painters who can make those adjustments quickly and thoughtfully while it's all wet and messy like toothpaste, but I'm not one of them.

MA Do you work from smaller to larger drawings?

WK Sometimes I do, but I usually take a large sheet and just start drawing. I also have what I call sketchbooks—but my sketchbooks, if you want to call them that, are books of words. The words become my sketches for drawings. If I look at all the notebooks I have kept, there are more words than drawings. The language is usually lists, single words, not full statements. A narrative usually comes out of the process of drawing, but I might use verbal suggestions to get the drawing going. Then the drawing just keeps developing.

MA Like stream-of-consciousness writings or the automatic drawings of the Surrealists?

WK Not quite so fluid. I wish it were. There is a lot of correcting and adjusting. Erasing is actually an important part of the process. The image comes into being as much from what I'm taking away as from what I'm putting down. Erasure becomes a kind of pentimento, an element of layering as you get in painting, but it is more ghostly in drawing. Erasure also makes palpable the activity of the work. It gives you a sense of the process both of making and thinking, which is not linear but a series of advances and reversals and lateral moves. Erasure begs the question of what used to be there. Why is it not there now? I'm always trying to think of new ways of erasing. For me, there are fundamentally two forms of erasure. One is erasing with a rubber eraser, erasing the lines and rubbing down to the paper support, and there are a lot of ways of doing that—using your hand in different ways and applying different kinds of pressure. A less obvious way is literally tearing images up and reconstituting them—fragmenting them and then sticking pieces back together and discovering a new image in that way, which is what I've been doing more lately.

I am wrong here. Tearing and sticking is not erasure. (Occasionally I will tear fragments of a shape away successively—a jagged removal of the wings.) Even as elements are changed, we will the continuation of the first element of recognition. Erasure and the traces it leaves are about the passage of time and hence memory. Fragmentation is about resilience and recognition.

MA So the drawing is always in a state of transformation. Would it be too simplistic to conclude that that is how you got involved in animation?

WK It probably would, although there is a connection between how I draw and the potential for a moving image. As long as I can remember I've drawn into drawings, probably because I never really see them as finished or I don't want to finish them. Some of the drawings are in fact continuous, like drawings that don't have an end. So in a sense the drawing has its own form of animation.

This evades the real issue: a need for provisionality, a need for judgment to be deferred and for redemption to always be possible. Animation is a way in which all stages of the drawing are legitimated and I don't have to judge when a drawing is finished.

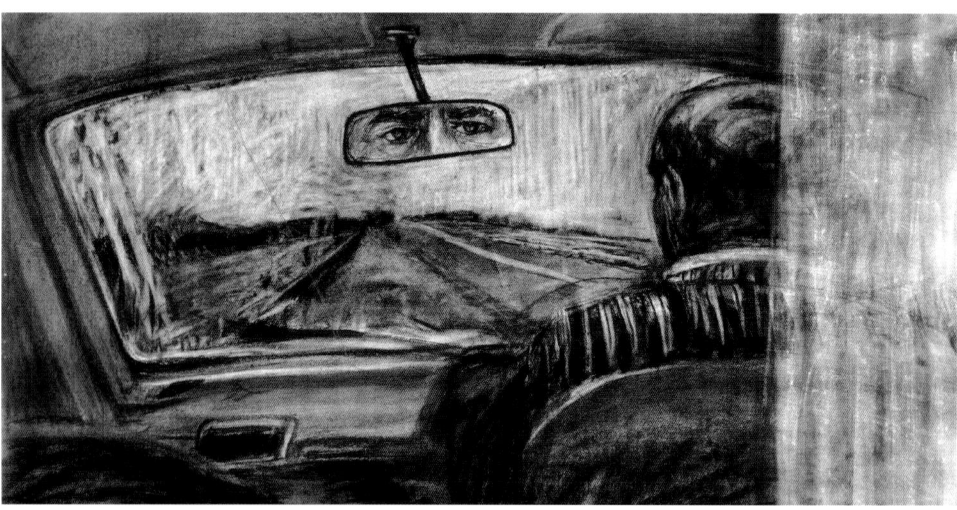

FIG. 48
William Kentridge
Drawing for the film *History of the Main Complaint* [Eyes in Rearview Mirror], 1995–96
Charcoal and pastel on paper
47 1/4 x 63 in. (120 x 160 cm)
Collection of J. Classens, Johannesburg

MA But was there ever a point when you were doing drawings and a recognition of sequencing came to mind, and you thought, "I should just do a film"? I guess I'm trying to establish a sequential relationship from your drawings to the animated films.

WK I see what you mean. Well, I'm thinking the chronology through in my head as we speak. On one level it was very natural for me to move from drawing to animation. I had been involved in theater and film production for a number of years, and that involvement is tangled up with the history of my drawing activity. However, art never seems to unfold in a logical way. But then when you look back, you start to see relationships that were there all the time. Right now I am thinking about an early film I worked on in which there were real actors and there was a drawing on the wall behind them. I remember thinking about seeing the actors perform and in the background the drawing was performing.

Then, not long ago, someone reminded me of something I did when I was fourteen that I had completely forgotten about. A friend had a Super 8 camera, and I had been doing a series of drawings that changed—little line drawings on top of one another, about fifty of them. I borrowed the camera and filmed them, frame by frame. It was like a movie flip book that lasted only a matter of seconds.

MA You did that when you were fourteen?

WK Yes. I'm not saying it was a great work of art, but it's funny how you start somewhere, forget where you started, and then remember again. But it is clear to me that the drawing always came first. Drawing is the primary element or at least the foundation of almost everything I do. And it's still the case today.

Of course the earliest animation was the schoolboy activity of drawing bouncing balls in the margin of successive pages of school textbooks. I think my father showed me how to do this. That is an animation technique that goes back to the 1920s. I wonder whether schoolchildren did this in the era before cinema animation. I have not seen in museums of the history of the moving image early-nineteenth-century textbooks with these marginalia.

MA So the charcoal animations are basically an extension of that teenage drawing project?

WK Not consciously, but I can't help thinking that it is connected. The charcoal animations actually started when a friend was filming a set I had been working on; he had to go off somewhere and said, "I'll leave the camera here for a week." He had been stop-frame filming different points in the making of this theater set. When I eventually looked at the film, I was struck by the effect of this set seeming to construct itself. I started to think about how I could apply the same process to drawing. My goal was to see how a drawing comes into being. So it was really about documenting a drawing, not making a film per se. I started by filming the blank page with the idea of filming each mark as it was added. The idea was that you would see a drawing drawing itself. When that was done I thought, "Well, I could continue with that process." In other words, I wouldn't have to stop when the drawing was finished. The drawing, through film, could continue almost indefinitely. I really just wanted to see a drawing continually making itself—marking, erasing, and eventually changing into different images. I wasn't thinking of it as animation. I was thinking of it as drawing.

MA You mentioned the concept of the flip book. It seems as if that might fit into the sequence of transforming a drawing into a moving image.

WK Again, not so directly. The flip book is a peculiar hybrid. It's a marvelous thing as a kind of primitive image technology. For me, drawing is about a certain kind of fundamental technology. The hand is a basic human tool, and you can extend that into the technology of the book, which allows you to flip the pages with your hands. Like magic, you get a new kind of drawing. I like the effect of the flip book, but in fact it is not how I prefer to work. It really is more like true animation, which people say I do, but I see it a little differently. In a flip book, the drawing on each page has to be a separate drawing. I see drawing as inherently animated. I like to work on a single sheet and erase and change, so the whole film might be one drawing rather than fifty. In the case of the flip book, you make a separate drawing for each page. A flip book is more like a physical film than a moving drawing. The point is that the flip book wasn't a drawing on its way to being a film. The flip book, the films, they are all drawings as far as I'm concerned.

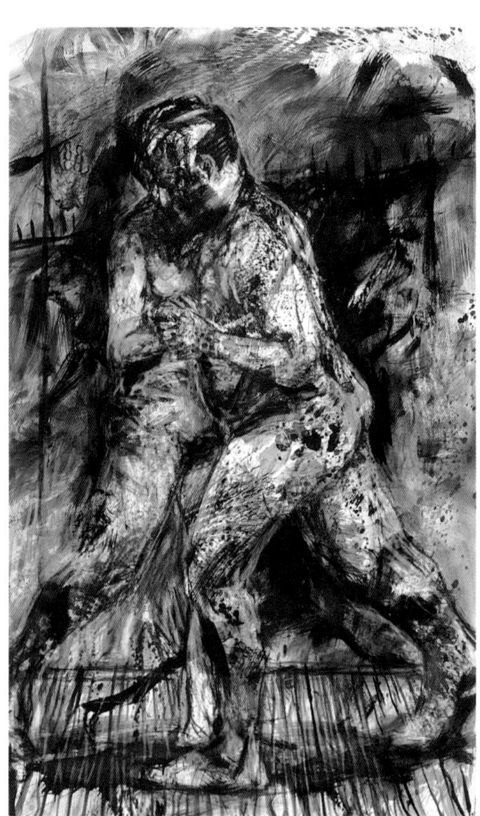

MA That's interesting, because your flip book *Cyclopedia of Drawing* (2004) isn't as seamless and smooth as most flip books. There is a certain jerkiness to the narrative that does seem more like the construction of a drawing. The image seems to jump out at you as it changes, almost like it is stopped and moving at the same time.

WK You are right. It doesn't actually work as a flip book. Going back to your question about sequencing, I have done some large drawings—there are four of them, I think—of a couple dancing. In the sequence they revolve around—a kind of pre-flip book on the wall. I wanted to continue the sequence but I ran out of studio space. I did those in 2005, long after my first film. In a way, they are a reversal of the process you are talking about. I had been doing a lot of films and I wanted very deliberately to turn a film back into a drawing—to retrace my steps back to stillness. The perfect point for me, and I think this is true for many visual artists, is that point between stillness and movement.

The tape ends here. I wonder what I meant. I would be very suspicious of this statement. A "perfect point." Trying to push T. S. Eliot into drawing. Smacks of Anglo-Catholicism. No. I would not go near this.

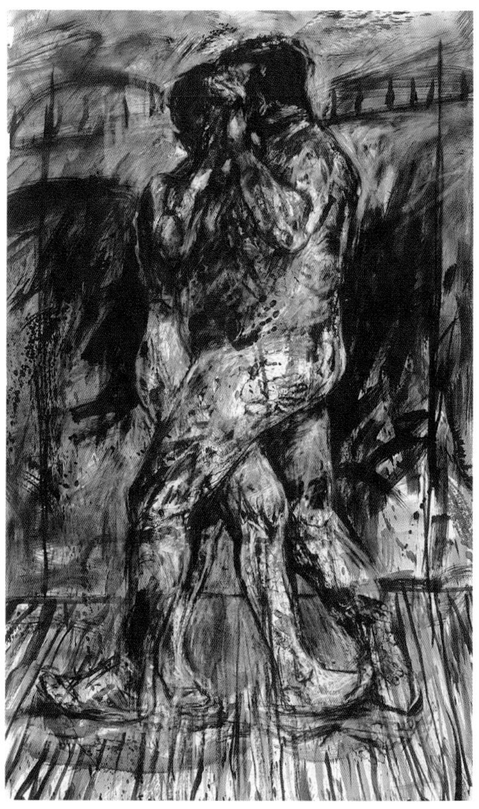

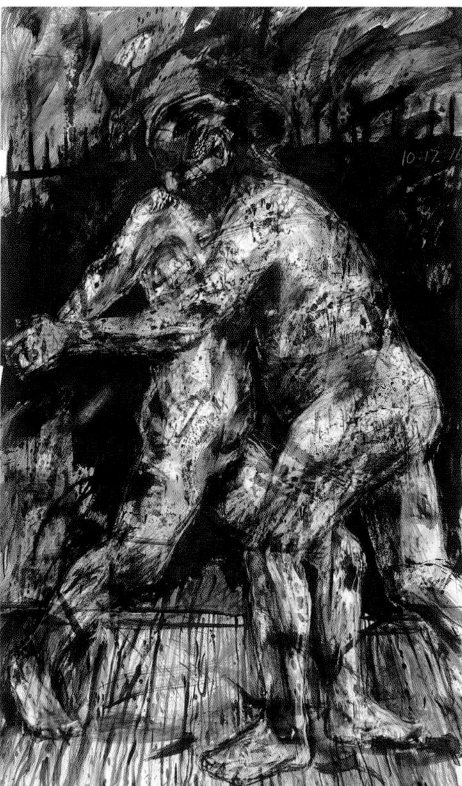

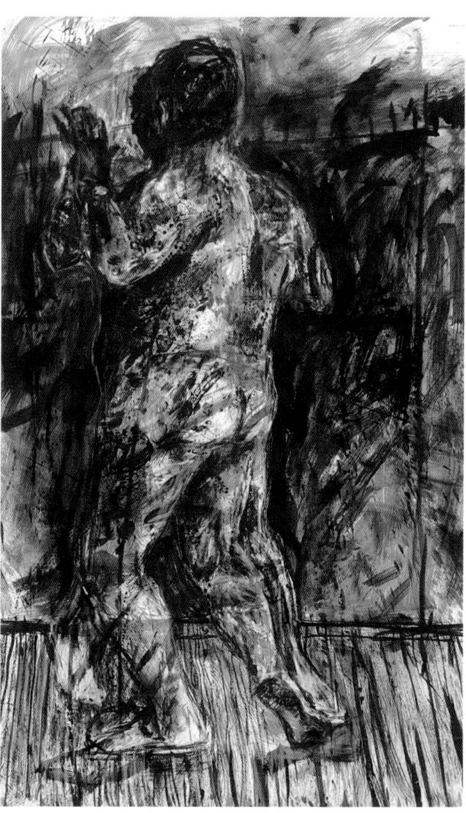

FIGS. 49–52 William Kentridge
***Middle-Aged Love* [1–4], 2005**
Charcoal, pastel, dry pigment, and gouache on paper
Each: 90 1/2 x 51 1/4 in. (230 x 130 cm)
Fundación Privada Sorigué, Spain, courtesy Galleria Lia Rumma

MA Do you think you are getting farther away from drawing in your recent multimedia installations and theater projects?

WK Part of the answer to that question is that it is simply a matter of viewpoint. I have come to think of drawing as a form of projection.

OK, I know this sounds tendentious. But I will not repudiate the statement. I know what I meant, but it is really the subject of another talk, another piece of writing.

So it isn't really a matter of making drawings of things in preparation for something else, but of making drawing literally into other things. If I imagine this sequence from drawing to moving image, I would talk about the anamorphic drawings and the use of a mirror to project and relocate the drawing. The anamorphic drawings are examples of how you can project drawing off the sheet of paper. You may not agree, but I think drawing is the first step of almost all imaging.

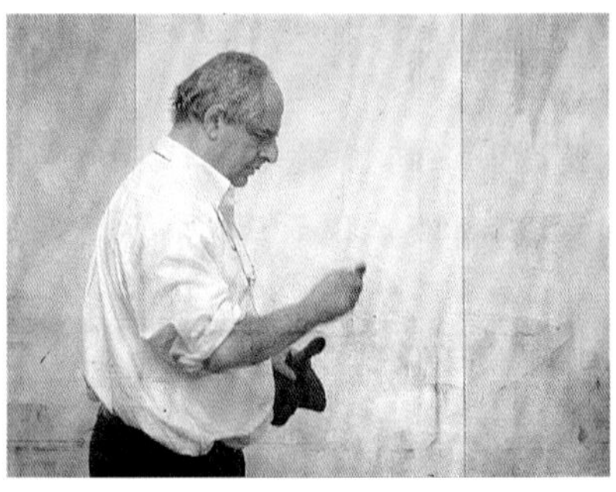

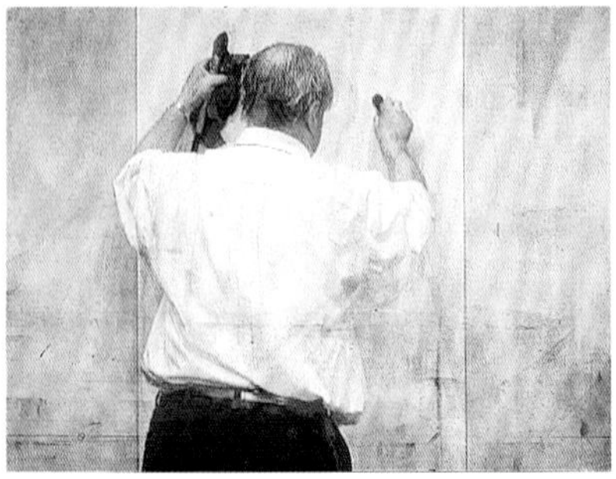

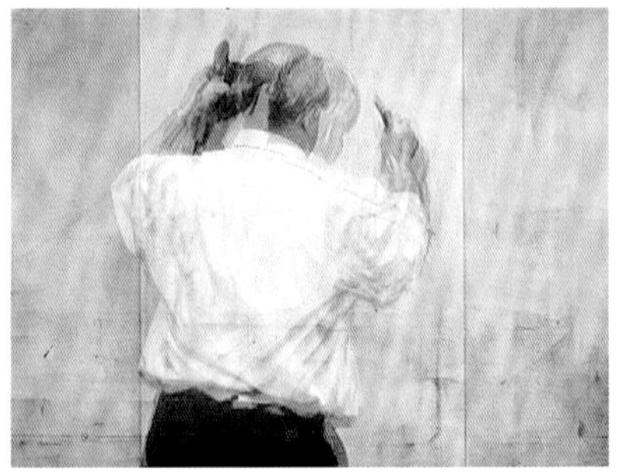

FIGS. 53–55
William Kentridge
Feats of Prestidigitation, from 7 Fragments for Georges Méliès, 2003
35mm animated film transferred to video, 1:50 min.
Collection of the artist, courtesy Marian Goodman Gallery, New York, and Goodman Gallery, Johannesburg

MA Giorgio Vasari said drawing was the purest form of thinking. Since most of us learn to draw before we paint or make sculpture, it becomes one of those first moments of beginning to understand the nature of representation.

WK Yes. When you are learning to draw you bend your head down and you become very intense about watching yourself draw. You put your face down to the paper and then you lift it up, and you start becoming aware of focal distances. Most people who spend any time drawing like to move the sheet of paper—turn it upside down or sideways or pin it to the wall. It seems to me at that point drawing becomes sculpture, because you are changing the relationship of your body to the object. The anamorphic drawings are a type of metaphor for those focal distances, and for how an image, depending on your position, can lose its stability. It has to do with different focal distances between the mirror and the surface of the paper, playing with these and the illusions they can create. So instead of the image appearing to just sit on the surface of the mirror as if it were another sheet of paper, it seems to recede behind the surface of the mirror. There is this three-dimensional depth—like a device you would marvel at in a childhood art class. It is childlike in the sense of trying to re-create the simple magic of certain effects you experience for the first time. The first time you made a drawing that you liked and it literally seemed to come alive off the page. If you take that anamorphic drawing and put it on a circular sheet of paper and throw down some charcoal marks and put a mirror in the center, it will turn into a landscape, one that comes alive as it moves.

But to answer the Vasari question: it's not that I think drawing the purest form of thinking. Rather that drawing as an activity gets close to being a visible external equivalent of an invisible internal process. Drawing (and all art making) is about negotiating the space between what we know and what we see.

MA We haven't discussed your background in theater very much. What role has that played in all this?

WK I learned a lot working in theater productions and have had a long association with a group called Junction Avenue Theatre Company. The productions were often political, but not dogmatic—mostly about the absurdities of apartheid, very Brechtian. It was almost like a support group of multidisciplinary people—artists, performers, psychologists, writers, everyone contributed to the narrative. At one point I thought I wanted to be an actor and went to theater school in Paris. Eventually I realized that I was not a very good actor, and that I had isolated myself a bit, focusing on just the performative part of theater. I realized that I liked working on different aspects of a production. But that wasn't really working either, because in the commercial world you need to focus to get work.

Between 1981 and 1985 I wasn't sure what I wanted to do. I had a lot of parts but it didn't seem to be coming together. I stopped everything at that point. I closed my studio. It was a critical time of assessing what it is I do well, or at least how a few of the different things I do well could find a place. It took a couple of years before I reopened my studio and started working again. When I did, I started drawing. I started working with charcoal and on a larger scale. Eventually, as I worked through the drawing, doing what I felt most comfortable doing, it began to develop into films, installations, and theater situations.

MA Why did you decide you weren't a good actor?

WK My range of gestures was too narrow and limited. Everything I did felt the same.

This assessment was not only mine.

It took a while, but I finally realized that I had a greater range of gestures and possibilities with drawing than with anything else, however modest drawing might seem to be. I didn't feel like there were limits with drawing. And I had this great epiphany that the question was not where drawing begins for an artist, but rather where it ends.

I do not remember this epiphany. It has taken me a little while to understand what I meant by this statement. In a crass interpretation, it would mean that anything could become drawing—writing a lecture is a type of drawing. But I think what I mean here is that the strategies of drawing—of working from blank paper and unclarity toward marks on paper that accumulate meaning—can be applied to many other forms.

LATER: No, I have no memory of saying any of this. It is on the tape, but God knows what I was thinking. There was no epiphany. Rather a long and painful time of failure. Failure to paint, failure to be an actor. I was reduced to drawing. It was the only thing I could do.

CHRONOLOGY

Compiled by Joshua Shirkey.

No title is listed for exhibitions simply called William Kentridge. *Film programs devoted solely to Kentridge's work are included under "Selected Solo Exhibitions and Reviews." Entries cite catalogues and selected reviews whenever possible. For additional books and periodicals, consult the bibliography on pages 257–59.*

Thanks are due to Anne McIlleron, Noemia Herdade-Gomes, and Amanda Glesmann for their assistance in gathering and verifying information.

WILLIAM KENTRIDGE

Born Johannesburg, 1955
BA, University of the Witwatersrand, Johannesburg, 1976
Studied at the Johannesburg Art Foundation, 1976–78; École Jacques Lecoq, Paris, 1981–82

SELECTED AWARDS

First Prize, *National Graphic Show,* South African Association of Arts, Bellville, 1981
Red Ribbon Award for Short Fiction, American Film Festival, New York, 1982
Olive Schreiner Prize for Drama, Cape Town, 1984
Blue Ribbon Award for Short Fiction, American Film Festival, New York, 1985
Merit Award, Cape Town Triennial, 1985
AA Vita Award, South African Arts Association, Pretoria, 1986
Standard Bank Young Artist Award, Grahamstown, South Africa, 1987
Winner, Weekly Mail Short Film Competition, Johannesburg, 1990
Rembrandt Gold Medal, Cape Town Triennial, 1991
Winner, Weekly Mail Short Film Competition, Johannesburg, 1991
Quarterly Vita Award, Johannesburg, 1992
Annual Vita Award, Johannesburg, 1993
Dalro Director Award, Johannesburg, 1993
Quarterly Vita Award, Johannesburg, 1993
Special Production Award, Vita Award for Best New South African Production, Johannesburg, 1993
Vita Award for Set Design of the Year, Johannesburg, 1993
Carnegie Prize, Carnegie Museum of Art, Pittsburgh, 2000
Honorary Doctor of Fine Arts, Maryland Institute of Contemporary Art, Baltimore, 2002
Der Kaiserring Kunstpreis der Stadt Goslar, Mönchehaus Museum für moderne Kunst, Goslar, Germany, 2003
6th Sharjah International Biennial Prize, United Arab Emirates, 2003
Honorary Doctor of Literature, University of the Witwatersrand, Johannesburg, 2004
Rosenberger Medal, University of Chicago, 2006
National Orders, South Africa, Order of Ikhamanga in Silver, 2007
Honorary Doctor of Fine Arts, Rhodes University, Grahamstown, South Africa, 2008
Oskar-Kokoschka-Preis, Vienna, 2008

SELECTED SOLO EXHIBITIONS AND REVIEWS

1979
Market Gallery, Johannesburg, November 4–December 1.
Emdon, Erica. "From the Courtyard." *Financial Mail,* November 23, 1979.

1981
Domestic Scenes, Market Gallery, Johannesburg, February 1–21.

1985
Cassirer Fine Art, Johannesburg, April 15–27.

1986
Cassirer Fine Art, Johannesburg, November 3–15. Traveled to South African Arts Association, Pretoria.

1987
In the Heart of the Beast, Vanessa Devereux Gallery, London, April 22–May 19.
Hilliard, Elizabeth. Review. *Arts Review* 39, no. 9 (May 8, 1987): 295.
Packer, William. "Rich Breeding Ground for Galleries." *Financial Times,* April 28, 1987.

1988
William Kentridge and Simon Stone, Gallery International, Cape Town, March 29–April 15.

Cassirer Fine Art, Johannesburg, November 6–19.

1989
Responsible Hedonism, Vanessa Devereux Gallery, London, May 14–June 20.

1990
Drawings and Graphics, Cassirer Fine Art and Market Gallery, Johannesburg, April 30–May 23.

Drawings, Gallery International, Cape Town, October 29–November 10.

T&I, FIG Gallery, Johannesburg.

1992
William Kentridge: Drawings for Projection, Goodman Gallery, Johannesburg, February 21–March 14. Traveled to Vanessa Devereux Gallery, London. Catalogue by Michael Godby.
Hall, Charles. Review. *Arts Review* 44 (June 1992): 224–25.

1993
Ruth Bloom Gallery, Los Angeles.

1994
William Kentridge: Felix in Exile, Goodman Gallery, Johannesburg, October 16–November 5.

1995
Memory and Geography, Studio Stefania Miscetti, Rome, June 15–July 28. Catalogue.

1996
Eidophusikon: Seven Colonial Landscapes and Drawings from Faustus in Africa!, Annandale Galleries, Sydney, March 27–April 20.

1997
William Kentridge: Applied Drawings, Goodman Gallery, Johannesburg, March 2–22.
Geers, Kendell. Review. *Star Tonight!* (Johannesburg), March 21, 1997.

1998
William Kentridge: Drawings for Projection, Drawing Center, New York, January 9–February 14.
Brooks, Rosetta. Review. *Artforum* 36, no. 8 (April 1998): 110.
Camhi, Leslie. "Mind Field." *Village Voice,* January 27, 1998, 89.
Rush, Michael. "The Enduring Avant-Garde: Jean-Luc Godard and William Kentridge." *PAJ: A Journal of Performance and Art* 20, no. 3 (September 1998): 48–52.
Smith, Roberta. Review. *New York Times,* February 6, 1998.

William Kentridge: WEIGHING . . . and WANTING, Museum of Contemporary Art, San Diego, January 25–April 12. Traveled to North Dakota Museum of Art, Grand Forks; MIT List Visual Arts Center, Cambridge, Massachusetts; Forum for Contemporary Art, Saint Louis; Salina Art Center, Kansas; Art Gallery of Ontario, Toronto; University of Michigan Museum of Art, Ann Arbor; Bowdoin College Museum of Art, Brunswick, Maine. Catalogue edited by Hugh M. Davies.
Gopnik, Blake. "The Conservative Mr. Kentridge." *Toronto Globe and Mail,* August 14, 2000.
Hume, Christopher. Review. *Toronto Star,* August 19, 2000.
Ollman, Leah. "A Laconic Film, Far from Silent." *Los Angeles Times,* February 8, 1998.
Pincus, Robert L. "Weighed in the Balance." *San Diego Union-Tribune,* February 5, 1998.
Plagens, Peter. "The Best of 1998." *Artforum* 37, no. 4 (December 1998): 98–99.
Sherman, Mary. "Hit List." *Boston Herald,* January 24, 1999.
Temin, Christine. "Three Shows at the List Face Up to Human Suffering." *Boston Globe,* January 31, 1999.

Stephen Friedman Gallery and A22 Gallery, London, March 6–April 18.

Palais des Beaux-Arts / Paleis voor Schone Kunsten, Brussels, May 15–August 23. Traveled to Kunstverein München, Munich; Museu d'Arte Contemporani de Barcelona; Serpentine Gallery, London; Neue Galerie Graz am Landesmuseum Joanneum, Austria; Centre de Vieille Charité, Marseille, France. Catalogue by Carolyn Christov-Bakargiev.
Bader, Joerg. Review. *Art Press* 246 (May 1999): 71–72.
Chambers, Eddie. "The Main Complaint." *Art Monthly* 227 (June 1999): 1–4.
Cork, Richard. "Sombre Visions of Africa." *Times* (London), April 28, 1999.
Cumming, Laura. "Blood and Charcoal." *Observer* (London), May 2, 1999.
Gayford, Martin. "London Surprises." *Spectator* (London), May 15, 1999.
Grünberg, Serge. Review. *Cahiers du cinema,* no. 537 (July–August 1999): 6.
Hauffen, Michael. Review. *Kunstforum* 142 (October–December 1998): 433–34.
Januszczak, Waldemar. "Root of the Problem." *Times* (London), April 25, 1999.

Leonard, Robert. Review. *Art/Text* 66 (1999): 85–86.
Lubbock, Tom. "Almost Black and White." *Independent* (London), May 4, 1999.
"Mit Gewalt und allen Tricks." *ART: das Kunstmagazin* 9 (September 1998): 91.
Packer, William. "Moving Drawings." *Financial Times*, April 24, 1999.
Pérez, Luis Francisco. "Movimiento estático de lo real." *Lapiz* 18, no. 152 (April 1999): 18–23.
Searle, Adrian. "Nasty, Comic and Crude." *Guardian* (London), April 20, 1999.
Serra, Catalina. "William Kentridge exhibe en el MACBA dolorosos filmes humanos." *El Pais*, January 26, 1999.
Sotiriadi, Tina. "William Kentridge: A Process of Remembering and Forgetting." *Third Text* 48 (Autumn 1999): 106–8.
Vogel, Sabine. "Wie man die schlechte Welt in den Kopf hineinbringt." *Frankfurter Allgemeine Zeitung*, October 2, 1998.
Ziegler, Erdmann. "Die Folklore von Folterern." *Die Tageszeitung*, September 5, 1998.

William Kentridge: New Editions, Cindy Bordeau Fine Art, Chicago, November 6–December 1.
Barandiarán, María José. Review. *New Art Examiner* 26, no. 6 (March 1999): 52–53.

Ulisse: Echo, Netherlands Architecture Institute, Rotterdam, December 16, 1998–March 30, 1999.

1999
Projects 68: William Kentridge, Museum of Modern Art, New York, April 15–June 8.
Desai, Anuj. "Looney, Tuned." *Black Book* (Spring 1999): 48–49.
Firstenberg, Lauri. Review. *Nka: Journal of Contemporary African Art* 11–12 (Fall–Winter 2000): 119.
Smith, Roberta. Review. *New York Times*, April 23, 1999.

William Kentridge: Recent Editions, Robert Brown Gallery, Washington, DC, May 1–June 12.

Galleria Lia Rumma, Naples, Italy, May 22–July 22.

Marian Goodman Gallery, Paris, September 18–November 13.
Bouruet-Aubertot, Véronique. Review. *Beaux Arts* 185 (October 1999): 31.
Breerette, Geneviève. Review. *Le Monde*, September 25, 1999.

William Kentridge: Stereoscope, Goodman Gallery, Johannesburg, October 16–November 20.
Elliott, Robyn. "Kentridge's Desperate State of Mind." *Business Day*, October 19, 1999.

Douglas F. Cooley Gallery, Reed College, Portland, Oregon, November 2–December 31.
Gragg, Randy. "Rough and Tumbling Visions in Charcoal." *Oregonian*, November 7, 1999.

2000
Insistent Memory Part I: William Kentridge, Samuel P. Harn Museum of Art, University of Florida, Gainesville, January 21–March 12.

Elizabeth Leach Gallery, Portland, Oregon, March 2–April 1.

William Kentridge et Kara Walker, Centre d'Art Contemporain Genève, Geneva, March 3–May 28.
Chauvy, Laurence. "William Kentridge et Kara Walker, entre scène, satire et video." *Le Temps* (Geneva), March 21, 2000.

Stephen Friedman Gallery, London, April 14–May 20.

William Kentridge: New Work, Marian Goodman Gallery, New York, May 30–July 14.
Koplos, Janet. Review. *Art in America* 88, no. 12 (December 2000): 116–17.
Sheets, Hilarie M. Review. *ARTnews* 99, no. 8 (September 2000): 170.

Goodman Gallery, Johannesburg, September 16–23.

William Kentridge: Procession, Annandale Galleries, Sydney, November 15–December 9.
Smee, Sebastian. "Follow the Conjurer." *Sydney Morning Herald*, November 25, 2000.

2001
Bowdoin College Museum of Art, Brunswick, Maine, January 28–March 18.

William Kentridge: Recent Editions, Robert Brown Gallery, Washington, DC, February 24–April 21.

Organized by New Museum of Contemporary Art, New York, and Museum of Contemporary Art, Chicago. Hirshhorn Museum and Sculpture Garden, Smithsonian Institution, Washington, DC, February 28–May 13. Traveled to New Museum of Contemporary Art; Museum of Contemporary Art; Contemporary Arts Museum, Houston; Los Angeles County Museum of Art; South African National Gallery, Cape Town. Catalogue by Neal Benezra et al. (copublished with Harry N. Abrams, New York).
Baker, George. Review. *Artforum* 40, no. 3 (November 2001): 143.
Belasco, Daniel. "Vexed Lives." *New York Jewish Week*, June 15, 2001, 35.
Bischoff, Dan. "Animator Traces South Africa Progress." *Newark Star-Ledger*, June 15, 2001.
Boschmann, Hella. "Zeichnen gegen das Unrecht." *Die Welt*, March 7, 2001.
Brunetti, John. Review. *Dialogue*, January–February 2002, 45–47.
Budick, Ariella. "Works of Remembrance." *New York Newsday*, June 10, 2001.
Campbell, Shane. Review. *New Art Examiner* 29, no. 4 (March–April 2002): 79–80.
Candela, Iria. Review. *Lapiz* 20, no. 175 (July 2001): 80.
Ciezaldo, Janina. Review. *Chicago Reader*, January 11, 2002, 22.
Clifford, Katie. Review. *ARTnews* 100, no. 6 (June 2001): 135.
Danto, Arthur C. "Drawing for Projection." *The Nation* 273, no. 3 (July 16, 2001): 43–45.
Douglas, Susan. Review. *C: International Contemporary Art* 71 (Fall 2001): 43–44.
Dreyer, Elfriede. Review. *De Arte* 68 (September 2003): 50–51.
Drohojowska-Philp, Hunter. "Ambivalent African." *Los Angeles Times*, July 14, 2002.
Falconer, Morgan. Review. *Art Review* 53 (April 2001): 77.
Farrell, Laurie Ann. Review. *African Arts* 35, no. 2 (Summer 2002): 81–83.
Gioni, Massimiliano. "New York Cut Up." *Flash Art* 34, no. 219 (July–September 2001): 71–73.
Glueck, Grace. "Apartheid and Its Bitter Aftertaste." *New York Times*, June 8, 2001.
Gopnik, Blake. "An Animated Darkness." *Washington Post*, March 11, 2001.
Hawkins, Margaret. "Self Examination." *Chicago Sun-Times*, November 16, 2001.
Howell, George. Review. *Art Papers* 25, no. 5 (September–October 2001): 43.
Johnson, Patricia C. "Kentridge's Narratives Are Bold, Moralistic." *Houston Chronicle*, March 2, 2002.
Joubert, Suzanne. Review. *Business Day*, February 3, 2003.
Klassmeyer, Kelly. "The Reluctant Spokesman." *Houston Press*, May 2, 2002.
Knaff, Devorah L. "Seeing Beyond South Africa." *Riverside Press-Enterprise*, August 25, 2002.
Knight, Christopher. "Work That Seems to Hold That Thought." *Los Angeles Times*, July 29, 2002.
McNatt, Glenn. "Traces of Memory Touch the Present." *Baltimore Sun*, July 1, 2001.
Milani, Joanne. "The Person in the Mirror." *Tampa Tribune*, July 8, 2001.
Naves, Mario. "Kentridge's Charcoals: I Saw the Movie." *New York Observer*, September 10, 2001.
Ogbechie, Sylvester Okwunodu. "Are We There Yet?" *African Arts* 35, no. 1 (Spring 2002): 1, 4–7.
O'Sullivan, Michael. "Kentridge's Troubling Shades of Truth." *Washington Post*, March 9, 2001.
Pollack, Barbara. "Art of Resistance." *Village Voice*, June 5, 2001, 44, 47.
Reif, Wanda. "Apartheid and Its Aftermath in Charcoal and Cinema." *Lancet* 357, no. 9266 (May 5, 2001): 1453–54.
Salopek, Paul. "South African Artist Soars from Years of Obscurity." *Chicago Tribune*, October 19, 2001.
Sausset, Damien. "Le monde torturé de William Kentridge." *Oeil* 527 (June 2001): 90.
Shaw-Eagle, Joanna. "Staring into Apartheid's Legacy." *Washington Times*, March 3, 2001.
Sheets, Hilarie M. "In a Kaleidoscope of Remembering and Forgetting." *New York Times*, June 17, 2001.
Sirmans, Franklin. "Cry Freedom." *Time Out New York*, June 21–28, 2001.
Sorkin, Jenni. Review. *Frieze* 63 (November–December 2001): 123.
Stein, Lisa. "Territory of Grief." *Chicago Tribune*, October 28, 2001.

Stevens. Mark. "Flowers on the Wall." *New York Magazine,* July 9, 2001, 45, 81.
Vayda, Priscilla Fleming. "Cross Hatchings." *Los Angeles Daily News,* July 31, 2002.
Velázquez de León, Mauricio. "Plasma el sufrimiento en obras cambientes." *Reforma,* June 16, 2001.
Weintraub, Linda. Review. *Tema Celeste* 87 (September–October 2001): 78.
Weiss, Hedy. "South African Landscapes." *Chicago Sun-Times,* October 18, 2001.
"William Kentridge's Graphic Pursuit." *Art on Paper* 5, no. 6 (July–August 2001): 23.
Zeaman, John. "A Country's Pain, Frame by Frame." *Hackensack Record,* June 8, 2001.

The 59th Minute: Video Art on the Astrovision by Panasonic; Shadow Procession, organized by Creative Time. Times Square, New York, May 21–June 30. Catalogue titled *Creative Time: The Book* by Anne Pasternak et al. (copublished with Princeton Architectural Press, New York, 2007).

William Kentridge: Prints, Gracie Mansion Gallery, New York, May 31–July 27.

Marian Goodman Gallery, Paris, September 8–October 27.
Fouquet, Ludovic. "Vidéo et le charbon." *Etc Montréal* 56 (December 2001–February 2002): 54–58.

William Kentridge's Soho Eckstein Cycle, San Francisco Cinematheque, October 18.
Baker, Kenneth. "Kentridge's Moving Sketches." *San Francisco Chronicle,* October 17, 2001.

2002

Galleria Lia Rumma, Milan, January 17–March 29.

William Kentridge: Stereoscope, Gus Fisher Gallery, University of Auckland, New Zealand, January 23–March 16.
McNamara, T. J. "Messages Surge through Gallery Air." *New Zealand Herald,* January 30, 2002.

William Kentridge: Graphics, Annandale Galleries, Sydney, May 1–June 22.

Points of Contact, Robert Brown Gallery, Washington, DC, closed July 5.
Dawson, Jessica. "Portraits of Tyranny." *Washington Post,* June 13, 2002.

William Kentridge: Zeno Writing, Marian Goodman Gallery, New York, November 8, 2002–January 4, 2003.
Chang, Chris. Review. *Film Comment* 39, no. 1 (January–February 2003): 17.
Mac Adam, Alfred. Review. *ARTnews* 102, no. 2 (February 2003): 126.
Naves, Mario. Review. *New York Observer,* January 6, 2003.
Saltz, Jerry. "History Drawing." *Village Voice,* December 25, 2002, 53.

2003

Goodman Gallery, Johannesburg, March 1–29.
Johnson, Ashley. Review. *Business Day,* March 26, 2003.

William Kentridge: Thinking in Water, Dieu Donné, New York, April 23–June 14.
"Thinking in Watermarks." *Art on Paper* 7, no. 7 (May–June 2003): 90.

William Kentridge: Journey to the Moon, 7 Fragments for Georges Méliès, Day for Night, Baltic Art Center, Visby, Sweden, June 6–August 31. Catalogue.

Mönchehaus Museum für moderne Kunst, Goslar, Germany, October 11, 2003–February 1, 2004.
Klett, Renate. "Liebe Kunstgenießer!" *Theater Heute* 12 (December 2003): 71.

William Kentridge: Learning the Flute, Kappatos Gallery, Athens, Greece, November 12, 2003–January 31, 2004.

Greg Kucera Gallery, Seattle.

2004

Castello di Rivoli Museo d'Arte Contemporanea, Italy, January 10–February 29. Traveled to K20/K21 Kunstsammlung Nordrhein-Westfalen, Düsseldorf, Germany; Museum of Contemporary Art, Sydney; Musée d'Art Contemporain de Montréal; Johannesburg Art Gallery; Miami Art Central, Florida. Catalogue edited by Carolyn Christov-Bakargiev (copublished with Skira Editore, Milan).
Anderson, Randall. Review. *Flash Art* 38 (May–June 2005): 150–51.
Barrowclough, Nikki. "Works in Progress." *Sydney Morning Herald,* September 4, 2004.
Diez, Renate. Review. *Arte* 365 (January 2004): 140–46.
Dittmar, Peter. "Melancholie der Schatten." *Die Welt,* April 27, 2004.
Fortescue, Elizabeth. "Little Box of Horrors." *Daily Telegraph* (Sydney), September 3, 2004.
Gordon, Margery. Review. *ARTnews* 105, no. 5 (May 2006): 171.
Higson, Rosalie. "Politics Poured into His Art." *Australian,* September 3, 2004.
Hill, Peter. "Backward Glances." *Sydney Morning Herald,* September 18, 2004.
Kothenschulte, Daniel. "Poesie der Pappkulisse." *Frankfurter Rundschau,* April 10, 2004.
Lehmann, Henry. "Suffocatingly Black Art from the Dark Continent." *Montreal Gazette,* February 19, 2005.
Low, Lenny Ann. "A Dabbler Makes His Mark." *Sydney Morning Herald,* September 2, 2004.
Mendelssohn, Joanna. Review. *Art & Australia* 42, no. 3 (Autumn 2005): 378–79.
Pérez León, Dermis. Review. *Art Nexus* 3, no. 54 (October–December 2004): 104–8.
Rocco, Moliterni. Review. *La Stampa,* January 9, 2004.
Rossmann, Andreas. "Proteus am Kap." *Frankfurter Allgemeine Zeitung,* April 17, 2004.
Sausset, Damien. Review. *Art Press* 299 (March 2004): 68–70.
Siegel, Katy. Preview. *Artforum* 42, no. 5 (January 2004): 79.
Suarez de Jesus, Carlos. "Pulling No Punches." *Miami New Times,* January 26, 2006.
Tansini, Laura. Review. *Art on Paper* 8, no. 4 (March–April 2004): 79.
Thea, Carolee. "The Human Procession." *Sculpture* 24, no. 3 (April 2005): 22–23.
Triff, Alfredo. "William Kentridge y sus sombrías siluetas." *Miami Nuevo Herald,* December 18, 2005.
Weinstein, Joel. "Sex and Empire." *Art Nexus* 5, no. 60 (March–May 2006): 36–37.

Spacex, Exeter, England, February 14–April 30.

William Kentridge: Tide Table and Learning the Flute, Marian Goodman Gallery, New York, March 4–April 10.
Bellini, Andrea. "New York Tales." *Flash Art* 37, no. 236 (May–June 2004): 114–16.
Hirsch, Faye. Review. *Art in America* 92, no. 11 (December 2004): 135–36.
Naves, Mario. "Words Alone Cannot Describe William Kentridge's Animated Film." *New York Observer,* April 5, 2004.
Rosenberg, Karen. "Ebb and Flow." *New York Magazine,* March 8, 2004, 103.

Journey to the Moon and 9 Drawings for Projection, Spier Amphitheatre, Stellenbosch, South Africa, March 6–7. Traveled to Old Fort at Constitution Hill, Johannesburg; Castello Maniace, Siracusa, Italy; Kliptown, Soweto, South Africa; Newton, Johannesburg; Barbican Centre, London; Zürcher Theater, Zurich; SKC, Belgrade, Serbia; Teatro Palladium, Rome; Deutsche Guggenheim, Berlin; Teatro Out Off, Milan; Sallis Benney Theatre, Brighton, England; Kennedy Center, Washington, DC.
Gurney, Kim. "Still Life in Motion." *Times* (Johannesburg), March 21, 2004.
Schoeman, Gerhard. Review. *ArtSouthAfrica* 3, no. 1 (Spring 2004): 65.

Organized by art3, Crac, Musée de Valence, Poudrière, écoles supérieures d'art de Valence et d'Annecy, and Château-Musée d'Annecy, France. Art3, Musée de Valence, and Crac, March 1–May 23. Traveled to Château-Musée d'Annecy. Artist's book titled *Cyclopedia of Drawing* (published by art3, Valence, and École d'art de l'agglomération d'Annecy, France).

Masters of Animation: William Kentridge, Australian Centre for the Moving Image, Melbourne, May 13–15.

Annandale Galleries, Sydney, August 25–October 30. Catalogue by Bill Gregory.

William Kentridge: Tide Table, Rose Art Museum, Brandeis University, Waltham, Massachusetts, September 7–December 12.
Boulanger, Susan. Review. *Art New England* 26, no. 2 (April–May 2005): 5, 59.
Temin, Christine. "Exhibits Present a Global Perspective." *Boston Globe,* November 28, 2004.

William Kentridge: Prints, Faulconer Gallery, Bucksbaum Center for the Arts, Grinnell College, Iowa, October 1–December 12. Traveled to College of Wooster Art Museum, Ebert Art Center, Ohio; Jane Voorhees Zimmerli Art Museum, Rutgers, the State University of New Jersey, New Brunswick; Corcoran Gallery of Art, Washington, DC; Smith College Museum of Art, Northampton, Massachusetts; Williams College Museum of Art, Williamstown, Massachusetts. Catalogue by Susan Stewart (second edition copublished with David Krut, Johannesburg, 2006).

Bischoff, Dan. "South African Artist's Conscience Is His Guide." *Newark Star-Ledger,* April 23, 2006.
Clements, French. "Images of a Dreamer." *Berkshire Eagle,* March 6, 2008.
Genocchio, Benjamin. "Searing Messages and Imaginative Flair." *New York Times,* June 18, 2006.
Godfrey, Tony. Review. *Print Quarterly* 22, no. 3 (September 2005): 330.
McQuaid, Cate. "Commenting on Society and Perception Itself." *Boston Globe,* August 3, 2008.
Ode, Susan. Review. *Art Papers* 29, no. 2 (March–April 2005): 52.
Tranberg, Dan. "South African Artist Appeals to Conscience." *Cleveland Plain Dealer,* February 26, 2005.

Marian Goodman Gallery, Paris, October 23–December 4.

William Kentridge: Selections on Paper, Metropolitan Museum of Art, New York, November 12, 2004–April 10, 2005.

Bischoff, Dan. "The Turmoil of Post-Apartheid South Africans." *Newark Star-Ledger,* November 28, 2004.

2005

William Kentridge's 9 Drawings for Projection, Museum of Modern Art, New York, February 15–20.

Halter, Ed. Review. *Village Voice,* February 15–21, 2006, 58.
Lee, Nathan. Review. *New York Times,* February 15, 2006.

Art Gallery of Western Australia, Perth, March 21–August 21.

William Kentridge: Preparing the Flute, Goodman Gallery, Johannesburg, June 4–July 18.

Carman, Jillian. Review. *ArtSouthAfrica* 4, no. 1 (Spring 2005): 62–63.
Johnson, Ashley. Review. *Business Day,* June 20, 2005.
Mkefa, Zingi. "Pure Magic from Kentridge." *Times* (Johannesburg), June 12, 2005.

William Kentridge: 9 Drawings for Projection, Prospect Park Bandshell, New York, June 23; Central Park Bandshell, New York, June 27.

William Kentridge: 9 Drawings for Projection, Massachusetts Museum of Contemporary Art, North Adams, June 25.

Jaeger, Luke. Review. *Art New England* 26, no. 6 (October–November 2005): 30.
Worrell, Kris. "Drawing from History." *Albany Times-Union,* August 20, 1999.

Model Arts and Niland Gallery, Sligo, Ireland, October 1–31. Traveled to Limerick City Gallery of Art, Ireland; Gallagher Gallery, Royal Hibernian Academy, Dublin. Catalogue by Francis McKee.

Dunne, Aidan. "Down-to-Earth Approach." *Irish Times,* October 17, 2005.
Leach, Cristin. "World View That's Not Just Black and White." *Times* (London), February 19, 2006.

"Sete Fragmentos para Georges Méliès" e outros trabalhos de William Kentridge, Museu do Chiado, Museu Nacional de Arte Contemporânea, Lisbon, October 7–December 31. Catalogue by Ruth Rosengarten.

Calvo, Guillermo. Review. *Arte y Parte* 59 (October–November 2005): 135.

William Kentridge: Black Box/Chambre Noire, Deutsche Guggenheim, Berlin, October 29, 2005–January 15, 2006. Traveled to Museum der Moderne Salzburg, Austria; Johannesburg Art Gallery. Catalogue by Maria-Christina Villaseñor.

Ansell, Gwen, and Judy Seidman. "Enlightenment's Shadow." *Business Day,* May 13, 2006.
Bourcier, Jean-Pierre. "Cimaises de Berlin." *La Tribune* (Paris), November 22, 2005.
Buhr, Elke. "Das Nashorn in der Schachtel." *Frankfurter Rundschau,* November 15, 2005.
Coulson, Michael. "Superb Execution." *Financial Mail,* June 2, 2006.
Dodd, Alex. Review. *Business Day,* May 8, 2006.
Dreyer, Elfriede. Review. *ArtSouthAfrica* 4, no. 1 (Spring 2005): 64–65.
Dubin, Steven C. "Theater of History." *Art in America* 95, no. 4 (April 2007): 128–31, 157.
Janku, Laura Richard. "Black Box: An Interview with William Kentridge." *ArtUS* 14 (July–September 2006): 8–11.
Lange, Christy. Review. *Frieze* 98 (April 2006): 172.
Molesworth, Charles. "Ethnography, Art, and Justice: The Example of William Kentridge." *Salmagundi* 152 (Fall 2006): 38–45.
Schoeman, Gerhard. Review. *ArtSouthAfrica* 5, no. 1 (Spring 2006): 63.
Sey, James. Review. *ArtSouthAfrica* 5, no. 1 (Spring 2006): 62.
Wahjudi, Claudia. Review. *Kunstforum* 179 (February–April 2006): 254–56.
Woeller, Marcus. "In der Dunkelkammer." *Die Tageszeitung,* November 11, 2005.

William Kentridge: Preparing the Flute, Galleria Lia Rumma, Naples, opened November 16.

William Kentridge: 7 Fragments for Georges Méliès, Museum of Contemporary Art, Los Angeles, December 11, 2005–February 26, 2006.

Ollman, Leah. "An Artist and His Studio Come Alive." *Los Angeles Times,* February 10, 2006.
Zellen, Jody. "Animated Journeys." *Afterimage* 33, no. 6 (May–June 2006): 42.

2006

William Kentridge: The Magic Flute, Drawings and Projections, Marian Goodman Gallery, New York, January 19–February 25.

Heuer, Megan. Review. *ARTnews* 105, no. 6 (June 2006): 144–45.
Panero, James. Review. *New Criterion* 24, no. 7 (March 2006): 36–37.

San Francisco Art Institute, January 25–March 25.

Baker, Kenneth. "Simple Images. Potent Impact." *San Francisco Chronicle,* February 25, 2006.

William Kentridge: 7 Fragments for Georges Méliès, National Gallery of Victoria, Melbourne, Australia, February 24–May 21.

Hill, Peter. "Grand Ambition Makes Art in Flickering Light." *Age* (Melbourne), March 18, 2006.

William Kentridge: 7 Fragments for Georges Méliès, Wexner Center for the Arts, Ohio State University, Columbus, April 7–August 6.

New Media Projects: William Kentridge, Nelson-Atkins Museum of Art, Kansas City, Missouri, April 21–July 9.

Marian Goodman Gallery, Paris, June 20–July 27.

Bailly, Bérénice. "Kentridge, c'est magique!" *Le Monde,* July 1, 2006.
Romney, Jonathan. Review. *Modern Painters* (September 2006): 109.

2007

William Kentridge: Works on Paper, 1980s and 1990s, Priska C. Juschka Fine Art, New York, February 1–March 3.

William Kentridge: Fragments for Georges Méliès and Black Box/Chambre Noire, Moderna Museet, Stockholm, February 3–April 15. Traveled to Malmö Konsthall, Sweden.

William Kentridge: Journey to the Moon, 7 Fragments for Georges Méliès, Day for Night, Hamburger Bahnhof Museum für Gegenwart, Berlin, February 7–May 6.
Althen, Michael. "Die außergewöhnliche Höflichkeit der Dinge." *Frankfurter Allgemeine Zeitung,* March 29, 2007.
Woeller, Marcus. "Punkt, Punkt, Komma, Strich." *Die Tageszeitung,* February 16, 2007.

William Kentridge: Works on Paper, Prichard Art Gallery, University of Idaho, Moscow, February 9–March 31.

William Kentridge: Selected Rare Graphics, Annandale Galleries, Sydney, March 21–April 21.

William Kentridge: New Editions, David Krut Projects, New York, March 24–April 21.

William Kentridge: What Will Come (has already come), Städelmuseum, Frankfurt, Germany, June 2–August 5. Traveled to Kunsthalle Bremen, Germany. Catalogue by Dennis Conrad.
Crüwell, Konstanze. "Das doppelte Rhinozeros." *Frankfurter Allgemeine Zeitung,* June 2, 2007.
——. "Eine Kunst des ungewissen Ausgangs." *Frankfurter Allgemeine Zeitung,* May 21, 2007.
Danicke, Sandra. "Fliegende Espressokannen im Kampf gegen Apartheid." *Frankfurter Rundschau,* June 1, 2007.
Lücken, Verena. Review. *Frankfurter Allgemeine Zeitung,* July 12, 2007.

William Kentridge: Prints, Edinburgh Printmakers, Scotland, July 21–September 8.

William Kentridge: WEIGHING… and WANTING, Eric and Ronna Hoffman Gallery of Contemporary Art, Lewis and Clark College, Portland, Oregon, November 1–December 16.

William Kentridge: Fragile Identities, University of Brighton Gallery and Regency Town House, England, November 7–December 31. Catalogue edited by Tom Hickey.
Searle, Adrian. "The Stone-Age Auteur." *Guardian* (London), November 20, 2007.

William Kentridge: What Will Come, Goodman Gallery, Johannesburg, November 10–December 14.

William Kentridge: Tapestries, Philadelphia Museum of Art, December 12, 2007–April 6, 2008. Catalogue edited by Carlos Basualdo (copublished with Yale University Press, New Haven, Connecticut, 2008).
Horler, Vivian. "Kentridge's Foray into Fibre." *Argus,* January 26, 2008.
Rice, Robin. "Weaving His Mark." *Philadelphia City Paper,* March 27, 2008.
Smith, Roberta. "Shadowy Nomads, Writ in Warp and Woof." *New York Times,* December 31, 2007.
Sozanski, Edward J. "A Statement in Thread." *Philadelphia Inquirer,* January 13, 2008.

2008

William Kentridge: Seeing Double, Marian Goodman Gallery, New York, January 16–February 16.
Cohen, David. "A Surfeit of Genius." *New York Sun,* February 7, 2008.
Princenthal, Nancy. Review. *Art in America* 96, no. 9 (October 2008): 191–92.
Wilkin, Karen. Review. *Hudson Review* 61, no. 2 (Summer 2008): 359–65.

William Kentridge: Everyone Their Own Projector, Marian Goodman Gallery, Paris, April 26–May 24. Artist's book (published by Captures/Éditions Valérie Cudel, Valence, France).

William Kentridge: Telegrams from the Nose, Annandale Galleries, Sydney, June 11–July 19.

Return, Teatro La Fenice, Venice, Italy, November 28–December 9.

William Kentridge: (REPEAT) from the Beginning/Da Capo, Palazzetto Tito, Fondazione Bevilacqua La Masa, Venice, Italy, November 30, 2008–January 16, 2009. Catalogue by William Kentridge et al. (copublished with Charta, Milan).

William Kentridge: I am not me, the horse is not mine, Iziko South African National Gallery, Cape Town, December 11, 2008–March 8, 2009. Catalogue by William Kentridge et al. (published by Goodman Gallery Editions, Johannesburg and Cape Town).

William Kentridge: (REPEAT) from the Beginning, Goodman Gallery Cape, Cape Town, December 11, 2008–January 17, 2009.

2009

Henry Art Gallery, Seattle, February 7–May 3.

SELECTED GROUP EXHIBITIONS, FILM FESTIVALS, AND REVIEWS

1978

Exhibition, Akis 101 Gallery, Johannesburg, November 1–30.

1981

National Graphic Show, South African Association of Arts, Bellville, South Africa.

1982

American Film Festival, New York.

1985

Cape Town Triennial, South African National Gallery, Cape Town, September 18–November 2. Traveled to King George VI Art Gallery, Port Elizabeth, South Africa; University of the Orange Free State Art Gallery, Bloemfontein, South Africa; William Humphreys Art Gallery, Kimberley, South Africa; Tatham Art Gallery, Pietermaritzburg, South Africa; Durban Art Gallery, South Africa; Pretoria Art Museum. Catalogue by Alan Crump and Deon Viljoen.

Eleven Figurative Artists, Market Gallery, Johannesburg, November 10–30.

American Film Festival, New York.

London Film Festival.

Paperworks Exhibition, Arts Society, Durban, South Africa.

Tributaries: A View of Contemporary South African Art/Quellen und Strömungen: Eine Ausstellung zeitgenössischer sudafrikanischer Kunst, Africana Museum, Johannesburg; traveled to BMW Museum, Munich. Catalogue edited by Ricky Burnett (published by BMW South Africa, Johannesburg).

1986

8th Durban International Film Festival, South Africa, March 23–April 18.

Visions, Market Gallery, Johannesburg, April 6–26.

Claes Eklundh, William Kentridge, Thomas Lawson, Simon/Neuman Galleries, New York, May 28–July 28.

But, This Is the Reality, Market Gallery, Johannesburg, July 20–August 2, August 11–13.

10th Cape Town International Film Festival.

1987

Three Hogarth Satires, University Art Galleries, Johannesburg, opened April 12. Traveled as *Hogarth in Johannesburg* to Cassirer Fine Art, Johannesburg. Catalogue titled *Hogarth in Johannesburg* by Michael Godby (published by Witwatersrand University Press, Johannesburg, 1990).

1989
South African Landscapes, Everard Read Gallery, Johannesburg, March 18–April 21.

African Encounters, Dome Gallery, Brooklyn, June 20–July 1. Traveled to Washington, DC.

Weekly Mail Film Festival, Johannesburg.

1990
12th Durban International Film Festival, South Africa, March 25–April 15.

Art from South Africa, Museum of Modern Art, Oxford, England, June 17–September 23. Traveled to Mead Gallery, University of Warwick, England; Aberdeen City Art Gallery, Scotland; Royal Festival Hall, London; Bolton Art Gallery, England; City Museum and Art Gallery, Stoke-on-Trent, England; Angel Row Gallery, Nottingham, England. Catalogue by David Elliott et al.

Planet Cinema, Johannesburg, June 23.

Zabalaza Festival, Institute of Contemporary Arts, London.

1991
Gala, Arts Association of Bellville, Cape Town, February 13–March 9.

Little Morals, Taking Liberties Gallery, Durban, South Africa.

Newtown Galleries, Johannesburg.

Weekly Mail Short Film Festival, Johannesburg.

1993
Robert Hodgins, William Kentridge, Deborah Bell, Goodman Gallery, Johannesburg, April 14–May 7. Traveled to Johannes Stegmann-Kunstgalery, University of the Orange Free State Art Gallery, Bloemfontein, South Africa.

Festival International du Film d'Animation et Marché International du Film d'Animation, Annecy, France, June 1–6.

Incroci del Sud: Affinities—Arte Contemporanea del Sudafrica/Contemporary South African Art, 45th Biennale di Venezia, Venice, Italy, June–December. Traveled to Sala 1, Rome; Stedelijk Museum, Amsterdam. Catalogue by Achille Bonita Oliva et al. (published by South African Embassy, Rome).

Edinburgh International Film Festival, August 14–29.

Best of Annecy Festival, Museum of Modern Art, New York. Traveled to Centre Georges Pompidou, Paris.

1994
Trackings: History as Memory, Document and Object—New Work by Four South African Artists, Art First, London, April 19–May 19.

Goodman in Grahamstown, Victoria Primary School, Grahamstown, South Africa, June 30–July 10. Catalogue.

Displacements: South African Works on Paper, 1984–1994, Block Museum of Art, Northwestern University, Evanston, Illinois, September 22–December 4.

1995
Africus, 1st Johannesburg Biennale, February 28–April 30. Catalogue edited by Christopher Till (published by Greater Johannesburg Transitional Metropolitan Council).
Bowie, David. "The Cleanest Work of All." *Modern Painters* 8, no. 2 (Summer 1995): 43–47.
Rosengarten, Ruth. "Inside Out." *Frieze* 23 (Summer 1995): 44–49.

Festival International du Film d'Animation et Marché International du Film d'Animation, Annecy, France, May 30–June 4.

Mayibuye I Afrika: Eight South African Artists, Bernard Jacobson Gallery, London, September 28–October 28.

On the Road: Works by Ten Southern African Artists, Delfina Studio Trust, London, October 5–November 12. Catalogue by Ivor Powell.

Orientation, 4th International Istanbul Biennial, November 10–December 10. Catalogue by René Block et al. (published by Istanbul Foundation for Cuture and the Arts).

Panoramas of Passage: Changing Landscapes of South Africa, Meridian International Center, Washington, DC. Traveled. Catalogue edited by Clive van den Berg.

1996
Common and Uncommon Ground: South African Art to Atlanta, City Gallery East, Atlanta, April 12–June 7. Catalogue.

Colours: Kunst aus Südafrika, Haus der Kulturen der Welt, Berlin, May 24–August 18. Catalogue by Alfons Hug et al.

Simunye: We Are One—Ten South African Artists, Adelson Galleries, New York, June 4–July 1.

Faultlines: Inquiries into Truth and Reconciliation, The Castle, Cape Town, June 16–July 31.

Jurassic Technologies Revenant, 10th Biennale of Sydney, July 27–September 22. Catalogue edited by Lynne Cooke.
MacDonald, Emma. "Sydney's Biennale Revisits Some Old Artistic Territory." *Canberra Times,* September 18, 1996.

Inklusion/Exklusion: Versuch einer neuen Kartografie der Kunst im Zeitalter von Poskolonialismus und globaler Migration, Reininghaus, Graz, Austria, September 22–October 26. Catalogue edited by Peter Weibel (copublished with DuMont, Cologne, 1997).

Don't Mess with Mister Inbetween: 15 artistas da Africa do Sul, Culturgest, Lisbon, September 25–November 10. Catalogue.

Campo 6: Il Villaggio a Spirale/The Spiral Village, Galleria Civica d'Arte Moderna e Contemporanea, Turin, Italy, September 28–November 3. Traveled to Bonnefanten Museum, Maastricht, Netherlands. Catalogue edited by Francesco Bonami (copublished with Skira Editore, Milan).

Festival du Dessin Animé et du Film d'Animation, Brussels.

1997
Samtidskunst fra Sør-Afrika/Contemporary Art from South Africa, Stenersenmuseet, Oslo, January 23–February 3. Traveled to Haugar Vestfold Kunstmuseum, Tønsberg, Norway; Søgne Gamle Prestegård, Norway; Bodø Kunstforening, Norway; Galleri Harstad, Norway; Stavanger Kunstforening, Norway; Haugesund Billedgalleri, Norway; Fylkesgalleriet i Sogn og Fjordane, Førde, Norway; Ål Kulturhus, Norway. Catalogue edited by Marith Hope (published by Riksutstillinger, Oslo).

Città natura: Mostra internazionale di arte contemporanea, various venues, Rome, April 21–June 23. Catalogue edited by Carolyn Christov-Bakargiev (published by Fratelli Palombi, Rome).
Blazwick, Iwona. "Citynature." *Art Monthly* 207 (June 1997): 7–10.

El individuo y su memoria, 6th Bienal de la Habana, Havana, May 3–June 8. Catalogue edited by Llilian Llanes Godoy (published by Association Française d'Action Artistique, Paris).

Documenta X, Kassel, Germany, June 21–September 28. Catalogue titled *Politics—Poetics: Documenta X—The Book* by Catherine David et al. (published by Hatje Cantz, Ostfildern-Ruit, Germany). Catalogue titled *Documenta X: Short Guide/Kurzführer* by Paul Sztulman et al. (published by Museum Fridericianum, Kassel).

Johnson, Ken. "A Post-Retinal Documenta." *Art in America* 85, no. 10 (October 1997): 80–88.

Morgan, Stuart. "The Human Zoo." *Frieze* 36 (September–October 1997): 70–77.

Ubu: ±101, Observatory Museum, Grahamstown, South Africa, July 3–13. Traveled to Gertrude Posel Gallery, Senate House, University of the Witwatersrand, Johannesburg. Catalogue by Rory Doepel (published by French Institute of South Africa and University of the Witwatersrand, Johannesburg).

TRUCE: Echoes of Art in an Age of Endless Conclusions, SITE Santa Fe, July 18–October 12. Catalogue edited by Francesco Bonami.

Mitchell, Charles Dee. "New Narratives." *Art in America* 85, no. 11 (November 1997): 42–47.

Wilson, Malin. Review. *Albuquerque Journal,* August 7, 1997.

New Art from South Africa, Talbot Rice Gallery, University of Edinburgh, Scotland, October 10–November 8. Catalogue by Duncan MacMillan.

Trade Routes: History and Geography, 2nd Johannesburg Biennale, October 12, 1997–January 18, 1998. Catalogue edited by Okwui Enwezor (published by Greater Johannesburg Metropolitan Council).

Les arts de la résistance, Galerie Michel Luneau, Nantes, France, October 17–November 22.

Lifetimes: Kunst aus dem südlichen Africa, Aktionsforum Praterinsel, Munich, Germany, November 21–December 3. Catalogue.

Delta, ARC Musée d'Art Moderne de la Ville de Paris, December 4, 1997–January 18, 1998.

Collaborations (1987–1997), Johannesburg Art Gallery.

Cram, Association of Visual Arts, Cape Town. Catalogue.

1998

Vertical Time, Barbara Gladstone Gallery, New York, January 10–February 21.

Cotter, Holland. Review. *New York Times,* January 30, 1998.

Festival du Dessin Animé et du Film d'Animation, Brussels, February 17–28.

FotoFest 1998, Vine Street Studios, Houston, March 1–31.

Johnson, Patricia C. "Images from Brazil, South Africa Impress." *Houston Chronicle,* March 25, 1998.

The Hugo Boss Prize 1998, Guggenheim Museum SoHo, New York, June 24–September 20. Catalogue by Nancy Spector et al.

Einzig, Barbara. "The Decay of Aura." *Artbyte* 1, no. 4 (October–November 1998): 54–58.

Glueck, Grace. "Contemporary Works Intended to Provoke." *New York Times,* July 17, 1998.

Projected Allegories, Contemporary Arts Museum, Houston, June 26–September 13.

FNB Vita Award Exhibition, Sandton Civic Gallery, Johannesburg, July 29–September 5.

Shoot at the Chaos: Age of Electronic Image, Wacoal Art Center, Spiral, Tokyo, September 17–October 4.

Breaking Ground, Marian Goodman Gallery, New York, September 25–November 7.

24th Bienal de São Paulo, Pavilhão Ciccillo Matarazzo, October 3–December 13. Catalogue edited by Paulo Herkenhoff and Adriano Pedrosa.

Dreams and Clouds: Konst från det nya Sydafrika/Contemporary Art from the New South Africa, Kulturhuset, Stockholm, October 3, 1998–January 10, 1999. Catalogue edited by Christina Björk.

Unfinished History, Walker Art Center, Minneapolis, October 18, 1998–January 10, 1999. Traveled to Museum of Contemporary Art, Chicago. Catalogue by Francesco Bonami and Douglas Fogle.

International Film Festival Rotterdam, Netherlands.

16th World Wide Video Festival, Amsterdam.

1999

La ville, le jardin, la mémoire, Académie de France à Rome, Villa Medici, May 27–September 5. Catalogue by Carolyn Christov-Bakargiev et al.

Wright, Stephen. Review. *Parachute* 97 (January–March 2000): 40–41.

<<REWIND>> FAST FORWARD.ZA: New Work from South Africa, Van Reekum Museum, Apeldoorn, Netherlands, June 5–September 7. Catalogue edited by Bozzie Rabie and Fritz Bless.

dAPERTutto/APERTO over ALL/APERTO par TOUT/APERTO über ALL, 48th Biennale di Venezia, Venice, Italy, June 12–November 7. Catalogue edited by Harald Szeemann and Cecilia Liveriero Lavelli (published by Marsilio, Venice).

AKT 1: Scenekunst og Billedkunst, Kunstforeningen, Copenhagen, June 19–August 15.

Claiming Art/Reclaiming Space: Post-Apartheid Art from South Africa, National Museum of African Art, Washington, DC, June 20–September 26.

O'Sullivan, Michael. "Art of Hardship and Healing in South Africa." *Washington Post,* July 16, 1999.

Beyond Borders, Coninx Museum, Zurich, September 15, 1999–January 28, 2000. Catalogue.

17th World Wide Video Festival, Amsterdam, September 15–20.

Tutku Ve Dalga/The Passion and the Wave, 6th International Istanbul Biennial, September 17–October 30. Catalogue edited by Paolo Colombo (published by Istanbul Foundation for Culture and Arts).

Antmen, Ahu, and Vasif Kortun. "The Istanbul Fall." *Flash Art* 32, no. 209 (November–December 1999): 84–87.

Kryza, Darlene. Review. *New Art Examiner* 27, no. 5 (February 2000): 40–41.

Tachikawa International Art Festival, Japan, October 3–November 23.

Drawing, Thinking, Gallagher Gallery, Royal Hibernian Academy, Dublin, October 9–November 7.

A Sangre y Fuego, Espai d'Art Contemporani de Castelló, Spain, October 14–December 5. Catalogue edited by Juan Vicente Aliaga.

Life Cycles, Galerie für zeitgenössische Kunst, Leipzig, Germany, October 24–December 5. Catalogue by Caroline Broadhead and Lynne Cooke.

Kunstwelten im Dialog: Von Gauguin zur globalen Gegenwart, Museum Ludwig, Cologne, November 5, 1999–March 19, 2000. Catalogue edited by Marc Scheps et al. (copublished with DuMont, Cologne).

Carnegie International 1999/2000, Carnegie Museum of Art, Pittsburgh, November 6, 1999–March 26, 2000. Catalogue edited by Madeleine Grynsztejn.

Leffingwell, Edward. "Carnegie Ramble." *Art in America* 88, no. 3 (March 2000): 86–93, 142.

Pincus, Robert L. "World-Class Exhibition." *San Diego Union-Tribune,* November 21, 1999.

Sorkin, Jenni. Review. *Art Monthly* 232 (December 1999–January 2000): 28–30.

Thomas, Mary. Review. *Pittsburgh Post-Gazette,* November 28, 1999.

Vidéo Art Plastique, Rencontres Hérouville Saint-Clair, France, November 24–December 5.

Prins Claus Prijzen ceremony, Koninklijk Paleis, Amsterdam, December 8.

Artery, Visual Arts Association and other venues, Cape Town.

International Film Festival Rotterdam, Netherlands.

2000

Ich ist etwas Anderes: Kunst am Ende des 20. Jahrhunderts, K20/K21 Kunstsammlung Nordrhein-Westfalen, Düsseldorf, Germany, February 19–June 18. Catalogue edited by Armin Zweite et al. (copublished with DuMont, Cologne).

Outbound: Passages from the 90s, Contemporary Arts Museum, Houston, March 4–May 7. Catalogue by Dana Friis-Hansen et al.

International Trickfilm-Festival, Stuttgart, Germany, March 16–21.

Man + Space, 3rd Kwangju Biennale, Biennale Hall, Kwangju, Korea, March 29–June 7. Catalogue edited by Oh Kwang-su.

Line of Connection, Galerie Mam, Douala, Cameroon, May 3–May 17.

Around 1984: A Look at Art in the 80s, P.S.1 Contemporary Art Center, New York, May 21–September 24.

Festival International du Film d'Animation et Marché International du Film d'Animation, Annecy, France, June 5–10.

Umedalen Skulptur 2000, Bildmuseet, Umeå, Sweden, June 6–September 3.

Das Lied von der Erde: Biennalen im Dialog, Kunsthalle Fridericianum, Kassel, Germany, June 10–October 3.

Illuminations: Contemporary Film and Video Art, Ackland Art Museum, University of North Carolina at Chapel Hill, June 25–October 8.

New Zealand International Film Festival, Wellington, July 7–23.

Mostra Africana de Arte Contemporânea, Serviço Social do Comércio Pompéia, São Paulo, August 16–September 17.

La beauté in fabula, Palais des Papes, Avignon, France, August–October.

3rd Shanghai Biennale, Shanghai Art Museum, November 6, 2000–January 6, 2001. Catalogue edited by Hou Hanru et al. (published by Shanghai Fine Arts Publishers).

7th Bienal de la Habana, Havana, November 14, 2000–January 6, 2001. Catalogue edited by Nelson Herrera Ysla (published by Centro de Arte Contemporáneo Wifredo Lam, Havana).

Das Gedächtnis der Kunst: Geschichte und Erinnerung in der Kunst der Gegenwart, various venues, Frankfurt, Germany, December 16, 2000–March 18, 2001. Catalogue edited by Kurt Wettengl (published by Historisches Museum, Frankfurt; Schirn Kunsthalle, Frankfurt; and Hatje Cantz, Ostfildern-Ruit, Germany).

A.R.E.A.: Art Region End of Africa, Reykjavík Art Museum—Kjarvalsstadir.

A Double View: Three Exhibitions, Tel Aviv Museum of Art, Israel.

Levine, Angela. "A Rift in the Canvas." *Jerusalem Post,* March 17, 2000.

Festival de Dessin Animé et du Film d'Animation, Brussels.

2001

The Short Century: Independence and Liberation Movements in Africa, 1945–1994, Museum Villa Stuck, Munich, February 15–April 22. Traveled to Haus der Kulturen der Welt, Berlin; Museum of Contemporary Art, Chicago; P.S.1 Contemporary Art Center and Museum of Modern Art, New York. Catalogue edited by Okwui Enwezor (copublished with Prestel, Munich).

Hanussek, Christian, and Isabell Lorey. "How African Is It?" *Texte zur Kunst* 11, no. 43 (September 2001): 190–98.

Works on Paper: From Acconci to Zittel, Victoria Miro Gallery, London, June 27–September 15.

Hieronymus Bosch, Museum Boijmans Van Beuningen, Rotterdam, Netherlands, September 1–November 11.

Yokohama 2001, 1st International Triennale of Contemporary Art, Yokohama, Japan, September 2–November 11. Catalogue by Kohmoto Shinji et al.

Lateral Thinking: Art of the 1990s, Museum of Contemporary Art, San Diego, September 16, 2001–January 13, 2002. Traveled to Colorado Springs Fine Art Center; Hood Museum, Dartmouth University, Hanover, New Hampshire; Dayton Art Institute, Ohio. Catalogue by Toby Kamps.

In fumo: Arte, fumetto, comunicazione da Warhol e Keith Haring a Murakami, Galleria d'Arte Moderna e Contemporanea, Bergamo, Italy, September 26, 2001–January 6, 2002. Catalogue by Giacinto di Pietrantonio (copublished with Lubrina Editore, Bergamo).

ARS 01: Avautuvia näköaloja/Unfolding Perspectives, Nykytaiteen museo Kiasma, Helsinki, September 30, 2001–January 20, 2002. Catalogue edited by Maaretta Jaukkuri and Virve Sutinen.

Animations, P.S.1 Contemporary Art Center, New York, October 14, 2001–January 13, 2002. Traveled to Kunst-Werke, Berlin. Catalogue edited by Klaus Biesenbach.

2002

International Film Festival Rotterdam, Netherlands, January 23–February 3.

The Divine Comedy: Francisco Goya, Buster Keaton, William Kentridge, Vancouver Art Gallery, Canada, January 24–April 25. Traveled to Art Gallery of Western Australia, Perth. Catalogue by Trevor Smith.

Duke, David Gordon. "Laughing 'Til It Hurts." *Vancouver Sun,* January 24, 2004.

Gandesha, Samir. Review. *Art Papers* 28, no. 3 (May–June 2004): 60.

Snell, Ted. Review. *Art & Australia* 40, no. 1 (Spring 2002): 62–63.

Passport to South Africa: Arte contemporanea sudafricana, Centro Trevi, Bolzano, Italy, February 8–March 12.

Stories: Erzählstrukturen in der zeitgenössischen Kunst, Haus der Kunst, Munich, March 28–June 23. Catalogue edited by Stephanie Rosenthal.

Screen Memories, Art Tower Mito, Japan, April 13–June 9.

Documenta 11, Kassel, Germany, June 8–September 15. Catalogue titled *Documenta 11_Platform 5: Exhibition* edited by Okwui Enwezor (published by Hatje Cantz, Ostfildern-Ruit, Germany).

Fanelli, Franco. "A Mighty Denunciation of Violence, Poverty, and Social Dissolution." *Art Newspaper* 13, no. 127 (July–August 2002): 23–25.

Haase, Amine. "Keine Zukunft ohne Vergangenheit, oder: Kunst als Mittel der Erkenntnis." *Kunstforum* 161 (August–October 2002): 52–67.

O'Toole, Sean. "Art of Apartheid." *Blueprint* 198 (August 2002): 52–56.

Wulffen, Thomas. Review. *Kunstforum* 161 (August–October 2002): 298–99.

Refuge, Henie Onstad Kunstsenter, Oslo, opened June 20. Catalogue.

Moving Pictures: Contemporary Photography and Video from the Guggenheim Museum Collections, Solomon R. Guggenheim Museum, New York, June 28, 2002–January 12, 2003. Traveled to Guggenheim Museum Bilbao, Spain. Catalogue by Lisa Dennison et al.

African Marketplace, Ivan Dougherty Gallery, University of New South Wales, Paddington, Australia, August 22–September 28.

Imagining the Book: International Contemporary Art Encounter, Bibliotheca Alexandrina, Alexandria, Egypt, September 12–21.

Premio Biella per l'incisione 2002, Museo del Territorio Biellese, Biella, Italy, September 29–November 3. Catalogue by Ida Gianelli et al.

Grafinnova 2002: International Exhibition of Prints and Drawings, Pohjanmaan Museo, Vaasa, Finland, October 6–December 12. Catalogue.

Tech/No/Zone: Contemporary Media Art, Museum of Contemporary Art, Taipei, October 12, 2002–January 12, 2003.

Global Priority, Jamaica Center for Arts and Learning, New York, October 19–December 21. Traveled to Pier Two, Kaohsiung, Taiwan; Herter Art Gallery, University of Massachusetts, Amherst.

Future Cinema: The Cinematic Imaginary after Film, Zentrum für Kunst und Medientechnologie, Karlsruhe, Germany, November 16, 2002–March 30, 2003. Traveled to Nykytaiteen museo Kiasma, Helsinki; NTT InterCommunication Centre, Tokyo. Catalogue edited by Jeffrey Shaw and Peter Weibel (copublished with MIT Press, Cambridge, Massachusetts).

Comer o no comer: O las relaciones del arte con la comida en el siglo XX, Centro de Arte de Salamanca, Spain, November 23, 2002–January 19, 2003. Catalogue edited by Darío Corbeira.

Apparition: The Action of Appearing, Arnolfini, Bristol, England, November 30, 2002–February 9, 2003. Traveled to Kettle's Yard, Cambridge, England. Catalogue by Roger Malbert and Lucy Steeds.

A Place of Your Own, RASA, Sint-Niklaas, Belgium. Traveled.

2003

Coexistence: Contemporary Cultural Production in South Africa, Rose Art Museum, Brandeis University, Waltham, Massachusetts, January 22–June 29. Traveled to South African National Gallery, Cape Town. Catalogue by Pamela Allara et al.

Banquete: Metabolismo y comunicación, Palau de la Virreina, Barcelona, January 29–March 30. Traveled to Zentrum für Kunst und Medientechnologie, Karlsruhe, Germany; Centro Cultural Conde Duque, Madrid, and MediaLabMadrid.

Arts in a Changing Horizon: Globalization and Formulas of Modernization, 6th Sharjah International Biennial, United Arab Emirates, April 4–May 9.

Trauer, Atelier Augarten, Zentrum für zeitgenössische Kunst der Österreichischen Galerie Belvedere, Vienna, April 16–July 27. Catalogue edited by Thomas Trummer.
Buchhart, Dieter. Review. *Kunstforum* 165 (June–July 2003): 347–49.

Transferts, Palais des Beaux-Arts/Paleis voor Schone Kunsten, Brussels, June 21–September 14. Catalogue edited by Toma Muteba Luntumbue (copublished with Africalia, Brussels).

For the Record: Drawing Contemporary Life, Vancouver Art Gallery, Canada, June 28–September 28. Catalogue by Dana Augaitis.

Gesellschaftsbilder/Images of Society, Kunstmuseum Thun, Switzerland, September 7–November 16. Catalogue edited by Madeleine Schuppli.

Artists and Maps: Cartography as a Means of Knowing, Ronna and Eric Hoffman Gallery of Contemporary Art, Lewis and Clark College, Portland, Oregon, September 14–October 19.

Reflection: Seven Years in Print, Miriam and Ira D. Wallach Art Gallery, Columbia University, New York, September 24–December 13. Catalogue by Faye Hirsch.

White: Whiteness and Race in Contemporary Art, Center for Art and Visual Culture, University of Maryland, Baltimore, October 9, 2003–January 10, 2004. Traveled to International Center of Photography, New York. Catalogue edited by Maurice Berger.
Jefferson, Margo. “Playing on Black and White.” *New York Times,* January 10, 2005.

Synopsis 3—Testimonies: Between Fiction and Reality, National Museum of Contemporary Art, Athens, Greece, October 10, 2003–March 14, 2004. Catalogue edited by Anna Kafetsi.
Stech, Fabian. Review. *Kunstforum* 169 (March–April 2004): 318–19.

Drawing Modern: Works from the Agnes Gund Collection, Cleveland Museum of Art, October 26, 2003–January 1, 2004. Catalogue by Carter E. Foster et al.

Supernova: Art of the 1990s from the Logan Collection, San Francisco Museum of Modern Art, December 13, 2003–May 23, 2004. Catalogue edited by Madeleine Grynsztejn (copublished with Distributed Art Publishers, New York).

2004

International Film Festival Rotterdam, Netherlands, January 21–February 1.

Memorials of Identity: New Media from the Rubell Family Collection, Art Gallery at Florida Gulf Coast University, Fort Myers, February 3–March 5. Traveled to Rubell Family Collection, Miami, Florida; Corcoran Gallery of Art and College of Art and Design, Washington, DC; Museo de Arte de Puerto Rico, San Juan; Nasher Museum of Art, Duke University, Durham, North Carolina; Haifa Museum of Art, Israel. Catalogue by Mark Coetzee and Luisa Lagos.
Bennett, Lennie. “Challenging Notions.” *St. Petersburg Times,* May 6, 2007.
Sung, Ellen. “Now Projecting at a Museum Near You.” *Raleigh News & Observer,* August 6, 2006.

Imagination Becomes Reality, Part III: Talking Pictures, Sammlung Goetz, Munich, February 20–June 3. Traveled to Zentrum für Kunst und Medientechnologie/Museum für Neue Kunst, Karlsruhe, Germany. Catalogue edited by Rainald Schumacher.

Public/Private: Tumatanui/Tumataiti, 2nd Auckland Triennial, New Zealand, March 20–May 30.

TREMOR: Contemporary South African Art/Art sud-africain contemporain, Palais des Beaux-Arts de Charleroi, Belgium, April 22–June 20. Catalogue edited by Emma Bedford (published by Centre d’Art Contemporain, Brussels).

X, Warren Siebrits Modern and Contemporary Art, Johannesburg, April 27–June 12. Catalogue by Warren Siebrits.

Reflecting the Mirror, Marian Goodman Gallery, New York, June 14–August 27.

Monument to Now: The Dakis Joannou Collection, DESTE Foundation for Contemporary Art, Athens, Greece, June 22, 2004–March 6, 2005. Catalogue edited by Jeffrey Deitch.

Afrika Remix, Museum Kunst Palast, Düsseldorf, Germany, July 24–November 7. Traveled to Hayward Gallery, London; Centre Georges Pompidou, Paris; Mori Art Museum, Tokyo; Moderna Museet, Stockholm. Catalogue edited by Simon Njami (published by Hayward Gallery and Hatje Cantz, Ostfildern-Ruit, Germany, 2005).

New Identities: Zeitgenönissische Kunst aus Südafrika, Museum Bochum, Germany, July 31–November 7. Traveled to Pretoria Art Museum, South Africa; Johannesburg Art Gallery. Catalogue edited by Hans Günter Golisnki and Sepp Hiekisch-Picard (copublished with Hatje Cantz, Ostfildern-Ruit, Germany).

61st Venice International Film Festival, Italy, September 1–11.

+positive, 2nd Biennale von kunst Meran, Merano, Italy, September 12, 2004–January 9, 2005. Catalogue by Valerio Dehò (copublished with Verlag für moderne Kunst, Nuremberg, Germany).

In Bed: Images from a Vital Stage, Toyota Municipal Museum of Art, Tokyo, October 5–December 26. Catalogue.

Trouble, Grand Café Centre d’Art Contemporain, Saint-Nazaire, France, November 6–December 31.

Moving Pictures, Artcore Gallery, Toronto, November–December.

Faces in the Crowd: Picturing Modern Life from Manet to Today/Volti nella folla: Immagini della vita moderna da Manet a oggi, Whitechapel Gallery, London, December 3, 2004–March 6, 2005. Traveled to Castello di Rivoli Museo d’Arte Contemporanea, Italy. Catalogue by Iwona Blazwick et al. (copublished with Skira Editore, Milan).

2005

DreamingNow, Rose Art Museum, Brandeis University, Waltham, Massachusetts, January 27–April 24. Catalogue edited by Raphaela Platow.

Prepossession, Ivan Dougherty Gallery, University of New South Wales, Paddington, Australia, March 4–April 9. Traveled to Golden Thread Gallery, Belfast, Northern Ireland.

The World Is a Stage: Stories behind Pictures, Mori Art Museum, Tokyo, March 29–June 15. Catalogue.

Daumenkino: The Flip Book Show, Kunsthalle Düsseldorf, Germany, May 7–July 17. Catalogue edited by Daniel Gethmann et al.

The Experience of Art, 51st Biennale di Venezia, Venice, Italy, June 12–November 6. Catalogue edited by María de Corral.
Smee, Sebastian. “Navigating the Currents.” *Australian,* June 25, 2005.
Vetrocq, Marcia E. “Be Careful What You Wish For.” *Art in America* 93, no. 8 (September 2005): 108–19, 168.

Modern Times, Mönchehaus Museum für Moderne Kunst, Goslar, Germany, June 25–September 18.

Rückkehr ins All, Hamburger Kunstalle, Germany, September 23, 2005–February 12, 2006. Catalogue edited by Christoph Heinrich and Markus Heinzelmann (copublished with Siemens Arts Program, Munich).
Schiff, Hajo. *Kunstforum* 178 (November 2005–January 2006): 291–94.

Deadend, Museum on the Seam, Jerusalem.

International Film Festival Rotterdam, Netherlands.
Romney, Jonathan. “Ant Astronomers and Man-Trees.” *Modern Painters* (April 2005): 41–42.

2006

Hadith: Conversation, Galerie Sfeir-Semler, Beirut, Lebanon, January 26–April 22.
Wilson-Goldie, Kaelen. "Exploring the Many Meanings of Hadith." *Daily Star* (Beirut), February 2, 2006.

Experimenta: Vanishing Point, CAST Gallery, North Hobart, Australia, January 28–February 26. Traveled to Devonport Regional Gallery, Australia; Northern Territory Centre for Contemporary Art, Darwin, Australia; Newcastle Region Art Gallery, Australia; Perth Institute of Contemporary Art, Australia; Art Gallery of South Australia, Adelaide; Ipswich Art Gallery, Australia; Gold Coast City Art Gallery, Australia; Albury Library Museum, Australia. Catalogue.
Smee, Sebastian. "Not One of Pavlov's Dogs." *Australian,* October 7, 2006.

There and Back: Africa, Casa Encendida, Madrid, March 31–June 11. Catalogue edited by Danielle Tilkin.

Glasgow International Festival of Contemporary Visual Art, Scotland, April 19–May 1.
Black, Catriona. "Festival's Make-Up Still Needs a Bit More Foundation." *Evening Times* (Glasgow), April 30, 2006.
Jeffrey, Moira. "Portrait of a Rock Star as an Artist." *Herald* (Glasgow), April 21, 2006.
Macmillan, Duncan. "Not Telling the Whole Story." *Scotsman,* April 25, 2006.

Contemporary Art on the Lake Maggiore, Isola Madre, Italy, June 11–September 18.

Polemos: L'Opera d'arte tra conflitto e superamento/The Work of Art between Conflict and Resolution, Forte di Gavi, Italy, July 2–October 1. Catalogue edited by Daniela Cristadoro (published by Silvana, Milan).
Russi, Viola Lilith. Review. *D'Ars* 45, no. 187 (September 2006): 46–51.

The Starry Messenger: Visions of the Universe, Compton Verney, Warwickshire, England, July 7–September 10. Catalogue edited by John Leslie.

Venice—Istanbul, Istanbul Museum of Modern Art, October 18, 2006–February 2, 2007.

2007

Fantasmagoría: Dibujo en movimiento, Museo Colecciones ICO, Madrid, January 18–March 18.

Collectors Choice, Annandale Galleries, Sydney, February 20–March 17.

Momentary Momentum: Animated Drawings, Parasol Unit Foundation for Contemporary Art, London, March 3–May 12.
Barrett, David. Review. *Art Monthly* 205 (April 2007): 27–28.
Searle, Adrian. "Dirty Gritty Things." *Guardian,* March 6, 2007.

Phantasmagoria: Specters of Absence, Museo de Arte del Banco de la República, Bogotá, Colombia, March 7–June 11. Traveled to Contemporary Museum, Honolulu; McColl Center for Visual Art, Charlotte, North Carolina; John and Mable Ringling Museum of Art, Sarasota, Florida; Fisher Gallery, University of Southern California, Los Angeles. Catalogue by José Roca (published by Independent Curators International, New York).
Bennett, Lennie. "Phantastic Vision." *St. Petersburg Times,* July 13, 2008.

Lift Off Part I, Goodman Gallery Cape, Cape Town, March 23–April 28.

Not Afraid of the Dark, Hangar Bicocca, Milan, March 29–May 27.

Paper Cuts, Hove Museum & Art Gallery, England, April 7–July 1.

Video Killed the Painting Star, Domus Artium 2002, Salamanca, Spain, April 20–May 27.

Geopoéticas: El vídeo como documento del lugar, Centro José Guerrero, Granada, Spain, June 5–July 22.

Artempo: Where Time Becomes Art, Palazzo Fortuny, Venice, Italy, June 8–November 5. Catalogue edited by Axel Vervoordt and Mattijs Visser (published by MER Paper Kunsthalle, Ghent, Belgium).

Stereo Vision, University of South Florida Contemporary Art Museum, Tampa, June 15–August 4.

Im Untergrund/Below Ground Level, Haus für Kunst Uri, Altdorf, Switzerland, June 30–September 2. Catalogue.

6th Bienal do Mercosul, Porto Alegre, Brazil, September 1–November 18. Catalogue.

Apartheid: The South African Mirror, Centre de Cultura Contemporània de Barcelona, September 26, 2007–January 13, 2008. Traveled to Centro Cultural Bancaja, Valencia, Spain. Catalogue edited by Pep Subirós.

Animated Painting, San Diego Museum of Art, October 13, 2007–January 13, 2008. Traveled to Centro Cultural Tijuana, Mexico; Faulconer Gallery, Grinnell College, Iowa. Catalogue edited by Betti-Sue Hertz.
Pincus, Robert L. "*Animated Painting* an Exploration of Hybrid Approaches." *San Diego Union-Tribune,* November 4, 2007.

Passage du temps: Collection François Pinault Foundation, Tri Postal, Lille, France, October 15, 2007–January 6, 2008. Catalogue.

Achtung Sprengerarbeiten (Caution! Blasting Operations!), Neue Gesellschaft für Bildende Kunst, Berlin, October 20–December 2. Catalogue.

Gehen, Bleiben: Bewegung, Körper, Ort in der Kunst der Gegenwart, Kunstmuseum Bonn, Germany, November 28, 2007–February 17, 2008. Catalogue edited by Volker Adolphs (copublished with Hatje Cantz, Ostfildern-Ruit, Germany).

About Beauty, Goodman Gallery Cape, Cape Town, December 13, 2007–January 5, 2008.
Corrigall, Mary. "Interrogating Our Accepted Ideas about Beauty." *Independent* (Cape Town), December 23, 2007.

2008

The Puppet Show, Institute of Contemporary Art, University of Pennsylvania, Philadelphia, January 18–March 30. Traveled to Santa Monica Museum of Art, California; Contemporary Museum, Honolulu; Contemporary Arts Museum, Houston; Frye Art Museum, Seattle. Catalogue edited by Ingrid Schaffner and Carin Kuoni.
Carlson, Ben. Review. *Modern Painters* 20, no. 2 (March 2008): 82–83.

Africa On, Galleria Lia Rumma, Milan, February 6–March 15.

Rumore: Un buco nel silenzio, Spazio Oberdan, Milan, February 28–May 25.

Multiple Choice: Contemporary Art from South Africa, Nomad Gallery, Brussels, May 7–June 22.

Paradies und zurück: Sammlung Rheingold in Schloss Dyck, Düsseldorf, Germany, May 19–December 31.

Sguardo periferico e corpo collettivo, Museion Museo d'arte moderna e contemporanea, Bolzano, Italy, May 24–September 21. Catalogue by Corinne Diserens et al.

Home Lands—Land Marks, Haunch of Venison, London, May 31–July 5. Catalogue edited by Tamar Garb.
Glover, Michael. "Shadows on the Land." *Independent,* June 9, 2008.

Revolutions—Forms That Turn, 16th Biennale of Sydney, June 18–September 7. Catalogue edited by Carolyn Christov-Bakargiev (published by Thames & Hudson, London).
Fortescue, Elizabeth. "The Extravagance of Art." *Daily Telegraph* (Sydney), June 21, 2008.
McDonald, John. "Place of Treats and Tortures." *Sydney Morning Herald,* July 12, 2008.

Turn and Widen, 5th Seoul International Media Art Biennale, Seoul Museum of Art, September 12–November 5.

Smoke, Pump House Gallery, London, October 5–December 15.

SELECTED THEATRICAL PRODUCTIONS, PERFORMANCES, AND REVIEWS

As many of Kentridge's theatrical productions have toured extensively or are performed periodically as part of the repertoires of certain companies, only premiere venues and dates are listed below.

1975

Ubu Rex, performance, collaboration with Junction Avenue Theatre Company, Nunnery Theatre, Johannesburg, May 20–31.

The Goat That Sneezed, performance, collaboration with Junction Avenue Theatre Company, Nunnery Theatre, Johannesburg, December.

1976

Fantastical History of a Useless Man, script (coauthor), set design, and performance, collaboration with Junction Avenue Theatre Company, Nunnery Theatre, Johannesburg, May 20–31. Traveled.

1977

Wooze Bear, set and graphic design (with Steven Sack), Nunnery Theatre, Johannesburg, July 18–22.

1978

Randlords and Rotgut, performance, collaboration with Junction Avenue Theatre Company, Nunnery Theatre, Johannesburg, February–March.

Travesties, set design and performance, Market Theatre, Johannesburg, opened May 25.

Play It Again, Sam, set design, Market Theatre, Johannesburg, October.

1979

Will of a Rebel, direction, collaboration with Junction Avenue Theatre Company, Nunnery Theatre, Johannesburg, March 19–31.

Security, performance, collaboration with Junction Avenue Theatre Company, Johannesburg, October and December.

1980

Dikhitsheneng, script and direction, collaboration with Junction Avenue Theatre Company, various community centers, Johannesburg.

1983

The Bacchae, set design, collaboration with Junction Avenue Theatre Company, Market Theatre, Johannesburg, September–October.

Emily's Wheelbarrow Show and the Infamous Mr. Sterntrap, script, Wits Theatre, Johannesburg, December 1983–January 1984.

1984

Catastrophe, direction, Wits Theatre, Johannesburg, September. Traveled.

A Noose for Scariot Impimpi, performance, various venues, Durban, South Africa.

1987

Sophiatown, design, collaboration with Junction Avenue Theatre Company, Market Theater, Johannesburg, opened February 19.

1992

Woyzeck on the Highveld, animation, set design, and direction, collaboration with Handspring Puppet Company, Graeme College, Grahamstown, South Africa, July 7–12. Traveled.

Accone, Daryl. "Animated Encounters in 3-D." *Star Tonight!* (Johannesburg), September 18, 1992.
Berman, Kathy. "Mixed Medium Marvel." *Vrye Weekblad,* September 17, 1992.
Blignault, C. "Making Sense of Darkness." *Vrye Weekblad,* September 18–24, 1992.
Blumenthal, Eileen. "String Theory." *American Theatre* 25, no. 7 (September 1, 2008): 50–56.
Corrigall, Mary. "Woyzeck as Poignant as Ever." *Independent* (Cape Town), March 16, 2008.
Daniel, Raeford. Review. *Weekly Mail* (Johannesburg), September 18–24, 1992.
Henry, Zane. "Visually Arresting, But Heartless." *Argus,* May 13, 2008.
Horler, Vivian. "Puppet Magic Saves Woyzeck." *Argus,* May 11, 2008.
Hough, David. "Requiem for Anti-Hero." *West Australian,* April 11, 2008.
Kaye, Helen. "Post-Apartheid Puppets." *Jerusalem Post,* May 28, 1996.
Kirchhoff, H. J. "Clues to the Complexity of Africa." *Toronto Globe and Mail,* April 16, 1994.
"Life's Drama Unfolds with Pull of String." *South China Morning Post,* December 18, 1995.
MacLiam, Garalt. "Exceptional Synthesis a Wonder to Behold." *Star Tonight!* (Johannesburg), September 11, 1992.
Mayne, Jane. "Authentic SA Classic." *Cape Times,* May 12, 2008.
Schmitt, Olivier. "Inattendus parfums d'Afrique du Sud." *Le Monde,* July 13, 1996.
Sichel, Adrienne. "Betwixt Reality and Illusion." *Star* (Johannesburg), March 11, 2008.
Smith, Sid. "Modern Twist." *Chicago Tribune,* September 16, 1994.
Van Gelder, Lawrence. "Woyzeck, as Puppet, Still Yanked Around by Life." *New York Times,* September 8, 1994.
Von Lucius, Robert. "Das Wunder in der Puppe." *Frankfurter Allgemeine Zeitung,* July 5, 1993.
Wagner, Wit. "South African Puppet Theatre Premieres." *Toronto Star,* April 15, 1994.

1995

Faustus in Africa!, animation, set design, and direction, collaboration with Handspring Puppet Company, Weimar, Germany, June 22–25. Traveled.

Anstey, Gillian. "International Critics in a Frenzy over SA Play." *Sunday Times* (Johannesburg), July 23, 1995.
Diehl, Siegfried. "Der ewige Comic zieht uns hinan." *Frankfurter Allgemeine Zeitung,* June 28, 1995.
Jones, Chris. "South African Politics Drives Puppet Version of Faust." *Chicago Tribune,* April 11, 1997.
Kaufman, Sarah. "The Soul of a Puppet." *Washington Post,* April 5, 1997.
Kurson, Bob. "The Devil's Handiwork." *Chicago Sun-Times,* April 11, 2007.
Nicodemus, Katja. "Zwischen Holz und Mensch." *Die Tageszeitung,* June 27, 1995.
Putz, Fred. Review. *Puppetry Journal* 49, no. 1 (Fall 1997): 8–9.
Wynants, Jean-Marie. "Faust s'impose en Afrique." *Le Soir,* May 9, 1996.

1996

Ubu and the Truth Commission, animation, set design, and direction, collaboration with Handspring Puppet Company, Weimar, Germany, June 17–22. Traveled. Catalogue by Jane Taylor (published by University of Cape Town Press, 1998).

Alberro, Alexander. Review. *Artforum* 37, no. 5 (January 1999): 122–23.
Billington, Michael. "It Matters, Too Much." *Guardian* (Manchester), June 12, 1999.
Brand, Robert. "Ubu's Exploits Hold a Mirror to SA's Violent Past." *Star* (Johannesburg), August 8, 1997.
Feingold, Michael. "Puppet States." *Village Voice,* September 22, 1998, 153.
Friedman, Hazel. "Massive New Ubu Show." *Mail & Guardian* (Johannesburg), December 20, 1996.
Heliot, Armelle. "Ubu en Afrique du Sud." *Le Figaro,* July 22, 1997.
Jones, Jonathan. "Pulling the Strings." *Guardian* (London), June 9, 1999.
Jordan, Mary. "Puppets Create a Hauntingly Powerful Effect." *Business Day,* August 28, 1997.
McNeil, Donald G., Jr. "Playwrights Are Doing an Autopsy on Apartheid." *New York Times,* August 5, 1997.
Oppelt, Phylicia. "Puppets with Punch." *Washington Post,* September 18, 1998.
Periale, Andrew. Review. *Puppetry Journal* 50, no. 2 (Winter 1998): 5.
Russo, Francine. "Ubu Raw." *Village Voice,* September 8, 1998, 138.
Shuttleworth, Ian. "Tangled Web Fails to Face Up to the Issues." *Financial Times,* June 23, 1999.
Sweeting, Adam. "Mildly Spiced." *Guardian* (London), June 12, 1999.
Taylor, Paul. "The Truth Is Out There." *Independent* (London), June 14, 1999.
"Truth and Reconciliation." *Art on Paper* 3, no. 2 (November–December 1998): 18–19.

1998

Il Ritorno d'Ulisse, animation, set design, and direction, collaboration with Handspring Puppet Company, Kaaitheater, Brussels, May 9–22. Traveled.

Conrad, Willa J. "Opera's Odd Odyssey." *Newark Star-Ledger,* February 27, 2004.

Davidson, Justin, and Ariella Budick. "Doing Justice to Opera Traditions—or Not." *New York Newsday,* March 5, 2004.

Eelen, Tom. "New York enthousiast over Poppenopera van William Kentridge." *De Tijd,* March 9, 2004.

Gilmore, Joanathan. "Bed and Puppet." *Artforum* 42, no. 10 (Summer 2004): 78.

Gurewitsch, Matthew. "Into the Heart of Darkness, with Puppets." *New York Times,* February 29, 2004.

Kimmelman, Michael. "In a Waterlogged City, Operatic Puppets and Shadows on a Curtain." *New York Times,* December 4, 2008.

——. "'Ulysses' Ponders the 'Fragility of Coherence.'" *International Herald Tribune,* December 4, 2008.

Midgette, Anne. "A Wanderer's Dreams of Home, through Puppet Artistry with Video Assist." *New York Times,* March 4, 2004.

Shineberg, Susan. "Opera, Strings Attached." *Age* (Melbourne), October 11, 2004.

Waleson, Heidi. "Puppets Take Manhattan." *Wall Street Journal,* February 24, 2004.

2001

Zeno at 4 A.M., animation and direction, collaboration with Handspring Puppet Company, Lunatheater, Brussels, May 18–23. Traveled.

Bédarida, Catherine. "Les ombres noires et blanches de l'inconscient." *Le Monde,* September 15, 2001.

Belasco, Daniel. "Split Infinitives." *New York Jewish Week,* November 9, 2001, 55.

Champenois, Michèle. "Eloge de l'insomnie par Kentridge." *Le Monde,* September 20, 2002.

Davidson, Justin. "Shadowy Pageant for the Sleepless." *New York Newsday,* November 16, 2001.

Preston, Rohan. "Shadow Opera." *Minneapolis Star-Tribune,* November 2, 2001.

Starbuck, Jennifer Parker, and Joshua Abrams. "Storytelling at the Kunsten Festival des Arts in Brussels." *Western European Stages* 14, no. 2 (Spring 2002): 31.

Weiss, Hedy. Review. *Chicago Sun-Times,* November 12, 2001.

2002

Confessions of Zeno, animation and direction, collaboration with Handspring Puppet Company, Kaaitheater, Brussels, May 14–17. Traveled.

Gardner, Belinda Grace. "Wahrheit im Schatten, Zweifel im Licht." *Die Welt,* October 2, 2002.

Heliot, Armelle. "Le miracle de Kentridge." *Le Figaro,* November 23, 2002.

Stadelmaier, Gerhard. "Zigarettenschall und -rauch." *Frankfurter Allgemeine Zeitung,* June 10, 2002.

Wolff, Marga. "Kampf mit dem Prinzip Macht." *Die Tageszeitung,* October 2, 2002.

2005

The Magic Flute, animation, set design (with Sabine Theunissen), and direction, La Monnaie/De Munt, Brussels, April 26–May 12. Traveled. Catalogue titled *William Kentridge: Flute* edited by Bronwyn Law-Viljoen (published by David Krut, Johannesburg, 2007).

Allison, John. Review. *Opera* 56, no. 7 (July 2005): 813–16.

Brug, Manuel. "Mozart in der Black Box." *Die Welt,* April 28, 2005.

Coulson, Michael. Review. *Business Day,* October 2, 2007.

Davidson, Justin. "A *Flute* Higher on Scenery than Singing." *New York Newsday,* April 12, 2007.

De Beer, Diane. "Adding Colour to the World of Opera." *Star* (Johannesburg), September 25, 2007.

Debrocq, Michel. "Bruxelles réenchante *La Flûte.*" *Le Temps* (Geneva), April 29, 2005.

Greig, Robert. "Kentridge Finds Perfect Tempo in Magic Flute." *Indedependent* (Cape Town), March 25, 2007.

Gurewitsch, Matthew. "An Artist in Many Media Tackles *The Magic Flute.*" *Wall Street Journal,* April 5, 2007.

Hirsch, Faye. Review. *Art in America* 95, no. 6 (June–July 2007): 205–6.

Holland, Bernard. "Awfully Nice, Tamino, But Check Out That Astral Sketchbook." *New York Times,* April 11, 2007.

Isaacson, Maureen. "A Profound Meditation on Kentridge's Multi-Dimensional Magic Flute." *Independent* (Cape Town), October 28, 2007.

Kirshnit, Fred. "*Flute* Visuals More Magical than Music." *New York Sun,* April 11, 2007.

Klaue, Magnus. "Mechaniker des Unbewußten." *Frankfurter Allgemeine Zeitung,* June 13, 2002.

Midgette, Anne. "Artist's Video Adds Magic to *Flute.*" *New York Times,* April 9, 2007.

Rohde, Gerhard. "Zauberflötenflimmerkiste." *Frankfurter Allgemeine Zeitung,* April 30, 2005.

Roux, Marie-Aude. "*La Flûte,* version désenchantée, par William Kentridge." *Le Monde,* May 7, 2005.

Schwankhart, Marianne. "There's Magic in the Wings." *Business Day,* October 1, 2007.

Schwartz, Stan. "The Modern *Magic Flute.*" *New York Sun,* March 26, 2007.

Thurman, Chris. "Kentridge's *Magic Flute* Is Dazzling." *Business Day,* September 22, 2007.

Tinazzi, Noël. "Une *Flûte* imagée." *La Tribune* (Paris), March 6, 2006.

Waleson, Heidi. "Kentridge's Visual Technology Makes Mozart's Fantasy a Reality." *Wall Street Journal,* April 11, 2007.

Wilson, Jonathan. "Shades of Gray." *ARTnews* 106, no. 4 (April 2007): 34.

2008

I am not me, the horse is not mine, performance, 16th Biennale of Sydney, June 17–18. Traveled.

SELECTED BIBLIOGRAPHY

BOOKS

Alemani, Cecilia. *William Kentridge.* Milan: Mondadori Electa, 2006.

Apter, Emily. *The Translation Zone: A New Comparative Literature.* Princeton: Princeton University Press, 2006.

Basualdo, Carlos, et al. *Cream: 10 Curators, 10 Writers, 100 Artists.* London: Phaidon, 1998.

Bell, Richard H. *Understanding African Philosophy: A Cross-Cultural Approach to Classical and Contemporary Issues.* New York: Routledge, 2002.

Bennett, Jill. *Empathic Vision: Affect, Trauma, and Contemporary Art.* Stanford, CA: Stanford University Press, 2005.

Berman, Esmé. *Painting in South Africa.* Johannesburg: Southern Book Publishers, 1993.

Blumberg, Marcia, and Dennis Walder, eds. *South African Theatre as/and Intervention.* Amsterdam: Rodopi, 1999.

Burton, Johanna, et al. *Vitamin D: New Perspectives in Drawing.* London: Phaidon, 2005.

Busca, Joëlle. *Perspectives sur l'art contemporain africain.* Paris: L'Harmattan, 2000.

Cameron, Dan, Carolyn Christov-Bakargiev, and J. M. Coetzee. *William Kentridge.* London: Phaidon, 1999.

Christov-Bakargiev, Carolyn. *William Kentridge.* Brussels: Société des Expositions du Palais des Beaux Arts/Vereniging voor Tentoonstellingen van het Paleis voor Schone Kunsten, 1998.

——, ed. *William Kentridge.* Rivoli, Italy: Castello di Rivoli; Milan: Skira Editore, 2004.

Cork, Richard. *Breaking Down the Barriers: Art in the 1990s.* New Haven, CT: Yale University Press, 2003.

Danto, Arthur C. *Unnatural Wonders: Essays from the Gap between Art and Life.* New York: Farrar, Straus and Giroux, 2005.

Davis, Geoffrey V. *Voices of Justice and Reason: Apartheid and Beyond in South African Literature.* Amsterdam: Rodopi, 2003.

Fuchs, Anne. *Playing the Market: The Market Theatre, Johannesburg.* Amsterdam: Rodopi, 2002.

Geers, Kendell, ed. *Contemporary South African Art: The Gencor Collection.* Johannesburg: Jonathan Ball, 1997.

Irvin, Polly. *Directing for the Stage.* Mies, Switzerland: RotoVision, 2003.

Kastner, Jeffrey, ed. *Land and Environmental Art.* London: Phaidon, 1998.

Kentridge, William, and Angela Breidbach. *William Kentridge: Thinking Aloud; Conversations with Angela Breidbach.* Kunstwissenschaftliche Bibliothek, vol. 28, edited by Christian Posthofen. Cologne: Walther König, 2006.

Lee, Donvé. *William Kentridge: Drawing Us into a New World.* Gallo Manor, South Africa: Awareness, 2006.

Perryer, Sophie, ed. *10 Years 100 Artists: Art in a Democratic South Africa.* Cape Town: Bell-Roberts, 2004.

Saltz, Jerry. *Seeing Out Loud: The* Voice *Art Columns, Fall 1998–Winter 2003.* Great Barrington, MA: The Figures, 2003.

Saltzman, Lisa. *Making Memory Matter: Strategies of Remembrance in Contemporary Art.* Chicago: University of Chicago Press, 2006.

Smith, Elizabeth A. T., et al. *Life Death Love Hate Pleasure Pain: Selected Works from the Museum of Contemporary Art, Chicago, Collection.* Chicago: Museum of Contemporary Art, 2002.

Steiner, Barbara, and Jun Yang. *Autobiography.* New York: Thames & Hudson, 2004.

Stewart, Susan. *The Open Studio: Essays on Art and Aesthetics.* Chicago: University of Chicago Press, 2005.

Stone, Jennifer Arlene. *Freud's Body Ego or Memorabilia of Grief: Lucian Freud and William Kentridge.* New York: Javaribook, 2003.

———. *Politeness of Objects: William Kentridge's Noiraille.* New York: Javaribook, 2005.

Taylor, Mark C., et al. *PressPLAY: Contemporary Artists in Conversation.* London: Phaidon, 2005.

Van Voolen, Edward. *Jewish Art and Culture.* Munich: Prestel, 2006.

Weintraub, Linda. *In the Making: Creative Options for Contemporary Art.* New York: Distributed Art Publishers, 2003.

William Kentridge. Chicago: Museum of Contemporary Art; New York: New Museum of Contemporary Art; New York: Harry N. Abrams, 2001.

Williamson, Sue. *Resistance Art in South Africa,* Cape Town: David Philip, 1989.

Williamson, Sue, and Ashraf Jamal. *Art in South Africa: The Future Present.* Cape Town: David Philip, 1996.

ESSAYS AND INTERVIEWS

Apter, Emily. "The Aesthetics of Critical Habitats." *October* 99 (Winter 2002): 21–44.

———. "Kentridge and the Big League." *Mail & Guardian* (Johannesburg), June 13, 1997.

Bédarida, Catherine. "Les anges et les démons sud-africains de William Kentridge." *Le Monde,* July 10, 1997.

Bester, Rory. "Felix in Exile: The Work of William Kentridge." *Nka: Journal of Contemporary African Art* 8 (Spring–Summer 1998): 28–33.

Bindman, Catherine. "Suspended Animation." *Art on Paper* 11, no. 4 (March–April 2007): 38–39.

Burgio, Valeria. "Animar y hacer humo la escritura: De *Zeno Writing* (2002) de William Kentridge a *La conciencia de Zeno* (1923) de Italo Svevo." *Revista de Occidente* 316 (September 2007): 38–61.

———. "Identità e pregiudizio: William Kentridge al di là del determinismo territoriale." *Africa e Mediterraneo: Cultura e società* 1, no. 55 (August 2006): 60–63.

Camhi, Leslie. "Drawing the Shades." *ARTnews* 100, no. 9 (October 2001): 150–53.

Coetzee, Yvette. "Visibly Invisible." *South African Theatre Journal* 12, nos. 1–2 (May–September 1998): 35–51.

Collinge, Jo-Anne. "Under Fire." *American Film,* November 1985, 30–38, 78.

Corrigal, Mary. "The Faces of Jozi." *Independent* (Cape Town), February 10, 2008.

Crawford, Ashley. "Kentridge's Mixed Media Probes a Divided Nation." *Age* (Melbourne), May 15, 2004.

Crüwell, Konstanze. "Zurück in die Zukunft." *Frankfurter Allgemeine Zeitung,* April 3, 2005.

Danicke, Sandra. "Ameisen im Weltraum." *Frankfurter Rundschau,* April 12, 2005.

Daniels, Glenda. "Kentridge Shifts Focus from Canvas to Centre Stage." *Business Day,* September 29, 2007.

Davis, Geoffrey, and Anne Fuchs. "'An Interest in the Making of Things': An Interview with William Kentridge." In *Theatre and Change in South Africa,* edited by Davis and Fuchs, 140–54. Amsterdam: Harwood, 1996.

De Waal, Shaun. "Drawing on History." Review of *William Kentridge,* by Dan Cameron et al. *Mail & Guardian* (Johannesburg), November 5, 1999.

Diserens, Corinne. "Unwilling Suspension of Disbelief." *Art Press* 255 (March 2000): 20–26.

Dubow, Jessica, and Ruth Rosengarten. "History as the Main Complaint: William Kentridge and the Making of Post-Apartheid South Africa." *Art History* 27, no. 4 (September 2004): 671–90.

Enright, Robert. "Achievements of Indecision: The Art of William Kentridge." *Border Crossings* 21, no. 1 (February 2002): 20–37.

Enwezor, Okwui. "On the Nature of Vision and Visuality in the Landscape of South Africa: William Kentridge Speaks with Okwui Enwezor." *FYI* (San Francisco) 1 (2006): 16–25.

———. "Swords Drawn." *Frieze* 39 (March–April 1998): 66–69.

———. "Truth and Responsibility: A Conversation with William Kentridge/Wahrheit und Verantwortung: Ein Gespräch mit William Kentridge." *Parkett* 54 (1998–99): 165–76.

Forbey, Sarah. "Ghosting Shadows." *Contemporary* 50 (2003): 50–51.

Franklin, Sirmans. "William Kentridge: Crowning a Star." *Flash Art* 31, no. 200 (May–June 1998): 74–75.

Godby, Michael. "Excavating Memory: Collage as a Strategy for the Recovery of History in the Work of Cecil Skotnes, William Kentridge, and Willie Bester." *Nka: Journal of Contemporary African Art* 6–7 (Summer–Fall 1997): 38–43.

———. "Memory and History in William Kentridge's *History of the Main Complaint.*" In *Negotiating the Past: The Making of Memory in South Africa,* edited by Sarah Nuttall and Carli Coetzee, 100–111. Cape Town: Oxford University Press, 1998.

———. "William Kentridge." *Revue Noire* 11 (December 1993–February 1994): 20–23.

———. "William Kentridge: Retrospective." *Art Journal* 58, no. 3 (Fall 1999): 74–85.

Goldberg, RoseLee. "Live Cinema and Life in South Africa: A Telephone Conversation in Chicago, October 21, 2001/Live-Kino und Leben in Südafrika: Telefongespräch vom 21. Oktober 2001 in Chicago." *Parkett* 63 (2001): 96–111.

Gossler, Horst. "Not Half Crazy." *Sunday Times* (Johannesburg), March 24, 1991.

Gunning, Tom. "Doubled Vision: Peering through William Kentridge's *Stereoscope*/Die Verdoppelung des Blicks in Kentridges *Stereoskop.*" *Parkett* 63 (2001): 66–81.

Hirsch, Faye. "William Kentridge." *Art on Paper* 7, no. 4 (January–February 2003): 68.

Homes, A. M. "The Best of 1998." *Artforum* 37, no. 4 (December 1998): 104–5.

hooks, bell. "Breaking Down the Wall." *Interview,* September 1998, 166–67, 182.

Hubbard, Sue. "Out with the Old, In with the New." *Contemporary* 26 (1999): 52–56.

———. Review of *William Kentridge,* by Dan Cameron et al. *Contemporary* 28 (2000): 75.

Kaplan, Cheryl. "The Time-Image." *PAJ: A Journal of Performance and Art* 27, no. 80 (May 2005): 28–44.

Kentridge, William. "Beckmann's *Death.*" In *Max Beckmann,* edited by Sean Rainbird, 181–83. London: Tate, 2003.

———. "*Fortuna*: Neither Programme nor Chance in the Making of Images." *Cycnos* 11, no. 1 (January 1994): 163–68.

———. "Landscape in a State of Siege." *Stet* 5, no. 3 (November 1988): 15–18.

———. "Out of Africa." *Interview,* May 2001, 80–81.

———. "Some Thoughts on Obsolescence," in "Artist Questionnaire: 21 Responses," edited by George Baker. *October* 100 (Spring 2002): 16–18.

———. "Two Thoughts on Drawing Beauty." In *Beautiful/Ugly: African and Diaspora Aesthetics,* edited by Sarah Nuttall, 95–101. Durham, NC: Duke University Press, 2006.

Kentridge, William, and Robin Rhode. "Free Forms." *Modern Painters* 20, no. 5 (June 2008): 64–69.

Klett, Renate. "The Voice of Africa." *Theater Heute* 9 (September 1995): 8–10.

Korber, Rose. Interview. *Ada* 14 (1995): 78.

Krauss, Rosalind. "'The Rock': William Kentridge's Drawings for Projection." *October* 92 (Spring 2000): 3–35.

Kröner, Magdalena. "William Kentridge: die Gestalt der Spur, die Gestalt des Erinnerns." *Kunstforum* 170 (May–June 2004): 208–17.

Kruger, Loren. "Making Sense of Sensation: Enlightenment, Embodiment, and the End(s) of Modern Drama." In *Modern Drama: Defining the Field,* edited by Ric Knowles et al., 80–101. Toronto: University of Toronto Press, 2003.

Labuscagne, Cobi. "Representing the South African Landscape: Coetzee, Kentridge, and the Ecocritical Enterprise." *Journal of Literary Studies* 23, no. 4 (December 2007): 432–43.

Marlow, Stuart. "The Dramaturgy of Political Violence: Challenges to Accepted Notions of Dramatic Discourse." In *Towards a Transcultural Future: Literature and Human Rights in a "Post"-Colonial World,* edited by Peter H. Marsden and Geoffrey V. Davis, 173–86. Amsterdam: Rodopi, 2004.

McLean, Ian. "Postcolonial Traffic: William Kentridge and Aboriginal Desert Painters." *Third Text* 17, no. 3 (September 2003): 227–40.

Mejias, Jordan. "Verwandlung." *Frankfurter Allgemeine Zeitung,* November 14, 2004.

Morris, Rosalind C. "William Kentridge." *Transition* 98 (2008): 115.

Ollman, Leah. "William Kentridge: Ghosts and Erasures." *Art in America* 87, no. 1 (January 1999): 70–75, 113.

O'Reilly, Sally. "Ways of Seeing." *Art Review* 21 (April 2008): 74–77.

Païni, Dominique. "Le retour du flâneur." *Art Press* 255 (March 2000): 33–41.

Poggi, Christine. "Mass, Pack, and Mob: Art in the Age of the Crowd." In *Crowds,* edited by Jeffrey T. Schnapp and Matthew Tiews, 159–202. Stanford, CA: Stanford University Press, 2006.

Powell, Ivor. Interview. *Weekly Mail* (Johannesburg), November 7, 1986.

———. "Kentridge's Free-Floating Art of Ambiguities." *Weekly Mail* (Johannesburg), April 26, 1990.

Randall, Peter. "Knowing and Seeing." Review of *William Kentridge,* by Dan Cameron et al. *Financial Mail,* December 17, 1999.

Rankin, Elizabeth. "Seeing Stereoscopically: Soho in Auckland." *De Arte* 66 (September 2002): 58–64.

Salas, Alexis. "The Materiality of Thought: A Telephone Interview with William Kentridge, May 9, 2006, 2:00 p.m. (CST)." *Chicago Art Journal* 16 (2006): 100–107.

Sassen, Robyn. "Mirroring a World Gone Mad: Beckmann and Kentridge." *De Arte* 61 (April 2000): 24–46.

———. Review of *William Kentridge: Thinking Aloud,* by William Kentridge and Angela Breidbach. *Times* (Johannesburg), September 10, 2006.

Schumacher, Rainald. "William Kentridge: Ubu Tells the Truth." *Neue Bildende Kunst* 4 (1998): 38–45.

Schwabsky, Barry. "Drawing in Time: Reflections on Animation by Artists." *Art on Paper* 4, no. 4 (March–April 2000): 36–41.

Solomon, Andrew. "The Artists of South Africa: Separate, and Equal." *New York Times,* March 27, 1994.

Stevens, Mark. "Moral Minority." *New York Magazine,* February 20, 2006, 71–74.

Stewart, Susan. "A Messenger / Ein Bote." *Parkett* 63 (2001): 82–95.

Talotta, Joseph. "Kentridge: International Icon, Still Working from Home." *Business Day,* December 2, 2005.

Taylor, Jane. "Spherical and Without Exits: Thoughts on William Kentridge's Anamorphic Film *What Will Come (Has Already Come)*." *Art & Australia* 45, no. 4 (Winter 2008): 609–15.

Thirion, Antoine. "Cinéma, âge de Pierre." *Cahiers du cinéma* 594 (October 2004): 88–89.

Thompson, Vanessa Leswin Laubscher. "Violence, Re-membering, and Healing: A Textual Reading of *Drawings for Projection* by William Kentridge." *South African Journal of Psychology* 36, no. 4 (2006): 813–29.

Tschechne, Martin. "Die Schatten der Erinnerung." *ART: das Kunstmagazin* 5 (May 1999): 72–79.

Vendrame, Simona. Interview. *Tema Celeste* 90 (March–April 2002): 38–43.

Waites, James. "Drawing on an African Experience." *Sydney Morning Herald,* March 27, 1996.

Walker, Andrew. "Art and Music in the Service of Love." *Independent* (Cape Town), October 7, 2007.

Wecker, Menachem. "Painting Apartheid's Silhouette." *New York Forward,* April 11, 2008, 18.

Weldman, Sabrina. "Les arts plastiques et le théâtre: Doubles jeux." *Beaux Arts* 277 (July 2007): 70–77.

Wilson-Goldie, Kaelen. "Artist Dossier: William Kentridge."*Art & Auction,* April 2002, 100–101.

Wright, Stephen. "William Kentridge: L'écran et le tracé." *Parachute* 98 (April–June 2000): 26–33.

AUDIOVISUAL MATERIALS

Certas Dúvidas de William Kentridge. DVD. Directed by Alex Gabassi. São Paulo: Associação Cultural Videobrasil, 2000. Rereleased as *William Kentridge: Certain Doubts Of,* 2007.

Gespleten Wereld: Portret van de Zuid-Afrikaanse kunstenaar William Kentridge. Television documentary. Directed by Jos van den Bergh. Hilversum, Netherlands: VPRO, 2001.

Point of View: An Anthology of the Moving Image. Set of eleven DVDs. Produced by Ilene Kurtz-Kretzschmar and Caroline Bourgeois. New York: New Museum of Contemporary Art, 2003.

William Kentridge. CD-ROM. Edited by David Krut. Johannesburg: David Krut, 1997.

William Kentridge: Drawing the Passing. Videocassette. Directed by Maria Anna Tappeiner and Reinhard Wulf. Johannesburg: David Krut, 1999.

William Kentridge: The End of the Beginning. Videocassette. Directed by Beata Lipman. Johannesburg: David Krut, 1994.

FILMOGRAPHY

Title/Tale, with Steven Sack and Jemima Hunt, 1978
Howl at the Moon, with Hugo Cassirer and Malcolm Purkey, 1981
Salestalk, 1984
David Goldblatt, 1985
Vetkoek/Fête Galante, 1985
Exhibition, 1987
Freedom Square and Back of the Moon, with Angus Gibson, 1988
Johannesburg, 2nd Greatest City after Paris, 1989
Monument, 1990
T&I, 1990
Mine, 1991
Sobriety, Obesity & Growing Old, 1991
Easing the Passing (of the Hours), with Deborah Bell and Robert Hodgins, 1992
Another Country, 1994
Felix in Exile, 1994
Memo, with Deborah Bell and Robert Hodgins, 1994
Memory & Geography, with Doris Bloom, 1994
History of the Main Complaint, 1996
Hotel, with Deborah Bell and Robert Hodgins, 1997
Ubu Tells the Truth, 1997
Ulisse: ECHO scan slide bottle, 1998
WEIGHING... and WANTING, 1998
Overvloed, 1999
Shadow Procession, 1999
Sleeping on Glass, 1999
Stereoscope, 1999
Medicine Chest, 2001
Automatic Writing, 2002
Zeno Writing, 2002
Day for Night, 2003
Journey to the Moon, 2003
Learning the Flute, 2003
7 Fragments for Georges Méliès, 2003
Tide Table, 2003
What Will Come (has already come), 2007
Breathe, Dissolve, Return, 2008
I am not me, the horse is not mine, 2008

CATALOGUE OF THE EXHIBITION

Note: many drawings associated with William Kentridge's films, theatrical productions, and installations do not bear individual titles. Whenever possible, brief descriptions of these works have been provided in brackets in the list below.

Unless otherwise indicated, each work will be shown at all tour venues.

PARCOURS D'ATELIER: ARTIST IN THE STUDIO

Artist and Model, from the series *Pit*, 1979 (pl. 1)
Monotype
27 1/2 x 19 2/3 in. (70 x 50 cm)
Collection of the artist, courtesy Marian Goodman Gallery, New York, and Goodman Gallery, Johannesburg

Self-portrait (Testing the Library), 1998 (pl. 2)
Charcoal on paper
26 x 20 in. (66 x 51 cm)
Collection of Brenda Potter and Michael Sandler
American venues only

Drawing for the film *Medicine Chest* [Self-Portrait], 2000–2001 (fig. 1)
Charcoal and pastel on paper
47 1/4 x 31 1/2 in. (120 x 80 cm)
San Francisco Museum of Modern Art, gift of Mary and Harold Zlot
San Francisco only

Untitled [Artist and Model Drawing], 2001 (pl. 3)
Gouache, dry pigment, charcoal, and pastel on paper
42 1/8 x 100 3/8 in. (107 x 255 cm)
Collection of Jennifer and David Stockman
American venues only

Untitled [Artist and Model Drawing], 2001 (pl. 4)
Gouache, dry pigment, charcoal, and pastel on paper
22 x 29 7/8 in. (55.9 x 75.9 cm)
Collection of Lisa and John Miller
American venues only

Untitled [Artist and Model Drawing], 2001 (pl. 5)
Gouache, dry pigment, charcoal, and pastel on paper
22 x 29 7/8 in. (55.9 x 75.9 cm)
Collection of Sally and Michael Gordon
American venues only

Untitled [Artist and Model Drawing], 2001 (pl. 6)
Gouache, dry pigment, charcoal, and pastel on paper
22 x 29 7/8 in. (55.9 x 75.9 cm)
Collection of Sally and Michael Gordon
American venues only

Untitled [Artist and Model Drawing], 2001 (pl. 7)
Gouache, dry pigment, charcoal, and pastel on paper
22 x 29 7/8 in. (55.9 x 75.9 cm)
Collection of Heidi L. Steiger
American venues only

Untitled (Video Transfers) [Woman Getting in Bathtub], 2002 (pls. 48–51)
Charcoal, dry pigment, and gouache on paper
Nine drawings, each: 31 1/2 x 23 7/8 in. (80 x 60.6 cm)
Courtesy Marian Goodman Gallery, New York
American venues only

Day for Night, 2003 (fig. 28)
16mm film transferred to video, 6:32 min.
Collection of the artist, courtesy Marian Goodman Gallery, New York, and Goodman Gallery, Johannesburg
Direction, drawing, and photography: William Kentridge
Editing: Catherine Meyburgh

Journey to the Moon, 2003 (pls. 28–47)
35mm and 16mm animated film transferred to video, 7:10 min.
Collection of the artist, courtesy Marian Goodman Gallery, New York, and Goodman Gallery, Johannesburg
Direction, drawing, and photography: William Kentridge
Editing: Catherine Meyburgh
Music: Philip Miller

7 Fragments for Georges Méliès, 2003
Installation of seven film fragments: *Invisible Mending* (pls. 8–13); *Moveable Assets* (figs. 44–46); *Autodidact*; *Feats of Prestidigitation* (figs. 53–55); *Tabula Rasa I* (pls. 18–23); *Tabula Rasa II* (pls. 24–27); and *Balancing Act* (pls. 14–17)
35mm and 16mm animated film transferred to video, 3:64 min.
Collection of the artist, courtesy Marian Goodman Gallery, New York, and Goodman Gallery, Johannesburg
Direction, drawing, and photography: William Kentridge
Editing: Catherine Meyburgh

THICK TIME: SOHO AND FELIX

Drawing for the film *Johannesburg, 2nd Greatest City after Paris* [Captive of the City], 1989 (pl. 59)
Charcoal on paper
37 4/5 x 59 2/5 in. (96 x 151 cm)
Collection of the artist, courtesy Marian Goodman Gallery, New York, and Goodman Gallery, Johannesburg

Drawing for the film *Johannesburg, 2nd Greatest City after Paris* [Soho Outside His Headquarters], 1989 (pl. 57)
Charcoal and pastel on paper
19 7/10 x 13 3/4 in. (50 x 35 cm)
Collection of the artist, courtesy Marian Goodman Gallery, New York, and Goodman Gallery, Johannesburg

Drawing for the film *Johannesburg, 2nd Greatest City after Paris* [Soho with Cigar], 1989 (pl. 58)
Charcoal on paper
39 2/5 x 51 1/5 in. (100 x 130 cm)
Collection of the artist, courtesy Marian Goodman Gallery, New York, and Goodman Gallery, Johannesburg

Johannesburg, 2nd Greatest City after Paris, 1989 (pls. 52–56)
16mm animated film transferred to video, 8:02 min.
Collection of the artist, courtesy Marian Goodman Gallery, New York, and Goodman Gallery, Johannesburg
Direction, drawing, and photography: William Kentridge
Editing: Angus Gibson
Sound design: Warwick Sony
Music: Duke Ellington; South Kaserne Choir
Production: Free Filmmakers Cooperative, Johannesburg

Drawing for the film *Monument* [Harry—Close-up of Head and Load], 1990 (pl. 65)
Charcoal on paper
59 x 47 1/4 in. (150 x 120 cm)
Collection of the artist, courtesy Marian Goodman Gallery, New York, and Goodman Gallery, Johannesburg

Monument, 1990 (pls. 60–64)
16mm animated film transferred to video, 3:11 min.
Collection of the artist, courtesy Marian Goodman Gallery, New York, and Goodman Gallery, Johannesburg
Direction, drawing, and photography: William Kentridge
Editing: Angus Gibson
Sound design: Catherine Meyburgh
Music: Edward Jordan
Production: Free Filmmakers Cooperative, Johannesburg

Drawing for the film *Sobriety, Obesity & Growing Old* [Her Absence Filled the World], 1991 (pl. 70)
Charcoal and pastel on paper
47 1/4 x 59 in. (120 x 150 cm)
Collection of the artist, courtesy Marian Goodman Gallery, New York, and Goodman Gallery, Johannesburg

Drawing for the film *Sobriety, Obesity & Growing Old* [Soho and Mrs. Eckstein in Pool], 1991 (fig. 5)
Charcoal and pastel on paper
47 1/4 x 59 in. (120 x 150 cm)
Collection of the artist, courtesy Marian Goodman Gallery, New York, and Goodman Gallery, Johannesburg

Mine, 1991 (pls. 66–69)
16mm animated film transferred to video, 5:50 min.
Collection of the artist, courtesy Marian Goodman Gallery, New York, and Goodman Gallery, Johannesburg
Direction, drawing, and photography: William Kentridge
Editing: Angus Gibson
Music: Antonin Dvořák, Cello Concerto in B Minor, op. 104
Production: Free Filmmakers Cooperative, Johannesburg

Sobriety, Obesity & Growing Old, 1991 (pls. 71–76)
16mm animated film transferred to video, 8:22 min.
Collection of the artist, courtesy Marian Goodman Gallery, New York, and Goodman Gallery, Johannesburg
Direction, drawing, and photography: William Kentridge
Editing: Angus Gibson
Music: Antonin Dvořák, String Quartet in F, op. 96; South Kaserne Choir; "M'appari" from Friedrich von Flotow, *Martha* (sung by Enrico Caruso)

Drawing for the film *Felix in Exile* [Constellation], 1994 (pl. 82)
Charcoal and pastel on paper
31 1/2 x 47 1/4 in. (80 x 120 cm)
Private collection, Johannesburg

Felix in Exile, 1994 (pls. 77–81)
35mm animated film transferred to video, 8:43 min.
Collection of the artist, courtesy Marian Goodman Gallery, New York, and Goodman Gallery, Johannesburg
Direction, drawing, and photography: William Kentridge
Editing: Angus Gibson
Sound design: Wilbert Schübel
Music: Philip Miller, String Trio for *Felix in Exile* (performed by Peta-Ann Holdcroft, Marjan Vonk-Stirling, and Jan Pustejovsky); Motsumi Makhene, "Go Tlapsha Didiba" (sung by Sibongile Khumalo)

Drawing for the film *History of the Main Complaint* [Consultation, Ten Doctors], 1996 (pl. 88)
Charcoal on paper
47 1/4 x 63 in. (120 x 160 cm)
Museum of Contemporary Art, Chicago, gift of Susan and Lewis Manilow
American venues only

Drawing for the film *History of the Main Complaint* [Title Drawing], 1996 (pl. 87)
Charcoal and pastel on paper
27 1/2 x 47 1/4 in. (70 x 120 cm)
Museum of Contemporary Art, Chicago, gift of Susan and Lewis Manilow
American venues only

History of the Main Complaint, 1996 (pls. 83–86)
35mm animated film transferred to video, 5:50 min.
Collection of the artist, courtesy Marian Goodman Gallery, New York, and Goodman Gallery, Johannesburg
Direction, drawing, and photography: William Kentridge
Editing: Angus Gibson
Sound design: Wilbert Schübel
Music: Claudio Monteverdi, "Ardo"

Drawing for the film *WEIGHING...and WANTING* [Industrial Landscape], 1997 (pl. 96)
Charcoal on paper
48 1/4 x 63 in. (122.6 x 160 cm)
Museum of Contemporary Art, San Diego, museum purchase
American venues only

Drawing for the film *WEIGHING...and WANTING* [Soho with Head on Rock], 1997 (pl. 95)
Charcoal, pastel, and gouache on paper
48 1/2 x 63 in. (123.2 x 160 cm)
Museum of Contemporary Art, San Diego, museum purchase
American venues only

WEIGHING...and WANTING, 1998 (pls. 89–94)
35mm animated film transferred to video, 6:20 min.
Collection of the artist, courtesy Marian Goodman Gallery, New York, and Goodman Gallery, Johannesburg
Direction, drawing, and photography: William Kentridge
Editing: Angus Gibson and Catherine Meyburgh
Sound design: Wilbert Schübel
Music: Philip Miller (performed by Peta-Ann Holdcroft, Marjan Vonk-Stirling, and Ivo Ivanov)

Drawing for the film *Stereoscope* [Felix Crying], 1998–99 (pl. 104)
Charcoal, pastel, and colored pencil on paper
47 1/4 x 63 in. (120 x 160 cm)
The Museum of Modern Art, New York, gift of The Junior Associates of the Museum of Modern Art, with special contributions from Anonymous, Scott J. Lorinsky, Yasufumi Nakamura, and the Wider Foundation
American venues only

Drawing for the film *Stereoscope* [Felix in Pool with Megaphone], 1998–99 (pl. 103)
Charcoal and pastel on paper
31 7/16 x 48 3/8 in. (79.9 x 122.9 cm)
Hirshhorn Museum and Sculpture Garden, Smithsonian Institution, Washington, D.C., Joseph H. Hirshhorn Purchase Fund 1999
American venues only

Drawing for the film *Stereoscope* [Soho at Desk on Telephone], 1998–99 (pl. 102)
Charcoal and pastel on paper
47 1/4 x 63 in. (120 x 160 cm)
Hirshhorn Museum and Sculpture Garden, Smithsonian Institution, Washington, D.C., Joseph H. Hirshhorn Purchase Fund 1999
American venues only

Stereoscope, 1999 (figs. 20, 27, pls. 97–101)
35mm animated film transferred to video, 8:22 min.
Collection of the artist, courtesy Marian Goodman Gallery, New York, and Goodman Gallery, Johannesburg
Direction, drawing, and photography: William Kentridge
Editing: Catherine Meyburgh
Sound design: Wilbert Schübel
Music: Philip Miller (performed by Peta-Ann Holdcroft, Marjan Vonk-Stirling, Ishmael Kambule, and Minas Berberyan)

Drawing for the film *Tide Table* [Huts Interior], 2003 (pl. 111)
Charcoal on paper
25 x 66 in. (63.5 x 167.6 cm)
Collection of Brenda Potter and Michael Sandler
American venues only

Drawing for the film *Tide Table* [Soho Sleeping], 2003 (pl. 110)
Charcoal on paper
47 1/4 x 63 in. (120 x 160 cm)
Courtesy the artist and Marian Goodman Gallery, New York

Tide Table, 2003 (pls. 105–9)
35mm animated film transferred to video, 8:50 min.
Collection of the artist, courtesy Marian Goodman Gallery, New York, and Goodman Gallery, Johannesburg
Direction, drawing, and photography: William Kentridge
Editing: Catherine Meyburgh
Sound design: Wilbert Schübel
Music: Franco et le T.P. O.K. Jazz, "Likambo Ya Ngana"; singers from the Market Theatre Laboratory

OCCASIONAL AND RESIDUAL HOPE: UBU AND THE PROCESSION

Arc Procession (Smoke, Ashes, Fable), 1990 (pl. 144)
Charcoal and pastel on paper
Three parts, overall: 70 x 151 1/5 in. (178 x 384 cm)
Collection of the artist, courtesy Marian Goodman Gallery, New York, and Goodman Gallery, Johannesburg

Ubu Tells the Truth, 1996
Portfolio of eight etchings: *Act I, Scene 2* (pl. 112); *Act II, Scene 1* (pl. 113); *Act II, Scene 5* (pl. 114); *Act III, Scene 4* (pl. 115); *Act III, Scene 9* (pl. 116); *Act IV, Scene 1* (pl. 117); *Act IV, Scene 7* (pl. 118); and *Act V, Scene 4* (pl. 119)
Hardground, softground, aquatint, drypoint, and engraving, ed. 44/50
Each: 10 x 12 in. (25 x 30.5 cm)
Printed by Caversham Press, Natal, South Africa
Collection of the artist, courtesy Marian Goodman Gallery, New York, and Goodman Gallery, Johannesburg

Ubu Drawing (Bicycle), 1997 (pl. 131)
Charcoal, gouache, pastel, and dry pigment on paper
63 1/3 x 43 1/2 in. (177 x 106 cm)
Collection of Kenneth and Sherry Endelson, Boca Raton, Florida
American venues only

Ubu Drawing (Sleeper), 1997 (pl. 130)
Charcoal, gouache, pastel, and dry pigment on paper
42 1/2 x 84 3/5 in. (108 x 215 cm)
Collection of Jimmy and Becky Mayer
American venues only

Ubu Tells the Truth, 1997 (figs. 10–11, 21, pls. 120–29)
35mm animated film with documentary photographs and 16mm archival film transferred to video, 8 min.
Collection of the artist, courtesy Marian Goodman Gallery, New York, and Goodman Gallery, Johannesburg
Drawing, photography, and direction: William Kentridge
Editing: Catherine Meyburgh
Music: Warrick Sony and Brendan Jury

Ubu Drawing (Dancing Man), 1998 (pl. 133)
Gouache, charcoal, dry pigment, and pastel on paper
93 x 48 1/2 in. (236.2 x 123.2 cm)
Collection of Aaron and Barbara Levine
American venues only

Ubu Drawing (Listening Man), 1998 (pl. 132)
Gouache, charcoal, dry pigment, and pastel on paper
75 1/2 x 42 1/2 in. (192 x 108 cm)
Collection of Donna and Howard Stone
American venues only

Shadow Procession, 1999 (pls. 135–43)
35mm animated film transferred to video, 7 min.
Collection of the artist, courtesy Marian Goodman Gallery, New York, and Goodman Gallery, Johannesburg
Direction, animation, and photography: William Kentridge
Editing: Catherine Meyburgh
Sound design: Wilbert Schübel
Music: Alfred Makgalemele

Portage, 2000 (pls. 146–47)
Collage on book pages
Eighteen panels, each: 10 4/5 x 9 1/4 in. (27.5 x 23.5 cm); 10 4/5 x 168 1/8 in. (27.5 x 427 cm) overall
Display table designed by the artist and fabricated by Gregor Jenkins
Collection of the artist, courtesy Marian Goodman Gallery, New York, and Goodman Gallery, Johannesburg

Procession on Anatomy of Vertebrates, 2000 (pl. 145)
Charcoal on book pages
11 x 70 in. (27.9 x 177.8 cm)
Collection of Brenda Potter and Michael Sandler
American venues only

Bridge, 2001 (pl. 148)
Bronze and books
23 5/8 x 36 3/4 x 7 1/2 in. (60 x 93.2 x 19 cm)
Display table designed by the artist and fabricated by Gregor Jenkins
Collection of the artist, courtesy Marian Goodman Gallery, New York, and Goodman Gallery, Johannesburg

Promenade II, 2002 (fig. 22)
Bronze
14 3/4 x 10 5/16 x 6 3/4 in. (37.5 x 26.2 x 17 cm)
Display table designed by the artist and fabricated by Gregor Jenkins
Collection of the artist, courtesy Marian Goodman Gallery, New York, and Goodman Gallery, Johannesburg

SARASTRO AND THE MASTER'S VOICE: THE MAGIC FLUTE

Learning the Flute, 2003 (pls. 149–50)
35mm animated film transferred to video and projected on blackboard, 8:02 min.
Blackboard: 50 2/5 x 65 3/5 in. (128 x 166.5 cm); 82 x 65 3/5 x 39 2/5 in. (208 x 166.5 x 100 cm) overall
The Museum of Modern Art, New York, Patricia P. Irgens Larsen Foundation Fund, 2004
Exhibition copy
Direction, drawing, and photography: William Kentridge
Editing: Catherine Meyburgh
Music: Wolfgang Amadeus Mozart, *The Magic Flute*

Drawing for the installation *Preparing the Flute*, 2004–5 (pl. 160)
Charcoal, pastel, and colored pencil on paper
31 3/4 x 47 5/8 in. (80 x 120 cm)
Courtesy the artist and Marian Goodman Gallery, New York

Drawing for the opera *The Magic Flute*, 2004–5 (pl. 155)
Charcoal and colored pencil on paper
48 x 48 in. (121.9 x 121.9 cm)
Collection of Brenda Potter and Michael Sandler
American venues only

Drawing for the opera *The Magic Flute*, 2004–5 (pl. 156)
Charcoal, pastel, colored pencil, and collage on paper
39 2/5 x 51 1/5 in. (100 x 130 cm)
Collection of Joel and Anne Ehrenkranz, New York
American venues only

Drawing for the opera *The Magic Flute*, 2004–5 (pl. 157)
Pastel on paper
29 7/8 x 44 1/4 in (75.9 x 112.4 cm)
Courtesy Marian Goodman Gallery, New York
American venues only

Drawing for the opera *The Magic Flute*, 2004–5 (pl. 159)
Charcoal, pastel, colored pencil, and collage on paper
31 1/2 x 47 1/4 in. (80 x 120 cm)
Private collection, Ross, California
American venues only

Drawing for the opera *The Magic Flute*, 2004–5 (pl. 161)
Charcoal, pastel, and colored pencil on paper
46 1/2 x 63 in. (118.1 x 160 cm)
Collection of Joan and Richard Barovick
American venues only

Drawing for the opera *The Magic Flute*, 2004–5 (pl. 162)
Charcoal, pastel, and colored pencil on paper
47 1/4 x 63 in. (120 x 160 cm)
Courtesy the artist and Marian Goodman Gallery, New York

Drawing for the opera *The Magic Flute* [Rhino on Stage], 2004–5 (pl. 158)
Charcoal, pastel, colored pencil, and collage on paper
32 5/8 x 52 1/2 in. (83 x 133.5 cm)
Private collection, New York
American venues only

Black Box/Chambre Noire, 2005 (fig. 29, pls. 163–69)
Model theater with drawings (charcoal, pastel, collage, and colored pencil on paper), mechanical puppets, and 35mm animated film transferred to video, 22 min.
141 3/4 x 78 3/4 x 55 in. (360 x 200 x 139.7 cm)
Commissioned by Deutsche Bank AG in consultation with the Solomon R. Guggenheim Foundation for the Deutsche Guggenheim, Berlin
Exhibition copy
Direction, animation, and photography: William Kentridge
Editing: Catherine Meyburgh
Music: Philip Miller (sung by Alfred Makgalemele and Vevangua Muuondjo)
Musical recordings in Namibia: Minette Mans and Philip Miller
Mechanical design: Jonas Lundquist
Programming: Ronald Hallgren
Lighting: Ann-Charlotte Fogelström

Preparing the Flute, 2005 (pls. 151–54)
Model theater with drawings (charcoal, pastel, and colored pencil on paper) and 35mm animated film transferred to video, 21:06 min.
95 x 44 x 60 1/2 in. (241.3 x 111.8 x 153.7 cm)
San Francisco Museum of Modern Art, fractional and promised gift of Doris and Donald Fisher
Exhibition copy
Direction, drawing, and photography: William Kentridge
Editing: Catherine Meyburgh
Music: Wolfgang Amadeus Mozart, *The Magic Flute*
Carpentry: Richard Forbes

Drawing for *Il Sole 24 Ore* [World Walking], 2007 (pl. 173)
Charcoal, gouache, pastel, and colored pencil on paper
84 x 59 in. (213.5 x 150 cm)
Collection of Doris and Donald Fisher
American venues only

Drawing for *What Will Come* [World on Its Hind Legs], 2007
Charcoal, gouache, and colored pencil on paper
84 x 59 in. (213.5 x 150 cm)
Collection of the artist, courtesy Marian Goodman Gallery, New York, and Goodman Gallery, Johannesburg
European venues only

What Will Come (has already come), 2007 (fig. 18, pls. 170–72)
Steel table, cylindrical steel mirror, and 35mm animated film transferred to video, 8:40 min.
41 1/4 x 48 x 48 in. (104.7 x 121.9 x 121.9 cm)
Norton Museum of Art, purchase, acquired through the generosity of the Contemporary and Modern Art Council and the R. H. Norton Trust, 2008
Exhibition copy
Direction, drawing, and photography: William Kentridge
Editing and sound design: Catherine Meyburgh
Music: Dmitri Shostakovich, Piano Trio no. 2; Giuseppe Micheli and Mario Ruccione, "Faccetta Nera"; "Mbila Solo," "Love Song," and "Song to the Emperor" (music from Ethiopia and Eritrea, composers and performers unknown)

LEARNING FROM THE ABSURD: THE NOSE

I am not me, the horse is not mine, 2008 (figs. 25–26, 35)
Installation of eight film fragments: *A Lifetime of Enthusiasm* (pls. 174–81); *The Horse Is Not Mine* (pls. 182–91); *Commissariat for Enlightenment* (pls. 192–96); *His Majesty the Nose* (pls. 197–201); *Prayers of Apology* (pls. 202–8); *That Ridiculous Blank Space Again (A One-Minute Love Story)* (pls. 209–18); *Country Dances I (Shadow)* (pls. 219–22); and *Country Dances II (Paper)* (pls. 223–39)
DVCAM and HDV transferred to video, 6:01 min.
Collection of the artist, courtesy Marian Goodman Gallery, New York, and Goodman Gallery, Johannesburg
Direction, drawing, and photography: William Kentridge
Editing: Catherine Meyburgh
Composer: Philip Miller
Animation assistants: Gerhard Marx and Catherine Walker
Music: Philip Miller, "Galop" (performed by Dan Selsick, Billy Middleton, Adam Howard, Ntkozo Zunga, Bethuel Mbonani, and Thulani Manaka); "Ngilahlekelelwe Ikhala Lami" (arranged by Philip Miller; music and lyrics by Richard Siluma and Thulani Manana; sung by Thulani Manana and Abanikazi Bomkhalanga)
Dancer: Thato Motlhaolwa
Workshop participants (Johannesburg, January 2008): Panayota Athanasiou, Zola Hashatsi, Rachel Jacobs, Alex-Ann Keppie, Wez-Lee Masilo Makgamatha, Mbovu Malinga, Thato Mathole, Onthatile Matshidiso, Hlomohang Mothetho, Thato Motlhaolwa, Miranda Ndou, Lesego Ngwato, Mzamo Nondlwana, Roberto Manuel Pombo, Eve Rakow, Motlalentwa Sehloho, Rabeka Silinda, Nqaba Thela, Claudine Ullman, and Nick Welch

PHOTOGRAPHY CREDITS

All artworks are reproduced by permission of the artist and the owners of the works named in the image captions. Additional photography credits appear below.

FRONT AND BACK COVER, FACE OF DVD, AND FRONTISPIECE

John Hodgkiss

PLATES

1, 8–81, 83–86, 88–95, 97–111, 113–29, 131, 134–53, 161, 163–70, 172, 174–239: John Hodgkiss; 2–7, 82, 112, 155–60, 162, 171, 173: courtesy Marian Goodman Gallery, New York; 96: Gary Conaughton Photography; 130: David Clarke; 154: Ian Reeves

FIGURE ILLUSTRATIONS

1: Frank Wing; 2–7, 10–18, 20–24, 27–31, 33, 36, 39–40, 42, 44–55: John Hodgkiss; 8: © 2008 Artists Rights Society (ARS), New York/VG Bild-Kunst, Bonn; 9: © Tate, London 2008; 19: Ben Blackwell; 25–26, 35: Jenni Carter; 34: Franz Wamhof, courtesy ZKM/VG Bild-Kunst, Bonn, 2008; 41: Herman Sorgeloos for Handspring Puppet Company, Cape Town; 43: Michele Crosera, courtesy Fondazione Teatro La Fenice

This catalogue is published by the San Francisco Museum of Modern Art and the Norton Museum of Art in association with Yale University Press. It accompanies the exhibition *William Kentridge: Five Themes*, organized by Mark Rosenthal.

Exhibition Schedule
San Francisco Museum of Modern Art
March 14–May 31, 2009

Modern Art Museum of Fort Worth
July 11–September 27, 2009

Norton Museum of Art, West Palm Beach, Florida
November 7, 2009–January 17, 2010

Museum of Modern Art, New York
February 28–May 17, 2010

Albertina, Vienna
October 30, 2010–January 30, 2011

Israel Museum, Jerusalem
March 5–May 29, 2011

Stedelijk Museum, Amsterdam
July 7–October 2, 2011

William Kentridge: Five Themes is organized by the San Francisco Museum of Modern Art and the Norton Museum of Art. Generous support for the exhibition is provided by the Koret Foundation. Additional support is provided by the National Endowment for the Arts.

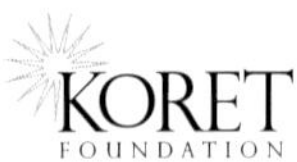

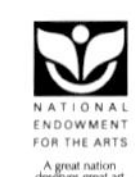

The San Francisco presentation is made possible by generous support from Doris and Donald Fisher, the Mimi and Peter Haas Fund, and Nancy and Steven H. Oliver.

The West Palm Beach presentation is made possible in part through the generosity of Mr. and Mrs. Ralph Saltzman, the Milton and Sheila Fine Endowment for Contemporary Art, The Dr. Henry and Lois Foster Endowment for the Exhibition of Contemporary Art, and The Contemporary and Modern Art Council of the Norton Museum of Art.

Library of Congress Cataloging-in-Publication Data
Kentridge, William, 1955–
William Kentridge : five themes / edited by Mark Rosenthal ; with contributions by Michael Auping . . . [et al.]. — 1st ed.
p. cm.
Published on the occasion of an exhibition held at the San Francisco Museum of Modern Art and six other institutions between Mar. 14, 2009 and Fall 2011.
Includes bibliographical references.
ISBN 978-0-300-15048-3
1. Kentridge, William, 1955—Themes, motives—Exhibitions. I. Rosenthal, Mark (Mark Lawrence). II. Auping, Michael. III. San Francisco Museum of Modern Art. IV. Title.
N7396.K45A4 2009
709.2—dc22
2008050305

Director of Publications Chad Coerver
Managing Editor Karen A. Levine
Publications Assistant Amanda Glesmann
Designers Abbott Miller and Kristen Spilman, Pentagram
Production Manager Amanda W. Freymann

Published in association with Yale University Press, New Haven and London
www.yalebooks.com

FRONT AND BACK COVER
Paper construction for *The Nose* (abandoned), 2007
Paper, india ink, gouache, dowel sticks, glue, wire, board, and rubber bands
23 5/8 x 13 1/2 x 4 3/8 in. (60 x 34 x 11 cm)
Courtesy the artist

FACE OF DVD
***Balancing Act*, from *7 Fragments for Georges Méliès*, 2003**
35mm and 16mm animated film transferred to video, 1:20 min.
Collection of the artist, courtesy Marian Goodman Gallery, New York, and Goodman Gallery, Johannesburg

FRONTISPIECE
Kentridge performing ***I am not me, the horse is not mine*** (2008) at the Biennale of Sydney, 2008

Drawn from encyclopedias, atlases, maps, and other sources, the images on pages 12, 66, 130, 170, and 204 were selected by William Kentridge expressly for this publication.

Photography credits appear on page 263.

Color separations by Professional Graphics Inc., Rockford, Illinois
Printed and bound in Italy by Conti Tipocolor